WAR, EMPIRE,
AND THE MILITARY

ESSAYS ON THE FOLLIES OF WAR AND U.S. FOREIGN POLICY

Books by Laurence M. Vance

The Other Side of Calvinism
A Brief History of English Bible Translations
The Angel of the Lord
Archaic Words and the Authorized Version
A Practical Grammar of Basic Biblical Hebrew
Double Jeopardy: The NASB Update
Christianity and War and Other Essays Against the Warfare State
King James, His Bible, and Its Translators
Greek Verbs in the New Testament and Their Principal Parts
War, Foreign Policy, and the Church
Guide to Prepositions in the Greek New Testament
The Myth of the Just Price and the Biblical Case for Laissez Faire
Guide to Nouns in the Greek New Testament
Guide to Adjectives in the Greek New Testament
Guide to Pronouns in the Greek New Testament
The Revolution that Wasn't
Rethinking the Good War
Galatians 1 & 2: Exposition, Commentary, Application
The Quatercentenary of the King James Bible
The War on Drugs Is a War on Freedom
War, Christianity, and the State: Essays on the Follies of
    Christian Militarism
Social Insecurity
War, Empire, and the Military: Essays on the Follies of War and
    U.S. Foreign Policy

WAR, EMPIRE,
AND THE MILITARY

ESSAYS ON THE FOLLIES OF WAR AND U.S. FOREIGN POLICY

by

Laurence M. Vance

Vance Publications
www.vancepublications.com

ISBN 978-0-9823697-8-4

Published and Distributed by: Vance Publications
P.O. Box 780671, Orlando, FL 32878
E-mail: vancepub@vancepublications.com
Website: www.vancepublications.com

Printed in the United States of America

TABLE OF CONTENTS

CHAPTER THREE
THE WAR IN IRAQ

CHAPTER FOUR
WORLD WAR II

CHAPTER FIVE
OTHER WARS

CHAPTER SIX
THE U.S. GLOBAL EMPIRE

CHAPTER SEVEN
U.S. FOREIGN POLICY

INTRODUCTION

These essays, although organized under seven headings, have one underlying theme: opposition to the warfare state that robs us of our liberty, our money, and in some cases our life. Conservatives who decry the welfare state while supporting the warfare state are terribly inconsistent. The two are inseparable. Libertarians who are opposed to war on principle, but support the state's bogus "war on terrorism," even as they remain silent about the U.S. global empire, are likewise contradictory.

Most of these 127 essays were published on the premier anti-state, anti-war, pro-market website, LewRockwell.com, during the period from January 2, 2004, to June 1, 2013. The vast majority of them first appeared on and were written exclusively for that website. LewRockwell.com is the brainchild of Lew Rockwell, the founder and chairman of the Ludwig von Mises Institute in Auburn, Ala., and a leading opponent of the central state, its wars, and its socialism. Most of the rest of the essays were originally published by the Future of Freedom Foundation, whose founder and president is the equally courageous Jacob Hornberger.

Forty-four of the essays contained in this work originally appeared in the second edition of the author's book *Christianity and War and Other Essays Against the Warfare State*, published in 2008. Nine of them appeared there and in the book's first edition, published in 2005. In addition to essays relating to Christianity and war and Christianity and the military, that book also included essays on war and peace, the military, the war in Iraq, other wars, and the U.S. global empire. Although a third edition was planned, two things served to redirect my intentions.

Because the second edition had already grown in size to seventy-nine essays in 432 pages and I had written so much on these subjects since its publication early in 2008, a third edition would just be too large of a book if I tried to include everything I had written on these subjects since the publication of the second edition. Additionally, since one part of the book and much additional material consisted of essays with a decidedly Christian theme, while the other part of the book and much additional material was more secular in nature, it seemed best to organize the existing and new material along these themes. So, instead of issuing an unwieldy one volume third edition, I opted to collect all of the former material into *War, Christianity, and the State: Essays on the Follies of Christian Militarism*, and issue the latter material in a companion volume titled *War, Militarism, and Empire: Essays on the Follies of War and U.S. Foreign Policy*.

Each essay is reprinted verbatim, with the exception of the correction of a few minor errors. It should be noted, however, that the original spelling, capitalization, and punctuation are followed in all quotations. Because they were published on the Internet, most of the essays originally contained numerous links to documentation and further information on the Web that the reader could click on if he desired. Because this feature is not possible in a printed format, the reader is encouraged to consult the online versions of each essay at LewRockwell.com or FFF.org where they are archived. Many of the essays also originally included pictures, which, for space considerations, are not included here.

Although many of these essays reference contemporary events, the principles discussed in all of them are timeless: war, militarism, empire, interventionism, and the warfare state. The essays in each chapter are listed in their order of publication. Each chapter as well as its individual essays can be read in any order, with the exception of the essays on "The U.S. Global Empire" in chapter 6, which are better read chronologically.

In chapter 1, "War and Peace," the evils of war and warmongers and the benefits of peace are examined. In chapter 2, "The Military," the evils of standing armies and militarism are discussed, including a critical look at the U.S. military. In chapter 3, "The War in Iraq," the wickedness of the Iraq War is exposed. In chapter 4, "World War II," the "good war" is shown to be not so good after all. In chapter 5, "Other Wars," the evils of war and the warfare state are chronicled in specific wars: the Crimean War (1854–1856), the Russo-Japanese War (1904–1905), World War I (1914–1918), the Persian Gulf War (1990–1991), and the war in Afghanistan (2001–). In chapter 6, "The U.S. Global Empire," the beginnings, growth, extent, nature, and consequences of the U.S. empire of bases and troops are revealed and critiqued. In chapter 7, "U.S. Foreign Policy," the belligerence, recklessness, and follies of U.S. foreign policy are laid bare.

The books listed at the close under "For Further Reading" include not only some of the more important books referenced in the essays, but other recommended works that relate in some way to war, the military, the U.S. global empire, and U.S. foreign policy. Most of them are available from Amazon.com. The inclusion of any book should not be taken as a blanket endorsement of everything contained in the book or anything else written by the author.

It is my desire in all of these essays to show, as Randolph Bourne said many years ago, that "war is the health of the state."

CHAPTER 1
WAR AND PEACE

CATO ON THE EVILS OF WAR AND STANDING ARMIES

To a classical historian, Cato refers to the Roman statesmen Cato the Elder (234–139 B.C.) and Cato the Younger (95–46 B.C.). To a fashion-conscious woman, Cato is a chain of clothing stores. To a beltway libertarian, Cato refers to the Cato Institute in Washington, D.C. But to the American colonists, Cato would have been a reference to the essays by John Trenchard (1662–1723) and Thomas Gordon (d.1750) that condemned tyranny and corruption in government while advancing the principles of liberty.

Cato's Letters is a collection of 144 essays by Trenchard and Gordon that appeared in the *London Journal* and the *British Journal* between 1720 and 1723. They were published together beginning in 1724 as *Cato's Letters: Or Essays on Liberty, Civil and Religious, and Other Important Subjects.* The essays were signed with the pseudonym Cato, after Cato the Younger, the foe of Julius Caesar and champion of liberty and republican principles. Cato the Younger was the great-grandson of Cato the Elder. His daughter married Brutus, one of the assassins of Julius Caesar. Cato's life was immortalized in the 1713 play, *Cato: A Tragedy,* by the English playwright and essayist Joseph Addison (1672–1719).

Cato's Letters was not the first collaboration of Gordon and Trenchard. They also wrote and published anonymously the London political weekly, *The Independent Whig,* in 1720. Previous to this, they authored two pamphlets: *The Character of an Independent Whig* and *Considerations Offered upon the Approaching Peace and upon the Importance of Gibraltar to the British Empire, being the Second Part of the "Independent Whig,"* both published in 1719.

While *Cato's Letters* were still being published in London, they began to be reprinted in the American colonies. Thirty-seven percent of library and booksellers' catalogs surveyed in the fifty years preceding the American Revolution listed *Cato's Letters.* Trenchard and Gordon were among the ten most quoted individuals during the period from 1760–1805. According to historian Clinton Rossiter, *Cato's Letters* were "the most popular, quotable, esteemed source of political ideas in the colonial

1

period." Bernard Bailyn further notes that to the American colonists, *Cato's Letters* "ranked with the treatises of Locke as the most authoritative statement of the nature of political liberty."

In light of the current debacle in Iraq that the United States is engaged in, our particular concern here is the statements in *Cato's Letters* relating to the evils of war and standing armies. Although Trenchard and Gordon did not say much, they said a mouthful. Their equally notable statements on liberty and property have already been examined elsewhere.

Cato on War

The classic statement on the evils of war appears in *Cato's Letters* No. 87:

> If we consider this question under the head of justice and humanity, what can be more detestable than to murder and destroy mankind, in order to rob and pillage them? War is comprehensive of most, if not all the mischiefs which do or ever can afflict men: It depopulates nations, lays waste the finest countries, destroys arts, sciences, and learning, butchers innocents, ruins the best men, and advances the worst; effaces every trace of virtue, piety, and compassion, and introduces confusion, anarchy, and all kinds of corruption in publick affairs; and indeed is pregnant with so many evils, that it ought ever to be avoided, when it can be avoided; and it may be avoided when a state can be safe without it, and much more so when all the advantages proposed by it can be procured by prudent and just methods.

In *Cato's Letters* No. 17, as an example of "what measures have been taken by corrupt ministers, in some of our neighbouring countries, to ruin and enslave the people over whom they presided," we read something strangely reminiscent of our own "leaders":

> They will engage their country in ridiculous, expensive, fantastical wars, to keep the minds of men in continual hurry and agitation, and under constant fears and alarm; and, by such means, deprive them both of leisure and inclination to look into publick miscarriages. Men, on the contrary, will, instead of such inspection, be disposed to fall into all measures offered, seemingly, for their defence, and will agree to every wild demand made by those who are betraying them.

> When they have served their ends by such wars, or have other

motives to make peace, they will have no view to the publick interest; but will often, to procure such peace, deliver up the strong-holds of their country, or its colonies for trade, to open enemies, suspected friends, or dangerous neighbours, that they may not be interrupted in their domestick designs.

This theme is continued in *Cato's Letters* No. 87:

I have often wondered at the folly and weakness of those princes, who will sacrifice hundreds of thousand of their own faithful subjects, to gain a precarious and slavish submission from bordering provinces, who will seek all opportunities to revolt; which cannot be prevented but by keeping them poor, wretched, and miserable, and consequently unable to pay the charges of their own vassalage; when, if the same number of men and the sums of money were usefully employed at home, which are necessary to make and support the conquest, they would add vastly more to their power and empire.

Cato preferred commerce to conquest:

All the advantages procured by conquest is to secure what we possess ourselves, or to gain the possessions of others, that is, the produce of their country, and the acquisitions of their labor and industry; and if these can be obtained by fair means, and by their own consent, sure it must be more eligible than to exhort them by force.

This is certainly more easily and effectually done by a well regulated commerce, than by arms: The balance of trade will return more clear money from neighbouring countries, than can be forced from them by fleets or armies, and more advantageously than under the odious name of tribute. It enervates rival states by their own consent, and obligates them, whilst it impoverishes and ruins them: It keeps our own people at home employed in arts, manufactures, and husbandry, instead of murdering them in wild, expensive, and hazardous expeditions, to the weakening their own country, and the pillaging and destroying their neighbours, and only for the fruitless and imaginary glory of conquest.

Cato on Standing Armies

Like the American Brutus, Cato also spoke out against the evils of standing armies. This subject was a particular concern of John Trenchard.

With Walter Moyle, Trenchard had previously written *An Argument Shewing that a Standing Army is Inconsistent with a Free Government, and Absolutely Destructive to the Constitution of the English Monarchy* (London, 1697). This was followed the next year by Trenchard's *A Short History of Standing Armies in England* (London, 1698). He was also the author of the anonymously-published work, *A Letter from the Author of the Argument Against a Standing Army, to the Author of the Ballancing Letter* [an essay defending standing armies] (London, 1697).

    Cato's Letters No. 94 and 95 are both devoted to the subject of standing armies. The subject is also mentioned in another essay titled "Considerations upon the Condition of an Absolute Prince." Sometimes it is standing armies in general that are warned against:

> Standing armies are standing curses in every country under the sun, where they are more powerful than the people.

> It is certain, that all parts of Europe which are enslaved, have been enslaved by armies; and it is absolutely impossible, that any nation which keeps them amongst themselves can long preserve their liberties; nor can any nation perfectly lose their liberties who are without such guests: And yet, though all men see this, and at times confess it, yet all have joined in their turns, to bring this heavy evil upon themselves and their country.

> I never yet met with one honest and reasonable man out of power who was not heartily against all standing armies, as threatening and pernicious, and the ready instruments of certain ruin: And I scarce ever met with a man in power, or even the meanest creature of power, who was not for defending and keeping them up: So much are the opinions of men guided by their circumstances! Men, when they are angry with one another, will come into any measures for revenge, without considering that the same power which destroys an enemy, may destroy themselves; and he to whom I lend my sword to kill my foe, may with it kill me.

> Great empires cannot subsist without great armies, and liberty cannot subsist with them. As armies long kept up, and grown part of the government, will soon engross the whole government, and can never be disbanded; so liberty long lost, can never be recovered. Is not this an awful lesson to free states, to be vigilant against a dreadful condition, which has no remedy.

At other times the reference is specific and contemporary:

When, in King William's reign, the question was in debate, Whether England should be ruled by standing armies? The argument commonly used by some, who had the presumption to call themselves Whigs, and owned in the Ballancing Letter (supposed to be written by one who gave the word to all the rest), was, that all governments must have their periods one time or other, and when that time came, all endeavours to preserve liberty were fruitless; and shrewd hints were given in that letter, that England was reduced to such a condition; that our corruptions were so great, and the dissatisfaction of the people was so general, that the publick safety could not be preserved, but by increasing the power of the crown: And this argument was used by those shameless men, who had caused all that corruption, and all that dissatisfaction.

I should be glad to know in what situation of our affairs it can be safe to reduce our troops to the usual guards and garrisons, if it cannot be done now. There is no power in Europe considerable enough to threaten us, who can have any motives to do so, if we pursue the old maxims and natural interest of Great Britain; which is, to meddle no farther with foreign squabbles, than to keep the balance even between France and Spain.

And once again it is commerce that "saves the trouble, expence, and hazard, of supporting numerous standing armies abroad to keep the conquered people in subjection; armies, who, for the most part too, if not always, enslave their own country, and ever swallow up all the advantages of the conquests."

The current U.S. policies of militarism and interventionism are directly contrary to the wisdom of Trenchard and Gordon in *Cato's Letters*. If the Founding Fathers considered these essays to be so important, why doesn't Bush and Company think likewise?

All quotations from Cato's Letters *are taken from the Liberty Fund edition edited by Ronald Hamowy, which is also available online.*

* * * * *

JEFFERSON ON THE EVILS OF WAR

The Jeffersonian principles of peace, commerce, honest friendship with all nations, and entangling alliances with none, as annunciated in Jefferson's First Inaugural Address, are no where more evident than in his opinion of war.

War and Peace

Jefferson was a man of peace. President Polk will ever be associated with the Mexican War, Lincoln with the Civil War, McKinley with the Spanish-American War, Wilson with World War I, Roosevelt with World War II, Johnson with Vietnam, Bush I with Gulf War I, and Bush II with the ongoing debacle in Iraq. But such is not the case with Jefferson. Even though he is usually considered to be one of the "great" presidents, he is not remembered as such because he was associated with a major war.

As a man of peace, he often made a contrast between the blessings of peace and the scourge of war:

> I love peace, and am anxious that we should give the world still another useful lesson, by showing to them other modes of punishing injuries than by war, which is as much a punishment to the punisher as to the sufferer.

> War has been avoided from a due sense of the miseries, and the demoralization it produces, and of the superior blessings of a state of peace and friendship with all mankind.

> I value peace, and I should unwillingly see any event take place which would render war a necessary resource.

> Having seen the people of all other nations bowed down to the earth under the wars and prodigalities of their rulers, I have cherished their opposites, peace, economy, and riddance of public debt, believing that these were the high road to public as well as private prosperity and happiness.

> Believing that the happiness of mankind is best promoted by the useful pursuits of peace, that on these alone a stable prosperity can be founded, that the evils of war are great in their endurance, and have a long reckoning for ages to come, I have used my best endeavors to keep our country uncommitted in the troubles which afflict Europe, and which assail us on every side.

> I do not believe war the most certain means of enforcing principles. Those peaceable coercions which are in the power of every nation, if undertaken in concert and in time of peace, are more likely to produce the desired effect.

We love and we value peace; we know its blessings from experience. We abhor the follies of war, and are not untried in its
distresses and calamities.

On several occasions, Jefferson presented his philosophy of peace
to some Indian tribes:

> The evils which of necessity encompass the life of man are
> sufficiently numerous. Why should we add to them by voluntarily
> distressing and destroying one another? Peace, brothers, is better
> than war. In a long and bloody war, we lose many friends, and
> gain nothing. Let us then live in peace and friendship together,
> doing to each other all the good we can.

> Born in the same land, we ought to live as brothers, doing to each
> other all the good we can, and not listening to wicked men, who
> may endeavor to make us enemies. By living in peace, we can help
> and prosper one another; by waging war, we can kill and destroy
> many on both sides; but those who survive will not be the happier
> for that.

> How much better is it for neighbours to help than to hurt one
> another. How much happier must it make them. If you will cease
> to make war on one another, if you will live in friendship with all
> mankind, you can employ all your time in providing food and
> clothing for yourselves and your families; your men will not be
> destroyed in war; and your women and children will lie down to
> sleep in their cabins without fear of being surprised by their
> enemies and killed or carried away. Your numbers will be
> increased instead of diminishing, and you will live in plenty and
> in quiet.

The Evils of War

Because Jefferson was a man of peace, he considered war to be a
great evil:

> I abhor war and view it as the greatest scourge of mankind.

> The insults & injuries committed on us by both the belligerent
> parties, from the beginning of 1793 to this day, & still continuing,
> cannot now be wiped off by engaging in war with one of them.

> I have seen enough of one war never to wish to see another.

One war, such as that of our Revolution, is enough for one life.

The most successful war seldom pays for its losses.

War is as much a punishment to the punisher as to the sufferer.

War is an instrument entirely inefficient toward redressing wrong; and multiplies, instead of indemnifying losses.

We have obtained by a peaceable appeal to justice, in four months, what we should not have obtained under seven years of war, the loss of one hundred thousand lives, an hundred millions of additional debt, many hundred millions worth of produce and property lost for want of market, or in seeking it, and that demoralization which war super-induces on the human mind.

Great sacrifices of interest have certainly been made by our nation under the difficulties latterly forced upon us by transatlantic powers. But every candid and reflecting mind must agree with you, that while these were temporary and bloodless, they were calculated to avoid permanent subjection to foreign law and tribute, relinquishment of independent rights, and the burthens, the havoc, and desolations of war.

War and the Nations

Jefferson did not consider a nation to be great because of its military might: "Wars and contentions, indeed, fill the pages of history with more matter. But more blessed is that nation whose silent course of happiness furnishes nothing for history to say." He considered war between nations to be "the consequence of a want of respectability in the national character." Regarding the attitude toward war of the people of the United States, Jefferson believed that "no country, perhaps, was ever so thoroughly against war as ours. These dispositions pervade every description of its citizens, whether in or out of office."

He knew firsthand the folly of getting involved in European wars:

Wars with any European powers are devoutly to be deprecated.

For years we have been looking as spectators on our brethren in Europe, afflicted by all those evils which necessarily follow an abandonment of the moral rules which bind men and nations together. Connected with them in friendship and commerce, we have happily so far kept aloof from their calamitous conflicts, by a steady observance of justice towards all, by much forbearance and multiplied sacrifices. At length, however, all regard to the rights of others having been thrown aside, the belligerent powers have beset the highway of commercial intercourse with edicts which, taken together, expose our commerce and mariners, under almost every destination, a prey to their fleets and armies. Each party, indeed, would admit our commerce with themselves, with the view of associating us in their war against the other. But we have wished war with neither.

It is much to be desired that war may be avoided, if circumstances will admit. Nor in the present maniac state of Europe, should I estimate the point of honor by the ordinary scale. I believe we shall on the contrary, have credit with the world, for having made the avoidance of being engaged in the present unexampled war, our first object.

The cannibals of Europe are going to eating one another again. A war between Russia and Turkey is like the battle of the kite and snake. Whichever destroys the other, leaves a destroyer the less for the world. This pugnacious humor of mankind seems to be the law of his nature, one of the obstacles to too great multiplication provided in the mechanism of the Universe. The cocks of the henyard kill one another up. Bears, bulls, rams, do the same. And the horse, in his wild state, kills all the young males, until worn down with age and war, some vigorous youth kills him, and takes to himself the harem of females. I hope we shall prove how much happier for man the Quaker policy is, and that the life of the feeder is better than that of the fighter; and it is some consolation that the desolation by these maniacs of one part of the earth is the means of improving it in other parts. Let the latter be our office, and let us milk the cow, while the Russian holds her by the horns, and the Turk by the tail.

He recognized that geography was one of the great advantages of the United States: "The insulated state in which nature has placed the American continent should so far avail it that no spark of war kindled in the other quarters of the globe should be wafted across the wide oceans which separate us from them." With a very few exceptions, the United States has always had to cross oceans to wage its wars.

Jefferson realized that the push for war comes, not from the people in the nations, but from the governments of the nations:

We have received a report that the French Directory has proposed a declaration of war against the United States to the Council of Ancients, who have rejected it. Thus we see two nations, who love one another affectionately, brought by the ill temper of their executive administrations, to the very brink of a necessity to imbrue their hands in the blood of each other.

The agents of the two people [United States and France] are either great bunglers or great rascals, when they cannot preserve that peace which is the universal wish of both.

The people now see that France has sincerely wished peace, and their seducers [federalists] have wished war, as well for the loaves and fishes which arise out of war expenses, as for the chance of changing the Constitution, while the people should have time to contemplate nothing but the levies of men and money.

No one wakes up in the morning with the desire to drop bombs on people in foreign countries that he does not know, have never injured him in any way, and are no threat to him or his family. This desire is always government induced and government sponsored. When it comes to mass murder, the state takes a backseat to no one.

Jefferson thought it beneficial for a nation to avoid war:

Never was so much false arithmetic employed on any subject, as that which has been employed to persuade nations that it is their interest to go to war. Were the money which it has cost to gain, at the close of a long war, a little town, or a little territory, the right to cut wood here, or to catch fish there, expended in improving what they already possess, in making roads, opening rivers, building ports, improving the arts, and finding employment for their idle poor, it would render them much stronger, much wealthier and happier. This I hope will be our wisdom.

Jefferson believed that the best policy for the United States toward other nations was one of friendship and nonintervention:

Unmeddling with the affairs of other nations, we had hoped that our distance and our dispositions would have left us free, in the example and indulgence of peace with all the world.

To cherish and maintain the rights and liberties of our citizens, and to ward from them the burthens, the miseries, and the crimes of war, by a just and friendly conduct toward all nations, were among the most obvious and important duties of those to whom the management of their public interests have been confided; and happy shall we be if a conduct guided by these views on our part, shall secure to us a reciprocation of peace and justice from other nations.

The desire to preserve our country from the calamities and ravages of war, by cultivating a disposition, and pursuing a conduct, conciliatory and friendly to all nations, has been sincerely entertained and faithfully followed.

He much preferred commerce to war: "War is not the best engine for us to resort to; nature has given us one in our commerce, which, if properly managed, will be a better instrument for obliging the interested nations of Europe to treat us with justice." The current U.S. foreign policy of belligerency, intervention, hegemony, and subjugation is a far cry from the example of Jefferson.

The Advent of War

It is true that Jefferson did believe in war under certain circumstances:

If ever there was a holy war, it was that which saved our liberties and gave us independence.

It is our duty still to endeavor to avoid war; but if it shall actually take place, no matter by whom brought on, we must defend ourselves. If our house be on fire, without inquiring whether it was fired from within or without, we must try to extinguish it. In that, I have no doubt, we shall act as one man.

Obviously, traversing oceans to bomb places that many Americans cannot even locate on a map would not fall into this category.

But even though Jefferson realized that war might take place, he had his doubts as to whether we would be better off at its conclusion: "If we are forced into war [with France], we must give up political differences of opinion, and unite as one man to defend our country. But whether at the close of such a war, we should be as free as we are now, God knows." If a war was necessary then it should not be undertaken "till our revenue shall be entirely liberated from debt. Then it will suffice for war, without creating new debt or taxes." But Jefferson opposed "taxing the industry of our fellow citizens to accumulate treasure for wars to happen we know not when and which might not perhaps happen but from the temptations offered by that treasure."

He also did not believe in the bloodthirsty doctrine of "total war" that the United States has engaged in since 1862. In a model treaty drawn up while he was in France, Jefferson contended that if contracting parties went to war, their trade should not be interrupted, prisoners were to be given good treatment, merchants were to be given time to settle their affairs and depart peacefully from enemy territory, and women, children, and scholars were to be considered non-combatants. (It is inconceivable that Jefferson, or any of the Founding Fathers, could ever have considered women serving in combat or semi-combat roles à la Jessica Lynch.)

On actually abolishing war, Jefferson was certainly no utopian, and stated: "I hope it is practicable, by improving the mind and morals of society, to lessen the disposition to war; but of its abolition I despair."

The Declaration of War

Jefferson was particularly concerned about the executive branch of government having the war power. Our modern Jeffersonian in Congress, Rep. Ron Paul (R–Tex.), was one of the few legislators to voice similar concerns as the U.S. was poised to invade Iraq. Here again is Jefferson:

> The power of declaring war being with the Legislature, the Executive should do nothing necessarily committing them to decide for war in preference of non-intercourse, which will be preferred by a great many.

> I opposed the right of the President to declare anything future on the question, Shall there or shall there not be war?

> Considering that Congress alone is constitutionally invested with the power of changing our condition from peace to war, I have thought it my duty to await their authority for using force in any degree which could be avoided. I have barely instructed the officers stationed in the neighborhood of the aggressions to protect our citizens from violence, to patrol within the borders actually delivered to us, and not to go out of them but when necessary to repel an inroad or to rescue a citizen or his property.

> As the Executive cannot decide the question of war on the affirmative side, neither ought it to do so on the negative side, by preventing the competent body from deliberating on the question.

> Congress [must] be called [if there] is a justifiable cause of war;

and as the Executive cannot decide the question of war on the affirmative side, neither ought it to do so on the negative side by preventing the competent body from deliberating on the question.

We have already given in example one effectual check to the Dog of war by transferring the power of letting him loose from the Executive to the Legislative body, from those who are to spend to those who are to pay.

The making reprisal on a nation is a very serious thing. Remonstrance and refusal of satisfaction ought to precede; and when reprisal follows, it is considered as an act of war, and never yet failed to produce it in the case of a nation able to make war; besides, if the case were important enough to require reprisal, and ripe for that step, Congress must be called on to take it; the right of reprisal being expressly lodged with them by the Constitution, and not with the Executive.

The question of war being placed by the Constitution with the Legislature alone, respect to that [makes] it [the Executive's] duty to restrain the operations of our militia to those merely defensive; and considerations involving the public satisfaction, and peculiarly my own, require that the decision of that question, whichever way it be, should be pronounced definitely by the Legislature themselves.

Standing Armies

Like the British Cato and the American Brutus, Jefferson was averse to standing armies:

There are instruments so dangerous to the rights of the nation and which place them so totally at the mercy of their governors that those governors, whether legislative or executive, should be restrained from keeping such instruments on foot but in well-defined cases. Such an instrument is a standing army.

Were armies to be raised whenever a speck of war is visible in our horizon, we never should have been without them. Our resources would have been exhausted on dangers which have never happened, instead of being reserved for what is really to take place.

Nor is it conceived needful or safe that a standing army should be kept up in time of peace.

The spirit of this country is totally adverse to a large military force.

In another statement regarding relations with the Indians, Jefferson again decried standing armies:

We must do as the Spaniards and English do. Keep them in peace by liberal and constant presents. Another powerful motive is that in this way we may leave no pretext for raising or continuing an army. Every rag of an Indian depredation will, otherwise, serve as a ground to raise troops with those who think a standing army and a public debt necessary for the happiness of the United States, and we shall never be permitted to get rid of either.

Conclusion

Jefferson was not alone in his views on the evils of war. Most of the Founding Fathers thought likewise:

Of all the enemies to public liberty, war is perhaps the most to be dreaded because it comprises and develops the germ of every other. ~ James Madison

There was never a good war or a bad peace. ~ Benjamin Franklin

Preparation for war is a constant stimulus to suspicion and ill will. ~ James Monroe

While there are knaves and fools in the world, there will be wars in it. ~ John Jay

The fiery and destructive passions of war reign in the human breast with much more powerful sway than the mild and benefi-cent sentiments of peace. ~ Alexander Hamilton

My first wish is to see this plague of mankind, war, banished from the earth. ~ George Washington

But today, instead of sages like Madison, Franklin, Monroe, Jay, Hamilton, Washington, and Jefferson, we have warmongers like Bush, Cheney, Libby, Feith, Wolfowitz, Rumsfeld, Perle, and Abrams. And instead of the wisdom of the Founding Fathers, the American public is fed a steady diet of David Frum, William Kristol, Sean Hannity, Jonah

Goldberg, Max Boot, Fox News, and the *War Street Journal*.

Jefferson was not perfect, and he was at times inconsistent, but overall his principles were sound. The senseless waste of American lives in Bush's Iraq fiasco could have been avoided if Jefferson's aversion to war had been followed instead of forsaken, as have the other sound principles of the Founders.

These quotations from Jefferson have been taken from a variety of sources. Most are from the now out-of-print volume, The Complete Jefferson, *edited and assembled by Saul K. Padover. However, other similar volumes of Jefferson's writings are available, and much is now available online, such as this collection of Jefferson's letters.*

* * * * *

BENJAMIN RUSH'S PEACE OFFICE

It sounds like a radical idea today, just like it must have sounded like a radical idea when it was first proposed over two hundred years ago. We certainly need it more today than we have needed it at any time in U.S. history. And no, it's not a balanced budget, campaign finance reform, or term limits for members of Congress.

One of the first three departments created in 1789 in the new executive branch of the government of the United States was the War Department. This department, which contained the army, existed side by side with the Department of the Navy (created in 1798) until both departments were reorganized in 1947 as the Department of Defense (DOD), along with the newly created Department of the Air Force. Judging from the interventionist and aggressive actions of the U.S. military since then, the DOD was certainly misnamed, and should more accurately be known as the Department of War.

If the DOD was not so busy providing security, guarding borders, patrolling coasts, and training troops in other countries, then perhaps it could have defended the country on September 11, 2001, or at least its headquarters, the Pentagon. It is obvious that the current purpose of the DOD is to fight those foreign wars that Jefferson warned us against. If the DOD is supposed to defend the country, then why do we need a Department of Homeland Security? According to one of the forgotten Founding Fathers, Benjamin Rush (1745–1813), who died on this date 193 years ago, we don't need either one.

Known as the Father of American Psychiatry, Rush (not to be

confused with that conservative windbag Rush Limbaugh) was a noted physician and Professor of Medicine at the University of Pennsylvania. But he was also a member of the Continental Congress and a signer of the Declaration of Independence. Near the end of his life, he served as Treasurer of the National Mint.

Rush was also a prolific author. In 1798 he collected twenty-five of his previous writings and published them in a volume he titled *Essays, Literary, Moral, and Philosophical* (Philadelphia: Printed by Thomas & Samuel F. Bradford, 1798). One of the essays had been previously published in *Banneker's Almanac*. This was the work of Benjamin Banneker (1731–1806), a noted black scientist, astronomer, and surveyor who published an almanac from 1792–1797. Rush's radical essay was called "A Plan of a Peace-Office for the United States."

A PLAN OF A PEACE-OFFICE FOR THE UNITED STATES

Among the defects which have been pointed out in the Federal Constitution by its antifederal enemies, it is much to be lamented that no person has taken notice of its total silence upon the subject of an *office* of the utmost importance to the welfare of the United States, that is, an office for promoting and preserving perpetual *peace* in our country.

It is to be hoped that no objection will be made to the establishment of such an office, while we are engaged in a war with the Indians, for as the *War-Office* of the United States was established in time of peace, it is equally reasonable that a *Peace-Office* should be established in the time of *war*.

The plan of this office is as follows:

I. Let a Secretary of the Peace be appointed to preside in this office, who shall be perfectly free from all the present absurd and vulgar European prejudices upon the subject of government; let him be a genuine republican and a sincere Christian, for the principles of republicanism and Christianity are no less friendly to universal and perpetual peace, than they are to universal and equal liberty.

II. Let a power be given to this Secretary to establish and maintain free-schools in every city, village and township of the United States; and let him be made responsible for the talents, principles, and morals, of all his schoolmasters. Let the youth of our country be carefully instructed in reading, writing, and arithmetic, and in the doctrines of a religion of some king: the Christian religion should be preferred to all others; for it belongs to this religion exclusively to teach us not only to cultivate peace with men, but to forgive, nay more—to love our very enemies. It belongs to it further to teach us that the Supreme Being alone possesses a power to take away human life, and that we rebel against his laws, whenever we undertake to execute death in any way whatever upon any of his creatures.

III. Let every family in the United States be furnished at the public expense, by the Secretary of this office, with a copy of an American edition of the BIBLE. This measure has become the more necessary in our country, since the banishment of the bible, as a school-book, from most of the schools in the United States. Unless the price of this book be paid for by the public, there is reason to fear that in a few years it will be me with only in courts of justice or in magistrates' offices; and should the absurd mode of establishing truth by kissing this sacred book fall into disuse, it may probably, in the course of the next generation, be seen only as a curiosity on a shelf in a public museum.

IV. Let the following sentence be inscribed in letters of gold over the doors of every State and Court house in the United States.

THE SON OF MAN CAME INTO THE WORLD, NOT TO DESTROY MEN'S LIVES, BUT TO SAVE THEM.

I. To inspire a veneration for human life, and an horror at the shedding of blood, let all those laws be repealed which authorize juries, judges, sheriffs, or hangmen to assume the resentments of individuals and to commit murder in cold blood in any case whatever. Until this reformation in our code of penal jurisprudence takes place, it will be in vain to attempt to introduce universal and perpetual peace in our country.

II. To subdue that passion for war, which education, added to human depravity, have made universal, a familiarity with the instruments of death, as well as all military shows, should be carefully avoided. For which reason, militia laws should every where be repealed, and military dresses and military titles should be laid aside: reviews tend to lessen the horrors of a battle by connecting them with the charms of order; militia laws generate idleness and vice, and thereby produce the wars they are said to prevent; military dresses fascinate the minds of young men, and lead them from serious and useful professions; were there no *uniforms*, there would probably be no armies; lastly, military titles feed vanity, and keep up ideas in the mind which lessen a sense of the folly and miseries of war.

III. In the last place, let a large room, adjoining the federal hall, be appropriated for transacting the business and preserving all the records of this *office*. Over the door of this room let there be a sign, on which the figures of a LAMB, a DOVE and an OLIVE BRANCH should be painted, together with the following inscriptions in letters of gold:

PEACE ON EARTH—GOOD-WILL TO MAN.
AH! WHY WILL MEN FORGET THAT THEY ARE BRETHREN?

Within this apartment let there be a collection of plough-shares and pruning-hooks made out of swords and spears; and on each of the walls of the apartment, the following pictures as large as the life:

1. A lion eating straw with an ox, and an adder playing upon the lips of a child.

2. An Indian boiling his venison in the same pot with a citizen of Kentucky.

3. Lord Cornwallis and Tippoo Saib, under the shade of a sycamore-tree in the East Indies, drinking Madeira wine together out of the same decanter.

4. A group of French and Austrian soldiers dancing arm and arm, under a bower erected in the neighbourhood of Mons.

5. A St. Domingo planter, a man of color, and a native of Africa, legislating together in the same colonial assembly.

To complete the entertainment of this delightful apartment, let a group of young ladies, clad in white robes, assemble every day at a certain hour, in a gallery to be erected for the purpose, and sing odes, and hymns, and anthems in praise of the blessings of peace.

One of these songs should consist of the following lines.

Peace o'er the world her olive want extends,
And white-rob'd innocence from heaven descends;
All crimes shall cease, and ancient frauds shall fail,
Returning justice lifts aloft her scale.

In order more deeply to affect the minds of the citizens of the United States with the blessings of peace, by *contrasting* them with the evils of war, let the following inscriptions be painted upon the sign which is placed over the door of the War Office.

1. An office for butchering the human species.

2. A Widow and Orphan making office.

3. A broken bone making office.

4. A Wooden leg making office.

5. An office for the creating of public and private vices.

6. An office for creating a public debt.

7. An office for creating speculators, stock jobbers, and bankrupts.

8. An office for creating famine.

9. An office for creating pestilential diseases.

10. An office for creating poverty, and the destruction of liberty, and national happiness.

In the lobby of this office let there be painted representations of all the common military instruments of death, also human skulls, broken bones, unburied and putrefying dead bodies, hospitals crowded with sick and wounded soldiers, villages on fire, mothers in besieged towns eating the flesh of their children, ships sinking in the ocean, rivers dyed with blood, and extensive plains without a tree or fence, or any object, but the ruins of deserted farm houses.

Above this group of woeful figures,—let the following words be inserted, in red characters to represent human blood,

"NATIONAL GLORY."

The Founding Fathers of the United States, even with all of their blemishes and inconsistencies, were miles ahead of the vermin called politicians we are presently cursed with. Contrary to George WMD Bush, who insists that he is "a war president" who makes "decisions with war on my mind," the other Founding Fathers often echoed Benjamin Rush's sentiments on the evils of war:

> Of all the enemies to public liberty, war is perhaps the most to be dreaded because it comprises and develops the germ of every other. ~ James Madison

> There was never a good war or a bad peace. ~ Benjamin Franklin

> Preparation for war is a constant stimulus to suspicion and ill will. ~ James Monroe

> While there are knaves and fools in the world, there will be wars in it. ~ John Jay

> The fiery and destructive passions of war reign in the human breast with much more powerful sway than the mild and beneficent sentiments of peace. ~ Alexander Hamilton

> My first wish is to see this plague of mankind, war, banished from the earth. ~ George Washington

It is both a grave injustice and a great display of ignorance that those who speak out for peace and against the evils of war are often labeled by blind Republican Bush apologists, crazed conservative armchair warriors, and wannabe-writer, e-mail debater, Christian warmongers as hippies, peaceniks, Quakers, traitors, leftists, anti-Americans, or antiwar weenies. Although their support for this war may eventually wane, they can be counted on to support the next one—to their "shame and everlasting contempt" (Daniel 12:2).

Benjamin Rush's "Plan of a Peace-office" was quoted in its entirety from The Selected Writings of Benjamin Rush *(New York: Philosophical Library, 1947, pp. 19–23.*

* * * * *

THE WARMONGER'S CHRISTMAS CAROLS

It begins soon after the Thanksgiving holiday. You hear them in stores. You listen to them on the radio. You sing them in church. You probably have some of them on a CD. I am referring, of course, to Christmas carols, like say: *God Rest Ye Merry Gentlemen, O Christmas*

Tree, O Come All Ye Faithful, It Came Upon the Midnight Clear, Angels from the Realms of Glory, O Little Town of Bethlehem, The First Noel.

Although Christmas is the time when people celebrate the birth of the Prince of Peace (Isaiah 9:6), if some people were honest they would have to acknowledge that they also honor Mars, the Roman god of war. And if this wasn't bad enough, they honor him every day of the year, not just on December 25. They honor Mars every time they claim to support the troops.

Americans are in love with the U.S. military. As the fiasco that is the war in Iraq has shown, it doesn't matter how senseless the war, it doesn't matter how many lies the war is based on, it doesn't matter how much the Bush administration manipulated intelligence, it doesn't matter how much the war costs, it doesn't matter how long the war lasts, it doesn't matter how many thousands of American soldiers are killed or injured, and it certainly doesn't matter how many hundreds of thousands of Iraqis are killed or injured—too many Americans can be found who still mindlessly repeat the refrain of "support the troops." Some American Christians chime in with their "obey the powers that be" mantra. Coupled with the melody of "we can't just cut and run" and the chorus of "it is better to fight them over there so we don't have to fight them over here," we have a four-part warmonger harmony.

Because it is the Christmas season, and the sound of Christmas carols is everywhere, I have taken the liberty to rewrite the traditional carols that I have mentioned above.

If Americans who are so enamored with the military were honest, this is what they should really be singing during this time of the year:

> God rest ye merry soldiers
> Let nothing you dismay,
> Remember, the U.S. military
> Still fights on Christmas day;
> To kill those darn Iraqis
> Because they have gone astray.
> O tidings of destruction and death,
> Destruction and death.
> O tidings of destruction and death.
>
> O Uniform! O Uniform!
> I can kill when I wear thee.
> O Uniform! O Uniform!
> I can kill when I wear thee.

Not only when the summer's here,
But also when 'tis cold and drear.
O Uniform! O Uniform!
I can kill when I wear thee.

O come all ye soldiers
Joyful and triumphant,
O come ye, O come ye to Baghdad.
Come and behold them,
Muslim worshippers of Allah.
O come, let us bomb them,
O come, let us maim them,
O come, let us kill them,
Ragheads galore.

It came upon the midnight clear,
That horrible sound of old,
Of soldiers flying near the earth,
With bombs to drop from their hold.
"Peace on the earth, goodwill to men
From America's mighty military!"
Iraq in solemn horror lay
To hear the bombs zing.

Soldiers from the U.S. military,
Fire your weapons o'er all Baghdad.
Ye who seek to kill for glory,
Now have a chance to make your heart glad:
Fire your weapon,
Fire your weapon,
Fire your weapon for Bush the king!

O little town of Baghdad
How still we see thee lie;
Above all thy destruction
The U.S. air force flies.
And in thy dark streets shineth
America's military might.
The bombs and bullets of all us here
Will be unleashed on thee tonight.

The first bullet, George Bush did say
Was for certain poor Iraqis in deserts as they lay,
In sand where they lay all night in a heap
On a March '03 night that was so deep.

Oh well, Oh well, Oh well, Oh well;
Now is the time for us to blow you to hell!

"How irreverent," says the supporter of the U.S. military. "Sacrilegious," says the defender of the war in Iraq. "Blasphemous," says the Christian warmonger. Is that so? Why is it not considered irreverent when people ask God to bless the troops? Why is it not considered sacrilegious when people pray that God would protect the troops? Why is it not considered blasphemous when Christians campaign for Bush and defend his war?

For those who refuse to listen to anything I say about the military because I never "served"—and would in fact prefer that I shred all the copies of my book, *Christianity and War and Other Essays Against the Warfare State*—I highly recommend the work of West Point graduate and Vietnam veteran Andrew Bacevich. His recent book is called *The New American Militarism: How Americans Are Seduced by War* (Oxford, 2005). I have previously written about his book in the context of the conservative Christian love affair with the U.S. military. There is still time to get the book in time for Christmas. If there is one book to give to current and former members of the military, as well as their enthusiasts, this is the book.

War brings out the worst in young men. What we tolerate from them, and what they tolerate from themselves, would normally be repugnant to any civilized person. It is tolerated because it is sanitized (in the minds of many) because a soldier wears a uniform, is surrounded by a great company of other soldiers, and kills by government decree.

The folly of this idea can be seen in the story of the reply given to Alexander the Great (356–323 B.C.) by a captured pirate that was recounted by Augustine (354–430) sixteen hundred years ago in his famous work, *The City of God*:

> Indeed, that was an apt and true reply which was given to Alexander the Great by a pirate who had been seized. For when that king had asked the man what he meant by keeping hostile possession of the sea, he answered with bold pride, "What thou meanest by seizing the whole earth; but because I do it with a petty ship, I am called a robber, whilst thou who dost it with a great fleet art styled emperor" (book IV, chapter 4).

Writing on the causes, consequences, and lawfulness of war, along with comments on the probable practical effects of adhering to the moral law in respect to war, Jonathan Dymond (1796–1828), one young in years but old in wisdom, stated:

> Another cause of our complacency with war, and therefore another cause of war itself, consists in that callousness to human misery which the custom induces. They who are shocked at a single murder on the highway, hear with indifference of the slaughter of a thousand on the field. They whom the idea of a single corpse would thrill with terror, contemplate that of heaps of human carcasses mangled by human hands, with frigid indifference. If a murder is committed, the narrative is given in the public newspaper, with many adjectives of horror—with many expressions of commiseration, and many hopes that the perpetrator will be detected. In the next paragraph, the editor, perhaps, tells us that he has hurried in a second edition to the press, in order that he may be the first to glad the public with the intelligence, that in an engagement which has just taken place, eight hundred and fifty of the enemy were killed. Now, is not this latter intelligence eight hundred and fifty times as deplorable as the first? Yet the first is the subject of our sorrow, and this—of our joy! The inconsistency and disproportionateness which has been occasioned in our sentiments of benevolence, offers a curious moral phenomenon.

He also wrote about why wars are often so popular:

> But perhaps the most operative cause of the popularity of war, and of the facility with which we engage in it, consists in this; that an idea of glory is attached to military exploits, and of honor to the military profession. The glories of battle, and of those who perish in it, or who return in triumph to their country, are favorite topics of declamation with the historian, the biographers, and the poet. They have told us a thousands times of dying heroes, who "resign their lives amidst the joys of conquest, and, filled with their country's glory, smile in death;" and thus every excitement that eloquence and genius can command, is employed to arouse that ambition of fame which can be gratified only at the expense of blood.

It is indeed "a curious moral phenomenon" that many Americans, the vast majority of whom claim to be a Christian of one sort or another, can sing traditional Christmas carols one minute and—by defending Bush and his war, glorifying the military, and repeating their mindless mantras—sing warmonger Christmas carols the next.

* * * * *

HOW TO PREVENT A WAR WITH IRAN

The saber rattling and drum beating for war with Iran are getting louder and louder every day.

Unfortunately, some Evangelicals are among the loudest voices crying for war with Iran. President Ahmadinejad is worse than Hitler, according to the Friends of Israel Gospel Ministry. In the March/April 2007 issue of *Israel My Glory*, published by this ministry, Elwood McQuaid, the executive editor, maintains that "annihilating the Jewish state is merely a warm-up. Although the lynchpin of Ahmadinejad's crusade is a first-strike success against his near neighbor Israel, the next move is westward to Europe and then on to finish off the hated United States." Another piece in the same issue of *Israel My Glory* quotes Benjamin Netanyahu as saying that "unless the United States stops Iran from acquiring nuclear weapons, America has only two to five years left." In the recent May/June 2008 issue, we see more of the same: "Replace the name Hitler with Mahmoud Ahmadinejad who rants against his selected scapegoats, Israel and the Jewish people, blaming them for every iniquity and offering the only 'acceptable' solution: genocide and annihilation of the Jewish state. His desire is not for a 1,000-year Reich but for a global, Islamic caliphate."

The American people cannot just stop their ears and expect that all the saber rattling, drum beating, and war crying will go away after the election of a new U.S. president. We already know that John McCain—who had no problem bombing Vietnam back to the Stone Age—is a crazed warmonger. But the election of Barack Obama instead of John McCain will not mean anything different when it comes to Iran. Obama considers the danger posed by Iran to be grave and real—so much so that his goal "will be to eliminate this threat." But regardless of who occupies the U.S. presidency, there is really only one sure-fire way to prevent a war with Iran.

The fact that Iran is not a threat to the United States will not stop us from going to war. Was Iraq a threat to the United States? Was Afghanistan? Was Vietnam? Germany couldn't cross the English Channel to invade Great Britain. How was Germany a real threat to the United States? Japan was goaded into/allowed to bomb Pearl Harbor, but was Japan really a threat to the United States? Were the Central powers a threat to the United States in 1917? Was Spain a threat to the United States in 1898? None of the many incursions of U.S. troops into other countries was because of a credible threat to the United States. To say that war with Iran is justifiable because Iran *might* someday *possibly* become a threat to the United States is ludicrous. Should we go into the ghettos of U.S. cities and jail or kill young boys because they *might* grow up and become a thug and *possibly* carjack someone?

The fact that Iran is not a threat to Israel will not prevent a war with Iran. Now, whether country A is or is not a threat to country B should have no bearing on U.S. military activities. Following the wisdom of Washington and Jefferson, the United States should not have entangling alliances with *any* country. Unfortunately, the United States has many entangling alliances, and we have intractably entangled ourselves in the Middle East. The fruit of years of an aggressive, interventionist, and imperialistic U.S. foreign policy is increased hatred of both the United States and Israel.

The fact that Iran does not have a nuclear weapon, and, according to the CIA's National Intelligence Estimate, has not been working on a nuclear weapon since 2003 will not stop the Bush administration from foolishly and immorally launching a preventive strike against yet another country. Bush has even said that the NIE "in no way lessens" the threat of Iran.

It doesn't matter if Iran's nuclear program is entirely for civilian use. The United States, or Israel, or both countries, could still try to destroy anything in Iran that could possibly be used in any kind of a nuclear program. Secretary of Defense Robert Gates recently claimed that Iran "is hellbent on acquiring nuclear weapons." But the fact that Iran's civilian nuclear program *may* really be for military use or *might* in the future be converted to military use is immaterial. Three of Iran's neighbors—Israel, Pakistan, and India—have such weapons. Plus nearby China and Russia. And of course, the great Satan, the United States, not only has more nukes than any other country, it is the only country that has used them and is now currently threatening Iran.

The fact that the U.S. military is already stretched to the breaking point—"dangerously thin," according to a recent survey of military officers—is of no consequence to Bush the decider in chief, who maintains that "all options are on the table." No one in his family will ever suffer the horrors of war. The price of gas, which is certain to rise much higher in the advent of war with Iran, is inconsequential to anyone in the Bush family.

The failure of the anti-Iran resolutions introduced in the Senate (S. Res. 580) and the House (H. Con. Res. 362) to pass will not prevent a war with Iran. Congress long ago abrogated its constitutional war-making authority to the president. If Bush announced today that he ordered U.S. forces to bomb, invade, and occupy Iran, the Congress—Democrats and

Republicans—would begin allocating billions of dollars for the war effort to support the troops.

Public opinion against war with Iran is not enough to prevent such a war from taking place. We know this because of the Iraq war. When Vice President Cheney was recently told that polls showed that about two-thirds of the American people believed that the Iraq war was not worth fighting, Cheney arrogantly replied: "So?" And furthermore, U.S. presidents may be evil, but they are not stupid (okay, with one exception). Every president knows that Americans are in love with the U.S. military. Americans will support the troops no matter who they are fighting against, even if they can't locate the country of our "enemy" on a map.

The repercussions of a war with Iran would be devastating, for as Tom Engelhardt recently explained, Iran has "a remarkable capacity to inflict grievous harm locally, regionally, and globally." Since most Americans are relatively unconcerned about the number of innocent Iranians that might be wounded or killed in any U.S. military action against Iran (all Muslims are terrorists; and besides, their skin is darker than ours) or even the number of U.S. soldiers who might be wounded or killed (they enlisted of their own free will; and besides, they are defending our freedoms), I will just mention one area in which grievous harm will occur: the price of oil. A war with Iran, as Engelhardt also noted, "would result in a global oil shock of almost inconceivable proportions." And this time, it would be clear to all from the beginning that the price of oil was directly related to the war.

Engelhardt doesn't think war with Iran is likely, and I hope he is right. But when it comes to this evil administration, nothing is out of the question, nothing is off limits, nothing is too far-fetched.

But if Bush the decider in chief is determined to multiply his war crimes by attacking Iran, or giving Israel a green light (or not issuing a red light) to do so with the promise of U.S. military backup, what can be done to prevent such a war from taking place? I see only one solution: the troops.

The troops? But they are the ones who will be doing the fighting. Exactly. Bush, Cheney, Gates, Petraeus, the secretaries, under secretaries, and assistant secretaries of the Army, Navy, and Air Force, and the members of the Joints Chiefs of Staff won't be lifting a finger against Iran. Only U.S. troops—the ones who will suffer and bleed and die for a lie—will be fighting an illegal, immoral war against Iran.

But because it is only the troops that will be doing the dirty work, and because the troops greatly outnumber their commanders in the field and the bureaucrats in the Pentagon, and because it's impossible for the

American people to support the troops in their war effort if the troops themselves refuse to prosecute the war—the troops refusing to fight is the only sure-fire way to prevent a war with Iran.

Now, for this to happen, it is apparent that the hearts and minds of the troops must be changed.

The troops need to see that Iran is not a threat to the United States, that Iran is not a threat to Israel, that Iran doesn't have a nuclear weapon, that Iran is perfectly justified if it obtained a nuclear weapon, that the U.S. military is stretched to the breaking point, that the president has no constitutional authority to begin a war with Iran, and that the American people will support them in their decision.

The troops need to see that an attack on Iran would be unnecessary, unwise, unjust, illegal, immoral, and in violation of the Constitution they swore to uphold. It would be anything but fighting to defend our freedoms.

The troops need to see that attacking Iran perverts the purpose of the military. Defending the United States against attack or invasion is admirable; attacking and invading foreign countries is not. In defense of the United States, the U.S. military should guard U.S. borders, patrol U.S. coasts, and enforce no-fly zones over U.S. skies. It should not do these things in other countries, and should certainly not induce other countries to do these things because of a threat by the United States.

The troops need to see that American foreign policy is responsible for much evil throughout the world. It is contrary to the wise, noninterventionist foreign policy of the Founding Fathers. So contrary in fact that the Founders wouldn't recognize what their constitutional, federated republic has become. Fighting an offensive, foreign war perpetuates an evil U.S. foreign policy.

The troops need to see that they are the ones who will be responsible for waging an unjust war. They are the ones who will be dropping the bombs and firing the bullets. They are the ones who will be doing the wounding and killing. They are the ones who will be destroying property and infrastructure.

The troops need to see that there are some orders that they just shouldn't obey—even if they come directly from their commander in chief. Why is it that Americans insist that German soldiers should have disobeyed any commands to kill Jews, but that American soldiers should always obey their superiors? In reality, however, Americans really don't believe that all orders should be obeyed. If an American soldier were ordered to kill the president or to kill his mother, we would condemn him if he obeyed. What we really expect of our soldiers is to unconditionally obey any order that involves the killing of any foreigner in any country. But this is something that no soldier with an ounce of morality should do.

If the troops *don't* see these things, then war with Iran will come should the president be dumb enough, and evil enough, to order an attack, an invasion, a regime change, or a preemptive strike.

But if the troops *do* see these things, war with Iran will be impossible. Bush, or any future president, can try to lie the country into war as much as he wants, but the troops refusing to fight an unjust war will prevent any conflict from occurring.

If a U.S. soldier really wants to be a hero, he should refuse to fight in any foreign war. "Cursed be he that taketh reward to slay an innocent person" (Deuteronomy 27:25).

* * * * *

SAYING NO TO WAR

Apologists and defenders of Bush's global war on terror have always had one thing they could fall back on should none of their other lame arguments for war, militarism, the suppression of civil liberties, an imperial presidency, and an aggressive foreign policy be convincing: to dissent when America is at war is to be un-American or anti-American.

Not any more.

This pathetic argument has been laid to rest once and for all by Murray Polner and Thomas E. Woods with the publication of *We Who Dared to Say No to War: American Antiwar Writing from 1812 to Now* (Basic Books, 2008). Polner, who has written for the *Nation*, and Woods, who has written for the *American Conservative*, are as opposite politically as two men can be. They are united in this book by one, great, noble idea—mass murder is wrong, even when undertaken by governments.

Polner and Woods claim to have assembled "some of the most compelling, vigorously argued, and just plain interesting speeches, articles, poetry, and book excerpts" in the American antiwar tradition. Their assertion is accurate. What will be a surprise to many Americans is that this tradition includes such anti-Americans as Daniel Webster, Henry Clay, William Jennings Bryan, Helen Keller, Senator Robert Taft, Governor Robert La Follette, and Presidents Abraham Lincoln and Dwight Eisenhower.

Yes, the book is an anthology, but an eminently readable one, and on a subject of grave importance. The format is quite simple: a brief introduction to each major war in American history is given followed by "some of the most memorable, if largely neglected, writings and speeches by those Americans who have opposed our government's addiction to war." Thus, the selections in the book cover the War of 1812, the Mexican War, the Civil War, the Spanish-American and Philippine-American Wars, World War I, World War II, the Vietnam War, and the Iraq War. The authors have also wisely included a chapter on the Cold War and a concluding chapter in which "Americans from the past two centuries address various aspects of war." The whole book actually addresses all aspects of war, including militarism, imperialism, empire, conscription, and government propaganda.

It is this latter point that is especially pertinent, for as the authors point out in their introduction: "The history of American war is littered with propaganda, falsehoods, a compliant media, the manipulation of patriotic sentiment—everything we've seen recently, we've seen before. Time and again."

Since each of the seventy selections in this anthology contains some nugget, I will have to limit my examples to one from each war.

During the War of 1812, Daniel Webster delivered a speech in Congress disparaging conscription as inconsistent with free government, civil liberty, and the Constitution:

> Where is it written in the Constitution, in what article or section is
> it contained, that you may take children from their parents, and
> parents from their children, and compel them to fight the battles of
> any war, in which the folly or the wickedness of Government may
> engage it?

During the Mexican War, future president Abraham Lincoln, then a member of the U.S. House of Representatives, gave a speech in Congress against the war in which he denounced President Polk as a "bewildered, confounded, and miserably perplexed man." Polner and Woods point out in their introduction to the Mexican War that "Congress voted 85 to 81 to censure President Polk, declaring that the war had been 'unnecessarily and unconstitutionally begun by the President of the United States.'"

The authors include in their chapter on the so-Civil War the speech of Ohio congressman Clement Vallandigham that was declared to be an act of treason and resulted in him being seized, tried before a military tribunal, and deported from the Union:

> I assert here, to-day, as a Representative, that every principal act
> of the Administration since has been a glaring usurpation of
> power, and a palpable and dangerous violation of that very

Constitution which this civil war is professedly waged to support.

Three-time Democratic Party candidate for president William Jennings Bryan is featured in the chapter on the Spanish-American and Philippine-American Wars. Although he initially supported the Spanish-American War, he objected to the later occupation of the Philippines:

> Those who would have this nation enter upon a career of empire must consider not only the effect of imperialism on the Filipinos but they must also calculate its effects upon our own nation. We cannot repudiate the principle of self-government in the Philippines without weakening that principle here.

Bryan later resigned as secretary of state under Woodrow Wilson because he felt that Wilson was not committed to avoiding American involvement in World War I.

Although Helen Keller could neither see nor hear, she was more perceptive than most members of Congress when it came to the United States entering World War I. In her speech before the Women's Peace Party of New York City in 1916 she told the truth about the war:

> Congress is not preparing to defend the people of the United States. It is planning to protect the capital of American speculators and investors in Mexico, South America, China and the Philippine Islands. Incidentally this preparation will benefit the manufactures of munitions and war machines.
>
> The clever ones, up in the high places know how childish and silly the workers are. They know that if the government dresses them up in khaki and gives them a rifle and starts them off with a brass band and waving banners, they will go forth to fight valiantly for their own enemies. They are taught that brave men die for their country's honor. What a price to pay for an abstraction—the lives of millions of young men; other millions crippled and blinded for life; existence made hideous for still more millions of human beings; the achievement and inheritance of generations swept away in a moment—and nobody better off for all the misery!

World War II, which many Americans consider to be "good" or "necessary," was neither. Polner and Woods describe in their introduction to this war the America First Committee (AFC), which "prevented the U.S. from becoming even more involved in the European war for some two years." The AFC included among its estimated eight hundred thousand members

Gerald Ford, John F. Kennedy, Frank Lloyd Wright, E. E. Cummings, Walt Disney, and Charles Lindbergh. The Committee was unfortunately disbanded after Japan attacked Pearl Harbor.

Given the almost universal American acceptance of the necessity of American involvement in World War II, this is the weakest chapter in the book, with the authors including only five selections, two of which concern the draft, and two others that were written before Pearl Harbor. Nevertheless, the other piece that is included is a classic. It is "Two Votes Against War: 1917 and 1941," by Jeannette Rankin, the only member of Congress to vote against U.S. involvement in both world wars. Rankin recounts how, when the first anniversary of the congressional vote to enter World War II came around, she "extended remarks in the record in which I brought out some points which may well be recalled at the present critical moment." She then proceeded to remind the Congress of a number of instances in which it was apparent that the United States was guilty of provoking Japan.

On World War II not being "good," Polner and Woods point out that it "resulted in some sixty million deaths, mainly nonmilitary." This alone is enough to make the war anything but good. On the war not being "necessary," I highly recommend the recently published *Human Smoke*, by Nicholson Baker, and *Churchill, Hitler, and the Unnecessary War*, by Pat Buchanan.

The Cold War is another war that most Americans felt was necessary. In their introduction to this chapter, Polner and Woods relate how during this period: "Soviet capabilities were consistently exaggerated." This should come as no surprise, as the U.S. government lies on a regular basis about all manner of things. Must reading in this chapter is "Those Who Protest: The Transformation of the Conservative Movement," by Robert LeFevre, businessman and founder of the Freedom School in Colorado Springs, Colorado. Here LeFevre explains how conservatives, who were originally in favor of peace, individualism, and smaller government, turned away from these ideals in the name of fighting communism. Although the Cold War has been over for twenty years, our authors correctly note its legacy: "The Soviet Union may be long gone, but the military-industrial complex that got such a boost from the Cold War, and the interventionist thinking that came to dominate policymaking circles, are as strong as ever." Thank conservatives.

The war in Vietnam divided Americans as no other. Polner and Woods include many excellent selections here, but I think the one that carries the most weight is that of General David Shoup, former commandant of the Marines. Since it is very short, I here give the general's remarks in their entirety:

> You read, you're televised to, you're radioed to, you're preached to, that it is necessary that we have our armed forces fight, get killed and maimed, and kill and maim other human beings including women and children because now is the time we must stop some kind of unwanted ideology from creeping up on this nation. The place we chose to do this is 8,000 miles away with water in between. . . .

> The reasons fed to us are too shallow and narrow for students, as well as other citizens. Especially so, when you realize that what is happening, no matter how carefully and slowly the military escalation has progressed, may be projecting us toward world catastrophe. Surely it is confusing. . . .

> I want to tell you, I don't think the whole of Southeast Asia, as related to the present and future safety and freedom of the people of this country, is worth the life or limb of a single American.

> I believe that if we had and would keep our dirty, bloody, dollar-crooked fingers out of the business of these nations so full of depressed, exploited people, they will arrive at a solution of their own. That they design and want. That they fight and work for. And if unfortunately their revolution must be of a violent type because the "haves" refuse to share with the "have-nots" by any peaceful method, at least what they get will be their own, and not the American style, which they don't want and above all don't want crammed down their throats by Americans.

The current war in Iraq—Bush's war—is also harshly criticized in this volume. In "Why Did Bush Destroy Iraq?," Paul Craig Roberts, assistant secretary of the treasury under Ronald Reagan, sums it up nicely:

> Every reason we have been given for the Iraqi invasion has proved to be false. Saddam Hussein had no weapons of mass destruction. Reports from UN weapons inspectors, top level U.S. intelligence officials, Secretary of the Treasury Paul O'Neill, and leaked top-secret documents from the British cabinet all make it unequivocally clear that the Bush regime first decided to invade Iraq and then looked around for a reason.

Although the concluding chapter in *We Who Dared to Say No to War* contains many hard-hitting essays, the opening selection of a speech by John Quincy Adams shows us just how far we have come in this country. I am referring, of course, to his famous statement that America "goes not abroad in search of monsters to destroy." U.S. foreign policy is about as far removed from that of the Founding Fathers as it could possibly be.

I should also mention the wonderful appendix in this book on "Great Antiwar Films," by Butler Shaffer.

The sad thing that *We Who Dared to Say No to War* manifests is that after all the lies and propaganda of one war have been exposed, Americans are all too willing to rally around their government, their president, and their troops for the next war.

This book is a stepping-stone to further enlightenment. How many Americans even know that the United States fought wars against Great Britain and Mexico between the Revolutionary War and the Civil War? How many Americans who know that the United States fought in World War I also know about the Spanish-American and the Philippine-American Wars that were fought just a few years earlier? And of course, how many Americans realize that there has been vocal opposition to these wars from all over the political spectrum?

All patriotic Americans should say no to war. They should say no to war and its evil stepchildren of militarism, imperialism, empire, nationalism, jingoism, gunboat diplomacy, torture, extraordinary rendition, domestic spying, conscription, nation building, regime change, the military-industrial complex, the warfare state, government propaganda, and an interventionist foreign policy. *We Who Dared to Say No to War* is a reminder that those who say no to such things are not alone.

* * * * *

THE CRIME THAT CANNOT BE WIPED AWAY

One of the great tragedies of history is that too many men have been all too willing to kill for the state. Even worse is that most of the killing has taken place in senseless and unjust wars.

Regardless of who orders them into battle, regardless of whether they are drafted, and regardless of the reasons they are told the war is necessary, it is the soldiers who do the actual fighting, maiming, and killing. This has been true throughout history.

Even if we accept Hannah Arendt's principle that "in general the degree of responsibility increases as we draw further away from the man who uses the fatal instrument with his own hands," the soldiers at the bottom still bear diffused responsibility for their actions. Responsibility is not all concentrated in the state's leaders.

To soothe their consciences as they kill and plunder for the state, soldiers justify their acts of death and destruction by the doctrine of concentrated responsibility. This is the idea that the responsibility for the murder and mayhem we call war is concentrated in the sovereign or the heads of state responsible for ordering the troops into battle. This has also been true throughout history.

We can see this in Shakespeare's play *Henry V*, written about 1599, which deals with events surrounding the Battle of Agincourt in 1415—an English victory against the French in the Hundred Years' War. In scene 1 of act 4, King Henry disguises himself and wanders about the English camp on the night before the battle begins.

Three soldiers—Bates, Court, and Williams—are standing around talking when they are approached by the king in disguise.

Court: "Brother John Bates is not that the morning which breaks yonder?"

Bates: "I think it be: but we have no great cause to desire the approach of day."

Williams: "We see yonder the beginning of the day, but I think we shall never see the end of it. Who goes there?"

King Henry V: "A friend."

Williams: "Under what captain serve you?"

King Henry V: "Under Sir Thomas Erpingham."

Williams: "A good old commander and a most kind gentleman: I pray you, what thinks he of our estate?"

King Henry V: "Even as men wrecked upon a sand, that look to be washed off the next tide."

Bates: "He hath not told his thought to the king?"

King Henry V: "No; nor it is not meet he should. For, though I speak it to you, I think the king is but a man, as I am: the violet

smells to him as it doth to me: the element shows to him as it doth
to me; all his senses have but human conditions: his ceremonies
laid by, in his nakedness he appears but a man; and though his
affections are higher mounted than ours, yet, when they stoop, they
stoop with the like wing. Therefore when he sees reason of fears,
as we do, his fears, out of doubt, be of the same relish as ours are:
yet, in reason, no man should possess him with any appearance of
fear, lest he, by showing it, should dishearten his army."

Bates: "He may show what outward courage he will; but I believe,
as cold a night as 'tis, he could wish himself in Thames up to the
neck; and so I would he were, and I by him, at all adventures, so we
were quit here."

King Henry V: "By my troth, I will speak my conscience of the
king: I think he would not wish himself any where but where he
is."

Bates: "Then I would he were here alone; so should he be sure to
be ransomed, and a many poor men's lives saved."

King Henry V: "I dare say you love him not so ill, to wish him here
alone, howsoever you speak this to feel other men's minds:
methinks I could not die any where so contented as in the king's
company; his cause being just and his quarrel honourable."

Williams: "That's more than we know."

Bates: "Ay, or more than we should seek after; for we know
enough, if we know we are the kings subjects: if his cause be
wrong, our obedience to the king wipes the crime of it out of us."

Williams: "But if the cause be not good, the king himself hath a
heavy reckoning to make, when all those legs and arms and heads,
chopped off in battle, shall join together at the latter day and cry all
'We died at such a place;' some swearing, some crying for a
surgeon, some upon their wives left poor behind them, some upon
the debts they owe, some upon their children rawly left. I am afeard
there are few die well that die in a battle; for how can they charita-
bly dispose of any thing, when blood is their argument? Now, if
these men do not die well, it will be a black matter for the king that

led them to it; whom to disobey were against all proportion of subjection."

King Henry V: "So, if a son that is by his father sent about merchandise do sinfully miscarry upon the sea, the imputation of his wickedness by your rule, should be imposed upon his father that sent him: or if a servant, under his master's command transporting a sum of money, be assailed by robbers and die in many irreconciled iniquities, you may call the business of the master the author of the servant's damnation: but this is not so: the king is not bound to answer the particular endings of his soldiers, the father of his son, nor the master of his servant; for they purpose not their death, when they purpose their services. Besides, there is no king, be his cause never so spotless, if it come to the arbitrement of swords, can try it out with all unspotted soldiers: some peradventure have on them the guilt of premeditated and contrived murder; some, of beguiling virgins with the broken seals of perjury; some, making the wars their bulwark, that have before gored the gentle bosom of peace with pillage and robbery. Now, if these men have defeated the law and outrun native punishment, though they can outstrip men, they have no wings to fly from God: war is his beadle, war is vengeance; so that here men are punished for before-breach of the king's laws in now the king's quarrel: where they feared the death, they have borne life away; and where they would be safe, they perish: then if they die unprovided, no more is the king guilty of their damnation than he was before guilty of those impieties for the which they are now visited. Every subject's duty is the king's; but every subject's soul is his own. Therefore should every soldier in the wars do as every sick man in his bed, wash every mote out of his conscience: and dying so, death is to him advantage; or not dying, the time was blessedly lost wherein such preparation was gained: and in him that escapes, it were not sin to think that, making God so free an offer, He let him outlive that day to see His greatness and to teach others how they should prepare.

Williams: "'Tis certain, every man that dies ill, the ill upon his own head, the king is not to answer it."

Bates: "But I do not desire he should answer for me; and yet I determine to fight lustily for him."

Nothing has changed. Soldiers think they can have the best of both worlds. They think they can kill with impunity in a just cause and with immunity in an unjust cause. But should some of the king's soldiers get a little reckless and cause some collateral damage, even though the king, like General Tommy Franks, says "we don't do body counts," they are the ones who are fully responsible since "the king is not bound to answer the particular endings of his soldiers." And as for soldiers determining to fight lustily for king and crown or for president and government or, as so many of them think, for flag and freedom or for God and country, there has never been a shortage of willing participants.

Are soldiers excused for the death and destruction they cause in an unjust and immoral war, like say, the war in Iraq? Just what is it that excuses them? Because their government tells them to do it? Because their commander in chief tells them to do it? Because their commanding officer tells them to do it? Because they wear a military uniform? Because they need to fight "over there" lest they have to fight "over here"? Because they are defending our freedoms? I have answered all of these questions in the negative here, here, here, here, and here. The terrible truth is that U.S. soldiers in Iraq are fighting and dying for a lie.

In King Henry's reply to Williams, he eludes taking blame by his elaborate analogy. But Henry is missing something here. Sending soldiers to fight in a foreign war is not the same as a father sending his son or a master sending his servant on a legitimate business trip. Bombing, invading, and occupying other countries, and otherwise fighting foreign wars, are illegitimate—even when done under the guise of defense, liberation, regime change, national interest, national security, or humanitarianism.

There are thousands of U.S. soldiers in Afghanistan, and thousands more on the way (thanks to the new war criminal in chief) who just a short time ago could neither spell Afghanistan nor locate it on a map. And as far as I know, no Afghan ever lifted a finger against an American until our troops landed on their soil. U.S. soldiers, like most soldiers throughout history, have been duped.

The crime of unjustly killing another human being cannot be wiped away. No matter what his religion, skin color, ethnicity, or nationality. No matter who tells you to drop the bomb, launch the missile, throw the grenade, or pull the trigger. And no matter what kind of uniform you are wearing.

* * * * *

THE FOLLY AND WICKEDNESS OF WAR

"History is indeed little more than the register of the crimes, follies, and misfortunes of mankind" ~ Edward Gibbon (1737–1794)

"Those who cannot remember the past are condemned to repeat it" ~ George Santayana (1863–1952)

"What experience and history teach is this—that people and governments never have learned anything from history, or acted on principles deduced from it" ~ Georg Hegel (1770–1831)

Writing in 1968, the historian Will Durant, in his *The Lessons of History*, remarked that "in the last 3,421 years of recorded history only 268 have seen no war." Unfortunately, the most recent century was the bloodiest on record.

Operation Barbarossa, the German invasion of the Soviet Union in June of 1941, was one of the most horrendous military campaigns, not only in the twentieth century, but in all of history. As related by Catherine Merridale in *Ivan's War: Life and Death in the Red Army, 1939–1945* (Metropolitan Books, 2006):

By December 1941, six months into the conflict, the Red Army had lost 4.5 million men. The carnage was beyond imagination. Eyewitnesses described the battlefields as landscapes of charred steel and ash. The round shapes of lifeless heads caught the late summer light like potatoes turned up from new-broken soil. The prisoners were marched off in their multitudes. Even the Germans did not have the guards, let alone enough barbed wire, to contain the 2.5 million Red Army troops they captured in the first five months. One single campaign, the defense of Kiev, cost the Soviets nearly 700,000 killed or missing in a matter of weeks. Almost the entire army of the pre-war years, the troops that shared the panic of those first nights back in June, was dead or captured by the end of 1941. And this process would be repeated as another generation was called up, crammed into uniform, and killed, captured, or wounded beyond recovery.

The folly of war cannot be limited to Germans and Russians; it can also be seen in the actions of Americans. During World War II, the Battle of Peleliu between the United States and Japan was folly on a grand scale. As part of General MacArthur's strategy to recapture the Philippines, it was thought to be necessary to neutralize the Japanese occupation of the island of Peleliu—550 miles east of the Philippines. It wasn't. After 1,794 U.S. Marines died, it was determined that the island had no strategic value.

Rather than being a "good war," World War II was an unnecessary bloodbath just like most of the previous wars in history.

I suppose that men have pointed out the folly and wickedness of war for as long as wars have been fought. But judging from the history of warfare, I suppose also that they have been in the minority.

Most people, I suppose, are familiar with the novelist Leo Tolstoy (1828–1910), the author of *War and Peace* and a harsh critic of both war and the state. Writing in 1894, Tolstoy powerfully described the folly and wickedness of war:

> Every war ... with all its ordinary consequences ... the murder with the justifications of its necessity and justice, the exaltation and glorification of military exploits, the worship of the flag, the patriotic sentiments ... and so on, does more in one year to pervert men's minds than thousands of robberies, murders, and arsons perpetrated during hundreds of years by individual men under the influence of passion.

Just think how many millions of innocent lives could have been spared from the horrors of both World Wars had the participants listened to Tolstoy.

But long before Tolstoy, someone in Britain penned an equally powerful missive titled "On the Folly and Wickedness of War." That someone was the preacher and educator Vicesimus Knox (1752–1821), a tireless advocate of civil liberties and adversary of offensive war. I have written about Knox previously ("Vicesimus Knox: Minister of Peace"). My purpose here, however, is to bring this long-forgotten work of Knox into the public domain. I recently discovered it in volume one of Knox's collected works, and have transcribed it below. The date of publication of "The Folly and Wickedness of War" must be around 1800 for it was reprinted, with a few changes, in *The Hive of Ancient and Modern Literature: A Collection of Essays, Narratives, Allegories, and Instructive Compositions*, selected by the Solomon Hodgson. The third edition of this book was issued at Newcastle in 1806. The first edition is supposed to have been published in 1799, but I have been unable to confirm this.

Here is "On the Folly and Wickedness and War," circa 1800:

The calamities attendant on a state of war seem to have prevented the mind of man from viewing it in the light of an absurdity, and an object of ridicule as well as pity. But if we could suppose a superior Being capable of beholding us, miserable mortals, without compassion, there is, I think, very little doubt but the variety of military manoeuvres and formalities, the pride, pomp, and circumstance of war, and all the ingenious contrivances for the glorious purposes of mutual destruction, which seem to constitute the business of many whole kingdoms, would furnish him with an entertainment like that which is received by us from the exhibition of a farce or puppet-show. But, notwithstanding the ridiculousness of all these solemnities, we, poor mortals, are doomed to feel that they are no farce, but the concomitant circumstances of a most woeful tragedy.

The causes of war are for the most part such as must disgrace an animal pretending to rationality. Two poor mortals take offence at each other, without any reason, or with the very bad one of wishing for an opportunity of aggrandizing themselves, by making reciprocal depredations. The creatures of the court, and the leading men of the nation, who are usually under the influence of the court, resolve (for it is their interest) to support their royal master, and are never at a loss to invent some colourable pretence for engaging the nation in the horrors of war. Taxes of the most burthensome kind are levied, soldiers are collected so as to leave a paucity of husbandmen, reviews and encampments succeed, and at last a hundred thousand men meet on a plain, and coolly shed each others blood, without the smallest personal animosity, or the shadow of a provocation. The kings, in the mean time, and the grandees, who have employed these poor innocent victims to shoot bullets at each other's heads, remain quietly at home, and amuse themselves, in the intervals of balls, hunting schemes, and pleasures of every species, with reading at the fire side, over a cup of chocolate, the dispatches from the army, and the news in the Extraordinary Gazette. Horace very truly observes, that whatever mad frolics enter into the heads of kings, it is the common people, that is, the honest artisan, and the industrious tribes in the middle ranks, unoffended and unoffending, who chiefly suffer in the evil consequences. If the old king of Prussia were not at the head of some of the best troops in the universe, he would be judged more worthy of being tried, cast, and condemned at the Old Bailey, than any shedder of blood who ever died by a halter. But he was a king; but he was a hero;—those names fascinate us, and we enrol the butcher of mankind among their benefactors.

When one considers the dreadful circumstances that attend even victories, one cannot help being a little shocked at the exultation which they occasion. I have often thought it a laughable scene, if there were not a little too much of the melancholy in it, when a circle of eager politicians have met to congratulate each other on what is called a piece of good news just arrived. Every eye sparkles with delight; every voice is raised in announcing the happy event. And what is the cause of all this joy? and for what are our windows illuminated, bonfires kindled, bells rung, and feasts celebrated? We have had a successful engagement. We have left a thousand of the enemy dead on the field of battle, and only half the number of our countrymen. Charming news! it was a glorious battle! But before you give a loose to your raptures, pause a while; and consider, that to every one of these three thousand, life was no less sweet than it is to you; that to the far greater part of them there probably were wives, fathers, mothers, sons, daughters, sisters, brothers, and friends, all of whom are at this moment bewailing that event which occasions your foolish and brutal triumph; a triumph perfectly consistent with the basest cowardice.

The whole time of war ought to be a time of general mourning, a mourning in the heart, a mourning much more sincere than on the death of one of those princes whose cursed ambition is often the sole cause of war. Indeed that a whole people should tamely submit to the evils of war, because it is the will of a few vain, selfish, ignorant, though exalted, individuals, is a phenomenon almost unaccountable. But they are led away by false glory, by their passions, by their vices. They reflect not; and indeed, if they did reflect, and oppose, what would avail the opposition of unarmed myriads to the mandate of a government supported by a standing army? Many of the European nations are entirely military; war is their trade; and when they have no employment at home, or near it, they blush not to let themselves out to shed any blood, in any cause of the best paymaster. Ye beasts of the forest, no longer allow that man is your superior, while there is found on the face of the earth such degeneracy!

Morality and religion forbid war in its motives, conduct, and consequences; but to many rulers and potentates, morality and religion appear as the inventions of politicians to facilitate subordination. The principal objects of crowned heads, and their minions, in countries subject to despotism, are the extension of empire, the augmentation of a revenue, or the total annihilation of their subjects' liberty. Their restraints in the pursuit of these objects are not those of morality and religion; but solely reasons of state and political caution. Plausible words are used, but they are only used to hide the deformity of the real principles. Wherever war is deemed desirable in an interested view, a specious pretext never yet remained unfound. Morality is as little considered in the beginning, as in the prosecution of war. The most solemn treaties and engagements are violated by the governing part of the nation, with no more scruple than oaths and bonds are broken by a cheat and a villain in the walks of private life. Does the difference of rank and situation make any difference in the atrocity of crimes? If any, it renders a thousand times more criminal than that of a thief, the villainy of them, who, by violating every sacred obligation between nation and nation, give rise to miseries and mischiefs most dreadful in their nature; and to which no human power can say, Thus far shall ye proceed, and no farther. Are not the natural and moral evils of life sufficient, but they must be rendered more acute, more numerous, and more imbittered by artificial means? My heart bleeds over those complicated scenes of woe, for which no epithet can be found sufficiently descriptive. Language fails in labouring to express the horrors of war amid private families, who are so unfortunate as to be situated on the seat of it.

War, however, it will be said, has always been permitted by Providence. This is indeed true; but it has been only permitted as a scourge. Let a spirit and activity be exerted in regulating the morals of a nation, equal to that with which war, and all its apparatus, are attended to, and mankind will no longer be scourged, neither will it be necessary to evacuate an empire of its members, for none will be superfluous. Let us, according to the advice of a pious divine of the present age, think less of our fleets and armies, and more of our faith and practice. While we are warriors, with all our pretensions to civilization, we are savages. But be it remembered, that nothing in this essay, or in any other composition of its author, was ever intended, or could be fairly understood, to discountenance a truly just and necessary war is the subject of his reprehension.

Will men ever learn from history that war is nothing but folly and wickedness? Will civilized, educated Christian Americans ever learn from history that war is nothing but folly and wickedness? Judging from the persistent Christian support for war, the warfare state, and the military, I am not optimistic.

* * * * *

THE WARMONGER'S LEXICON

Defenders of U.S. wars and military interventions look like the majority of Americans. They also dress like them, eat like them, work like them, play like them, and talk like them. However, it is sometimes impossible to communicate with or make sense of them because some things they say have their own peculiar definition.

This differs from military doublespeak.

To really understand these defenders of U.S. wars and military interventions, one needs a warmonger's lexicon. To get started, I propose the following entries:

Just war: any war the United States engages in.
Good war: any war in which the United States is on the winning side.
Defensive war: any war the United States starts.

George Bush: the Messiah, but especially when he was fighting against Muslims.
Barack Obama: Satan, but not when he is fighting against Muslims.

Insurgent: anyone who dares to fight against U.S. troops occupying his country.
Militant: see insurgent.
Enemy combatant: see militant.
Freedom fighter: an insurgent, militant, or enemy combatant supported by the United States when he fights against some other country.

Weapons of mass destruction: weapons that foreigners can use to attack Americans.
Advanced weapons systems: weapons that Americans can use to attack foreigners.

Allies: countries that support U.S. foreign policy.
Enemies: countries that don't support U.S. foreign policy.

Patriot: any American who supports U.S. foreign wars.
Traitor: any American who opposes U.S. foreign wars.

Hero: any American soldier who fought in any war against any

country for any reason.
Coward: any American who doesn't support U.S. soldiers fighting in senseless foreign wars.

American: supporting large defense budgets.
Un-American: opposing large defense budgets.

Threat to American security: see un-American, coward, and traitor.

Veteran: God's chosen people.
Non-veterans: second-class citizens.

Muslim: terrorist.
Terrorist: Muslim.

Soldier: public servant.
Civilian: freeloader.

Isolationist: any American who opposes U.S. wars, empire, and/or foreign policy.

Zionist: someone who favors U.S. military intervention in the Middle East.
Anti-Semite: someone who opposes U.S. military intervention in the Middle East.

Pacifist: enemy of the United States.
Draft dodger: see pacifist.

Dead U.S. soldier: fallen hero.
Dead foreign civilian: collateral damage.

Torture: torture of Americans by foreigners.
Enhanced interrogation techniques: torture of foreigners by Americans.
Extraordinary rendition: U.S. supported torture of foreigners by foreigners.

U.S. interests: anything the United States wants to be interested in.

When it comes to defenders of U.S. wars and military interventions, learn their language so you won't be intimidated or deceived by them, but don't waste too much of your time with them. There is nothing more frustrating than discussing the finer points of something like just war theory and then finding out thirty minutes later that the warmonger you thought you were having a meaningful conversation with and in basic agreement with believes that all the wars the United States has engaged in are just wars.

* * * * *

CHAPTER 2

THE MILITARY

BRUTUS ON THE EVILS OF STANDING ARMIES

Recognizing his friend Brutus among his assassins, Julius Caesar (in the words of William Shakespeare) uttered the immortal phrase "Et tu, Brute? "This Latin sentence meaning "Even you, Brutus?" is the only Brutus that most Americans have ever heard of.

But whether one has heard of Brutus from the study of Shakespeare's play Julius Caesar or from a World history course, there is a Brutus in American history that most Americans have never heard of.

The Brutus of American history is one of the forgotten Anti-Federalists. It was their principled opposition to the Constitution that led to the adoption of the Bill of Rights. But because the Federalists prevailed, the writings of the Anti-Federalists have largely been forgotten.

Every student of American government has studied the eighty-five essays written between October 1787 and August 1788 in favor of the adoption of the new Constitution. Known collectively as *The Federalist*, they were all signed Publius (after the ancient Roman statesman), but authored by Alexander Hamilton, James Madison, and John Jay.

Brutus was the name signed to sixteen essays written in opposition to the new Constitution replacing the Articles of Confederation. They were all published in the *New York Journal* from October 1787 to April 1788. None of the essays have titles, and most were addressed to the people or the citizens of the State of New York. The first essay of Brutus actually appeared nine days before the first essay of *The Federalist*. The essays signed Brutus are generally ascribed to Robert Yates (1738–1801), a New York judge who served on the committee that drafted the first constitution for New York State. Yates, along with John Lansing (1754–1829) and Alexander Hamilton, was a delegate to the Constitutional Convention in Philadelphia. Yates and Lansing withdrew from the Convention early and opposed the adoption of the Constitution by the state of New York.

One subject that Brutus speaks on at length is the evils of standing armies. In four of his sixteen essays (numbers 1, 8, 9, 10), he explains how the establishment and maintenance of standing armies breeds fear, is destructive to liberty, and should be viewed as a scourge to a country instead of a benefit.

On the subject of war itself, Brutus believed that only a defensive war was justifiable. He recognized that the countries of Europe were plagued by destructive wars:

> The European governments are almost all of them framed, and administered with a view to arms, and war, as that in which their chief glory consists; they mistake the end of government—it was designed to save mens lives, not to destroy them. We ought to furnish the world with an example of a great people, who in their civil institutions hold chiefly in view, the attainment of virtue, and happiness among ourselves. Let the monarchs, in Europe, share among them the glory of depopulating countries, and butchering thousands of their innocent citizens, to revenge private quarrels, or to punish an insult offered to a wife, a mistress, or a favorite: I envy them not the honor, and I pray heaven this country may never be ambitious of it. The czar Peter the great, acquired great glory by his arms; but all this was nothing, compared with the true glory which he obtained, by civilizing his rude and barbarous subjects, diffusing among them knowledge, and establishing, and cultivating the arts of life: by the former he desolated countries, and drenched the earth with human blood: by the latter he softened the ferocious nature of his people, and pointed them to the means of human happiness.

In his first essay, Brutus brings up the subject of standing armies in his discussion of the dangers of a consolidated central government over a large territorial republic:

> It might be here shown, that the power of the federal legislative, to raise and support armies at pleasure, as well in peace as in war, and their controul over the militia, tend, not only to a consolidation of the government, but the destruction of liberty.

> In despotic governments, as well as in all the monarchies of Europe, standing armies are kept up to execute the commands of the prince or the magistrate, and are employed for this purpose when occasion requires: But they have always proved the destruction of liberty, and [as] abhorrent to the spirit of a free republic. In England, where they depend upon the parliament for their annual support, they have always been complained of as oppressive and unconstitutional, and are seldom employed in executing of the laws; never except on extraordinary occasions, and then under the direction of a civil magistrate.

A free republic will never keep a standing army to execute its laws. It must depend upon the support of its citizens. But when a government is to receive its support from the aid of the citizens, it must be so constructed as to have the confidence, respect, and affection of the people. Men who, upon the call of the magistrate, offer themselves to execute the laws, are influenced to do it either by affection to the government, or from fear; where a standing army is at hand to punish offenders, every man is actuated by the latter principle, and therefore, when the magistrate casts, will obey: but, where this is not the case, the government must rest for its support upon the confidence and respect which the people have for their government and laws.

He concludes that if the people have "no confidence in their legislature, suspect them of ambitious views, be jealous of every measure they adopt, and will not support the laws they pass," then the government will be "nerveless and inefficient, and no way will be left to render it otherwise, but by establishing an armed force to execute the laws at the point of the bayonet—a government of all others the most to be dreaded."

In his eighth essay, Brutus raises the subject of standing armies in his discussion of the new federal government being authorized to raise and support armies:

Let us then enquire, whether standing armies in time of peace, would be ever beneficial to our country—or if in some extraordinary cases, they might be necessary; whether it is not true, that they have generally proved a scourge to a country, and destructive of their liberty.

He then reprints the text of a speech against standing armies recently delivered in the British Parliament, because, as he says, it "is so full to the point, and so much better than any thing I can say":

"I have always been, and always shall be against a standing army of any kind; to me it is a terrible thing, whether under that of a parliamentary, or any other designation; a standing army is still a standing army by whatever name it is called; they are a body of men distinct from the body of the people; they are governed by different laws, and blind obedience, and an entire submission to the orders of their commanding officer, is their only principle; the nations around us, sir, are already enslaved, and have been enslaved by those very means; by means of their standing armies they have every one lost their liberties; it is indeed impossible that the liberties of the people in any country can be preserved where a numerous standing army is kept up. Shall we then take our measures from the example of our neighbours? No, sir, on the contrary, from their misfortunes we ought to learn to avoid those rocks upon which they have split."

"It signifies nothing to tell me that our army is commanded by such gentlemen as cannot be supposed to join in any measures for enslaving their country; it may be so; I have a very good opinion of many gentlemen now in the army; I believe they would not join in any such measures; but their lives are uncertain, nor can we be sure how long they will be kept in command, they may all be dismissed in a moment, and proper tools of power put in their room. Besides, sir, we know the passions of men, we know how dangerous it is to trust the best of men with too much power. Where was a braver army than that under Jul. Caesar? Where was there ever an army that had served their country more faithfully? That army was commanded generally by the best citizens of Rome, by men of great fortune and figure in their country, yet that army enslaved their country. The affections of the soldiers towards their country, the honor and integrity of the under officers, are not to be depended on. By the military law the administration of justice is so quick, and the punishment so severe, that neither the officer nor soldier dare dispute the orders of his supreme commander; he must not consult his own inclination. If an officer were commanded to pull his own father out of this house, he must do it; he dares not disobey; immediate death would be the sure consequence of the least grumbling: and if an officer were sent into the court of request, accompanied by a body of musketeers with screwed bayonets, and with orders to tell us what we ought to do, and how we were to vote: I know what would be the duty of this house; I know it would be our duty to order the officer to be hanged at the door of the lobby; but I doubt, sir, I doubt much, if such a spirit could be found in the house, or in any house of commons that will ever be in England."

"Sir, I talk not of imaginary things? I talk of what has happened to an English house of commons, from an English army; not only from an English army, but an army that was raised by that very house of commons, an army that was paid by them, and an army that was commanded by generals appointed by them; therefore do not let us vainly imagine, that an army, raised and maintained by authority of parliament, will always be so submissive to them. If an army be so numerous as to have it in their power to overawe the parliament, they will be submissive as long as the parliament does nothing to disoblige their favourite general; but when that case happens, I am afraid, that in place of the parliament's dismissing the army, the army will dismiss the parliament."

Brutus concludes from this speech that "if this great man's reasoning be just, it follows, that keeping up a standing army, would be in the highest degree dangerous to the liberty and happiness of the community—and if so, the general government ought not to have authority to do it; for no government should be empowered to do that which if done, would tend to destroy public liberty."

In his ninth essay, Brutus faults the proposed constitution for its lack of a bill of rights. He acknowledges that the framers of the new constitution believed in prohibiting or restricting the general government from exercising certain powers. Nevertheless, he wonders why, if there are sections in the proposed constitution that prohibit bills of attainder and restrict the suspension of the writ of habeas corpus, that there is no prohibition or restriction against standing armies since they are likewise just as harmful:

> Let us apply these remarks to the case of standing armies in times of peace. If they generally prove the destruction of the happiness and libertys of the people, the legislature ought not to have power to keep them up, or if they had, this power should be so restricted, as to secure the people against the danger arising from the exercise of it.

> That standing armies are dangerous to the liberties of a people was proved in my last number—If it was necessary, the truth of the position might be confirmed by the history of almost every nation in the world. A cloud of the most illustrious patriots of every age and country, where freedom has been enjoyed, might be adduced as witnesses in support of the sentiment. But I presume it would be useless, to enter into a laboured argument, to prove to the people of America, a position, which has so long and so generally been received by them as a kind of axiom.

> Some of the advocates for this new system controvert this sentiment, as they do almost every other that has been maintained by the best writers on free government.—Others, though they will not expressly deny, that standing armies in times of peace are dangerous, yet join with these in maintaining, that it is proper the general government should be vested with the power to do it. I shall now proceed to examine the arguments they adduce in

support of their opinions.

A writer, in favor of this system, treats this objection as a ridiculous one. He supposes it would be as proper to provide against the introduction of Turkish janizaries, or against making the Alcoran a rule of faith.

But, why is this provision so ridiculous? because, says this author, it is unnecessary. But, why is it unnecessary? ["]because, the principles and habits, as well as the power of the Americans are directly opposed to standing armies; and there is as little necessity to guard against them by positive constitutions, as to prohibit the establishment of the Mahometan religion." It is admitted then, that a standing army in time of peace, is an evil. I ask then, why should this government be authorised to do evil? If the principles and habits of the people of this country are opposed to standing armies in time of peace, if they do not contribute to the public good, but would endanger the public liber[ty] and happiness, why should the government be [vested] with the power? No reason can be given, why [rulers] should be authorised to do, what, if done, would oppose the principles and habits of the people, and endanger the public safety, but there is every reason in the world, that they should be prohibited from the exercise of such a power. But this author supposes, that no danger is to be apprehended from the exercise of this power, because, if armies are kept up, it will be by the people themselves, and therefore, to provide against it, would be as absurd as for a man to "pass a law in his family, that no troops should be quartered in his family by his consent." This reasoning supposes, that the general government is to be exercised by the people of America themselves—But such an idea is groundless and absurd. There is surely a distinction between the people and their rulers, even when the latter are representatives of the former.—They certainly are not identically the same, and it cannot be disputed, but it may and often does happen, that they do not possess the same sentiments or pursue the same interests. I think I have shewn, that as this government is constituted, there is little reason to expect, that the interest of the people and their rulers will be the same.

The idea that there is no danger of the establishment of a standing army, under the new constitution, is without foundation.

It is a well known fact, that a number of those who had an agency in producing this system, and many of those who it is probable will have a principal share in the administration of the government under it, if it is adopted, are avowedly in favour of standing armies. It is a language common among them, "That no people can be kept in order, unless the government have an army to awe them into obedience; it is necessary to support the dignity of government, to have a military establishment." And there will not be wanting a variety of plausible reason to justify the raising one, drawn from the danger we are in from the Indians on our frontiers, or from the European provinces in our neighbourhood. If to this we add, that an army will afford a decent support, and agreeable employment to the young men of many families, who are too indolent to follow occupations that will require care and industry, and too poor to live without doing any business we can have little reason to doubt, but that we shall have a large standing army, as soon as this government can find money to pay them, and perhaps sooner.

Brutus then directly engages Hamilton, who had written several essays in *The Federalist* trying to answer objections to standing armies:

A writer, who is the boast of the advocates of this new constitution, has taken great pains to shew, that this power was proper and necessary to be vested in the general government.

He first attempts to shew, that this objection is futile and disingenuous, because the power to keep up standing armies, in time of peace, is vested, under the present government, in the legislature of every state in the union, except two. Now this is so far from being true, that it is expressly declared, by the present articles of confederation, that no body of forces "shall be kept up by any state, in time of peace, except such number only, as in the judgment of the United States in Congress assembled, shall be deemed requisite to garrison the forts necessary for the defence of such state." Now, was it candid and ingenuous to endeavour to persuade the public, that the general government had no other power than your own legislature have on this head; when the truth is, your legislature have no authority to raise and keep up any forces?

He next tells us, that the power given by this constitution, on this head, is similar to that which Congress possess under the present confederation. As little ingenuity is manifested in this representation as in that of the former.

I shall not undertake to enquire whether or not Congress are vested with a power to keep up a standing army in time of peace; it has been a subject warmly debated in Congress, more than once, since the peace; and one of the most respectable states in the union, were so fully convinced that they had no such power, that they expressly instructed their delegates to enter a solemn protest against it on the journals of Congress, should they attempt to exercise it.

But should it be admitted that they have the power, there is such a striking dissimilarity between the restrictions under which the present Congress can exercise it, and that of the proposed government, that the comparison will serve rather to shew the impropriety of vesting the proposed government with the power, than of justifying it.

It is acknowledged by this writer, that the powers of Congress, under the present confederation, amount to little more than that of recommending. If they determine to raise troops, they are obliged to effect it through the authority of the state legislatures. This will, in the first instance, be a most powerful restraint upon them, against ordering troops to be raised. But if they should vote an army, contrary to the opinion and wishes of the people, the legislatures of the respective states would not raise them. Besides, the present Congress hold their places at the will and pleasure of the legislatures of the states who send them, and no troops can be raised, but by the assent of nine states out of the thirteen. Compare the power proposed to be lodged in the legislature on this head, under this constitution, with that vested in the present Congress, and every person of the least discernment, whose understanding is not totally blinded by prejudice, will perceive, that they bear no analogy to each other. Under the present confederation, the representatives of nine states, out of thirteen, must assent to the raising of troops, or they cannot be levied: under the proposed constitution, a less number than the representatives of two states, in the house of representatives, and the representatives of three states and an half in the senate, with the assent of the president, may raise any number of troops they please. The present Congress are restrained from an undue exercise of this power, from this consideration, they know the state legislatures, through whose authority it must be carried into effect, would not comply with the requisition for the purpose, if it was evidently opposed to the public good: the proposed constitution authorizes the legislature to carry their determinations into execution, without the intervention of any other body between them and the people.

In his tenth essay, which is devoted exclusively to the evils of standing armies, Brutus begins with a discussion of how a standing army can subvert the very government whose authority it is supposed to be under:

> The liberties of a people are in danger from a large standing army, not only because the rulers may employ them for the purposes of supporting themselves in any usurpations of power, which they may see proper to exercise, but there is great hazard, that an army will subvert the forms of the government, under whose authority, they are raised, and establish one, according to the pleasure of their leader.

To prove his point, he then adduces the historical examples of Rome and Britain:

> We are informed, in the faithful pages of history, of such events frequently happening.—Two instances have been mentioned in a former paper. They are so remarkable, that they are worthy of the most careful attention of every lover of freedom.—They are taken from the history of the two most powerful nations that have ever existed in the world; and who are the most renowned, for the freedom they enjoyed, and the excellency of their constitutions:—I mean Rome and Britain.
>
> In the first, the liberties of the commonwealth was destroyed, and the constitution overturned, by an army, lead by Julius Cesar, who was appointed to the command, by the constitutional authority of that commonwealth. He changed it from a free republic, whose fame had sounded, and is still celebrated by all the world, into that of the most absolute despotism. A standing army effected this change, and a standing army supported it through a succession of ages, which are marked in the annals of history, with the most horrid cruelties, bloodshed, and carnage;—The most devilish, beastly, and unnatural vices, that ever punished or disgraced human nature.
>
> The same army, that in Britain, vindicated the liberties of that people from the encroachments and despotism of a tyrant king, assisted Cromwell, their General, in wresting from the people, that liberty they had so dearly earned.
>
> You may be told, these instances will not apply to our case.—But those who would persuade you to believe this, either mean to

deceive you, or have not themselves considered the subject.

Continuing his argument, Brutus contrasts Caesar and Cromwell with George Washington:

> I firmly believe, no country in the world had ever a more patriotic army, than the one which so ably served this country, in the late war.

> But had the General who commanded them, been possessed of the spirit of a Julius Cesar or a Cromwell, the liberties of this country, had in all probability, terminated with the war; or had they been maintained, might have cost more blood and treasure, than was expended in the conflict with Great-Britain. When an anonimous writer addressed the officers of the army at the close of the war, advising them not to part with their arms, until justice was done them—the effect it had is well known. It affected them like an electric shock. He wrote like Cesar; and had the commander in chief, and a few more officers of rank, countenanced the measure, the desperate resolution had been taken, to refuse to disband. What the consequences of such a determination would have been, heaven only knows.—The army were in the full vigor of health and spirits, in the habit of discipline, and possessed of all our military stores and apparatus. They would have acquired great accessions of strength from the country.—Those who were disgusted at our republican forms of government (for such there then were, of high rank among us) would have lent them all their aid.—We should in all probability have seen a constitution and laws, dictated to us, at the head of an army, and at the point of a bayonet, and the liberties for which we had so severely struggled, snatched from us in a moment. It remains a secret, yet to be revealed, whether this measure was not suggested, or at least countenanced, by some, who have had great influence in producing the present system.—Fortunately indeed for this country, it had at the head of the army, a patriot as well as a general; and many of our principal officers, had not abandoned the characters of citizens, by assuming that of soldiers, and therefore, the scheme proved abortive. But are we to expect, that this will always be the case? Are we so much better than the people of other ages and of other countries, that the same allurements of power and greatness, which led them aside from their duty, will have no influence upon men in our country? Such an idea, is wild and extravagant.—Had we indulged such a delusion, enough has appeared in a little time past, to convince the most credulous, that the passion for pomp,

power and greatness, works as powerfully in the hearts of many of our better sort, as it ever did in any country under heaven.—Were the same opportunity again to offer, we should very probably be grossly disappointed, if we made dependence, that all who then rejected the overture, would do it again.

Brutus concludes:

From these remarks, it appears, that the evil to be feared from a large standing army in time of peace, does not arise solely from the apprehension, that the rulers may employ them for the purpose of promoting their own ambitious views, but that equal, and perhaps greater danger, is to be apprehended from their overturning the constitutional powers of the government, and assuming the power to dictate any form they please.

Brutus again directly engages Hamilton, who had argued in *The Federalist* that we needed a standing army in peacetime to guard against Indians and to repel an invasion from abroad:

The advocates for power, in support of this right in the proposed government, urge that a restraint upon the discretion of the legislatures, in respect to military establishments in time of peace, would be improper to be imposed, because they say, it will be necessary to maintain small garrisons on the frontiers, to guard against the depredations of the Indians, and to be prepared to repel any encroachments or invasions that may be made by Spain or Britain.

The amount of this argument striped of the abundant verbages with which the author has dressed it, is this:

It will probably be necessary to keep up a small body of troops to garrison a few posts, which it will be necessary to maintain, in order to guard against the sudden encroachments of the Indians, or of the Spaniards and British; and therefore, the general government ought to be invested with power to raise and keep up a standing army in time of peace, without restraint; at their discretion.

I confess, I cannot perceive that the conclusion follows from the premises. Logicians say, it is not good reasoning to infer a general conclusion from particular premises: though I am not much of a Logician, it seems to me, this argument is very like that species of reasoning.

When the patriots in the parliament in Great-Britain, contended with such force of argument, and all the powers of eloquence, against keeping up standing armies in time of peace, it is obvious, they never entertained an idea, that small garrisons on their frontiers, or in the neighbourhood of powers, from whom they were in danger of encroachments, or guards, to take care of public arsenals would thereby be prohibited.

The advocates for this power farther urge that it is necessary, because it may, and probably will happen, that circumstances will render it requisite to raise an army to be prepared to repel attacks of an enemy, before a formal declaration of war, which in modern times has fallen into disuse. If the constitution prohibited the raising an army, until a war actually commenced, it would deprive the government of the power of providing for the defence of the country, until the enemy were within our territory. If the restriction is not to extend to the raising armies in cases of emergency, but only to the keeping them up, this would leave the matter to the discretion of the legislature; and they might, under the pretence that there was danger of an invasion, keep up the army as long as they judged proper—and hence it is inferred, that the legislature should have authority to raise and keep up an army without any restriction. But from these premises nothing more will follow than this, that the legislature should not be so restrained, as to put it out of their power to raise an army, when such exigencies as are instanced shall arise. But it does not thence follow, that the government should be empowered to raise and maintain standing armies at their discretion as well in peace as in war. If indeed, it is impossible to vest the general government with the power of raising troops to garrison the frontier posts, to guard arsenals, or to be prepared to repel an attack, when we saw a power preparing to make one, without giving them a general and indefinite authority, to raise and keep up armies, without any restriction or qualification, then this reasoning might have weight; but this has not been proved nor can it be.

It is admitted that to prohibit the general government, from keeping up standing armies, while yet they were authorised to raise them in case of exigency, would be an insufficient guard against the danger. A discretion of such latitude would give room to elude the force of the provision.

It is also admitted that an absolute prohibition against raising troops, except in cases of actual war, would be improper; because it will be requisite to raise and support a small number of troops to garrison the important frontier posts, and to guard arsenals; and it may happen, that the danger of an attack from a foreign power may be so imminent, as to render it highly proper we should raise an army, in order to be prepared to resist them. But to raise and keep up forces for such purposes and on such occasions, is not included in the idea, of keeping up standing armies in times of peace.

Brutus then refutes yet another argument of Hamilton:

The same writer who advances the arguments I have noticed, makes a number of other observations with a view to prove that the power to raise and keep up armies, ought to be discretionary in the general legislature; some of them are curious; he instances the raising of troops in Massachusetts and Pennsylvania, to shew the necessity of keeping a standing army in time of peace; the least reflection must convince every candid mind that both these cases are totally foreign to his purpose—Massachusetts raised a body of troops for six months, at the expiration of which they were to disband of course; this looks very little like a standing army. But beside, was that commonwealth in a state of peace at that time? So far from it that they were in the most violent commotions and contents, and their legislature had formally declared that an unnatural rebellion existed within the state. The situation of Pennsylvania was similar; a number of armed men had levied war against the authority of the state, and openly avowed their intention of withdrawing their allegiance from it. To what purpose examples are brought, of states raising troops for short periods in times of war or insurrections, on a question concerning the propriety of keeping up standing armies in times of peace, the public must judge.

Brutus also raises the subject of conscription in his discussion of the evils of standing armies. After informing his readers that the power to raise armies under the proposed constitution is "indefinite and unlimited, and authorizes the raising of forces, as well in peace as in war," he wonders whether "the clause which impowers the Congress to pass all laws which are proper and necessary, to carry this into execution, will not authorise them to impress men for the army." For "if the general legislature deem it for the general welfare to raise a body of troops, and they cannot be procured by voluntary enlistments, it seems evident, that it will be proper and necessary to effect it, that men be impressed from the militia to make up the deficiency."

The views of Brutus on the evils of standing armies were by no means novel. How quickly do Americans forget that one of the complaints of the Colonists against King George III in the Declaration of Independence was that "he has kept among us, in times of peace, Standing Armies without the consent of our legislatures." It should also be pointed out that Brutus did not merely attack the idea of a free state having a standing army, he proposed a solution to the problem of how to entrust the government with sufficient authority to provide for the cases of an enemy attack, guard arsenals, and garrison the frontier posts, while at the same time providing "a reasonable and competent security against the evil of a standing army." His solution was to add the following clause to the new constitution:

> As standing armies in time of peace are dangerous to liberty, and have often been the means of overturning the best constitutions of government, no standing army, or troops of any description whatsoever, shall be raised or kept up by the legislature, except so many as shall be necessary for guards to the arsenals of the United States, or for garrisons to such posts on the frontiers, as it shall be deemed absolutely necessary to hold, to secure the inhabitants, and facilitate the trade with the Indians: unless when the United States are threatened with an attack or invasion from some foreign power, in which case the legislature shall be authorised to raise an army to be prepared to repel the attack; provided that no troops whatsoever shall be raised in time of peace, without the assent of two thirds of the members, composing both houses of the legislature.

Brutus believed that not only would a clause like this "afford sufficient latitude to the legislature to raise troops in all cases that were really necessary," it would at the same time provide "competent security against the establishment of that dangerous engine of despotism a standing army."

The statements of Brutus on the evils of standing armies are also applicable to the current U.S. foreign policy of interventionism, for if a standing army is despotic in its own country, there is no telling how much more it may be when transplanted to a foreign country.

All quotations from the essays of Brutus are taken from Regnery edition of The Anti-Federalists: Selected Writings and Speeches, *edited by Bruce Frohnen.*

* * * * *

THE PROBLEM WITH BRAC

The Base Realignment and Closure (BRAC) Commission has just given President Bush its military base realignment and closure recommendations. On the surface, closing obsolete military bases in the United States sounds like a good thing. The Bush administration has even estimated that 20 to 25 percent of military bases are surplus, and that their closure could result in savings of over $3 billion a year. So, given that saving the taxpayers money is the goal, what possible problem could there be with the BRAC Commission?

There is one major problem with the BRAC Commission—a fatal flaw that calls the whole process into question. It is not that the military is being downsized. It is not that the United States might be rendered more vulnerable to a terrorist attack. It is not that no cost savings will ultimately be realized since the Defense Department budget will still increase no matter how many bases are closed. It is not that communities will suffer economically when a local base is shut down. It is not that local dignitaries have to shamelessly grovel before the BRAC Commission to keep their bases off the closure list. It is not that members of Congress have to suddenly come up with reasons why the base in their district is so strategically important.

The problem, in a word, is empire: the U.S. empire of troops and bases that encircles the globe. The only concern of the BRAC Commission is bases in the United States and its territories. The fact that the United States now has troops in 150 countries or territories is of no concern to the Pentagon, the president, the Congress, or the BRAC Commission.

Base closings in the United States began in the early 1960s. Back then the Department of Defense (DOD) was able to close obsolete bases without the involvement of Congress or any other government agency. Congress attempted to involve itself in the process in 1965, but President Johnson vetoed a bill that would have required the Pentagon to report any base closure programs to Congress.

In 1977, Congress passed, and President Carter signed, a law (PL 95-82) that required the Defense Department to notify Congress of any proposed base closings or reductions. The 1983 Grace Commission recommended the creation of an independent commission to study the need for base realignments and closures. These two events laid the groundwork for the modern BRAC Commission.

In 1988, the Commission on Base Realignment and Closure was created to recommend to Congress and the DOD military bases for realignment or closure. This first round of BRAC (as it is called) resulted in the closure, partial closure, or realignment of 145 military installations.

The next three BRAC rounds, which took place in 1991, 1993, and 1995, were carried out differently, as well as the round currently in progress. Under the new guideless adopted in 1990, it is the job of the Defense Department to draw up an initial list of bases to be closed or realigned and submit it to the BRAC Commission. Although the original BRAC Commission had twelve members, the Commission currently consists of nine members, all appointed by the president and congressional leaders and confirmed by the Senate. Working from that list, but also with the authority to add additional bases not recommended by the DOD, the Commission then recommends to the president which bases should be closed or realigned. The president reviews the BRAC recommendations, but can only accept or reject the recommendations in their entirety. If its recommendations are rejected, the BRAC Commission can resubmit a revised list. Congress, however, can still block the implementation of the package of BRAC recommendations, even if approved by the president.

There is no question that most of the bases recommended for closure by the BRAC Commission should be closed. If the Pentagon, the BRAC Commission, and the commander in chief all agree on the need for a particular base to be closed, and Congress acquiesces, it is hard to justify keeping it open. But before any bases in the United States are closed, a hard look needs to be made at the hundreds of U.S. military installations on foreign soil. If the purpose of the military is to defend the country, then why is the United States closing bases at home and expanding them abroad? Foreign military bases are for offense, empire, imperialism, intervention—not for defense. The conclusion is inescapable: the U.S. military does very little to actually defend the country. If it did then it would patrol our coasts and guard our borders instead of patrolling the Persian Gulf and guarding the borders of Iraq.

According to the latest DOD "Base Structure Report" for fiscal year 2005, the U.S. military has 770 military installations in thirty-nine countries. Is there some rational explanation why we should close military bases in America and maintain 106 military sites in South Korea? Is there any reason why the United States needs 302 military sites in Germany and 111 sites in Japan sixty years after World War II has ended?

There is no doubt that many bases in the United States are obsolete or unnecessary. And there is no doubt that closing or realigning these bases would result in significant cost savings. But the foreign bases should be closed first, the troops brought home to stay, and then, and only then, should the BRAC process proceed.

* * * * *

THE ARMED FORCES DAY OF RECKONING

The third Saturday in May has, since 1950, been designated Armed Forces Day. Harry Truman, who was the president at the time, remarked that the U.S. military was "vital to the security of the nation and to the establishment of a desirable peace." On the occasion of the first Armed Forces Day while he was president, Dwight Eisenhower stated: "It is fitting and proper that we devote one day each year to paying special tribute to those whose constancy and courage constitute one of the bulwarks guarding the freedom of this nation and the peace of the free world." Since today is Armed Forces Day, it is perhaps the best day to say—as unpopular as it may be—that rather than contributing to the peace of the world, the U.S. military has become the greatest force for evil in the world. Instead of being a force for peace, the U.S. military, through its numerous wars, interventions, and occupations, is a force for instability, death, and destruction.

Yes, I know, I am a liberal, a communist, a Quaker, a pacifist, a peacenik, a traitor, a coward, an appeaser, an America-hater, and an antiwar weenie.

Prior to the creation of Armed Forces Day after the unification of the various branches of the military into the Department of Defense, each branch of the military had its own special day. Army Day was April 6, Navy Day was October 27, Air Force Day was August 1, and Marine Corps Day was November 10. Only Marine Corps Day is still observed. Although the Coast Guard also participates in Armed Forces Day, it has its own day (August 4), and is actually part of the Department of Homeland Security.

Like perhaps many Americans, I did not realize that May 20 was Armed Forces Day until I was sent a Patriot Petition via e-mail from *The Patriot Post*, advertised as "The Conservative E-Journal of Record."

The e-mail encouraged me to:

> Please join fellow Patriots and sign the Petition to pray for our Armed Forces and let them know you stand with them as One Nation Under God. Please forward this invitation to friends, family members and fellow American Patriots.

> Please sign this Petition to pray for our Armed Forces and forward this invitation to friends, family members and fellow American Patriots. We intend to collect as many petition signatures as possible so that brave Patriots in uniform know that we stand behind them, united in prayer.

Let your voice be heard! Please join fellow Patriots in support of the Petition to pray for our Armed Forces.

The petition is called "A Call to prayer for our Armed Forces," and reads as follows:

We, your fellow Americans, resolve and commit to pray for you, our uniformed Patriots standing in harm's way around the world in defense of our liberty, every day. We further resolve and commit to pray for your families awaiting your safe return. We thank God for you, your courage, tenacity and vigilance.

The words of George Washington's First Inaugural Address are fitting: "The preservation of the sacred fire of liberty, and the destiny of the republican model of government, are justly considered deeply, perhaps as finally, staked on the experiment entrusted to the hands of the American people." We, the American people, then turn that trust to God, who in His sovereign wisdom gave us the freedom we enjoy.

You Patriots—American Soldiers, Sailors, Airmen, Marines and Coastguardsmen—have plowed the ground for liberty. We remain the proud and the free because you have stood bravely in harm's way, and remain on post today. For this, we, the American People, offer our heartfelt thanks. We commit to continually pray for you and your families.

I agree. We should pray for the men and women in the U.S. military. The Bible says that "supplications, prayers, intercessions, and giving of thanks" should "be made for all men" (1 Timothy 2:1).

But how should we pray for them? Should we pray that God bless the troops while they drop their bombs, throw their grenades, launch their missiles, fire their mortars, and shoot their bullets? Should we pray that the troops are protected while they injure, torture, maim, and kill others? Should we pray that the troops are successful when they drive their tanks into a city and reduce it to rubble?

Why not? What do you think has been happening in Iraq for the past three years?

Yes, we should pray for the troops. We should pray that the troops come home. We should pray that the troops come home now. We should pray that the blood of not one more American soldier is shed on foreign soil. We should pray for the healing of the thousands of U.S. soldiers who have been injured in the senseless Iraq war. We should pray for an end to this unconstitutional, immoral, and unjust war. We should pray that Congress ends funding for this war. We should pray that Bush leaves office a disgraced commander in chief. We should pray that young, impressionable students are not ensnared by military recruiters. We should pray that pastors stop recommending military service to their young men (and women). We should pray that families stop supplying cannon fodder to the military. We should pray that the troops actually start defending this country instead of every other country. We should pray for a change in U.S. foreign policy that can make this all possible.

But as long as the U.S. military is garrisoning the planet, there is another group of people that we should pray for: the people our armed forces are putting in harm's way. Pray that they will not be at home when the bombs start dropping and the bullets start flying.

The U.S. military is not "plowing the ground for liberty" or "standing in defense of our liberty." The military, as the coercive arm of the U.S. government, is at once the world's policeman, bully, and troublemaker. The United States has, for over a hundred years, intervened in the affairs of other countries in every corner of the globe. This has been documented by a number of individuals in a variety of places.

Zoltan Grossman of Evergreen State College in Olympia, Washington, has compiled a partial list of over 100 U.S. military foreign interventions from 1890 to 2006. Global Security has a report of U.S. military operations broken down into five periods from the eighteenth century to the post cold war period. At the 2002 annual meeting of the Southern Political Science Association in Savannah, Georgia, one of the papers documented 176 U.S. military operations since the Cold War. Although the Department of Defense admits to having 702 military installations in foreign countries, it has been documented by Chalmers Johnson that this number is far too low and perhaps actually numbers around 1,000. I have recently chronicled the presence of U.S. troops in 155 countries or territories.

No wonder former U.S. Attorney General William Ramsey Clark has said that "the greatest crime since World War II has been US foreign policy." I don't often agree with Martin Luther King Jr., but he was right when he said during the Vietnam War that "the greatest purveyor of violence in the world today is my own government." And Murray Rothbard, the twentieth century's greatest proponent of liberty, was certainly correct when he claimed that "empirically, taking the twentieth century as a whole, the single most warlike, most interventionist, most imperialist government has been the United States."

Professor Grossman has astutely characterized U.S. military

interventions:

- First, they were explained to the U.S. public as defending the lives and rights of civilian populations. Yet the military tactics employed often left behind massive civilian "collateral damage."
- Second, although nearly all the post-World War II interventions were carried out in the name of "freedom" and "democracy," nearly all of them in fact defended dictatorships controlled by pro-U.S. elites.
- Third, the U.S. always attacked violence by its opponents as "terrorism," "atrocities against civilians," or "ethnic cleansing," but minimized or defended the same actions by the U.S. or its allies.
- Fourth, the U.S. often portrays itself as a neutral peacekeeper, with nothing but the purest humanitarian motives.
- Fifth, U.S. military intervention is often counterproductive even if one accepts U.S. goals and rationales.

How much wiser were the Founding Fathers than Bush, Cheney, Rumsfeld, and Rice! If more Americans heeded the wisdom of the Founders, a militaristic United States would never have been tolerated. It was James Madison, the "father of the Constitution," who warned the country back in 1787:

> A standing military force, with an overgrown Executive will not long be safe companions to liberty. The means of defence against foreign danger, have been always the instruments of tyranny at home. Among the Romans it was a standing maxim to excite a war, whenever a revolt was apprehended. Throughout all Europe, the armies kept up under the pretext of defending, have enslaved the people.

George Washington likewise warned against "those overgrown military establishments which, under any form of government, are inauspicious to liberty, and which are to be regarded as particularly hostile to republican liberty." He believed that "the great rule of conduct for us in regard to foreign nations is in extending our commercial relations, to have with them as little political connection as possible." He counseled that our true foreign policy should be "to steer clear of permanent alliances with any portion of the foreign world." Here is Thomas Jefferson's "Quaker" foreign policy:

> Peace has been our principle, peace is our interest, and peace has

saved to the world this only plant of free and rational government now existing in it. However, therefore, we may have been reproached for pursuing our Quaker system, time will affix the stamp of wisdom on it, and the happiness and prosperity of our citizens will attest its merit. And this, I believe, is the only legitimate object of government, and the first duty of governors, and not the slaughter of men and devastation of the countries placed under their care, in pursuit of a fantastic honor, unallied to virtue or happiness; or in gratification of the angry passions, or the pride of administrators, excited by personal incidents, in which their citizens have no concern.

I am for free commerce with all nations, political connection with none, and little or no diplomatic establishment. And I am not for linking ourselves by new treaties with the quarrels of Europe, entering that field of slaughter to preserve their balance, or joining in the confederacy of Kings to war against the principles of liberty.

How well I remember the outrage in this country when the U.S. government shot, gassed, and burned men, women, and children in 1993 at the Branch Davidian compound near Waco, Texas. So why no outrage when the U.S. military does the same thing in other countries?

The only explanation is that many Americans, and especially many conservative, evangelical, and fundamentalist Christians, are blindly in love with the U.S. military.

It is my hope and prayer that this Armed Forces Day serve as day of reckoning as to the true nature of the U.S. military. The troops must be brought home, not just from Iraq, but from every corner of the globe. The military must be scaled back to coincide with a return to the noninterventionist foreign policy of the Founders. U.S. soldiers should be limited protecting our shores, guarding our borders, and patrolling our coasts. The peace of the world depends on it.

* * * * *

WHO IS RESPONSIBLE?

"I oppose the war far more than you do. The fault is not that of soldiers sent to war. Only an immature idiot like yourself would make that claim. Your comments on what soldiers are good for is an embarrassment. They are heroes, you are an ass." ~ One of my critics

Who is responsible for the death and destruction in Iraq? A critic of mine believes that the U.S. soldiers who kill people and break things are not responsible for their actions. I strongly disagree.

No one questions whether the Russian soldiers who executed 21,000 Polish Army reservists in the Katyn Forest Massacre are responsible for their actions. No one questions whether the German soldiers who invaded Poland are responsible for their actions. No one questions whether the Turkish soldiers who massacred thousands of Armenians in 1915 are responsible for their actions. Why is it then that few Americans—even those opposed to the war—question whether U.S. soldiers are responsible for their actions?

Not only are U.S. soldiers not viewed as responsible for the death and destruction that they bring, we continually see signs and yellow ribbons expressing support for the troops. We also frequently hear from church pulpits that we should pray for the troops. Sometimes this is expanded to praying for the safety of the troops while they are defending our freedoms, but it is usually just the nebulous refrain: "pray for the troops."

Although many defenders of the Iraq war have tried, usually under the umbrella of "just war" theory, it can't be said that the actions of U.S. soldiers in this war are so different from the actions of Russians, Germans, and Turks that they should be commended instead of condemned. Labeling the U.S. invasion and occupation of Iraq a just war does not make it one. By no stretch of the imagination can the U.S. invasion and occupation of Iraq be called a just war. In fact, the war violates every "just war" principle ever invoked to justify a war. So why aren't U.S. soldiers viewed as responsible for the death and destruction in Iraq—even by many of those who see this as an unjust war?

Those who say the troops are not responsible are, consciously or unconsciously, saying one of four things (or perhaps even all four).

Some say the troops are not responsible because they are just following the orders given them by their superiors. U.S. soldiers were told to invade and occupy Iraq. They were told to hunt down "terrorists." They were told to load their planes and their weapons. They were told to drop their bombs and fire their bullets. Even some who oppose the war would agree. They maintain that although Bush the liar in chief and Rumsfeld the secretary of lies are war criminals, the individual soldier is not responsible because the chain of command goes all the way back to them. But I thought it was only God who should be obeyed 100 percent of the time without question? These people are hypocrites. No supporter of the war in Iraq who uses the "obeying orders" defense would allow a German officer at the Nuremberg Trials to get away with saying that he was just obeying Hitler's orders. Do those who use the "obeying orders" defense actually believe that a soldier should never question the morality of his orders? Should a soldier shoot unarmed civilians because a Lt. Calley orders him to do so? Why not? He would just be obeying orders. Being told to clean or paint a piece of equipment is one thing; being told to bomb or shoot a person is another.

Others say the troops are not responsible because, as citizens of the United States, soldiers, like everyone else, must do as the state dictates. Many evangelical Christians agree, and join in this chorus of statolatry with their "obey the powers that be" mantra. No soldier is responsible for the death and destruction he inflicts as long as it is state-sanctioned death and destruction. Those who consistently hold this opinion have made the state their god; those who don't should not be taken seriously.

Many say the troops are not responsible because they are American troops. Unlike the soldiers of any other country, U.S. soldiers are always liberators and peacekeepers, never invaders and occupiers. True, the United States has troops scattered all over the globe in 155 countries or territories, but America is a benevolent hegemon. Here too many evangelical Christians concur. They view the United States as the God-anointed protector of Israel that enjoys a special relationship with God. The war in Iraq is a modern-day crusade. The U.S. military is the Lord's army that fights against the Muslim infidel. The inevitable conclusion to this aberrant nationalism can be seen in a statement from a critic of mine who considers me to be a "traitor": "Every war that has ever been fought and ever will be fought by the United States has been just and has been for honor." The government and the military could not ask for a more loyal piece of cannon fodder than this ultimate warmonger, although he himself won't be the one going overseas—it will be the young men in his neighborhood who will be sacrificed for the state.

And then there are those who say the troops are not responsible because we are at war. As Rush Limbaugh recently said: "When our nation is at war, your duty is to support it, not offer your precious little opinion." War not only makes for strange bedfellows (like the United States and Soviet Russia in WWII), it can used to cover a multitude of sins. In fact, under the cloak of war, the vilest crimes can be covered up or excused. In the minds of many Americans, a soldier in a uniform is a sanctified individual. In his review of *My Battle of Algiers* in *National Review*, Christopher Levenick makes a chilling observation about military uniforms and those soldiers guilty of torturing their opponents: "Indeed, it is not uncommon to learn that such men are capable of living out the rest of their lives without any sense of guilt for their actions. It remains a basic truth of human nature that a uniform is all that many men need to dissociate themselves from the evil they commit."

Although the U.S. government and the general public don't hold the troops responsible for their actions (unless they do something particularly evil that becomes an embarrassment), U.S. soldiers need to realize that it is they themselves who will ultimately be held responsible when they stand before God Almighty and give account of their deeds. U.S. soldiers fighting in Iraq need to recognize some things that are true and some things that are not true:

- The war is a crime against the Iraqi people.
- The war violates every just war principle ever formulated.
- U.S. military interventions are detrimental to world peace.
- U.S. foreign policy creates enemies and terrorists.
- God never appointed the United States to be the world's policeman.
- The war is not in the best interests of the United States.
- U.S. forces in Iraq are not retaliating for 9/11.
- U.S. forces in Iraq are not defending our freedoms.
- U.S. forces in Iraq are not fighting terrorism.
- U.S. forces in Iraq are not defending the United States.

Until U.S. soldiers concede that the war was a grave mistake, they will keep on fighting. Until U.S. soldiers accept responsibility for their actions, they will keep on killing. Until U.S. soldiers understand that the state is a lying, stealing, and killing machine they will continue their state-sanctioned death and destruction. Until U.S. soldiers realize that they are but cannon fodder for the state, they will keep dying for a lie. And until young men and women acknowledge that the U.S. military has become—through its wars, interventions, and occupations—the greatest force for evil in the world, they will keep joining the military to get that enlistment bonus or that money for college.

No one is holding a gun to the head of any soldier and commanding him to fight. Yes, it is true that U.S. soldiers who refuse to continue to participate in the state's interventions, invasions, and occupations might be dishonorably discharged, court-martialed, sent to prison, mistaken for a left-wing antiwar activist, called a coward, branded as anti-American, labeled a traitor, shunned by family, termed a quitter, ridiculed by veterans, or ostracized by fellow soldiers. Perhaps all of the above. But doing what's right is oftentimes not an easy thing to do. There are frequently adverse consequences to doing the right thing.

But even if a gun was held to a soldier's head and he was commanded to fight, does that mean he should give in? Don't the negative consequences of refusing to fight that I mentioned above pale in comparison to losing one's life? My answer is still the same: Do what's right. If it's not right to invade and occupy another country, then don't do it. If it's not right to kill people and break things, then don't do it. The consequences be damned.

I have prescribed a bitter pill, and some will have a hard time digesting it. I am afraid that Christopher Levenick is right. The illicit love affair that many Americans—and especially many conservative, evangelical, and fundamentalist American Christians—have with the U.S. military means that it all comes down to a uniform. God help us when the absence or presence of a uniform is all that it takes to hold or not hold someone responsible for the destruction of person and property. God help us.

* * * * *

SUPPORTING THE TROOPS

Now more than any time in history, the majority of Americans are in love with the military. It doesn't seem to matter how many countries the United States has bases in. It doesn't seem to matter how many countries the United States has troops stationed in. It doesn't seem to matter that the United States has had troops in some countries since the end of World War II. It doesn't seem to matter what the reason is for each war or intervention. It doesn't seem to matter how many foreign civilians are killed or injured. It doesn't seem to matter how many billions of dollars are spent by the military. It doesn't seem to matter what the troops are actually doing—Americans generally believe in supporting the troops no matter what.

I don't support the troops. I don't support the troops in this war, and I won't support them in the next one with Iran or any other country.

The typical view of the U.S. military held by the average American is the one expressed by the American Legion:

> At this moment, America's finest young men and women are serving in harms way on our behalf in places thousands of miles from our shores. In Iraq, they liberated oppressed people. In Afghanistan, the Philippines, parts of the Middle East and even here at home, they are preventing another Sept. 11. In over 130 countries, the U.S. military is finding and eliminating terrorists

committed to destroying our way of life.

This is gibberish. Every sentence contains at least one lie, and the parts that are true (troops thousands of miles away in over 130 countries) are undesirable. These are the people whose patriotic juices flow when they see a bumper sticker that says: "If You Can Read, Thank a Teacher. If You Can Read in English, Thank a Marine." They might even have their own bumper sticker that boldly proclaims: "My Son Is in the Air Force." These are the people who think that I am only able to write what I do because some Americans in the past donned a military uniform and fought the communists in Vietnam. These are the people who think that everything the military does is somehow in defense of our freedoms.

Many Americans, however, are not that gullible. They have a healthy distrust of government. They are not in favor of the U.S. military participating in U.N. peacekeeping operations, nation building, or regime changes. And while some might favor the military being used to assist in humanitarian relief efforts, others would be opposed to any interventions on foreign soil.

It is understandable that those in the former group who hold a glorified view of the military might think that it is treasonous to not support the troops in whatever military or humanitarian endeavor the president sends them on, but it is strange to see those in the latter group likewise say that they support the troops. At the SupportYourTroops website we are even told:

> Regardless of your opinions on war or U.S. foreign policy, we
> hope you take some time to show YOUR troops that you support
> them.

But why should we? It is ludicrous to say you oppose the war but support the troops. It is the troops that invaded a foreign country. It is the troops that are occupying a foreign country. It is the troops that are dropping the bombs. It is the troops that are throwing the grenades. It is the troops that are launching the missiles. It is the troops that are firing the mortars. It is the troops that are shooting the bullets. It is the troops that are destroying homes and infrastructure. It is the troops that are injuring, maiming, and killing people, including thousands of civilians.

If more Americans who don't support U.S. wars and interventions would also quit expressing support for the troops then perhaps more of the troops would quit participating in these wars and interventions.

But what about the Iraqis? They have killed, injured, or maimed thousands of U.S. soldiers. Of course they have. What do you think we would do to foreign troops that invaded our soil? But did we not remove their oppressive dictator? Indeed we did. But there are some things about removing Saddam Hussein that should be noted. First, wasn't he also an oppressive dictator in the 1980s? Why is it that he was our friend up until the Persian Gulf War? Second, Hussein was a greater "threat" to U.S. interests under the regime of Bush I than he was under Bush II. Why wasn't he taken out in 1991 after we routed his armies? Third, why are U.S. troops still in Iraq three years after they toppled Hussein's regime? What happened to "victory" and "Mission Accomplished?" Fourth, how would Americans feel if another country said that we needed to submit to a regime change? As much as Americans loathe George Bush, they would be outraged. And fifth, whose responsibility was it to remove Saddam Hussein from power? It certainly wasn't the responsibility of the United States. The kind of government they have and the type of leader they have is the sole business of the Iraqi people. If Saddam was so bad, any Iraqi could have put a bullet in his head and gone down in history as a hero. Even Saddam had to sleep at night. Ridding the country of Saddam Hussein was not worth the life of one American. Not one. What comfort it must be to the mother of a dead American soldier to know that although her son is dead and Saddam Hussein is alive, healthy, and eating three meals a day—he has been deposed!

I have been accused by an emotional wreck of a mother of boys in the military of hating American troops fighting in Iraq and wanting them to come home in body bags because I don't support the troops. I have never said or thought anything of the kind. I feel sorry for American troops sent to fight without the proper equipment or training. I feel sorry for American troops sent to fight for bogus reasons. I feel sorry for American troops sent to fight without a clear mission. I feel sorry for American troops sent to fight for a liar in chief.

I especially feel sorry for those U.S. soldiers who now realize that the United States had no business invading Iraq regardless of how quickly the war might have ended or how few casualties we might have suffered. I realize that they feel trapped in a war machine run by a deranged psychotic with no regard for their welfare. But as I have recently expressed, the troops are still responsible for their actions. A man does not throw his morality out the window just because he puts on a uniform, as one of my critics recently suggested.

In spite of everything I have said about not supporting the troops, there are in fact some ways in which I fully support them. I support bringing the troops home—today, not tomorrow or next week or next month—right now. I support providing the troops with gainful employment. I support allowing the troops to be conscientious objectors—the more the better. I support allowing the troops to leave the military—in droves. I support giving the troops medical treatment for their injuries. I support giving the troops mental help for emotional problems related to being in combat.

And when they are all home—from Iraq and everywhere else in the world—I support using the troops to actually patrol our coasts and guard our borders. I support the troops so much that I don't want them sent to fight any more foreign wars.

Support the troops!

* * * * *

NO, YOU CAN'T HAVE MY DAUGHTER

The military is getting desperate. Morale is at an all time low, enlistments are way down, casualties are way up, more U.S. soldiers have been killed in Iraq than people were killed in the September 11th attacks, and there is no end to the war in sight.

My daughter, a high school senior, was just sent in the mail a slick advertisement from the Army National Guard "introducing up to 20,000 new reasons to join the National Guard."

Every one of them is a dollar bill.

In addition to the pictures of U.S. currency on the front of the envelope, there are pictures of six smiling Guard members on the back. Inside is a reply card, some information on what the Guard has to offer, and a letter from a colonel who is the Guard's chief recruiter.

On the reply card is a redemption code to get a free iTunes music download and the promise of a free Army National Guard t-shirt and an American Soldier DVD. Inside the envelope there is an information card about the National Guard's College First Enlistment Option:

- Have the time *and* money to focus on college
- Up to two years of non-deployment following completion of Initial Active Duty Training
- Up to a $20,000 Enlistment Bonus
- 100% Tuition Assistance
- $20,000 Student Loan Repayment for Pre-existing Loans
- Additional Educational Assistance of up to $350 per month

Sounds like an impressive package, but I afraid that I will have to say no, you can't have my daughter.

Call me old-fashioned, call me traditional, call me chauvinistic, call me over-protective, call me misogynic, but the National Guard is no place for a young woman. I will not waste my time saying that men and women are different and that women have no business being in any branch of the military, but I will say this. I previously wrote about the fifty-four female American soldiers who have been killed in Iraq. Nine of them were in the National Guard. That number is now up to sixty, including a member of the National Guard, Sgt. Denise A. Lannaman, 46, of Bayside, N.Y., who died on October 1 from a non-combat related incident. Of all the places for a young American woman to die, a battlefield in Iraq certainly shouldn't be one of them. In my previous article I said: "What kind of military do we have that sends women to die overseas? What kind of society do we have that would accept a woman with children flying a military helicopter in Iraq or anywhere else?" I stand behind those two statements. Women now comprise about 16 percent of the enlisted ranks and 19 percent of the officer corps, and those numbers are getting higher.

Another reason the National Guard can't have my daughter is that the Guard is being used as cannon fodder. The opening paragraphs of the letter from the Guard's chief recruiter say about the Guard:

> For nearly 370 years, America has relied on its National Guard to defend our shores and serve our citizens in times of need.
>
> In the wake of Hurricane Katrina, over *41,000 National Guard* members from 42 states across America rushed to storm-ravaged areas to save lives, maintain law and order and support recovery efforts.

But is this what the National Guard is being used for? An increasing number of Guard members are being sent to the quagmire in Iraq. After the Army recently announced that it would keep the current level of troops in Iraq—about 120,000—through 2010, the Army chief of staff, Gen. Peter J. Schoomaker, said that "the Army will have to rely on the National Guard and Reserves to maintain the current level of deployments." According to Defense Department, the number of members of the Guard and Reserve that have been placed on active duty in support of the partial mobilization for the Army National Guard and Army Reserve is 80,234. The total number of National Guard and Reserve personnel from all branches of the military is now up to 100,694. A cumulative roster of all National Guard and Reserve personnel who are currently mobilized can be seen here. Military analyst William Lind has stated about this misuse of the National Guard:

> One of the likely effects of the disastrous war in Iraq will be the
> destruction of an old American institution, the National Guard.
> Desperate for troops as the situation in Iraq deteriorates, Secretary
> of Defense Rumsfeld is using the National Guard in a mission for
> which it was never intended: carrying on a "war of choice"
> halfway around the world. Most Guardsmen enlisted expecting to
> help their neighbors in natural disasters, or perhaps maintain order
> locally in the event of rioting. They never signed up for Vietnam
> II.

Over one third of the U.S. troops in Iraq are National Guard members.
And more than half of the U.S. casualties there were members of either
the Guard or Reserve.

Still another reason the National Guard can't have my daughter is
because of the number of sexual assaults involving members of the
military. An Associated Press investigation in August revealed that "more
than 100 young women who expressed interest in joining the military in
the past year were preyed upon sexually by their recruiters." The AP
found that "more than 80 military recruiters were disciplined last year for
sexual misconduct with potential enlistees. The cases occurred across all
branches of the military and in all regions of the country." According to
the DOD's Sexual Assault Report for 2005: "The Services received 2,374
reports of alleged cases of sexual assault involving members of the Armed
Forces." Restricted reports were filed in 327 cases, which means that
although victims are allowed "to receive services from sexual assault
program staff, healthcare, providers, and chaplains," no investigation is
conducted and no notification is given to command authorities or military
criminal investigative organizations. Out of the remaining 2,047 cases that
were subject to investigation, 661 were still pending at the end of the year.
The number of sexual assaults involving military personnel is evidently
a significant problem. The Sexual Assault Report informs us that the
military services established sexual assault program offices at all major
installations and collaborated with DoD to train more than 1,000 Sexual
Assault Response Coordinators and Victim Advocates to conduct those
programs. They have also trained more than 1,000,000 service members
and have integrated sexual assault awareness instruction into initial entry
training and professional military education.

All of the time and money wasted on this training was only
necessary because of the feminization of the military.

It is certainly true that any young woman over the age of eighteen has a perfect legal right to enlist in the National Guard. And it is certainly true that those who join do so of their own free will. It is up to us fathers to teach them about the true nature of this war and the U.S. military. And if not fathers, then mothers, brothers, sisters, clergymen, or friends. Someone must look out for these young women. The military recruiters certainly won't.

* * * * *

DEADLY OATHS

"I, _____, do solemnly swear (or affirm) that I will support and defend the Constitution of the United States against all enemies, foreign and domestic; that I will bear true faith and allegiance to the same; and that I will obey the orders of the President of the United States and the orders of the officers appointed over me, according to regulations and the Uniform Code of Military Justice. So help me God." ~ U.S. Military Enlistment Oath (U.S. Code, Title 10, Subtitle A, Part II, Chapter 31, § 502).

Okay (so I have been told), perhaps the war in Iraq is an unconstitutional, unjust, illegal, immoral, and unnecessary war of aggression. But what's a soldier to do? He can't just walk away. It's too far to swim across the Atlantic. And besides, there is no draft. Every soldier joined the military of his own free will. He committed himself to serve for a certain number of years. He just can't quit. He isn't allowed to change his job. It doesn't matter what his opinion of the war is now, he took an oath to obey the president and his officers.

Shall we do evil [continue to fight this war] that good [keep an oath] may come (Romans 3:8)?

Some Christians would say yes, and then try to justify their decision with Scripture:

If a man vow a vow unto the LORD, or swear an oath to bind his soul with a bond; he shall not break his word, he shall do according to all that proceedeth out of his mouth (Numbers 30:2).

But is vowing a vow to God the same as vowing a vow to obey the president? Is swearing an oath to the Lord the same as swearing an oath to obey U.S. military officers? Obviously not. The president is not God, except in the mind of some Christian warmongers. And neither is the U.S. military, except to these Christian warmongers.

Taking an oath to obey one's commander in chief and officers can result in the death of innocents. There are two examples of deadly oaths in the Bible.

In the Old Testament, there is the case of Jephthah, who hastily sacrificed his daughter:

> And Jephthah vowed a vow unto the LORD, and said, If thou shalt without fail deliver the children of Ammon into mine hands,
> Then it shall be, that whatsoever cometh forth of the doors of my house to meet me, when I return in peace from the children of Ammon, shall surely be the LORD's, and I will offer it up for a burnt offering.
> So Jephthah passed over unto the children of Ammon to fight against them; and the LORD delivered them into his hands.
> And he smote them from Aroer, even till thou come to Minnith, even twenty cities, and unto the plain of the vineyards, with a very great slaughter. Thus the children of Ammon were subdued before the children of Israel.
> And Jephthah came to Mizpeh unto his house, and, behold, his daughter came out to meet him with timbrels and with dances: and she was his only child; beside her he had neither son nor daughter.
> And it came to pass, when he saw her, that he rent his clothes, and said, Alas, my daughter! thou hast brought me very low, and thou art one of them that trouble me: for I have opened my mouth unto the LORD, and I cannot go back.
> And she said unto him, My father, if thou hast opened thy mouth unto the LORD, do to me according to that which hath proceeded out of thy mouth; forasmuch as the LORD hath taken vengeance for thee of thine enemies, even of the children of Ammon.
> And she said unto her father, Let this thing be done for me: let me alone two months, that I may go up and down upon the mountains, and bewail my virginity, I and my fellows.
> And he said, Go. And he sent her away for two months: and she went with her companions, and bewailed her virginity upon the mountains.
> And it came to pass at the end of two months, that she returned unto her father, who did with her according to his vow which he had vowed: and she knew no man. And it was a custom in Israel,
> That the daughters of Israel went yearly to lament the daughter of Jephthah the Gileadite four days in a year (Judges 10:30–40).

In the New Testament, there is the case of Herod, who rashly had John the Baptist executed:

But when Herod heard thereof, he said, It is John, whom I beheaded: he is risen from the dead.

For Herod himself had sent forth and laid hold upon John, and bound him in prison for Herodias' sake, his brother Philip's wife: for he had married her.

For John had said unto Herod, It is not lawful for thee to have thy brother's wife.

Therefore Herodias had a quarrel against him, and would have killed him; but she could not:

For Herod feared John, knowing that he was a just man and an holy, and observed him; and when he heard him, he did many things, and heard him gladly.

And when a convenient day was come, that Herod on his birthday made a supper to his lords, high captains, and chief estates of Galilee;

And when the daughter of the said Herodias came in, and danced, and pleased Herod and them that sat with him, the king said unto the damsel, Ask of me whatsoever thou wilt, and I will give it thee.

And he sware unto her, Whatsoever thou shalt ask of me, I will give it thee, unto the half of my kingdom.

And she went forth, and said unto her mother, What shall I ask? And she said, The head of John the Baptist.

And she came in straightway with haste unto the king, and asked, saying, I will that thou give me by and by in a charger the head of John the Baptist.

And the king was exceeding sorry; yet for his oath's sake, and for their sakes which sat with him, he would not reject her.

And immediately the king sent an executioner, and commanded his head to be brought: and he went and beheaded him in the prison,

And brought his head in a charger, and gave it to the damsel: and the damsel gave it to her mother (Mark 6:16–28).

So what should a soldier do once he realizes that the war in Iraq is an unconstitutional, unjust, illegal, immoral, and unnecessary war of aggression? Should he continue to fight and bleed and die for a lie because he swore to obey his commander in chief and officers?

One option available to soldiers is to seek conscientious objector status. According to Department of Defense Directive 1300.6, a conscientious objector has "a firm, fixed and sincere objection to participation in war in any form or the bearing of arms, by reason of religious training and belief." But this directive goes on to define "religious training and belief" as:

Belief in an external power or being or deeply held moral or ethical belief, to which all else is subordinate or upon which all else is ultimately dependent, and which has the power or force to affect moral-well-being. The external power or being need not be of an orthodox deity, but may be a sincere and meaningful belief that occupies in the life of its possessor a place parallel to that filled by the God of another, or, in the case of deeply held moral or ethical beliefs, a belief held with the strength and devotion of traditional religious conviction. The term "religious training and belief" may include solely moral or ethical beliefs even though the applicant himself may not characterize these beliefs as "religious" in the traditional sense, or may expressly characterize them as not religious.

The Central Committee for Conscientious Objectors has a guide to military discharges and GI rights. The Center on Conscience & War works to defend and extend the rights of conscientious objectors. Iraq Veterans Against the War supports all those resisting the war, including conscientious objectors and others facing prosecution for refusing to fight. Contact information for veterans who have firsthand experience with the conscientious objection process, and have volunteered to give advice and support to soldiers seeking conscientious objector status, can be seen here.

Something akin to conscientious objector status was granted to Jews in the Old Testament. When it was time for the people of Israel to go out to battle against their enemies (Deuteronomy 20:1), exceptions were made for those who just "planted a vineyard" (Deuteronomy 20:6), those who just "betrothed a wife" (Deuteronomy 20:7), and those who were "fearful and fainthearted" (Deuteronomy 20:8).

But there is another part of the U.S. military enlistment oath that is being overlooked—the part that reads: "I will support and defend the Constitution of the United States against all enemies, foreign and domestic; that I will bear true faith and allegiance to the same."

Months before the invasion of Iraq, Congressman Ron Paul (R–Tex.) pointed out on the House floor the unconstitutional nature of the upcoming war. So what will it be Mr. Patriotic, Constitution-Loving American? Bush and Rumsfeld or the Constitution?

Daniel Ellsberg, who released the Pentagon Papers to the press in 1971, recently wrote in *Harper's Magazine* about his conflict of loyalties:

In 1964 it never even occurred to me to break the many secrecy agreements I had signed, in the Marines, at the Rand Corporation, in the Pentagon. Although I already knew the Vietnam War was a mistake and based on lies, my loyalties then were to the secretary of defense and the president (and to my promises of secrecy, on which my own career as a president's man depended). I'm not proud that it took me years of war to awaken to the higher loyalties owed by every government official to the rule of law, to our soldiers in harm's way, to our fellow citizens, and, explicitly, to the Constitution, which every one of us had sworn an oath "to support and uphold."

It took me that long to recognize that the secrecy agreements we had signed frequently conflicted with our oath to uphold the Constitution. That conflict arose almost daily, unnoticed by me or other officials, whenever we were secretly aware that the president or other executive officers were lying to or misleading Congress. In giving priority, in effect, to my promise of secrecy—ignoring my constitutional obligation—I was no worse or better than any of my Vietnam-era colleagues, or those who later saw the Iraq war approaching and failed to warn anyone outside the executive branch.

There are several groups of people that would be better off if fewer American soldiers sought to uphold their deadly oath.

The latest report on the number of Iraqis killed since the U.S. invasion claims that the number of dead Iraqis is now around 655,000. Naturally, President Bush doesn't believe the report to be credible. Well, then how about the very conservative estimate by the Iraq Body Count research group that puts the number of Iraqi civilian deaths between 44,661 and 49,610? And then there are the thousands of deaths in Afghanistan. It really doesn't matter what the actual numbers are. To many Americans the dead Iraqis and Afghans are just terrorists and ragheads. More sophisticated defenders of the war will dismiss the dead Iraqis and Afghans as just collateral damage.

And what about the toll of the wars in Iraq and Afghanistan on Americans?

100,000 veterans of these wars are receiving disability compensation of some kind.

30,000 veterans of these wars have received treatment for post-traumatic stress disorder.

3,144 veterans of these wars never made it home to receive either of the above.

How many more American soldiers must die for a lie before the insanity that is the Global War on Terrorism is ended?

* * * * *

BEWARE OF CHILD PREDATORS

There is a new breed of child predator on the loose. You won't find him featured on America's Most Wanted or appearing on the FBI's Ten Most Wanted list. Up until now parents who were concerned about child predators could check their state's Sex Offender Registries or the Child Predator Watch List. But now we can thank *Ladies Home Journal* magazine for informing parents about this dangerous new predator in an article that appears in the latest issue (February 2007) called "This Man Wants Your Children."

I don't normally read *Ladies Home Journal*. In fact, I don't think I had ever read a single copy until I happened recently to look through the latest issue. Unfortunately, *Ladies Home Journal* has enlisted in the service of the state. The purpose of its thirteen-page child predator article was not to warn parents about predators at all—it was to promote them.

You see, "This Man Wants Your Children" was not about sex offenders—even though some of them are sex offenders—it was about Army recruiters; specifically, Sergeant First Class Chad Christenson, one of the top Army recruiters in the country. Indeed, Sgt. Christenson was the Army's "Recruiter of the Year" in 2005.

We learn a number of things in this article about recruiters and recruiting. The 2005 military recruiting budget was about $4 billion. Since the recruiting numbers were way down in 2005, "the Army added 1,000 new recruiters, doubled the maximum sign-in bonus from $20,000 to $40,000, relaxed standards and raised the maximum-age limit." Then there was the new $200 million ad campaign for 2006. We are also told that "in 2005 the Army officially investigated 836 allegations of recruiter misconduct." The Army now accepts lower entrance scores on aptitude tests, grants more "moral waivers" to allow convicted criminals to enlist, and allows non-citizens to gain their citizenship after only one year of active duty. The enlistment age has been raised from 35 to 40 to 42. Older women who want to enlist will find that the physical fitness requirements are now less rigorous—they must now be able to do three push-ups. Oh, and the Army now has a MySpace profile.

Thanks to the No Child Left Behind Act of 2001, which mandates that "public high school administrators are required to allow military recruiters access to students or risk losing federal funding," Christenson preys on high school students. He is stationed in Texas, "the state that contributed more 2005 and 2006 Army enlistees than any other." He is paid about $64,000 to "show young Texans how the Army can enrich their lives." I know public high school teachers that make half of that and private high school teachers who make less than half of that. Christenson says the Army changed his life—"It made me who I am." But who he is?

We read in this article about some of the people Christenson persuades to join the Army. One recruit tells him that he wants to serve in the infantry. His reason: "It's a moral thing with me. After what happened on 9/11, I can't live with myself if I don't go to war." Does Christenson tell the young man that the war in Iraq has nothing to do with 9/11? Why not? "We have no evidence that Saddam Hussein was involved with September the 11th," said Christenson's commander in chief in answer to a reporter's question on September 17, 2003, after hundreds of U.S. soldiers had already died for a lie. Another recruit is a forty-one-year-old mother of five. Does Christenson tell her that it would better if she stayed home with her family? Does he tell her about the female U.S. soldiers who have been killed in Iraq? Why not? I have posted their names and pictures here.

What else is Christenson not telling young men and women about the U.S. military? Is he telling them that the military does very little to actually defend the country? Is he telling them that the military is not defending our freedoms? Is he telling them that the military is protecting the shores, guarding the borders, and patrolling the coasts of other countries instead of our own? Is he telling them that the military is garrisoning the planet with its military bases? Is he telling them that the war in Iraq has lasted longer than the war against Nazi Germany? Is he telling them that the military has troops in over 150 different regions of the world?

Why not?

Sgt. Christenson is supposed to be an honest man. We are told in the *Ladies Home Journal* article that he is "familiar with the dark side of recruiting, of course—the improprieties brought on by the pressure to meet quotas," but that "he scrupulously avoids the sorts of ethical lapses—such as misleading potential recruits (or their parents) about the chances of going to Iraq—that have tripped up other recruiters." This means that he doesn't tell students that the war in Iraq is over in order to get them to enlist—like some Army recruiters did. So why doesn't he tell young men and women the whole story?

I wonder how many people would join the Army if the gentleman in this picture were a recruiter? Since he left his legs in Iraq—or what was left of them—for what will go down in history as the lie of the century, perhaps he would be more inclined to give a little more information to potential recruits than Sgt. Christenson. Instead of talking about the amount of a sign-in bonus, he could talk about the more than 3,000 U.S.

soldiers that have been killed in Iraq. Instead of speaking about the free health care that the military provides, he could speak about the hundreds of disabled soldiers who are missing body parts like he is. Instead of discussing the amount of money available from the military for college, he could discuss the costs of the war in Iraq—now over $200 million a day. Instead of mentioning the structure and stability that the military provides, he could mention the tens of thousands—and perhaps hundreds of thousands—of Iraqis who have been killed since the U.S. invaded Iraq almost four years ago. Instead of conversing about how the military has lowered enlistment standards, he could converse about the evils of an interventionist U.S. foreign policy that sends young men to die for a lie. And instead of informing potential soldiers about the variety of positions available in the military, he could inform them about the animosity that exists between the Sunni and Shiite Muslims that has now erupted —thanks to the United States—into a civil war.

Perhaps some disabled soldiers who now realize that they gave their limbs in vain should sue the U.S. military under the Americans with Disabilities Act for the right to be a recruiter. I wonder what employing handicapped soldiers would do for enlistment quotas?

Protect your children and the children of everyone you know: Warn them about child predators—and especially those in uniform.

* * * * *

THE ANTI-FEDERALISTS ON STANDING ARMIES

> "He has kept among us, in times of peace, Standing Armies without the Consent of our legislatures." ~ Declaration of Independence

The opponents of the Constitution, which history has mischaracterized as *Anti-Federalists,* had numerous reasons for rejecting the proposed Constitution. Although their central argument concerned the danger to liberty from a strong central government, they also wrote extensively against the Constitution's provision for a standing army and federal control over the militia.

In Article I, Section 8, of the Constitution, it states that The Congress shall have Power

> To raise and support Armies, but no Appropriation of Money to
> that Use shall be for a longer Term than two Years;

To provide and maintain a Navy;

To make Rules for the Government and Regulation of the land and naval Forces;

To provide for calling forth the Militia to execute the Laws of the Union, suppress Insurrections and repel Invasions;

To provide for organizing, arming, and disciplining the Militia, and for governing such Part of them as may be employed in the Service of the United States, reserving to the States respectively, the Appointment of the Officers, and the Authority of training the Militia according to the discipline prescribed by Congress;

The Anti-Federalists Were Opposed to a Standing Army in Peacetime

The Anti-Federalist who called himself "Centinel" wrote a series of letters that appeared in the Philadelphia *Independent Gazetteer* in late 1787 and early 1788. He referred to standing armies in his second letter as "that grand engine of oppression."

The "Federal Farmer" wrote a series of letters that were published in the Poughkeepsie *Country Journal* in late 1787 and early 1788. In his third letter, he lamented that under the new Constitution Congress "will have unlimited power to raise armies, and to engage officers and men for any number of years." He then voiced his objection to standing armies:

> I see so many men in American fond of a standing army, and especially among those who probably will have a large share in administering the federal system; it is very evident to me, that we shall have a large standing army as soon as the monies to support them can be possibly found. An army is not a very agreeable place of employment for the young gentlemen of many families.

He also stated in his thirteenth letter that "we all agree, that a large standing army has a strong tendency to depress and inslave the people."

Essays signed "Old Whig" also appeared in Philadelphia's *Independent Gazetteer* the same time as the letters from the "Federal Farmer." In his second essay, he remarked that "this generation in America have seen enough of war and its usual concomitants to prevent all of us from wishing to see any more of it;—all except those who make a trade of war." In his fifth essay, in the course of explaining how rulers can violate the rights of conscience, "Old Whig" stated that "*the unlimited power of taxation* will give them the command of all the treasures of the continent; *a standing army will* be wholly at their devotion."

"Cato" wrote a series of letters that appeared in the *New York Journal* between September 1787 and January 1788. One of his complaints against the proposed new government was that "standing armies may be established, and appropriation of money made for their support, for two years."

Those in the Pennsylvania ratification convention who objected to the proposed Constitution published their views in the *Pennsylvania Packet and Daily Advertiser* on December 18, 1787, as *The Address and Reasons of Dissent of the Minority of the Convention of Pennsylvania to Their Constituents*. In their address, these Pennsylvania delegates remarked that one of the helps to Congress completing "the system of despotism" is "when a numerous standing army shall render opposition vain." The delegates in the minority also stated that in case the new government "must be executed by force," the framers of the Constitution "have therefore made a provision for this purpose in a permanent STANDING ARMY, and a MILITIA that may be subjected to as strict discipline and government." They objected to a standing army because

> A standing army in the hands of a government placed so independent of the people, may be made a fatal instrument to overturn the public liberties; it may be employed to enforce the collection of the most oppressive taxes, and to carry into execution the most arbitrary measures. An ambitious man who may have the army at his devotion, may step up into the throne, and seize upon absolute power.

The Anti-Federalist who signed his 1788 essays in the Baltimore *Maryland Gazette* "A Farmer" gave historical examples in his second essay to show that "both political and civil liberty have long since ceased to exist in almost all the countries that now employ standing troops, and that their slavery has in every instance been effected and maintained by the instrumentality and invariable obedience of these living machines to their chief." He mentions not only that in England "a standing army is declared to be contrary to their constitution, and a militia the only natural and safe defense of a free people," but also that in America "the constitutions of all the States positively forbid any standing troops at all, much less laws for them." For example:

> Massachusetts: "And as in times of peace, armies are dangerous to liberty, they ought not to be maintained without the consent of the

legislature."

Pennsylvania & North Carolina: "And as standing armies in the time of peace, are dangerous to liberty, they ought not to be kept up."

Maryland & Delaware: "That standing armies are dangerous to liberty, and ought not to be raised or kept without consent of the legislature."

"A Farmer" also mused in this essay: "I was persuaded that the grave would have closed on my bones, before this question would be publicly proposed in America.—Are we then to look up to a standing army for the defence of this soil from foreign invasion?" In his sixth essay, he included as a "great and manifest" defect in the proposed government "the manifest danger to public liberty from a standing army, without limitation of number, in time of peace."

The Anti-Federalist who used the name of "John DeWitt" wrote extensively about the evils of standing armies in a series of essays published in the Boston *American Herald* in late 1787:

They shall have also the power of raising, supporting and establishing a standing army in time of peace in your several towns, and I see not why in your several houses."

Where lies the security of the people? What assurances have they that either their taxes will not be exacted but in the greatest emergencies, and then sparingly, or that standing armies will be raised and supported for the very plausible purpose only of cantoning them upon their frontiers? There is but one answer to these questions.—They have none.

The advocates at the present day, for a standing army in the New Congress pretend it is necessary for the respectability of government. I defy them to produce an instance in any country, in the Old or New World, where they have not finally done away the liberties of the people.—Every writer upon government,—Lock, Sidney, Hamden, and a list of other have uniformly asserted, that standing armies are a solecism in any government; that no nation ever supported them, that did not resort to, rely upon, and finally become a prey to them.

It is universally agreed, that a militia and a standing body of troops never yet flourished in the same soil. Tyrants have uniformly

depended upon the latter, at the expense of the former. Experience
has taught them, that a standing body of regular forces, where ever
they can be completely introduced, are always efficacious in
enforcing their edicts, however arbitrary.

There is no instance of any government being reduced to a
confirmed tyranny without military oppression; and the first policy
of tyrants has been to annihilate all other means of national
activity and defence, and to rely solely upon standing troops.

It is very true, that the celebrated Mr. Wilson, a member of the
Convention, and who we may suppose breathes, in some measure,
the spirit of that body, tells you, it [a standing army] is for the
purpose of forming cantonments upon your frontiers, and for the
dignity and safety of your country, as it respects foreign nations.
No man that loves his country could object to their being raised for
the first of these causes, but for the last it cannot be necessary.
GOD has so separated us by an extensive ocean from the rest of
mankind, he hath so liberally endowed us with privileges, and so
abundantly taught us to esteem them precious, it would be
impossible, while we retain our integrity and advert to first
principles, for any nation whatever to subdue us.

DeWitt also equated the "revenue, excise, impost and stamp officers" that
would be introduced under the new Constitution with a standing army.

Patrick Henry (1736–1799), in his June 5 speech in the Virginia
ratifying convention against adopting the Constitution, likewise deni-
grated standing armies: "A standing army we shall have, also, to execute
the execrable commands of tyranny; and how are you to punish them?
Will you order them to be punished? Who shall obey these orders? Will
your mace-bearer be a match for a disciplined regiment?"

"Brutus" wrote more about the evils of standing armies than any
other Anti-Federalist. Sixteen of his essays were published in the *New
York Journal* from October 1787 to April 1788. In four of these essays
(numbers 1, 8, 9, 10), he explains how the establishment and maintenance
of standing armies breeds fear, is destructive to liberty, and should be
viewed as a scourge to a country instead of a benefit. Since I have already
explored at length the opinions of "Brutus" on this subject in a previous
article ("Brutus on the Evils of Standing Armies"), I only present here
something he said in his ninth essay on this subject:

That standing armies are dangerous to the liberties of a people was
proved in my last number—If it was necessary, the truth of the

position might be confirmed by the history of almost every nation in the world. A cloud of the most illustrious patriots of every age and country, where freedom has been enjoyed, might be adduced as witnesses in support of the sentiment. But I presume it would be useless, to enter into a laboured argument, to prove to the people of America, a position, which has so long and so generally been received by them as a kind of axiom.

The "Impartial Examiner" wrote essays for the Virginia *Independent Chronicle* in 1788. He twice refers to standing armies in his first essay:

It has ever been held that standing armies in times of peace are dangerous to a free country; and no observation seems to contain more reason in it. Besides being useless, as having no object of employment, they are inconvenient and expensive. The soldiery, who are generally composed of the dregs of the people, when disbanded, or unfit for military service, being equally unfit for any other employment, become extremely burthensome. As they are a body of men exempt from the common occupations of social life, having an interest different from the rest of the community, they wanton in the lap of ease and indolence, without feeling the duties, which arise from the political connection, though drawing their subsistence from the bosom of the state. The severity of discipline necessary to be observed reduces them to a degree of slavery; the unconditional submission to the commands of their superiors, to which they are bound, renders them the fit instruments of tyranny and oppression.—Hence they have in all ages afforded striking examples of contributing, more or less, to enslave mankind;—and whoever will take the trouble to examine, will find that by far the greater part of the different nations, who have fallen from the glorious state of liberty, owe their ruin to standing armies.

You will advert to the dangerous and oppressive consequences, that may ensue from the introduction of standing armies in times of peace; those baneful engines of ambition, against which free nations have always guarded with the greatest degree of caution.

The Anti-Federalists Were Opposed to Federal Control over the Militia

The "Impartial Examiner," in his first essay, referenced above, explained his preference for a militia over a standing army:

It has been urged that they are necessary to provide against sudden attacks. Would not a well regulated militia, duly trained to discipline, afford ample security? Such, I conceive, to be the best, the surest means of protection, which a free people can have when not actually engaged in war. This kind of defence is attended with two advantages superior to any others; first, when it is necessary to embody an army, they at once form a band of soldiers, whose interests are uniformly the same with those of the whole community, and in whose safety they see involved every thing that is dear to themselves: secondly, if one army is cut off, another may be immediately raised already trained for military service. By a policy, somewhat similar to this, the Roman empire rose to the highest pitch of grandeur and magnificence.

What did the Anti-Federalists mean by a militia?

In the Virginia Declaration of Rights, which was written by George Mason (1725–1792) and adopted by the Virginia Constitutional Convention in 1776, it states:

> That a well-regulated militia, composed of the body of the people, trained to arms, is the proper, natural, and safe defense of a free state; that standing armies, in time of peace, should be avoided as dangerous to liberty; and that in all cases the military should be under strict subordination to, and governed by, the civil power.

The militia was always regarded as such until the Militia Act of 1903, which created the modern National Guard, and the rise of gun-control advocates, who try to keep guns out of the hands of the citizenry by redefining the Second Amendment as merely affirming the states' right to form National Guard-like militias. But the militia, as it is still defined in Title 10 of the U.S. Code, "consists of all able-bodied males at least 17 years of age and, except as provided in section 313 of title 32, under 45 years of age who are, or who have made a declaration of intention to become, citizens of the United States and of female citizens of the United States who are members of the National Guard."

A well-regulated and well-armed militia under the control of the several states was viewed by the Anti-Federalists as being essential to secure the liberties of the people. They opposed not only a regular standing army, but also a federalized militia that would serve the same function.

In his fifth essay, referred to above, the Anti-Federalist who called himself "Old Whig" stated that our future rulers can invade our rights of conscience because of the authority which is given them over the *militia*, by virtue of which they may, if they please, change all the officers of the militia on the continent in one day, and put in new officers whom they can better trust; by which they can subject all the militia to strict military laws, and punish the disobedient with death, or otherwise, as they shall think right: by which they can march the militia back and forward from one end of the continent to the other, at their discretion.

But "Old Whig" had another problem with federal control over the militia:

Let us instance one thing arising from this right of organizing and governing the militia. Suppose a man alledges that he is conscientiously scrupulous of bearing Arms.—By the bill of rights of Pennsylvania he is bound only to pay an equivalent for his personal service.—What is there in the new proposed constitution to prevent his being dragged like a Prussian soldier to the camp and there compelled to bear arms?

The "Federal Farmer," in his eighteenth and last letter, which was published in the Poughkeepsie *Country Journal* in January of 1788, argued that only state militias could protect the powers and liberties of the states against a federal government with a standing army. He believed that "the powers to form and arm the militia, to appoint their officers, and to command their services, are very important; nor ought they in a confederated republic to be lodged, solely, in any one member of the government." To put a check on the federal government, "the militia of any state shall not remain in the service of the union, beyond a given period, without the express consent of the state legislature."

The Address of the minority in the Pennsylvania ratification convention was very strongly opposed to federal control over state militias:

The absolute unqualified command that Congress have over the militia may be made instrumental to the destruction of all liberty, both public and private; whether of a personal, civil or religious nature.

First, the personal liberty of every man, probably from sixteen to sixty years of age, may be destroyed by the power Congress have in organizing and governing of the militia. As militia they may be subjected to fines to any amount, levied in a military manner; they may be subjected to corporal punishments of the most disgraceful and humiliating kind; and to death itself, by the sentence of a court martial. To this our young men will be more immediately subjected, as a select militia, composed of them, will best answer the purposes of government.

Secondly, the rights of conscience may be violated, as there is no exemption of those persons who are conscientiously scrupulous of hearing arms. These compose a respectable proportion of the community in the state. This is the more remarkable, because even when the distresses of the late war and the evident disaffection of many citizens of that description inflamed our passions, and when every person who was obliged to risk his own life must have been exasperated against such as on any account kept back from the common danger, yet even then, when outrage and violence might have been expected, the rights of conscience were held sacred.

Thirdly, the absolute command of Congress over the militia may be destructive of public liberty; for under the guidance of an arbitrary government, they may be made the unwilling instruments of tyranny. The militia of Pennsylvania may be marched to New England or Virginia to quell an insurrection occasioned by the most galling oppression, and aided by the standing army, they will no doubt be successful in subduing their liberty and independency. But in so doing, although the magnanimity of their minds will be extinguished, yet the meaner passions of resentment and revenge will be increased, and these in turn will be the ready and obedient instruments of despotism to enslave the others; and that with an irritated vengeance. Thus may the militia be made the instruments of crushing the last efforts of expiring liberty, of riveting the chains of despotism on their fellow-citizens, and on one another. This power can be exercised not only without violating the Constitution, but in strict conformity with it; it is calculated for this express purpose, and will doubtless be executed accordingly.

These Pennsylvania delegates closed their arguments against the Constitution by offering fourteen propositions to their state convention. The eleventh one concerns the subject at hand:

That the power of organizing, arming and disciplining the militia (the manner of disciplining the militia to be prescribed by Congress) remain with the individual states, and that Congress shall not have authority to call or march any of the militia out of their own state, without the consent of such state, and for such length of time only as such state shall agree.

The Anti-Federalists Were Not Alone

It is not just the Anti-Federalists who were opposed to standing armies. James Madison, "The Father of the Constitution," voiced his concern as well:

> A standing military force, with an overgrown Executive will not long be safe companions to liberty. The means of defence against foreign danger, have been always the instruments of tyranny at home. Among the Romans it was a standing maxim to excite a war, whenever a revolt was apprehended. Throughout all Europe, the armies kept up under the pretext of defending, have enslaved the people.

> Of all the enemies to public liberty, war is perhaps the most to be dreaded because it comprises and develops the germ of every other. War is the parent of armies; from these proceed debts and taxes; and armies, and debts, and taxes are the known instruments for bringing the many under the domination of the few.

Thomas Jefferson not only included standing armies in the Declaration of Independence as a component of British tyranny, he likewise despairingly described them elsewhere:

> There are instruments so dangerous to the rights of the nation and which place them so totally at the mercy of their governors that those governors, whether legislative or executive, should be restrained from keeping such instruments on foot but in well-defined cases. Such an instrument is a standing army.

> Were armies to be raised whenever a speck of war is visible in our horizon, we never should have been without them. Our resources would have been exhausted on dangers which have never happened, instead of being reserved for what is really to take place.

> Nor is it conceived needful or safe that a standing army should be kept up in time of peace.

Newspapers editorialized after the American Revolution against standing armies, referring to them as "that great support of tyrants" and as a "manifest danger to public liberty." This is because, as Lew Rockwell has well said, "America was born in love of liberty and opposition to a standing army. The two go together."

The Evil of a Standing Army

The contemporary historian of the American Revolution, Mercy Otis Warren, in her *History of the Rise, Progress, and Termination of the American Revolution* (1805), described the true beginning of the American Revolution as when British troops arrived in Boston in 1768: "The troops arrived from Halifax. This was indeed a painful era. The American war may be dated from this hostile act; a day which marks with infamy the councils of Great Britain."

Yet, the Federalist President Washington federalized the militia to suppress the 1794 Whiskey Rebellion, substituting an American army for a British one, and the Union Army occupied the South after the so-called Civil War. Advocates of a large standing army generally consider the former to be an isolated incident and the latter to be justified. Some even point to the Posse Comitatus Act of 1878, which limits the power of the national government to use the military for law enforcement purposes. True, but *except* when troops are used to quell domestic violence, *except* when troops are participating in the war on drugs, *except* when troops are engaged in homeland security activities, *except* when troops are used in major public emergencies, *except* when troops are utilized in the fight against illegal immigration, and *except* when troops are employed in fighting terrorism.

Proponents of a standing army are forgetting that governments have used standing armies, not just at home, but abroad as well. Both are equally destructive to liberty, for foreign wars demand enormous expenditures of the taxpayers' money, require the sacrifice of life or limb of thousands of the country's young men, and result in the suppression of civil liberties at home. This is why labor leader Samuel Gompers, a member of the Anti-Imperialist League, formed in 1898 in the midst of the Spanish-American War, could say:

> I propose stating as succinctly as possible the grounds of our opposition to the so-called policy of imperialism and expansion. We cannot annex the Philippines without a large increase in our standing army. A large standing army is repugnant to republican institutions and a menace to the liberty of our own people. If we annex the Philippines, we shall have to conquer the Filipinos by force of arms, and thereby deny to them what we claim to ourselves—the right to self-government.

Rather than America's military heritage being one of how the military has defended the country from attack, it is instead one of invasion, destabilization, occupation, subjugation, oppression, death, and destruction. Instead of the U.S. military defending our freedoms, the military has been at once the world's policeman, fireman, social worker, bully, and busybody. Rather than the presence of the U.S. military guaranteeing peace and stability throughout the world, the presence of the U.S. military more often than not is the cause of war and instability around the globe. Instead of existing to defend the country, U.S. troops exist to serve as the president's personal attack force, ready to obey his latest command to deploy to any country for any reason.

There are over 700 U.S. military bases on foreign soil. There are U.S. troops stationed in 159 different regions of the world in every corner of the globe. Foreign military bases and the stationing of troops abroad are for offensive military actions, not defensive ones. U.S. troops need to come home and then go home. But only a change in U.S. foreign policy can stop the evil that is America's standing army.

All quotations from the Anti-Federalists are taken from Regnery edition of The Anti-Federalists: Selected Writings and Speeches, *edited by Bruce Frohnen.*

* * * * *

DOD 101

"Hence likewise they will avoid the necessity of those overgrown Military establishments, which under any form of Government are inauspicious to liberty, and which are to be regarded as particularly hostile to Republican Liberty." ~ George Washington, Farewell Address

The Department of Homeland Security was established by the Homeland Security Act of 2002 (PL 107-296). It became operational in January of 2003. It is the third largest cabinet department in the federal government, with 180,000 employees and a budget of $46 billion. The mission statement of the Homeland Security Department includes this statement: "We will prevent and deter terrorist attacks and protect against and respond to threats and hazards to the nation."

Why, then, do we need a Department of Defense? And conversely, if the mission of the Defense Department is to defend the country, then why do we need a Department of Homeland Security?

The truth of the matter is that the Department of Defense, which couldn't defend its own headquarters, is misnamed. Rather than guarding our borders, patrolling our coasts, and protecting our citizens, the DOD is focused on—because of our interventionist foreign policy—invading the next country and fighting the next foreign war.

This is not exactly the picture one gets from DOD 101: An Introductory Overview of the Department of Defense, found on the Department's website.

According to the opening paragraph of DOD 101, the Department of Defense is America's oldest, largest, busiest, and most successful company. Although the DOD was actually created in 1949, two of its divisions are in fact quite old. The War Department was established in 1789 and the Navy Department in 1798. In 1947 the Department of War became the Department of the Army and the Department of the Air Force was created. These three departments were all united under the umbrella of the Department of Defense in 1949. Although the DOD should never be termed a company, it is indeed very large, employing over 1.3 million people on active duty, 669,281 civilian personnel, and 1.1 million in the National Guard and Reserve. There is also no question that the DOD is quite busy. But is the DOD America's most successful company? The DOD failed to protect the country on September 11th, 2001. The DOD failed to protect its headquarters on the same date. The only thing of late that the DOD has been successful at is bombing, maiming and killing foreigners, and spending over $200 million a day of the taxpayers' money on a failed war.

Under the heading of "Our Global Infrastructure," DOD 101 informs us that

> The Defense Department manages an inventory of installations and facilities to keep Americans safe. The Department's physical plant is huge by any standard, consisting of more than several hundred thousand individual buildings and structures located at more than 5,000 different locations or sites. When all sites are added together, the Department of Defense utilizes over 30 million acres of land.

There is no mention of the fact that there are over 700 U.S. military bases on foreign soil.

However, we are told in "Worldwide Presence" that "Department of Defense employees work in more than 163 countries. 450,925 troops and civilians are overseas both afloat and ashore. We operate in every time zone and in every climate." That is quite an admission. The presence of U.S. troops in foreign countries is something that I have written about many times (most recently here). For those critics of mine who continue to deny that my figures are accurate, will you also question this admission by the DOD?

To show just how large the DOD is, the next section of DOD 101 compares the military budget and the number of DOD employees to the budgets and numbers of employees of Wal-Mart, Exxon-Mobil, GM, and Ford. But is it a good thing that the DOD spends more money and employs more people than the largest U.S. corporations? No one who works for Wal-Mart, Exxon-Mobil, GM, or Ford costs the taxpayers a dime. The military budget for fiscal year 2006 is stated to be $419 billion. But not only did the DOD actually spend $499 billion, economist Robert Higgs has estimated that the true amount spent by the United States on defense during fiscal year 2006 was actually $934 billion. This means that defense-related spending for fiscal year 2008 will actually top $1 trillion for the first time in history, accounting for about one-third of the total federal budget.

Under the heading of "We Hire the Best," we are told that "the Department of Defense mission is accomplished seeking out our nation's best and brightest." Is that why the Army has relaxed standards, lowered the physical fitness requirements for women, increased waivers for medical problems, and raised the maximum-age limit to 42? Is that why the Army now accepts lower entrance scores on aptitude tests, grants more "moral waivers" to allow convicted criminals to enlist, allows more applicants with gang tattoos, and allows non-citizens to gain their citizenship after only one year of active duty? And now it has come to light that military recruiters have helped applicants cheat on drug tests.

According to DOD 101 section "We Instill Values," the core values of the Defense Department are leadership, professionalism, and technical know-how. Furthermore, "We constantly build and reinforce core values that everyone wearing a uniform must live by: duty, integrity, ethics, honor, courage, and loyalty." But are these the only values that the military instills? There is no mention in this section about other values like mistreating non-combatants, destroying civilian property, torturing prisoners, and not reporting the abuses perpetrated by fellow soldiers.

Not only does DOD 101 compare the Defense Department to a company, it also uses the language of the corporate world. Under the heading of "Who We Work For," we are informed that the chief executive officer is the president, the members of Congress serve as the board of directors, and the American people are the stockholders. But what kind of a corporation ever forced people to own its stock?

The section titled "Services Train and Equip" contains some startling admissions. The Army is said to defend "the land mass of the

United States, its territories, commonwealths, and possessions." But then we are told that the Army "operates in more than 50 countries." Although our Navy's aircraft carriers are "stationed in hotspots that include the Far East, the Persian Gulf, and the Mediterranean Sea," there is no mention of our Navy patrolling our coasts. The Air Force "routinely participates in peacekeeping, humanitarian, and aeromedical evacuation missions, and actively patrols the skies above Iraq [and] Bosnia." We also read that "Air Force crews annually fly missions into all but five nations of the world." One would get the impression in reading DOD 101 that the Air Force doesn't do anything related to defending the United States. The National Guard and Reserve are also mentioned in this section. In addition to providing "wartime military support" and undertaking "humanitarian and peacekeeping operations," the Guard and Reserve "are essential to, and are integral to the Homeland Security portion of our mission." Here is an admission by the DOD that the security of the homeland is only a portion of its mission. There is no mention, of course, about reenlistment rates for the Guard and Reserve being at an all-time low because of the war in Iraq.

In the section titled "Unified Commanders," we read about the Northern Command, which "oversees the defense of the continental United States." But why do we have a European Command, which "covers more than 13 million square miles and includes 93 countries and territories, to include Iceland, Greenland, the Azores, more than half of the Atlantic ocean, the Caspian sea, and Russia"? There is also a Central Command, which "oversees the balance of the Mid-East, parts of Africa and west Asia, and part of the Indian Ocean," a Southern Command, which "guards U.S. interests in the southern hemisphere, including Central America, South America, and the Caribbean," and a Pacific Command, which "covers 50 percent of the Earth's surface including Southwest Asia, Australia."

The longest section in DOD 101 is titled "September 11, 2001: Day of Terror." Here we discover that although "there are currently 70 nations supporting the global war on terrorism," to date "21 nations have deployed more than 16,000 troops to the U.S. Central Command's region of responsibility." No countries are listed, probably because the "coalition of the willing" includes such world powers as Albania, Armenia, Azerbaijan, Bosnia-Herzegovina, Bulgaria, Czech Republic, Denmark, El Salvador, Estonia, Georgia, Kazakhstan, Latvia, Lithuania, Macedonia, Moldova, Mongolia, Poland, and Romania. We are also told that "though there has been significant progress, the war on terror continues." I don't know what the DOD means by progress, unless it is referring to the over 3,400 soldiers who died for a lie in Iraq, the 152,000 veterans who filed disability claims after fighting in the war on terror, the 70 female U.S. soldiers who have now been killed fighting in Iraq, or the estimated 655,000 Iraqis who have died since the U.S. invasion of Iraq.

The next part of DOD 101 is called "Homeland Security and Homeland Defense." This section contains more lies than any other:

> The Department of Defense contributes to homeland security through its military missions overseas.

> Ongoing military operations abroad have reduced the terrorist threat against the United States.

> The Department of Defense is responsible for homeland defense.

I think rather that the Department of Defense contributes to the instability of the world through its military missions overseas. I believe instead that ongoing military operations abroad have increased terrorism. And if the Department of Defense is responsible for homeland defense, then why do we need a Department of Homeland Security?

Under the heading "What We Do," the closing paragraph reads: "Whether it's saving lives, protecting property or keeping the peace, the U.S. military stands at the ready to keep America strong and free." Saving lives? Protecting property? Keeping the Peace? Does the Defense Department really think that Americans are that naïve? In actuality, the DOD does just the opposite: wasting lives, destroying property, and destroying the peace.

The purpose of the U.S. military should be to defend the United States. That's it. Nothing more. Using the military for anything else perverts the purpose of the military. It is not the purpose of the U.S. military to spread democracy or goodwill, remove dictators, change a regime, fight communism or Islam, train foreign armies, open foreign markets, protect U.S. commercial interests, provide disaster relief, or provide humanitarian aid. The U.S. military should be engaged exclusively in defending the United States, not defending other countries, and certainly not attacking them. Now that is real DOD 101.

* * * * *

DO VIOLENCE TO NO MAN

> "And the soldiers likewise demanded of him, saying, And what shall we do? And he said unto them, Do violence to no man,

neither accuse any falsely; and be content with your wages" (Luke 3:14)

This message of John the Baptist to soldiers is more critical today than at any other time in American history.

When John the Baptist began his ministry in "all the country about Jordan" (Luke 3:3), the multitude of people who came to him were told to "bring forth therefore fruits worthy of repentance" (Luke 3:8) and to give to those in need (Luke 3:11). He then instructed the publicans not to collect any more than they were required to. And finally, he said to the soldiers what is quoted above.

In his seminal article, "None Dare Call It Genocide," Lew Rockwell has courageously termed the U.S. invasion of Iraq genocide:

- More than one million people have been murdered in Iraq since the U.S. invasion.
- Nearly half of households report having lost a family member to a killing of some sort.
- The total number of dead exceeds the hugely well-publicized Rwandan genocide in 1994.
- The further geographically you move from US troop activity, the more peaceful the area is.
- The US has unleashed bloodshed in Iraq that is rarely known even in countries we think of as violent and torn by civil strife.

And all this is after the "500,000 children and old people killed by the US-UN anti-civilian sanctions in the 10 previous years."

Who is responsible all the death and destruction in Iraq? Who is dropping the thousands of tons of bombs? Who is firing the guns to the tune of 250,000 bullets for every Iraqi "insurgent" killed? Who has paved the way for the sectarian violence that makes it unsafe to walk down the street, go to the market, or attend a wedding?

Who is responsible for this genocide in Iraq?

It isn't George Bush; he hasn't fired a shot outside of his Texas ranch since his days in the National Guard. It isn't Dick Cheney; he targets only hunters. It isn't the current secretary of defense, Robert Gates; he hasn't been on active duty since 1969. It isn't the former secretary of defense, Donald Rumsfeld; he left active duty back in 1957. It isn't the Republican-controlled Congress that funded the war for several years or the Democratic-controlled Congress that is funding it right now; most members of Congress have never set foot on Iraqi soil. It isn't Wolfowitz,

Feith, Perle, Abrams, Powell, Rice and the other architects of the Iraq War; most of them have left the Bush administration to follow other pursuits. It isn't the chickenhawks who quibble about strategy; they would probably faint at the sight of blood. It isn't the Values Voters who support killing Iraqis while claiming to be pro-life; they are too busy campaigning for constitutional amendments against abortion and same-sex marriage. It isn't the conservative warmongers who warn us about Islamofascism; they prefer to let others do their dirty work. It isn't the armchair warriors who call for more bombs and bullets with Iraqi names on them; they never personally directed any towards Iraqis. It isn't the neocons; most of them have never even been in the military.

The terrible truth is that the U.S. military is responsible—the troops, the Army, the Navy, the Air Force, the Marine Corps—U.S. soldiers. They may have been just following orders, obeying the powers that be, wearing a uniform, serving in the military, supporting their commander in chief, or fighting a war—but they are still responsible.

As unpleasant as it sounds, as horrible as it is, and as much as we don't want to admit it: It is the U.S. military that is responsible for the destruction, brutality, and murder in Iraq. It doesn't matter if a soldier joined the military with the best of intentions, it doesn't matter how careful he is to minimize civilian casualties, it doesn't matter if he thinks he is defending our freedoms—he is still participating in what Lew Rockwell dares to call genocide. U.S. soldiers need to stop en masse their waging of this war. Short of a commander in chief who practices a non-interventionist foreign policy, the war won't end any other way.

I fully realize that many U.S. soldiers are in a position where they feel they must shoot first and ask questions later, kill or be killed. But they must acknowledge that the reason for this is that they are invaders and interlopers, and do whatever it takes to get out of Iraq—regardless of the consequences. If it is done for no other reason than to save their own neck, fine; they should just stop fighting and get out of Iraq any way they can.

For the soldiers currently in the United States who face the possibly of going to Iraq the solution is a much simpler one: Don't go. Go AWOL, go to jail, get court-martialed, get dishonorably discharged, lose your rank, lose your retirement—just don't go. Make the military drag you there kicking and screaming.

Are you a soldier in Iraq? Do violence to no man. Do you know a soldier in Iraq? Tell him to not accuse someone falsely of being a terrorist. Are you thinking about enlisting in the military? Be content with your wages and don't covet the Army's $20,000 signing bonus to be a hired killer. Isn't it time, after the loss of a million Iraqis and almost 4,000 U.S.

soldiers, to say enough is enough?

* * * * *

SHOULD ANYONE JOIN THE MILITARY?

I have maintained in a number of articles over the past several years that no Christian—whether he terms himself a conservative, an evangelical, a fundamentalist, or a Bible-believer—has any business in the U.S. military, including the National Guard and the chaplaincy.

Although the same goes for anyone else who names the name of Christ, I have always emphasized these particular Christian groups because of the unholy relationship that exists between them and the military.

But what about American Jews, Muslims, Buddhists, and Hindus? Would it be okay if they joined the military? And what about the members of the various cults and sects that abound in the United States? Is the military a good place for them? And let's not forget about atheists, agnostics, infidels, witches, Satanists, and the irreligious. Should they be discouraged from joining the military as well?

Should anyone join the military?

Here are seven reasons why I think that no one, regardless of his religion or lack of it, should join today's military.

1. Joining the military may cost you your limbs, your mind, or even your life. There is no end in sight to the Iraq war. Over 3,800 U.S. soldiers have been killed in Iraq. Many thousands more have been wounded. Hundreds of these have had limbs amputated. An increasing number of soldiers are committing suicide. Untold numbers suffer from post-traumatic stress disorder. Some soldiers will spend the rest of their lives unable to work or drive a car. Others will live out their days as physical and/or emotional basket cases. What makes you think that you or one of your loved ones will not be sent to Iraq or will emerge unscathed in body and mind? Don't trust the recruiter who tells you that you won't be sent to Iraq. They are getting so desperate for cannon fodder that they are blatantly lying to potential recruits.

2. Joining the military may have an adverse effect on your family. The breakup of marriages and relationships because of soldiers being deployed to Iraq and elsewhere is epidemic. Multiple duty tours and increased deployment terms are the death knell for stable families. It is devastating to a young child to be deprived of his father for months at a time. It is a national disgrace that we send single mothers in the National

Guard off to war who must then leave their small children in the care of friends or relatives. Yes, I know they joined the military of their own free will, but it still shouldn't be done. What makes you think that the military will never send you away from your family for an extended period of time? You know that the possibility exists, so why gamble with your family? And then, as if being away from your family wasn't bad enough on you and them, some soldiers come home with such physical and/or mental problems that they are unable to return to civilian life. Debt, doctors, and divorce lawyers soon consume their finances. It is U.S. military families that are the unseen victims of the war in Iraq.

   3. Joining the military does not mean that you will be defending the country. The purpose of the U.S. military should be to defend the United States. Period. Yet, one of the greatest myths ever invented is that the current U.S. military somehow defends our freedoms. First of all, our freedoms are not in danger of being taken away by foreign countries; if they are taken away it will be by our own government. It is not a country making war on us that we need to fear, it is our government making war on the Bill of Rights. And second, how is stationing troops in 150 different regions of the world on hundreds of U.S. military bases defending our freedoms? It is not the purpose of the U.S. military to change regimes, secure the borders of other countries, or spread democracy at gunpoint. The Department of Defense should first and foremost be the Department of Homeland Security.

   4. Joining the military means that you will be helping to carry out an evil, reckless, and interventionist U.S. foreign policy. For many, many years now, U.S. foreign policy has resulted in the destabilization and overthrow of governments, the assassination of leaders, the destruction of industry and infrastructure, the backing of military coups, death squads, and drug traffickers, imperialism under the guise of humanitarianism, support for corrupt and tyrannical governments, interference in the elections of other countries, taking sides or intervening in civil wars, engaging in provocative naval actions under the guise of protecting freedom of navigation, thousands of dubious covert actions, the dismissal of civilian casualties as collateral damage, the United States being the arms dealer to the world, and the United States bribing and bullying itself around the world as the world's policeman, fireman, social worker, and busybody.

   5. Joining the military means that you will be expected to unconditionally follow orders. There will be no questioning of the purpose or morality of an order. You will often times not be in a position to know whether an order is in fact dubious or immoral. You will be expected to, without reservation, drop that bomb, fire that weapon, launch that missile, and throw that grenade, as well as kill people and destroy their property. Do you question whether that prisoner should be transported to some secret CIA prison to undergo "enhanced interrogation techniques"? Too bad. Do you question whether the United States should have troops in 150 different places around the globe? Sorry. Do you question whether the United States should launch a preemptive strike? Banish the thought. Do you question whether the United States should effect a regime change? Keep your mouth shut. But wouldn't military effectiveness unravel if the troops didn't obey orders? Let's hope so. Every act of American military intervention was made possible because the troops blindly followed the orders of their superiors. If they had refused to do anything that was not related to actually defending the country, then there would not have been any overseas deployments, land mines buried, bombs dropped, preemptive strikes, or missiles launched. The result of this would have been not only less anti-American sentiment, but fewer terrorists, fewer dead foreign civilians, and fewer dead American soldiers.

6. *Joining the military means that you will be pressured to make a god out of the military.* Am I exaggerating? Here is a note I recently received from a veteran:

Mr. Vance,

I, perhaps, have some insights why soldiers or Christian soldiers do not refuse to fight.

I enlisted in the Marines when I was 17. I went to boot camp 2 months after graduating from a Jesuit high school in 88. I served until 94. In that time I graduated from boot camp as Series Honorman, was meritoriously promoted twice, was platoon high shooter a few times, and volunteered for as much advance and rear party (so I could stay in the field) duties I could. At the time, I was not a Christian and worshipped the USMC.

Boot camp was an interesting experience. They instill ones duty to first the Marines (before I went to combat, I made sure I had a good picture of me standing proudly in front of the Marine Colors) then your comrades. At the end of boot camp we would have done anything for the drill instructors and our comrades. There was a saying, ours is not to reason why, but to do and die. There are few people that have the where-with-all to go against this. Plus, the intellectual foundation required for resistance (which, even though I went to a Jesuit prep school, I didn't have) is constantly attacked.

The honor of our former Marines and duty to current Marines must be upheld.

The attitude, when in these situations, is that you must make "them" objects. Otherwise you might hesitate and it could get yourself or your comrades killed. This attitude pretty much trumps everything else.

Luckily, I got out, found Antiwar.com and then LewRockwell. com.

Best Regards.
SM

Idolatry is certainly something that any non-religious person should be averse to.

7. *Joining the military means that you may be put into a position where you will have to kill or be killed.* What guarantee do you have that you will always be in a non-combat role? You are responsible for the "enemy" soldiers you kill as they defend their homeland against U.S. aggression. It may soothe your conscience if you attempt to justify your actions by maintaining it is self-defense, but it is hardly self-defense when you travel thousands of miles away to engage in an unnecessary and unjust war. You are responsible for the civilians you kill. Dismissing them as collateral damage doesn't change the fact that you killed someone who was no threat to you or your country. You are responsible for every soldier and civilian you kill: not Bush, not Cheney, not Rumsfeld, not Gates, not your commanding officers, and not Wolfowitz, Feith, Hadley, Perle, Abrams, Tenet, Powell, Rice, and the other architects of the Iraq War. Bush and company will not be firing a single shot. You will be expected to do their dirty work and live with it the rest of your life. "Thou shalt not kill" is not just a tenet of the Judeo-Christian tradition; it is part of the moral code of every civilization, pagan or religious.

Should anyone join the military? Certainly not today's military. And until a major change in U.S. foreign policy occurs, not tomorrow's military either. So be all you can be: Just don't be it in the U.S. military.

* * * * *

DON'T ENLIST

Over 181,000 people joined the U.S. military during the fiscal 2007 recruiting year. This is more than joined the military during fiscal years 2006 and 2005. All four of the services met or exceeded their recruiting goals for 2007, as did four of the six reserve components.

Why?

Why are all these people joining the military? Why, in spite of multiple duty tours, ever-increasing deployment terms, an increase in sexual assaults, post-traumatic stress disorder, the breakup of military families, and the suicide rate, and almost daily reports of U.S. military personnel being killed or maimed in Iraq, are so many men and women joining the military?

It could have something to do with the military:

- Spending over $4 billion a year on recruiting
- Raising the maximum enlistment age
- Accepting lower entrance scores on aptitude tests
- Granting more medical waivers
- Giving more moral waivers
- Permitting ex-convicts to enlist
- Relaxing the physical fitness requirements
- Loosening weight restrictions
- Allowing non-citizens to gain their citizenship after one year of active duty

But it could also have to do with the military:

- Giving enlistment bonuses
- Providing tuition assistance
- Granting educational allowances
- Assisting with student loan repayment
- Offering assignment incentive pay

Then there is the career training, the world travel, the thirty days of vacation every year, and the free medical and dental care. And who can forget the GI Bill, VA loans, and the generous retirement benefits.

After the September 11th terrorist attacks, many people joined the military because they believed the president when he said: "Freedom was attacked, freedom will be defended." Others, ignorant of the blowback we reaped after decades of an interventionist foreign policy, joined the military because they thought they were actually going to take part in defending the United States against unjust aggression. Some actually supposed that by joining the military they were participating in a religious crusade against Isalmofacism.

But what about now? After almost five years of needless destruction, senseless deaths, and billions of wasted dollars, after all the lies of the Bush administration have been exposed, after the principle of "blowback" has been thoroughly explained and proved, after the genocide that the Iraq War has become—why do American men and women continue to join the U.S. military?

There are some things that they know. They know that they may be put in harm's way. They know that being deployed will take a toll on their family. They know that they may be put into a situation where they will have to kill or be killed. They know that there is no end in sight to the war.

There are also some things that they may not know but should. They should know that many generals with much more military knowledge and experience than any recruiter they know have denounced this war. They should know that by joining the military they are helping to carry out the foreign policy of an evil empire that stirs up strife and creates terrorists. They should know that the military does very little to actually defend the country. They should know that if they die fighting in Iraq that it will be for a lie.

So why do thousands of people continue to join the military? In most cases, the decision is a financial one—just like the decision to sell crack or become a prostitute. But until joining the military receives the same stigma as those activities, enlistments will continue. Because we are in the middle of an unpopular war, because there is no draft, and because the majority of people who join today's military do so for financial reasons, the conclusion is inescapable: They are mercenaries, they are contract killers—they are killers for hire. "The love of money is the root of all evil" (1 Timothy 6:10).

* * * * *

VETERANS DAY

We have too many veterans. We have too many living veterans. We have too many dead veterans. We have too many wounded veterans. We have too many disabled veterans. We have too many veterans who have fought in wars. We have too many veterans who have never fired a shot. Any way you look at it, we have too many veterans.

Veterans Day began as Armistice Day—a day to commemorate the signing of the armistice on the 11th hour of the 11th day of the 11th month that ended fighting on the Western Front in World War I, "the war to end all wars." A few years after World War II, the holiday was changed to Veterans Day as a tribute to all soldiers who fought for their country. Veterans Day has now become a day to honor, not just those who have served in the military during wartime, but those who have served during peacetime or are serving now. It has also become a day—even though we have Armed Forces Day—to recognize all things military.

Why?

Why do most Americans hold veterans and current members of the U.S. military in such high esteem? Why is there such a military mindset in the United States?

One reason people feel this way is because they falsely believe that those who serve in the military are somehow defending our freedoms. They are convinced that it is the military that stands between a free society and subjugation by some foreign power. They think that it is because of the military that we still have our First Amendment rights. It is inevitable that whenever I write about the military I receive an e-mail or two from a current or former member of the military who closes his rebuke (which usually argues that I have the freedom to write the "trash" that I write because of the U.S. military) with this simplistic cliché: "If you can read this e-mail, thank a teacher. If you can read it in English, thank a Marine." Has anyone ever thought this through? Are we are supposed to believe that the German army that couldn't cross the English Channel to invade Great Britain and make its population speak German was going to cross the Atlantic Ocean to invade the United States and make us all speak German if it wasn't for the Marines? Or was it Japanese that the Marines kept us from speaking? Or perhaps it was Spanish because of the tremendous threat we faced from Spain during the Spanish-American War? Were we in danger of having to speak Russian during the Cold War? Looking at the history of U.S. military interventions, there is one thing we can thank the Marines for: We can thank the Marines for helping to carry out an evil, interventionist U.S. foreign policy. Thanks a lot jarheads. Semper Fi and all that jazz. Our freedoms, our liberties, and our Constitution that all Marines swear to uphold are under attack by our government. The state is a greater enemy than any foreign country or ruler. If the Marines are to really defend our freedoms, then they should be deployed to Washington, D.C. After they oversee the closure of most federal agencies and expel the bureaucrats from the city, they can protect the Constitution (with fixed bayonets) from its daily assault by the members of Congress. In that case I would even say with you: "The few, the proud, the Marines."

Another reason the military is held in such high esteem is that most American wrongfully assume that the military is actually engaged in defending the country. They don't know about the hundreds of U.S. military bases on foreign soil. They don't realize that there are thousands of U.S. troops stationed abroad to defend *other* countries. They have no idea that the United States has troops in 150 different regions of the world. Instead, they think that it is because of the military fighting terrorists "over there" that we don't have to fight them "over here." The threat of a conquest of America by foreign invasion is nonexistent. And if we were attacked with nuclear weapons, even the Marines would be helpless to defend us. Although the purpose of the U.S. military should only be to defend the United States from genuine attacks and credible enemies, it has primarily been used to intervene in the affairs of other countries. When all of the troops come home and start guarding our borders and patrolling our coasts then, and only then, can we say that the military is defending the country. Even the Coast Guard, which actually patrols our coasts, is tainted—thanks to another unconstitutional, unwinnable war that the government is engaged in that is more destructive than the "enemy" we are fighting: the war on drugs.

Still another reason for the military mindset is that members of the military are viewed as "public servants." Members of Congress like to brag about how they have been in public service their whole life. Some policemen and firemen have jumped on the "public service" bandwagon as well. But if you want to be a policeman or a fireman, fine, just don't expect us get excited about the fact that you have a job. And plenty of jobs are just as dangerous. Veterans are looked upon as special because they "served" in the military. It didn't take any special education, experience, or accomplishments to land a job in the military—they just signed on the dotted line. We don't bestow any special honors on bricklayers, mechanics, and accountants; yet, we see plenty of bumper stickers that say things like: "My son is in the Air Force." We never see "My son is a plumber" or "My son is a garbage collector" or "My son is a waiter"? And why not? The people in those occupations don't drop bombs on anyone. They "serve" some important needs of society. Shouldn't we honor them as least as much as soldiers?

It is unfortunate that some of the most vocal defenders of today's military are Christians. It is even worse that churches fawn over current and former members of the military on Veterans Day. In response to my recent article "Should Anyone Join the Military?," I was chastised by two detractors.

The first asked if I could read the Old Testament and still say that no one should serve in the military. I was also told that God instructed the Jews and others to destroy people. It is not hard for me to read the Old Testament and still say that no one should serve in the military. America is not Israel, and the U.S. military is not God's army. And telling me that God instructed the Jews and others to destroy people is like telling George Bush that he is the decider. There is no denying that God instructed the Jews and others to destroy people. But George Bush is not God, America is not the nation of Israel, and God didn't command the U.S. military to kill anyone.

My other detractor appealed to Alphonsus Liguori and maintained that as the sword maker has no control over the product, so "the soldier does not commit an actual sin unless he chooses to break a moral law while in the military." It is "the leaders or military officers who sin when they issue immoral orders." Military service is "morally neutral." But what kind of morality is this? It certainly isn't Christian. What kind of morality says that it would be okay to kill someone in an unjust war in his own country who was no threat to you or your country because you are wearing a military uniform? Oh, I forgot: Just don't break a moral law while you are killing him.

It is high time that Americans stop elevating members of the military to a position of honor. It is long past the time when veterans have done anything honorable. We should abolish Veterans Day. And because of our shameful foreign policy and militarism during the twentieth century, we should abolish any Armistice Day celebration as well.

* * * * *

HAVE A NON-MILITARY CHRISTMAS

Are you having a merry Christmas or a military Christmas?

Most Americans will be having a merry Christmas this year. Families will get together, trees will be decorated, lights will be hung, gifts will be exchanged, children will get the latest toys, eggnog will be served, cookies will be baked, massive amounts of food (and spirits) will be consumed, employees will receive a paid day off, parades will be marched in, Christmas movies will be watched, churches will be attended, carols will be sung, the biblical Christmas story will be read.

Some Americans, however, will be having a military Christmas this year. Even if they partake of some of the above activities, they will still be having a military Christmas. This is for one of two reasons. It could be because families are separated due to someone in the family being in the military and deployed overseas. But it could also be that someone is no longer in the family because he or she was killed fighting in Iraq or Afghanistan. Almost four thousand U.S. soldiers have died in Iraq and almost five hundred have died in Afghanistan.

Both of these situations could have and should have been prevented from happening.

Every year at this time, and especially every Christmas since we invaded Iraq, we hear much ado about how U.S. troops overseas are lonely, how they miss their families, how they have to spend Christmas away from home, and, of course, how the troops are making our Christmas celebrations possible by keeping us safe from terrorism and defending our freedoms.

I am not moved.

U.S. troops have absolutely no business overseas, period. They should not be fighting in Iraq, drinking beer in Germany, or playing golf in Okinawa. Everyone in the military joined voluntarily, knowing that he might be deployed overseas. Yet, even in the midst of an unpopular debacle of a war in Iraq, over 181,000 people still joined the military this past year.

What we don't hear much about this time of year is the emotional pain and heartache felt by parents, grandparents, spouses, siblings, and children who have to suffer through a military Christmas because one of their loved ones is either thousands of miles away or dead—courtesy of the U.S. military.

One thing we certainly never hear about is the grieving loved ones of all the foreigners we have killed in their own country. The Marine Corps Toys for Tots program distributes toys as Christmas gifts to needy children in communities all across the United States. Too bad no toys are distributed to the children of dead Iraqis. Just like no toys were ever distributed to the children of dead Vietnamese.

The tragic thing about a military Christmas is that it is so unnecessary. None of our troops should be deployed on foreign soil. None of our troops should be killed fighting a foreign war. My heart goes out to those families who have lost loved ones fighting this senseless, immoral war in Iraq. They will forever have a military Christmas. I realize that the best we can hope for is that no one else in America has to suffer through a military Christmas. But that is infinitely better than the current situation of a deadly war and troops stationed in 159 different regions of the world.

I wish you a non-military Christmas.

* * * * *

HEROES OR DUPES?

Americans love their war heroes. It doesn't matter where the war was fought, why it was fought, how it was fought, or what the war cost. Every battlefield is holy; every cause is just; every soldier is a potential hero. But what is it that turns an ordinary soldier into a war hero? Since it obviously depends on the criteria employed, is it possible that American war heroes are not heroes at all? Could it be that, rather than being heroes, they are instead dupes?

Democrats who loathe John McCain because he is a Republican and Republicans who consider him to be a lukewarm conservative are united in their belief that, whatever his politics, McCain is a genuine war hero because he spent five years as a prisoner of the North Vietnamese. But one does not have to be a prisoner of war to be considered a war hero. The Department of Defense maintains a website that highlights "the military men and women who have gone above and beyond the call of duty in the Global War on Terror." Every soldier who died fighting in the debacles in Iraq and Afghanistan, otherwise known as Operation Iraqi Freedom and Operation Enduring Freedom, is also considered to be a war hero.

After McCain graduated from the Naval Academy in 1958, he became a naval aviator. During the Vietnam War he rained down death and destruction on the people of Vietnam during twenty-three bombing missions. After being shot down, he was imprisoned instead of receiving the death sentence his bombs delivered to the Vietnamese. So why is he considered a war hero? If he got what he deserved, there would be 58,257 names on the Vietnam Veterans Memorial in Washington, D.C. instead of 58,256. Pilots like McCain who drop napalm from the safety of their cockpit are lauded as heroes by the government, the media, and Americans ignorant enough or gullible enough to swallow the myth that there can be heroism in the performance of evil. McCain was even well received by the Vietnamese government in 2000 when he traveled to Vietnam in pursuit of a bilateral trade agreement.

Begun in September of 2006, the DOD "Heroes' Archive" contains the names of 116 U.S. soldiers who performed some heroic deed fighting in Iraq or Afghanistan. Of the four soldiers currently featured, two were awarded the Bronze Star, one was awarded the Purple Heart and the Distinguished Service Cross, and the fourth was awarded the Bronze Star, the NATO Medal, the Afghan Campaign Medal, and the Outstanding Service Medal. Now, unlike General Petraeus, at least these soldiers earned their metals during real combat. Yet, the fact remains, as Catholic

Eastern Rite priest Charles McCarthy has recently stated, "Murder decorated with a ribbon is still murder."

Both IraqWarHeroes.org and AfghanistanWarheroes.org are "dedicated to our deceased Heroes that have served in Iraq & Afghanistan." The list of "deceased Heroes" contains the names of 4,591 U.S. soldiers who have died in Iraq and Afghanistan. I don't know where these sites are getting their information from. The "Casualties in Iraq" page at Antiwar.com shows a total of 4,528 deaths. But regardless of the exact number, the point is that every soldier who died fighting in the war on terror is said to be a hero. It doesn't matter if they were killed by enemy fire, roadside bombs, friendly fire, disease, accident, or carelessness—they are all heroes. But since the war in Iraq is senseless, immoral, and criminal does it really matter how these soldiers died? Again, I refer the reader to Father McCarthy:

> Authentic heroism is freely taking a grave risk in order to try to do good.

> Evil does not become a scintilla less evil because a person put his or her life in jeopardy to do it and is subsequently designated a hero.

This means that whatever we call U.S. soldiers fighting in Iraq, we should not call them heroes.

Some of these "heroes" are mercenaries. The "large Armies of foreign Mercenaries to complete the works of death, desolation, and tyranny" that our Founding Fathers protested against in the Declaration of Independence are now fighting for the United States in Iraq. Since 9/11, the United States has granted citizenship to over 32,000 foreign soldiers. All it takes now is one year of service in the military to be granted citizenship.

Many of these "heroes" are killers for hire. For them, the enlistment bonuses, the tuition assistance, the student loan repayment plans, the assignment incentive pay, the career training, the thirty days of vacation each year, the free medical and dental care, and the generous retirement benefits are enough to erase any concerns about the morality of traveling thousands of miles away from U.S. soil to kill people they have never met or seen, and that posed no threat to America or Americans.

Most of these "heroes," however, are dupes. They think they are fighting for our freedoms when instead they are helping to destroy our freedoms. They think they are retaliating for 9/11 when instead they are paving the way for another terrorist attack. They think they are preventing terrorism when instead they are making terrorists. They think they went to Iraq to fight al-Qaeda when instead al-Qaeda came to Iraq because of them. They think they are protecting Israel when instead they are contributing to increased hatred of Israel. They think that our cause is just when instead it violates every just war principle ever formulated. They think they are fighting injustice when instead they are committing a crime against the Iraqi people. They think they are defending the United States when instead they are helping to destroy it.

One of the saddest cases of a duped hero is that of Marine Staff Sergeant Marcus Golczynski. He died fighting in Iraq on March 27 of last year while assigned to the Marine Forces Reserve's Third Battalion, 24th Marine Regiment, Fourth Marine Division, in Nashville, Tennessee. He had been in the Marine Reserves for twelve years, and was thirty years old when he died.

About a week before he died, Golczynski sent home this e-mail:

> I want all of you to be safe. And please don't feel bad for us. We are warriors. And as warriors have done before us, we joined this organization and are following orders because we believe that what we are doing is right. Many of us have volunteered to do this a second time due to our deep desire to finish the job we started. We fight and sometimes die so that our families don't have to. Stand beside us. Because we would do it for you. Because it is our unity that has enabled us to prosper as a nation.

At his funeral in Lewisburg, Tennessee, the eight-year-old son he left behind was presented with the flag from his father's casket. This was captured in a heart-rending photograph that has circulated around the Internet. But Golczynski was not the only one who was duped. Instead of being outraged about his son's death, his father said that "we owe a debt of gratitude that we will never be able to pay." And instead of resenting the government that sent the father of her son to fight and die in a senseless foreign war, his wife said that her husband "made the sacrifice for my freedom."

The terrible truth, of course, is that Sergeant Golczynski, like all of the other soldiers who died in Iraq, died for a lie. He was duped by his commander in chief who said our cause was just. He was duped by the secretary of defense who said the war would be over quickly. He was duped by his commanding officers who said he should obey orders. He was duped by veterans who said he was fighting for our freedoms. He was duped by Republicans who said he needed to follow the president's leadership. He was duped by politicians who said we should trust them.

He was duped by pundits who said we had to fight them "over there" lest we have to fight them "over here." He was duped by preachers who said we should obey the powers that be. He was duped by Christians who said we must fight against Islamo-fascism. He was duped by Americans who said he was a hero. He was duped by the lying and killing machine known as his own government.

Marcus Golczynski was not alone. Millions of Americans were duped as well. Millions of Americans remain duped. The fact that McCain can talk about being in Iraq for a hundred years and still be greeted by cheering crowds and receive millions of votes says a lot about just how much Americans are duped.

The love affair that Americans have with all things military must be ended. The United States has become a rogue state, a pariah nation, an evil empire—all made possible by the dupes in the U.S. military we call heroes.

* * * * *

THE MOST UNNECESSARY JOB IN THE WORLD

Garbage collector, septic tank cleaner, janitor—the most necessary jobs are often the least glamorous. Some jobs, however, are not only unglamorous; they are completely unnecessary. Marine Colonel Steve Beck has the most unnecessary job in the world. He is a Casualty Assistance Calls Officer. He is the one who comes knocking with a message that no military family wants to hear.

Colonel Beck's story is told in a just-released book by journalist Jim Sheeler. *Final Salute: A Story of Unfinished Lives* (Penguin Press, 2008) is a continuation of Sheeler's Pulitzer Prize-winning *Rocky Mountain News* series written about his experiences in following Beck over the course of a year on his visits to the families of fallen Marines. Sheeler was recently interviewed about his book on NPR's *Fresh Air*.

Beck learned each dead Marine's name and nickname. He embraced their grieving mothers. He attended the funerals. He shed his own tears when he returned to his family. All after unintentionally serving as the death angel. According to Beck, the families always know why he pays them a visit: "The curtains pull away. They come to the door. And they know. They always know."

This is a sad and depressing book. Not just because of the pain it records that was experienced by the wives, parents, and children of dead Marines, but because their pain was so unnecessary. And because the events recounted in the book were so unnecessary, the more I read the angrier I became. Although I never finished the book, and don't even recommend that anyone read it, I feel compelled to mention it because, if nothing else, it serves to remind us just how unnecessary and senseless this war in Iraq is.

There is absolutely no reason why Steve Beck or anyone else in the military should have to notify the next of kin of a dead soldier that their loved one was killed fighting in Iraq. No American soldier had any business setting foot in Iraq, harming an Iraqi, dropping bombs on Iraq, or supporting in any way the troops that invaded Iraq. There is absolutely no reason why the United States had to invade and destroy Iraq. Not to retaliate for 9/11, not to find weapons of mass destruction, not to defend the United States, not to protect our freedoms, not to fight terrorism, not to destroy al-Qaeda, not to overthrow Saddam Hussein, not to bring democracy to Iraq, not to secure access to oil, not to protect Israel. And since there is absolutely no reason why the United States had to invade and destroy Iraq, there is absolutely no reason why any American soldiers had to die. And since there is absolutely no reason why any American soldier had to die, there is absolutely no reason why Colonel Beck had to deliver the most terrible news the family of someone in the military ever had to hear.

Even worse is the terrible truth that no soldier who died in Iraq died an honorable death and made the ultimate sacrifice for his country. They died in vain. They died for a lie. They died while instigating, perpetrating, participating in, or otherwise being a part of war crimes, mass murder, and genocide.

Instead of moving Americans to demand an end to this senseless war and the unnecessary duties of Casualty Assistance Calls Officers, I fear that this book will just make them feel sorry for the families of dead Marines. Look for it to perpetuate the love affair that Americans have with all things military.

* * * * *

WAR HERO OR WAR CRIMINAL?

"The date was Oct. 26, 1967. I was on my 23rd mission, flying right over the heart of Hanoi in a dive at about 4,500 feet, when a Russian missile the size of a telephone pole came up—the sky was full of them—and blew the right wing off my Skyhawk dive bomber." ~ John McCain

Over and over again it has been said or inferred that one of the reasons John McCain deserves to be president is because he is a war hero. Even Barack Obama has called McCain "a genuine American hero."

Make that an American war criminal.

John McCain graduated (near the bottom of his class) from the Annapolis Naval Academy in 1958. After flight training in my city of residence, Pensacola, Florida (where he admits he frequented strip clubs), to "become an aviator and an instrument of war for my country," McCain spent some time on aircraft carriers in the Caribbean and Mediterranean Seas before volunteering for combat duty. In 1967 Lieutenant Commander McCain began bombing runs over North Vietnam from the deck of the USS *Forrestal*. After a bad fire that put the ship out of commission, McCain switched to bombing North Vietnam from the deck of the USS *Oriskany* (which was recently sunk off the coast of Pensacola to make an artificial reef). McCain was shot down on his twenty-third bombing mission over North Vietnam and then held as a prisoner of war for five years. After his release in 1973, McCain resumed his naval service until his retirement as a captain with a disability pension in 1981.

All wars are not created equal. An unjust war is criminal, and soldiers who participate in it are murderers. No North Vietnamese gook (McCain referred to them as gooks in a *U.S. News & World Report* interview in 1973) had ever posed a threat to the United States or harmed an American until the United States intervened with military advisors, military aid, the CIA, intelligence missions, puppet governments, and finally, U.S. troops—thousands and thousands of U.S. troops.

How could John McCain possibly be considered a war hero? He was not captured, imprisoned, and tortured because he was defending U.S. soil against invading enemy forces. Had this been the case, I would be the first one to congratulate him as a war hero.

McCain is a war criminal because he rained down death and destruction on the people of Vietnam during twenty-three bombing missions. It doesn't matter if the "incident" in the Gulf of Tonkin really happened—U.S. ships had no business being within a thousand miles of North or South Vietnam. There can be no heroism in the performance of evil. If McCain had been executed by the Vietnamese after being shot down, would he not have deserved it? What would you do to the pilot who just ejected and landed in your backyard after bombing your house? Why is it that war criminals are always foreigners? If McCain is a war hero then so are the September 11th hijackers. At least they had a reason to attack the United States.

The real American heroes are the men who refused to go to

Vietnam and participate in an immoral, unconstitutional, and unjust war. U.S. soldiers who refuse to deploy to Iraq or Afghanistan because it is another immoral, unconstitutional, and unjust war (not just because they don't want to get killed) are real heroes as well.

In an interview with *60 Minutes* in 1997, McCain mentioned the confession his North Vietnamese captors forced him to write: "I was guilty of war crimes against the Vietnamese people. I intentionally bombed women and children." The truth, of course, is that what McCain wrote under duress is actually an accurate statement.

Although while in the Navy McCain earned the Silver Star, Bronze Star, Legion of Merit, Purple Heart, and the Distinguished Flying Cross, there is one designation he earned that he doesn't wear on his chest: WAR CRIMINAL.

* * * * *

THE BLAME GAME

Soon after the Virginia Tech massacre in April of 2007, a myriad of articles and blogs began to appear, each seeking to blame someone or something for the actions of the shooter. One cynical blogger has compiled a list of links to seventy-three articles espousing just as many theories on who or what was to blame for what remains the deadliest shooting rampage by an individual in U.S. history.

The blame game is also being played when it comes to fighting the wars in Iraq and Afghanistan. Some say Cheney is to blame. Others blame Bush the commander in chief or the Bush administration collectively. No, say some others, it is the fault of the big oil companies or the defense contractors. Still others maintain that the neocons are to blame, or perhaps the Project for the New American Century. It's all about religion, insist some. It is the fault of the Zionists, the Israel Lobby, the Muslims, or the warmonger faction of the Evangelicals. None of these is right, says another, Congress and Congress alone is to blame. No, others reply, the blame lies with Saddam Hussein or Osama bin Laden or al-Qaeda. A few still think it is all the fault of those 9/11 hijackers.

The same thing goes for the Vietnam War. Johnson is to blame. LBJ should share the blame with Nixon. The fault lies with the hawks in the Johnson and Nixon administrations. McNamara should receive most of the blame. Eisenhower and Kennedy sent in military advisers so they are responsible. We should blame the Vietcong or Ho Chi Minh or Mao, says the super-patriot. When all else fails the Vietnam War can be blamed on the politicians. Maybe no men are to blame at all: Communism is to blame.

But what about U.S. troops? Don't the ones doing the actual fighting get any of the blame? After all, neither Bush nor Cheney has killed anyone in Iraq or Afghanistan. Just like neither Johnson nor Nixon bombed Vietnam or Cambodia.

Judging from some of the responses I received to my recent article "War Hero or War Criminal?," some people believe that U.S. troops should not be blamed for the death and destruction they dispense—even in an unconstitutional, immoral, and unjust war:

> If your country calls you to service you should go... it is not a soldier's job to determine the moral virtue of military policy. ~ Critic No. 1

> I cannot accept that those who fight these wars are responsible (morally or otherwise) for them. The politicians and leaders who argue for and encourage such wars are wholly responsible. ~ Critic No. 2

> I can't criminalize all of our soldiers, marines, and airmen because the political basis for the war was unjust. ~ Critic No. 3

This isn't the first time I have received mail like this. I get basically the same song whenever I write about the military and mention U.S. troops being responsible for the death and destruction they mete out:

> The politicians are the ones you should be opposing, not the soldiers. The soldiers are there to do what they are told. They perform terrible acts because they are told to do so.

> A soldier don't make the decisions. They are told. You are simply a limp d**k sorry communist a**hole. Morality is for the simple pukes like you and not for the soldier.

> I can agree with you on the point of not fighting illegal and unjust wars. But those are not the soldiers fault.

> I oppose the war far more than you do. The fault is not that of soldiers sent to war.

> The soldier does not commit an actual sin unless he chooses to break a moral law while in the military.... Military service is

morally neutral.

The song is a little different each time, but the chorus is the same: The troops are just following orders so don't criticize the troops. Some are ambivalent about the troops, but would never condemn them. Others will strongly denounce the war in Iraq, but never disparage the troops fighting it. Still others not only are not critical of the troops, they enjoin us with signs, ribbons, and exhortations to respect, support, and pray for the troops. Everyone gets livid if you make any critical remarks about the troops (unless they do something particularly evil that embarrasses the United States).

Unless one believes that the state is God or that the state should always be obeyed unconditionally, I fail to see how soldiers should get such a free pass. And what a free pass this is: killing with impunity and immunity.

Have U.S. troops been deceived by the U.S. government about the necessity of sending them halfway around the world? Definitely. Have they been duped about the nature of threats to the United States? No doubt. Have they been pawns in the game of U.S. imperialism? Certainly. But does this excuse them from being responsible for killing people and destroying their property when not directly engaged in the defense of the United States? Of course not. Ignorance is no excuse—just try to claim ignorance the next time a cop gives you a speeding ticket. And public school education or not, how could they possibly be ignorant, given the history of U.S. foreign interventions in the twentieth century?

But not only is ignorance no excuse, it is a point that is rarely raised by my detractors. My critics are united in their belief that morality is put off when a uniform is put on. Not so? Then what else are we to conclude? If U.S. soldiers should not be blamed for their killing of tens of thousands Iraqis, Afghans, Vietnamese, and Cambodians (who never lifted a finger against the United States until U.S. troops starting bombing them) because they should just do what their government tells them without regard to the morality of killing foreigners in their own country (again, who never lifted a finger against the United States until U.S. troops starting bombing them), then it is the uniform that makes all the difference. No one but the most ardent anti-Islamo-fascist super-patriot would excuse me, a civilian not in the employ of the U.S. government, if I boarded a plane for Iraq, landed, kicked in a few front doors, and opened fire—even if I tried to justify my actions by saying that I was fighting terrorism. But U.S. troops are lauded for "defending our freedoms" as they do this very thing.

I can hear the howls of protest from those who say that they are being misunderstood. U.S. troops cannot just kill indiscriminately. A uniform does not mean that all morality goes out the window. U.S. troops can only kill whom the U.S. government says to kill; they can only destroy whatever property the U.S. government says to destroy.

I see. No soldier is responsible for the death and destruction he inflicts as long as it is state-sanctioned death and destruction. I guess Voltaire was right: "It is forbidden to kill; therefore all murderers are punished unless they kill in large numbers and to the sound of trumpets."

But is there *anything* U.S. soldiers shouldn't do if commanded by the government? Few would say there isn't. So, morality is not just for liberal, commie, pacifist, traitor, simple pukes like me after all. Morality *does* come into play—even in wartime. The problem is that some people have such a flawed view of the military that it has warped their morality. They would make a difference between the U.S. government ordering an American soldier to go to Iraq and kill a man clutching a gun and the U.S. government ordering the same soldier to go and kill a woman cradling a baby.

But why? No U.S. soldier has any business killing in either case. And no U.S. soldier has any business in Iraq in either case. The only reason an Iraqi would be pointing a gun at an American soldier in the first place is because the soldier traveled thousands of miles from the United States to invade and occupy Iraq at the behest of his government.

If no actions of soldiers obeying orders should be criticized because "it is not a soldier's job to determine the moral virtue of military policy," then what are we to do if U.S. troops are used against American citizens? What will those who think that soldiers should always do as they are told do when these same soldiers are ordered to march through *their* neighborhood and break down *their* front doors while participating in the war on drugs, the war on terror, the war on illegals, or the war on dissent? Will they still insist that "military service is morally neutral"? If so, then they are fools; if not, then they must believe that U.S. troops are not immune from criticism.

There exists a terrible inconsistency when it comes to troops following orders. To be consistent, no one in America should get upset with individual soldiers from other countries bombing, maiming, injuring, or killing Americans, military or civilian. They should be honored as war heroes for defending the freedoms of the people in their countries. Our anger and hatred should be limited to the politicians and leaders of the countries that order them to wage war against the United States. Why should U.S. soldiers always be considered liberators, peacekeepers, and defenders, but foreign soldiers invaders, occupiers, and attackers?

I also think that many people, including some veterans, are naïve about the military.

First, some soldiers (I didn't say all soldiers or even most soldiers) don't need to wait for an order from the U.S. government to kill. They just plain like killing what they consider to be ragheads, sand niggers, or camel jockeys, and have fun while they are doing it ("hedonists with guns" is how one Marine Corps veteran described it to me).

Second, most young people today join the military, not because they are willing to follow orders to keep the country safe, but because they are willing to follow orders to get enlistment bonuses, tuition assistance, educational allowances, help with student loan repayment, incentive pay, career training, world travel, thirty days of leave, free medical and dental care, the GI Bill, VA loans, and a pension.

Third, many soldiers covet the prestige that comes with being a soldier. Here is an e-mail I recently received from a veteran with many years of "service":

> Soldiers love the opportunity to wear something that others don't have, something that makes them stick out in a crowd and makes them part of a special group. This is why they volunteer for Airborne, Special Forces and Ranger units, where they can wear berets with colors that make them stand out, and wear shoulder patches that make them the envy of others. They want badges, shoulder tabs, patches, etc., to signify their completion of difficult courses and combat tours. If an Army GI doesn't have a patch yet on his right shoulder (signifying combat duty overseas with that unit), he feels naked around those who do. The cure? Get a combat tour and get that patch.

Uniform or no uniform, committing acts of aggression is immoral no matter who tells you to commit them. It's high time that we started blaming the soldiers for the death and destruction they mete out. Perhaps then they won't be so willing to fight in unconstitutional, unnecessary, and immoral wars.

* * * * *

I WAS JUST FOLLOWING ORDERS

George Bush is an arrogant, egotistical, hypocrite. But he is not alone. Every U.S. president, secretary of state, diplomat, congressman, military commander, and other advocate of the highly interventionist

American foreign policy of the last fifty years is just as arrogant, just as egotistical, and just as hypocritical.

A few days before he ordered U.S. dupes to invade Iraq back in 2003, Bush the decider delivered an address to the nation from the White House. As usual, the speech was full of lies:

> The United States and other nations did nothing to deserve or invite this threat.

> In a free Iraq, there will be no more wars of aggression against your neighbors, no more poison factories, no more executions of dissidents, no more torture chambers and rape rooms.

> Intelligence gathered by this and other governments leaves no doubt that the Iraq regime continues to possess and conceal some of the most lethal weapons ever devised.

Some observations. First, if it means anything, fifty years of U.S. intervention in the Middle East means that the United States invited any "threat" that we faced from that region of the world. Second, if in a free Iraq there will be no more aggression and torture, then, since the United States has an aggressive foreign policy and is guilty of torture, can we call America a free country? And third, speaking of the most lethal weapons ever devised (which, of course, we know that Iraq never had), the United States not only has more of these weapons than any other country, we are the only country to have used them.

But it gets worse. In this same speech Bush instructed foreign soldiers to do something that he would never want American soldiers to do:

> And all Iraqi military and civilian personnel should listen carefully to this warning. In any conflict, your fate will depend on your action. Do not destroy oil wells, a source of wealth that belongs to the Iraqi people. Do not obey any command to use weapons of mass destruction against anyone, including the Iraqi people. War crimes will be prosecuted. War criminals will be punished. And it will be no defense to say, "I was just following orders."

So, the former commander in chief believes that soldiers should sometimes disobey orders from their commanding officers. I have no doubt that the current commander in chief believes likewise. But what about American soldiers? Can they ever disobey orders? What would happen if they refused to obey an order? What if they refused an order to deploy to

Iraq or Afghanistan? What if they refused an order to launch a cruise missile, drop a bomb, throw a grenade, or pull a trigger? What if they refused an order to harshly interrogate a prisoner? We know what would happen: A U.S. soldier would be called a traitor and a coward; he would be ridiculed and ostracized; he would face court-martial or time in the brig; he would be called un-American and un-patriotic.

But what if an American soldier thought an order was unjust? Wouldn't he be excused?

First Lt. Ehren Watada wasn't. In fact, when he publicly refused to fight in Iraq, the Army tried to court-martial him, but it ended in a mistrial. Although a new court-martial date was later set, rescheduled, and postponed, a federal judge ruled that the Army could not prosecute Watada a second time because that would be double jeopardy. A federal appeals court judge recently allowed the Army to drop its appeal. Watada could still face charges of "conduct unbecoming an officer" for public statements he made against Bush and the war.

But if soldiers should always obey orders then why aren't Iraqi soldiers defending their homeland lauded as heroes? Aren't U.S. soldiers who obeyed orders to invade Iraq all said to be heroes? Why the double standard?

And what a double standard it is. This is American exceptionalism at its worse and most deadly.

No soldier in any of the world's other 193 countries is supposed to follow an order to fire a weapon at an American soldier, sink an American ship, shoot down an American plane, drop a bomb on American territory, invade American soil, mine an American harbor, occupy an American city, torture an American, or kill an American. Those that do are considered terrorists, insurgents, and enemy combatants, all worthy of torture.

But if an American soldier is ordered to launch a preemptive strike against Iraq, he should just follow orders. If an American soldier is ordered to bomb Afghanistan, he should just follow orders. If an American soldier is ordered to drop napalm in the jungles of Vietnam, he should just follow orders. If an American soldier is ordered to invade Korea, he should just follow orders. If an American soldier is ordered to put down an insurrection by Filipinos, he should just follow orders. If an American soldier is ordered to firebomb a German or Japanese city, he should just follow orders. If an American soldier is ordered to help the CIA remove a foreign leader, he should just follow orders. If an American soldier is ordered to intervene in some country's civil war, he should just follow orders. If an American soldier is ordered to destroy a city and kill its inhabitants in a country that he cannot locate on a map, he should just follow orders.

Just think what it would mean to the peace of the world, not to mention the U.S. defense budget, if American soldiers limited their activities to actually defending the United States—guarding American borders, patrolling American coasts, protecting American citizens, enforcing no-fly zones in American skies—and refusing to follow orders to do otherwise.

That would truly be an America First foreign policy, a constitutional foreign policy, a Jeffersonian foreign policy, a Ron Paul foreign policy.

Since it is soldiers the world over who do the actual fighting, we would all be better off if none of them followed orders, including Americans.

* * * * *

RUSH IS WRONG

"The intent of the committee is to neuter the United States of America. They've done it by rewarding a pacifist." ~ Rush Limbaugh

In addition to being a Nobel laureate, Barack Obama is many things. After his election, I wrote in *Liberty* of his radical associations, his life spent in the service of racial preference, his aberrant Christianity, and his plan to further redistribute the wealth of taxpayers to taxeaters. I haven't changed my mind. The black conservative Alan Keyes simply calls him "a radical communist." Obama may personify the extreme left wing of the Democratic Party, but a pacifist he is not.

Just days after taking office, Obama killed his first victims in Pakistan via predator drone. Over 120,000 U.S. troops are still in Iraq. And not only has Obama already escalated the war in Afghanistan, he is contemplating an additional troop surge. The United States still maintains an empire of troops and bases around the world. Obama has threatened to take military action against Iran.

Although conservatives have bemoaned Obama's plan to decrease defense spending ever since he took office, it turns out that defense spending is up for fiscal year 2010, which began October 1. Back on May 7, Obama sent to Congress his proposed defense budget. He requested a base of $533.8 billion and an additional $130 billion to continue the wars in Iraq and Afghanistan. According to a Department of Defense press release: "The base budget represents an increase of $20.5 billion over the $513.3 billion enacted for fiscal 2009" (Bush's last defense budget). And according to Secretary of Defense Robert Gates: "This budget provides the balance necessary to institutionalize and finance our capabilities to fight the wars we are in today and the scenarios we are most likely to face in the years ahead, while at the same time providing a hedge against other risks and contingencies."

Obama's first defense budget (FY 2010) is almost as much as the rest of the world's defense spending combined. The U.S. Navy's battle fleet is larger than the next 13 foreign navies combined.

So much for Obama "destroying your country as a superpower" and "emasculating this country," as Rush Limbaugh also intoned.

The Senate just passed by a vote of 93—7 a $636 billion appropriations bill (H.R. 3326) for the Department of Defense for fiscal year 2010. This bill previously passed the House by a vote of 400—30. This means that 34 out of 40 Republicans in the Senate and 170 out of 178 Republicans in the House agreed with the president on the defense budget. What a bunch of pacifists.

Thanks to the work of economist Robert Higgs, we know that the real U.S. defense budget is really over a trillion dollars, and has been for several years.

There are 120 U.S. soldiers who have been killed in Operation Iraqi Freedom since Obama became president. I'll bet these soldiers who died for a lie wish Obama were a pacifist. In Afghanistan, there are 231 soldiers who have been killed in Operation Enduring Freedom since Obama became president. Of the 872 U.S. soldiers who have died in Afghanistan, over one fourth of them (231) died during the short time that Obama has been in office. I'm sure that these soldiers likewise wish Obama were a pacifist. And if it were possible to ask them now and they said otherwise because they swallowed the line that they died "defending our freedoms," there is probably someone in their family who would rather Obama were a pacifist so their son, grandson, father, brother, cousin, or nephew would still here. But if not, then there are millions of Americans like me who don't think anything in Iraq or Afghanistan is worth one drop of American blood. Yet, we are the ones who are considered by conservative warmongers to be traitors and America haters.

Since Obama took office earlier this year conservatives and Republicans have shown the world that there is something they love more than their movement or their party—war. Leading the way are Republican politicians (McCain, Gingrich, Huckabee), conservative pundits (Limbaugh, Hannity, O'Reilly, Scarborough, Kristol, Coulter), conservative intellectuals (Kagan, Hanson, Boot), conservative organizations (Heritage, AEI, FOX), and conservative publications (*Weekly Standard*, *WSJ*, *National Review*).

Reagan misspoke when he said: "The very heart and soul of conservatism is libertarianism." The very heart and soul of conservatism is war. Patriotism, Americanism, and being a real conservative are now equated with support for war, torture, and militarism. Although conservatism today is generally defined by opposition to Obama, the president can count on conservatives and Republicans to support any further military actions he undertakes.

Rush is wrong. Obama is no pacifist. And too bad. Just think of all the Americans that would not have been killed in senseless foreign wars if McKinley, Wilson, Roosevelt, Truman, Johnson, Nixon, and Bush had been pacifists.

* * * * *

MILITARY DOUBLESPEAK

In George Orwell's novel *Nineteen Eighty-Four*, the government had three slogans emblazoned on The Ministry of Truth building: war is peace, freedom is slavery, ignorance is strength. True, the dystopian society depicted by Orwell existed only in his mind. Yet, the doublespeak that existed in that made-up society has increasingly been adopted by governments—our government.

It is a tragic thing that the U.S. government employs doublespeak to deceive the American people; it is even more tragic that most Americans accept government doublespeak as the gospel truth.

There is no greater instance of government doublespeak than when it comes to the military. Here are some examples:

- Serving in the military: getting money for college from the taxpayers.
- Deploying to Iraq or Afghanistan: occupying a sovereign country.
- The global war on terrorism: a cash machine for privileged government contractors.
- Conscription: slavery.
- Stop-loss policy: backdoor draft.
- Dress blues: government-issued costume.

- Troop surge: escalation of a war we are losing.
- Flying sorties: bombing civilians and their property.
- Stationed overseas: helping to maintain the U.S. global empire of troops and bases.
- Enhanced interrogation techniques: torture by the United States.
- Extraordinary rendition: U.S. sanctioned torture by other countries.
- Fighting terrorism: making terrorists.
- Fighting our enemies: making more enemies.
- Defending our freedoms: destroying our freedoms.
- Insurgents: foreigners who resent having their country invaded or occupied.
- Sanctions: killing children without bombs and bullets.
- Military chaplain: trying to serve two masters.
- Military appreciation service: idolatry.
- Praying "God bless our troops": blasphemy.
- Supporting the troops: supporting foreign invasions and occupations.
- Precision bombing: civilian killer.
- Cluster bomb: child civilian killer.
- Land mine: American IED.
- Terrorist: someone who plants a bomb that doesn't wear an Air Force uniform.
- Enemies of the United States: countries that oppose U.S. hegemony.
- Enemy combatant: someone turned over to U.S. troops in Afghanistan by someone eager to collect a bounty.
- Axis of evil: countries with oppressive governments that our oppressive government doesn't like.
- Allies: countries with oppressive governments that our oppressive government likes.
- Anti-Semite: someone who opposes U.S. military intervention in the Middle East.
- Military recruiter: pimp for duped young men who want to sell their services to the government.
- Bomber pilot: long-distance killer.
- Persistent conflict: perpetual warfare.
- U.S. interests: an excuse to police the world.
- U.S. foreign policy: imperialism.
- National security: national police state.
- Collateral damage: the slaughter of unarmed civilians by

American bullets and bombs.
- Die for our freedoms: die for a lie.
- War hawk: warmonger.
- Regime change: meddling in the affairs of other countries.
- Congressional supporters of large military budgets: pimps to hook up government and defense contractors.
- Military spokesman: military propagandist.
- Commander in chief: the chief war criminal.

I'm sure there are other words and terms that have been or will be devised or brought to bear to justify the actions of the U.S. military. Reject them, and denounce them for what they are: military doublespeak.

* * * * *

DO ANTIWAR LIBERTARIANS HATE THE MILITARY?

Americans love the U.S. military—and especially American conservatives. Even among those who treasure the Constitution, oppose an interventionist foreign policy, and no longer support the war in Iraq, the U.S. military is still held in high esteem.

Support for the military among conservative Christians is just as bad—and perhaps even worse. Many Christians have a military fetish. Support for the military has been elevated to an article of faith by many evangelicals.

It doesn't seem to matter where U.S. troops go, why they go, how long they stay, how much it costs to keep them there, how many foreigners die at their hands, and what they do when they are there—stanch support for the military is inherent in any conservative platform, secular or religious.

Conservatives get indignant when you question the institution of the military. To question the military in any way means that one is unpatriotic, unappreciative, and un-American.

I have written about these things many times over the years. So then, why another article on the U.S. military? On Saturday, December 12, I posted the following picture on the LRC blog with the comment: "Hey Marines, how about some toys for this tot in Afghanistan." The picture of this Afghan child was taken at the International Red Cross Orthopedic rehabilitation center on December 10 in Herat, Afghanistan. According to the UN mine information network, an average of sixty-two people are killed or injured by mines each month in Afghanistan.

Well, the "Conservative, Pro-military" blogger at political-byline.com went ballistic. In a post titled: "Why I left the libertarian ranks: Exhibit A—Hatred of the United States Military," Patrick (he doesn't give his last name), who blogs from "the southern suburbs of Detroit," opines:

> I present this as "Exhibit A", to the fact that the libertarian movement has been infiltrated by Anti-War leftists who hate America, our Military and why they should be stripped of their citizenship and deported out of our fine Country and into another country; like say, North Korea, Venezuela or maybe even Communist China. Not to be rude about this, but it just so happens, that if that dumb kids fellow Countrymen had not giving refuge and comfort to those who would seek to destroy America—Namely Osama Bin Laden and Al-Qaeda; the damned kid would still possibly have his damned leg. Not to mention the fact that on September 11, 2001, our Country was attacked by Islamic terrorists who did more than just destroy a leg. It killed 2,996 of our people.

> However, of course, you cannot tell this to the likes of Lew Rockwell and his bastard gang of leftists who hate this damn Country; they still believe that George W. Bush ordered those planes into the trade center towers. What really troubles me, is that the author of this posting is none other than Dr. Lawrence Vance, who is supposedly a Born-Again Christian. How anyone can harbor such hatred for this Country and our Nation's Military and still claim to be ANY kind of a Christian is beyond me.

In an update, Patrick adds that "libertarian leftists, their Paleo-Conservative counterparts, and their cousins the Anti-War socialist left" are all in bed together because of their views on foreign policy and their "inbred hatred of war and of anything military."

I normally don't pay too much attention to gnats, and especially when they take the form of bloggers that no one has ever heard of. My interest in this "Conservative, Pro-military" blogger lies solely in the fact that he is not alone. There are millions of disciples of Limbaugh, Hannity, Beck, and O'Reilly who feel the same way he does. I would therefore like to reply to his post, clarify some things, and make some recommendations.

In addition to the incorrect spelling of my name, there are a number of fallacies evident in the screed by Patrick the "Conservative, Pro-military" blogger.

First and foremost is the claim that antiwar libertarians hate the military. I don't recall ever writing anywhere that I hated the military. And neither do I remember reading where some other antiwar libertarian said that he hated the military. I hate many things that the military does, and think I have good reasons for doing so, as I mention below. I certainly don't hate any individual members of the military or any other organization. I can't speak for all antiwar libertarians, but here are some things I hate about the military:

- I hate the military fighting without a constitutional congressional declaration of war.
- I hate the military garrisoning the planet with bases.
- I hate the military targeting impressionable high school students (thanks to the NCLB act).
- I hate military recruiters lying to potential recruits.
- I hate the military fighting foreign wars.
- I hate the military fighting unjust wars of aggression.
- I hate the military invading and unleashing violence and civil unrest in Iraq and Afghanistan.
- I hate the military bombing and destroying Iraq and Afghanistan.
- I hate the military killing hundreds of thousands of Iraqis and Afghans.
- I hate the military maintaining troops in Germany, Italy, and Japan when World War II ended in 1945.
- I hate the military stationing troops in 150 different regions of the world.
- I hate the military recruiting terrorists and feeding insurgencies by its foreign occupations.
- I hate military chaplains praying with troops before they unleash death and destruction.
- I hate the military doing anything other than actually defending the country.
- I hate the military perpetuating the myth that they are defending our freedoms when the more the troops defend our freedoms the more our freedoms are taken away.
- I hate the military perpetuating the myth that I couldn't write the things I do if it weren't for the U.S. military when the truth is I wouldn't need to write the things I do if it weren't for the actions of the U.S. military.

(To their credit, some members of the military don't practice these last two points. They know they enlisted because they needed a job or wanted money for college. They are not stupid enough to think that they are defending anyone's freedom to do anything. Oftentimes, it is chicken-hawks and armchair warriors who talk the loudest about the troops defending our freedoms.)

I would love it if the functions of the U.S. military were limited to defending the United States, securing U.S. borders, guarding U.S. shores, patrolling U.S. coasts, and enforcing no-fly zones over U.S. skies instead of serving as the president's personal attack force to bomb, invade, occupy, and otherwise bring death and destruction to any country he deems necessary.

I would be thrilled to death if all the troops stationed overseas came home, all foreign bases were closed, and no more American soldiers died fighting foreign wars.

In addition to his statements about the military, Patrick the "Conservative, Pro-military" blogger is guilty of the following.

He equates the U.S. government and military with the country. If one disapproves of the warfare state then he must hate America. But why is it that a conservative can disapprove of the welfare state and not be considered anti-American? What is so sacrosanct about the military?

He refers to Lew Rockwell and myself and other antiwar libertari-ans as leftists when we are anti-leftists who despise FDR and his New Deal, LBJ and his Great Society, and every other liberal program and left-wing income redistribution scheme.

He thinks that to be antiwar is to be left wing. This is absurd. See the article by Gary Benoit of the John Birch Society (certainly not a leftist organization) titled: "Anti-war Stance Is Right, Not Left."

He sees everything in terms of a left/right paradigm. I recommend that he read Murray Rothbard's "Left and Right: The Prospects for Liberty" and Lew Rockwell's *The Left, the Right, and the State*.

He refers to the antiwar socialist left like it is alive and well when the reality is that it is hardly in existence anymore since the inauguration of their leader to the presidency and his escalation of the war in Afghani-stan.

He makes the ridiculous statement that we believe Bush ordered the planes into the trade center towers. I think Bush was too stupid to know what was happening on September 11. And if he is subtly implying that I am a 9/11 Truther, then he is mistaken, although I don't believe much of what the government says about what happened on 9/11—or any other day for that matter.

He wonders how anyone can be a Christian and harbor such hate for the country and its military. Here he is ascribing things to me that are simply not true, as I explain above. Actually, the wonder of wonders is how Christians can be so enamored with the military. See my *Christianity and War and Other Essays Against the Warfare State* and my LRC article archive for the articles I have written since the publication of the book.

The most disturbing statement by Patrick the "Conservative, Pro-military" blogger is that antiwar libertarians should be "stripped of their citizenship and deported out of our fine Country and into another country; like say, North Korea, Venezuela or maybe even Communist China." This exposes him as the red-state fascist that he is. As bad as genuine leftists are, I don't recall any of them ever calling for conservatives or libertarians to be stripped of their citizenship and deported. But apparently our blogger doesn't think that deportation is punishment enough. In a note to someone in the military who wrote to him in defense of my "Toys for Tots" post, Patrick says: "Pat Tillman, another Anti-War twirp [twerp] that got what was coming to him."

I took a lot of heat for this statement I made in a recent article: "The very heart and soul of conservatism is war. Patriotism, Americanism, and being a real conservative are now equated with support for war, torture, and militarism." Patrick, the "Conservative, Pro-military" blogger at politicalbyline.com, is exhibit A of why this is true.

* * * * *

SHOULD THE U.S. MILITARY GO TO HAITI?

There is no doubt that the death toll from the earthquake in Haiti will be horrendous. There is no disagreement about the destruction from the earthquake being catastrophic. There is also no disputing that the situation in Haiti is very grave. One thing that must, however, be challenged is the notion that the U.S. military should go to Haiti.

A military assessment team has already landed in Haiti from the U.S. Southern Command. The Secretary of Defense has made it clear that "he will help provide 'anything and everything' the military command needs to aid the mission." But should the U.S. military go to Haiti?

The short answer is simply: of course not. The long answer is what follows.

If the U.S. military goes to Haiti it would not be the first time. The American military occupied the country from 1915—1934 and intervened in Haitian affairs other times before and since this occupation. The most recent intervention was in 2004 after a coup ousted the president of Haiti,

Jean-Bertrand Aristide.

But, it is argued, U.S. military intervention in Haiti *this time* would be for purely humanitarian reasons. I agree. However, I still believe the U.S. military has no business going to Haiti.

The main reason the U.S. military has no business going to Haiti is simply that the purpose of the military should be to defend the United States against attack or invasion. Nothing more (like invading other countries), and nothing less (like failing to defend its own headquarters on 9/11). Using the military to establish democracy, spread goodwill, change regimes, train foreign armies, open foreign markets, enforce no-fly zones, protect U.S. commercial interests, serve as peacekeepers, furnish security in other countries, contain communism, and *provide disaster relief and humanitarian aid* perverts the purpose of the military.

There are some other reasons as well for the U.S. military not going to Haiti.

First, private U.S. and international relief agencies exist for things like this. It is a myth that nothing will be done soon enough and good enough without the help of the U.S. military. An even greater myth is that without the help of governments there would not be enough money, supplies, and personnel to help the people in areas hit by natural disasters. The American people especially are a generous people. They donate millions of dollars for relief efforts whenever and wherever a disaster strikes and would probably give even more if they knew their government was not getting involved.

Second, disaster relief and humanitarian aid, whether provided by the state department or the defense department, is still a form of foreign aid. This is funded by taking money out of the pockets of American taxpayers and giving it to countries that most Americans can't locate on map. How many Americans have any idea that the country of Haiti shares the island of Hispaniola with the country of the Dominican Republic? No American should be forced to "contribute" to the aid of another country. If foreign aid is wrong in principle then foreign aid is still wrong when a country is hit by a famine, a flood, a cyclone, a tsunami, *or an earthquake*. So, just like the United States shouldn't have given foreign aid to Myanmar under the guise of disaster relief, so the United States shouldn't give foreign aid to Haiti.

And third, U.S. military relief efforts in Haiti are a PR bonanza for the military. It is certain to counter, at least for a few weeks, the fact that we are engaged in two unpopular wars. And it certainly will help to quash the news that our Predator drone attacks have killed more civilians than militants. Humanitarian intervention by the U.S. military fosters the illusion that the military is somehow benevolent and praiseworthy instead of aggressive and contemptible.

There is one good thing I can say about U.S. military intervention in Haiti. At least for a change the military would be saving life instead of taking it, rebuilding property instead of destroying it, restoring basic services instead of wrecking them, spreading goodwill instead of terror, and making friends instead of terrorists.

As much as I deplore U.S. military interventions for any reason, I would love to see all U.S. forces leave Iraq and Afghanistan and deploy to Haiti instead.

* * * * *

THE FEW, THE PROUD, THE HIGH SCHOOL STUDENTS

Thank you George Bush and the 186 Republicans in the House and 43 Republicans in the Senate who passed the No Child Left Behind Act in 2001.

Buried in Title IX—General Provisions, Part E—Uniform Provisions, Subpart 2—Other Provisions of the No Child Left Behind Act in Section 9528—Armed Forces Recruiter Access to Students and Student Recruiting Information, is the following provision relating to military recruiters and high school students:

(a) POLICY —

(1) ACCESS TO STUDENT RECRUITING INFORMA-TION—Notwithstanding section 444(a)(5)(B) of the General Education Provisions Act and except as provided in paragraph (2), each local educational agency receiving assistance under this Act shall provide, on a request made by military recruiters or an institution of higher education, access to secondary school students names, addresses, and telephone listings.

(2) CONSENT—A secondary school student or the parent of the student may request that the student's name, address, and telephone listing described in paragraph (1) not be released without prior written parental consent, and the local educational agency or private school shall notify parents of the option to make a request and shall comply with any request.

(3) SAME ACCESS TO STUDENTS—Each local educational agency receiving assistance under this Act shall provide military

recruiters the same access to secondary school students as is provided generally to post secondary educational institutions or to prospective employers of those students.

(b) NOTIFICATION—The Secretary, in consultation with the Secretary of Defense, shall, not later than 120 days after the date of enactment of the No Child Left Behind Act of 2001, notify principals, school administrators, and other educators about the requirements of this section.

(c) EXCEPTION—The requirements of this section do not apply to a private secondary school that maintains a religious objection to service in the Armed Forces if the objection is verifiable through the corporate or other organizational documents or materials of that school.

(d) SPECIAL RULE—A local educational agency prohibited by Connecticut State law (either explicitly by statute or through statutory interpretation by the State Supreme Court or State Attorney General) from providing military recruiters with information or access as required by this section shall have until May 31, 2002, to comply with that requirement.

Since I never filled out an opt out form, my son received a small packet in the mail with the following note from the Marine Corps Recruiting Command:

Dear High School Student,

When our nation was founded, Marines were there to secure freedom. Today, it is up to young men and women like you to continue defending our way of life.

Training will offer demanding challenges, but it will also give you the skill and courage to fight for what's right. You will earn the title Marine and take your place among 234 years of honor. It will be up to you to uphold the freedoms of life, liberty and the pursuit of happiness for future generations.

PRESERVE THE AMERICAN WAY OF LIFE.

Complete and mail in the enclosed card today. We will send you an information kit and your choice of free Marine Corps dog tags, duffle bag or skullcap. You can get more information right now at

MARINES.COM/GOAL or contact us at 1-8-MARINES and give code "GOAL."

Semper Fidelis,
Fenton Reese
Sergeant Major, United States Marine Corps
Sergeant Major, Marine Corps Recruiting Command

P.S. Show your Marine Corps pride—hang the enclosed poster in your school locker or bedroom.

Included in the packet was a card to fill out with pictures at the top of the dog tags, duffle bag, and skullcap mentioned in the note. An extra card was also included to "have a friend join you." The card requests not only one's name and address, but also one's e-mail address, phone number, cell number, date of birth, school name, and last grade completed. The poster mentioned in the note has two sides. The first side contains the image of a sword with "United States Marines" on it. The other side contains images of thirty-two different Marine Corps recruiting posters, some apparently from World War I.

First of all, why would any young woman want to join the Marines? Among other reasons, several of which I discussed in "No, You Can't Have My Daughter," there is the risk of death or sexual assault. Since the beginning of the so-called war on terror, there have been over 100 U.S. female military personnel killed in Iraq and 20 in Afghanistan. Of all the places for a young American woman to die, a war zone in Iraq or Afghanistan shouldn't be one of them. And of all the ways for a young American woman to die, getting blown up by an IED shouldn't be one of them. Sexual assaults in the military are on the increase—as acknowledged by the Defense Department.

And second, why would any young man want to join the Marines? Just look at all the lies in the brief note from the Marine Corps Recruiting Command.

- Lie no. 1: "Today, it is up to young men and women like you to continue defending our way of life."
- Lie no. 2: "Training will offer demanding challenges, but it will also give you the skill and courage to fight for what's right."
- Lie no. 3: You will earn the title Marine and take your place among 234 years of honor.
- Lie no. 4: It will be up to you to uphold the freedoms of life, liberty and the pursuit of happiness for future generations.

The unvarnished truth is that Marines in Iraq and Afghanistan are not currently defending our way of life, they are not currently fighting for what is right, they are not currently worthy of honor, and they are not currently upholding any freedoms for future generations.

If you doubt the truth of what I'm saying, then I refer you to not just my book and my article archive, but to ex-Marine James Glaser, ex-Army Michael Gaddy, ex-Air Force Mike Reith, and the veterans who signed my "Letter to a Christian Young Man Regarding Joining the Military."

By the way, my son will not be sending in the reply card—or getting the dog tags, duffle bag or skullcap.

* * * * *

THERE THEY CRUCIFIED HIM

"And when they were come to the place, which is called Calvary, there they crucified him, and the malefactors, one on the right hand, and the other on the left." ~ Luke 23:33

They didn't just crucify him; they scourged him, stripped him, put a purple robe on him, put a crown of thorns on his head, mocked him, smote him with their hands, spit on him, cast lots for his garments, smote him on the head, feigned worship to him, and nailed him to a cross.

Crucifixion was an ancient, brutal, gruesome, painful, humiliating, and public method of execution. The "him" referenced above who was crucified is, of course, Jesus Christ. He was crucified even though he was declared to be without fault, not worthy of death, and a just person.

Who in the world would do such a thing? Who would nail the Son of God to a cross and crucify him?

Then the soldiers, when they had crucified Jesus, took his garments, and made four parts, to every soldier a part; and also his coat: now the coat was without seam, woven from the top throughout. (John 19:23)

Of all the horrible things that soldiers have done throughout history, this is certainly the most reprehensible.

Oh, but they were just following orders.

Apologists for the wars in Iraq and Afghanistan, most people who are indifferent to these wars, and even many of those who oppose them all generally agree on one thing: We should never condemn the soldiers; they are just following orders.

I have often been chastised, even by those who condemn the wars in Iraq and Afghanistan, denounce the abuses of the U.S. government, and oppose an interventionist U.S. foreign policy, because I have criticized the institution of the military and the soldiers who mete out death and destruction on its behalf:

Soldiers, I am told:

- Are trained to kill people and break things
- Are required to follow the orders of their officers
- Must never question the orders they are given
- Must follow orders to maintain discipline and effectiveness

I agree completely.

The problem here is two fold: These things are true and the people who recite them the most don't actually believe them.

It is because these things are true of soldiers that no American should enlist in the military and fight for what Will Grigg calls "the world's most powerful terrorist syndicate, the United States Government." When someone joins the military of a country like the United States with such an interventionist foreign policy and an empire of troops and bases that encircles the globe, he will be expected to not only uphold and maintain the policy and the empire, but carry it out and expand it by military force. When someone works for the policeman, fireman, bully, busybody, and social worker of the world—the U.S. military—he will be expected to participate in acts of military intervention.

But, some will reply in retreat, there are some things that soldiers shouldn't do when ordered to do them by their superiors—like commit war crimes.

My point exactly.

But if that is so then soldiers would not be doing what they are trained to do, would not be following the orders of their superiors, would not be never questioning the orders they are given, and would not be maintaining discipline and effectiveness.

You can't have it both ways.

And what are the wars in Iraq and Afghanistan anyway but crimes against not only the Iraqi and Afghan peoples, but also the thousands of U.S. soldiers who gave their lives in vain and for a lie.

In spite of the blame game that is played when it comes to soldiers being culpable for their actions, they are responsible and will have to answer to a higher power than their commanding officers. That higher power may be their religion, philosophy, moral code, or conscience, but unless they have made a god out of the military, it will be something.

Christ forgave those who crucified him; millions of Koreans, Vietnamese, Laotians, Cambodians, Iraqis, and Afghans killed by the U.S. military are not only not so forgiving, they never even had the chance.

* * * * *

THE MARINES ARE LOOKING FOR A FEW GOOD HIGH SCHOOL STUDENTS

The theme this time is defense. And this time, along with the *About the Corps* "opportunity book," it is a choice between folding speakers, a T-shirt, or a wristband instead of dog tags, a duffle bag, or a skullcap.

The Marine Corps recruiting literature that came in the mail to my son this time, thanks once again to the No Child Left Behind Act, contained no poster to show Marine Corps pride and no note from the Sergeant Major at the Marine Corps Recruiting Command, just a simple fold-out brochure. I wrote about the packet with the poster and the note in "The Few, the Proud, the High School Students."

On the cover of the brochure is a picture of a child with the caption: "THE ONES YOU DEFEND." When you open to the first page you see four Marines with rifles walking through a forest—no doubt in some foreign backwater that most Americans would have a hard time finding on a map—with the caption: "THE ONES WHO DEFEND YOU." Page 2 contains two short paragraphs:

> You choose to become a Marine to defend the people at home and the American way of life. As you earn this coveted title, you build an unbreakable bond with the men and women who earn it alongside of you. You learn that by protecting each other, you serve all of your families, friends and neighbors at home. You join a proud tradition of warriors who have defended our country this way for 234 years.

> To find out how you can become part of the Corps, return the enclosed card. We'll send you more information and your choice of Marine Corps folding speakers, T-shirt or wristband. Or learn more today: Call us a 1-800-MARINES and give code "BOND" or visit MARINES.COM/BOND.

The back page has pictures of the folding speakers, T-shirt, and wristband under a large headline that reads: "DEFEND THE PEOPLE YOU CARE ABOUT."

Attached to the brochure (not enclosed) are two reply cards—one for the high school student that reads: "WILL YOU DEFEND THE ONES YOU LOVE?" and one for a friend that reads: "KNOW A FRIEND WHO WILL DEFEND YOU?" New to these reply cards is a question at the bottom: "How likely is it that you will be serving in the military in the next four years?" The choices are definitely, probably, probably not, and definitely not.

The theme of defense shows up on all four pages of the recruiting brochure plus the two reply cards. But how much of what the U.S. military does is actually related to defense? What do the following practices of the military have to do with the defense of the United States?

- Providing disaster relief in foreign countries
- Dispensing humanitarian aid in foreign countries
- Supplying peacekeepers in foreign countries
- Enforcing UN resolutions in foreign countries
- Nation building in foreign countries
- Spreading goodwill in foreign countries
- Launching preemptive strikes in foreign countries
- Fighting wars in foreign countries
- Establishing democracy in foreign countries
- Changing regimes in foreign countries
- Assassinating people in foreign countries
- Stationing troops in foreign countries
- Maintaining bases in foreign countries
- Containing communism in foreign countries
- Training armies in foreign countries
- Opening markets in foreign countries
- Enforcing no-fly zones in foreign countries
- Rebuilding infrastructure in foreign countries
- Reviving public services in foreign countries
- Promoting good governance in foreign countries
- Invading foreign countries
- Occupying foreign countries
- Unleashing civil unrest in foreign countries

All the while, of course, perpetuating the myth that the military is defending our freedoms.

The Department of Defense couldn't even defend its own headquarters on September 11th. It was too busy occupying, defending, and building golf courses in other countries.

Most of the defense services that are actually provided today by the U.S. military are done in other countries. Although World War II ended in 1945, the United States still has tens of thousands of soldiers stationed in Germany, Italy, and Japan. I recently documented that the U.S. military has over 700 foreign military bases with troops stationed in 148 countries and 11 territories in every corner of the globe.

The U.S. military should be limited to defending the United States, securing U.S. borders, guarding U.S. shores, patrolling U.S. coasts, and enforcing no-fly zones over U.S. skies instead of defending, securing, guarding, patrolling, and enforcing in other countries. The U.S. military should be engaged exclusively in defending the United States, not defending other countries, and certainly not attacking, invading, or occupying them. Using the military for any other purpose than the actual defense of the United States perverts the purpose of the military.

The Marines may be looking for a few good high school students, but my son is not available. Is yours? Do you want your son to be a bomber pilot for Obama? Aside from the military's lack of actually providing defense services, I have given other reasons for people not to join the military here, here, here, here, and here.

By the way, my son will not be sending in the reply card this time either—or getting the folding speakers, T-shirt, or wristband.

* * * * *

THINGS THE MARINE CORPS FORGOT TO MENTION

The Marine Corps recruiting literature sent to high school students is a little different each time. The first time I saw it the theme was preserving the American way of life. The student who sent in the reply card was entitled to receive dog tags, a duffle bag or a skullcap. I wrote about this in "The Few, the Proud, the High School Students." The theme the second time I saw it was defense. Offered this time was a choice between folding speakers, a T-shirt, or a wristband. I wrote about this in "The Marines Are Looking for a Few Good High School Students." Although it has been said that the third time's the charm, I'm afraid the Marine Corps has failed once again to ensnare my son.

The recruiting literature that arrived in the mail this time, thanks yet again to the No Child Left Behind Act, consisted of an envelope with a short note and two reply cards—all of which have pictures of the free

Marine Corps gear being offered this time: a duffle bag, sunglasses, or a watch. The note says that in order to become a Marine you have to want certain things:

- You have to want to push your mind and body to its limits, and prove you can overcome obstacles even at the brink of exhaustion.
- You have to want to protect freedom, democracy and every state in this nation—more than you want a day off.
- You have to be willing to do what is hard because you believe it is what's right.
- You have to want to be a Marine.

With the exception of the lie that is the second item listed above—the thousands of Marines in Iraq and Afghanistan are doing nothing of the kind—these things are true. The problem is what the Marine Corps forgot to mention.

What is not mentioned is that in order to become a Marine you also have to want certain other things:

- You have to want to intervene in the affairs of other countries.
- You have to want to do anything but actually defend the United States.
- You have to want to obey *without reservation* the orders of your superiors.
- You have to want to perpetuate the lie that the military defends our freedoms.
- You have to want to invade other countries that have not attacked the United States.
- You have to want to occupy other countries that resist being invaded.
- You have to want to kill foreigners that resist being invaded and occupied.
- You have to want to maintain the U.S. global empire of troops and bases.

If a high school student *doesn't* want to do any of these things, then he has no business joining the Marine Corps. The Marine Corps is not preserving the American way of life, defending anyone's freedoms, or protecting every state in the nation.

Parents, do you want your children to do these things? Pastors, do you want your young adults to do these things? Teachers, do you want your students to do these things? Brothers and sisters, do you want your siblings to do these things? Grandparents, do you want your grandchildren to do these things? Friends, do you want your friends to do these things? Friends don't let friends join the military—and neither do parents, pastors, teachers, brothers, sisters, and grandparents if they actually take the time to do a little research about the military. I recommend they start with DOD 101.

If my arguments don't carry any weight because I never "served" in the military, then consider the words of U.S. Marine Corps Major General Smedley Butler (1881–1940)—a Congressional Medal of Honor winner who could never be accused of being a pacifist and the author of *War Is a Racket*:

> War is just a racket. A racket is best described, I believe, as something that is not what it seems to the majority of people. Only a small inside group knows what it is about. It is conducted for the benefit of the very few at the expense of the masses.

> I believe in adequate defense at the coastline and nothing else. If a nation comes over here to fight, then we'll fight. The trouble with America is that when the dollar only earns 6 percent over here, then it gets restless and goes overseas to get 100 percent. Then the flag follows the dollar and the soldiers follow the flag.

> I wouldn't go to war again as I have done to protect some lousy investment of the bankers. There are only two things we should fight for. One is the defense of our homes and the other is the Bill of Rights. War for any other reason is simply a racket.

> It may seem odd for me, a military man, to adopt such a comparison. Truthfulness compels me to. I spent 33 years and 4 months in active service as a member of our country's most agile military force—the Marine Corps. I served in all commissioned ranks from second lieutenant to Major General. And during that period I spent most of my time being a high-class muscle man for Big Business, for Wall Street and for the bankers. In short, I was a racketeer for capitalism.

Butler also recognized the mental effect of military service:

> Like all members of the military profession I never had an original thought until I left the service. My mental faculties remained in

suspended animation while I obeyed the orders of higher-ups. This is typical with everyone in the military service.

Three mailings of Marine Corps recruiting literature this semester are enough. It is time to submit an opt-out form. A sample one is available here.

Oh, and in case you were wondering, my son will yet again not be sending in the reply card—or getting the duffle bag, sunglasses, or watch.

* * * * *

U.S. PRESIDENTS AND THOSE WHO KILL FOR THEM

"The Czar can send any of his officials to Siberia, but he cannot rule without them, or against their will." ~ John Stuart Mill

What kind of a man would kill someone he didn't know for someone else he didn't know? I suppose our opinion of such an individual would depend on the circumstances. Most people would condemn a hit man for hire even as they would praise a man who came to the defense of a little old lady in a parking lot who was being attacked with deadly force by a gang of thugs.

But what kind of a man would kill someone he didn't know, who had never harmed or threatened him, his family, his friends, or anyone he knew for someone he didn't know, who didn't know him, and had never been harmed or threatened by the person he wanted killed?

And even worse, who would do such a thing at a moment's notice, without giving it a second thought, laugh while he did it, brag about it afterward, and then expect to be lauded as a hero?

It pains me to say that the answer is a soldier in the U.S. military.

Since World War II, the nature and role of the U.S. military has drastically changed. Now, although I believe World War II to be neither necessary (see Pat Buchanan's *Churchill, Hitler, and the Unnecessary War*) nor good (see my *Rethinking the Good War*), and although I realize that U.S. troops, especially since the time of Theodore Roosevelt, have often been sent to countries the United States was not at war with, World War II is still a notable turning point. It marks the end of congressional declarations of war and the permanent establishment of the military as the president's personal army instead of the defender of the country against attack or invasion.

On five different occasions, the United States has declared war on other countries a total of eleven times. The first was Great Britain in 1812 (the War of 1812). The second was Mexico in 1848 (the Mexican War). The third was Spain in 1898 (the Spanish-American War). The fourth was Germany and Austria-Hungary in 1917 (World War I). The fifth was Japan, Germany, and Italy in 1941 (World War II) and Bulgaria, Hungary, and Romania in 1942 (World War II).

That Congress issued these declarations of war doesn't mean that they should have been issued. It just means that it was recognized that a major military engagement called for a real declaration of war by the Congress according to Article I, Section 8, of the Constitution.

The Founders were united on keeping the power to instigate war out of the hands of the executive. I have given Jefferson's thoughts on the matter here. The reason for this limitation can be seen in a letter from Madison to Jefferson: "The constitution supposes, what the History of all Governments demonstrates, that the Executive is the branch of power most interested in war, and most prone to it. It has accordingly with studied care vested the question of war in the Legislature."

The executive power of the king of Great Britain to wage war at the time of the American Revolution should be contrasted with the limitation of the U.S. president's power under the Constitution. As relayed by constitutional scholar Edwin Vieira, Sir William Blackstone explained in his *Commentaries on the Laws of England* that the English king was "the generalissimo, or the first in military command within the kingdom" and exercised "the sole prerogative of making war and peace," "the sole power of raising and regulating fleets and armies," and "the sole supreme government and command of the militia." In the Constitution, the powers the king could exercise were assigned to Congress. As found in Article I, Section 8, the Congress has the power

- To declare War
- To raise and support Armies
- To provide and maintain a Navy
- To make Rules for the Government and Regulation of the land and naval Forces
- To provide for calling forth the Militia to execute the Laws of the Union, suppress Insurrections and repel Invasions
- To provide for organizing, arming, and disciplining, the Militia, and for governing such Part of them as may be employed in the Service of the United States

The president is merely the commander in chief, subject to the power of Congress to do all of the above. Even that great advocate of presidential power, Alexander Hamilton, acknowledged in *Federalist* no. 69 that the president's authority as commander in chief, although "nominally the same with that of the King of Great Britain," was "in substance much inferior to it." The danger of giving the president war powers was recognized by none other than Abraham Lincoln. He wrote in an 1848 letter on the Mexican War to his law partner William Herndon: "Allow the President to invade a neighboring nation whenever he shall deem it necessary to repel an invasion, and you allow him to do so whenever he may choose to say he deems it necessary for such purpose, and you allow him to make war at pleasure." Too bad Honest Abe didn't heed his own advice in 1861.

Since World War II, the U.S. military has been exclusively used by the president for purposes other than the actual defense of the country: providing disaster relief, containing communism, invading countries, occupying countries, enforcing UN resolutions, nation building, etc. The fact that some of these actions were termed defense doesn't make them so.

It all began with the Korean "police action." Korea was divided at the 38th parallel after World War II. U.S. forces withdrew from Korea in 1949, as Soviet forces had done the previous year. After North Korea invaded the South in June of 1950, President Truman ordered American troops into combat in Korea to contain communism and save the United Nations. Said Truman: "Here was history repeating itself. Here was another probing action, another testing action. If we let the Republic of Korea go under, some other country would be next, and then another. . . and the United Nations would go the way of the League of Nations." There was not the slightest pretense of consulting Congress. The president informed the leaders of both parties only a few moments before he issued a statement to the press. The Democratic majority in Congress closed ranks behind the president. Only a few Republican senators demurred, most notably Senator Robert Taft: "The President is usurping his powers as Commander in Chief. There is no legal authority for what he has done. If the President can intervene in Korea without congressional approval, he can go to war in Malaya or Indonesia or Iran or South America." Over 36,000 American soldiers suffered and bled and died for their president to confirm the division of Korea.

Believing that Truman had made a tactical blunder in committing U.S. troops without consulting Congress, President Eisenhower in 1955 sought a congressional resolution authorizing the employment of American forces in any manner necessary to defend Formosa [Taiwan]. It passed both houses of Congress almost unanimously. Representative Eugene Siler (R–Kent.) voted against the blank-check resolution because he had promised his constituents that he would never help to "engage their boys in war on foreign soil." Eisenhower sought another resolution in 1957 in response to perceived Soviet expansionism and instability in the Middle East. This time, instead of rallying around a *Republican* president, some Democrats in Congress resisted. In the end, 19 senators and 61 representatives voted against what has been called the Eisenhower Doctrine.

John F. Kennedy likewise sought two congressional resolutions during his presidency, both in 1962. The first was in response to the threat of Cuban communism in the western hemisphere; the second was in response to a crisis in Berlin in which Khrushchev challenged the right of the United States to maintain troops in West Berlin. These resolutions left it to the president to determine how and when the terms of the resolutions would be applied.

Next came the infamous Tonkin Gulf Resolution sought by President Johnson in 1964. Although the United States had already been providing military aid to South Vietnam, supporting a puppet regime, undertaking reconnaissance missions and naval sabotage operations against North Vietnam, and supplying thousands of military advisors, it was this resolution that gave President Johnson a blank check to send U.S. ground troops to Vietnam at his command. Johnson provoked a North Vietnamese attack on U.S. ships in the Gulf of Tonkin and then falsely claimed that North Vietnam had launched a second attack. Johnson ordered retaliatory air strikes against the phantom attack and announced on national television that the U.S. response would be "limited and fitting." After the election in which Johnson held himself out as the peace candidate, he sent thousands of U.S. troops to die in the jungles of Vietnam. There were no dissenting votes in the House. Only two senators opposed this blank-check delegation of power. Senator Gruening (D–Alas.) objected to "sending our American boys into combat in a war in which we have no business, which is not our war, into which we have been misguidedly drawn, which is steadily being escalated." Senator Wayne Morse (D–Oreg.) remarked: "I believe that history will record that we have made a great mistake in subverting and circumventing the Constitution of the United States, article 1, section 8 thereof by means of this resolution." Johnson himself recognized that the Tonkin Gulf Resolution gave him the power to do whatever he wanted in Vietnam. "The sky's the limit," he said. The War Powers Act, passed over Nixon's veto in 1973, was an attempt by Congress to limit the power of the president to conduct military actions. In actuality, however, it ceded powers to the president not authorized by the Constitution. It gives the president a free hand to engage U.S. troops in offensive military actions without the prior consent of Congress.

In 1991, George H. W. Bush went to war in Iraq the first time to drive Iraq out of Kuwait. This was after April Glaspie, the U.S. Ambassador to Iraq, told Saddam Hussein: "We have no opinion on your Arab-Arab conflicts, such as your dispute with Kuwait. Secretary Baker has directed me to emphasize the instruction, first given to Iraq in the 1960s, that the Kuwait issue is not associated with America." This was also after John Kelly, the Assistant Secretary of State for Near Eastern Affairs, testified to Congress that the "United States has no commitment to defend Kuwait and the US has no intention of defending Kuwait if it is attacked by Iraq." Yet, soon after Iraq invaded that bastion of democracy known as Kuwait, Bush the elder sent 500,000 U.S. troops without the Persian Gulf region. Then, in January of 1991, Congress issued a resolution authorizing the president to use military force against Iraq. The actual title was "Joint Resolution to Authorize the Use of United States Armed Forces Pursuant to United Nations Security Council Resolution 678." This was "in order to achieve implementation of Security Council Resolutions 660, 661, 662, 664, 665, 666, 667, 669, 670, 674, and 677." Only two Republicans in the Senate and three in the House voted against the resolution.

Passed soon after the attacks of September 11, 2001, the "Joint Resolution to Authorize the Use of United States Armed Forces Against Those Responsible for the Recent Attacks Launched Against the United States" has resulted in the quagmire known as the war in Afghanistan. This resolution authorized the president "to use all necessary and appropriate force against those nations, organizations, or persons he determines planned, authorized, committed, or aided the terrorist attacks that occurred on September 11, 2001, or harbored such organizations or persons, in order to prevent any future acts of international terrorism against the United States by such nations, organizations or persons." The problem with this blank check is that the president cashed it and invaded a country with a long history of religious, ethnic, and factional squabbling that was not home to any of the 9/11 hijackers, was no threat to the United States, and had never harmed any Americans. We now know that Representative Barbara Lee (D–Calif.) was right about this resolution: "It was a blank check to the president to attack anyone involved in the September 11 events—anywhere, in any country, without regard to our nation's long-term foreign policy, economic and national security interests, and without time limit."

In 2002, Congress presented President George W. Bush with the

"Authorization for Use of Military Force Against Iraq Resolution of 2002." This gave him a blank check go to war in Iraq the second time ~~because of 9/11~~ ~~because of Iraq's weapons of mass destruction~~ ~~because Iraq was a threat to the United States~~ ~~because Iraq had bought uranium from Africa~~ ~~because Saddam Hussein was connected with al-Qaeda~~ ~~because Saddam Hussein tried to kill his dad~~ because he made the decision at the first meeting of his National Security Council ten days into his presidency (a student at the University of Illinois once documented 27 reasons put forth by the Bush administration or war hawks in Congress before the war began). Only one Republican in the Senate and six in the House voted against this resolution.

In addition to these eight congressional resolutions authorizing the president to initiate military action, there were other occasions besides the Korean conflict in which the president sent U.S. troops abroad. Eisenhower sent Marines to Lebanon in 1958, Johnson sent Marines to the Dominican Republic in 1965, Nixon invaded Cambodia in 1970 and did not withdraw all U.S. troops from Vietnam until March of 1973 even though the Gulf of Tonkin Resolution was repealed in January of 1971, Reagan invaded Grenada in 1983, Bush invaded Panama in 1989, and Clinton sent troops to Bosnia in 1995 and Kosovo in 1999. As usual, much of the opposition to presidential warmongering was merely political. According to Representative John Duncan (R–Tenn.), a rare Republican opponent of the Iraq war from the beginning, "Eighty percent of House Republicans voted against the bombings in the former Yugoslavia under President Clinton. I am convinced that at least the same percentage would have opposed the war in Iraq if it had been started by a Democratic president."

And now, in addition to traditional military conflicts, Robert Gates, the secretary of defense under the current and former president, envisions new roles for the military:

> Army soldiers can expect to be tasked with reviving public services, rebuilding infrastructure and promoting good governance. All these so-called nontraditional capabilities have moved into the mainstream of military thinking, planning, and strategy—where they must stay.

A military not strictly for defense of U.S. borders, shores, coasts, and skies is nothing more than the president's personal attack force staffed by mercenaries willing to obey his latest command to bomb, invade, occupy, and otherwise bring death and destruction to any country he deems necessary. As the Future of Freedom Foundation's Jacob Hornberger has so courageously pointed out, U.S. troops

> serve not as a defender of our freedoms but instead simply as a loyal and obedient personal army of the president, ready and prepared to serve him and obey his commands. It is an army that stands ready to obey the president's orders to deploy to any country in the world for any reason he deems fit and attack, kill, and maim any "terrorist" who dares to resist the U.S. invasion of his own country. It is also an army that stands ready to obey the president's orders to take into custody any American whom the commander in chief deems a "terrorist" and to punish him accordingly.

> Just listen to President Obama:

> I—like any head of state—reserve the right to act unilaterally if necessary to defend my nation.

> Still, we are at war, and I'm responsible for the deployment of thousands of young Americans to battle in a distant land. Some will kill, and some will be killed.

And now Obama, like Bush before him, claims the power to order the assassination of anyone—including American citizens—anywhere in the world, via sharpshooter or Predator drone, based only on the suspicion that they are somehow associated with terrorism. That is assassination without charge, without evidence, without witnesses, without trial.

Although God only knows the extent of what the U.S. military at the president's behest is now doing in Yemen, we know what has been happening in Iraq and Afghanistan.

In Iraq, trigger-happy U.S. Army helicopter pilots and U.S. Special Forces slaughtered civilians and then covered up their crimes until a video was leaked exposing their collateral murder.

In Afghanistan, the DOD has finally admitted that U.S. Special Forces killed two pregnant Afghan women and a girl earlier this year. American troops recently shot up a large passenger bus, killing and wounding civilians. Of the more than thirty people who have been killed and the eighty who have been wounded in convoy and checkpoint shootings in Afghanistan since last summer, not one was found to have been a threat. "We have shot an amazing number of people, but to my knowledge, none has ever proven to be a threat," said Gen. Stanley A. McChrystal. And then there are prisoner executions. These and other crimes in Afghanistan—like eradicating wedding parties—have been chronicled by Tom Engelhardt here.

Yet, despite 4,409 American soldiers who have died for a lie in Iraq and 1,144 American soldiers who have died in vain in Afghanistan, Americans continue to foolishly rally around their commander in chief and his army instead of showing contempt for him and it.

In Donald Rayfield's chilling book *Stalin and His Hangmen: The Tyrant and Those Who Killed for Him* (Random House, 2004), he recounts the destruction of the Soviet Union under Stalin:

> From January 1928 Stalin gathered the power, as well as the will, to destroy the lives not only of Lenin's Politburo, but of millions of peasants, intellectuals, and workers.

> Stalin, the party, and OGPU were not worried. Apparently, putting a dozen foreign technologists on trial hurt Soviet prestige, but enslaving and exterminating millions of Russian and Ukrainian peasants did not.

> Stalin's expedition to Siberia in 1928 was a trial run for a crime against humanity. In the next two years, requisition and dispossession under the names of collectivization and "dekulakization" would lay waste virtually all the arable lands of the USSR. Arrests, deportations, and killings escalated, probably beyond what even Stalin and Menzhinsky had anticipated, into a holocaust unmatched in Europe between the Thirty Years' War of the seventeenth century and Hitler. Stalin's attack on the peasantry ravaged Russian agriculture and the Russian peasant to such an extent that for perhaps a century Russia would be incapable of feeding itself. It introduced irrational and unquestioned rule by fear and turned people back into beasts of burden. Stalin was now using OGPU to repress not counterrevolutionaries but a peaceful population.

> Arrests and executions carried out by OGPU soared: 162,726 persons were arrested in 1929, mostly for "counterrevolutionary activity," 2,109 were shot, some 25,000 were sent to camps and as many again into exile. In 1930 arrests doubled to a third of a million and executions increased tenfold to 20,000. The camps received over 100,000. By 1934 there would be half a million slave laborers.

> Allowing for famine, violence, hypothermia, and epidemics caused by the disruption, the number of excess deaths between

1930 and 1933 attributable to collectivization lies between a conservative 7.2 and a plausible 10.8 million.

As Stalin was condemning the last of the old Bolshevik guard to death, he was also preparing his own remedy for dissidence and free thought in the general population. The ensuing "Great Terror" raged across the Soviet Union from spring 1937 to autumn 1938 and resulted in around 750,000 executions and twice as many sentences to lingering death in the camps.

In 1937, some time before Hitler, Stalin's NKVD hit on gassing as a means of mass execution. Trucks advertising bread drove around the Urals, pumping exhaust gases into the rear compartment where naked prisoners lay roped together in stacks, until their loads were ready for the burial pits.

In 1937 Stalin authorized the use of active physical torture and the horrors at the Lubianka were replicated in dozens of provincial centers.

In southern Russia and the Caucasus, even before Stalin authorized torture, the sadism was such that the living envied the dead; few of those tortured were fit for the GULAG.

The camps could not keep up with the mass arrests; those detained in grotesquely overcrowded prisons often died of typhus, dysentery, heart, malnutrition, or torture before they could be executed.

Collectivization had brutalized victims and perpetrators to such a degree that civilized society no longer existed in the USSR. The cruelty and passivity it induced in Soviet citizens made it possible for Stalin and his hangmen to proceed to an even more violent campaign in the party and among the urban population.

Although Stalin himself was a notorious liar, forger, robber, sadist, adulterer, pervert, terrorist, revolutionary, and murderer who once seduced a thirteen-year-old girl, provoked his son to shoot himself, and whose own wife had ten abortions before she killed herself, this well-read seminarian turned murderer didn't kill millions of people by himself.

Stalin and his hangmen were peas in the same pod:

> Iagoda brought to Stalin his grimmest associates. Stanislaw Messing, Gleb Bokii, and Efim Evdokimov, who had personally tortured, executed, and raped.

Most NKVD men, like Ezhov, drowned fear for their own fates in alcohol and sadism: they hated the innocents who were slow to confess, for the interrogator who failed to secure a statement might follow his prisoner to the executioner.

Ezhov sent those he spared the bullet into the GULAG, which he expanded into a hitherto unimaginable inferno. When Iagoda fell, over 800,000 slaves were working in the GULAG, while NKVD prisons held another quarter of a million and many hundreds of thousands of exiles working in conditions indistinguishable from slavery.

Ezhov's last competent agent was Sergei Shpigelglas, who specialized in liquidating defectors and émigrés. Shpigelglas's final action was to murder Trotsky's son, Lev Sedov, as the latter convalesced from an appendectomy. . . . Shpigelglas also left such a blatant trail of blood that he damaged Franco-Soviet and Swiss-Soviet relations.

Sometimes, in a cruel twist of fate, Stalin's hangmen were on the receiving end of other hangmen:

Ezhov was taken to the secret prison of Sukhanovka outside Moscow, which he himself had had converted from a monastery and in which the church had been converted to an execution chamber with an oil-fired crematorium where the altar had been. Ezhov had hysterics; he was beaten.

Ezhov was taken in the dead of night to a slaughterhouse he himself had built near the Lubianka. Dragged screaming to a special room with a sloping cement floor and a log-lined wall, he was shot by the NKVD's chief executioner.

Particularly notable, and particularly evil, among Stalin's hangmen was the sadistic killer and sexual degenerate Lavrenti Beria:

Beria had proved himself as the Stalin of the Caucasus, murdering and terrorizing like Ezhov and Stalin combined.

Nobody in Stalin's circle was so fastidious as to object to working with such a murderous, devious, ambitious, and utterly unscrupulous lecher.

Beria's rise was speeded by sudden deaths among his colleagues, and he acquired a reputation for murder and falsification.

Lakoba's mother was bludgeoned to death by Beria's hangman Razhden Gangia. Beria slaughtered almost the entire Lakoba clan, keeping the children in prison until they were old enough to execute.

Like Ezhov, Beria seduced or raped women by first arresting their husbands, lovers, or fathers. Unlike Ezhov, he made his sexual predilections public.

Beria curb-crawled Tbilisi, abducting schoolgirls.

Beria inspired loathing among his party colleagues, many as murderous as he, largely because of his predilection for their wives, mistresses, and daughters.

Stalin wanted a more pliable, not a more humane, NKVD, and on occasion gave Beria orders to kill without arrest, let alone trial.

Worse were the massacres perpetrated on Beria's orders in the newly acquired Western Ukraine: perhaps 100,000 civilian prisoners were shot in Lwow as the Red Army retreated.

Other deaths were ordered from Moscow: in November 1941, in eight days, 4,905 persons were shot on Beria's orders.

As for Beria's legendary sexual proclivities, he was certainly guilty of many rapes—usually by blackmail rather than force— and of violating young girls.

It was Beria who recommended to Stalin on March 5, 1940, that the Polish officers be shot in what is known as the Katyn Forest Massacre. It was Beria who presided over the deportation or extermination of ethnic minorities in the Soviet Union during World War II. It was Beria's men who, in their determination to deport the Chechens quickly, "burned the villagers alive in barns, stables, and mosques." It was Beria who was supposed to install a Soviet regime in each of the conquered territories after the war.

Beria, one of the few hangmen to outlive Stalin, was, like some Christians, fond of torture:

Beria went on executing army officers. Some, like Bliukher, were beaten with a brutality exceeding even Ezhov's. Bliukher died on

November 9, 1938, under interrogation, blind in one eye, of a
blood clot in the lung, after his abdominal organs had been
reduced to pulp.

Javakhishvili was beaten in Beria's presence until he signed a
confession; he was shot on September 30. His property was
looted, his archives destroyed, his brother shot, his widow turned
into a recluse for the next forty-five years.

Beria let Rodos loose on the central Asian party leadership in
spring and summer 1939. Working in the specially equipped
Moscow prison of Lefortovo and scorning the usual truncheons,
drugs, or electrodes, he trampled victims with his boots or urinated
in their mouths.

The director of a theater was falsely imprisoned as a British spy who had
plotted to kill Beria. After he was tortured until mute and paralyzed, he
was shot, with "Beria's final touch being an auction of all his goods in the
theater."

Beria got it in the end. He had the gall to complain that he was
going to be gotten rid of "without trial or investigation, after five days'
incarceration, without one interrogation." Witnesses accused him of
engineering murders and having sex with minors. His own hangmen give
graphic accounts of prisoners beaten on Beria's orders and by his own
hand. He was tried in secret with no defense lawyers. He was finally shot
after his mouth was stuffed with a towel. Even Khrushchev considered
Beria utterly ruthless and depraved.

Soldiers who kill for U.S. presidents are not unlike the hangmen
who killed for the tyrant Stalin. No, I wouldn't equate even the worst U.S.
presidents with Stalin; and no, the typical U.S. soldier is not the equal of
one of Stalin's hangmen. But what does it say about Americans that so
many *who are not as bad as Stalin's hangmen* are willing, like those in
the picture below boarding a plane for Afghanistan, to bomb, kill, maim,
and destroy on the command of the man who occupies the Oval Office
who is not as bad as Stalin? And what does it say about Americans that
so many *who claim to follow Judeo-Christian ethics* are willing to bomb,
kill, maim, and destroy on the command of the man who occupies the
Oval Office *who claims to follow Judeo-Christian ethics*?

Soldiers who go to Iraq and Afghanistan, like those who went to
Korea, Vietnam, and all the other countries where U.S. forces had no
business going, go as part of the president's personal army. They are not
defending the country. They are not protecting Americans. They are not

spreading democracy. They are not safeguarding the American way of life. They are not resisting terrorism. They are not fighting over there so we don't have to fight over here. They are not stabilizing the region. They are not looking after American interests. They are not liberating the oppressed. They are not holding back the Muslim hordes. And they certainly aren't defending anyone's freedoms.

The Korean War should have been a wake-up call. Each of the 36,000 American soldiers who died in Korea and came home in a flag-draped coffin, a body bag, or not at all should have sent a resounding message to the American people. But instead, it doesn't seem to matter where U.S. troops go, why they go where they go, how long they stay, how much it costs to keep them there, how many foreigners die at their hands, how much hatred against America is stirred up, and what the troops actually do when they are there—support for the troops as they follow their commander in chief is sacrosanct.

What kind of a man operates a Predator drone for the military? What kind of a man tortures for the CIA? What kind of a man kills for the president? What is it that makes them any different from Stalin's hangmen?

Contrast the modern-day soldier who is willing to kill for U.S. presidents with Benjamin Salmon (1889–1932). Soon after the United States declared war on Germany during World War I, Salmon wrote to President Wilson:

> Regardless of nationality all men are brothers. God is "our father who art in heaven." The commandment "Thou shalt not kill" is unconditional and inexorable. . . . The lowly Nazarene taught us the doctrine of non-resistance, and so convinced was he of the soundness of that doctrine that he sealed his belief with death on the cross. When human law conflicts with Divine law, my duty is clear. Conscience, my infallible guide, impels me to tell you that prison, death, or both, are infinitely preferable to joining any branch of the Army.

Salmon soon began writing letters, giving speeches, and distributing pamphlets against the "Great War." He returned his Army registration questionnaire with a note explaining why he was refusing to fill it out: "Let those who believe in wholesale violation of the commandment, 'Thou Shalt not Kill' make a profession of faith by joining the army of war. I am in the army of peace, and in this army, I intend to live and die." He was subsequently arrested, tried, and convicted. While out on appeal, he was then re-arrested for refusing to report for induction into the Army.

After being charged with desertion and spreading propaganda, Salmon was court-martialed on July 24, 1918, and sentenced to death. The sentence was later commuted to 25 years. All charges could have been dismissed if Salmon had agreed to make a deal and serve as a clerk in the Army, but he refused to cooperate with what he said was an institution "antithetical to Christianity."

The armistice soon ended the war, but not Salmon's prison time in Leavenworth. After suffering in solitary confinement for five months, he was transferred to a military prison in Utah where he was beaten, starved, and stripped; that is, he was treated like some U.S. prisoners at Abu Ghraib. After spending two weeks on a hunger strike, Salmon was force-fed and then sent to a mental hospital. Thanks in part to the ACLU, he was dishonorably discharged in 1920—from an army he never joined.

Although initially denounced by the *New York Times* and forsaken by his own church, Salmon persevered in his refusal to kill for Wilson. God only knows how many Americans have willingly killed for U.S. presidents since then.

* * * * *

THANK A VET?

We've all seen the bumper stickers: "My son is in the Air Force," "If You Can Read This in English, Thank a Marine," "Proud Vietnam Veteran," "Fly Navy," and of course, "Thank a Vet."

Why should we?

Why should we call them heroes, give them military discounts, grant them veterans preference, express our support for them with ribbons on our cars, honor them with a holiday, hold military appreciation church services for them, and thank them for their "service"?

Veterans Day began as Armistice Day to commemorate the signing of the armistice that ended World War I. It had nothing to do with honoring current and former members of the military like Veterans Day is celebrated today. And if the sole purpose of Armistice Day was to honor World War I veterans, it should never have been celebrated since no American soldier did anything honorable by intervening in a European foreign war. And it doesn't matter if he was drafted or not.

Britain's last World War I combat veteran, Harry Patch, died last year at the age of 111. He boasted that he hadn't killed anyone in combat. "War isn't worth one life," Patch said, it is "calculated and condoned slaughter of human beings." In his autobiography *The Last Fighting*

Tommy, Patch wrote that "politicians who took us to war should have been given the guns and told to settle their differences themselves, instead of organising nothing better than legalised mass murder." In the last years of his life, Patch warned some young naval recruits that they shouldn't join.

Frank Buckles, age 109, is the only American veteran of World War I still living. When asked while being honored for his service at a 2007 Veterans Day ceremony at Arlington National Cemetery what he thought about being there while the United States was at war, he replied: "I'm no authority, but I'm not in favor of war unless it's an emergency." I think that Buckles is more of an authority on the horrors of war and the folly and wickedness of war than the current members of the Joint Chiefs.

It is only because World War I did not turn out to be the "war to end all wars" that the holiday was changed to Veterans Day as a tribute to all soldiers who fought for their country.

Although I believe World War II to be neither necessary nor good, I come not on this Veterans Day to criticize the "greatest generation," who, it turns out, were also great at pillaging and carousing.

For reasons I explained in "U.S. Presidents and Those Who Kill for Them," World War II marks the permanent establishment of the American military as the president's personal attack force to kill by his decree Koreans, Vietnamese, Laotians, Cambodians, Grenadians, Panamanians, Yugoslavs, Serbians, Afghans, Iraqis, Somalis, Yemenis, and Pakistanis. Next on the list is Iranians. Sometimes these presidential decrees are rubberstamped by a congressional authorization to use force, but they are always preceded by presidential lies and warmonger propaganda.

So why should a Vietnam veteran be proud? He was typically young, ignorant, deceived, and drafted. He may have fought obediently, valiantly, selflessly, and fearlessly, but since he had no business fighting in Vietnam in the first place, I have nothing to thank him for. And I certainly can't thank him for preventing the Viet Cong from turning America into a socialist republic. Besides, LBJ beat Ho Chi Minh to that anyway. Many Vietnam veterans have written me and expressed shame, remorse, anger, and resentment—not pride—for having been duped into going thousands of miles away from American soil to intervene in another country's civil war. In fact, I have found that it is those who are not Vietnam veterans who are the most vociferous defenders of the war in Vietnam.

The most undeserved and oftentimes disgusting outpouring of thankfulness I have ever seen is over those who have fought or are fighting in Iraq and Afghanistan. The praise and adoration of those fighting in "the front lines in the war on terror" reaches its apex on

Veterans Day, which has become a day to defend U.S. wars and recognize all things military. These soldiers certainly have done nothing worthy of thanks. Sure, they have rebuilt infrastructure—after bombing it to smithereens. They no doubt removed a brutal dictator—and unleashed American brutality in the process. And yes, they have rescued orphan children—after blowing their parents and brothers and sisters to kingdom come.

What is there to thank our soldiers for? They are not defending our freedoms. They are not keeping us safe from our enemies. They are not protecting us from terrorists. They are not guaranteeing our First Amendment rights. They are not defending U.S. borders. They are not guarding U.S. shores. They are not patrolling U.S. coasts. They are not enforcing no-fly zones over U.S. skies. They are not fighting "over there" so we don't have to fight "over here." They are not avenging 9/11. They are not safeguarding the American way of life. Oh, and they are not ensuring that I have the liberty to write what I do about the military.

What, then, should we thank our soldiers for? Should we thank them for fighting an unconstitutional war, an unscriptural war, an immoral war, an offensive war, an unjust war, or a senseless war? Should we thank our veterans for helping to carry out an aggressive, reckless, belligerent, and interventionist foreign policy? Should we thank the military for sucking $1 trillion out of the federal budget?

But, some will say, these soldiers are just doing their jobs. They can't help it if the U.S. military sends them to fight in an unjust war in Iraq or Afghanistan. They are just following orders. They didn't enlist in the military to kill people.

What would any sane man think about a doctor who takes a job at a hospital knowing that the hospital instructs its doctors to euthanize old and sickly patients—and then says he was just doing his job, following orders, and didn't take the job to kill people?

Why are soldiers treated so differently? Why do they get a pass on committing or supporting those who commit murder and mayhem?

But, someone else says, the military has lowered its recruiting standards and is scraping the bottom of the barrel. Many soldiers are ignorant about the true nature of the military and U.S. foreign policy. Why should we fault them for their ignorance? Why should they be criticized for unjustly killing Iraqis or Afghans or Pakistanis? They are just following orders.

Let's go back to the doctor I mentioned. Suppose that after he takes a job in ignorance at what he thinks is a reputable hospital he is instructed to euthanize old and sickly patients? What should he do? I don't know of anyone who would say anything else but that he should quit his job or at least refuse to euthanize anyone.

Again, why are soldiers treated so differently? Why do they get a pass on committing or supporting those who commit murder and mayhem?

But, comes another reply, soldiers have a term of enlistment. They can't just quit their jobs. Doctors can walk away from their jobs at any time. Then I guess it all comes down to morality: Be a mercenary and kill for the state or refuse to do so and suffer the consequences of dishonorable discharge and/or imprisonment.

It is high time that Americans stop holding veterans and current members of the military in such high esteem. It is scientists, engineers, inventors, businessmen, industrialists, software developers, and entrepreneurs that made America great—not veterans of foreign wars. It is doctors, iron workers, taxi drivers, bricklayers, writers, electricians, and cooks that positively contribute to society—not soldiers.

I would like to be able to thank a vet—on Veterans Day and every other day of the year—but I'm still searching for a reason.

* * * * *

SHOULD GAYS AND LESBIANS SERVE IN THE MILITARY?

With the vote in Congress to repeal "Don't Ask, Don't Tell," some conservative Christians are upset that gays and lesbians will be able to serve openly in their beloved institution. "Will the last masculine institution fall?" asked Dave Welch of the U.S. Pastor Council back in December, although I don't know how masculine an institution the military is when there are 200,000 women serving in it.

Well, apparently it will fall, but only sixty days after the secretary of defense "has received DOD's comprehensive review on the implementation of such repeal, and the President, Secretary, and Chairman of the Joint Chiefs of Staff (JCS) certify to the congressional defense committees

- that they have considered the report and proposed plan of action,
- that DOD has prepared the necessary policies and regulations to exercise the discretion provided by such repeal, and
- that implementation of such policies and regulations is consistent with the standards of military readiness and effectiveness, unit cohesion, and military recruiting and retention."

These Christians may have a point; and then again they may not. What I find strange is that few of the Christians objecting to gays and lesbians serving openly in the military have a problem with anything the military does. They never question the military launching preemptive strikes in foreign countries, invading foreign countries, occupying foreign countries, fighting wars in foreign countries, assassinating people in foreign countries, changing regimes in foreign countries, spreading democracy at the point of a gun in foreign countries, enforcing no-fly zones in foreign countries, intervening in the affairs of foreign countries, stationing troops in over 150 foreign countries, and maintaining over 1,000 bases in foreign countries.

Should gays and lesbians serve in the military? Once in the military, they will be expected to blindly follow the orders of their superiors and not exercise independent thought. They will often times not be in a position to know whether an order is in fact dubious or immoral. They will be expected to, without reservation, drop that bomb, fire that weapon, launch that missile, and throw that grenade, as well as directly kill people and destroy their property.

Should gays and lesbians serve in the military? Once in the military, there is no guarantee that they will be in a non-combat role, regardless of what the lying military recruiters say. There is a chance they could be sent to Iraq or Afghanistan, or covertly to Yemen or Pakistan, where they could die in vain and for a lie. They might be put into a position where they will have to kill or be killed. They might come home from Iraq with limbs amputated, like hundreds already have. They might come home from Afghanistan with serious brain injuries, post-traumatic stress disorder, and thoughts of suicide, unable to ever again hold down a job.

Should gays and lesbians serve in the military? Once in the military, they will not be defending our freedoms, protecting us from terrorists, fighting for what is right, or guaranteeing our way of life. Their work will not be limited to the defense of U.S. borders, shores, coasts, and skies. They will instead be expected to serve as the president's personal attack force to bomb, invade, occupy, and otherwise bring death and destruction to any country he deems necessary and that may never have attacked or threatened the United States. And then they will be expected to kill foreigners that resist being bombed, invaded, and occupied.

Should gays and lesbians serve in the military? Once in the military, they will be helping to carry out a reckless and belligerent foreign policy that stirs up hatred against the United States and creates terrorists. They will be expected to carry out a foreign policy that perverts the use of the military and is contrary to the Founding Fathers' policy of nonintervention in the affairs of other countries.

Should gays and lesbians serve in the military? Perhaps some more pressing questions are should heterosexuals serve in the military? Should Christians serve in the military? Should atheists serve in the military? Should anyone serve in the military?

* * * * *

OUR MEN AND WOMEN IN UNIFORM

Our men and women in uniform have stood in the forefront of the war on terror since soon after 9/11.

Our men and women in uniform are our first line of defense against terrorists.

Our men and women in uniform keep us safe from Muslim extremists.

Our men and women in uniform are heroes.

Our men and women in uniform are true public servants.

Our men and women serve voluntarily so we don't have to.

Our men and women in uniform should not have to suffer abuse while they try to do their jobs.

Our men and women in uniform did not ask to perform their job as they do.

Our men and women in uniform are just following orders.

Our men and women must follow the chain of command.

Our men and women in uniform have families that must endure their unusual schedules.

Our men and women in uniform should be thanked when we see them in airports.

Our men and women in uniform help defend our freedoms.

Our men and women in uniform help ensure that we remain the "land of the free and the home of the brave."

Our men and women in uniform should be supported with our prayers.

Our men and women in uniform seek to harm no one.

Our men and women in uniform work in a very stressful environment.

Our men and women in uniform should not be criticized; all criticism of their actions should be directed at the government.

Our men and women in uniform are not directly responsible for any harm they might cause; it is the politicians that are ultimately responsible.

Our men and women in uniform deserve the support of all Americans regardless of political party or philosophy.

Support our men and women in uniform—support your local TSA agent.

N.B.: Although I don't believe a line of what I wrote, this is more than just an April Fool's joke. My purpose is simply to show how utterly ridiculous it is to support the troops while criticizing the TSA.

* * * * *

THANK YOU FOR YOUR SERVICE

It is without question that Americans are in love with the military. Even worse, though, is that their love is unqualified, unconditional, unrelenting, and unending.

I have seen signs praising the troops in front of all manner of businesses, including self-storage units, bike shops, and dog grooming.

Many businesses offer discounts to military personnel not available to doctors, nurses, and others who save lives instead of destroy them.

Special preference is usually given to veterans seeking employment, and not just for government jobs.

Many churches not only recognize veterans and active-duty military on the Sunday before holidays, they have special military appreciation days as well.

Even many of those who oppose an interventionist U.S. foreign policy and do not support foreign wars hold the military in high esteem.

All of these things are true no matter which country the military bombs, invades, or occupies. They are true no matter why the military does these things. They are true no matter what happens while the military does these things. They are true no matter which political party is in power.

The love affair that Americans have with the military—the reverence, the idolatry, the adoration, yea, the worship—was never on display like it was at the post office the other day.

While at the counter shipping some packages, a U.S. soldier, clearly of Vietnamese origin in name and appearance, dressed in his fatigues, was shipping something at the counter next to me. The postal clerk was beaming when he told the soldier how his daughter had been an MP in Iraq. Three times in as many minutes I heard the clerk tell the soldier—with a gleam in his eye and a solemn look on his face—"Thank you for your service." The clerk even shook the soldier's hand before he left.

I could not believe what I was seeing and hearing, and I am no stranger to accounts of military fetishes in action.

Aside from me not thanking that soldier for his service—verbally or otherwise—I immediately thought of four things.

One, what service did this soldier actually render to the United States? If merely drawing a paycheck from the government is rendering service, then we ought to thank every government bureaucrat for his service, including TSA goons. Did this soldier actually do anything to defend the United States, secure its borders, guard its shores, patrol its coasts, or enforce a no-fly zone over U.S. skies? How can someone blindly say "thank you for your service" when he doesn't know what service was rendered?

Two, is there anything that U.S. soldiers could do to bring the military into disfavor? I can't think of anything. Atrocities are dismissed as collateral damage in a moment of passion in the heat of battle by just a few bad apples. Unjust wars, we are told, are solely the fault of politicians not the soldiers that do the actual fighting. Paul Tibbets and his crew are seen as heroes for dropping an atomic bomb on Hiroshima. Before he died, Tibbets even said that he had no second thoughts and would do it again. I suspect that if the United States dropped an atomic bomb tomorrow on Afghanistan and Pakistan, killing everyone and everything, and declaring the war on terror over and won, a majority of Americans would applaud the Air Force crew that dropped the bomb and give them a ticker-tape parade.

Three, why is it that Americans only thank American military personnel for their service? Shouldn't foreign military personnel be thanked for service to their country? What American military worshippers really believe is that foreign military personnel should only be thanked for service to their government when their government acts in the interests of the United States. Foreign soldiers are looked upon as heroic if they refuse to obey a military order to shoot or kill at the behest of their government as long as such an order is seen as not in the interests of the United States. U.S. soldiers, however, are always expected to obey orders, even if it means going to Iraq, Afghanistan, Pakistan, Yemen, or Libya under false pretenses.

And four, what is a Vietnamese man—who most certainly has relatives, or friends or neighbors of relatives, that were killed or injured by U.S. bombs and bullets during the Vietnam War—doing joining the U.S. military where he can be sent to shoot and bomb foreigners like the

U.S. military did to his people?

And aside from these four things, I'm afraid I must also say: Sorry, soldiers, I don't thank you for your service.

- I don't thank you for your service in fighting foreign wars.
- I don't thank you for your service in fighting without a congressional declaration of war.
- I don't thank you for your service in bombing and destroying Iraq and Afghanistan.
- I don't thank you for your service in killing hundreds of thousands of Iraqis and Afghans.
- I don't thank you for your service in expanding the war on terror to Pakistan and Yemen.
- I don't thank you for your service in occupying over 150 countries around the world.
- I don't thank you for your service in garrisoning the planet with over 1,000 military bases.
- I don't thank you for your service in defending our freedoms when you do nothing of the kind.
- I don't thank you for your service as part of the president's personal attack force to bomb, invade, occupy, and otherwise bring death and destruction to any country he deems necessary.

Thank you for your service? I don't think so.

* * * * *

CURSED BE UNCONDITIONAL OBEDIENCE

Like all members of the military profession I never had an original thought until I left the service. My mental faculties remained in suspended animation while I obeyed the orders of higher-ups. This is typical with everyone in the military service." ~ Major General Smedley Butler

"If soldiers were to begin to think, not one of them would remain in the army." ~ Frederick the Great

"I find in existence a . . . dangerous concept that the members of the armed forces owe their primary allegiance and loyalty to those who temporarily exercise the authority of the executive branch of the Government, rather than to the country and its Constitution

they are sworn to defend. No proposition could be more dangerous." ~ General Douglas MacArthur

"There is one thing in the world more wicked than the desire to
command, and that is the will to obey." ~ W. K. Clifford, mathe-
matician and philosopher

After almost ten years of fighting in Afghanistan, the deadliest day
for U.S. forces was just a few weeks ago on Saturday, August 6. On that
day thirty U.S. military personnel were killed when their helicopter was
shot down. The majority of those killed were said to be elite Navy Seals
from the same unit that killed Osama bin Laden.

The question that was never asked about this event by any major
news media outlet is a question that I (and a few others) have been asking
since the war in Afghanistan began: What is the U.S. military doing in
Afghanistan?

The ones who bear the most responsibility for the 9/11 attacks are
the pilots who flew the planes, none of whom were from Afghanistan. No
American was ever harmed by anyone in Afghanistan until the U.S.
military invaded and occupied that country. The United States even
supported the Muslim insurgents and Afghan militants when they were
freedom-fighting Mujahideen fighting against the Soviets when they
invaded Afghanistan.

Tens of thousands of Afghans are now dead who had never
threatened America and had nothing to do with 9/11. Over 1,700
American soldiers are also dead, and many thousands more have
life-altering injuries.

So, what is the U.S. military doing in Afghanistan?

The purpose of the U.S. military should be limited to defending the
United States, securing its borders, guarding its shores, patrolling its
coasts, and enforcing a no-fly zone over its skies. Period. To do otherwise
is to pervert the purpose of the military.

This means the purpose of the U.S. military should never be to
defend other countries, secure their borders, guard their shores, patrol their
coasts, and enforce no-fly zones over their skies.

This also means that the purpose of the U.S. military should never
be to provide disaster relief, dispense humanitarian aid, supply peacekeepers, enforce UN resolutions, spread goodwill, rebuild infrastructure,
establish democracy, nation build, change regimes, eradicate drugs,
contain communism, open markets, keep oil pipelines flowing, revive
public services, build schools, or train armies in any foreign country.

This also means that the purpose of the U.S. military should never be to remedy oppression, human rights violations, sectarian violence, ill treatment of women, forced labor, child labor, religious or political persecution, poverty, genocide, famine, or injustice in any foreign country.

And it certainly also means that the purpose of the U.S. military should never be to launch preemptive strikes in foreign countries, fight wars in foreign countries, drop bombs on foreign countries, assassinate people in foreign countries, torture people in foreign countries, takes sides in a civil war in foreign countries, station troops in foreign countries, maintain bases in foreign countries, attack foreign countries, invade foreign countries, occupy foreign countries, or unleash civil unrest in foreign countries.

Clearly, no U.S. soldier, sailor, or marine had any business stepping foot in Afghanistan in 2001 or flying a helicopter there in 2011. Those who returned in a coffin (if enough of their body parts could be found) died unnecessarily, duped, in vain, and for a lie.

So again I ask: What is the U.S. military doing in Afghanistan?

The only answer is unconditional obedience. Although some U.S. soldiers, because of misguided zeal, may have wanted to go to Afghanistan after 9/11, few would choose to go now if it were their decision to make. But soldiers were told to go and they went, and soldiers are still being told to go.

They didn't consider the history of Afghanistan. They didn't consider the purpose of the military. They didn't consider U.S. foreign policy. They didn't consider Chalmers Johnson. They didn't consider the wisdom of the Founding Fathers. They didn't consider the Constitution. They didn't consider the Soviet Union's failed attempt to subdue Afghanistan. They didn't consider their families. They didn't consider the cost to U.S. taxpayers. They didn't consider their own mental and physical health. They didn't consider the thousands of dead or maimed Afghan civilians.

Even worse, those that did consider some or all of these things went to Afghanistan anyway. They may not have even bought in the baloney about fighting for our freedoms or fighting them "over there" so we don't have to fight them "over here," but they went anyway.

Unconditional obedience.

If you want to see a perfect example of unconditional obedience on display, then just look at the recent interview on the Diane Rehm show about "Navy Seals and U.S. Strategy in Afghanistan."

After announcing that U.S. forces were continuing their investigation into the shooting down of the helicopter in Afghanistan, Diane introduced her guests in the studio, Thom Shanker, the Pentagon correspondent for the *New York Times* and Paul Pillar of the Center for Peace and Security Studies at Georgetown University, and by phone from Plymouth, Massachusetts, former Navy SEAL lieutenant commander Anthony O'Brien. Joining the panel later by phone was Lawrence Korb, senior fellow at the Center for American Progress and former assistant secretary of defense in the Reagan administration.

The second caller to the show was someone named Don, who made this comment:

> I just wanted to comment real quick. Any time you have generals on the air and they're pressured to give some reasons why we're in this war in Afghanistan, they always fall back to a main reason being women's rights, so girls can go to school, you know, for all the Taliban oppression. And I was just wondering if your panelists thought that that was really a legitimate reason, that we should have our military spending billions of dollars a year in this country to fight for women's rights.

Diane referred the caller to Anthony O'Brien, who gave this reply:

> I agree with the caller's premise. The primary reason why you engage the military at the strategic level is for the national security interest of the United States of America. And as much as I'm a fighter for the rights of women, it is—it's not our duty in the military, primarily, to protect the women or stop drug trades, et cetera. However, the president is the boss, and he calls the shots. And if—whether it be President Bush or President Obama, when they tell us where to go and when, we give a snappy salute, and we do what we're told.

Diane then sought a comment from Thom Shanker:

> Well, I just want to give Anthony a snappy salute 'cause his answer is perfect. I mean, we hear so often these conversations among civilians: why are we there, I don't want us there or the opposite, we should be there. The military does not assign itself these missions. They follow the orders of the elected civilian leadership who are representing, Diane, your caller and everybody else. So that is where the responsibility for these decisions resides at the end of the day.

My only comment is simply this: Only God deserves unconditional obedience.

Unconditional obedience is why Nazis killed Jews in concentration camps, Japanese pilots bombed Pearl Harbor, East German border guards killed their fellow citizens fleeing over the Berlin Wall to the West, and Soviet soldiers invaded Afghanistan before U.S. soldiers did.

Cursed be unconditional obedience.

* * * * *

FREEDOMS I WISH THE MILITARY WERE DEFENDING

Freedom itself was attacked this morning by a faceless coward, and freedom will be defended." ~ George W. Bush, September 11, 2001

We have heard it repeated loudly and continuously since 9/11—the troops are defending our freedoms. This claim is made so often and by so many different segments of society that it has become another meaning-less national dictum—like "God Bless America" or "In God We Trust."

This cliché is actually quite insidious. It is used as a mantra to justify or excuse anything the U.S. military does.

U.S. troops are engaged in unconstitutional, undeclared wars—but the troops are defending our freedoms. U.S. drone strikes killed civilians in Pakistan—but the troops are defending our freedoms. U.S. bombs landed on a wedding party in Afghanistan—but the troops are defending our freedoms. U.S. soldiers murdered Afghan civilians and kept some of their body parts—but the troops are defending our freedoms. U.S. helicopter pilots gunned down Iraqi civilians—but the troops are defending our freedoms. U.S. soldiers killed civilians for sport—but the troops are defending our freedoms. U.S. troops carelessly killed civilians and then covered it up—but the troops are defending our freedoms.

But as I have pointed out many times in my articles on the military, and others like Jacob Hornberger of the Future of Freedom Foundation have been arguing for years (see here and here), the troops are doing everything but defending our freedoms. In fact, the more the troops defend our freedoms by bombing, invading, and occupying other countries, the more enemies they make of the United States and the more our freedoms get taken away in the name of "fighting terrorism" or "national security."

Not in any particular order, and in varying degrees of significance, here are some freedoms I wish the military were defending:

- The freedom to fly without being sexually violated.
- The freedom to purchase a gun without a waiting period.
- The freedom to grow, sell, and smoke marijuana.
- The freedom to sell goods and services for whatever amount a buyer is willing to pay.
- The freedom to make more than six withdrawals from one's savings account each month.
- The freedom to drink alcohol as a legal, voting adult under twenty-one years of age.
- The freedom to purchase Sudafed over the counter.
- The freedom to gamble without government approval.
- The freedom to deposit more than $10,000 in a bank account without government scrutiny.
- The freedom to not be stopped at a checkpoint and have one's car searched without a warrant.
- The freedom to sell any good or offer any service on Craigslist.
- The freedom to fill in a "wetland" on one's own property.
- The freedom to cut someone's hair for money without a license.
- The freedom to home-brew over 100 gallons of beer per year.
- The freedom to advertise tobacco products on television.
- The freedom to smoke Cuban cigars.
- The freedom to not wear a seatbelt.
- The freedom to be secure in our persons, houses, papers, and effects, against unreasonable searches and seizures.
- The freedom to keep the fruits of one's labor.
- The freedom of an employer and an employee to negotiate for any wage.
- The freedom to discriminate against anyone for any reason.
- The freedom to videotape the police in public.
- The freedom of businesses to hire and fire whomever they choose.
- The freedom to not be brutalized by the police.
- The freedom to not be arrested for victimless crimes.
- The freedom to sell raw milk.
- The freedom to not have one's child subject to unnecessary vaccinations.
- The freedom to not have one's child unjustly taken by Child Protective Services.
- The freedom to not be subject to the Patriot Act.
- The freedom for kids to set up neighborhood lemonade stands.
- The freedom to not have every facet of business and society

regulated.
- The freedom to stay in one's home during a hurricane.
- The freedom to not have our e-mail and phone conversations monitored.
- The freedom to travel to and trade with any country.
- The freedom to be left alone.

Certainly there are hundreds of things that could be added. We no longer live in a free country. We are increasingly living in a police state, a warfare state, and a national security state. Our freedom is not absolute. The only reason the United States is still considered "the land of the free and the home of the brave" is because we are relatively free, with the degree of freedom varying depending on which country America is compared to.

Would I rather live somewhere else? No, I wouldn't, but that is a ridiculous question. First of all, if the typical German, Italian, Swede, Korean, Australian, or Spaniard were asked if he would rather live somewhere else you would probably get the same answer. And second, although a prisoner would rather live in a clean prison than a dirty prison and a safe prison rather than a violent prison, he would prefer to not be a prisoner in the first place.

I conclude with three brief thoughts. One, I want the military to defend our freedoms. But fighting foreign wars only reduces our freedoms. After all, it is still true that war is the health of the state. Two, if the military is going to defend our freedoms, then we need freedoms to defend. Our freedoms must be restored before the military can defend them. And three, the greatest threat to our freedoms is the U.S. government, not the governments of China, Syria, Libya, Yemen, Iraq, Afghanistan, Russia, Cuba, Venezuela, or Iran.

* * * * *

HOW TO REDUCE MILITARY SUICIDES

Since the invasion of Iraq in 2003, I have been quite vocal in my opposition to most of what is done by the U.S. military in the name of defending our freedoms and other nonsense. Because of this I have been accused over the years of not appreciating and not supporting the troops (I plead guilty) and indifference to and wishing harm to the troops (I plead not guilty).

However, on this latter point it needs to be said that it is only natural to expect that foreigners on the receiving end of U.S. military invasions, occupations, bombings, and killings would retaliate against U.S. troops. Just think of what Americans would do if these things were done to them.

So, on the one hand, as Herbert Spencer wrote over a hundred years ago in his essay on patriotism: "When men hire themselves out to shoot other men to order, asking nothing about the justice of their cause, I don't care if they are shot themselves." But on the other hand, as an American, I don't want to see any American soldiers harmed, and especially those that were duped into fighting some unnecessary and senseless foreign war.

The solution to the dilemma is to not send American soldiers overseas to fight foreign wars, which are inherently unjust. This keeps foreigners from having to shoot invading American soldiers and American soldiers from having to shoot resisting foreigners.

The difference between a warmongering Republican or conservative (like every major conservative talk show host and every major Republican presidential candidate except Ron Paul) and yours truly is that I don't want anyone on either side to die.

One way that American soldiers are increasingly dying is at their own hands. More U.S. military personnel have died because they committed suicide than from suicide bombers detonating explosive devices near U.S. troops in Iraq and Afghanistan. I would like to see military suicides reduced.

According to a new policy brief titled "Losing the Battle: The Challenge of Military Suicide," published by the Center for a New American Security (CNAS), from 2005-2010, "service members took their own lives at a rate of approximately one every 36 hours." The Army had a record number of thirty-three suicides in July of 2010. That is eight times more soldiers dead by suicide than were killed in Iraq that month. That is over half the number of soldiers killed in the much-more-dangerous occupation of Afghanistan that month. The report also says that the Veterans Administration estimates "that a veteran dies by suicide every 80 minutes." Although only 1 percent of Americans have served in the military, veterans account for 20 percent of all suicides.

According to the report:

- The mental health screening process following deployment is flawed.
- Suicide among service members and veterans threatens the health of the all-volunteer force.
- America is losing its battle against suicide by veterans and

service members. And, as more troops return from deployment, the risk will only grow.

- Soldiers who deploy are more likely to die by suicide. Data have long indicated definitive links between suicide and injuries suffered during deployment.
- Additional factors that heighten risk include chronic pain and post-traumatic stress disorder (PTSD) symptoms such as depression, anxiety, sleep deprivation, substance abuse and difficulties with anger management. These factors are also widely associated with deployment experience in Afghanistan and Iraq.

The report also noted that military hazing caused some of the suicides and that excess prescription medication in the military community was also a problem.

At an event launching the CNAS report, Vice Chief of Staff of the Army Peter Chiarelli said that trying to reduce the number of suicides in the Army has been "the most difficult challenge" in his forty years in the military. One of the authors of the report, Dr. Margaret Harrell said that the battle against suicide was being lost "multiple times a day."

According to the Department of Defense Suicide Event Report (DoDSER) for calendar year 2010, 295 service members died by suicide in 2010 (Air Force—59, Army—160, Marine Corps—37, Navy—39). There were 863 known suicide attempts. The suicide rate for divorced service members was 55 percent higher than the suicide rate for married service members. Most of those who successfully committed suicide were white, male, and under 25 years old. The number of suicides in 2009 was 309; the number in 2008 was 268.

According to the Final Report of the Department of Defense Task Force on the Prevention of Suicide by Members of the Armed Forces, in the nine-year period from 2001 to 2009, more than 1,900 members of the military took their own lives. This is more soldiers than have died fighting in Afghanistan since the war on terror was launched.

Although I am not a physician, a psychologist, a psychiatrist, or a mental health or suicide prevention counselor, I can think of four things that would reduce military suicides. And not only that, these things would also save the taxpayers money, improve America's image in the world, keep us safer, and make it honorable to serve in the military.

One, stop fighting foreign wars.

When soldiers are sent to fight unnecessary, unjust foreign wars (is there any other kind?), there will always be questions in their minds about why they are fighting in a place they couldn't locate without a map and against a people that never harmed an American until Americans first stuck their noses in their business. And we wonder why soldiers get depressed and suicidal?

The aforementioned CNAS report found a direct connection between deployment and suicide. Some soldiers don't even wait until they get home to suffer chronic pain, PTSD, depression, and unemployment—they kill themselves in Iraq or Afghanistan.

The fewer foreign wars our soldiers are told to fight (the ones who have to do the actual fighting are never asked for their opinion), the fewer cases of traumatic brain injury, loss of limbs, depression, PTSD, anxiety, substance abuse, and chronic pain our soldiers will needlessly have to suffer with.

I just can't see U.S. soldiers getting depressed and suicidal or suffering PTSD and sleep loss over having to kill enemy soldiers who actually tried to attack the United States.

Two, end the empire.

Why does the United States still have tens of thousands of troops in Germany, Japan, and South Korea? Why does the United States have any troops at all in Djibouti, Australia, and Argentina? Why does the United States have 250,000 troops in foreign countries? Why does the United States have troops in 160 countries and territories? Why is it now so commonly accepted that someone in the military is being deployed to Germany or Japan?

Military life is destructive to children, families—and service members. The strain of separation or relationship breakups, or the guilt over temptations succumbed to, can certainly lead to suicide.

Sailors on Navy ships in Jacksonville should sail down around the Florida Keys and up through the Gulf of Mexico to Texas and then turn around and go back and see their families. No landing in Mexico, the Caribbean, or South America—for any reason. That will do more to keep America safe than sailing in the Persian Gulf or the Gulf of Tonkin. And it will certainly do more for morale and military families than overseas deployments.

Three, end most roles for women in the military.

"Your mother wears army boots" used to be a derogatory remark. Now it is true for 207,308 women in the U.S. military. This is about 15 percent of the 1,425,115 total members of the military. (All figures are as of September 30, 2011.) And these numbers don't include the Coast Guard. Women comprise an even higher percentage in the Guard and Reserve.

Over 200,000 women have served in Iraq and Afghanistan. There have been 111 female U.S. soldiers killed in Iraq. There have been 30 female U.S. soldiers killed in Afghanistan, the most recent one being Sarina Butcher, aged 19, who died on November 1, 2011. It is a terrible tragedy that we send young men to die in senseless foreign wars; it is a horrendous evil that we send young women.

Call me a sexist, a chauvinist, and a misogynist all you want, but no woman has any business flying a helicopter in Iraq, like twenty-seven-year old Army captain Kimberly Hampton, who died when the OH-58 Kiowa Warrior helicopter she was piloting was shot down. (No man does either, but that is not my point here.)

According to Allan Carlson, the U.S. Department of Defense is the nation's largest child-care system. Up to 40 percent of military pregnancies occur among unmarried military personnel. The 10 percent of military personnel who are "service couples," with both husband and wife in uniform, are 64 percent more likely to be divorced by age 24 than comparable civilian couples. Carlson made the case many years ago for the "Bachelor Army" in *Policy Review* (the Fall 1993 issue in which it appeared is apparently not online).

Things will only get worse since the Military Leadership Diversity Commission, established by Congress two years ago, recommended that the Pentagon do away with the policy that bans women from serving in combat units.

According to the previously mentioned DoDSER, one fourth of attempted suicides in the military are by women. Relationship issues are a factor in both male and female military suicides.

Four, stop perverting the purpose of the military.

As I have said in one form or another on many occasions:

The U.S. military should be limited to defending the United States, securing U.S. borders, guarding U.S. shores, patrolling U.S. coasts, and enforcing no-fly zones over U.S. skies instead of defending, securing, guarding, patrolling, and enforcing in other countries. The U.S. military should be engaged exclusively in defending the United States, not defending other countries, and certainly not attacking, invading, or occupying them. Using the military for any other purpose than the actual defense of the United States perverts the purpose of the military.

Soldiers should know without a doubt that what they are doing is moral, just, and right. Limiting the military to actually protecting the United States is the surest way to do this.

This means no more offensive wars. No more nation building. No more spreading democracy at the barrel of a gun. No more policing the world. No more providing disaster relief. No more dispensing humanitarian aid. No more preemptive strikes. No more bombing. No more extraordinary renditions. No more enhanced interrogation techniques. No more peacekeeping operations. No more enforcing UN resolutions. No more regime changes. No more assassinations. No more overseas deployments. No more foreign military bases. No more containing communism. No more opening markets. No more enforcing no-fly zones. No more training foreign police and armies. No more invasions. No more occupations. No more foreign wars.

I support the troops. I support the troops not being put into positions where they face unnecessary danger. I support the troops not fighting senseless foreign wars. I support the troops not being separated from their families. I support the troops not being sent to kill foreigners. I support the troops not being stationed on overseas bases. I support the troops not being misused by presidents, politicians, and military brass. I support the troops not being killed as invaders and occupiers. And I support the troops not killing themselves.

* * * * *

BLUE ANGEL BUDGET BLUES

The Navy's Blue Angels flight-demonstration team is in trouble. And not because their commander resigned earlier this year after flying his F/A-18 Hornet below minimum altitude at an air show in Virginia and causing a month-long safety stand-down.

Headquartered at the Pensacola Naval Air Station, the Blue Angels have been flying and thrilling audiences for more than 60 years. The team began after World War II with the desire of Adm. Chester Nimitz to maintain peacetime support for naval aviation and highlight the Navy and Marines, from which the Blue Angels gets its pilots, for potential recruits who didn't live near a Naval base.

The Air Force has a similar demonstration team called the Thunderbird's, while the Army has the Golden Knights parachute team.

The Blues, as the Blue Angels squadron is known, made 70 performances at 35 locations around the United States in 2011 during a show season that runs from March through November. More than 100,000 people attended the recent Blue Angels end-of-season show at the Pensacola Naval Air Station. The Navy says that about 11million people each year watch the Blue Angels six blue and gold jets twist, turn, drop, and climb in perfect formation for a carefully choreographed 45-minute show. As one who lived for many years in Pensacola, I can testify that seeing the Blue Angels fly is impressive.

However, all of this comes at a price. There have been 26 Blue Angels pilots who have been killed in air-show or training accidents, most recently in 2007 when a pilot lost control of his plane and crashed during an air show in South Carolina. The other cost is that borne by American taxpayers. The Pentagons budget for the Blue Angels is $37 million.

But the mission of the Blue Angels is purely promoting naval aviation and recruiting instead of actually contributing to national defense, so some have begun to call for the squadrons elimination because of the budget deficit and potential cuts in military spending.

Laura Peterson, a spokeswoman for Taxpayers for Common Sense, says the money could be better spent on other programs. Some readers of the *Air Force Times* newspaper, obviously read mainly by current and former members of the Air Force, recently listed eliminating the Blue Angels and similar programs as one way to cut defense spending.

Others intimately connected with the Navy naturally disagree.

Capt. Greg McWherter, the Blue Angels commander, claims that the Blues fill a vital national security role by improving morale, helping with recruiting and presenting a public face for the nations 500,000 sailors and Marines. He sees Blue Angels performances as inspiring young people to join the military and thus ensuring that the Navy and the Marine Corps is strong 10 to 15 years from now. Ray Davis, the U.S. Navy secretary, says the Blue Angels are important because they showcase the incredible skill level of U.S. military. The Blues are ambassadors for not just the Navy but for the entire American military across this country and around the world. Rep. Jeff Miller, whose district includes the Pensacola Naval Air Station and who is on the House Armed Services Committee, points to the popularity of the Blue Angels as proof that the program will be kept alive: You can ask the hundreds of thousands of people who come out each weekend and see them fly and know they aren't going anywhere.

The potential cuts to the defense budget are due to sequestration because the Congressional Joint Select Committee on Deficit Reduction (the so-called Supercommittee) failed to come to an agreement on how to reduce the federal budget deficit by $1.5 trillion *over ten years*. That is only $150 billion a year, split between security and nonsecurity programs, but exempting the Cerberus of the welfare state: Social Security, Medicaid, and Medicare.

The Budget Control Act of 2011 mandates that if the Supercommittee fails to specify spending cuts, then a cut of $1.2 trillion *over ten years* will automatically take place. That is $120 billion a year. Any idiot except a member of Congress could cut $120 billion a year in federal spending for ten years without thinking about it for more than ten minutes. By anyone's estimate, the U.S. government is spending more than $10 billion a month on the wars in Iraq and Afghanistan. There is your $120 billion a year. How hard was that?

But it turns out that the cuts to the defense budget are not real cuts at all; they are reductions in the rate of spending increases. Federal spending and federal debt are both still forecast to grow at a rate faster than the U.S. economy.

As the freshman, junior senator from Kentucky, Rand Paul, recently explained,

> The interesting thing is there will be no cuts in military spending. This may surprise some people, but there will be no cuts in military spending because were only cutting proposed increases. If we do nothing, military spending goes up 23 percent over 10 years. If we sequester the money, it will still go up 16 percent. So spending is still rising under any of these plans. In fact, if you look at both alternatives, spending is still going up. Were only cutting proposed increases in spending....
>
> Defense spending will go up $100 billion over ten years even if we sequester $600 billion, because the curve of spending in our country is going up at about 7.5percent a year. All spending goes up.

His father, Rep. Ron Paul (R–Tex.), has long called for real cuts not in *defense* spending, but in *offense* spending, which is what the budget of the Department of Defense is mostly spent on.

The war party, that is, the Republican Party, is livid over the proposed cuts to the Pentagons budget.

Mitt Romney says the cuts are undermining troop capacity, delaying the building of aircraft carriers and cutting the capacity of the U.S. to defend itself. Senators John McCain (R–Ariz.) and Lindsey Graham (R–S.C.) both members of the Senate Armed Services Committee maintain that the cuts represent a threat to the national security interests of the United States, and cannot be allowed to occur. The chairman of the House Armed Services Committee, Buck McKeon (R–Calif.), insisted that he would not be the armed services chairman who presides over crippling our military. Sen. Pat Toomey (R–Penn.) a member of the Supercommittee wants to reconfigure the automatic spending cuts mandated by the Budget Control Act to prevent cuts to the defense budget.

But we have been this way before. Earlier this year it was reported by *Defense News* that Barack Obama wanted to cut defense spending by $400 billion by 2023. The aforementioned Buck McKeon whose district includes Edwards Air Force Base and whose top two donors were Lockheed Martin and Northrup Grumman expressed his opposition then as well: I have grave concerns about the White House announcing a $400 billion cut to national security spending while our troops are fighting in three different theaters. I guess ending senseless foreign wars never occurred to him. But as it turns out, the $400billion cut was a reduction only in the rate of growth: The goal will be to hold growth in the defense base budget below inflation, which would save $400billion by 2023, said the White House.

And what is this nonsense about cutting spending by $1.2trillion over ten years or $400billion by 2023? Politicians always talk in terms of other years after the next fiscal year because they want to make their numbers look bigger. But it is ludicrous to talk about anything that will happen in ten years, in the year 2023, or in any other year after the next fiscal year. The present Congress cannot bind any future Congress to do anything. A politician might as well say that he plans to cut $100trillion from the federal budget by 2095.

The very heart and soul of conservatism is not libertarianism, as Ronald Reagan once claimed it was; the very heart and soul of conservatism is war and militarism. The Blue Angels have no need to worry as long as Republicans continue to equate reductions in the rate of increases in the defense budget with cuts that threaten national security.

* * * * *

A BUDDING RED-STATE FASCIST

Madeleine McAulay is, by her own admission, a one-of-a-kind, politics-obsessed teenager, a teenage political maverick, a common-sense conservative, and a supporter of Sarah Palin. But she is also a budding red-state fascist.

Madeleine blogs at Faith Hope & Politics. Her upcoming book, *The Makings of a Political Maverick*, is "a key into the intriguing mind of a teenage, Conservative." It is "a reflection of a young life that is so engulfed in politics."

I hate to pick on a sixteen-year-old girl. She is clearly far superior in intelligence than most of the kids her age that I had the misfortune of "teaching" when I taught high school. I would never have noticed her website had not a reader of my recent Veteran's Day article directed me to her "tribute to American Soldiers, past and present, in honor of Veteran's Day on 11/11/11" called "Thank You Soldiers, Past and Present," as well as an earlier post of hers called "Dear American Soldiers."

Poor Madeleine didn't have a chance. In introducing her Veteran's Day tribute she says: "Thank you to all of those who have served. I would like to especially thank, my Mom's Parents, my Dad's Dad, my Dad, and my Uncle Jerry for their service." No wonder she is a budding red-state fascist.

In the middle of her "Dear American Soldiers" post, Madeleine quotes this poem from the site Military-Money-Matters.com:

It Is the Soldier

It is the Soldier, not the minister
Who has given us **freedom of religion**.

It is the Soldier, not the reporter
Who has given us **freedom of the press**.

It is the Soldier, not the poet
Who has given us **freedom of speech**.

It is the Soldier, not the campus organizer
Who has given us **freedom to protest**.

It is the Soldier, not the lawyer
Who has given us the **right to a fair trial**.

It is the Soldier, not the politician
Who has given us the **right to vote**.

It is the Soldier who salutes the flag,
Who serves beneath the flag,
And whose coffin is draped by the flag,
Who allows the protester to burn the flag.

This is too much for even the editor of Military-Money-Matters.com, who comments at the beginning of his explanation of the poem's authorship:

> There are blogs and comments across the internet debating the content of the poem, some picking it apart by attempting to apply the words literally. Sadly, those who do so will never understand the true meaning of the poem—that without our military members willing to defend them, those freedoms we cherish would quickly disappear.
>
> So, while technically soldiers do not "give" us those freedoms, they do guarantee them. Those types of people just will never "get it," at least not until it's too late, and then they'll wonder what happened, and why the military didn't stop it.

But do U.S. soldiers even guarantee these things? Of course they don't. No U.S. soldier stationed in Germany, Japan, or South Korea is defending or guaranteeing our freedoms. No U.S. soldier fighting in Iraq or Afghanistan is protecting or guaranteeing our rights.

Since U.S. soldiers have begun fighting in Iraq and Afghanistan, our freedoms have been eviscerated. First it was the Patriot Act and the TSA. And now the U.S. government claims the power and the right to intern indefinitely anyone—including American citizens—anywhere in the world, including on American soil and to kill anyone—including American citizens—anywhere in the world, including on American soil. Just ask José Padilla. Just ask Anwar al-Awlaki. Oh, never mind, he's dead. He was killed, along with his sixteen-year-old son, by Predator drone strike.

Is there anyone in Iraq who wanted to take away our freedom of religion? Is there anyone in Afghanistan who wanted to take away our freedom of the press? Is there anyone in Pakistan who wanted to take away our freedom of speech? Is there anyone in Yemen who wanted to take away our freedom to protest? Is there anyone in Iran who wants to take away our right to a fair trial? Is there anyone anywhere who wants to take away our right to vote?

According to then CIA director and now Secretary of Defense Leon Panetta, there may be fewer than 50 al-Qaeda fighters in Afghanistan. Suppose they all hated our freedom of religion, freedom of the press, freedom of speech, and freedom to protest. Suppose they also hated our rights to a fair trial and to vote. Is that worth 1,800 more dead U.S. soldiers? Why am I, who supposedly hates all things military, the one who is concerned about the senseless deaths of American troops?

It is the U.S. government that we need to be more concerned about taking away our freedom of religion, freedom of the press, freedom of speech, freedom to protest, right to a fair trial, and right to vote than the government or the people of Iraq, Afghanistan, Pakistan, Iran, Venezuela, Cuba, Yemen, Syria, or North Korea. James Madison was right: "If tyranny and oppression come to this land, it will be in the guise of fighting a foreign enemy."

What really gets me upset at those adults who have influenced Madeleine are her remarks about Ron Paul that she made in commenting on the CNN Republican debate: "Ron Paul had a decent debate. He made great points regarding health care and economic prosperity, but when it came to Foreign Policy I couldn't disagree more." This reminds me of a comment I saw at the end of an article recently. Someone had posted that their ideal candiate would have the foreign policy views of Newt Gringrich and the views of Ron Paul on everything else. Sorry Madeleine, but militarism, imperialism, and foreign wars are inimical to liberty on the domestic front and foster American fascism.

* * * * *

OUTRAGE OVER BODY PARTS OF WAR DEAD IS MISDIRECTED

There didn't seem to be a lot of outrage last month when it was reported by the *Washington Post* that the Dover Air Force Base mortuary had for years been disposing of the unidentified remains of U.S. soldiers by cremating them and then dumping the ashes in a landfill in King George County, Virginia.

The Dover mortuary receives the remains of all U.S. military personnel killed in Iraq, Afghanistan, and other overseas locations. More than 6,000 U.S. soldiers have died in foreign wars since 2001. The mortuary engaged in the landfill disposal practice from 2003 to 2008. Relatives of the dead soldiers were not informed about the method of disposal. Since June 2008, the Navy has disposed of cremated remains at sea.

Waste Management, the owner of the landfill, said it was not informed about the origin of the ashes it disposed of.

The disclosure by the *Washington Post* came after several federal investigations documenting "gross mismanagement" at Dover Air Force Base. The Air Force has admitted that its mortuary lost an ankle, improperly stored and tracked other remains, and sawed off a dead

Marine's arm to fit his body into a casket. Three mortuary supervisors were disciplined, but not fired, after an 18-month investigation.

Now the Air Force has said that it dumped more human remains in the Virginia landfill than it previously acknowledged. It turns out that the cremated, incinerated partial remains consisting of 976 fragments from 274 identified American soldiers and 1,762 pieces of unidentified remains were deposited in the landfill. The Air Force had previously maintained that it "could not estimate how many troops might have had their remains sent to a landfill." The Air Force has decided not to notify the relatives of the 274 soldiers because "each of the families signed forms stipulating that they did not wish to be notified if additional remains were subsequently recovered or identified." Only if family members come forward and request the information will the Air Force disclose it. Naturally, the military regrets "any additional grief to families that past practices may have caused."

Family members of the fallen are, of course, outraged. But they are not alone. Joe Davis, of the Veterans of Foreign Wars (VFW), said, "The latest reports suggest the military hasn't been transparent." He further explained that "these kids are being put in body bags with all the parts that can possibly be retrieved, and then a month, two months later, somebody might be patrolling down that same alley way and find a finger. Consulting the families is the thing to do." The top Democrat and Republican on the House Oversight Committee, which is investigating the Dover Air Force Base mortuary, said they found the most recent *Washington Post* revelations "appalling." The committee is now going to broaden its probe to include all military burial practices over the past decade.

It is not really comforting to know that all the pieces of your loved one are buried in a coffin instead of being dumped in a landfill. The pieces that could be found, that is.

No, the outrage over the disposal of body parts of U.S. war dead is misdirected.

Where is the outrage of family members who have lost loved ones against George W. Bush for lying Americans into the wars in Iraq and Afghanistan and against Barack Obama for escalating the Afghan War and expanding the bogus war on terror to other countries? The United States has lost almost 5,000 soldiers in Iraq and more than 1,800 in Afghanistan. That translates into many thousands of grandmothers, grandfathers, mothers, fathers, sisters, brothers, aunts, uncles, nieces, nephews, and cousins who have lost family members in foreign wars, and for no good reason. There are some notable mothers—such as Cindy Sheehan—and fathers—Andrew Bacevich—who have spoken out. But for the most part, relatives of the fallen are content to perpetuate the myth that their loved ones died fighting for their freedoms.

Where is the outrage of the VFW over the thousands of U.S. soldiers who have died while becoming veterans of a foreign war? There are U.S. troops stationed in more than 150 countries and territories doing everything but actually defending the land, coasts, borders, and skies of the United States. Vietnam veteran and peace advocate James Glaser has documented the 65 official foreign military actions since World War II that have been approved by Congress to qualify the combatants for membership in the VFW—and that was before the wars in Iraq and Afghanistan. Better that the VFW loose all of its membership than that more American soldiers die in vain and for a lie in foreign wars.

Where is the outrage of members of Congress over the hundreds of billions of dollars wasted on foreign wars? Why aren't Bush and Dick Cheney being investigated along with the Dover Air Force Base mortuary?

But that's not all.

Where is the outrage of Democrats over the silence of most in their party (with the notable exception of Dennis Kucinich) regarding not only the failure of their president to end Bush's wars, but regarding his drone attacks and extra-judicial murder?

Where is the outrage of liberals over the dearth of criticism from progressives (with the notable exception of Glenn Greenwald) of Obama's dictatorial view of presidential power and murderous foreign policy?

Where is the outrage of Republicans over all of the major Republican presidential candidates (except Ron Paul) who want the United States to stay in Iraq, continue fighting in Afghanistan, expand the war on terror, and provoke Iran?

Where is the outrage of conservatives over the leading conservative talk-show hosts (Rush Limbaugh, Mark Levin, Sean Hannity, Bill O'Reilly) who want the United States to continue its reckless foreign policy of policing the world—at the expense of U.S. taxpayers, and soldiers and their families?

Regardless of whom U.S. military personnel are fighting, how they die, and where they are fighting, the Pentagon owes it to the families of the fallen to do all that it can to ensure that the remains of military personnel are handled, accounted for, and buried properly. But an even greater responsibility of the Pentagon is to actually defend the country and not engage in senseless and unjust foreign wars that needlessly sacrifice U.S. troops.

* * * *

THE REAL PROBLEM WITH THE NATIONAL DEFENSE AUTHORIZATION ACT

For each of the past forty-eight years, Congress has passed the misnamed National Defense Authorization Act to set forth the budget of the Defense Department. President Obama just signed into law the latest version of the NDAA, but not without some controversy.

The House originally passed this 1145-page bill (H.R.1540) back on May 26 by a vote of 322–96. Only six Republicans voted against the bill (Justin Amash, John Campbell, Jason Chaffetz, John Duncan, Tom McClintock, & Ron Paul).

The 926-page Senate version of the bill (S.1867) was passed on December 1 by a vote of 93–7. Only three Republicans voted against the bill (Tom Coburn, Mike Lee, & Rand Paul). The Senate then incorporated the measure in a now 908-page H.R.1540 as an amendment.

The original House bill contained an affirmation in section 1034 that the president has "the authority to detain belligerents," until "the termination of hostilities," including persons who "(A) are part of, or are substantially supporting, al-Qaeda, the Taliban, or associated forces that are engaged in hostilities against the United States or its coalition partners; or (B) have engaged in hostilities or have directly supported hostilities in aid of a nation, organization, or person described in subparagraph (A)."

But it is the Senate version that, as amended in two ways, raised such a firestorm of controversy.

Conservative, religious, and animal-rights groups were upset with a provision in the Senate bill seen as legalizing sodomy and bestiality in the military. The Senate bill simply says, buried in division A—DEPARTMENT OF DEFENSE AUTHORIZATIONS, title V—MILITARY PERSONNEL POLICY, subtitle E—Military Justice and Legal Matters Generally, section 551—REFORM OF OFFENSES RELATING TO RAPE, SEXUAL ASSAULT, AND OTHER SEXUAL MISCONDUCT UNDER THE UNIFORM CODE OF MILITARY JUSTICE, (d) REPEAL OF SODOMY ARTICLE, that "Section 925 of such title (article 125 of the Uniform Code of Military Justice) is repealed." This is a reference to title 10, subtitle A, part II, chapter 47, subchapter 10, section 925 of U.S. Code, which states:

> (a) Any person subject to this chapter who engages in unnatural carnal copulation with another person of the same or opposite sex or with an animal is guilty of sodomy. Penetration, however slight, is sufficient to complete the offense.

(b) Any person found guilty of sodomy shall by punished as a court-martial may direct.

Section 125 of the UCMJ adds this explanation:

> It is unnatural carnal copulation for a person to take into that person's mouth or anus the sexual organ of another person or of an animal; or to place that person's sexual organ in the mouth or anus of another person or of an animal; or to have carnal copulation in any opening of the body, except the sexual parts, with another person; or to have carnal copulation with an animal.

The Senate bill also directed that the two other mentions of sodomy in U.S. Code title 10, subtitle A, part II, chapter 47, subchapter 8, section 843, and subchapter 10, section 918, be excised.

Civil libertarians of all stripes were upset with a provision in the Senate bill that would codify the power of the president to use the military to indefinitely intern anyone, without charges or trial, anywhere in the world—including American citizens on U.S. soil.

The most worrisome sections of the bill are found in division A, title X, subtitle D, sections 1031 and 1032. I give here the sections in their entirety because we will return to them later:

> SEC. 1031. AFFIRMATION OF AUTHORITY OF THE ARMED FORCES OF THE UNITED STATES TO DETAIN COVERED PERSONS PURSUANT TO THE AUTHORIZATION FOR USE OF MILITARY FORCE.
>
> (a) IN GENERAL.—Congress affirms that the authority of the President to use all necessary and appropriate force pursuant to the Authorization for Use of Military Force (Public Law 107-40) includes the authority for the Armed Forces of the United States to detain covered persons (as defined in subsection (b)) pending disposition under the law of war.
>
> (b) COVERED PERSONS.—A covered person under this section is any person as follows:
>
> (1) A person who planned, authorized, committed, or aided the terrorist attacks that occurred on September 11, 2001, or harbored those responsible for those attacks.
>
> (2) A person who was a part of or substantially supported al-Qaeda, the Taliban, or associated forces that are engaged in

hostilities against the United States or its coalition partners, including any person who has committed a belligerent act or has directly supported such hostilities in aid of such enemy forces.

(c) DISPOSITION UNDER LAW OF WAR.—The disposition of a person under the law of war as described in subsection (a) may include the following:

(1) Detention under the law of war without trial until the end of the hostilities authorized by the Authorization for Use of Military Force.

(2) Trial under chapter 47A of title 10, United States Code (as amended by the Military Commissions Act of 2009 (title XVIII of Public Law 111-84)).

(3) Transfer for trial by an alternative court or competent tribunal having lawful jurisdiction.

(4) Transfer to the custody or control of the person's country of origin, any other foreign country, or any other foreign entity.

(d) CONSTRUCTION.—Nothing in this section is intended to limit or expand the authority of the President or the scope of the Authorization for Use of Military Force.

(e) AUTHORITIES.—Nothing in this section shall be construed to affect existing law or authorities, relating to the detention of United States citizens, lawful resident aliens of the United States or any other persons who are captured or arrested in the United States.

(f) REQUIREMENT FOR BRIEFINGS OF CONGRESS.—The Secretary of Defense shall regularly brief Congress regarding the application of the authority described in this section, including the organizations, entities, and individuals considered to be ''covered persons'' for purposes of subsection (b)(2).

SEC. 1032. REQUIREMENT FOR MILITARY CUSTODY.

(a) CUSTODY PENDING DISPOSITION UNDER LAW OF WAR.—

(1) IN GENERAL.—Except as provided in paragraph (4), the Armed Forces of the United States shall hold a person described

in paragraph (2) who is captured in the course of hostilities authorized by the Authorization for Use of Military Force (Public Law 107-40) in military custody pending disposition under the law of war.

(2) COVERED PERSONS.—The requirement in paragraph (1) shall apply to any person whose detention is authorized under section 1031 who is determined—

(A) to be a member of, or part of, al-Qaeda or an associated force that acts in coordination with or pursuant to the direction of al-Qaeda; and

(B) to have participated in the course of planning or carrying out an attack or attempted attack against the United States or its coalition partners.

(3) DISPOSITION UNDER LAW OF WAR.—For purposes of this subsection, the disposition of a person under the law of war has the meaning given in section 1031(c), except that no transfer otherwise described in paragraph (4) of that section shall be made unless consistent with the requirements of section 1033.

(4) WAIVER FOR NATIONAL SECURITY.—The Secretary of Defense may, in consultation with the Secretary of State and the Director of National Intelligence, waive the requirement of paragraph (1) if the Secretary submits to Congress a certification in writing that such a waiver is in the national security interests of the United States.

(b) APPLICABILITY TO UNITED STATES CITIZENS AND LAWFUL RESIDENT ALIENS.—

(1) UNITED STATES CITIZENS.—The requirement to detain a person in military custody under this section does not extend to citizens of the United States.

(2) LAWFUL RESIDENT ALIENS.—The requirement to detain a person in military custody under this section does not extend to a lawful resident alien of the United States on the basis of conduct taking place within the United States, except to the extent permitted by the Constitution of the United States.

(c) IMPLEMENTATION PROCEDURES.—

(1) IN GENERAL.—Not later than 60 days after the date of the enactment of this Act, the President shall issue, and submit to Congress, procedures for implementing this section.

(2) ELEMENTS.—The procedures for implementing this section shall include, but not be limited to, procedures as follows:

(A) Procedures designating the persons authorized to make determinations under subsection (a)(2) and the process by which such determinations are to be made.

(B) Procedures providing that the requirement for military custody under subsection (a)(1) does not require the interruption of ongoing surveillance or intelligence gathering with regard to persons not already in the custody or control of the United States.

(C) Procedures providing that a determination under subsection (a)(2) is not required to be implemented until after the conclusion of an interrogation session which is ongoing at the time the determination is made and does not require the interruption of any such ongoing session.

(D) Procedures providing that the requirement for military custody under subsection (a)(1) does not apply when intelligence, law enforcement, or other government officials of the United States are granted access to an individual who remains in the custody of a third country.

(E) Procedures providing that a certification of national security interests under subsection (a)(4) may be granted for the purpose of transferring a covered person from a third country if such a transfer is in the interest of the United States and could not otherwise be accomplished.

(d) EFFECTIVE DATE.—This section shall take effect on the date that is 60 days after the date of the enactment of this Act, and shall apply with respect to persons described in subsection (a)(2) who are taken into the custody or brought under the control of the United States on or after that effective date.

FBI Director Robert Mueller, Secretary of Defense Leon Panetta, and Director of National Intelligence James Clapper have all publicly opposed the bill. All three wrote letters to Congress on the matter. Mueller wrote that the "presumption of military detention" would "inhibit our ability to convince arrestees to cooperate." Panetta warned that the bill "imposes a whole new restraint on the flexibility we need to pursue our counterterrorism efforts." A group of twenty-six retired generals and admirals wrote to senators that the new provisions in the NDAA would "do more harm than good."

Thirty-two Democratic members of Congress sent their own letter to the House and Senate Armed Services Committee leaders in protest of these provisions, saying:

> The Senate-passed version of the NDAA, S. 1867, contains Section 1031, which authorizes indefinite military detention of suspected terrorists without protecting U.S. citizens' right to trial. We are deeply concerned that this provision could undermine the Fourth, Fifth, Sixth, Seventh, and Eighth amendment rights of U.S. citizens who might be subjects of detention or prosecution by the military.

One signer of the letter, Rep. Martin Heinrich, stated: "These provisions are deeply concerning and would risk putting American citizens in military detention, indefinitely. In short, this authority is at complete odds with the United States Constitution."

The ACLU urged the president to veto the bill. The *New York Times* editorialized against the bill.

A contributor to *Forbes* maintained that the NDAA is "the greatest threat to civil liberties Americans face."

Republican representative Justin Amash termed the bill "one of the most anti-liberty pieces of legislation in our lifetime."

Republican senator Rand Paul said: "If you allow the government the unlimited power to detain citizens without a jury trial, you are exposing yourself to the whim of those in power. That is a dangerous game."

Paul, as mentioned, was one of only three Republican senators to vote against the bill. The other warmongering, police statist Senate Republicans are typified by Lindsey Graham, who stated: "It is not unfair to make an American citizen account for the fact that they decided to help Al Qaeda to kill us all and hold them as long as it takes to find intelligence about what may be coming next. And when they say, 'I want my lawyer,' you tell them, 'Shut up. You don't get a lawyer.'"

The version of the NDAA just signed into law by President Obama is a result of a conference committee between the House and the Senate to work out a compromise on their version of H.R.1540. The House passed the final measure on December 14 by a vote of 283–136. The

Republican vote was 190–43. The Senate approved the final measure on December 15 by a vote of 86–13. But this time Republican senators Coburn, Lee, and Paul were joined by senators Mike Crapo, Jim DeMint, and James Risch.

So, what became of the sodomy and indefinite detention provisions?

The Senate attempt to strip the sodomy language out of the UCMJ was turned back by the House. According to the conference report (H.REPT. 112-329):

> The Senate amendment contained a provision (sec. 551) that would amend section 920 of title 10, United States Code (Article 120 of the Uniform Code of Military Justice (UCMJ)), to separate Article 120, UCMJ, into three separate articles applying to the offenses of rape and sexual assault, sexual offenses against children; and other non-consensual sexual misconduct offenses. The provision would also repeal section 125 of title 10, United States Code (Article 125 of the UCMJ), the offense of sodomy. The House bill contained no similar provision. The House recedes with an amendment that would delete the repeal of section 125 of title 10, United States Code (Article 125 of the UCMJ).

But regarding the dangerous provisions in sections 1031 and 1032, the Senate bill won out.

According to the conference report:

> The House bill contained a provision (sec. 1034) that would affirm that the United States is engaged in an armed conflict with al-Qaeda, the Taliban, and associated forces.

> The Senate amendment contained a provision (sec. 1031) that would affirm the authority of the Armed Forces of the United States to detain certain covered persons pursuant to the Authorization for Use of Military Force (Public Law 107-40). The provision would not affect existing law or authorities relating to the detention of United States citizens, lawful resident aliens of the United States, or any other persons who are captured or arrested in the United States.

> The House recedes.

The original language in S.1867 is thus retained verbatim in the new version of the NDAA.

And regarding section 1032, the conference report says:

The Senate amendment contained a provision (sec. 1032) that would require military custody for foreign al-Qaeda terrorists who are captured in the course of hostilities authorized by the Authorization for Use of Military Force (Public Law 107-40), subject to a national security waiver. Under the provision, the President would have broad authority to issue implementation procedures, including but not limited to deciding who makes a determination of coverage, how the determination is made, and when it is made.

The House bill contained no similar provision.

The House recedes with an amendment providing that nothing in this provision shall be construed to affect the existing criminal enforcement and national security authorities of the Federal Bureau of Investigation or any other domestic law enforcement agency with regard to a covered person, regardless whether such covered person is held in military custody. The law enforcement and national security tools that would not be affected in any way by this provision include, but would not be limited to, Grand Jury subpoenas, national security letters, and actions pursuant to the Foreign Intelligence Surveillance Act (Public Law 95-511). The amendment would also authorize the President, rather than the Secretary of Defense, to waive the requirements of the provision.

The conferees note that while section 1021 of this bill would apply to "al Qaeda, the Taliban, or associated forces that are engaged in hostilities against the United States or its coalition partners," this section would apply to "al Qaeda or an associated force that acts in coordination with or pursuant to the direction of al Qaeda." The conferees agree that while the Taliban is covered by section 1021, it is not covered by this section.

(It should be noted that the original sections 1031 and 1032 are numbered 1021 and 1022 in the new bill.)

So, the main thing that is different about the new version of the NDAA is the insertion of the following paragraph between "Implementation Procedures" and "Effective Date":

(d) AUTHORITIES.—Nothing in this section shall be construed to affect the existing criminal enforcement and national security authorities of the Federal Bureau of Investigation or any other domestic law enforcement agency with regard to a covered person, regardless whether such covered person is held in military custody.

There are only two other changes. Under (a)(4) "Waiver for National Security," instead of the secretary of defense submitting a wavier to Congress it is the president. And under (c)(2)(C), there is an inconsequential change in wording. An "interrogation session" is now called just an "interrogation."

I rarely agree with Democratic members of the House of Representatives, but Rep. Alcee Hastings from my state of Florida, during debate in the House over the conference report, gets it right it:

> This legislation establishes an authority for open-ended war anywhere in the world and against anyone. It commits us to seeing a "terrorist" in anyone who ever criticizes the United States in any country, including this one. The lack of definitions as to what constitutes "substantial support" and "associated forces" of al Qaeda and the Taliban mean that anyone could be accused of terrorism.
>
> While this measure includes an exemption for United States citizens, it does not protect them from indefinite detention. In one fell swoop, we have set up a situation where American citizens could have their Fourth, Fifth, Sixth, Seventh, and Eighth Amendment rights violated on mere suspicions.
>
> We won't defeat terrorism by using the military to lock up innocent people for the rest of their lives on the mere suspicion of wrongdoing. We will not defeat terrorism by claiming the entire world as a battlefield. And we will not defeat terrorism by replacing our rule of law with reckless, uncontrolled, and unaccountable powers.

Likewise, here are the comments of consistent war opponent Rep. Dennis Kucinich:

> Mr. Speaker, this bill authorizes permanent warfare anywhere in the world. It gives the President unchecked power to pursue war. It diminishes the role of this Congress.
>
> This legislation authorizes the military to indefinitely detain individuals without charge or trial, including the detention of U.S. citizens on U.S. soil.

In short, what this bill does is it takes a wrecking ball to the United States Constitution and gives enormous power to the government or the State.

In his article, "Three Myths about the Detention Bill," civil libertarian par excellence Glenn Greenwald concludes:

> In sum, there is simply no question that this bill codifies indefinite detention without trial (Myth 1). There is no question that it significantly expands the statutory definitions of the War on Terror and those who can be targeted as part of it (Myth 2). The issue of application to U.S. citizens (Myth 3) is purposely muddled—that's why Feinstein's amendments were rejected—and there is consequently no doubt this bill can and will be used by the U.S. Government (under this President or a future one) to bolster its argument that it is empowered to indefinitely detention even U.S. citizens without a trial.

But as correct and necessary as they are, the objections of civil libertarians regarding the indefinite detention of American citizens that the NDAA codifies, are not the real problem with the bill. Much more insidious is the bill itself and the $669 billion it allocates for "defense" spending.

In the "Constitutional Authority Statement" that accompanies H.R.1540, the chairman of the House Armed Services Committee, Buck McKeon (R–Calif.), has the audacity to say:

> Congress has the power to enact this legislation pursuant to the following:
>
> The constitutional authority on which this bill rests is the power of Congress to "provide for the common defense," "raise and support armies," and "provide and maintain a navy," as enumerated in Article I, Section 8 of the United States Constitution.

The U.S. military is used to provide disaster relief, dispense humanitarian aid, supply peacekeepers, enforce UN resolutions, launch preemptive strikes, nation build, spread goodwill, change regimes, eradicate drugs, rebuild infrastructure, contain communism, open markets, keep oil pipelines flowing, revive public services, establish schools, train foreign armies, invade foreign countries, occupy foreign countries, spread democracy, kill tens of thousands of people that were no threat to the United States, and secure the borders, guard the shores, patrol the coasts, enforce no-fly zones in the skies, and otherwise defend other countries. I doubt that the Framers of the Constitution envisioned any of these things when they said: "provide for the common defense," "raise and support armies," and "provide and maintain a navy." The purpose of the military has been perverted beyond all recognition. Because the military spends more for offense than defense, that the defense budget is actually for defense is clearly a myth.

Another myth is that defense spending keeps us safe. The United States spends more on defense than the rest of the world combined. It maintains an empire of over 1,000 foreign military bases and hundreds of thousands of troops in 150 countries and territories around the globe. The United States is the policeman, fireman, social worker, security guard, mediator, and babysitter of the world. It has "entangling alliances" with many countries that require it to go to war and expend blood and treasure in defense of other nations. But as Congressman Ron Paul, speaking recently on Face the Nation, maintained: "Those troops overseas aggravate our enemies, motivate our enemies. I think it's a danger to national defense, and we can save a lot of money cutting out the military expenditures that contribute nothing to our defense."

Yet another myth about the defense budget is that it is the only thing spent on defense. As economic historian Robert Higgs has shown, real defense spending is actually about $1 trillion.

Still another myth is that the defense budget includes spending on wars in Iraq and Afghanistan. Here is a list of U.S. spending on these foreign wars through fiscal year 2010 that was in addition to the defense budget:

- FY2001 Emergency Supplemental Appropriations Act for Recovery from and Response to Terrorist Attacks on the United States, P.L. 107-38 9/18/01, $13.9 billion
- FY2002 Department of Defense and Emergency Terrorism Response Act, P.L. 107-117, 1/10/02, $3.4 billion
- FY2002 Emergency Supplemental, P.L. 107-206, 8/2/02, $14.1 billion
- FY2002 Regular Foreign Operations, P.L. 107-115, 1/10/02, $0.2 billion
- FY2003 Consolidated Appropriations, P.L. 108-7, 2/20/03, $10.4 billion
- FY2003 Emergency Supplemental, P.L. 108-11, 4/16/03, $66.0 billion
- FY2003 DOD Appropriations, P.L. 107-248, 10/23/02, $7.1 billion

- FY2004 Emergency Supplemental, P.L. 108-106, 11/6/03, $86.1 billion
- FY2004 Foreign Operations Appropriations, P.L. 108-199, 1/23/04, $0.5 billion
- FY2005 DOD Appropriations Act, P.L. 108-287, 8/5/04, $27.8 billion
- FY2005 Consolidated Appropriations, P.L. 108-447, 12/8/04, $1.0 billion
- FY2005 Supplemental Appropriations, P.L. 109-13, 5/11/05, $79.0 billion
- FY2006 Interior & Related Agencies Appropriations, P.L. 109-54, 8/2/05, $0.2 billion
- FY2006 Foreign Operations Appropriations, P.L. 109-102, 11/14/05, 1.0 billion
- FY2006 Science, State, & Related Agencies Appropriations Act, P.L. 109-108, 11/22/05, $0.1 billion
- FY2006 Military Quality of Life & Veterans Affairs, P.L. 109-114 11/30/05, $0.4 billion
- FY2006 DOD Appropriations Act, P.L. 109-148 12/30/05, $50.8 billion
- FY2006 Emergency Supplemental, P.L. 109-234 6/15/06, $69.2
- FY2007 DOD Appropriations Act, P.L. 109-289 9/29/06, $70.5 billion
- FY2007 Continuing Resolution, P.L. 110-5, 2/15/07, $1.8 billion
- FY2007 Supplemental, P.L. 110-28, 5/25/07, $98.7 billion
- FY2008 Continuing Resolution, P.L. 110-92 9/29/07, $5.2 billion
- FY2008 DOD Appropriations Act, P.L. 110-116, 11/13/07, $11.6 billion
- FY2008 Consolidated Appropriations Act, P.L. 110-161, 12/26/07, $73.2 billion
- FY2008 Supplemental Appropriations Act, P.L. 110-252, 6/30/08, $163.2 billion
- FY2009 Continuing Appropriations Act, P.L. 110-329, 9/30/08, $4.0 billion
- FY2009 Omnibus Appropriations Act, P.L. 111-8, 3/11/09, $1.1 billion
- FY2009 Supplemental Appropriations Act, P.L. 111-32, 6/24/09, $82.5 billion
- FY2010 Consolidated Appropriations Act, P.L. 111-117,

  12/16/09, $8.2 billion
- FY2010 DOD Appropriations Act, Title IX, P.L. 111-118, 12/19/09, $127.3 billion
- FY2010 Supplemental, P.L. 111-212, 7/27/10, $34.2 billion

The most insidious myth about the defense budget is that it is tool of congressmen to enhance their chances for reelection while lining the pockets of defense contractors. In his book *Washington Rules: America's Path to Permanent War*, retired U.S. Army colonel Andrew Bacevich explains:

> Each year the Pentagon expends hundreds of billions of dollars to raise and support U.S. military forces. This money lubricates American politics, filling campaign coffers and providing a source of largesse—jobs and contracts—for distribution to constituents. It provides lucrative "second careers" for retired U.S. military officers hired by weapons manufacturers or by consulting firms appropriately known as "Beltway Bandits" (p. 228).

Two of Old Right journalist John T. Flynn's eight points he considers to be the main marks of the fascist State are:

- Militarism is a mainstay of government spending
- Military spending has imperialist aims

The U.S. economic system is not based on free market capitalism; it is based on that most insidious form of crony capitalism known as military fascism.

The NDAA, sans indefinite detention, or in whatever form it is found, is a bill for continued militarism, imperialism, and empire, and a terrible waste of the taxpayers' money.

* * * * *

MARINES, WHY DO YOU DO THIS TO YOUR FAMILIES?

From September 27, 2010, to April 11, 2011, the approximately 1,000 Marines of the 3rd Battalion, 5th Regiment, based at Camp Pendleton, and known as the "Darkhorse" Battalion, suffered the loss of 25 men in the Sangin district of Helmand province in Afghanistan in support of Operation Enduring Freedom. An estimated 470 enemy fighters were killed. A favorable ratio to be sure, but still 495 deaths too many.

Beginning this past October 30 and ending on November 5, NPR Pentagon correspondent Tom Bowman did a seven-part series for All Things Considered on the Darkhorse Battalion called "'Darkhorse' Battalion and the Afghan War." Here is how the series was introduced:

> A year ago, nearly 1,000 U.S. Marine officers and enlisted men of the 3rd Battalion, 5th Regiment deployed to restive Helmand province in southern Afghanistan. By the time their tour ended in April 2011, the Marines of the 3/5—known as "Darkhorse"—suffered the highest casualty rate of any Marine unit during the past 10 years of war. This week, NPR tells the story of this unit's seven long months at war—both in Afghanistan and back home.

Disgust, anger, sorrow, pity—this is how I felt after listening to some of the shows in the series. I recently listened to the whole series as well as a 50-minute version. A timeline of the deadly Afghan mission is online here. The seven shows with their descriptions as provided by NPR are as follows:

"Afghan Success Carries A Price For Commander," October 30

> In Afghanistan, Lt. Col. Jason Morris led the 3rd Battalion, 5th Regiment, which suffered the highest casualty rate of any Marine unit during the past 10 years of war. The "Darkhorse Battalion" commander says the unit's mission was a success—but he will live with the burden of those deaths.

"An Afghan Hell On Earth For 'Darkhorse' Marines," October 31

> October 31, 2011 A year ago, the Marines of the 3rd Battalion, 5th Regiment arrived in Sangin, a Taliban haven in southern Afghanistan, for a seven-month deployment. Known as "Darkhorse," the battalion sustained a higher casualty rate than any other Marine unit during the 10-year Afghan war.

"As Casualties Grew, So Did Marine Families' Fears," November 1

> When the Marines of the 3rd Battalion, 5th Regiment deployed to Afghanistan, they left behind families who were desperate for information and grew frightened as the death toll grew. For 25 families, the news they received was the worst possible.

"Strategy Behind A Marine Unit's Dangerous Mission," November 2

The Marines of Darkhorse Battalion suffered a high rate of casualties during their seven-month deployment to southern Afghanistan. Their mission was to go after the Taliban in a place called Sangin—a crossroads of insurgency and drug trafficking. At the time, officials in the military and all the way up to the secretary of defense asked why the Darkhorse Battalion was taking so many casualties. NPR Pentagon correspondent Tom Bowman is reporting all week on the battalion. On Wednesday, he speaks with Guy Raz about the strategy in Sangin: whether the Marines made mistakes and what they did to reduce causalities and complete the mission.

"A Marine's Death, And The Family He Left Behind," November 3

November 3, 2011 When Marine Cpl. Derek Wyatt left for Afghanistan, his wife, Kait, was pregnant with their first child. Three months later, Derek was dead. A day after his death, Kait was induced, so she could give birth and attend his funeral.

"For Wounded Marines, The Long, Hard Road Of Rehab," November 4

Dozens of Marines from Darkhorse Battalion returned home with missing limbs and other injuries that will last a lifetime. Learning to cope with their injuries and figure out their futures is a slow, arduous process.

"The Darkhorse Battalion and the Afghan War," November 5

This past week, All Things Considered has been sharing stories about the Darkhorse Battalion—that's the Marine unit that suffered the highest casualty rate of any Marine unit during the 10-year Afghan war. NPR Pentagon correspondent Tom Bowman wraps up the series today, as he tells weekends on All Things Considered guest host Laura Sullivan about some of the people he met—both on the battlefield and on the home front.

Here are the names of the fallen from the Darkhorse Battalion. Most were in their twenties.

Oct. 8, 2010: Lance Cpl. John Sparks

Oct. 13, 2010: Lance Cpl. Joseph Rodewald, Lance Cpl. Phillip
Vinnedge, Cpl. Justin Cain, and Pfc. Victor Dew
Oct. 14, 2010: Lance Cpl. Alec Catherwood, Lance Cpl. Irvin
Ceniceros, and Lance Cpl. Joseph Lopez
Oct. 15, 2010: Lance Cpl. James Boelk
Oct. 16, 2010: Sgt. Ian Tawney
Nov. 4, 2010: Lance Cpl. Matthew Broehm and Lance Cpl.
Brandon Pearson
Nov. 6, 2010: Lance Cpl. Randy Braggs
Nov. 9, 2010: 1st Lt. Robert Kelly
Nov. 10, 2010: Lance Cpl. James Stack
Nov. 24, 2010: Lance Cpl. Arden Buenagua
Nov. 25, 2010: 1st Lt. William Donnelly
Dec. 2, 2010: Sgt. Matthew Abbate
Dec. 6, 2010: Cpl. Derek Wyatt and Pfc. Colton Rusk
Dec. 7, 2010: Sgt. Jason Peto
Dec. 17, 2010: Lance Cpl. Jose Maldonado
Dec. 24, 2010: Lance Cpl. Kenneth Corzine
Dec. 28, 2010: Cpl. Tevan Nguyen
Jan. 20, 2011: Sgt. Jason Amores

In addition to the 25 Marines that died in Helmand province, there were
184 that were badly wounded, including 34 that lost limbs.

But I want to focus, not on what the Marines of the Darkhorse
Battalion endured in Afghanistan, but on what they did to their families
back home. In case you don't have the time to listen, here are some
excerpts from the NPR series:

> Back home, the families were frantic, wondering what was
> happening. Morris' wife, Jane Conwell, started getting a hundred
> emails each day. One wife was convinced she heard the doorbell
> ring in the middle of the night, that Marine officers were there to
> announce her husband's death. "The families, especially the
> spouses, really almost lost their minds," Morris says.

> At home in California, Ashley Tawney remembers waking up
> from a nap on her couch. It was the middle of an October after-
> noon. The house she and Ian had recently bought had several
> French doors. Through the glass of one of them, she watched two
> Marine officers pass by. She didn't have to open the door to see
> them standing there. "It was just a real solemn ... very eerie sight.
> It's just like the movies, just like the movies," she recalls. To this
> day, she doesn't know how she made it to the front door. "I, like,
> floated over there or something," she says. "And everything was

kind of in slow-motion. And I opened the door, and then they started off with the whole spiel ... and I was just in shock." "I remember my cat was playing with the chaplain's uniform. ... Then they started to do the paperwork ... the whole, me going to Dover to meet his body, and that's when it hit me, and I just covered my face with my hand and was like, 'Oh my God, oh my God.' There's no goodbye and there's no nothing. I couldn't fathom that he was gone," she says.

"It was just talking about an IED explosion and how many people were injured. There was one KIA. I remember making the comment to some of my colleagues, like, wow, my son's unit, somebody died, that really hits close to home," he recalls. Boelk went about his day. Five hours went by. "Then I got a call from our daughter. And she said there were two Marines at our house, and immediately, kind of lost my composure at work, obviously. There was just total silence in the office. Of course, what can they say? I just shut off my computers and picked up my bags, and told them I had to go home," Boelk says.

Last year, on Dec. 6, Kait Wyatt was up early, making breakfast, when the doorbell rang at her home on the Camp Pendleton Marine base. She opened the door. Two Marines stood there. "I wanted it to be them telling me that he was OK, that he was hurt or something along those lines. But I knew," Kait recalls. "I automatically knew Derek had passed away," she says. Her husband, Cpl. Derek Wyatt, was serving in Afghanistan with the 3rd Battalion, 5th Regiment, known as "Darkhorse." Kait was pregnant: She was due to give birth in just a couple of weeks, in mid-December. The Marines began the ritual, and Kait, who was 22 at the time, began to sob.

"Liam was sleeping, and I got the phone call. 'Is this Mrs. Romo ... Jacob Romo's wife?' And I knew right away who it was," she said. "I started to hyperventilate, and I need to breathe because I'm pregnant. And the guy was very sweet, he was so sweet. All I needed to get out was, 'Is he alive?' 'Yes, he's alive.' And I could calm down and take a couple of breaths." The Marine who called her was reading from a statement—something about a bilateral amputee. At first, she wasn't sure what that meant. And then she was told his legs were gone.

So we talked to some of these wives, and, you know, some of them would wake up in the middle of the night thinking a doorbell rang, thinking there were Marine officers there to say that their husband had been killed. It's very, very difficult for them. So I think that's what surprised me the most.

Marines, why do you do this to your families?

Based on the words of various Marines interviewed or talked about in this series, I say to those who made it through what I wish I could also say to twenty-five young men who didn't:

> If you just wanted to feel the trill of leading men in battle, then shame on you. If you just couldn't find a job so you enlisted in the Marines, then shame on you. If you just wanted to experience the mental and physical challenge, then shame on you. If you just enlisted because your father was a Marine, then shame on you. If you just wanted to go to war, then shame on you. If you just thought you were defending our freedoms, then shame on you. If you just wanted to die a hero, then shame on you. If you just felt you had to complete the mission, then shame on you. If you just enlisted because you thought your government needed you, then shame on you. If you thought there was just no better job than being a Marine, then shame on you.

I have no doubt that the Marines of the Darkhorse Battalion fought valiantly. I am not questioning their manhood, courage, or determination. But I also have no doubt that each of the deaths of those twenty-five Marines from the Darkhorse Battalion was preventable, unnecessary, and senseless.

Lance Cpl. Josue Barron, who lost an eye, a leg, and some of his close friends, at the end of a discussion about whether everything that happened in Afghanistan was "worth it," said: "It was worth it. If I say it wasn't worth it, what about my friends that died? I'm disrespecting them, like they died for nothing."

Sorry, Josue, as much as you may not want to face it, and no matter how many times you tell yourself that it was "worth it," your friends died in vain just like those unfortunate U.S. soldiers who died in Iraq. Likewise, the only thing that the Marines in Afghanistan died for was a lie.

The most maddening and depressing thing out of all that I have heard from this series on the Darkhorse Battalion is the closing paragraph from Tom Bowman's 50-minute report:

> Darkhorse Battalion will deploy again sometime next year, but this time they're going on what's known as a Marine Expeditionary Unit. They'll head on ships across the Pacific making port calls

and being ready for anything from a humanitarian disaster to a rescue operation. The families are relived, but many of the Marines we spoke with just want to go back to Afghanistan.

Go back to Afghanistan? Marines, why do you do this to your families? I plead with you to heed the words of U.S. Marine Corps Major General Smedley Butler (1881–1940), a two-time Congressional Medal of Honor winner who came to the conclusion that:

> War is a racket. It always has been. It is possibly the oldest, easily the most profitable, surely the most vicious. It is the only one international in scope. It is the only one in which the profits are reckoned in dollars and the losses in lives.

Shame on you for putting the Marines above your families. Shame on you for making a god out of the Marines.

* * * * *

GO AHEAD AND JOIN

For years I have cautioned against joining. I have written about the pitfalls of doing so. Yet, the criticism I have received has been relentless. There is no harm in joining, I am told; the personnel don't make the policies, they just do as they are told and take the good with the bad. If something is unjust, it is said, then those who join don't have to participate. I am wrong to condemn the entire organization, it is further alleged; the few bad apples in the group have clouded my vision and prejudiced me against the entire outfit.

Okay, I give up. I am weary of answering the negative e-mail. I am tired of getting cursed. Go ahead and join. That's right. Go ahead and join.

And not only that. Encourage your friends to join. Encourage your neighbors to join. If you are a pastor or youth leader, then encourage young people under your care to join. It will build character and foster discipline, I have always been told. Encourage your sons and daughters to join. Encourage your brothers and sisters to join. Encourage your aunts and uncles to join. Encourage your grandchildren to join. Kids can even encourage their parents to join. Sure, there might be some separation from your family, but if it's for a good cause, then the children will just have to put up with it. But whatever you do, make sure you thank those who do join.

If you just want to get some money for college, then go ahead and join.

If you think you can get by without killing anyone unjustly, then go ahead and join.

If you think God will be pleased because you're just obeying orders, then go ahead and join.

If you think the organization does some good, then go ahead and join.

If one of your relatives was a member, then go ahead and join.

If you think you can just be a driver, then go ahead and join.

If you think you won't get killed, then go ahead and join.

If you don't mind killing for hire as long as your victim deserves it, then go ahead and join.

If you think you won't suffer a life-threatening injury, then go ahead and join.

If you think the organization has an illustrious history, then go ahead and join.

If you think you can just provide medical care, then go ahead and join.

If you want to draw a salary instead of work by the hour, then go ahead and join.

If you think you can do some good as a chaplain, then go ahead and join

If you think you'll learn some valuable skills, then go ahead and join.

If you think you'll like to travel, then go ahead and join.

If you think God has called you to do so, then go ahead and join.

If you are looking for good benefits, then go ahead and join.

If you think there will be opportunities for advancement, then go ahead and join.

If you think you can influence the organization for good, then go ahead and join.

If you think the organization is a divine institution, then go ahead and join.

If you want a chance to serve, then go ahead and join.

If you want some respect just for being part of the organization, then go ahead and join.

If you haven't been able to find a steady job, then go ahead and join.

Go ahead and join. Go ahead and join the Mafia.

* * * * *

FUTURE KILLER

Thanks to the No Child Left Behind Act, passed by some of the very Republicans who are now calling for its repeal, "each local educational agency receiving assistance under this Act shall provide, on a request made by military recruiters or an institution of higher education, access to secondary school students names, addresses, and telephone listings."

But students at some high schools don't need to be conned by military recruiters into enlisting in the military—their parents will do it for them.

In Fairfax County, Virginia, some parents say that spring graduation ceremonies should recognize students who have chosen to enlist in the military instead of go to college. They are pressing the county school board "to acknowledge that volunteering for the armed forces is a commitment worthy of a public display of respect, with red, white, and blue 'honor cords' that graduates would wear around their necks as they receive diplomas."

Honor cords are generally reserved for members of academic honor societies. If schools are going to give out honor cords to students for non-academic reasons, then they ought to be giving them out to recognize those students who have decided to pursue taxi driving, plumbing, and other practical occupations instead of joining the military.

Some parents, however, don't wait until high school to influence their children to join the military.

One of the benefits I enjoy as a writer for LewRockwell.com is the information I receive from perceptive readers, and especially veterans. Some of these veterans are so radically anti-war and anti-military that they make me look like a lightweight. A veteran and friend in Pennsylvania who is always on the lookout for military propaganda was browsing in the gift section of a Cracker Barrel restaurant and came across a T-shirt that he thought I would be interested in. He has since gone back and purchased it and mailed it to me. Here is a picture of it.

There is a sticker on the shirt that says "official licensed product of the U.S. Army." If the shirt looks small it's because it is designed for a toddler. But you don't need to go to Cracker Barrel to get one. You can purchase the shirt online at armedforcesgear.com in size 3T or 4T. "How cute will they look in their Army Future Soldier T-Shirt," says the ad copy.

But if the Army told the truth (the Army didn't tell the truth to the family of Pat Tillman), it would change the wording on the T-shirt from

Future Soldier to Future Killer.

It's not just that toddlers who wear these shirts might end up accused of murdering Afghan civilians like Army sergeant Robert Bales, it's that they have a good chance of being sent to kill in some foreign war in the first place. None of the killings in Iraq and Afghanistan were justified since U.S. troops had no business traveling thousands of miles away to invade, bomb, and occupy countries that were not a threat to the United States. These wars were criminal from the very beginning.

As others and I have said again and again, U.S. troops aren't defending our freedoms, guaranteeing our First Amendment rights, keeping us safe from our enemies, protecting us from terrorists, avenging 9/11, safeguarding the American way of life, fighting "over there" so we don't have to fight "over here," defending this great nation, or any of the other phony-baloney slogans used as excuses for fighting unjust and immoral wars.

But as bad as it is to be a Future Killer is, it's not just a Future Killer that these kids might become. There is a good change that they might also become a:

- Future suicide
- Future victim of sexual assault
- Future substance abuser
- Future basket case
- Future traumatic brain injury case
- Future disabled veteran
- Future paraplegic
- Future quadriplegic
- Future death in vain
- Future cannon fodder

Parents, do your children a favor: encourage them to be all they can be without being in the Army.

* * * * *

JOIN OR NOT JOIN?

I don't normally visit websites like Military.com. The glorification of all things military just doesn't appeal to me, as you can well imagine if you have read any of my articles on the military.

Military.com is said to be "the online presence of Military Advantage." It "is committed to the mission of connecting the military community to all the advantages earned in service to America." It was founded in 1999 "to revolutionize the way the 30 million Americans with military affinity stay connected and informed." It is now the largest military and veteran membership organization, with more than 10 million members.

I did happen to visit the site recently after I came across an article by Marco O'Brien, a contributing editor at Military.com titled "5 Reasons to Join the Military Now!" Imagine my surprise when I happened to see another piece of his titled "Reasons To Not Join the Military."

To join or not join, that is the question. But of course, O'Brien's reasons to not join the military are no reasons at all, as we shall presently see.

Although I have given many reasons on many different occasions for joining or not joining the military, I thought I would present the reasons O'Brien gives for joining or not joining and then offer my own.

In "5 Reasons to Join the Military Now!" O'Brien first lists a general reason, followed by an explanation, and then followed by a military solution. To keep this from getting too long, I will list his general reasons and provide the main part of his solutions (I have corrected a few typos). You can read his entire piece online if interested.

> Reason 1—The Job Market
> Solution—Not only is the military hiring, but the military is actually increasing its numbers over the next several years. No experience is necessary and all entry-level jobs come with great pay and benefits!
>
> Reason 2—Rising Cost of College
> Solution—The Military's Tuition assistance program pays up to 100% of the first $4,500 each year of your tuition costs while serving on active duty. In addition there is the MGIB and the Post 9/11 G.I Bill.
>
> Reason 3—Health Care
> Solution—The military has a great health care plan for individuals and families. How about full coverage with little or no costs to service members or their families? Top-notch health care for free, it doesn't get much better than that.
>
> Reason 4—You want to own a home someday!
> Solution—Military service men and women have a unique avenue to obtain home loans through the Veteran's Administration.
> Reason 5—You aren't getting any younger!

Solution—Join Now!—If you enter active duty at the age of 18 you can be retired from the military at age 38. Don't be one of those people who look back and regret not joining when they were young.

In "Reasons To Not Join the Military," O'Brien lists five reasons, each followed by an explanation. Because this is relatively short, I will reproduce the entire piece:

1. You want an education and have at least $40,000 dollars just sitting around for you to use. Education is very expensive and $40,000 is actually a very conservative estimate for a 4-year degree. If you don't want to take advantage of the military paying 100% of your tuition while on active duty and giving you upwards of $50,000 dollars through the GI Bill to use on active duty or up to 10 years after you get out, then the military is not for you.

2. You absolutely do not want to have a job that gives you any kind of vacation time! If you are one of those people who never likes being away from the work place then the military is not for you. The military gives you 30 days of paid vacation every year starting with your first year. It could take 20 years with some civilian companies to build up that much time off.

3. You get a scared feeling every time you even think about leaving your hometown. Some people like where they live and have no desire to travel the world at someone else's expense. The military has installations all over the world and gives its members opportunities to travel like no other company in the world.

4. You would feel way too guilty receiving free medical care for you and your family! Being riddled with guilt can be pretty terrible. If you can't imagine ever having free health care for you, let alone for your wife and kids then the military is not for you. Imagine how bad you would feel accepting the military's world-class health care and not paying a dime for it.

5. You want to be really old when you finally retire from a company. There's good news and bad news here. If you join the military at 18 years old you can retire and start collecting your retirement at 38 years old, now that is the bad news you won't be really old when you retire from the military. The good news is you are only 38 years old and can go and work at another job until you are really old. The military's 20-year retirement is an awesome

benefit if you want to retire young.

These could, of course, be rephrased as five reasons to join the military: education benefits (see Reason 2 above), employment (see Reason 1 above), travel, free health care (see Reason 3 above), early retirement (see Reason 5 above).

In each of his short articles, O'Brien makes a good case for joining the military *from a financial point of view*. But there are other reasons to join or not join the military that he has not mentioned.

Here are five reasons to join the military from a slightly different perspective:

1. To kill people. Young men have been killing people by the thousands for years in their video games. I guess that is why the military uses these games as recruiting tools. The aphorism "Join the Army, travel the world, meet interesting people, and kill them" has never been truer. Just ask the hundreds of thousand of dead Iraqis and Afghans.

2. To build your ego. You can wear your uniform in an airport and be thanked for your service by throngs of people you have never seen before. You can wear your uniform to church the Sunday before Memorial Day, the Fourth of July, or Veterans Day and be asked to stand while someone asks God to bless the troops. And when you leave the military, just telling people you are a veteran will bring forth shouts of glory, laud, and honor.

3. To be part of the president's personal attack force. Since World War II, the U.S. military has been exclusively used by the president for purposes other than the actual defense of the country. Soldiers that went to Iraq and Afghanistan, like those that went to Korea, Vietnam, and all the other countries where the U.S. military had no business going, go as part of the president's personal army. And if they join for financial reasons—as recommended by Marco O'Brien—then they are simply mercenaries like the British hired to fight Americans during the Revolutionary War.

4. To commit random acts of depravity and violence. Want to urinate on dead bodies? Want to bomb wedding parties? Want to kill civilians for sport? Want to rape foreign women? Want to take body parts as trophies? Want to destroy a town and its entire

infrastructure? Want to pose for photos with murdered civilians? Want to torture and humiliate prisoners? Then the military is the place for you.

5. To pervert the purpose of the military. Invading countries, occupying other countries, enforcing UN resolutions, nation building, establishing democracy, changing regimes, training foreign armies, opening markets, supplying peacekeepers, assassinating people, maintaining no-fly zones, providing disaster relief, dispensing humanitarian aid, and fighting foreign wars—that is, anything but actually "defending our freedoms"—perverts the purpose of the military.

And here are five real reasons to not join the military:

1. To be killed. There are almost 5,000 U.S. military personnel who came home from Iraq in a flag-draped coffin or a body bag—if there were enough pieces of them to be picked up in the desert sands. Another 2,000 U.S. troops died in Afghanistan. And for what? Absolutely nothing. They all died in vain and for a lie. Why be added to those casualties?

2. To destroy your family. Multiple duty tours and increased deployment terms are the death knell for stable families. Do you think it is good to deprive a child of his father, and in many cases his mother, for months at a time? What makes you think that the military will never send you away from your family for an extended period of time? What makes you think that you and your family will be able to "handle it"? U.S. military families are the unseen victims of the wars in Iraq and Afghanistan.

3. To never have another independent thought. You will be expected to blindly follow the orders of your superiors without questioning their purpose or morality. You will often times not be in a position to know whether an order is in fact dubious or immoral. You will be expected to, without reservation, drop that bomb, fire that weapon, launch that missile, and throw that grenade, as well as kill people and destroy their property.

4. To suffer severe injuries. Many thousands of U.S. military personnel have been wounded in the wars in Iraq and Afghanistan.

Hundreds have had limbs amputated. Untold numbers suffer from post-traumatic stress disorder (PTSD). Some soldiers will spend the rest of their lives unable to work or drive a car. Others will live out their days as physical and/or emotional basket cases. What makes you think that you will not be sent to Afghanistan, Yemen, or some other God-forsaken place the U.S. military has no business being and emerge unscathed in body and mind?

5. To commit suicide. The suicide rate among active duty and veterans of the military is at an all-time high. No one joins the military with the intention of committing suicide, but dealing with broken relationships, strained families, chronic pain, PTSD, depression, deaths of fellow soldiers, substance abuse, multiple deployments, and/or adjusting to life after the military can come with a price that some are not willing to pay.

To join or not join, that is the question. Your life and the life of your family depend on your decision. After you join, you may never be stationed overseas, never face enemy fire, never be in danger, have a wonderful family, made a comfortable living, see the world, retire after twenty years, and then get a good job with a government contractor—and then again you may not do any of these things. You may die in a training accident before you are old enough to drink. Whatever you do, don't listen to the promises of the lying pimps known as military recruiters.

* * * * *

SO WAS IT WORTH IT?

Believe it or not, I like getting e-mails from military veterans.

I do admit, though, that this might seem like the last thing anyone would expect after looking through my LRC article archive and reading all the negative things I have written about the U.S. military.

I have termed U.S. soldiers invaders, occupiers, killers, destroyers, criminals, and murderers. I have placed the responsibility on them for their actions. I have charged them with helping to carry out an evil U.S. foreign policy as the president's personal attack force. I have blamed them for putting their families through unimaginable and unnecessary suffering. I have said of the U.S. soldiers who died in Iraq and Afghanistan that they died unnecessarily, duped, for a lie, in vain, and in vain again.

Yet, in spite of this, most of the mail I receive from veterans is positive—and especially from Vietnam veterans. Most of them realize that they were young, ignorant, deceived pawns of the U.S. government and the military industrial-industrial complex, whether they volunteered or were drafted. Most of them also acknowledge that no American soldier had any business going to Vietnam in the first place. Many of them say they still have bad memories of the people they killed and the things they did that are known only to them and God. None of them have ever written to me and said they were proud to be a Vietnam veteran. I know there are some proud Vietnam veterans out there, for I have seen their hats and bumper stickers, but not the Vietnam veterans that have written me.

It seems as though the further back the war, the more anti-war the veterans are. I don't think I've ever gotten a single note from any World War II veteran that expressed anything but disgust and/or regret for fighting in the "good war."

But this works both ways.

Some of the most vile hate mail I have ever received has come from veterans or active duty military personnel who have fought in Iraq or Afghanistan. Although this type of e-mail more often originates from armchair warriors, red-state fascists, reich-wing nationalists, bloodthirsty conservatives, or war-crazed Republicans who have never been in the military themselves, there is nothing more pathetic or tragic than a self-righteous soldier who claims he fought in Iraq or Afghanistan on my behalf so I could have the freedom to write the anti-American attacks on the very military that is keeping me safe from terrorists.

I recently received a lengthy response to my article "Marines, Why Do You Do This To Your Families?" from a Marine veteran of Iraq or Afghanistan, I'm not sure which (he said one reason he joined the military was "for the Iraqi and Afghani people"). Because the writer was polite, didn't threaten to do me bodily harm, didn't tell me to "go f___ yourself," didn't call me unpatriotic or anti-American, and didn't tell me to leave the country and go to North Korea or Cuba, I thought I would respond to something he said at the conclusion of his letter:

So was it worth it? Ask the women who now have fundamental human rights for the first time. Ask the children who can now attend school and get an education (schools that groups of insurgents haven't hidden a cache of weapons and explosives underneath). Ask the farmer who can now grow crops to feed his family, and his village, rather than poppy fields to create opium to line Al Qaeda's pocket (because if he didn't, they would systemat-ically kill his family until he complied). Ask the people of Iraq who no longer have to worry about Saddam Hussein's regime of terror.

I have no doubt that most of the women who now have fundamental human rights, children who can now attend school, farmers who can now grow crops, and people of Iraq who were maltreated by Saddam Hussein think that the U.S. invasions of Iraq and Afghanistan were "worth it."

But for others it simply wasn't worth it.

First of all, I only said "most" people in Iraq and Afghanistan think it was worth it because some of them who lost arms, legs, or loved ones to U.S. bombs, bullets, or drone strikes, saw the dead bodies of people they knew missing body parts because U.S. soldiers took trophies of their kills, or saw photographs of smiling U.S. soldiers next to civilians they murdered for sport might not be so enthusiastic about the U.S. invasion and occupation of Iraqi and Afghanistan.

Secondly, thousands of American soldiers have lost arms, legs, and/or genitals. How many of them think their injury was "worth it" for the cause of women's rights in Afghanistan? Thousands of American soldiers suffer from PTSD or a traumatic brain injury and will never live a normal life. How many of them think their injury was "worth it" so children in Iraq can attend school? Thousands of American soldiers are paralyzed or require constant medical care. How many of them think their injury was "worth it" so farmers in Afghanistan can grow their crops? Thousands of American soldiers can't tell us what they think about women's rights, children's education, and farmer's livelihoods in Iraq or Afghanistan because they committed suicide. More U.S. military personnel died by their own hand this year than in battle with "terrorists" or "insurgents."

Thirdly, the long-term costs of the wars in Iraq and Afghanistan will exceed $4 trillion dollars. How many American taxpayers think that restoring the rights of women in Afghanistan and educating children in Iraq was worth $4 trillion? How many of descendants of American taxpayers fifty years from now still paying the war bill will think it was "worth it"?

Fourthly, there are 4,400 U.S. soldiers who died in Iraq and 2,100 who have died so far in Afghanistan. Each one of those dead American soldiers has a son, a daughter, a father, a mother, a brother, a sister, an aunt, an uncle, a grandmother, a grandfather, a niece, a nephew, a cousin, and/or a friend who won't see them this Christmas. How many of them think it was worth it? How many parents of dead American soldiers think that women in Afghanistan now having fundamental human rights makes the death of their son "worth it"? How many children of dead American soldiers think that children in Iraq now being able to attend school makes the death of their father "worth it"? How many grandparents of dead American soldiers think that farmers in Afghanistan now being able grow crops makes the death of their grandson "worth it"? How many friends of dead American soldiers think that because people in Iraq are no longer maltreated by Saddam Hussein that the death of their friend was "worth it"?

And finally, there are tens of thousands of Iraqis and Afghans who don't think the U.S. invasions of Iraq and Afghanistan were "worth it" because they are now dead thanks to direct action of the U.S. military, sectarian violence unleashed by the U.S. military, or collateral damage courtesy of the U.S. military.

It doesn't matter what "good" has come from the U.S. invasions of Iraq and Afghanistan. None of it is worth an American soldier stubbing his toe or breaking a fingernail. And people question my patriotism?

* * * * *

THE TWELVE DAYS OF CHRISTMAS (MILITARY VERSION)

On the first day of Christmas, the military gave to me...
A list of foreign wars it's fighting to keep me free.

On the second day of Christmas, the military gave to me...
Two prosthetic limbs.
And a list of foreign wars it's fighting to keep me free.

On the third day of Christmas, the military gave to me...
A $3 trillion war bill.
Two prosthetic limbs.
And a list of foreign wars it's fighting to keep me free.

On the fourth day of Christmas, the military gave to me...
Four preemptive strikes.
A $3 trillion war bill.
Two prosthetic limbs.
And a list of foreign wars it's fighting to keep me free.

On the fifth day of Christmas, the military gave to me...
Five no-fly zones.
Four preemptive strikes.

A $3 trillion war bill.
Two prosthetic limbs.
And a list of foreign wars it's fighting to keep me free.

On the sixth day of Christmas, the military gave to me...
Six thousand dead American soldiers.
Five no-fly zones.
Four preemptive strikes.
A $3 trillion war bill.
Two prosthetic limbs.
And a list of foreign wars it's fighting to keep me free.

On the seventh day of Christmas, the military gave to me...
Seven grenades exploding.
Six thousand dead American soldiers.
Five no-fly zones.
Four preemptive strikes.
A $3 trillion war bill.
Two prosthetic limbs.
And a list of foreign wars it's fighting to keep me free.

On the eighth day of Christmas, the military gave to me...
Eight bombers bombing.
Seven grenades exploding.
Six thousand dead American soldiers.
Five no-fly zones.
Four preemptive strikes.
A $3 trillion war bill.
Two prosthetic limbs.
And a list of foreign wars it's fighting to keep me free.

On the ninth day of Christmas, the military gave to me...
Nine Predator drones.
Eight bombers bombing.
Seven grenades exploding.
Six thousand dead American soldiers.
Five no-fly zones.
Four preemptive strikes.
A $3 trillion war bill.
Two prosthetic limbs.
And a list of foreign wars it's fighting to keep me free.

On the tenth day of Christmas, the military gave to me...
Ten thousand fatherless American children.
Nine Predator drones.
Eight bombers bombing.
Seven grenades exploding.
Six thousand dead American soldiers.
Five no-fly zones.
Four preemptive strikes.
A $3 trillion war bill.
Two prosthetic limbs.
And a list of foreign wars it's fighting to keep me free.

On the eleventh day of Christmas, the military gave to me...
Eleven regime changes.
Ten thousand fatherless American children.
Nine Predator drones.
Eight bombers bombing.
Seven grenades exploding.
Six thousand dead American soldiers.
Five no-fly zones.
Four preemptive strikes.
A $3 trillion war bill.
Two prosthetic limbs.
And a list of foreign wars it's fighting to keep me free.

On the twelfth day of Christmas, the military gave to me...
Twelve thousand new terrorists it created.
Eleven regime changes.
Ten thousand fatherless American children.
Nine Predator drones.
Eight bombers bombing.
Seven grenades exploding.
Six thousand dead American soldiers.
Five no-fly zones.
Four preemptive strikes.
A $3 trillion war bill.
Two prosthetic limbs.
And a list of foreign wars it's fighting to keep me free.

* * * * *

I QUESTION YOUR PATRIOTISM

I have been called a lot of things since I began writing about ten years ago on the folly of the wars in Iraq and Afghanistan, the evils of the U.S. military, and the belligerence of U.S. foreign policy.

Many of the things I have been called I can't repeat because they are so vile and filthy. However, the negative e-mails have tapered off quite a bit over the years since these wars have turned out to be such debacles.

One charge that has been consistently leveled against me is that I am unpatriotic because I don't "support the troops" as they invade and occupy other countries and mete out death and destruction to "insurgents" and "terrorists." But who is really being unpatriotic? I think it is long past time that we question the patriotism of those who do "support the troops" in their foreign wars, occupations, interventions, and escapades.

Let's take the case of Syria.

For months now we have heard how the United States must "do something" and intervene in Syria to end the brutal regime of Bashar al-Assad and stop the violence that has led to the deaths of 40,000 people since the outbreak of an anti-regime revolt last year. The familiar cry that dictator x might use chemical weapons on his own people is being resurrected to garner support for U.S. intervention.

The U.S. Senate, by a vote of 92–6, recently voted to "require a report on military activities to deny or significantly degrade the use of air power against civilian and opposition groups in Syria." This amendment (S.AMDT.3262) to the National Defense Authorization Act requires that

> not later than 90 days after the date of the enactment of this Act, the Secretary of Defense shall, in consultation with the Chairman of the Joint Chiefs of Staff, submit to the congressional defense committees a report identifying the limited military activities that could deny or significantly degrade the ability of President Bashar al-Assad of Syria, and forces loyal to him, to use air power against civilians and opposition groups in Syria.

Its purpose is to "advance the goals of President Obama of stopping the killing of civilians in Syria and creating conditions for a transition to a democratic, pluralistic political system in Syria."

The U.S. military is sending Patriot air defense missiles and 400 U.S. troops to operate them at two batteries in "undisclosed locations" in Turkey as part of a NATO force meant to protect Turkish territory from potential Syrian missile attack.

The aircraft carrier the USS *Eisenhower* is reportedly off the coast of Syria along with the USS *Iwo Jima* Amphibious Ready Group.

There are also reports that more than 3,000 U.S. military personnel have secretly returned to Iraq via Kuwait in response to the civil war in Syria that has spilled over into northern Iraq. The Pentagon is denying this report, which means it is probably true.

Never mind that the "evil dictatorship" of Assad was once supported by the United States.

Never mind that the CIA "renditioned" people to Syria to be tortured.

Never mind that the United States just concluded a disastrous war in Iraq and is still conducting another disastrous one in Afghanistan.

Never mind that some Syrian rebel groups have ties to al-Qaeda.

Never mind that some Syrian rebels are foreign jihad mercenaries.

Never mind that some Syrian rebels have openly murdered Syrian Christians for not supporting the overthrow of the secular Syrian government.

Never mind that some Syrian rebels have committed acts of terrorism that have killed children.

Never mind that some Syrian rebel groups have tested their own chemical weapons.

Never mind that the United States and NATO developed their own chemical weapons years ago.

Never mind that George Washington—230 years ago—warned against making "entangling alliances" such as NATO.

But even if all of these things are not true, even if President Assad is another Hitler, even if the rebels have the purest of motives, and even if the Assad regime is targeting civilians, executing POWs, raping women, killing children, torturing political opponents, using chemical weapons, instituting pogroms, engaged in ethnic cleansing, and committing genocide—the U.S. government has no authority whatsoever to intervene in any way. No U.S. soldier, sailor, airman, Marine, military advisor, CIA operative, contractor, or State Department employee has any business going anywhere near Syria. It is not the purpose of the U.S. government to be the policeman, security guard, mediator, or babysitter of the world.

What happens in Syria is the concern of Syrians and perhaps Syria's immediate neighbors. Nothing that happens in Syria should be the concern of the United States.

Americans individually or collectively may despise the Assad regime, they may pray for the rebels, they may long for Assad's overthrow, they may sell weapons to the rebels, they may donate money to the rebels, they may go help the rebels fight against the Syrian government, they may undertake humanitarian relief efforts, they may marry Syrian widows, they may adopt Syrian orphans, they may employ Syrian refuges—they may even take the side of Assad against the rebels. But the U.S. government should do absolutely nothing.

How patriotic am I? Nothing that happens in Syria is worth one drop of blood from one American soldier or one dollar from one American taxpayer. Nothing and not one. Not a paper cut. Not a scrape. And not one red cent. I am so patriotic that I don't support U.S. troops getting within a thousand miles of Syria.

Since the U.S. military is nothing more than the personal attack force of the president, there is a chance that the president will order U.S. forces to intervene in Syria. If this happens, even most who oppose intervention will suddenly and vocally "support the troops" should Syria be their next military adventure.

But because the use of American troops should be limited to the defense of the United States, there should be no respect or support for any U. S. soldier who goes to fight in Syria. He didn't have to join the president's personal attack force. He can refuse to go and suffer the consequences or he can refuse to fight like soldiers did during the Christmas Truce of 1914.

To those Americans who think it will be "worth it" to "support the troops" as the United States expends blood and treasure in Syria: I question your patriotism.

* * * * *

SOLDIERS IN FANTASYLAND

Disney World in central Florida recently opened a large expansion and renovation of its Fantasyland area. Kids can ride Dumbo the Flying Elephant, the Mad Tea Party, the Many Adventures of Winnie the Pooh, and Peter Pan's Flight. Although adults can ride too, the difference is that they know these things are all fantasy—or at least they are supposed to.

Some American adults have not only ridden the rides at Fantasyland, they live in Fantasyland. Their conception of what the U.S. military accomplished in Iraq and Afghanistan belongs in a ride in Fantasyland. It is wishful thinking. It is pure fantasy.

It is bad enough when civilian American adults live their lives in Fantasyland; it is even worse when soldiers do.

I recently responded to a former soldier who had written to me concerning my article, "Marines, Why Do You Do This To Your Families?" I quoted this paragraph from his letter:

> So was it worth it? Ask the women who now have fundamental human rights for the first time. Ask the children who can now attend school and get an education (schools that groups of insurgents haven't hidden a cache of weapons and explosives underneath). Ask the farmer who can now grow crops to feed his family, and his village, rather than poppy fields to create opium to line Al Qaeda's pocket (because if he didn't, they would systematically kill his family until he complied). Ask the people of Iraq who no longer have to worry about Saddam Hussein's regime of terror.

For the sake of argument, I did not dispute the soldier's claims. Instead, I pointed out that for many, many others besides these women, children, farmers, and Iraqis, the U.S. invasion and occupation of Iraq and Afghanistan was not worth it at all. I did the same thing in my article about the end of the Iraq War, "Was It Worth It?":

> Okay, suppose it's all true—and then some. Suppose it's even better than anyone could have imagined. What if Iraq is now a model democracy for the rest of the world? What if Iraq now has a constitution that rivals our own? What if there is now no more sectarian violence in Iraq? What if Iraq now has a free market? What if Iraq is now an American ally? What if Iraq is now a friend of Israel? What if Iraqis now have freedom of speech and freedom of religion? What if Iraq now respects the rights of women and minorities? What if all Iraqi children are now in school? What if Baghdad is really the best city on earth instead of the worst?
>
> Would it now be worth the life of your son? Can you look your son in the face and tell him that you would have sacrificed him to bring about these changes in Iraq? And if your son had the misfortune of dying in Iraq, how do you think he would feel if he could now hear you say that his death was worth it?

So, this time, let's take an interactive ride through the Fantasyland that some soldiers (and their supporters) live in.

In the soldiers' Fantasyland, they see women who now have fundamental human rights for the first time. In reality things are otherwise. According to "Women in Afghanistan: A Human Rights Tragedy a Decade after September 11," published by the Revolutionary Association of the Women of Afghanistan (RAWA):

> Over a decade after the September 11, 2001, attacks in the United States and the military campaign in Afghanistan, there is some good news, but still much bad news pertaining to women in Afghanistan. The patterns of politics, military operations, religious fanaticism, patriarchal structures and practices, and insurgent violence continue to threaten girls and women in the most insidious ways. Although women's rights and freedoms in Afghanistan have finally entered the radar of the international community's consciousness, they still linger in the margins in many respects. Overall, the situation for girls and women in Afghanistan remains bleak.

> The situation for Afghan girls and women remains deplorable, despite concerted efforts to improve their freedoms, rights, and quality of life. In a June 2011 global survey, Afghanistan was named as the "world's most dangerous country in which to be born a woman.

In the soldiers' Fantasyland, they see children who can now attend school and get an education. In reality things are otherwise. According to a recent NPR story:

> In Afghanistan, girls are required by law to go to school. However, many of them never do. Death threats, acid attacks and bombings by Taliban militants and other extremists lead many parents who support female education to keep their daughters at home. Sometimes, it's the families themselves who stand in the way. School officials in conservative communities say relatives are often more interested in marrying off their daughters or sisters than in helping them get an education.

According to the UN's Inter-Agency Information and Analysis Unit, in Iraq "one in three girls aged 12–14 is not enrolled in school, while one in ten of the same age group has never attended school, according to the Iraq Knowledge Network Survey. Traditional cultural and social factors often remain obstacles to improvements in girls' access to education."

In the soldiers' Fantasyland, they see farmers who can now grow crops to feed their families and their villages rather than poppy fields to create opium. In reality things are otherwise. Heroin production by Afghan farmers rose between 2001 and 2011 from just 185 tons to 5,800 tons. It increased by 61 per cent last year alone. But that's not the worst of it:

> Some 15 per cent of Afghanistan's Gross National Product now comes from drug-related exports.

> The UN says there are now 17 provinces in Afghanistan affected by poppy cultivation, up from 14 a year ago. Experts say the Taliban's involvement in the drugs trade ranges from direct assistance—such as providing farmers with seed, fertiliser and cash advances—to distribution and protection.

> Ironically, the Taliban had overseen a significant fall in heroin production in the months before the invasion. Their leader Mullah Mohammed Omar—collaborating with the UN—had decreed that growing poppies was un-Islamic, resulting in one of the world's most successful anti-drug campaigns. As a result of this ban, opium poppy cultivation was reduced by 91 per cent from the previous year's estimate of 82,172 hectares. The ban was so effective that Helmand Province, which had accounted for more than half of this production, recorded no poppy cultivation during the 2001 season. However, with the overthrow of the Taliban opium fields returned, despite the destruction of crops by coalition forces and initiatives to persuade farmers to switch to other produce.

In the soldiers' Fantasyland, they see Iraqis who no longer have to worry about Saddam Hussein's regime of terror. In reality things are otherwise. Iraqis now have to worry about a despotic Islamic state under Sharia law instead of the secular government that existed under former U.S. subcontractor Saddam Hussein. Article 2 of the Iraqi constitution reads:

> Islam is the official religion of the State and it is a foundation source of legislation.

> No law may be enacted that contradicts the established provisions of Islam.

And then there are the first three articles of the constitution of the Islamic Republic of Afghanistan:

> Afghanistan shall be an Islamic Republic, independent, unitary and indivisible state.

The sacred religion of Islam is the religion of the Islamic Republic of Afghanistan.

No law shall contravene the tenets and provisions of the holy religion of Islam in Afghanistan.

Iraq and Afghanistan were invaded and occupied by U.S. troops who killed hundreds of thousands and died by the thousands to install militant Islamist governments with new constitutions that formally enshrine Sharia Law.

U.S. soldiers (and their supporters) are living in Fantasyland if they think that their actions did any "real and permanent good" in Iraq and Afghanistan.

The question, then, is why do so many U.S. soldiers (and their supporters) continue to live in Fantasyland? It is time that they begin to face reality. The wars in Iraq and Afghanistan are not just wars; they are monstrous evils. U.S. soldiers were not and are not defending anyone's freedoms, keeping Americans safe from terrorists, fighting "over there" so we don't have to fight "over here," or defending the country in any way. U.S. soldiers are attackers, invaders, trespassers, occupiers, aggressors, and, yes, killers.

It is time to leave Fantasyland. As Jacob Hornberger, president of the Future of Freedom Foundation puts it: "After 10 years of invasion, occupation, torture, killings, incarcerations, renditions, assassinations, death, destruction, anger, hatred, and the constant threat of terrorist retaliation, it's time to admit that the military invasion of Afghanistan, like that of Iraq, was horribly wrong."

* * * * *

NO, I HAVE NEVER BEEN IN THE MILITARY

It happens every time I write an article about war. It happens every time I write an article about the military. It happens every time I even mention war or the military.

The question may take a variety of forms but it is really always the same: "Have you ever been in combat" "Have you ever been in the military?" "Have you ever served?"

Because I have never been in combat, been in the military, or "served," my answer is, of course, always in the negative.

Those who ask such questions have one purpose: to discredit everything I say about the military. In their mind, it is either that I can't possibly have sufficient knowledge of what it is like in the military to be able to criticize it or I have no right to criticize the military because I have never been in it, or both.

But rather than hang my head in shame and sheepishly acknowledge that I have never been in the military, I lift it up high and shout No, I have never been in the military. I have never experienced the "glories" of combat. I have never had the "honor" of serving. Thank God I was never in the military.

No, I have never been in the military. I have never sung filthy cadences that glorify rape and killing.

No, I have never been in the military. I have never put my family through unnecessary hardship.

No, I have never been in the military. I have never helped to carry out an evil, reckless, and interventionist U.S. foreign policy.

No, I have never been in the military. I have never destroyed a country's industry and infrastructure that was no threat to the United States.

No, I have never been in the military. I have never enforced a UN resolution.

No, I have never been in the military. I have never killed someone that I didn't know, who was no threat to me, my family, my city, my state, or my country.

No, I have never been in the military. I have never been a plumber, but I know it is a dirty, smelly job. I have never been a roofer, but I know it is hazardous work. I have never been a prostitute, but I know it is an immoral activity.

No, I have never been in the military. I have never experienced PTSD because I had serious doubts about the justness of what I was fighting for.

No, I have never been in the military. I have never experienced the desire to commit suicide.

No, I have never been in the military. I have never unnecessarily been in a situation where I had to kill or be killed.

No, I have never been in the military. I have never been part of an organization that was a global force for evil.

No, I have never been in the military. I have never embraced the values that are all too prevalent in the military: adultery, fornication, promiscuity, drug abuse, alcohol abuse, pornography, sodomy, divorce, sexual assault, sexual harassment, suicide.

No, I have never been in the military. I have never had to be on guard against being sexually assaulted.

No, I have never been in the military. I have never been an accomplice to murder.

No, I have never been in the military. I have never killed a civilian and called it collateral damage.

No, I have never been in the military. I have never fought a police action for the UN.

No, I have never been in the military. I have never played golf on a U.S. military base thousands of miles away in a country that could provide for its own defense.

No, I have never been in the military. I have never violated the Constitution I swore to uphold.

No, I have never been in the military. I have never urinated on a dead body.

No, I have never been in the military. I have never been all that I can be in an organization that was the greatest purveyor of violence in the world today.

No, I have never been in the military. I have never expressed blind, unconditional obedience to someone's orders.

No, I have never been in the military. I have never cursed like a sailor.

No, I have never been in the military. I have never fought an undeclared war.

No, I have never been in the military. I have never committed random acts of depravity and violence.

No, I have never been in the military. I have never killed civilians for sport.

No, I have never been in the military. I have never participated in state-sponsored terrorism.

No, I have never been in the military. I have never posed for photos with murdered civilians.

No, I have never been in the military. I have never tortured and humiliated prisoners.

No, I have never been in the military. I have never worn a uniform in an airport and grinned from ear to ear when a group of people cheered me as I walked by.

No, I have never been in the military. I have never stopped having independent thoughts.

No, I have never been in the military. I have never transported anyone to some secret CIA prison to undergo "enhanced interrogation techniques."

No, I have never been in the military. I have never piloted a drone over Pakistan and killed people like I was playing a video game.

No, I have never been in the military. I have never been part of the president's personal attack force.

No, I have never been in the military. I have never unleashed violence and civil unrest in another country.

No, I have never been in the military. I have never deprived my child of his father while I made multiple duty tours with increased deployment terms.

No, I have never been in the military. I have never fought an unjust war of aggression.

No, I have never been in the military. I have never cut off someone's body part as a trophy.

No, I have never been in the military. I have never died in vain or for a lie.

No, I have never been in the military. I have never dropped a bomb on a wedding party.

No, I have never been in the military. I have never traveled thousands of miles from the United States to fight in a senseless foreign war.

No, I have never been in the military. I have never dwelled in one of the filthiest moral environments on the face of the earth.

No, I have never been in the military. I have never helped to keep in business the worldwide network of brothels around U.S. military bases.

No, I have never been in the military. I have never traveled the world, met interesting people, and killed them.

No, I have never been in the military. I have never told people that I was defending their freedoms when I was doing nothing of the kind.

No, I have never been in the military. I have never agreed to kill people to get money for college.

No, I have never been in the military. But when men that have been in combat, and have been in the military, and have served confirm what I say about the military and add their own criticisms of the military to it, they are not listened to either.

No, I have never been in the military. But I will continue to criticize it and persuade people to not join it. How could any thinking person do otherwise?

* * * * *

HERO OR MURDERER?

Chris Kyle, a former Navy SEAL, and the U.S. military's most lethal sniper, was deliberately and fatally shot recently by another veteran while on a gun range.

According to *Star and Stripes*, Kyle had been awarded two Silver Stars, five Bronze Stars with Valor, and two Navy and Marine Corps Achievement Medals. He is officially credited with more than 150 kills during four tours in Iraq; he is unofficially credited with up to 255. Kyle won't say just how many people he has killed.

"I don't care about the medals," Kyle told the Star-Telegram in a 2012 interview. "I didn't do it for the money or the awards. I did it because I felt like it was something that needed to be done and it was honorable."

I blogged about Kyle twice last year, once in January and once in February. I included this quote from him:

> It was my duty to shoot the enemy, and I don't regret it. My regrets are for the people I couldn't save: Marines, soldiers, buddies. I'm not naive, and I don't romanticize war. The worst moments of my life have come as a SEAL. But I can stand before God with a clear conscience about doing my job.

And also this excerpt from his book, *American Sniper: The Autobiography of the Most Lethal Sniper in U.S. Military History*:

> Savage, despicable evil. That's what we were fighting in Iraq. That's why a lot of people, myself included, called the enemy "savages." There really was no other way to describe what we encountered there. People ask me all the time, "How many people have you killed?" My standard response is, "Does the answer make me less, or more, of a man?" The number is not important to me. I only wish I had killed more. Not for bragging rights, but because I believe the world is a better place without savages out there taking American lives. Everyone I shot in Iraq was trying to harm Americans or Iraqis loyal to the new government.

Will Grigg also wrote about Kyle in 2012.

After Kyle's death, I blogged that "You reap what you sow." However, what really got apologists for the U.S. military in a tizzy was this tweet by Ron Paul: "Chris Kyle's death seems to confirm that 'he who lives by the sword dies by the sword.'"

Conservatives, naturally, because they are in love with all things military, were quite upset. But others expressed their "concerns" as well.

Medal of Honor recipient Dakota Meyer chastised Dr. Paul, calling his tweet "insane," and calling Kyle "a modern, American war hero."

Another veteran said that "Ron Paul has been reading too much Laurence Vance."

Senator Rand Paul responded: "Chris Kyle was a hero like all Americans who don the uniform to defend our country. Our prayers are with his family during this tragic time."

Some libertarians weren't too happy with Paul's "social media strategies, or basic skills of persuasion."

Wannabe-libertarian Glenn Beck ("I'm becoming more and more Libertarian every day") termed Paul's statement "despicable," "ugly," and "offensive."

But there is nothing honorable or heroic about anything Chris Kyle did in Iraq. He defended no American's freedoms. He didn't fight "over there" so no American would have to fight "over here." Soldiers who kill for the state in unjust wars are murderers, not heroes. As Future of Freedom Foundation president and Army veteran Jacob Hornberger recently wrote: "Since the U.S. government was the aggressor in the war on Iraq, that means that no U.S. soldier had the moral authority to kill even one single Iraqi. Every single soldier who killed an Iraqi or who even participated in the enterprise was guilty of murder in a moral, religious, and spiritual sense."

Here is a simple test to determine whether a soldier is a murderer or a hero. There are only fifteen questions and only one of two responses is possible so you should be able to keep track of your answers.

1. A soldier from a country thousands of miles away travels to the United States and throws grenades at Americans. Hero or murderer?

2. A soldier from a country thousands of miles away travels to the United States and incinerates Americans with a flamethrower. Hero or murderer?

3. A soldier from a country thousands of miles away travels to the United States and blows up Americans with a land mine. Hero or murderer?

4. A soldier from a country thousands of miles away travels to the United States and blasts Americans to kingdom come with a tank. Hero or murderer?

5. A soldier from a country thousands of miles away travels to the United States and drops bombs on Americans. Hero or murderer?

6. A soldier from a country thousands of miles away travels to the United States and cuts Americans in half with a machine gun. Hero or murderer?

7. A soldier from a country thousands of miles away travels to the United States and launches missiles at Americans. Hero or murderer?

8. A soldier from a country thousands of miles away travels to the United States and shoots Americans with a pistol. Hero or murderer?

9. A soldier from a country thousands of miles away travels to the United States and maims Americans with mortar fire. Hero or murderer?

10. A soldier from a country thousands of miles away travels to the United States and fires rocket propelled grenades at Americans. Hero or murderer?

11. A soldier from a country thousands of miles away travels to the United States and shreds the flesh of Americans with cluster bombs. Hero or murderer?

12. A soldier from a country thousands of miles away travels to the United States and burns Americans to a crisp with napalm. Hero or murderer?

13. A soldier from a country thousands of miles away travels to the United States and destroys Americans with attack helicopters. Hero or murderer?

14. A soldier from a country thousands of miles away travels to the United States and kills Americans as a sniper. Hero or murderer?

15. A soldier from a country thousands of miles away travels to the United States via drone and performs targeted killings of Americans. Hero or murderer?

I don't know of a single American who wouldn't say, and say it fifteen times, that these foreign soldiers were murderers.

But why is it that when American soldiers do these things they are heroes but when foreign soldiers do them they are murderers?

Time for another test. Again, there are only fifteen questions and only one of two responses is possible so you should be able to keep track of your answers.

1. Should we excuse foreign soldiers because they wore a government-issued uniform?

2. Should we excuse foreign soldiers because they were just following orders?

3. Should we excuse foreign soldiers because they joined the military to serve their country?

4. Should we excuse foreign soldiers because they were patriotic?

5. Should we excuse foreign soldiers because their government said America needed a regime change?

6. Should we excuse foreign soldiers because they joined the military because they couldn't find a job?

7. Should we excuse foreign soldiers because they were just obeying their commander in chief?

8. Should we excuse foreign soldiers because they didn't make their country's foreign policy?

9. Should we excuse foreign soldiers because they were drafted?

10. Should we excuse foreign soldiers because their government said there were communists in America?

11. Should we excuse foreign soldiers because they joined the military because their father had been in the military?

12. Should we excuse foreign soldiers because they just did what they were told?

13. Should we excuse foreign soldiers because their government told them they were fighting a defense war?

14. Should we excuse foreign soldiers because their politicians are the ones responsible for their actions?

15. Should we excuse foreign soldiers because they thought they were

defending the freedoms of civilians in their country?

Then why do we excuse American soldiers for these same reasons? U.S. foreign policy is aggressive, reckless, belligerent, and meddling. We don't need a foreign policy that strikes a balance. We don't need a foreign policy that we can afford. We don't need a foreign policy that is like Reagan's. We don't need a foreign policy that is less interventionist. We need a wholesale repudiation of the past century of an evil and murderous U.S. foreign policy.

* * * * *

MURDER IS STILL MURDER

Murder decorated with a ribbon is still murder." ~ Emmanuel Charles McCarthy

In my previous article ("Hero or Murderer?") I said that a soldier from a country thousands of miles away who travels to the United States and kills Americans is a murderer. But I also said that American soldiers who do the same thing are not heroes but murderers. I said that foreign soldiers should not be excused no matter who told them to go or why they went. But I also said that American soldiers should not be excused either.

Aside from a few comments that said I was "filled with hate" or "a totally f**ked up anti-American," I received a few sincere inquiries about my statement that we shouldn't excuse foreign soldiers because they were drafted.

So, what if a soldier is drafted? Should we hold draftees to the same standard as those who voluntarily enlist? Are conscripts not accountable or less accountable than those who sent them to war? Can we hold soldiers responsible for actions done under fear of punishment, imprisonment, or death? A few brief thoughts.

First of all, when people raise the issue of soldiers being drafted, it is usually in the context of excusing American soldiers from killing in unjust wars. Conscripted foreign fighters are rarely accorded the same consideration. And no wonder, for no one wants to be seen as excusing Nazi atrocities. But murder is still murder. If it is murder when foreign soldiers do it, then it is murder when American soldiers do it.

Second, the draft ended in the United States in 1973. Since murder is still murder, hypothetical questions about the draft are irrelevant when U.S. troops have been fighting in Afghanistan longer than they fought in

World War II. The chances of the draft being reinstituted are next to nothing, despite the efforts of Rep. Charles Rangel, who wants to not only reinstate the draft, but include women in it as well. And besides, no draft is needed. All the branches of the armed forces have met their enlistment quotas for several years now. There is no shortage of Americans willing to invade, occupy, and kill for the state should they be told to do so once in the military.

Third, I certainly agree with those who say we should blame the president, the politicians, the ruling class, the neoconservatives, the Joint Chiefs, the military brass, the defense contractors, and the Congress for sending U.S. soldiers to fight unjust foreign wars, as if a foreign war could be just. But draft or no draft, I have nothing but contempt for the architects of U.S. foreign wars, the presidents who instigate or continue these wars, the neocons who welcome these wars, the liberals who defend these wars (when a Democratic president is conducting them), the conservatives who defend these wars (when a Republican president is conducting them), the military officers who use these wars to advance their careers while not actually doing any fighting themselves, the Congressmen who vote to fund these wars, the defense contractors who profit from these wars, and the Christians who pray for the troops in these wars. They are all moral monsters, and are accomplices to murder. But that doesn't change that fact that since murder is still murder, soldiers who do the actual killing are still murderers.

Fourth, if your family were on the receiving end of foreign troops bombing, shooting, maiming, and killing, would it matter to you if they were drafted? Does it make the death of your family less horrible? Would it be comforting to know that the killers of your family were drafted? I don't think so. Murder is still murder. The question, then, is why are Americans so quick to excuse U.S. soldiers should they be drafted? How do you think foreigners feel that lose family members because of U.S. bombs and bullets?

Fifth, if the U.S. government drafted someone into the military, told him to kill your father, and he did it, would you feel sorry for him because he was drafted? Would you try to find excuses for his actions? Again, I don't think so. Murder is still murder. And again, why are Americans so quick to excuse U.S. soldiers should they travel overseas to kill someone else's father just because they were drafted?

Sixth, consider the following scenarios? What would your response be if representatives of the U.S. government, members of the Bloods or the Crips, a policeman, or just some individual puts a gun in your hand and tells you to kill a member of your family? I can't imagine anyone who would do it. But what if one of the same groups or individuals puts a gun in your hand and tells you to kill some other American that you didn't know? I still have a hard time imagining anyone actually doing it. But what if in each instance you had a gun to your head and were told to kill or be killed? I would like to think that most everyone would take a bullet to the head rather than kill a member of his own family. I'm not so sure, however, what would happen in the latter case. But since murder is still murder, the proper moral response would be to do what was right and suffer the consequences; that is, to take the bullet. Now, I said all that to say this. What would the proper moral response be if someone were to be drafted, given a uniform, handed a gun, sent to fight in an unjust conflict, and put in a situation where he must kill or be killed? I say to take the bullet. But really, it doesn't have to go this far. The draft can be opposed. The uniform can be torn up. The gun can be thrown away. The trip overseas can be refused. But if all of this resistance comes to naught, then the proper moral response is, again, to take the bullet. Does wearing a uniform, traveling to another country, killing someone you don't know, or committing murder because you are threatened with death make murder not murder?

And seventh, if murder is still murder and fighting in an unjust war is criminal, then soldiers who participate in it are war criminals and murderers. The real military heroes are those who refuse to kill for the state in immoral, unjust wars, not those who become decorated war heroes. As Emmanuel Charles McCarthy has also said: "There is no such thing as heroism in the execution of evil."

Murder is still murder.

* * * * *

TIMBUKTU NOT OUT OF REACH OF U.S. TROOPS

Although it is a real city north of the Niger River on edge of the Sahara Desert in the West African country of Mali, Timbuktu has long served as a metaphor for an exotic, mysterious, and distant land. To travel from "here to Timbuktu" suggests a long, arduous, and adventurous journey to a place far away.

Timbuktu has both economic and religious significance. By the 14th century, it was a flourishing center for the trans-Saharan gold and salt trade. The city was a center of Islamic learning from the 13th to the 17th centuries. Three of western Africa's oldest mosques were built there. Thousands of manuscripts have been collected in Timbuktu over the course of many centuries. The city was designated a UNESCO World Heritage site in 1988.

France is the one European country that has always been connected with the region. A 10,000 franc prize was offered by a French society in 1824 to the first non-Muslim to go to Timbuktu and return with information about it. A Frenchman who disguised himself as a Muslim claimed the prize in 1828. France took control of Mali in the 1890s. And although the Independent Republic of Mali was formed on September 22, 1960, French is still the country's official language. After its independence, Mail was ruled by a series of corrupt and dictatorial regimes until a constitution was adopted and a democratic, multi-party presidential election was held in 1992.

More recently, however, a rebellion began in northern Mali in January 2012 led by the National Movement for the Liberation of Azawad (Timbuktu is in Azawad). A military coup in March 2012 ousted Mali's president and suspended the constitution. In April 2012, Timbuktu was captured, sharia law was implemented, and the independence of Azawad was declared. In October 2012, the United Nations Security Council passed a French resolution approving an African-led force to assist Mali in combating rebel forces. French soldiers intervened in January 2013 and, with Malian soldiers, reclaimed Timbuktu with little resistance. The French president and Mali's interim president then made a public appearance in Timbuktu. In February 2013, the National Movement for the Liberation of Azawad renounced its claim of independence and began helping French and African Union forces. Fighting continues between Islamic militants and the French-backed Mali government forces.

U.S. Marines may have gone to the halls of Montezuma and the shores of Tripoli, they may have fought in every clime and place, they may have taken a gun in the snow of far-off northern lands and sunny tropic scenes, but now they have a chance to go to Timbuktu.

In a letter late last month to the Speaker of the House of Representatives and the president pro tempore of the Senate, Barack Obama informed them that he had deployed U.S. troops to Niger to conduct intelligence collection and sharing with French forces:

> On February 20, 2013, the last elements of a deployment of approximately 40 additional U.S. military personnel entered Niger with the consent of the Government of Niger. This deployment will provide support for intelligence collection and will also facilitate intelligence sharing with French forces conducting operations in Mali, and with other partners in the region. The total number of U.S. military personnel deployed to Niger is approxi-

mately 100. The recently deployed forces have deployed with weapons for the purpose of providing their own force protection and security.

I directed this deployment of U.S. forces in furtherance of U.S. national security interests, and pursuant to my constitutional authority to conduct U.S. foreign relations and as Commander in Chief and Chief Executive.

I am providing this report as part of my efforts to keep the Congress fully informed, consistent with the War Powers Resolution (Public Law 93-148). I appreciate the support of the Congress in this action.

Niger, which signed a status of forces agreement with the United States last month that governs the presence of American troops in the country, borders on Mail. The president of Niger has voiced concern about the spillover of violence and refugees from Mali.

Defense Department officials told NBC News that "a first wave will include two Raptor surveillance drones and 250 to 300 military personnel, including remote pilots and security and maintenance crews." The Pentagon has already acknowledged that the United States has transported French soldiers, cargo, and military equipment into Mali and refueled French fighter jets there. A spokesman for the U.S. Africa Command (which is headquartered in, of all places, Stuttgart, Germany) said in an e-mail message, "Africa Command has positioned unarmed remotely piloted aircraft in Niger to support a range of regional security missions and engagements with partner nations." Although the United States already has surveillance aircraft stationed at several places around Africa, the only permanent U.S. military base on the continent is located in Djibouti, which is more than 3,000 miles from Mali.

There are four glaring problems with this latest escapade of the U.S. military.

One, the Constitution nowhere authorizes the president to initiate the deployment of U.S. forces. There is no such thing as presidential war power. The Founding Fathers did not entrust to one man the power to take the nation to war. Article I, Section 8 of the Constitution grants to Congress the power to "declare war," "raise and support armies," "provide and maintain a navy," "make rules for the government and regulation of the land and naval forces," "provide for calling forth the militia to execute the laws of the Union, suppress insurrections, and repel invasions," and "provide for organizing, arming, and disciplining, the militia." Article II,

Section 2 of the Constitution makes the president the "Commander-in-Chief of the Army and Navy of the United States, and of the militia of the several States, when called into the actual service of the United States." Obama has things backwards, just like his predecessors:

> George H.W. Bush: "I didn't have to get permission from some old goat in Congress to kick Saddam Hussein out of Kuwait."

> George W. Bush: "As your president, I am responsible for the decision to go into Iraq."

The fact that Congress has for many years consistently gone along with the president's usurpation of power makes it neither right nor constitutional.

Two, have Americans forgotten what happened the last time the United States came to the aid of the French military? In a word: Vietnam. France began meddling in Vietnam as far back as the late 1850s. Before 1900, Cambodia, Vietnam, and Laos were forcibly made into the French colony of French Indochina. Naturally, a nationalist movement for independence soon developed. When Vietnam was occupied by Japan during World War II, the League for the Independence of Vietnam, or Viet Minh—with the help of the United States—fought a guerrilla war against both the Japanese and Vietnam's French administrators. Independence was proclaimed after World War II, but the United States supported the French reconquest of Indochina. After the war, the Vietnamese began a guerrilla war against French colonial rule. But instead of supporting an independent Vietnam, or at least not taking sides, the United States intervened in behalf of the French with funding and weapons, but to no avail. In 1954, after a military defeat, France granted Cambodia, Laos, and Vietnam their independence. But that didn't end American intervention in Vietnam; it was only the beginning. When civil war erupted in Vietnam after a failed attempt at unification in 1956, the United States sent military "advisors," then troops, and then more troops. More than 3 million were deployed during the course of the war. That does not mean that U.S. intervention in Mali will turn into another Vietnam, but it does mean that there are always unforeseen consequences of U.S. military interventions. The war in Iraq was supposed to be a cakewalk, not last longer than five months, and cost "only" about $50 billion, with Iraq's vast oil reserves helping to defray the costs.

Three, sending U.S. troops thousands of miles from American soil, to conduct intelligence collection, and to assist another country in a military escapade is a perversion of the use of the military. It is beyond dispute that the purpose of any country's having a military is to defend its borders, skies, and shores from aggression by other countries. But since World War II, the U.S. military has been exclusively used by the president for purposes other than the actual defense of the country. U.S. soldiers who go to Niger, Mali, or Timbuktu, like those who went to Iraq, Afghanistan, Korea, Vietnam, Panama, Grenada, Haiti, Bosnia, Kosovo, Somalia, and all the other countries where the U.S. military had no business going, go as part of the president's personal attack force. The actions of the U.S. military should extend no further than defending the United States, securing its borders, guarding its shores, patrolling its coasts, and enforcing a no-fly zone over its skies. To do otherwise is to pervert the purpose of the military. It is not the purpose of the U.S. military to defend other countries, secure their borders, guard their shores, patrol their coasts, or enforce no-fly zones over their skies. And it is certainly not the proper use of the military to attack, invade, or occupy foreign countries. But that's not all. The U.S. military should never be used for disaster relief, humanitarian aid, nation building, training foreign armies, assisting foreign armies, establishing democracy, enforcing UN resolutions, regime change, containing communism, fighting the drug war, policing the world, or righting all the wrongs that exist in foreign societies.

And four, talking about national security interests and signing status of forces agreements do not change the fact that U.S. foreign policy is fundamentally, perpetually, and hopelessly interventionist. The United States would never tolerate another country's engaging in an American-style foreign policy. Most Americans probably don't realize that the United States already has troops in many countries in North Africa (Algeria, Egypt, Libya, Morocco, Sudan, Tunisia) and sub-Saharan Africa (Angola, Botswana, Burkina, Burundi, Cameroon, Chad, Congo, Djibouti, Ethiopia, Gabon, Ghana, Guinea, Ivory Coast, Kenya, Liberia, Madagascar, Malawi, Mali, Mauritania, Mauritius, Mozambique, Niger, Nigeria, Rwanda, Senegal, Sierra Leone, South Africa, Tanzania, Togo, Uganda, Zaire, Zambia, Zimbabwe) long before this latest deployment of more troops to Niger. There are no soldiers from any of these countries, or any other country, stationed in the United States. And although there are at least 1,000 U.S. military bases in foreign countries, there are no foreign military bases in the United States.

Timbuktu is not out of reach of U.S. troops. And a future U.S. military installation in Timbuktu is not out of the question.

* * * * *

WAR HEROES

Throughout American history, soldiers have always been held in high esteem. It doesn't matter where or why a particular war was fought—current and former members of the military have always been put on a pedestal.

We are expected to heap glory, laud, and honor upon them. We are expected to reverence and idolize them. We are expected to post signs expressing our support for them. We are expected to greet them in airports. We are expected to let them serve as role models for our children. We are expected to recognize them at sporting events. We are expected to pray for them during church services. We are expected to let them recruit in schools. We are expected to give them discounts at our businesses. We are expected to give them preference in employment. We are expected to thank them for their service.

To not participate is to be ungrateful for their sacrifice; to object to the attention paid to them is to be unpatriotic. Indeed, to question the military in any way—its size, its budget, its efficiency, its bureaucracy, its contractors, its weaponry, its missions, its effectiveness, its wars, its interventions, and especially its personnel—is to question America itself.

The adulation given to soldiers is especially true if they have been in combat. And this is increasingly the case since the beginning of the wars in Iraq and Afghanistan over ten years ago. Never before in American history has such military idolatry gripped the country. Never before have so many Christians bowed before the golden calf of the U.S. military. It has gotten to the point where any soldier who went to Iraq or Afghanistan is a war hero.

It should come as no surprise, then, that some men have taken advantage of Americans' infatuation with soldiers and all things military.

According to Mary Schantag, a Marine widow who launched the nonprofit Fake Warriors Project in 1998 with her late husband Chuck, her group, along with partners at similar sites, has revealed more than 4,000 hoaxers who falsely claimed military service or battlefield glory. Mrs. Schantag "uses Internet background searches and files Freedom of Information Requests with government agencies to corroborate a suspicious veteran's claimed history. She also taps her personal connections with Navy SEALS, Army Special Forces, even military chaplains to double check her detective work."

Just recently, retired Army Staff Sgt. Fred Campbell, one of 10 veterans who operate a virtual detective agency called Guardian of Valor, and who suffers from paralysis on one side as a result of his military service, helped expose military impersonator "Danny Crane," a fraud who in public routinely wore two Purple Hearts, a Distinguished Flying Cross and an Air Medal—none of them earned. In reality, Crane "served less than three months in the Army—never in combat—conned the Department of Veterans Affairs out of $7,000 by claiming he was half blind, had once been shot in the back, suffered from Post Traumatic Stress Disorder and had 24 metal plates inserted in his face." Assistant U.S. Attorney Amanda Kaiser said Crane concocted the persona of "the most decorated man in Florida." Crane was recently sentenced to one year and one day in federal prison.

While I certainly don't condone the lies and stupidity of "Danny Crane," impersonating a war hero is not the greatest of all sins. All the people that were awed by the sight of someone in a military uniform with a bunch of medals are deceiving themselves just as they were deceived. If Americans paid more attention to where the U.S. military goes, how long it stays, what it does when it is there, and how much of their tax money it spends on offense instead of defense, then a fraud like that perpetrated by "Danny Crane" would never have happened.

If soldiers were viewed as makers of widows and orphans, then the last thing the sight of a soldier in uniform would bring to mind would be a hero. If soldiers were viewed as willingly participating in the invasion, occupation, and destruction of countries that were no threat to the United States, then the sight of someone in a military uniform would bring forth feelings of revulsion instead of respect. If soldiers were viewed as ignorant but willing pawns for the state that just couldn't find other jobs, then they would be pitied instead of praised. If soldiers were viewed with indifference as just men who have jobs where uniforms are required, they would be looked at no differently than cooks, mechanics, or doormen.

Lucas Tomlinson, a producer for Fox News who happens to be a U.S. Naval Academy graduate and a Navy veteran, recently lamented the absence of military flyovers at Major League Baseball's "Opening Day" festivities due to budget cuts. "Millions of Americans were left without a critical opportunity to not only showcase our military might, but perhaps the first opportunity to see the military in action and think of a future of service in it," he wrote. "The military needs to do its part to inspire the next generation of heroes," he added, thus further cementing and perpetuating the military hero myth.

For a real hero, consider the case of skydiving instructor Orvar Arnarson, part of a skydiving group from Iceland that travels to Florida annually. Footage from his helmet camera shows that he was trying to help another man open his parachute just before they both recently plunged to their deaths. "He was a hero," said Pasco County detective William Lindsey of Arnarson. "He died a hero." Indeed he did, and he wasn't even wearing a military uniform.

* * * * *

SHOULD WE HONOR VIETNAM VETERANS?

Perhaps it's just my imagination, but it seems like the longer the United States military remains mired in Afghanistan, the more recognition is being given to Vietnam veterans.

The U.S. Congress and some states have in the last few years issued resolutions declaring March 30th as "Welcome Home Vietnam Veterans Day." March 30, 1973, is the date when all U.S. troops withdrew from Vietnam.

At an event to recognize Vietnam Veterans on March 30 at the Vietnam War Memorial near the Florida State Capitol, Vietnam Veteran Robert Jordan said: "When I see these young guys come home from Iraq and Afghanistan and everybody shaking their hands [and] all that, I shake their hands [and] I give them a lot of respect, but there is a part of me that says where is mine?" "The worst thing that can happen to us is that America forgets what we did," said another Vietnam Veteran.

The Vietnam Traveling Memorial Wall, a 3/5 scale of the Vietnam Veterans Memorial Wall in Washington, D.C., made an appearance in Melbourne, Florida, for a week late last month. I have never seen it or the Wall in Washington, D.C., but I have visited the one half scale version of the Wall in Pensacola, Florida, known as the Wall South. Like the memorial in Washington, D.C., these other "Walls" are inscribed with the names of the over 58,000 Americans who died fighting the Vietnam War. (None of the names of the millions of Vietnamese who died as a result of the war will be found on the Wall.)

The purpose of the Vietnam War Memorial is to honor those who fought in the war. One Vietnam veteran I quoted above says he wants respect; the other says that Americans should never forget what Vietnam Veterans did.

I for one will never forget what Vietnam Veterans did—they traveled half way around the world to fight an unjust, immoral, and unnecessary war against people they didn't know who were no threat to them, their families, or the United States. The Vietnam War was a monstrous evil in every respect. And as Nick Turse documents over and over again in his new book *Kill Anything that Moves: The Real American*

War in Vietnam, the whole war was one murderous My Lai incident, with lots of rape, torture, and mutilation thrown in.

So, why should we honor or respect Vietnam Veterans? Because, as Turse documents, they killed, poisoned, raped, beat, tortured, burned, mutilated, abused, drowned, and sexually exploited the Vietnamese? Of, of course not (it is said), only a few bad apples did those things.

How about because they blindly obeyed the state? How about because they were deceived, ignorant, young, and/or foolish? How about because they had no idea what they were getting into? How about because they were pawns of the state? No (it is said), these reasons are insulting to those who "served," "answered the call," and "fought for our freedoms."

How about because of their courage, sacrifice, bravery, guts, and valor? How about because they did it for "duty, honor, country"? Nice try, but as Fred Reed recently wrote: "There is no honor in going to someone else's country and butchering people you don't know because some political general, which is to say some general, told you to; A hit man for the Mafia is exactly as honorable."

How about because they thought they were serving their country? How about because they thought they were being patriotic? How about because they were lied to? How about because they were drafted? Okay, these things may be true, but that is not why people say we should honor our Vietnam veterans.

The reason we are supposed to honor Vietnam veterans is because . . . they fought in Vietnam. Just like the reason we are supposed to honor Iraq and Afghanistan war veterans is because they fought in those countries. The mindset of most Americans is that we should honor every U.S. soldier who fought in any war for any reason.

Because of the nature of the Vietnam War, Vietnam veterans *as a group* should not be honored any more than Iraq and Afghanistan war veterans *as a group* should be honored. That means they shouldn't be honored at all.

There are, however, some individual Vietnam Veterans that should be honored—but not because they fought in the Vietnam War. We can honor those who acknowledge that their participation in the war was a terrible mistake. We can honor those who regret the lives they took and the property they destroyed. We can honor those who now realize that the war was a great evil. We can honor those refused to kill once they arrived in Vietnam. We can honor those who have publicly denounced the war. We can honor those who have returned to Vietnam and apologized to the Vietnamese. We can honor these individual Vietnam veterans—but not because of anything they did while fighting in Vietnam.

I don't know how many of these honorable Vietnam veterans there are, but at least a hundred have written to me expressing regret, anger, sorrow, remorse, and/or shame because they fought in Vietnam. They don't want to be honored for participating in an unjust and immoral war. They don't want to be thanked for their service. They don't want to be respected like Iraq and Afghanistan veterans unfortunately are. They don't want to remember what they did.

The Vietnam veterans that we shouldn't honor are the ones who wear their 25th Infantry Vietnam cap everywhere they go and demand that we respect them, honor them, and not forget their "service." These we can pity, educate, and help—if they will let us.

The brutal truth about every U.S. soldier who died in Vietnam is that he died for a mistake. The only lasting thing about the death of any American in Vietnam is his name on a wall. I doubt that Nick Turse's book is sold in the gift shop at the Vietnam Veterans Memorial Wall, but is should be.

Should we honor Vietnam Veterans? It all depends.

* * * * *

IS IT OKAY TO KILL?

Is it okay to kill? I don't mean a bug in your house, a snake in your garage, or a deer in the woods. Deer tastes good; you may not know if that snake in your garage is poisonous; and bugs are home invaders.

I mean is it okay to kill a man, a human being, a person? Again, I don't mean someone trying to kill you, rob your business, rape your wife, harm your children, or break into your house. Killing someone might be perfectly justified in those circumstances if it involves defense against aggression.

Specifically, is it okay to kill someone who has not threatened or committed violence or aggression against you, your family, your friends, your neighborhood, anyone you know, or any American you don't know?

No? Then—

- What if he is not an American?
- What if he lives thousands of miles away from America?
- What if he adheres to a religion that is different from that of most Americans?
- What if he is a darker color than most Americans?
- What if he speaks a language that most Americans don't

understand?
- What if he has habits that seem peculiar to most Americans?
- What if he holds to a political ideology that doesn't resemble America's?
- What if he smells different than most Americans?

Does someone having one or more of these characteristics alone mean it is okay to kill him?

Another no? Then—

- What if the U.S. government says he is a terrorist?
- What if the U.S. government says he is an insurgent?
- What if the U.S. government says he is a communist?
- What if the U.S. government says he is an extremist?
- What if the U.S. government says he is a potential threat?
- What if the U.S. government says he hates our freedoms?
- What if the U.S. government says he is the enemy?
- What if the U.S. government says he is a bad guy?

Does the U.S. government merely saying any of these things make it okay to kill him?

No again? Then—

- What if the U.S. government says it is a matter of national security?
- What if the U.S. government says it is in the national interest?
- What if the U.S. government says it is of strategic concern?
- What if the U.S. government says it has secret information that makes it necessary?
- What if the U.S. government says it is part of the president's grand strategic vision?
- What if the U.S. government says it is essential to maintaining hegemony?
- What if the U.S. government says it is just a part of fighting terrorism?
- What if the U.S. government says it is important to foreign policy objectives?

Does the U.S. government merely saying any of these things make it okay to kill him?

Still no? Then—

- What if the U.S. military gives you a nice uniform?
- What if the U.S. military gives you a gun and ammunition?
- What if the U.S. military pays for your college education?
- What if the U.S. military provides you with free medical and dental care?
- What if the U.S. military offers you citizenship in exchange for service?
- What if the U.S. military gives you an enlistment bonus?
- What if the U.S. military gives you generous combat pay?
- What if the U.S. military assists you with repaying your student loans?
- What if the U.S. military offers you liberal retirement benefits?

Does the U.S. military doing any of these things make it okay to kill him? Of course not? Then—

- Why are some so quick to make apologies for U.S. military personnel who kill for the state in unjust wars?
- Why are some so quick to excuse U.S. military personnel who kill while not defending the United States?
- Why are some so quick to justify U.S. military personnel who kill people thousands of miles away that are no threat to the United States?
- Why are some so quick to defend U.S. military personnel who kill people that resent and resist being invaded, bombed, occupied, or "liberated"?
- Why are some so quick to blame the government, the politicians, and the defense contractors and exempt the U.S. military personnel who do the actual killing?

For years now I have heard the excuses. But what are these apologists, excusers, justifiers, defenders, and exempters really saying?

- It is okay to kill for the U.S. government in an unjust war if you can't find a job.
- It is okay to kill for the U.S. government in an unjust war if you can't make it in college.
- It is okay to kill for the U.S. government in an unjust war if you are economically disadvantaged.
- It is okay to kill for the U.S. government in an unjust war if your father was in the military.

- It is okay to kill for the U.S. government in an unjust war if you are patriotic.
- It is okay to kill for the U.S. government in an unjust war if you are ignorant.
- It is okay to kill for the U.S. government in an unjust war if you are poor.
- It is okay to kill for the U.S. government in an unjust war if you are uneducated.
- It is okay to kill for the U.S. government in an unjust war if you have no resources available.
- It is okay to kill for the U.S. government in an unjust war if you think you are doing the right thing.
- It is okay to kill for the U.S. government in an unjust war if you were raised to never question the military.
- It is okay to kill for the U.S. government in an unjust war if you were never taught otherwise.
- It is okay to kill for the U.S. government in an unjust war if you are just obeying orders.
- It is okay to kill for the U.S. government in an unjust war if you think you are avenging 9/11.
- It is okay to kill for the U.S. government in an unjust war if you think you are defending our freedoms.

I have been given every one of these excuses at least ten times. The first part of the excuse is generally omitted, but why should it be? Is not this exactly what people are saying?

None of this means that the despicable creatures in the U.S. government who send American boys to war, and the equally loathsome creatures outside of the U.S. government who cheer them on, are not to be condemned as well. But those aren't the people that are applauded in airports, called heroes, and thanked for their service.

But why is it that these excuses only seem to be valid for American soldiers? Why is it that soldiers from other countries aren't lauded as heroes for killing Americans if they offer up one of the excuses that are commonly used to justify killings carried out by American soldiers?

Some agree with everything I have said thus far, but think that if soldiers are draftees then it changes everything. I know this is the case because they write and tell me. I have written about the culpability of drafted soldiers in my article "Murder Is Still Murder." But again, why is it that it is only drafted American soldiers who can kill with impunity? I don't think that apologists for draftees realize what they are saying. To excuse the actions of soldiers because they were drafted is to say that the state can somehow sanctify murder.

Although the U.S. military is looking for a few good men to unjustly kill for the state, it is not okay to kill, even if the military advertises itself as a global force for good.

* * * * *

HAPPY MILITARY APPRECIATION DAY

The Fourth of July is supposed to be celebrated as American Independence Day – the day when the thirteen original colonies seceded from the British Empire and its oppressive taxation, spying, regulating, and attacks on due process (sound familiar?).

As John Adams wrote to his wife about celebrating the nation's independence:

The Second Day of July 1776 [the date the resolution of independence was approved by Congress], will be the most memorable Epocha, in the History of America. I am apt to believe that it will be celebrated, by succeeding Generations, as the great anniversary Festival. It ought to be commemorated, as the Day of Deliverance by solemn Acts of Devotion to God Almighty. It ought to be solemnized with Pomp and Parade, with Shews, Games, Sports, Guns, Bells, Bonfires and Illuminations from one End of this Continent to the other from this Time forward forever more. You will think me transported with Enthusiasm but I am not. I am well aware of the Toil and Blood and Treasure, that it will cost Us to maintain this Declaration, and support and defend these States. Yet through all the Gloom I can see the Rays of ravishing Light and Glory. I can see that the End is more than worth all the Means. And that Posterity will tryumph in that Days Transaction, even altho We should rue it, which I trust in God We shall not.

There is one thing that Adams forgot to mention: adoration of the military. The Fourth of July is now nothing but Military Appreciation Day Number 2.

Military Appreciation Day Number 1 is Memorial Day. This holiday was first observed in honor of Union soldiers who died during the War to Prevent Southern Independence. It was initially called Decoration Day because the tombs of the dead soldiers were decorated. Originally celebrated in select localities, the holiday was first widely observed on

May 30, 1868, because of an earlier proclamation by General John Logan of the Grand Army of the Republic, an organization of Union veterans. New York, in 1873, was the first state to officially recognize the holiday. After World War I, the holiday was expanded to include U. S. soldiers who died in any war. It is now just a day to honor all things military.

Military Appreciation Day Number 3 is Veterans Day. This holiday began as Armistice Day – a day to commemorate the signing of the armistice on the 11th hour of the 11th day of the 11th month that ended fighting on the Western Front in World War I, "the war to end all wars." A few years after World War II, the holiday was changed to Veterans Day as a tribute to all soldiers who fought for their country. Veterans Day has now become a day to honor, not just those who have served in the military during wartime, but those who have served during peacetime or are serving now. It is now just a day to honor all things military.

Independence Day is now wholly given over to praising soldiers, thanking veterans, reciting ridiculous slogans and poems about the military, and heaping glory, laud, and honor ad nauseam on the troops.

Nothing confirms this more than an e-mail that was forwarded around the country beginning the week before the Fourth of July. It begins:

> Happy 4th of July!.... Let's get this started NOW! So it will be out there on the fourth!

After the Pledge of Allegiance, which no one should waste his time reciting, there are these three statements:

> For all of our other military personnel, where ever they may be.
> Please Support all of the troops defending our Country.
>
> And God Bless our Military who are protecting our Country for our Freedom.
> Thanks to them, and their sacrifices, we can celebrate the 4th of July.
>
> We must never forget who gets the credit for the freedoms we have, of which we should be eternally grateful.

Wherever they me be? Like I have said on several occasions, most Americans don't care where the troops go, how long they stay, and what they do when they get there. Defending our country? Are there any U.S. troops that are actually defending the country? It seems to me like they are all overseas somewhere or on ship sailing where it has no business. God bless our military? How blasphemous to ask God to bless the greatest force for evil in the world. Protecting our country for our freedom? U.S. soldiers don't protect anyone's freedom – just ask this former soldier. The military doesn't protect our freedom; it stands by while our freedom is eroded and taken away. Thanks to the military we can celebrate the 4th of July? The U.S. military has never had anything to do with celebrating the 4th of July. Even the first Fourth of July was not in any way dependent on the U.S. military in any way. The Fourth of July celebrates the Declaration of Independence, not the day the Revolutionary War ended. Never forget who gets the credit? It is God who gets all the credit for any freedoms we had or still have. It is the God of heaven that we are eternally grateful for, certainly not the U.S. military – employees of the U.S. government. The greatest threat to freedom has always been our own government, not some foreign country or terrorist organization. And as James Madison said: "If tyranny and oppression come to this land, it will be in the guise of fighting a foreign enemy." Since the U.S. military is not strictly used for the defense of U.S. borders, shores, coasts, and skies, it is nothing more than the president's personal attack force staffed by mercenaries willing to obey his latest command to bomb, invade, occupy, and otherwise bring death and destruction to any country he deems necessary.

The three statements are followed by this poem:

I watched the flag pass by one day.
It fluttered in the breeze.
A young Marine saluted it,
And then he stood at ease.

I looked at him in uniform;
so young, so tall, so proud.
With hair cut square and eyes alert,
He'd stand out in any crowd.

I thought how many men like him
had fallen through the years.
How many died on foreign soil;
how many mothers' tears?

How many pilots' planes shot down?
How many died at sea?

How many foxholes were soldiers' graves?
NO, FREEDOM ISN'T FREE!

I heard the sound of Taps one night,
when everything was still.
I listened to the bugler play
And felt a sudden chill.

I wondered just how many times
That Taps had meant 'Amen.'
When a flag had draped a coffin
of a brother or a friend.

I thought of all the children,
of the mothers and the wives,
of fathers, sons and husbands
With interrupted lives.

I thought about a graveyard
At the bottom of the sea.
Of unmarked graves in Arlington .
NO FREEDOM ISN'T FREE!

Right, freedom isn't free; but wrong, freedom isn't provided by the U.S. military. I have asked the same questions as those in the poem: "How many died on foreign soil?" "How many mothers' tears?" I too have thought about the children, the mothers, the wives, the fathers, the sons, the husbands, and the unmarked graves in Arlington. The conclusion I have reached is this: What a senseless, unnecessary waste of life for any U.S. soldier to die on foreign soil or be buried in an unmarked grave.

The poem was followed by these four statements:

Enjoy Your Freedom and God Bless Our Troops.

When you receive this, please stop for a moment and say a prayer for our servicemen.

Of all the gifts you could give a U.S. Soldier, prayer is the very best one.

Only two defining forces have ever offered to die for you. Jesus Christ and the American GI. One died for your soul, the other for your freedom. You might want to pass this on ... as many seem to forget both of them.

I will enjoy the freedom I have left, until the government takes it away. I will not ask God to bless our troops. I will say a prayer for our servicemen, but it will be a prayer that they come home and stop fighting unjust foreign wars, not a war prayer. Perhaps the most nauseating thing in this e-mail is the last statement that equates soldiers with Christ. As I have said elsewhere: Do soldiers imitate Christ when they bomb and shoot, when they invade and occupy, when they plunder and pillage, or when they maim and kill?

So, until Military Appreciation Day Number 3 comes around, happy Military Appreciation Day Number 2.

* * * * *

SERVICE OR EMPLOYMENT?

"There is no higher calling than service in our Armed Forces." ~ George W. Bush

"The debt to the heroic men and valiant women in the service of our country can never be repaid." ~ Harry S. Truman

The idea that U.S. military personnel are serving the country just by virtue of being in the military is so ingrained in American thinking that being in the military is simply referred to as being in "the service."

Callers to some radio shows who identify themselves as being in the military are thanked for their service. Well-wishers in airports thank returning soldiers for their service. Signs outside of churches on the Sunday before one of the three military appreciation days (Memorial Day, Fourth of July, and Veterans Day) thank veterans for their service. Signs outside of businesses thank the troops for their service every day of the year. Even postal clerks thank military personnel for their service.

This "military service" mindset leads to some absurd conclusions, like this one I received from a critic: "Enjoy your right to express such intellectually bankrupt ideas. It is through the sacrifices of veterans that you enjoy this right. I just suggest that you exercise it a bit more wisely." Or this one: "They continue to stand guard for us, so that if someone comes to take away your freedom to write your nice little remarks about them, they stop them dead in their tracks." Or this bumper sticker: "If You Can Read, Thank a Teacher. If You Can Read in English, Thank a

Marine." Or this one: "If You Can't Get Behind Our Troops, Feel Free to Stand in Front of Them."

According to the Department of Defense, there were 155,754 Americans who joined the military during the most recent fiscal year. All four branches of the military exceeded their recruitment goals, as they did the previous fiscal year. Additionally, there were 100,654 Americans who joined the Army or Air National Guard or the Army, Navy, or Marine Corps Reserve.

Are these men (and women) who recently joined the military serving "us" or just getting a paycheck? Oh, they may be serving Uncle Sam; they may be serving an evil empire; they may be serving the president; they may be serving a rogue state; they may be serving themselves-but they certainly aren't serving "us."

My problem with many in the military, and many more chicken-hawks and armchair warriors out of the military, is not just that military personnel are the president's personal attack force or that they are a global force for imperialism or that they help maintain an empire or that they fight senseless foreign wars or that they help carry out an evil, interventionist foreign policy or that brothels flourish wherever U.S. military bases are. My problem is the charade, the masquerade, the subterfuge, the deceit, the scam, the ruse that is military "service."

Military service is a job, nothing more. Forget all the nonsense about duty, honor, country, the flag, the few, the proud, patriotism, 9/11, terrorism, and service. The military is an employment program. If those in and out of the military would just come clean and drop the service pretense, then I wouldn't pay any more attention to them than I do clerks who work for the Social Security Administration—except, of course, when they unjustly kill for the government.

Why are people looked upon as a special because they "served" in the military? What need in society have they met? What is something productive they have done? Because the military does everything but actually defend the country against real threats, the answer is very little if anything at all. Military personnel should be viewed as just another faceless government bureaucrat or clerk.

So, to those in the military, and to those who moan incessantly about the troops not being appreciated for their service, I would just say this: Stop the deception; end the ruse. The military is an employer. The troops don't defend our freedoms. When they die overseas they die in vain and for a lie. They don't protect my right to write anymore than they protect your right to watch television, walk your dog, or play poker.

* * * * *

CHAPTER 3

THE WAR IN IRAQ

EIGHT FACTS ABOUT IRAQ

The Bush administration, its accomplices in the news media, and the conservative talk show hacks who do the bidding of the Republican party have sold America a bill of goods. The invasion of Iraq was justified, we have been led to believe, because Saddam Hussein was the reincarnation of Adolph Hitler, Iraq was in the position of Germany on the eve of World War II, and the "elite" Republican Guard was the equivalent of the German Wehrmacht. According to the president himself: "We will end a brutal regime, whose aggression and weapons of mass destruction make it a unique threat to the world."

Right-wing Christians too, who ought to know better, have also been duped because of their misplaced trust in the state just because it is currently controlled by the Republican party (the same Republican party that is expanding government at a rate not seen since the Democratic administrations of Lyndon Johnson and Franklin Roosevelt).

Located at the northern tip of the Persian Gulf, and encompassing the land of ancient Mesopotamia, as well as the biblical Tigris and Euphrates rivers, the country of Iraq, which until recently could not be located on a map by most Americans, is now the focus of all Americans. But because most Americans are woefully ignorant of history, and especially the history of U.S. intervention into other countries; and because most Christians are just as ignorant of history, and especially Christians who spend all their time believing what they read in the newspaper, hear on the radio, and see on television, some facts about Iraq are in order.

Fact Number 1: *There was no country of Iraq until it was created by the British in 1920.* In 1534 the Ottoman Turks conquered the area of what is now Iraq. Here the Ottoman empire ruled until its defeat in World War I because Turkey sided with the Central powers. After World War I, the French and British divided up the formerly Ottoman-controlled lands in the Middle East. France was given a League of Nations mandate over Syria and Lebanon; Great Britain was given the same over Palestine, Transjordan, and Iraq. The modern state of Iraq was created out of the three Ottoman provinces of Basra, Mosul, and Baghdad. The defeat of the Turks may have brought to an end the Ottoman empire, but it began a century of Western imperialism.

Fact Number 2: *The United States already sponsored two previous regime changes in Iraq.* Under their League of Nations mandate, the British installed King Faisal as the ruler of Iraq. But even after its independence, Iraq was still controlled by Britain. Faisal's dynasty lasted until his grandson Faisal II was executed in a 1958 coup. The Hitler in Iraq in the early 1960s was Abd al-Karim Qasim. After deposing the Western-allied Iraqi monarchy in 1958, Qasim was seen by the U.S. as a counter to Gamal Abdel Nassar of Egypt. But after he was perceived as too much of a threat to Western oil interests, Qasim was killed in February 1963 in a CIA-sponsored coup by the anti-Communist Baath party. American firms soon began doing business with Baghdad. All was not well, however, in the Baath party, for in 1968 an internal coup brought to power General Ahmad Hassan al-Bakr, who was succeeded by Saddam Hussein in 1979. These regime changes in Iraq were both accompanied by bloody reprisals.

Fact Number 3: *Saddam Hussein was an ally of the United States until the first Persian Gulf War.* The U.S.–Hussein connection actually goes all the way back to the late 1950s. Hussein was part of a group that tried to assassinate Abd al-Karim Qasim after he seized power in 1958. Fleeing Iraq, he eventually settled in Cairo, Egypt, where he was courted by the CIA. During the 1980s, when Iraq was at war with Iran, military intelligence was provided to Iraq because the United States sought to do whatever was necessary to prevent Iraq from losing its war with Iran. The U.S. problem with Iran stemmed from decades of American intervention that backfired when radical Shiite Muslims overthrew the Shah and installed the Ayatollah Khomeini. The United States has a bad habit of collaborating with tyrants who later come back to bite us. Who can forget that Joseph Stalin, one of the bloodiest killers who ever lived, was our "ally" in World War II?

Fact Number 4: *Iraq got its "weapons of mass destruction" from the United States.* This started after the Baath party coup of 1963, when the U.S. sent arms to the new regime. But during the Iran–Iraq War of the 1980s, when, under the successive administrations of Reagan and Bush I, Saddam Hussein was our ally against Iran, it was not just arms that were provided to Iraq. According to the 1992 U.S. Senate committee report on U.S. Chemical and Biological Warfare-Related Dual-Use Exports to Iraq, "The United States provided the government of Iraq with 'dual use' licensed materials which assisted in the development of Iraqi chemical, biological and missile-system programs." This included anthrax, VX nerve gas, West Nile fever germs, botulism, salmonella, and E coli.

Fact Number 5: *Iraq was a liberal Muslim state.* Iraq is made up of three major groups: the Kurds, the Shiites, and the Sunnis. The Shiites, which are in the majority, are the more radical Muslims. The ruling Baath party was more closely associated with the more moderate Sunnis, which make up about 35 percent of the population. Unlike Saudi Arabia, Iran, and most other Muslim states, Iraq was not controlled by a fundamentalist Muslim government, something that is now a possibility. One could even purchase a drink in Baghdad. The Baath government tolerated both Jews and Christians, something not to be seen in Muslim countries like Indonesia, Turkey, and Iran.

Fact Number 6: *Iraq was not responsible for the 9-11 attacks on the United States.* Many Americans who supported the war with Iraq did so because they were led to believe that the U.S. was retaliating for the terrorist attacks on September 11. Yet, none of the hijackers of the airplanes on September 11 were from Iraq (or Afghanistan). They were mainly from Saudi Arabia, our supposed Muslim ally in the Middle East. No connection has ever been proved between Iraq and al-Qaeda or Saddam Hussein and Osama bin Laden. There is even evidence that the invasion of Iraq was planned before the September 11 attacks. A September 2000 document issued by the Project for the New American Century (PNAC) titled "Rebuilding America's Defenses: Strategies, Forces and Resources For A New Century," drawn up by Dick Cheney, Donald Rumsfeld, and Paul Wolfowitz, shows that Bush's cabinet intended to take military control of the Persian Gulf region regardless of whether Saddam Hussein was in power.

Fact Number 7: *Iraq was not a threat to the United States.* Although Bush's initial justification for war was that Iraq was a "threat to the United Nations" (certainly no reason for the U.S. to go to war), this was soon shifted to Iraq being a threat to the United States. But even though Secretary of Defense Donald Rumsfeld insisted that "no terrorist state poses a greater and more immediate threat to the security of our people and the stability of the world than the regime of Saddam Hussein in Iraq," the condition of Iraq said otherwise. Not only was Iraq's army considerably weaker than it was during the first Persian Gulf War—a war in which Iraq only managed to kill 148 Americans—but Iraq had no navy or air force. Iraq's economy was in ruin after a decade of sanctions—sanctions that destroyed its water supplies. The GNP of Iraq was not even 15 percent of that of the state of Washington. The only time in history when Iraq did actually attack the United States—an Iraqi warplane attacked a U.S. ship in the Persian Gulf in 1987 resulting in the killing of dozens of U.S. sailors—we did nothing because Iraq apologized for its "mistake." No, the greatest threat to freedoms of the American people is not Iraq. The greatest threat to the freedoms of the American people is not some country six thousand miles away; it is our own government. How is it that in a country with such a heritage of individual liberty like the United States, one can smoke in a restaurant in Baghdad, but not in Manhattan? How is it that in a country with a Christian heritage like the United States, one can buy a gun in Baghdad, but not in Washington, D. C.? If Iraq's neighboring countries did not feel the need to send troops to Baghdad, then why did we?

Fact Number 8: *Iraq is the Mideast's second largest oil producer*. Although this is a fact that everyone knows, it is downplayed by all proponents of the war with Iraq. But if oil has nothing to do with the U.S. intervening in Iraq, then why hasn't the U.S. intervened in Sudan, where 2 million Christians have been killed during the past decade? What about the persecution of Christians in Indonesia? Why hasn't the U.S. intervened in Zimbabwe, where the Marxist tyrant Robert Mugabe has been confiscating the country's farmland? Why has Fidel Castro—90 miles away from our shores—been untouched for 40 years? Why didn't the U.S. instigate a "regime change" when Idi Amin was killing thousands of his own black people in Uganda in the 1970s? Why didn't the U.S. instigate a "regime change" when the Tutsis were slaughtered by the Hutu government of Rwanda in 1994? Would things have been different if Sudan, Indonesia, Zimbabwe, Cuba, Uganda, and Rwanda had significant oil reserves?

These sobering facts, unknown to Americans who get all their news from ABC, CBS, NBC, CNN, FOX, and CNBC, should cause every citizen, and especially every Christian, to question the motives of the state the next time it is insisted that we should invade another country. They should also cause all Americans to question the necessity of the United States maintaining 184 military bases in over 100 countries around the world. God never appointed the United States to be the world's policeman.

* * * * *

WAR ON HIS MIND

It has been just over two years since President Bush—in commander-in-chief mode—landed on the *USS Lincoln* and spoke these words in front of a "Mission Accomplished" banner:

> Major combat operations in Iraq have ended. In the Battle of Iraq,
> the United States and our allies have prevailed. And now our
> coalition is engaged in securing and reconstructing that country.

But the mission was not accomplished, for out of the 1,614 American combat deaths in Iraq, 1,477 occurred *after* Bush's "Mission Accomplished" speech. How many more Americans must die before Bush's "mission" is accomplished?

When the number of Americans killed in Iraq surpassed the 1,000 mark in September of 2004, Bush said of the families of the dead during a campaign rally: "My promise to them is that we will complete the mission so that their child or their husband or wife has not died in vain." Then in January of 2005, Bush invoked his mission once again: "American troops will be leaving as quickly as possible, but they won't be leaving until we have completed our mission." But how many more Americans must die before Bush's "mission" is completed?

As long as Bush is in office, there will be no "mission accomplished" or "mission completed." Like his predecessors Lincoln, Wilson, Roosevelt, and Johnson, Bush is now a war president—and seems to relish his role in this elite society. It has been a little over a year now since Bush uttered the following words during an interview in the Oval Office with Tim Russert for NBC's "Meet the Press" that was broadcast on February 8, 2004:

> I'm a war president. I make decisions here in the Oval Office in
> foreign-policy matters with war on my mind.

Since Bush made this admission, I have written four articles in which I mentioned the number of American troops that have been killed in Bush's "splendid little war" against Iraq. On July 9, 2004, in "The Horrors of War," I related that before the phony transfer of power to the Iraqis on June 28, 855 American troops had died. On November 5, 2004, in "For Whom Would Jesus Vote," I pointed out that Bush's undeclared, unconstitutional, immoral war had resulted in the deaths of over 1,100 American soldiers. On May 2, 2005, in "What's Wrong with the U.S. Global Empire?" I said that there were 1,569 military deaths in Iraq. And most recently, on May 9, 2005, in "The Warmonger's Beatitudes," I used the figure of 1,601 dead Americans. The death count is now up to 1,614, with no end in sight.

At the rate things are going, by the time Bush's second term comes to a close, the number of American serviceman killed in Iraq will surpass the number of Americans killed in the World Trade Center attacks. Depending on the source of your information, the official death toll in the New York City terrorist attacks was 2,752 (NYC), 2,774 (AP), or 2,784 (*USA Today*). Since some of those killed were foreigners, the actual number of Americans killed will be less than any of the above figures.

Perhaps it is time for President Bush to have American soldiers on his mind instead of war on his mind. American soldiers that could be guarding our borders, patrolling our coasts, and actually defending us from terrorist attacks instead of dying halfway around the world trying to impose American-style democracy on a country and a people that have never been so inclined.

It is the American people that need to have war on their mind. How many more billions of dollars will have to be spent before the American people demand an end to this obscene waste of their money? How much higher does the body count have to go before the American people are outraged enough to demand an end to this senseless war? Every new casualty should be met with increasing contempt for the state and its wars. Bringing democracy to Iraq and ridding the country of Saddam Hussein is not worth the life of one American. What kind of government they have and who is to be their "leader" is the business of the Iraqi people, not the United States.

I continue to be amazed that those who oppose the war and don't want to see the blood of Americans shed on foreign soil are labeled as un-patriotic and anti-American. Real patriots don't want to see their country hated because of interventionism and militarism. Real patriots don't want to see even one American used as cannon fodder for the state. Real patriots want their country to be admired not scorned.

And yet, Americans continue to support and make apologies for the state and its wars. In spite of growing opposition to the war in Iraq, I am not very optimistic about the American people as a whole demanding the complete withdrawal of American troops and American influence from Iraq. And here are some reasons why.

First, oil: As long as drilling for oil in the United States is demonized and there is oil in the Middle East, the United States can be counted on to intervene in Iraq and everywhere else in the Middle East.

Second, Vietnam: The deaths of 58,000 young American men, the wounding of 304,000 more, and the permanent disabling of 75,000 of those wounded—all in the jungles of Vietnam—should have forever turned the American people away from supporting another foreign war. It didn't.

Third, September 11th: As long as many Americans continue to believe that Iraq was behind the September 11th attacks (a belief that even the president does not hold), there will never be sufficient enough outrage at anything that happens in Iraq.

Fourth, the U.S. empire: The stationing of U.S. troops abroad is so pervasive (we now have troops in 150 different regions of the world), and has gone on for so long (we still have troops in Japan and Germany even though WWII ended in 1945), that the American people don't seem to mind when the latest overseas U.S. military adventure is announced.

Fifth, the military: Abu Ghraib notwithstanding, the military is still held in high esteem by too many of the American people even though very little of what the military actually does has anything to do with defending the country.

Sixth, the Religious Right: Conservative Christians, who would know better if they spent as much time reading their Bible and studying history as they did reading the *Weekly Standard* and listening to Republican propaganda from their pulpits, should be the first to denounce any new foreign war that will lead to the deaths of thousands of innocent people. Yet, many of them continue to defend anything the president does with the lame excuse that "he is a Christian."

What is really tragic about this president is that the things he thinks of when war is not on his mind are things like faith-based welfare schemes, the Medicare prescription drug benefit, steel tariffs, and Social Security "privatization." It would be nice to have a president with the protection of life, liberty, and property on his mind. A president who actually followed the Constitution he swore to uphold, like "the last good Democrat," Grover Cleveland.

Even though Bush will leave office in a few years and cease being a war president, and even though the war will some day be forgotten, there are some people that will always have war on their mind—the parents, children, and spouses of the U.S. servicemen who lives continue to be wasted in a country the average American could not, until just a short time ago, even locate on a map.

* * * * *

IT IS A SIMPLE MATTER

Why are U.S. troops still in Iraq? After all the lies about this war have been exposed, one would think that the American people would be shouting from the housetops for an end to the senseless loss of life of young American soldiers, now numbering 1,827.

So why are U.S. troops still in Iraq? The excuse often given when someone doesn't want to do something is that the action in question is just too complicated to be carried out.

The war in Iraq is no different.

Douglas Feith, the Undersecretary of Defense for Policy, in a recent interview on NPR, said that withdrawal from Iraq is "not a simple matter." Feith, who will shortly be leaving his post to spend more time with his family, follows Secretary of Defense Donald Rumsfeld and Deputy Defense Secretary Paul Wolfowitz in civilian authority at the Pentagon, and is considered to be a principal architect of U.S. postwar strategy in Iraq. Feith has not been without his critics, even within the establishment. Retired Army general Tommy Franks called him "the stupidest guy on the face of the Earth."

But, Mr. Feith, it is a simple matter. Stop making excuses for the fact that you don't want U.S. troops to leave Iraq. The withdrawal of all U.S. and coalition forces from Iraq is a simple matter. And don't dismiss me as an idealist with my head in the clouds. I am not naïve enough to think that the entire U.S. military could leave Iraq tomorrow. However, a journey of a thousand miles begins with a single step.

There is no one correct plan to withdraw from Iraq. But in my opinion, to withdraw the U.S. military from Iraq in not only a safe, reasonable, and timely manner, but also in a just manner, the following simple steps should be taken.

Step one: Announce to Iraq that our invasion was a horrible mistake, as was our intervention in the region for the last fifty years. Tell Iraq that we intend to withdraw every American soldier as soon as possible. Apologize for the tens of thousands of Iraqis that were killed by our bullets, bombs, or sanctions.

Step two: Stop all killing, bombing, patrols, arrests, imprisonments, and interrogations. Maintain a defensive position until exiting the country.

Step three: Perform the logistics necessary to leave the country. Tell the troops to start packing.

Step four: Apologize to our troops for sending them to Iraq, and especially our wounded. Apologize to the families of all our soldiers killed in Iraq. Release from confinement all U.S. soldiers imprisoned for refusing to fight, like Sgt. Kevin Benderman.

Step five: Announce to every country that was a member of our "coalition," and especially to Great Britain, that they made a horrible mistake in following our lead in invading Iraq. Tell them that they should immediately withdraw all their forces from Iraq. Let them know that we intend to withdraw as soon as possible and that if they choose to remain in Iraq then they do so without our protection. The United States should also apologize to every country that it demonized for not supporting our invasion of Iraq.

Step six: Announce to Iraq that there will be no future military interventions or interference with the government of the country. If the government of Iraq wants to hire former members of the U.S. military to train their military and police forces or contractors to rebuild the country then that is their business. No U.S. troops will be stationed in Iraq to guard Halliburton employees. Americans who work in Iraq will do so at their own risk. Offer to purchase as much oil as Iraq can supply to give the country funds to rebuild its infrastructure.

Step seven: Use every available truck, plane, and ship to get the troops out. Squad by squad, platoon by platoon, company by company, battalion by battalion, squadron by squadron, brigade by brigade, division by division, corps by corps—it doesn't matter, just get the troops out.

Once these seven steps are carried out, there are two other steps that those of us who want to return to the nonintervention policy of the Founding Fathers would like to see taken:

Step eight: Put the world on notice—withdrawal from your country is next.

Step nine: Tell the defense contractors to start diversifying.

Mr. Feith may not agree with these steps. He may think that they could not be carried out. He may even dismiss me as a simpleton. But one thing is certain; these steps would not result in the deaths of any more American soldiers—unlike any of the plans circulating in the Bush administration.

* * * * *

IT'S NOT MY WAR!

"Yes, this is Bush's war, but it is also America's war, our war." ~ Pat Buchanan

If there is anything this war is not, it is not my war. I have opposed it from the beginning. I have denounced it from the beginning. I have never wavered in my disagreement with the president who instigated it, my disgust for the Congressmen who funded it, my loathing for the conservatives who promoted it, my abhorrence of the Christians who defended it, and my pity for the soldiers who were duped by military recruiters to participate in it.

But I am not alone. I know that there are hundreds, thousands, and perhaps millions of Americans who have condemned the Iraq war from the beginning.

The difference between my opposition to the war and that of many others is that my opposition is based on principle—not because Bush lied about Saddam Hussein's intentions, weapons, and al-Qaeda connection.

There is no question that this is Bush's war, but he is not alone. There is no shortage of conservative talk show hosts, congressmen, pundits, politicians, political appointees, and Christian "leaders" who have not only defended Bush and his war, but continue to defend him and it despite growing dissatisfaction with the way things are going in Iraq. The body count of dead American soldiers, now over 1,900, does not seem to bother this diverse group of conservatives much at all. Conservatives who denounced Clinton's abuse of the military when he ordered cruise missile strikes on Afghanistan and Sudan during the Monica Lewinsky fiasco would again be calling for Clinton's impeachment if 1,900 American soldiers died on his watch. The typical conservative is not opposed to war at all as long as it is launched by a Republican president who claims to be one of them.

But is it America's war? Buchanan himself cites a *Newsweek* report that "support for Bush's handling of the war has fallen below 40%, to 34%, with 61% now disapproving of his leadership." This is the American government's war, but it is not the American people's war. The same is true of any of our government's wars. If we were invaded by foreign troops, an armed American populace (except in cities with draconian gun control laws) would rise up to repel the invaders. The U.S. military would not be of much help since so many of our troops are overseas.

I am very surprised that this statement by Buchanan has only garnered a little attention. He made the comments in reply to Democratic strategist Bob Shrum on the MSNBC Hardblogger site. Buchanan also said this:

> And while American soldiers have not lost a single battle, we are not winning the war. But this, it seems to me, is not cause for gloating or mockery of the president. The question is: What do we do now? How do we bring our troops home with honor, and leave behind in Iraq something that does not dishonor their sacrifice. If running for the exit ramp would do that, I would favor it, but I do not believe it.

Mockery would be too good for this president. Bush deserves far worse.

There is no way to bring our troops home with honor. The damage has already been done. The death and destruction that our troops have wrought in Iraq has dishonored America for years to come. The best thing U.S. troops could do is run for the "exit ramp," as long as it is done in a safe, reasonable, timely, and just manner, as I have described in my exit plan.

Yes, the war in Iraq is Bush's war. But it is also Sean Hannity's war, Rush Limbaugh's war, Michael Savage's war, Bill O'Reilly's war, and Neal Boortz's war. It is David Frum's war, Max Boot's war, Jonah Goldberg's war, Lawrence Kaplan's war, and Bill Kristol's war. It is the war of the *Wall Street Journal*, *National Review*, The Claremont Institute, and the *Weekly Standard*. It is Donald Rumsfeld's war, Dick Cheney's war, Lewis Libby's war, Douglas Feith's war, Paul Wolfowitz's war, Condoleezza Rice's war, and Richard Pearle's war. And yes, it is also the war of Jerry Falwell, Cal Thomas, James Dobson, Pat Robertson, Ralph Reed, Donald Wildmon, Tim LaHaye, D. James Kennedy, John Hagee, and other so-called Christian leaders who serve as both apologists and cheerleaders for the Republican Party.

But it's not my war!

* * * * *

DO THEY THINK IT'S WORTH IT?

"The work in Iraq is difficult and it is dangerous. Like most Americans, I see the images of violence and bloodshed. Every picture is horrifying, and the suffering is real. Amid all this violence, I know Americans ask the question: Is the sacrifice worth it? It is worth it, and it is vital to the future security of our country." ~ President Bush

The president uttered these words before a friendly audience at Fort Bragg, North Carolina—not in front of a crowd of wounded U.S. troops. The official number of these troops is 16,155, although unofficial estimates range up to almost 50,000. It is easy for Mr. Bush and supporters of this war, both inside and outside the government, to say that it's worth it. But perhaps we should get another opinion. Why don't we ask the wounded U.S. troops if they think it's worth it?

This twenty-year-old young man was trapped for twenty minutes in a fiery ammunition truck in Iraq. He was left with disfiguring burns on his face, head, arms and legs. This is what he looks like after more than two dozen surgeries. Does he think it's worth it? For the rest of his life kids will laugh at him and call him Frankenstein or a freak. For the rest of his life he will have to look at his face in the mirror in the morning. For the rest of his life people will silently stare at him—thinking that he reminds them of someone they saw in a horror movie. Finding a girlfriend or even a job will be a difficult thing. Does he think the war in Iraq is worth the price of his face?

This soldier lost his left hand and will probably lose his right arm. Does he think it's worth it? For the rest of his life he will not be able to open a door or a can of coke. For the rest of his life he will not be able to go to the bathroom by himself. For the rest of his life he will not be able to turn on the radio or type an e-mail. Picking up his kids, if he ever has any, will be very difficult. Does he think the war in Iraq is worth the price of his hands?

This soldier will have to have his feet removed. Does he think it's worth it? For the rest of his life he will not be able to walk or drive a car. For the rest of his life he will not be able to participate in any sports. For the rest of his life he will be confined to a wheelchair. Running and playing with his kids, if he ever has any, will be impossible. Does he think the war in Iraq is worth the price of his feet?

The Pentagon frowns on photographers and the press from seeing, watching, or taking photos of wounded U.S. troops arriving from Iraq via Ramstein Air Base in Germany and being transported to Walter Reed Army Medical Center and Bethesda Naval Medical Center. What if the American people were allowed to see thousands of pictures of wounded U.S. troops instead of just the three I have included here? What if they could see the grieving parents, spouses, children, and friends that God sees? How quickly public opinion would be turned against Bush and his war!

A month before Bush made his Fort Bragg speech in which he said the Iraq war was worth it, a CNN/USA Today/Gallup poll recorded that 57 percent of those polled said they did not believe it was worth going to war in Iraq, versus 41 percent who said it was. As more and more Americans conclude that the war is not worth it, both in lives and in dollars, Bush's approval rating goes down further and further. We can only hope that these numbers continue on their upward and downward paths until the former number reaches one hundred and the latter number reaches zero. But until that day comes, how many more faceless, handless, and feetless soldiers will have to suffer?

There is a group of U.S. troops that we can't ask about the war being worth it. They died for a lie. They will never enjoy the finer things in life like eating a good meal, walking on the beach, visiting a museum, or relaxing under a shade tree. They will no longer know the love of a parent, a spouse, or a child. They will never have any more children and will never see their grandchildren. They will never buy a house, retire from a job, or take a vacation. They're dead Mr. Bush. Do they think the war in Iraq was worth their life?

The president now acknowledges that he is "responsible for the decision to go into Iraq." This means that he is responsible for the scarred faces, the missing hands, the missing feet, and the coffins of dead Americans. Will there be any repercussions? Perhaps not in this life, but certainly at the Judgment.

* * * * *

IS ANYONE LISTENING?

They should know better. Supporters of this war, apologists for this war, defenders of this war, participants in this war—they should all know better. The evidence is there, but is anyone listening?

Democrats, Republicans, Libertarians, Objectivists—they should know better. Catholics, Protestants, Evangelicals, Fundamentalists, Jews—they should know better. Ministers, teachers, doctors, managers, fast food workers, housewives should know better. Marines, soldiers, sailors, airmen, guardsmen, and reservists—they should know better. Flag wavers, patriots, veterans, yellow ribbon wearers, "God and country" and "God bless America" Christians—they should know better. All Americans should know better. The evidence is there, but is anyone listening?

They have the word of Pentagon insiders. They have the word of Bush administration insiders. They have the word of the Army War College. They have the word of army generals. They have the word of members of Congress. They have the word of the Founding Fathers. They have the word of war veterans. They have the word of Iraq war veterans. They have the word of the vice president. They even have the word of the president himself. The evidence is there, but is anyone listening?

Karen Kwiatkowski retired as a USAF lieutenant colonel after spending her final four and a half years working at the Pentagon. She accelerated her retirement "because of the ethical difficulties brought on by witnessing the misuse of intelligence in order to support an agenda for an unnecessary, unwarranted war of choice against Iraq." She describes the current U.S. military and civilian leadership as "politicized, emasculated, obedient to the bureaucracy and ignorant of the Constitution." Is anyone listening to Colonel Kwiatkowski?

Lawrence Wilkerson, a former colonel in the U.S. Army, a decorated Vietnam vet, and a life-long Republican who served as chief of staff to former Secretary of State Colin Powell, has recently stated that Powell's February 2003 speech before the United Nations that sought to justify the impending war against Iraq was "a hoax on the American people, the international community, and the United Nations Security Council." He further stated that "there were major doubts inside the intelligence community about everything that was being said about the Iraq threat, even as Powell's speech was being planned and delivered."

Jeffrey Record, a professor in the Department of Strategy and International Security at the U.S. Air Force's Air War College in Montgomery, Alabama, and former professional staff member of the Senate Armed Services Committee, writes in *Bounding the Global War on Terrorism*, published by the Strategic Studies Institute of the Army War College, that the war in Iraq "has created a new front in the Middle East for Islamic terrorism and diverted attention and resources away from securing the American homeland against further assault by an undeterrable al-Qaeda." The nature and parameters of the global war on terror (GWOT) "remain frustratingly unclear." The declared objectives of the GWOT are "unrealistic." The goals of the GWOT are "politically, fiscally, and militarily unsustainable." The GWOT is "strategically unfocused, promises much more than it can deliver, and threatens to dissipate scarce U.S. military and other means over too many ends." Is anyone listening to Professor Record?

Lieutenant General William Odom (Ret.) calls the war in Iraq "the greatest strategic disaster in our history, not in terms of its present body count, but rather because of its radiating consequences for the region and the world." Invading Iraq "was never in the U.S.' interests and has not become so." Brigadier General Andrew Gatsis (Ret.), who was awarded numerous medals for bravery during the Korean and Vietnam Wars, says about the war:

> We never should have gone in there in the first place since we weren't immediately threatened. There were no weapons of mass destruction; Saddam Hussein's regime had no connection to Osama bin Laden and al-Qaeda, and wasn't responsible for the attacks on the Pentagon and the World Trade Center; and there wasn't any evidence to back up the claim that Iraq was building nuclear weapons capability. All the reasons given by the administration to justify this war have been shown to be false.
>
> We invaded a country that posed no threat to us. What's different

about what we have done in Iraq and what Hitler did when he sent his forces into Czechoslovakia in 1939? This war in Iraq has already cost the lives of 2,200 Americans, wounded over 15,000 more, and left at least 30,000 Iraqis dead, most of whom were non-combatants caught in crossfires or victimized by Islamist terrorists. And look at the billions of dollars being poured into this flawed effort. It saddens me to see all of this happen to our troops—and all for an unjust cause.

Is anyone listening to these generals?

Representative John Murtha (D–Penn.), a decorated Marine combat veteran and the first Vietnam veteran elected to Congress, has recently called for the withdrawal of American forces from Iraq, concluding that the war has increased both terrorism and instability in the Middle East. He now terms the war "a flawed policy wrapped in illusion." On the Republican side of the aisle, there is the heroic Representative Ron Paul (R–Tex.), an Air Force veteran who has opposed the war from the beginning. Is anyone listening to these congressmen?

The Founding Fathers of this country issued numerous warnings about the dangers of wars. We know that Thomas Jefferson said: "Never was so much false arithmetic employed on any subject, as that which has been employed to persuade nations that it is their interest to go to war." But let's hear the "father of the Constitution," James Madison, on how the state uses war to strip its citizens of their liberties:

> If tyranny and oppression come to this land, it will be in the guise of fighting a foreign enemy.

> The means of defense against foreign danger historically have become the instruments of tyranny at home.

> Of all the enemies to public liberty, war is perhaps the most to be dreaded because it comprises and develops the germ of every other. War is the parent of armies; from these proceed debts and taxes; and armies, and debts, and taxes are the known instruments for bringing the many under the domination of the few.

> The loss of liberty at home is to be charged to the provisions against danger, real or imagined, from abroad.

Is anyone listening to the Founding Fathers?

Veterans for Peace, which includes veterans from World War II, Korea, Vietnam, the Gulf War, and other conflicts, as well as peacetime veterans, is calling for the impeachment of President Bush and Vice-President Cheney. In a letter sent to each member of Congress, Veterans for Peace stated that "this administration's war on Iraq, in addition to being increasingly unpopular among Americans, is an unmistakable violation of our Constitution and federal law which you have sworn to uphold. In our system, the remedy for such high crimes is clear: this administration must be impeached." The president of the group further says that "we believe that when our government conducts a war of aggression on Iraq and commits a growing and appalling series of what must legally be considered war crimes and crimes against humanity in the execution of that war, it violates Article VI of the U.S. Constitution, the War Crimes Act of 1996 (18 U.S.C. § 2441), and numerous international treaties which are legally binding on our nation."

Tim Goodrich, one of the founders of Iraq Veterans Against the War, charges the president with "deceit, lack of planning, and arrogance." He says that

> for a real victory plan, the best course of action would be an immediate withdrawal of our troops from Iraq. Our continued presence only serves to fuel terrorism, not defeat it. Not only would an immediate withdrawal prevent the unnecessary deaths of more of our country's honorable military personnel, but it would also increase the security of our nation by allowing our troops to do what they signed up for; defending the country.

Is anyone listening to Iraq war veterans?

After the First Gulf War, then secretary of defense and now vice president, Dick Cheney, in a speech at the Washington Institute for Near East Policy in April of 1991, said about Saddam Hussein and Iraq:

> I think that the proposition of going to Baghdad is also fallacious. I think if we were going to remove Saddam Hussein we would have had to go all the way to Baghdad, we would have to commit a lot of force because I do not believe he would wait in the Presidential Palace for us to arrive. I think we'd have had to hunt him down. And once we'd done that and we'd gotten rid of Saddam Hussein and his government, then we'd have had to put another government in its place.
>
> What kind of government? Should it be a Sunni government or Shi'i government or a Kurdish government or Ba'athist regime? Or maybe we want to bring in some of the Islamic fundamentalists? How long would we have had to stay in Baghdad to keep that

government in place? What would happen to the government once U.S. forces withdrew? How many casualties should the United States accept in that effort to try to create clarity and stability in a situation that is inherently unstable?

I think it is vitally important for a President to know when to use military force. I think it is also very important for him to know when not to commit U.S. military force. And it's my view that the President got it right both times, that it would have been a mistake for us to get bogged down in the quagmire inside Iraq.

Cheney also made a speech in Seattle at the Discovery Institute in 1992, and said:

And the question in my mind is how many additional American casualties is Saddam worth?

And the answer is not very damned many. So I think we got it right, both when we decided to expel him from Kuwait, but also when the president made the decision that we'd achieved our objectives and we were not going to go get bogged down in the problems of trying to take over and govern Iraq.

All of a sudden you've got a battle you're fighting in a major built-up city, a lot of civilians are around, significant limitations on our ability to use our most effective technologies and techniques.

Once we had rounded him up and gotten rid of his government, then the question is what do you put in its place? You know, you then have accepted the responsibility for governing Iraq.

Now what kind of government are you going to establish? Is it going to be a Kurdish government, or a Shi'ia government, or a Sunni government, or maybe a government based on the old Baathist Party, or some mixture thereof? You will have, I think by that time, lost the support of the Arab coalition that was so crucial to our operations over there.

I would guess if we had gone in there, I would still have forces in Baghdad today, we'd be running the country. We would not have been able to get everybody out and bring everybody home.

Is anyone listening to the vice president? Is the vice president even listening to himself?

As the whole world now knows, and President Bush has himself acknowledged, two of the major reasons given for undertaking this war in the first place were simply not true. Iraq was not responsible for the September 11th attacks. "We have no evidence that Saddam Hussein was involved with September the 11th," said the president in answer to a reporter's question on September 17, 2003, after hundreds of U.S. soldiers had already died for a lie. There were no weapons of mass destruction. "It is true that most of the intelligence turned out to be wrong," said Mr. Bush in a speech on December 14, 2005, at the Woodrow Wilson Center in Washington, D.C., after the death count had by then passed the 2,000 mark. Is anyone listening to the president? Are any soldiers listening to their commander in chief?

I am afraid that too many people have the same mindset as the president, who says that even "knowing what I know today, I'd make the decision again. Removing Saddam Hussein makes this world a better place and America a safer country."

Since human lives are at stake—American lives and the lives of the U.S. government's enemy of the week—those in the military ought to be more diligent than the average American in finding out about the justness of a war. And American soldiers who claim to be Christians ought to be even more thorough in their investigation. Is anyone in the military listening?

* * * * *

WEAPONS OF MASS DISTRACTION

> "Saddam Hussein is a man who told the world he wouldn't have weapons of mass destruction, but he's got them." ~ President Bush, November 3, 2002

> "Simply stated, there is no doubt that Saddam Hussein now has weapons of mass destruction. There is no doubt he is amassing them to use against our friends, against our allies, and against us." ~ Vice President Dick Cheney, August 26, 2002

It was three years ago, on March 20, 2003, and 2,317 American soldiers' lives ago, that the United States invaded Iraq and launched an unconstitutional, unjust, illegal, immoral, and unnecessary war of aggression because of Iraq's "weapons of mass destruction." But as everyone now knows, except for a few diehard armchair warriors, Bush the Messiah apologists, Republican Party loyalists, and pathetic Christian warmongers who refuse to acknowledge the facts, Iraq neither had any of these weapons nor was in a position to threaten anyone with them.

In the "Authorization for Use of Military Force Against Iraq Resolution of 2002," which passed the House on October 10 by a vote of 296-133, passed the Senate the next day by a vote of 77-23, and was signed into law (PL 107-243) by President Bush on October 16, there are six references to Iraq's "weapons of mass destruction":

> Whereas Iraq, in direct and flagrant violation of the cease-fire, attempted to thwart the efforts of weapons inspectors to identify and destroy *Iraq's weapons of mass destruction* stockpiles and development capabilities,

> Whereas in 1998 Congress concluded that *Iraq's* continuing *weapons of mass destruction* programs threatened vital United States interests and international peace and security,

> Whereas the current *Iraqi* regime has demonstrated its capability and willingness to use *weapons of mass destruction* against other nations and its own people;

> Whereas *Iraq's* demonstrated capability and willingness to use weapons of mass destruction,

> Whereas United Nations Security Council Resolution 678 authorizes the use of all necessary means to enforce United Nations Security Council Resolution 660 and subsequent relevant resolutions and to compel *Iraq* to cease certain activities that threaten international peace and security, including the development of *weapons of mass destruction* and refusal or obstruction of United Nations weapons inspections

> Whereas the United States is determined to prosecute the war on terrorism and *Iraq's* ongoing support for international terrorist groups combined with its development of *weapons of mass destruction* in direct violation of its obligations under the 1991 cease-fire and other United Nations Security Council resolutions

But it was all a lie. There were no weapons of mass destruction (unless you count the weapons the United States sold Iraq in the 1980s when Saddam Hussein was our "friend").

According to the Duelfer Report—the final report on Iraq's weapons of mass destruction by the Pentagon and CIA organized Iraq

Survey Group—Iraq had no deployable weapons of mass destruction on the eve of the U.S. invasion in March 2003, and had not produced any since 1991.

Bush's callous response to the continued absence of weapons of mass destruction was a comedy routine at the March 2004 Radio and Television Correspondents Association Dinner in which photos were shown of the president looking for weapons of mass destruction in the Oval Office and saying: "Those weapons of mass destruction have got to be somewhere." Although there was much laughter at the president's remarks, some people were not laughing.

Iraq's weapons of mass destruction were nothing more than weapons of mass distraction.

The president laughed because the weapons of mass destruction were just a ruse. It was old news before the Downing Street Memo was made public that Bush wanted to invade Iraq soon after the September 11th attacks, despite his father's warning:

> Trying to eliminate Saddam, extending the ground war into an occupation of Iraq, would have violated our guideline about not changing objectives in midstream, engaging in "mission creep," and would have incurred incalculable human and political costs. . . . We would have been forced to occupy Baghdad and, in effect, rule Iraq. . . . There was no viable "exit strategy" we could see, violating another of our principles. Furthermore, we had been consciously trying to set a pattern for handling aggression in the post Cold War world. Going in and occupying Iraq, thus unilaterally exceeding the United Nations' mandate, would have destroyed the precedent of international response to aggression that we hoped to establish. Had we gone the invasion route, the United States could conceivably still be an occupying power in a bitterly hostile land (George H. W. Bush, *A World Transformed*, 1999, p. 489).

The case has even been made that the die was cast at the first meeting of the new National Security Council in January of 2001 after Bush assumed the office of president. From then on it was merely a question of when, not if, the invasion of Iraq would take place.

But even before Bush was elected, the September 2000 publication, *Rebuilding America's Defenses: Strategies, Forces and Resources For A New Century*, by the neocon Project for the New American Century (PNAC), shows that the attack on September 11th merely provided an "opportunity" for the United States to take military control of the Middle

East. September 11th was the Bush administration's "Pearl Harbor." The roots of this go back, not just to the need for a new enemy after the demise of the Cold War (first Saddam Hussein, and now militant Islam), but to the U.S. government's overthrow of the democratically elected prime minister of Iran in 1953.

But what if Iraq did possess those dreaded weapons of mass destruction? Would possession alone have justified the U.S. invasion? Would possession in conjunction with other factors have justified the U.S. invasion?

Absolutely not.

Let's make this easy and focus on just the most lethal of all weapons of mass destruction—nuclear weapons. Even if Iraq possessed nuclear weapons, there is absolutely no reason why the United States would be justified in attacking and invading a sovereign country—no matter what we thought of that country's ruler, system of government, economic policies, religious intolerance, or human rights record.

First of all, who is the United States to say that a country should or shouldn't have nuclear weapons? When did the countries of the world appoint America to be the world's policeman, legislator, guardian, or sovereign?

Second, there are four countries which are not signers of the Nuclear Non-Proliferation Treaty: India, Pakistan, Israel, and North Korea (North Korea initially ratified but then withdrew from the treaty in 2003). All four of these countries have nuclear weapons, although Israel has not publicly acknowledged the extent of its nuclear capabilities. When is the United States going to attack and invade these countries to remove their stockpiles of nuclear weapons?

Third, there are four countries (France, China, Russia, & the UK) besides the United States which are permitted by the Nuclear Non-Proliferation Treaty to have nuclear weapons (because they possessed them at the time the treaty was promulgated). Why does the United States tolerate the massive amount of nuclear weapons in those countries and at the same time worry about some other country acquiring a few nuclear warheads? It can't be because those four countries are "friends" of the United States. Only the United Kingdom can be so classified. And now some warmongers want us to go to war with Iran, which has signed and never violated the Nuclear Non-Proliferation Treaty.

Fourth, every country in the world is justified in obtaining nuclear weapons to protect themselves against the one country that was the first county to develop nuclear weapons, the only county to use nuclear weapons, and the country that has the largest stockpile of nuclear weapons—the United States of America.

But, say the aforementioned armchair warriors, Bush apologists, Republican loyalists, and Christian warmongers, the difference between Iraq and all these other countries is that Iraq was a threat to the United States, its neighbors in the Middle East, and the state of Israel. First of all, the idea that Iraq was in any way a threat to the United States (other than by switching its oil export currency to euros) is so ludicrous that I will not waste any keyboard strokes to discuss it. Second, Iraq was a shell of a country after years of sanctions, with no navy or air force and an army that was considerably weaker than it was during the first Persian Gulf War. And third, Israel had enough tanks, ships, submarines, armored fighting vehicles, helicopter gunships, combat aircraft, bombs, rockets, missiles, heavy guns, and enough other assorted weaponry to destroy Iraq many times over if Saddam Hussein actually posed a credible threat to Israel's security.

By distracting the American people with the red herring of weapons of mass destruction, Bush and company were able to garner the support of the majority of the American public for what has turned out to be an absolute disaster for Iraqi people and a quagmire for the United States. We can only hope and pray that Bush leaves office in disgrace—preferably before January 19, 2009, the last full day of his second term.

* * * * *

DYING FOR A LIE

> "A thing is not necessarily true because a man dies for it." ~ Oscar Wilde

All Americans know that Memorial Day is a federal holiday. Most Americans know that it commemorates U. S. soldiers who died in military service for their country. Many Americans believe that U. S. soldiers died defending our freedoms. Few Americans believe that they died for a lie.

Memorial Day was first observed in honor of Union soldiers who died during the War to Prevent Southern Independence. It was initially called Decoration Day because the tombs of the dead soldiers were decorated. Originally celebrated in select localities (to this day several cities claim to be the birthplace of Memorial Day, although the federal government recognizes Waterloo, NY, as the official birthplace), the holiday was first widely observed on May 30, 1868, because of an earlier proclamation by General John Logan of the Grand Army of the Republic, an organization of Union veterans:

> The 30th of May, 1868, is designated for the purpose of strewing with flowers, or otherwise decorating the graves of comrades who died in defense of their country during the late rebellion, and whose bodies now lie in almost every city, village, and hamlet churchyard in the land. In this observance no form of ceremony is prescribed, but posts and comrades will in their own way arrange such fitting services and testimonials of respect as circumstances may permit.

New York, in 1873, was the first state to officially recognize the holiday. After World War I, the holiday was expanded to include U. S. soldiers who died in any war. Until this time, Southern states did not observe the holiday: they preferred to honor their Confederate dead on separate days. Although Congress in 1971 declared Memorial Day to be a national holiday celebrated on the last Monday in May, to this day some Southern states still maintain a day to honor their Confederate dead.

The focus this Memorial Day will be on those men and women who have died in the current Iraq war, although it is likely that only a small minority of Americans realize that 2,464 U.S. soldiers have died thus far. The 117,000 U.S. soldiers who died in that war to end all wars, World War I, are ancient history. Few can name even one of the 405,000 U.S. soldiers who died in that "good war," World War II, so that Eastern Europe could be turned over to the mass murderer Stalin. The 54,000 U.S. soldiers who died in what is called America's forgotten war, the Korean War, are certainly long forgotten. The 58,000 U.S. soldiers who died in Vietnam so their names could be inscribed on a wall are remembered by very few.

They died in vain; they died for a lie.

This does not mean that they were not brave, heroic, well-meaning, or patriotic. They may have fought with the best of intentions; they may have sacrificed themselves for others; they may have been sincere in their belief that they were fighting for a good cause; but they died for a lie.

The first lie is that war is necessary. After commanding forces that firebombed Tokyo, which killed as many civilians as the atomic bomb dropped a few months later, General Curtis LeMay remarked: "We knew we were going to kill a lot of women and kids when we burned that town. Had to be done." But regardless of what happened beforehand, or what might have happened in the future, since when does slaughtering 100,000 people at one time ever have to be done? War should not be considered as an alternative; it is always the worst possible solution. As psychologist

Alfred Adler has said: "War is not the continuation of politics with different means, it is the greatest mass-crime perpetrated on the community of man." War is not inevitable; it is never an absolute necessity. As Adler's successor Lydia Sicher once said: "Wars are inevitable... as long as we believe that wars are inevitable. The moment we don't believe it anymore it is not inevitable."

The second lie is that it is the people in a country that want war. Surprisingly, it was Ronald Reagan who recognized that "governments make wars, not people." It is up to the government to convince its citizens that the citizens of another country are "the enemy." After all, as one columnist remarked: "When people have friends and customers in other lands, they tend to take a dim view of their government dropping bombs on them." Governments abuse the concept of patriotism to convince the populace that "the enemy" should be bombed, maimed, and killed. Hermann Goering recognized that all a government has to do to get the people to support a war is to "denounce the pacifists for lack of patriotism and exposing the country to danger." Real patriotism is not wanting to see the blood of your country's soldiers shed in some desert or jungle halfway around the world fighting the enemy of the week, month, or year. Patriotism, as Charles de Gaulle explained, "is when love of your own people comes first; nationalism, when hate for people other than your own comes first." It is the old men who make wars, and then send the young men to fight them; it is the members of Congress with no children in the military who agitate for war.

The third lie is that there are winners and losers in a war. No side ever really wins a war. As Jeannette Rankin, the only member of Congress to vote against U.S. entry into both World Wars, said: "You can no more win a war than you can win an earthquake." Every side loses something in a war. English mystery writer, Agatha Christie, certainly showed more wisdom than most members of Congress when she said: "One is left with the horrible feeling now that war settles nothing; that to win a war is as disastrous as to lose one." The consequences of a war are never as expected. One reason, as recognized by Thomas Jefferson, is that "war is an instrument entirely inefficient toward redressing wrong; and multiplies, instead of indemnifying losses."

The fourth lie is that war can be good for a nation's economy. This myth of war prosperity was exploded by Ludwig von Mises: "War prosperity is like the prosperity that an earthquake or a plague brings. The earthquake means good business for construction workers, and cholera improves the business of physicians, pharmacists, and undertakers; but no one has for that reason yet sought to celebrate earthquakes and cholera as stimulators of the productive forces in the general interest." More recently, Robert Higgs has called this "The Fallacy that Won't Die." But didn't unemployment fall during World War II? Of course it did. How could it not fall when the government conscripted 16 million men into the armed forces? But what about GDP during World War II? Naturally, it increased, but only because of the increased output of military goods and services. Tell the grieving parents of their only son, who never gave them any grandchildren, about how much greater their standard of living will now be because of the war that took their son.

The fifth lie is that the U.S. military defends our freedoms. The military is too busy policing the world to defend our freedoms. We have U.S. troops in 155 countries or territories of the world. How are the 69,395 U.S. troops in Germany defending our freedoms? How are the 35,307 U.S. troops in Japan defending our freedoms? How are the 32,744 U.S. troops in Korea defending our freedoms? How are the 12,258 U.S. troops in Italy defending our freedoms? How are the 11,093 U.S. troops in the United Kingdom defending our freedoms? How are the _____ U.S. troops in _____ defending our freedoms? To appease his conservative base on the illegal immigration issue, President Bush recently called for the stationing of some National Guard troops along the border with Mexico. The National Guard units that have been deployed to Iraq should not be assigned to guard the Mexican border. They should be sent home to their jobs and their families, and only used for genuine emergencies on U.S. soil. Stationing U.S. soldiers along the Mexican border would be defending our freedoms a thousand times more than putting them along any German or Italian border.

Contrary to these lies, the truth about war, in the words of Major General Smedley Butler, is that "war is a racket. It always has been. It is possibly the oldest, easily the most profitable, surely the most vicious." Ambrose Bierce once made a callous statement about war that nevertheless comes to pass whenever the United States intervenes in another country: "War is God's way of teaching Americans geography."

The aphorism that truth is the first casualty of war has often been spoken but rarely learned from. This is because, as Charles Lindbergh said: "In a time of war, truth is always replaced by propaganda." This war in particular was started and maintained by more government lies than perhaps any other war in our history.

What were our objectives in this war? Finding weapons of mass destruction? Finding chemical and biological weapons? Removing Saddam Hussein? Imposing democracy to Iraq? Bringing stability to the Middle East? Forcing Iraq to comply with UN resolutions? Protecting the nation of Israel? Dismantling al-Qaeda? Freeing Muslim women from oppression? Enforcing the no-fly zone imposed on Iraq after the first Persian Gulf War?

If one stated objective was found to be a lie another could quickly be offered in its place. The number and scope of these objectives shows that there were no legitimate obtainable objectives. So why did we invade and occupy Iraq? I call your attention to two documents. Just two. Both of these documents are readily available online.

The first document is called *Uncovering the Rationales for the War on Iraq: The Words of the Bush Administration, Congress, and the Media from September 12, 2001 to October 11, 2002.* It was written by Devon M. Largio in 2004 as a thesis for a bachelor's degree in political science at the University of Illinois. It is a total of 212 pages. Print it out and read it in its entirety. If you don't have time to read it right now then at least read her executive summary. Largio documents twenty-seven rationales given for the war by the Bush administration, war hawks in Congress, and the media between the September 11th attacks and the October 2002 congressional resolution to use force in Iraq. It was "the Bush administration, and the President himself" that "established the majority of the rationales for the war and all of those rationales that make up the most prominent reasons for war." The result of this investigation shows that Bush is a bigger liar than Clinton ever was, and, even worse, his lies are more deadly.

The second document is called *Iraq on the Record: The Bush Administration's Public Statements on Iraq.* It was prepared for Representative Henry Waxman (D–Calif.) by the U.S. House of Representatives Committee on Government Reform—Minority Staff, Special Investigations Division. It is dated March 16, 2004. It is a total of 36 pages. Print it out and read it in its entirety. An executive summary appears on pages *i–iv.* The report is "a comprehensive examination of the statements made by the five Administration officials most responsible for providing public information and shaping public opinion on Iraq: President George Bush, Vice President Richard Cheney, Defense Secretary Donald Rumsfeld, Secretary of State Colin Powell, and National Security Advisor Condoleezza Rice." Here is the report's conclusion:

> Because of the gravity of the subject and the President's unique access to classified information, members of Congress and the public expect the President and his senior officials to take special care to be balanced and accurate in describing national security threats. It does not appear, however, that President Bush, Vice President Cheney, Secretary Rumsfeld, Secretary Powell, and

National Security Advisor Rice met this standard in the case of
Iraq. To the contrary, these five officials repeatedly made misleading statements about the threat posed by Iraq. In 125 separate
appearances, they made 11 misleading statements about the
urgency of Iraq's threat, 81 misleading statements about Iraq's
nuclear activities, 84 misleading statements about Iraq's chemical
and biological capabilities, and 61 misleading statements about
Iraq's relationship with al Qaeda.

Every U.S. soldier who died in Iraq died for a lie. They may have
died for Bush, Cheney, Rumsfeld, Rice, the U.S. global empire, the U.S.
government, the military-industrial complex, or Halliburton, but none of
them died for the American people or our freedoms.

If they died for a lie, then the liars should be held accountable. But
don't look for Congress to do anything. How can we expect a Congress
that continues to fund this war to hold the Bush administration accountable for its lies? Every member of Congress that continues to vote to fund
this war is complicit in these lies. How many more dead American
soldiers and billions of dollars will it take before Congress finally says
enough is enough? How many American soldiers not currently in Iraq
who are enjoying this Memorial Day holiday will be sent to Iraq to die for
a lie before the next observance of Memorial Day?

* * * * *

Fifty-Four Dead Women

Dead women. Fifty-four dead women. Has it really come to this?
We know that American women die everyday. They die in hospitals,
nursing homes, bedrooms, and cars. They die by accident, disease,
murder, suicide, or natural causes. But why should any American women
die in Iraq fighting a war?

Yes, women. It is horrible enough when young men in the prime of
their life have their arms and legs torn to shreds because of an encounter
with an "improvised explosive device," but it is absolutely hideous that
we as a country countenance young women—young American women,
some of them with children—dying the same grisly type of death. True,
they enlisted in the military of their own free will. But where are the
fathers, the brothers, and the pastors of these misguided and impressionable girls? What kind of slime do we have for military recruiters that
would prey on these women?

As I have argued many, many times before, no American

soldiers—men or women—should be fighting in Iraq in the first place. Some Americans are aware that 2,475 U.S. soldiers have been killed in Iraq; few Americans probably realize that 54 of them were women.

The following table lists all of the women who have been killed to date in the Iraq war. The date given is the date of death, beginning with the most recent. Clicking the link on the name will bring up the official DOD news release about the woman's death. Then follows a photo of the dead woman, her rank, her branch of service, and the cause of her death:

04/08/06, NavarroArellano, Juana, 24, Lance Corporal, Marines
    Hostile: small arms fire
03/16/06, Pinson, Amanda N., 21, Sergeant, Army
    Hostile: mortar attack
03/11/06, Duerksen, Amy A., 19, Private 1st Class, Army
    Non-hostile: weapon discharge
03/01/06, Priest, Tina M., 20, Private 1st Class, Army
    Non-hostile: unspecified
01/07/06, Campbell, Jaime L., 25, 1st Lieutenant, National Guard
    Non-hostile: helicopter crash
12/24/05, Maravillosa, Myla L., 24, Sergeant, Army Reserve
    Hostile: RPG attack
12/23/05, Reali, Regina C., 25, Sergeant, Army Reserve
    Hostile: IED attack
12/10/05, Atkins, Julia V., 22, Sergeant, Army
    Hostile: IED attack
10/28/05, Banaszak, Debra A., 35, 1st Lieutenant, National Guard
    Non-hostile: unspecified
09/28/05, Jacobson, Elizabeth Nicole, 21, Airman 1st Class, Air Force
    Hostile: IED attack
08/14/05, Green, Toccara R., 23, Specialist, Army
    Hostile: IED attack
07/19/05, Johnson, Lavena L., 19, Private, Army
    Non-hostile: weapon discharge
07/14/05, Jameson, Tricia L., 34, Staff Sergeant, National Guard
    Hostile: IED attack
06/23/05 Valdez, Ramona M., 20, Corporal, Marines
    Hostile: suicide car bomb
06/23/05 Charette, Holly A., 21, Lance Corporal, Marines
    Hostile: suicide car bomb
06/23/05 Clark, Regina R., 43, Petty Officer 1st Class, Naval
    Hostile: suicide car bomb

06/05/05 French, Carrie L., 19, Specialist, National Guard
    Hostile: IED attack
06/03/05 Villar, Linda J., 41, Civilian, Dept. of the Army
    Hostile: mortar attack
04/18/05 Huff, Sam W., 18, Private 1st Class, Army Reserve
    Hostile: IED attack
04/15/05 Ramirezgonzalez, Aleina, 33, Specialist, Army
    Hostile: mortar attack
03/04/05 Salem, Adriana N., 21, Specialist, Army
    Non-hostile: vehicle accident
03/01/05 Robles, Lizbeth, 31, Specialist, Army
    Non-hostile: vehicle accident
02/16/05 Bell-Johnson, Katrina Lani, 32, Specialist, Army
    Non-hostile: vehicle accident
02/09/05 Housby, Jessica M., 23, Sergeant, National Guard
    Hostile: IED attack
01/29/05 Heald, Barbara, 60, Civilian, Dept. of the Army
    Hostile: rocket attack
12/13/04 Time, Tina Safaira, 22, Sergeant, Army Reserve
    Non-hostile: vehicle accident
12/04/04 Gasiewicz, Cari Anne, 28, Sergeant, Army
    Hostile: IED attack
10/11/04 Osbourne, Pamela G., 38, Sergeant, Army
    Hostile: rocket attack
10/06/04 Cawvey, Jessica L., 21, Specialist, National Guard
    Hostile: IED attack
09/05/04 Morrison, Shawna M., 26, Sergeant, National Guard
    Hostile: mortar attack
07/22/04 Reed, Tatjana, 34, Sergeant, Army
    Hostile: IED attack
07/11/04 Tarango-Griess, Linda, 33, Sergeant 1st Class, National Guard
    Hostile: IED attack
06/06/04 Hobart, Melissa J., 22, Private 1st Class, Army
    Non-hostile: illness
05/20/04 Jackson, Leslie D., 18, Private 1st Class, Army
    Hostile: IED attack
05/08/04 Rubalcava, Isela, 25, Specialist, Army
    Hostile: mortar attack
04/09/04 Witmer, Michelle M., 20, Specialist, National Guard
    Hostile: IED attack
04/07/04 Felder, Tyanna S., 22, Specialist, Army

Hostile: IED attack
03/09/04 Holland, Fern L., 33, Civilian, Dept. of the Army
    Hostile: unspecified
03/07/04 Jones, Gussie M., 41, Captain, Army
    Non-hostile: illness
02/16/04 Frye, Nichole M., 19, Private 1st Class, Army Reserve
    Hostile: IED attack
01/31/04 McGeogh, Holly J., 19, Private 1st Class, Army
    Hostile: IED attack
01/31/04 Hines, Keicia M., 27, Sergeant, Army
    Non-hostile: vehicle accident
01/02/04 Hampton, Kimberly N., 27, Captain, Army
    Hostile: helicopter crash
12/14/03 Voelz, Kimberly A., 27, Staff Sergeant, Army
    Hostile: IED attack
11/08/03 Jimenez, Linda C., 39, Sergeant, Army
    Non-hostile: accident
11/07/03 Swartworth, Sharon T., 43, Chief Warrant Officer, Army
    Hostile: helicopter crash
11/02/03 Vega, Frances M., 20, Specialist, Army
    Hostile: helicopter crash
11/02/03 Lau, Karina S., 20, Private 1st Class, Army
    Hostile: helicopter crash
10/26/03 Bosveld, Rachel K., 19, Private 1st Class, Army
    Hostile: mortar attack
10/01/03 Ramos, Tamarra J., 24, Specialist, Army
    Non-hostile: unspecified
10/01/03 Gutierrez, Analaura Esparza, 21, Private 1st Class, Army
    Hostile: grenade
09/15/03 Peterson, Alyssa R., 27, Specialist, Army
    Non-hostile: weapon discharge
07/09/03 Valles, Melissa, 26, Sergeant, Army
    Non-hostile: weapon discharge
03/23/03 Piestewa, Lori Ann, 23, Private 1st Class, Army
    Hostile: ambush

Along with a pacifist dog and an antiwar weenie, I have been called a coward for not supporting the war in Iraq. But even if the war is necessary, what kind of coward would countenance sending women to their deaths in Iraq when it is not necessary that any women go? If this war is really necessary then why don't members of Congress go and fight or at least encourage their sons to enlist instead of sending women? How many members of the Senate and House Armed Services Committees are even aware of the number of female U.S. soldiers killed in Iraq? What kind of military do we have that sends women to die overseas? What kind of society do we have that would accept a woman with children flying a military helicopter in Iraq or anywhere else? Where were all the Bush apologists, Republican loyalists, Christian warmongers, and other supporters of this war when women were dying in Iraq? I suppose they were seated next to the armchair warriors.

Dead women. Fifty-four dead women. It is a terrible tragedy that we send young men to die in this senseless war in Iraq; it is a horrendous evil that we send young women.

* * * * *

LIMBAUGH LUNACY

Defenders of Bush and his war of aggression in Iraq are getting desperate—and especially their self-appointed leaders. You can tell by the ridiculous arguments that they are beginning to use.

One of the biggest apologists for Bush and the Republican Party is the self-proclaimed "doctor of democracy," Rush Limbaugh. Not only does he believe that the U.S. military in Afghanistan is "doing the Lord's work over here," he is also an outspoken supporter of the war in Iraq. In Limbaugh's mind, opponents of the Iraq war are all leftists. He apparently has little regard for the first amendment when Republicans are in power, for he recently told dissenters: "When our nation is at war, your duty is to support it, not offer your precious little opinion."

On his August 23rd radio talk show (read the complete transcript here), Limbaugh used the most preposterous argument to date in defense of the war in Iraq:

> Now, the number of highway deaths in this country, 43,443 in 2005, is 40 to 50 times our troop losses in Iraq and Afghanistan combined. Well, ten or 20 times at least. And a whole lot more deaths per month than any civil war in Iraq, if there was or is a civil war in Iraq. I don't know whatever happened to "if it bleeds, it leads," but there's a whole lot more bleeding on our highways than in the war zone in Iraq out there, and a whole lot more dying going on in the American highway system than there is in the so-called civil war in Iraq. I don't hear a word from John Kerry who served in Vietnam or John Murtha or Joe Biden or Howard Dean.

For every Cindy Sheehan, there are 40 to 50 mothers who have suffered far worse heartbreak. Cindy's son gave his life for his country, not for going to the drugstore.

In fact, the roadway deaths is at a highest level in 15 years, 43,443 Americans every year, ladies and gentlemen, and we're here turning ourselves into rags, pretzeling ourselves into contortions over the combat deaths in Iraq, regardless and mindless of the heroic mission that is taking place.

This is lunacy in broadcasting. I think Rush's Viagra and Oxy-Contin are having a severe drug interaction. The "highway deaths" argument is so irrational that it almost seems like a waste of time to even consider it. Yet, I have been asked about it several times, even before Limbaugh's most recent use of it.

I have not been a regular listener to Rush's show since the early Clinton years. One of my faithful readers happened to tune in on August 23rd and notified me about Limbaugh's latest pathetic attempt to justify the wars in Iraq and Afghanistan. After reading the transcript of the August 23rd show, I thought of six things that I would say in response to this argument. I am sure that others have or will probably come up with more, but since I was just asked about it, and since many of Rush's loyal dittoheads will now accept and parrot his argument, I thought I would make mine public now.

First, why highway deaths? Why not compare the number of dead U.S. soldiers in Iraq and Afghanistan to the number of deaths in the United States resulting from dog bites or drowning in the bathtub or getting caught in a piece of machinery? The answer should be obvious. War proponents need a high number so as to discount the number of dead U.S. soldiers.

Second, does this mean that if 43,444 U.S. soldiers were to die in Iraq and Afghanistan, because it is one more than were killed in auto accidents, that troop losses would suddenly be too high? Or does it mean that if 43,442 U.S. soldiers were to die, because it is one less than were killed in auto accidents, that troop losses would be acceptable?

Third, if the number of highway deaths is the standard for this war, then what about previous wars? We lost 405,000 U.S. soldiers in that "good war," World War II. I suppose then that since troop losses in World War II exceeded traffic deaths that we should say that World War II was an unjust war.

Fourth, if the number of highway deaths is the standard for this war, then what about future wars? Can we say that as long as traffic deaths exceed battle deaths by at least one that any amount of troop losses is acceptable?

Fifth, how comforting this "highway deaths" argument must be to a mother or father who just lost a son! How it must console a grieving wife who just lost her husband! How it must assuage the anguish of a child who just lost his father! Defenders of Bush's wars wouldn't use such a ridiculous, irrational argument if it was their son or grandson who was killed.

And finally, most traffic deaths in the United States were accidents and could not be prevented. That's why we use the term "auto accidents." But the death of every single U.S. soldier killed in battle Iraq and Afghanistan, including those who died from disease and accidents, was preventable. Every death was preventable because there was no reason for the United States to launch these wars in the first place. The shedding of the blood of even one American is not worth anything "good" that has happened in Iraq or Afghanistan. It is supporters and defenders of Bush's wars who are anti-American. Real patriots don't want to see even one American used as cannon fodder for the state. Real patriots want their country to be admired not scorned. Real patriots want their country to be a blessing to the world instead of a curse.

Rush is wrong: Cindy's son gave his life for a lie. He was bush-whacked.

* * * * *

THEY WON'T BE HOME FOR CHRISTMAS

There are 2,969 Americans who won't be home for Christmas today. They won't be home for Christmas next year either. In fact, they won't ever be home for Christmas again. No, it's not because they're homeless or broke. It's not because they're an atheist or a humbug. And it's not because they're celebrating Hanukkah or Kwanzaa. I'm sure most of them would want to celebrate Christmas with their families, but they can't. Not this year, next year, or any year in the future. The plain truth is they have an irreversible and unalterable condition that prevents them from ever coming home—for Christmas or otherwise.

They're dead.

It would be bad enough if they died of a heart attack or cancer. It would be even worse if they died in a hunting or automobile accident. But these 2,963 Americans didn't die from a disease or an accident. Their deaths were unnecessary even as they were preventable. They didn't die because they were fighting terrorism or defending our freedoms or preserving the American way of life. They died for a lie.

They died for the lie that the United States had the right to institute a regime change in Iraq. They died for the lie that Iraq had weapons of mass destruction. They died for the lie that democracy had to be imposed on Iraq at the point of a gun. They died for the lie that the United States had to force Iraq to comply with UN resolutions. They died for the lie that the Iraqis would greet us as liberators. They died for the lie that Iraq was behind the September 11th attacks. They died for the lie that there was an Iraq–al-Qaeda connection. They died for the lie that Saddam Hussein was the next Hitler. They died for the lie that the United States should launch a preemptive strike. They died for the lie that it is possible to have a global war on terrorism. They died for the lie that the president should be given congressional authorization to use military force against Iraq. They died for the lie that the United States should be the world's policeman. They died for the lie that the United States should have a global empire of troops and bases. They died for the lie that the war in Iraq would be a cakewalk. They died for the lie that we had to fight them over there so we did not have to fight them over here. They died for the lie that Iraq was a threat to the United States.

In spite of all the senseless deaths of American soldiers because of these lies, the war in Iraq is still being defended by Republican Party loyalists, Religious Right zealots, conservative talk show hosts and their duped listeners, and other apologists for the Bush administration like the warmongers who write for the *Wall Street Journal*, the *Weekly Standard*, *National Review*, and RedState.com.

The difference now is that the arguments of warmongers have shifted. The focus is no longer on whether the United States should have gone to war in Iraq, but on whether we should quit waging war (i.e., destroying Iraq and killing Iraqis). The new choruses are: "We can't just cut and run," "Talk of retreat gives comfort to the enemy," "We need to develop an exit strategy," "We owe it to the Iraqi people," "We must stay the course." And of course, there is still the old refrain of "Support our troops."

The war in Iraq is lost. Although the president won't admit that we are losing, he did recently acknowledge: "We're not winning." But the war has been lost for some time now. Even many who supported the initial invasion would agree with those of us who opposed the war from the very beginning that the point has long since passed the place where the United States could claim "victory" in Iraq. That point can now be measured in years. Wasn't it in 2003 that Bush made the claim, in front of a "Mission Accomplished" banner, that "the United States and our allies have prevailed"? Although the death of every American soldier in Iraq has been a tragic waste of human life, every day that this senseless war continues makes the deaths of U.S. servicemen even more of a heartrending tragedy.

The continual stream of dead American soldiers from Iraq, all of whom died an unnecessary death, is similar to the senseless slaughter that occurred in the closing hours of World War I *after the armistice had been signed.*

Rumors of an imminent armistice had been rife for days. Shortly after 5:00 a.m. on November 11, 1918, in a rail car in a dark forest in France, the final draft of the armistice was signed. It was to take effect in the eleventh month, on the eleventh day, at the eleventh hour. Word of the armistice was sent out to commanders on all fronts. The message was transmitted from the Eiffel Tower. The headline of the early edition of the *New York Times* declared: "Armistice Signed, End of the War!" Of course, not everyone in command of troops received word right away, but those that did often sent men to their deaths anyway, as Joseph Persico shows us in *Eleventh Month, Eleventh Day, Eleventh Hour: Armistice Day, 1918, World War I and Its Violent Climax*:

> Of sixteen American divisions engaged on the western front on armistice morning, the commanders of seven judged the war essentially over upon receiving word of the signing and stopped; but the commanders of nine divisions decided that the war must go on until the last minute, with predictable results to the lives entrusted to them.

> Captain Harry Truman, following his orders, had said nothing to the crew of Battery D about an armistice until his watch read precisely 11 A.M.

> As a historian of the division would later put it, "Our regimental wireless had picked up sufficient intercepted messages during the early hours of the morning to make it certain that Armistice had been signed at 5 o'clock that morning; and the fact that the prearranged attack was launched after the Armistice was signed . . . caused sharp criticism of the high command on the part of the troops engaged, who considered the loss of American lives that morning as useless and little short of murder."

> Pershing had known in advance the conditions that Foch would demand of the Germans. Thus, he knew that the enemy would be

compelled within fourteen days to withdraw from territory they now occupied and pull back inside Germany. Consequently, any ground gained between the signing of the armistice and 11 A.M., at whatever cost in lives, would be handed over at no cost within two weeks. Still, Foch had said to keep up the pressure until the last, and Pershing was all too willing to oblige. Before the signing, he too had ordered all attacks planned and in progress to go forward, even those set for November 11. According to Pershing's chief of staff, the objective was "to take every advantage of the situation." After the signing, Pershing merely passed along Foch's order to stop the fighting at 11 A.M. What was to happen in the hours between the signing and the end was not addressed. Pershing, who had no love for the armistice, was not about to tell his subordinates to stop.

After receiving word only to stop at eleven, American commanders found themselves left in a decisional vacuum as to what to do until then. They had two choices: to stop fighting, save lives, and risk censure for not pressing on to the very last; or to keep fighting, spend lives, avoid potential disobedience, and perhaps gain victories, even promotion. To many of the professional caste, the choice was obvious. The approach of a momentous hour in history aroused their competitive instincts. What laurels were yet to be won in the time remaining? Whose final burst to the finish line would be most brilliant? . . . How a general viewed his duty would determine over the final five hours whether a doughboy would live out the normal ages of man or die at the first stage of manhood.

Although strict orders against fraternization were given, "a trade began to flourish as at no time since the Christmas truce of 1914: cigarettes for sausages, chewing gum for rye bread, coffee for chocolate." World War I, which lasted for 1,560 days, averaged every day about 2,250 dead and 5,000 wounded. On the last day of the war, mainly in the six hours after the armistice was signed, Persico conservatively estimates that there were "10,944 casualties, of which 2,738 were deaths." That is more casualties than those on D-Day.

Persico remarks that had Ferdinand Foch, the French chief Allied negotiator, heeded the plea of Matthias Erzberger, the German negotiator who later signed the armistice, "to stop fighting on November 8 while negotiations were under way, likely, 6,750 lives would have been spared and nearly 15,000 maimed, crippled, burned, blinded, and otherwise injured men would instead have gone home whole." Worse yet: "All this sacrifice was made over scraps of land that the Germans, under the armistice, were compelled to surrender within two weeks."

If the fighting had stopped then there might be around today some descendants of George Price, the last Canadian killed in the war, G. E. Ellison, the last Briton killed in the war, Joseph Trebuchon, the last Frenchman killed in the war, and Henry Gunther, the last American killed in the war. Henry died one minute before the armistice took effect. A VFW post in Baltimore honors his memory.

President Bush recently called for more troops to be sent into the Iraq quagmire. The war will require "additional sacrifices" next year, he warned. What he means is that more young men must die because of, as Congressman John Murtha (D–Penn.) has described Bush's war: "A flawed policy wrapped in illusion."

There is no more a vain, wasteful, unnecessary, senseless, preventable death than that of U.S. soldiers dying for a lie in Iraq. Pastors, teachers, and parents should do everything in their power to discourage young people from joining the military. The government pimps known as military recruiters are certainly doing everything in their power to encourage it.

How many families will be told tomorrow by the U.S. government that their father, husband, son, grandson, brother, cousin, uncle, or nephew died in Iraq on Christmas Day? How many fathers, husbands, sons, grandsons, brothers, cousins, uncles, and nephews in the military right now won't be home for Christmas next year? Sadly, I'm afraid, it won't be until one of *their* relatives or friends doesn't make it home for Christmas before many Americans become outraged over this evil war.

* * * * *

FOUR YEARS, FOUR PLANS

"The situation in Iraq is unacceptable to the American people—and it is unacceptable to me." ~ President George W. Bush

As of today, March 20, the debacle that is the war in Iraq has now dragged on for four years. The United States defeated Nazi Germany in less time than we have been fighting ill-equipped terrorists, insurgents, and "ragheads." One would think that if "the situation" was so unacceptable that some significant plans would be made for changing it.

Think again.

Ever since it has became evident that Bush's "Mission Accom-

plished" accomplished nothing in Iraq but more destabilization, disinte-
gration, destruction, and death (over 3,000 American soldiers have now
been killed since Bush proclaimed "Mission Accomplished"—some
mission), there has been a lot of hot air expended from many who initially
supported the war but now say that we need a plan for ending it.

Although its seems as though every politician and pundit has an
idea to end the war, the real plans for ending the war in Iraq can be
reduced to just four.

The Republican Plan

This is a Republican war. Although some Democrats voted for the
"Authorization for Use of Military Force Against Iraq Resolution of
2002," which passed the House by a vote of 296-133, passed the Senate
by a vote of 77-23, and was signed into law (PL 107-243) by President
Bush on October 16, 2002, the Republicans didn't need any Democratic
votes to get the measure passed. Only six principled Republicans in the
House voted against the resolution (John Duncan, John Hostettler, Amo
Houghton, James Leach, Constance Morella, & Ron Paul). Only one
Republican in the Senate voted against it—Lincoln Chafee of Rhode
Island.

The Republican Plan, whether it is termed "stay the course,"
"surge," "escalation," "supporting democracy," "nation building," "new
way forward," or "other options," is a plan to continue the war for some
indefinite period. Sure, say the Republicans, we want to end the war
someday, but since that day might be far into the future, we shouldn't set
any definite dates for withdrawing from Iraq lest the region "descend into
total chaos" or we "embolden radical Muslims" or we "validate the
terrorists' strategy." As the war drags on, additional troops may be sent to
die one year followed by troop withdrawals in the next—it really doesn't
matter. The Republican Plan is a plan that prescribes perpetual war for
perpetual peace.

Many conservatives and Republicans who now say they oppose the
war and want to end it are only saying so because of how badly the war
has turned out. Many of them are already talking about the inevitability
of war with Iran, Syria, North Korea, and other "rogue states" that make
up the "axis of evil." When those wars don't go as planned, these same
conservatives and Republicans may begin opposing them as well, but will
never call for a change in America's belligerent foreign policy.

The vast majority of Republicans in Congress have no principles
other than party loyalty. It doesn't matter what the cause, if a Republican

president says we need to go to war then we must "support the president" and "support the troops."

What would happen if Bush suddenly changed course and announced a total withdrawal of all U.S. forces from Iraq? Limbaugh, Hannity, and the Hannitized dittoheads who hang on their every word would then line up behind the president like cattle before a stunning box. Anyone who then wanted to continue the war would be denounced as a warmonger who was being disloyal to the president.

But are the Democrats any better?

The Democratic Plan

The Democrats who control Congress also have a plan to end the war. See the Republican plan. Really.

Although the Democratic plan might be termed "supporting the troops," "phased withdrawal," "change of mission," "setting benchmarks," "a new direction," "mission shifting," "timetable for troop withdrawal", or "redeployment"—all backed, of course, by nonbinding resolutions—I suspect that most of the Democratic opposition to the war is not out of principle, but out of political considerations. After all, eighty-one Democrats in the House and twenty-nine Democrats in the Senate voted for the "Authorization for Use of Military Force Against Iraq Resolution of 2002."

True, there are a few principled Democrats who have consistently opposed the war from the beginning. Senator Robert Byrd comes to mind, who stated soon after the war began:

> Regarding the situation in Iraq, it appears to this senator that the American people may have been lured into accepting the unprovoked invasion of a sovereign nation, in violation of longstanding International law, under false premises. There is ample evidence that the horrific events of September 11 have been carefully manipulated to switch public focus from Osama bin Laden and Al Qaeda, who masterminded the September 11 attacks, to Saddam Hussein, who did not. The run-up to our invasion of Iraq featured the President and members of his Cabinet invoking every frightening image they could conjure, from mushroom clouds, to buried caches of germ warfare, to drones poised to deliver germ-laden death in our major cities. We were treated to a heavy dose of overstatement concerning Saddam Hussein's direct threat to our freedoms.

Byrd also recently said about Bush's troops surge: "At the outset of this war, the Bush administration believed, apparently, that democracy could be exported through the barrel of a gun. That belief was wrong then; it is wrong still today. Twenty thousand more troops won't make it right."

But as Justin Raimondo wrote after the November elections: "The idea that the Democratic capture of Congress means that we've reclaimed American foreign policy for the people is a charming idea, but unfortunately it is very far from the truth." Not only do the Democrats in Congress have no intention of cutting off funding for the war, they plan to increase funding. Said the chairman of a defense spending panel overseeing war funds, Representative John Murtha (D–Penn.)—who once called Bush's Iraq policy "a flawed policy wrapped in illusion"—"There will be $98 billion for the military part." This is about $5 billion more than what Bush has requested.

No impeachment of Bush, no denouncement of Bush as a war criminal, no slashing of the military budget, no cutting off funding for the war, and no change in America's foreign policy.

The Curtis LeMay Plan

Curtis LeMay (1906–1990) was the infamous Air Force general who was responsible for the fire-bombing of Tokyo during World War II. On the first night alone, sixteen square miles of the city were incinerated and 100,000 people were killed. According to LeMay: "Killing Japanese didn't bother me very much at that time. . . . I suppose if I had lost the war, I would have been tried as a war criminal. . . . Every soldier thinks something of the moral aspects of what he is doing. But all war is immoral and if you let that bother you, you're not a good soldier."

Although he ran for vice president on the Wallace ticket in 1968, LeMay is instead remembered for his approach to the "problem" of North Vietnam: "My solution to the problem would be to tell them frankly that they've got to draw in their horns and stop their aggression, or we're going to bomb them back into the Stone Age."

He also said:

There are no innocent civilians.

If you kill enough of them, they stop fighting.

I think there are many times when it would be most efficient to use nuclear weapons.

So how would the LeMay plan work in Iraq? Simple. First, get every available M1 Abrams tank. Then purchase some Caterpillar D9 armored bulldozers from the Israeli Defense Forces. Next, line up half of the tanks and bulldozers on the southwestern border of Iraq with Saudi Arabia and the other half on the northeastern border of Iraq with Iran. Then it is "Gentlemen, start your engines," followed by every tank and bulldozer slowly moving toward Mesopotamia, destroying everything and everybody that gets in the way.

Am I in favor of this plan? Of course not. Would it be immoral? Absolutely.

The LeMay Plan is a truly bipartisan plan that would please all Democratic/Republican and liberal/conservative warmongers. This is the plan to "unleash hell" that many "Red State" Republicans are wanting. It is a plan of "total war" that General Sherman would be proud of.

The LeMay Plan is a plan that those who follow Objectivism can call their own. It was bad enough when the president of the Ayn Rand Institute, Yaron Brook, advocated back in December of 2004 that the United States military should "be a lot more brutal," "bring this war to the civilians," and turn "Fallujah into dust," but now, writing in the premier issue of the *Objective Standard*, he states:

> Doing whatever is necessary in war means doing whatever is necessary. Once the facts are rationally evaluated, if it is found that using tactical nuclear weapons against Iran's nuclear facilities or flattening Fallujah to end the Iraqi insurgency will save American lives, then these actions are morally mandatory, and to refrain from taking them is morally evil.

The morally evil LeMay plan is a plan that many Americans want or at least wouldn't question, but are afraid to express their support for publicly.

The LeMay Plan is also an ecumenical plan that would please bloodthirsty Christian warmongers who want the U.S. military to do their bidding so they don't have to get their hands dirty. The Christians who write me and say that we should "kill 'em all and let Allah sort 'em out" would be ecstatic. John Hagee and the other members of the Christian axis of evil would jump for joy. Syndicated columnist Cal Thomas, who says that "this war should be stepped up and fought like World War II," would have his wish. It is unfortunate that some Christians would be among the first people to justify such a plan of death and destruction. I have previously examined some reasons why this is so in my article "Killing Heartily in the Name of the Lord."

The Right Plan

The right plan is the immediate withdrawal of all U.S. forces from Iraq. Today. Now. Not when Iraq has a stable government, not when the "sectarian violence" comes to an end, not when the next U.S. president takes office, not next year, not next month, not next week, not tomorrow—today, right now. Could the entire U.S. military leave Iraq today? Of course not. But there are some things that definitely could be done. We could announce to the world that our invasion was a terrible mistake. We could apologize for the death and destruction we caused. We could tell our "coalition partners" that we led them astray. Could all the killing, bombing, and shooting stop today? Yes. Could the troops start packing? Of course. Could every available truck, plane, and ship fuel up and get ready to transport U.S. troops? Certainly.

An immediate withdrawal is the right plan because the war was a grave injustice and a monstrous wrong from the very beginning. We withdrew all of our forces from Lebanon in 1984. We withdrew all of our forces from the Philippines in 1992. We withdrew all of our forces from Somalia in 1994. We can withdraw all our forces from Iraq in 2007.

When I wrote an article last year on the occasion of the third anniversary of the war, I reported that 2,317 American soldiers had died so far in this immoral and unnecessary war. The number is now up to 3,218. How many current and future American soldiers will die before the fifth anniversary comes and goes? Will any of them be your friends or relatives?

* * * * *

THE MORALITY OF THE IRAQ WAR

The following is the unabridged text of my opening remarks in a debate concerning the morality of the Iraq War with Mark Overstreet, vice president and professor at Criswell College in Dallas, Tex. The debate was held on SoapBox Radio on June 9, 2007.

The question of the morality of the Iraq War is not a difficult one. It is, in fact, an open and shut case. The war was immoral from the very beginning. It is still immoral right now. And anything short of immediately withdrawing U.S. troops merely continues the immorality.

The mission of the U.S. military in Iraq can never be moral, just, and consistent with the principles of Christianity. No Christian has any business defending, supporting, or participating in the war in Iraq. If there is any religion that should be opposed to the evils of war it is Christianity. And if there is any group within Christianity that should be the most consistent, the most vocal, and the most scriptural in its opposition to the offensive, preemptive, open-ended, "shock and awe" campaign known as the Iraq War, it is conservative Christians who look to the Bible as their sole authority.

There are a number of reasons why I believe the war in Iraq is immoral. It is immoral because it is not defensive, because of its incredible cost, because 3,500 U.S. soldiers have died for a lie, because of the tremendous death and destruction that we have meted out to Iraqis, and because the state can't sanctify murder.

The war in Iraq is immoral because it is not defensive. The essence of war is killing people and destroying property. It is never moral to kill someone and destroy his property unless one is acting in self-defense. The war in Iraq is anything but self-defense. The United States invaded a sovereign country thousands of miles away that had not attacked us. Before we invaded Iraq, not one American had been killed by an Iraqi since the last time we invaded. But have not the Iraqis killed, injured, or maimed thousands of U.S. soldiers? Of course they have. We would do the same thing to foreign troops that invaded our soil. We can call the invasion of Iraq regime change, nation building, or gunboat diplomacy, but we certainly cannot call it self-defense. But what about the September 11th terrorist attacks? What about them? President Bush himself has acknowledged that Iraq was not behind the September 11th terrorist attacks and was not connected with al-Qaede. A report drawn up by Cheney, Rumsfeld, and Wolfowitz for the Project for the New American Century a year before the 2001 terrorist attacks shows that Bush's minions were waiting for what they called a "new Pearl Harbor" that could be used to justify the United States taking military control of Iraq. But what about Iraq's weapons of mass destruction? Do you mean the weapons the United States sold Iraq during the 1980s when Iraq was our ally or do you mean the non-existent weapons of mass destruction that Bush used to justify invading Iraq before he acknowledged that "most of the intelligence turned out to be wrong"?

The war in Iraq is immoral because of its incredible cost. Although then Secretary of Defense Donald Rumsfeld said that the war would cost $50 billion, it is now costing the American taxpayers over $200 million a day. Congress just appropriated $100 billion to continue fighting the war this year. The final cost of the war is projected to be has high as $2 trillion. And who knows what the cost will be to provide a lifetime of medical care to the thousands of wounded and mangled U.S. troops. There comes a time when it must be said that enough is enough. With the national debt fast approaching $9 trillion, this is a war that we cannot afford.

The war in Iraq is immoral because 3,500 U.S. soldiers have died for a lie. The U.S. military does not defend our freedoms. Instead, it serves as the world's policeman, fireman, social worker, bully, and busybody. Rather than guarding our borders, patrolling our coasts, and protecting our citizens, the Defense Department—which couldn't defend its own headquarters—is focused on fighting the next foreign war. There are over 700 military bases on foreign soil, with U.S. troops stationed in 159 different regions of the world. Instead of the U.S. military helping to guarantee peace and stability throughout the world, the presence of the U.S. military more often than not is the cause of war and instability around the globe. Because of what the military has become, Christians in the military, if they want to act consistently with the principles of Christianity, need to do just one thing: get out of the military.

The war in Iraq is immoral because of the tremendous death and destruction that we have meted out to Iraqis. After the United States invaded Iraq the first time during the 1991 Gulf War, we imposed brutal economic sanctions on Iraq that lead to the deaths of half a million infants and children. Osama bin Laden listed these sanctions against Iraq as one of the main reasons for the September 11th attacks on the United States. I believe the CIA term for what we experienced is blowback. The scriptural principle is "whatsoever a man soweth that shall he also reap." But even if Iraq had not been devastated by U.S. sanctions and yet still had been directly responsible for the September 11th attacks, I fail to see how that justifies reducing the country to rubble and killing—according to the latest estimates—600,000 people, most of whom were supposedly people who had been brutalized by Saddam Hussein.

The war in Iraq is immoral because the state can't sanctify murder. State sanctified murder—can there be such a thing? Will it be an adequate defense at the Judgment? The state is responsible for more deaths throughout history than those caused by all individuals and organizations combined. In the twentieth century alone, tens of millions of people were murdered by their own governments. Trusting the state when it comes to the necessity of going to war is ludicrous. Blind obedience to the state is not a tenet of New Testament Christianity. Killing for the state in some foreign war violates the biblical precept against killing. Limiting the biblical prohibition against killing to just murder doesn't legitimize killing in war. Because the war in Iraq was not defensive, U.S. soldiers—many of whom would claim to be Christians—cannot claim to be acting in self-defense when they gun down Iraqis. They are invaders and occupiers, not liberators and peacekeepers. It is unfortunate that many Americans have the idea that a terrorist is anyone who detonates a bomb but doesn't wear an air force uniform. The Bible says in Colossians 3:23: "And whatsoever ye do, do it heartily, as to the Lord, and not unto men." Bombing, killing, maiming, and interrogating for the state cannot be done heartily in the name of the Lord. Christians who do these things in the service of the state do them unto men—men like Bush, Cheney, Rumsfeld, Wolfowitz, Perle, Powell, and the other architects of the Iraq war—they do not do them for the glory of God or even for the American people. The war in Iraq has made not made us more secure. To the contrary, it has intensified the hatred that many foreigners around the world have for Americans, and has created terrorists faster than we can kill them.

The majority of the American people are now against this war. Perhaps not out of principle, but at least they are against it—for whatever their reason. Yet, support for the war among many conservative Christians continues. I know that among Americans, and even among Christian Americans, conservative Christians are usually in the minority on many issues. But being in the minority on a particular issue doesn't necessarily mean that one is in the right. Just look at one person who is in the minority: George W. Bush. Here is a professing Christian who believes that Muslims and Christians worship the same God and a Republican president who has done more to expand the power of government than any other Republican president since Abraham Lincoln.

But whether we are in the minority or the majority, conservative Christians should oppose this war, not because the war did not go as planned, not because we don't want another Vietnam, not because we have suffered too many casualties, not because too many Iraqi civilians have been killed, not because the war is too expensive, not because the conflict in Iraq has descended into a civil war, not because there are too many insurgents, and not because the troop surge is not working—we should oppose the war because it was a grave injustice, a monstrous wrong, and a great evil from the very beginning.

* * * * *

COUNTING THE COST

"For which of you, intending to build a tower, sitteth not down first, and counteth the cost, whether he have sufficient to finish it?

Lest haply, after he hath laid the foundation, and is not able to
finish it, all that behold it begin to mock him,
Saying, This man began to build, and was not able to finish.
Or what king, going to make war against another king, sitteth not
down first, and consulteth whether he be able with ten thousand to
meet him that cometh against him with twenty thousand?
Or else, while the other is yet a great way off, he sendeth an
ambassage, and desireth conditions of peace." (Luke 14:28–32)

What has cost the U.S. taxpayers almost half a trillion dollars, and
now costs $275 million every day, $11 million each hour, $191,000 every
minute, and $3,180 each second? If you answered, "The war in Iraq," then
you are right. But if you think that the U.S. government had any idea of
what the cost of the war would be thus far, or what the cost will be to
continue fighting the war, or what total cost will be when and if the U.S.
military is completely withdrawn from Iraq, then you are wrong.

What was supposed to be a cakewalk costing about $50 billion has
turned into a debacle that may cost the taxpayers over $2 trillion.

Before the invasion of Iraq, then Secretary of Defense Donald
Rumsfeld replied to questions about the length of a war against Iraq,
saying: "The Gulf War in the 1990s lasted five days on the ground. I can't
tell you if the use of force in Iraq today would last five days, or five
weeks, or five months, but it certainly isn't going to last any longer than
that."

A year after the invasion, General Peter Schoomaker, the Army
chief of staff, stated that the war against terrorism will "never go away in
our lifetime."

When asked about the timing of the war at a press conference a
week after the invasion, President Bush replied: "However long it takes.
That's the answer to your question and that's what you've got to know.
It isn't a matter of timetable, it's a matter of victory." Four years after the
invasion, Bush still maintained his aversion to timetables, vetoing a
war-spending bill because it contained a withdrawal timetable. Now we
are told that Bush's model for Iraq is South Korea, a country where the
U.S. has had troops since the end of our war there—in 1953.

The Bush Administration initially claimed that the war in Iraq
would cost "only" about $50 billion. To make that number more palatable,
Deputy Secretary of Defense Paul Wolfowitz claimed that "Iraq's vast oil
reserves would help defray the costs." The director of the Office of
Management and Budget, Mitch Daniels, and the Secretary of Defense,
Donald Rumsfeld, believed that some of the war's cost would be paid for
by other countries like the last time the United States invaded Iraq. Both

of these ideas turned out to be erroneous.

In an interview with the *Wall Street Journal* in 2002, the director of the White House's National Economic Council, Lawrence Lindsey, predicted that the Iraq War would cost between $100 and $200 billion. Naturally, the Bush Administration wasn't very happy with those figures, and Lindsey soon lost his job. Lindsey, of course, turned out to be wrong—but only because his estimate was way too low. Now, after four years and billions of dollars, we can only wish that Lindsey had been correct.

Before the second anniversary of the war had passed, the Congressional Budget Office estimated that the cost of fighting the war for the years 2005-2015 would be an *additional* $448.

Just a year later, economists Linda Bilmes (Harvard) and Joseph E. Stiglitz (Columbia) estimated that the war would ultimately cost between $1 and $2 trillion—ten times what Lindsey had estimated. But in an article published late last year, Bilmes and Stiglitz make the case that their original estimate was too low. They now say that because "the cost of the war—in both blood and money—has risen even faster than our projections anticipated," the cost of the war, if one considers "the sum of the current and future budgetary costs along with the economic impact of lives lost, jobs interrupted and oil prices driven higher by political uncertainty in the Middle East," will now *exceed* $2 trillion. And this is just the cost for the United States. The way things are going in Iraq, is there any doubt that Bilmes and Stiglitz will have to revise upward their figures once again? Is there any doubt that this $2 trillion figure will one day seem way too low?

The latest war-funding bill passed by Congress was signed into law by the president on May 25, 2007. H.R. 2206 (PL 110-28), the "U.S. Troop Readiness, Veterans' Care, Katrina Recovery, and Iraq Accountability Appropriations Act, 2007," provides another $100 billion to fund the wars in Iraq and Afghanistan through the end of September. [Buried in the bill is also a $2.10 per hour increase in the federal minimum wage over the next two years.] This war-funding bill was preceded by the following:

- Department of Defense Appropriations Act, 2007 (PL 109-289), $70 billion
- Emergency Supplemental Appropriations Act for Defense, the Global War on Terror, and Hurricane Recovery, 2006 (PL 109-234), $66 billion
- Department of Defense Appropriations Act, 2006 (PL 109-148),

$51 billion
- Emergency Supplemental Appropriations Act for Defense, the Global War on Terror, and Tsunami Relief, 2005 (PL 109-13), $75.9 billion
- Department of Defense Appropriations Act, 2005 (PL 108-287), $2.1 billion
- Emergency Supplemental Appropriations Act for Defense and for the Reconstruction of Iraq and Afghanistan, 2004 (PL 108-106), $64.9 billion
- Emergency Wartime Supplemental Appropriations Act, 2003 (PL 108-11), $62.6 billion
- Consolidated Appropriations Resolution, 2003 (PL 108-7), $10 billion
- 2002 Supplemental Appropriations Act for Further Recovery From and Response To Terrorist Attacks on the United States (PL 107-206), $13.8 billion
- Department of Defense and Emergency Supplemental Appropriations for Recovery from and Response to Terrorist Attacks on the United States Act, 2002 (PL 107-117), $3.4 billion
- 2001 Emergency Supplemental Appropriations Act for Recovery from and Response to Terrorist Attacks on the United States (PL 107-38), $13.6 billion

In addition to the billions of dollars these acts gave to the Defense Department for military operations, there were also billions of additional dollars allocated for foreign aid, base security, embassy operations, reconstruction, veterans' health care, and other costs related to fighting the global war on terror.

The latest analysis on the cost of the war is the Congressional Research Service (CRS) report for Congress titled *The Cost of Iraq, Afghanistan, and Other Global War on Terror Operations Since 9/11*, by Amy Belasco, a specialist in national defense in the Foreign Affairs, Defense, and Trade Division of the CRS.

With a national debt fast approaching $9 trillion dollars, the cost of continuing the futile attempt to secure Iraq and make it a democracy is a cost that the U.S. economy cannot bear. Back before the war started, Bush tried to justify his impending invasion of Iraq by appealing to the effects of not going to war. Another terrorist attack would, said the president, "Cripple our economy." But it is the war in Iraq that has crippled our economy. The price of a barrel of crude oil was under $25 in 2003. Does anyone in his right mind think that U.S. intervention in the Middle East has not had something to do with the price of oil more than doubling since the invasion of Iraq?

There are, of course, many other costs of fighting the war in Iraq. The morale and readiness of the military are at historic lows. The Guard and Reserve forces have been decimated. Military hardware and equipment are worn out. The reputation of America in the eyes of the world, although previously sullied, is now at rock bottom. New terrorists are being created faster than we can kill them. Countless numbers of American families have suffered because of multiple duty tours and ever-increasing deployment terms. Thousands of American soldiers will need a lifetime of medical and/or psychiatric care. The cost of this war to the children of Iraq is incalculable.

One of the most important costs of fighting this war is the number of U.S. soldiers who have died for a lie. As I write these words, the death toll stands at 3,645. The first time I ever mentioned in an article the number of U.S. troops killed in Iraq the figure was "only" 855. I believe now what I believed then: every death was both unnecessary and preventable. Every life lost was not just lost; every life lost was utterly wasted, thrown away. Bush and company have blood on their hands— American blood and Iraqi blood. Just as Johnson, Nixon, and their cronies were never held accountable for the crime of Vietnam, so Bush and company may never be held accountable for their war crimes—in this life. They will certainly give an account to Almighty God for their sins when we are rid of them here.

The great tragedy of this war, like most wars throughout history, is that all the death and destruction, all the carnage, all the broken homes, all the money wasted, all the suffering, all the ruined lives, all the power the state has gained, all the liberty the people have lost—all of it could have been prevented if only Bush and company had counted the cost.

* * * * *

ENDING THE WAR

As we approach the fifth anniversary of the war in Iraq, there is no end of the war in sight.

The Republicans, although some of them might be upset with how the war has turned out, are still a bunch of crazed warmongers. They have shown that they love war as long as it is a Republican war. And as we already knew, Republicans love the military-industrial complex and the security-industrial complex.

The Democrats who began their control of Congress last year have done nothing to stop the war. They have continually caved into Bush's demands for more money for the war. They have no plans to impeach the war criminals who lied us into war. Of course, if it was a Democratic president who had started the war, they would be all for it.

None of the current or former presidential candidates (except Ron Paul) have any real plans to end the war. Some want to escalate it. Some want to change its course. Others talk of gradually withdrawing some troops. They are all (except Ron Paul) dedicated to continuing Bush's "war on terror" and maintaining the U.S. empire of troops and bases that encircles the globe.

The American people, the majority of whom say that they no longer support the war, have shown by their yellow ribbons, their "I Support the Troops" signs, and their voting patterns in the presidential caucuses and primaries that they are not as opposed to the war as they claim.

Evangelical Christians continue to be among the most vocal supporters of the war. Even Christians who have become disillusioned about the war, can be found—because of their love affair with the U.S. military—talking out of both sides of their mouth. They condemn the war but then urge us to condone it when they recite their "pray for the troops" mantra. "Out of the same mouth proceedeth blessing and cursing. My brethren, these things ought not so to be" (James 3:10).

There are other signs as well. The temporary troop surge will apparently now never end. And the secretary of Defense wants to expand the army by some 65,000 soldiers. Then there are the permanent bases and the fortified embassy.

Can this war be stopped? Can anyone stop this war?

Since we can't rely on Congress or political candidates or the typical American or even Christians who supposedly follow the "Prince of Peace," there is only one way I see to end this war.

The only ones who can end this war, and end it now, once and for all, are the troops themselves. After all, it is the troops that are doing the actual fighting, bleeding, dying—not the Congress. It is the troops that are bringing death, destruction, and heartache to the people of Iraq—not the political candidates. It is the troops that are dropping the bombs—not the typical American. It is the troops that are firing the bullets—not Christian warmongers.

I was told by one of my critics that he agreed with me on the point of not fighting illegal and unjust wars, but that doing so was not the fault of the soldiers. Well then, whose fault is it? No one is doing the fighting except the soldiers. It doesn't matter who told them to fight or what the reason is that they were told to fight. If the troops stop warring, the war will stop. It will not gradually come to and end, it will grind to a halt.

First, we don't need any more fresh meat sent to Iraq. Every soldier, sailor, airman, or Marine ordered to Iraq should refuse to go. Everyone in the Guard or Reserve should refuse to go. Every serviceman home on leave should refuse to go back. Second, every member of the military in Iraq should refuse to drop a bomb, go on a patrol, fire his weapon, or do anything offensive. And third, every soldier in Iraq should try to come home on the first plane or the first ship he can commandeer. Don't sit there and tell me that it won't work. It is a simple matter. In each of these scenarios, there will be too few telling too many that they must continue fighting the war.

Now, what will it take for this to come to pass? The hearts and minds of the troops must be changed. They must realize that by fighting in Iraq they are not defending our freedoms, avenging the United States for 9/11, stopping al-Qaeda, fighting terrorism, protecting Israel, or fighting them "over there" so we don't have to fight them "over here."

They are not liberating Iraq or bringing democracy to Iraq. They are in fact engaging in a war crime and perpetrating genocide against the Iraqi people.

And as I wrote about the troops being responsible for their actions:

> Until U.S. soldiers concede that the war was a grave mistake, they will keep on fighting. Until U.S. soldiers accept responsibility for their actions, they will keep on killing. Until U.S. soldiers understand that the state is a lying, stealing, and killing machine they will continue their state-sanctioned death and destruction. Until U.S. soldiers realize that they are but cannon fodder for the state, they will keep dying for a lie.

These are hard sayings. But until each individual soldier stops and asks the question: "What am I doing in Iraq?" (or as the case may be: "What the ____ am I doing in Iraq?"), there is no chance of this war coming to an end.

The troops are our only hope. Whatever steps they take to end this war, I applaud them. Whatever resistance they give the warfare state, I support them. Dear reader, I hope you will do likewise.

* * * * *

FIVE YEARS AND COUNTING

As of today, March 20, the debacle that is the war in Iraq has now dragged on for ~~one~~ ~~two~~ ~~three~~ ~~four~~ five years. How many more years will I have to begin an article on this date with those words?

I really don't know what else can be said about this war. It is immoral, aggressive, unjust, unconstitutional, unscriptural, unnecessary, wasteful, and pointless. It has made more terrorists and more enemies of the United States than Osama bin Laden could make in ten lifetimes. It was based on a mountain of lies, misrepresentations, and manipulated intelligence. It was the worst possible response to the 9/11 terrorist attacks. It "may well turn out to be," according to Lt. Gen. William Odom, former director of the National Security Agency, "the greatest strategic disaster in U.S. history."

As long as this war continues, there are more than years that we will be counting.

When I wrote about the war on its third anniversary, 2,317 American soldiers had already been killed. When I wrote about the war last year on its fourth anniversary, the total number of dead American soldiers had risen to 3,218. As I write about the war on this its fifth anniversary, that number has now increased to 3,992. How many wasted American lives will it take before the American people say enough is enough? It took almost 60,000 in Vietnam.

We can continue to count the cries of grieving family members who have lost or will lose a father, a son, a husband, a grandson, a nephew, or a brother. Unfortunately, it is also true that some will instead lose a mother, a daughter, a granddaughter, a niece, or a sister. It is bad enough to lose someone to a disease, an accident, or a natural death, but I can't think of anything worse than losing a loved one who was fighting in some senseless foreign war. There will be no comfort in the knowledge that one's loved one died for his country for a noble cause. Every soldier who died (or will die) in Iraq died for Bush's legacy, the warfare state, the military-industrial complex, and the U.S. global empire. They all died for a lie.

Even as America sinks deeper and deeper into a recession, we can also continue to count the incredible cost of this war. The trillion-dollar defense budget doesn't include the cost of fighting the war in Iraq (or the forgotten war in Afghanistan). We have already spent over half a trillion dollars on the war. The total cost of the war is now expected to exceed $3 trillion. The budget of the Department of Defense for fiscal year 2008 included $141 billion for the "supplemental" budget to wage the "global war on terrorism" plus $93 billion to fund the war for the remainder of fiscal year 2007. Regardless of all the other reasons not to fight this war, we simply can't afford to spend the $10 million or so an hour that it costs to fight it. Ending the war would be the greatest "stimulus package" the government could ever provide to the American people.

One thing we can try to count, but probably won't be able to, is the lies of presidents, congressmen, political appointees, journalists, pundits, talking heads, radio talk-show hosts, military brass, and, sadly, evangelical leaders, when it comes to justification for the war. A new study just released found that Bush and top officials in his administration issued hundreds of false statements about the threat from Iraq in the two years following the 9/11 attacks. You can see them all here in their context and with their source referenced. Stay tuned: more lies to follow.

Will U.S. troops still be in Iraq after five more years? If John McCain has his way, we only have ninety-five more years to go. If that sounds unthinkable, just remember that we still have troops in Japan, Germany, and Italy even though World War II ended in 1945.

* * * * *

THEY DIED IN VAIN

When the number of Americans killed in Iraq surpassed the 1,000 mark in September of 2004, President Bush said of the families of the dead during a campaign rally: "My promise to them is that we will complete the mission so that their child or their husband or wife has not died in vain." Well, the death count of U.S. soldiers has now reached 4,000, and the completion of the mission is nowhere in sight.

This should come as no surprise since Bush's promise to complete the mission was a lie before he even uttered the words. Back in 2003, in front of a "Mission Accomplished" banner, the president announced: "Major combat operations in Iraq have ended. In the Battle of Iraq, the United States and our allies have prevailed. And now our coalition is engaged in securing and reconstructing that country."

And even before we invaded Iraq to begin the war, the Bush administration was awash in lies, as study after study after study has documented.

But not only has Bush's mission not been completed, it has never been defined. So, just what is this mission that remains to be completed lest the deaths of U.S. soldiers be in vain?

Is Bush's mission to liberate Iraq from a tyrannical ruler? Saddam Hussein was captured in December of 2003, but we kept on fighting. Saddam Hussein is now dead, but we keep on fighting. There is no denying that Hussein was a tyrannical ruler, but since when is it the business of the United States to rid the world of tyrannical rulers? What would be our attitude if another country said that we needed a regime change? And what about all the other tyrannical rulers in the world? Why do we turn a blind eye to them? And even worse, why does the United States ally with tyrants? We allied with the brutal Stalin during World War II against Hitler, but then we allied with someone that both Bushes considered to be Hitler's reincarnation—Saddam Hussein—against Iran. Why do some Iraqis say that they prefer living under Saddam's rule to the U.S. occupation of their country? How ungrateful these Iraqis are for their liberation!

Is Bush's mission to make Iraq a democracy? What kind of democracy can be made at the point of a gun? And no one who knew anything about the history of the Arab peoples would even think of attempting to impose a democracy on them. And again, since when is it the business of the United States what form of government a country has? There are still a few hereditary monarchies in existence around the world. How undemocratic is that? Should we overthrow them and institute democracies? Don't we have a moral imperative to invade China and force those commies to become democrats? The United States sure is particular about which countries are due for democratic governments. And not only have we not made Iraq into a democracy, we have unleashed a religious civil war.

Is Bush's mission to remove a threat to the United States? With no air force or navy, and an economy in ruins after a decade of sanctions, Iraq was never a threat to the United States. Iraq was never even a threat to the United States when we invaded it the first time in 1991. If Iraq's neighboring countries didn't think it necessary to send troops to Iraq, then why should we even consider it? Bush has admitted that there were no weapons of mass destruction in Iraq. Only theocratic warmongers like Mike Huckabee think they were moved to Jordan or Syria. But it doesn't even matter how many weapons of mass destruction that Iraq had or didn't have. Many countries have weapons of mass destruction and could potentially target the United States. Why single out Iraq? Doesn't Russian still have thousands of nuclear devices that are or could be pointed at us? Why don't we demand that Russia destroy its nuclear facilities and allow UN inspectors to verify their destruction? After being pummeled by the United States military for five years, is there any country in the world that is not a threat to the United States it is Iraq. Yet, we continue making war on Iraq.

Is Bush's mission to retaliate for the 9/11 attacks? Many Americans still think that the invasion of Iraq was payback for 9/11 even though

Bush himself has said that Iraq was not responsible. But what if Iraq was responsible? The number of dead American soldiers has long ago surpassed the number of Americans who died on 9/11. The number of suffering relatives of dead American soldiers has long ago surpassed the number of suffering relatives of Americans who died on 9/11. The number of wounded American soldiers has long ago surpassed the number of Americans who were wounded on 9/11. The sum of money spent on the war has long ago surpassed the money spent to replace airplanes and rebuild buildings destroyed on 9/11. Some payback. But even if it were true that no price would be too high to take vengeance for the 9/11 attacks, taking vengeance on Iraq is no vengeance at all since Iraq was not responsible.

Is Bush's mission to maintain the free flow of oil? Iraq's oil reserves are second only to Saudi Arabia. How much oil has been pumped from beneath Iraq's desert sands recently? The price of a barrel of oil has quadrupled since Bush invaded Iraq. Most countries have no natural oil reserves. When they need oil they buy it from other countries that have it. What have we gotten for decades of intervention in the Middle East? Three dollar a gallon gas, that's what. Wouldn't it be easier to just buy oil from oil-producing states instead of trying to control the Middle East? What makes this even worse is that the United States has its own oil reserves—reserves that the government prohibits companies from tapping into. Since when is the United States entitled to another country's oil at a particular quantity and price?

Now, if Bush's mission were to destroy civil liberties, shred the Constitution, enrich defense and security contractors, construct permanent bases in Iraq, establish an imperial presidency, confirm him as a war president, build his legacy, expand the national debt, wreck the economy, and further increase the power of the warfare state then I would certainly say that the mission has been completed.

But at what cost?

The terrible cost of Bush's mission is the lives of 4,000 American soldiers. None of these soldiers had to die. They didn't die for their country. They didn't die for our freedoms. They didn't die for a noble cause. Every one of them died for George W. Bush's bogus mission. They all died in vain. Their lives were wasted.

Barack Obama and John McCain even admitted this, if only for a brief moment. Obama told an Iowa audience early last year that "we ended up launching a war that should have never been authorized, and should never been waged, and on which we have now spent $400 billion, and have seen over 3,000 lives of the bravest young Americans wasted."

He later said his remark was "a slip of the tongue." McCain soon afterward let it slip that Americans have every right to be frustrated because "we've wasted a lot of our most precious treasure, which is American lives, over there." He then back-tracked and said that he should have "used the word 'sacrificed.'"

Four thousand American soldiers have died in vain. Their lives were wasted, just like the over 58,000 American lives that were wasted in Vietnam. How many more American soldiers must die in vain before the American people, and especially their loved ones, realize that their lives were wasted?

But where is the outrage? Every relative of every American soldier killed in this war should be outraged. Every member of the military sent to fight this senseless war should be outraged. Every taxpayer forced to pay for this unnecessary war should be outraged. Every American who was deceived by the architects of this war should be outraged.

True, some are indeed outraged. But what we continue to see too much of is outrage—directed not at the president that manages the war, the Congress that funds the war, or the military that fights the war—but at those "pacifist dogs" and "pinko traitors" who dare to say that every death in Iraq was unnecessary, senseless, and pointless. They all died in vain.

* * * * *

WHAT HAPPENED TO THE WAR?

As of today, March 20, it has now been six years since the United States invaded Iraq. Yes, the United States still has tens of thousands of troops in Iraq, although we don't hear much about the war any more. What happened to the war?

The war should have been an issue in the election. It wasn't. And thanks to the disaster that is the Republican revolution that wasn't, it didn't even have to be. We hardly heard about the war after the Democratic and Republican presidential conventions. Republicans were perfectly willing to exchange one war criminal for another. Many Democrats only opposed the war because it was a Republican war. And now that Obama is president, no one from either party seems to mind that he wants to send 17,000 more U.S. troops to Afghanistan.

The war is still an immoral, aggressive, unjust, unconstitutional, unnecessary, and senseless war that that violates every "just war" principle ever formulated. It was a manufactured war based on manipulated intelligence, bogus claims of weapons of mass destruction, and an assortment of other lies.

The war is still making terrorists and enemies of the United States. Although Fred Barnes wrote (in the *Weekly Standard*) that the invasion of Iraq was "the greatest act of benevolence one country has ever done for another," we know that it was instead, as Lt. Gen. William Odom, former director of the National Security Agency, described it: "The greatest strategic disaster in U.S. history."

The war is still draining the treasury. The cakewalk that was supposed to cost $50 billion has bled U.S. taxpayers for almost a trillion dollars. About $12 billion was spent fighting the Iraq war each month last year. It costs about $390,000 to deploy one soldier to Iraq for one year. The cost for a lifetime of support and medical care for each severely wounded American soldier is in the millions.

The war is still resulting in the deaths of Iraqis—thanks to the U.S. invasion and occupation and the genocide we unleashed. The latest estimate of the number of Iraqis who have died in the war instigated by the Bush administration, and continued by the Obama administration, is about 1 million. Additionally, there are the millions of Iraqis who are wounded, disabled, displaced, homeless, refugees, widows, or orphans.

The war is still destroying the lives of American soldiers and their families. Many thousands of U.S. soldiers have been severely wounded. Hundreds of these have had limbs amputated. Untold numbers suffer from post-traumatic stress disorder. Defense Department doctors have recently reported that there may be as many as 360,000 U.S. soldiers who have suffered wartime brain injuries. Some returning soldiers will spend the rest of their lives unable to hold down a job. Others will live out their days as physical and/or emotional basket cases.

The war is still killing American soldiers. When I wrote about the war on its third anniversary, 2,317 American soldiers had died for a lie. On the fourth anniversary, that number had risen to 3,218. On the fifth, 3,992. The number of dead American soldiers is now up to 4,259. Although the total number of American deaths per year is falling, there are two ways in which American deaths are rising: military suicides and the war Afghanistan. There were more American soldiers who killed themselves in January of this year than died fighting in Iraq and Afghanistan. Military suicides are not only up for the fourth year in a row, they are at the highest level they have ever been. The number of American soldiers killed in Afghanistan is now up to 666. God only knows how many men from Obama's 17,000-troop surge will be added to that number. Yet, none of these soldiers had to die. They died neither for our

freedoms nor the freedoms of anyone else. They all died in vain.
What happened to the war? Nothing happened to the war. It is still
just as wrong as ever. It is still just as deadly ever. I'm afraid that most
Americans, like Rhett Butler, just don't give a damn. As William Lloyd
Garrison once said: "The apathy of the people is enough to make every
statue leap from its pedestal and hasten the resurrection of the dead."

* * * * *

THE FORGOTTEN WAR

The civil war in Korea from 1950 to 1953 that the United States
foolishly intervened in, and, for the first time for a major conflict, without
a congressional declaration of war, is known as the Forgotten War. The
number of American soldiers killed in this senseless war is over 36,000.
Yet, Korea remains divided at the 38th parallel to this day just like it was
before the war began. Talk about dying in vain. None of these soldiers
died in defense of the United States; all of them died for the United
Nations, for the foolish policies of Harry Truman, and for the failed
diplomacy of World War II.

Most Americans have no idea that there are still over 24,000 U.S.
troops stationed in South Korea (some no doubt the grandchildren of the
soldiers who fought in the Korean War). Fewer still probably know
anything about the war that put them there in the first place.

There is another war that, incredibly, is fast becoming a forgotten
war: the war in Iraq. I lamented last year at this time that we didn't hear
much about the war in Iraq anymore. Even though candidate Barack
Obama pledged in 2007 that the first thing he would do if elected was
bring the troops home and end the war, the war wasn't an issue in the
2008 election. And before the electoral vote was even counted, Democratic opposition to the war had evaporated.

Now, on the seventh anniversary of the unconstitutional, immoral,
aggressive, unjust, unnecessary, manufactured, manipulated, and senseless
war that is the war in Iraq, the escalation of the war in Afghanistan has
eclipsed any mention of the ongoing war in Iraq. And this in spite of the
fact that there are still 130,000 U.S. troops in Iraq.

When I wrote about the Iraq war on its third anniversary, 2,317
American soldiers had died for a lie. On the fourth anniversary, that
number had risen to 3,218. On the fifth, it was up to 3,992. Last year, on
the sixth anniversary of the war, the number of dead American soldiers
rose to 4,259. Currently, the death toll is at 4,385, with 157 of those

deaths since Obama became the new commander in chief.

But, it is said, look how the number of deaths per year has fallen. Agreed. But that is no consolation to the father, mother, wife, or child of the soldiers who died in vain and for a lie yesterday, last week, or last month.

Although combat deaths are decreasing in Iraq (but certainly not in Afghanistan), *increasing* among returning soldiers are suicides, PTSD, broken families, substance abuse, unemployment, horrible memories, lingering injuries, shattered dreams, acts of violence, and criminal activity. And of course, the war is still costing the American taxpayers billions of dollars a week.

But even if only one American soldier had died since last month, even if only one American soldier had died since the last anniversary of the war, even if only one American soldier had died since Obama took office, and even if only one American had died since the beginning of the war, that would still be one too many.

Only the grossly naïve still think that those fighting and dying in Iraq are doing so for our freedoms or to keep us safe from terrorism. The truth is rather that since the war on terrorism began our freedoms have steadily deteriorated and we have created more terrorists.

Before the United States invaded Iraq, not one American had been killed by an Iraqi since the previous time we invaded that country. But no U.S. soldier had to die in either war against Iraq. Bringing "democracy" to Iraq, ridding the country of Saddam Hussein, and destroying Iraq's weapons of war were not worth the life of one American. They were not worth the shedding of one drop of American blood.

But that's not all. No Iraqi soldiers had to die, no Iraqi civilians had to die, and no Iraqi children had to die between the wars because of brutal U.S. sanctions.

Yet, Americans who have lamented the senseless deaths of American soldiers, not to mention the deaths of countless numbers of Iraqis, and denounced this war from the beginning are the ones who have been labeled unpatriotic, un-American, communists, and traitors. This callous disregard for human life—American and Iraqi—is appalling, and especially among those who call themselves pro-lifers.

If you love what is left of our republic and want America to be loved instead of hated, blessed instead of cursed, admired instead of despised, and emulated instead of attacked, then you should want the United States to get out of Iraq and the Middle East—and stay out. Oh, it might take years, even decades, to restore America to favor in the eyes of world, but we must start sometime if it ever has a chance of coming to pass.

Do I think U.S. troops will ever leave Iraq? I can answer that with a question: Does the United States still have troops in South Korea?

* * * * *

WHAT IF IRAQ HAD WEAPONS OF MASS DESTRUCTION?

The recent revelation that the man most responsible for the myth that Iraq had weapons of mass destruction—Rafid Ahmed Alwan al-Janabi, a.k.a "Curveball"—lied should forever put that falsehood to rest.

It was Curveball's fabrications that formed the basis of Secretary of State Colin Powell's claims about Iraq's alleged weapons programs in his speech before the United Nations Security Council in February of 2003 on the eve of the U.S. invasion of Iraq. That is the speech that Lawrence Wilkerson, a former colonel in the U.S. Army, a decorated Vietnam vet, and a lifelong Republican who served as Powell's chief of staff, called "a hoax on the American people, the international community, and the United Nations Security Council." That is the speech that Powell himself said, in a February 2005 interview with Barbara Walters, was a "blot" on his record.

As the world knows all too well, one of the main justifications for the unconstitutional, unjust, and unnecessary war of aggression against Iraq was that Iraq had "weapons of mass destruction." In the "Authorization for Use of Military Force Against Iraq Resolution of 2002," there are six references to Iraq's supposed "weapons of mass destruction."

Before that resolution was passed, Vice President Dick Cheney had stated that there was no doubt that Saddam Hussein had those weapons and was amassing them "to use against our friends, against our allies, and against us." And soon after the resolution was passed, President Bush himself insisted that Saddam was lying to the world about not having weapons of mass destruction because "he's got them."

We know, of course, from the Duelfer Report—the final report on Iraq's weapons of mass destruction by the Pentagon and CIA-organized Iraq Survey Group—that Iraq had no deployable weapons of mass destruction on the eve of the U.S. invasion in March 2003, and had not produced any since 1991. Bush even admitted as much in 2005 when he acknowledged that "most of the intelligence turned out to be wrong."

And we also know that the whole idea of Iraq's having weapons of mass destruction was a ruse anyway. We know this not only from sources like the Downing Street Memo, made public in 2005, that Bush wanted to invade Iraq soon after the 9/11 attacks, but also from Bush's secretary of defense, Donald Rumsfeld. In Rumsfeld's new book, *Known and Unknown: A Memoir* (Sentinel, 2011), he writes about meeting with President Bush just fifteen days after 9/11 and being asked to "take a look at the shape of our military plans on Iraq." According to Russ Baker, author of *Family of Secrets: The Bush Dynasty, the Powerful Forces That Put It in the White House, and What Their Influence Means for America* (Bloomsbury Press, 2008), before he was even elected president, Bush was fixated on the political capital that fighting a war would bring, political capital that his father had "wasted" after he invaded Iraq the first time.

Because the evidence that Iraq had weapons of mass destruction was so shaky, a wide variety of other ruses were given in defense of the war. A study back in 2004 documented 27 rationales given for the war by the Bush administration, war hawks in Congress, and the media between 9/11 and the October 2002 congressional resolution to use force in Iraq and concluded that it was "the Bush administration, and the President himself" that "established the majority of the rationales for the war and all of those rationales that make up the most prominent reasons for war."

Many Americans actually believed, and perhaps still believe, that the invasion of Iraq was in retaliation for the 9/11 attacks. But as Bush himself even acknowledged in 2003: "We have no evidence that Saddam Hussein was involved with September the 11th."

But what if Iraq had weapons of mass destruction? What if every other rationale for the war against Iraq was a lie, but Iraq really did have weapons of mass destruction? What should the United States have done? Should the U.S. government have allowed Saddam Hussein to possess such weapons? Should it have allowed him to threaten neighboring Muslim countries? Should it have stood back and allowed him to brutalize the Iraqi people? Should it have allowed him to be a potential danger to U.S. ally Israel? Because of the gravity of the matter, should the United States have risked invading Iraq just in case weapons of mass destruction might have been there?

The answers are so what, nothing, yes, yes, yes, yes, and no.

First of all, with no navy or air force, and an economy in ruins after a decade of brutal U.S. sanctions, Iraq was never a threat to the United States. Iraq was not even a threat to the United States when U.S. and coalition forces invaded it the first time in 1991.

Second, if Iraq's neighboring Islamic countries didn't think it necessary to invade Iraq because of a perceived threat, then why should the United States have even considered it?

Third, Israel had enough tanks, helicopters, fighter jets, ships, bombs, and bullets to destroy Iraq many times over if that country actually posed a credible threat to its security. If Israel did think it necessary to launch a preemptive strike against Iraq (like it had done in 1981 when it took out an Iraqi nuclear reactor under construction), then why should the United States have even considered it?

Fourth, the United States cannot right every wrong in the world. It is not in the interests of the American people for the U.S. government to expend blood and treasure to take sides against those regimes that are persecuting or mistreating their own people or foreigners. It is not in the interests of the American people for the U.S. government to take sides during a civil war. Any American who wants to do these things on his own dime and in risk of his own life is perfectly free to do so. He should just not expect other Americans who prefer to keep their money in their pocket and their loved ones out of a flag-draped coffin to do his bidding.

And fifth, and most important, even if Iraq possessed nuclear, chemical, and biological weapons, there is absolutely no reason why the United States would be justified in attacking and invading Iraq or any other sovereign country—no matter what we thought of that country's rulers, system of government, economic policies, military capabilities, treatment of women, religious intolerance, violations of civil liberties, human rights record, or nuclear program.

And on this last point in particular, who is the United States to say that a country should or shouldn't have nuclear weapons? When did the countries of the world appoint America to be the world's policeman or guardian? Why does the United States tolerate the massive amount of nuclear weapons stockpiled in France, China, Russia, Israel, India, Pakistan, and the United Kingdom? Shouldn't the United States invade those countries as well? Isn't every county in the world justified in obtaining nuclear weapons to protect themselves against the one country that was the first and only country to actually use them—the United States of America?

What should the United States have done if Iraq had weapons of mass destruction? Absolutely nothing. I think that the 4,438 U.S. soldiers who died in Iraq in vain and for a lie might agree—if they still had the chance.

* * * * *

WHEN WILL THE IRAQ WAR REALLY END?

Although the war in Iraq has already ended twice, the United States still has troops stationed there, fighting there—and dying there.

Wars sometimes don't end when they should have or could have.

The Treaty of Ghent that ended the war of 1812 between the United States and Great Britain was signed on December 24, 1814. Yet, the last battle of the war—the Battle of New Orleans—was fought on January 8, 1815. It seems that news traveled a lot slower back then. The result, of course, was unnecessary deaths on both sides.

The armistice that ended World War I was signed at 5:00 a.m. in a rail car in France, but did not take effect until 11:00 a.m. Conservative estimates put the casualty count during the six hours between the signing of the armistice and its becoming effective at "10,944 casualties, of which 2,738 were deaths" (Joseph Persico, *Eleventh Month, Eleventh Day, Eleventh Hour: Armistice Day, 1918, World War I and Its Violent Climax* [Random House, 2004]). Again, we have unnecessary deaths, not that the other deaths during World War I were somehow necessary.

As of March 20, the war in Iraq has lasted for eight years—more than twice as long as the U.S. war against Nazi Germany in World War II. I first wrote about the Iraq war on its third anniversary ("Weapons of Mass Distraction") when 2,317 American soldiers had already died for a lie. When I wrote about the war on its fourth anniversary ("Four Years, Four Plans"), that number had risen to 3,218. On the fifth, ("Five Years and Counting"), the number was up to 3,992. On the sixth ("What Happened to the War?"), it was up to 4,259. Last year, on the war's seventh anniversary ("The Forgotten War"), that number had risen to 4,385. Now, on the eighth anniversary of this immoral war, the number of U.S. soldiers who have died in vain is up to 4,439, with 211 of those senseless deaths occurring since Obama took over as the chief war criminal.

Yes, the death count per day, week, month, year, or however you want to figure it keeps getting lower. But since there are now more U.S. troops in Afghanistan than Iraq, guess what is happening to the number of U.S. soldiers in Afghanistan who are coming home in flag-draped coffins? That number is up to 1,505.

But even if no more U.S. soldiers needlessly die in Iraq and the number remains at 4,439, that is still 4,439 soldiers too many. Even if only one American soldier had died since the beginning of the war, and even if the war had only cost 1 dollar, that is still one soldier and 1 dollar too many.

I mentioned that the war in Iraq has already ended twice.

The first time was on May 1, 2003, when President Bush announced—in front of a "Mission Accomplished" banner—that "the United States and our allies have prevailed" and "major combat operations in Iraq have ended."

This was followed by the deaths of 4,300 more U.S. soldiers.

The second ending of the Iraq war was on August 31, 2010, when President Obama proclaimed that "the American combat mission in Iraq has ended" and "Operation Iraqi Freedom is over, and the Iraqi people now have lead responsibility for the security of their country."

Yet, since the transition to "Operation New Dawn" took place on September 1, twenty-one more American soldiers have died.

And just what have our troops died for? It certainly wasn't to keep us safe from terrorism. It was acknowledged by the U.S. government in the National Intelligence Estimate as far back as 2006 that the war in Iraq increased the threat of terrorism rather than diminished it.

When will the Iraq War really end? How many more American soldiers, Iraqi "insurgents," and Iraqi civilians must die before it does? How many more billions of U.S. taxpayer dollars must be wasted before that time comes?

* * * * *

WHY THEY DIED IN VAIN

Since the beginning of the war in Iraq, I have unequivocally maintained several things about the deaths of U.S. troops. Every one of the 4,450 U.S. soldiers who has died so far in Iraq has died unnecessarily, senselessly, for a lie, and in vain.

This latter point struck a nerve with a reader of a recent article of mine on the Iraq war, "What If Iraq Had Weapons of Mass Destruction?," that was reprinted by LibertarianChristians.com. Although my critic didn't "necessarily disagree" with some of my conclusions, he did "disagree on one major point":

The soldiers did not die in vain. There is now a chance for freedom in a country that did not have it, if that is in vain then we all must question our purpose here on earth. I would not insult their families or their honor by reprinting such an inflammatory statement.

Does this mean there was no "chance for freedom" in Iraq before the United States invaded? A look at what has happened to oppressive regimes in the Middle East this year should answer that question. One bullet put by an Iraqi into the head of Saddam Hussein could have given Iraq a "chance for freedom." There was always a "chance for freedom" in Iraq. And even if there wasn't, who is to say that the deaths of hundreds of thousands of Iraqis and thousands of U.S. troops is a price that should have been paid to give Iraq a "chance for freedom"? Is my critic willing to sacrifice one of his children so Iraq can have a "chance for freedom"? I don't think so.

Look at what has happened to our freedoms in this country since 9/11 and since the troops started defending our freedoms by fighting in Iraq. Our freedoms have gone down the drain. Is it worth giving up our freedoms—like the freedom to travel without being sexually molested—so that Iraqis can have a "chance for freedom"?

Although I don't discount the brutality of Saddam Hussein's regime, some Iraqis who used to have legs, jobs, fathers, mothers, children, freedom to worship, and freedom to not be blown up by a suicide bomber don't think much of Iraq's newfound "chance for freedom."

And why is it that no totalitarian country has a "chance for freedom" unless the United States intervenes militarily or otherwise?

As much as I don't like to write it and as much as Americans don't want to read it, U.S. soldiers killed in Iraq died in vain. This means that their deaths were ineffectual, unsuccessful, and futile. Their deaths were without real significance, value, or importance. Their deaths were without effect, to no avail, and to no purpose.

I realize that this truth might be especially painful to the thousands of Americans who have lost loved ones in Iraq. I am not insensitive to the fact that every American soldier killed in Iraq was someone's father, husband, son, brother, uncle, nephew, grandson, and, in about a hundred cases, someone's mother, wife, daughter, sister, aunt, niece, or granddaughter. This painful truth should embolden those who have lost loved ones to never support or encourage any relative, friend, acquaintance, neighbor, coworker, business associate, or fellow church member ever joining the military.

I would like to mention three reasons why I believe U.S. soldiers killed while fighting in Iraq died in vain.

U.S. soldiers killed while fighting in Iraq died in vain because their mission in that conflict was undefined and unfinished.

When the number of U.S. soldiers killed in Iraq hit the 1,000 milestone in September of 2004, President Bush said of the families of those killed: "My promise to them is that we will complete the mission so that their child or their husband or wife has not died in vain." Yet, back in October of 2003, in front of a "Mission Accomplished" banner, Bush had already announced: "Major combat operations in Iraq have ended. In the Battle of Iraq, the United States and our allies have prevailed." But if the United States prevailed and ceased major combat operations, then what was Bush doing talking about completing the mission?

Just what was our mission in Iraq? To remove Saddam Hussein? To defend our freedoms? To dismantle al-Qaeda? To remove a threat to the United States? To liberate Iraq? To respond to an attack on the United States? To bring stability to the Middle East? To force Iraq to comply with UN resolutions? To free Muslim women from oppression? To impose democracy on Iraq? To retaliate for 9/11? To maintain the free flow of oil? To protect Israel? To destroy weapons of mass destruction?

A study back in 2004 documented 27 rationales given for the war by the Bush administration, war hawks in Congress, and the media between 9/11 and the October 2002 congressional resolution to use force in Iraq and concluded that it was "the Bush administration, and the President himself" that "established the majority of the rationales for the war and all of those rationales that make up the most prominent reasons for war." Another 2004 study—this one prepared for Representative Henry Waxman (D–Calif.) by the U.S. House of Representatives Committee on Government Reform—concluded that Bush, Cheney, Rumsfeld, Powell, and Rice

> repeatedly made misleading statements about the threat posed by Iraq. In 125 separate appearances, they made 11 misleading statements about the urgency of Iraq's threat, 81 misleading statements about Iraq's nuclear activities, 84 misleading statements about Iraq's chemical and biological capabilities, and 61 misleading statements about Iraq's relationship with al Qaeda.

U.S. soldiers killed while fighting in Iraq died in vain because the military they were in was engaged in an unjust war and immoral war.

Labeling the U.S. invasion and occupation of Iraq a just war does not make it one. A just war must be defensive, be in proportion to the gravity of the situation, have obtainable objectives, be preceded by a public declaration, be declared only by legitimate authority, and only be undertaken as a last resort. By no stretch of the imagination can the U.S. invasion and occupation of Iraq be called a just war. In fact, the war violates every "just war principle" ever invoked to justify a war.

What is the purpose of the U.S. military? I think it is beyond dispute that the U.S. military should be engaged exclusively in defending the United States, not defending other countries, not attacking other countries, not invading other countries, and not occupying other countries.

Using the military for other purposes perverts the role of the military. Any other purposes, including not only enforcing UN resolutions, nation building, establishing democracy, changing regimes, training foreign armies, opening markets, and maintaining no-fly zones, but even providing disaster relief and dispensing humanitarian aid, perverts the purpose of the military.

Even if the United States went into Iraq with the best of intentions and most purest of motives (which of course it didn't), is it the job of the U.S. military to free the oppressed peoples of the world from their autocratic rulers and totalitarian states? Absolutely not. Not only can't it be done, it would be a never-ending mission that would perpetually shed U.S. blood and spend U.S. treasure.

U.S. soldiers killed while fighting in Iraq died in vain because of the Islamic state they inadvertently helped set up.

Yes, an Islamic state. A socialistic Islamic state under Sharia law in place of the secular government that existed.. Did any advocate for more war and bloodshed in the Middle East ever read article 2 of the new Iraqi constitution? This article stands the beloved American principle of separation of church and state on its head:

> Islam is the official religion of the State and it is a foundation source of legislation.

> No law may be enacted that contradicts the established provisions of Islam.

And what about articles 30, 31, and 34? These articles establish an Iraqi Great Society that would make LBJ proud:

> The State shall guarantee to the individual and the family—especially children and women—social and health security, the basic requirements for living a free and decent life, and shall secure for them suitable income and appropriate housing.

> The State shall guarantee social and health security to Iraqis in cases of old age, sickness, employment disability, homelessness, orphanhood, or unemployment, shall work to protect them from ignorance, fear and poverty, and shall provide them housing and special programs of care and rehabilitation, and this shall be regulated by law.

> Every citizen has the right to health care. The State shall maintain public health and provide the means of prevention and treatment

by building different types of hospitals and health institutions.

Free education in all its stages is a right for all Iraqis.

This is the constitution created by the United States-created and funded Coalition Provisional Authority (CPA), not Al-Qaeda, Islamic extremists, militants, terrorists, insurgents, the Muslim Brotherhood, or Islamo-fascists. The administrator of the CPA reported directly to the U.S. secretary of defense—not to Osama bin Laden, a Muslim cleric or imam, or the Supreme Leader of Iran.

Why doesn't Congressman Peter King investigate this?

U.S. soldiers killed while fighting in Iraq died in vain. They didn't die defending anyone's freedoms. They didn't die protecting the United States. They didn't die fighting "over there" so we wouldn't have to fight "over here." They didn't die to keep American safe from terrorists. They didn't die to avenge 9/11.

They may have been sincere, patriotic, and altruistic. They may have fought bravely, heroically, and passionately. They may have died sacrificially, willingly, and eagerly. But they died for the imperial presidency (Bush or Obama), the U.S. empire, the U.S. military, the U.S. military-industrial complex, the national-security state, and a belligerent, reckless, and meddling U.S. foreign policy.

It is not honorable for a U.S. soldier to die fighting some unnecessary foreign war. It is in fact a shameful thing. All Americans ought to be ashamed of their government, its foreign policy, and the way it uses its military.

Why is it that those who opposed this monstrous war from the beginning are not considered the true patriots? Is it anti-American to think that it wasn't worth one drop of blood from one American soldier to give Iraq a "chance for freedom"? How much more pro-American could one get? Real patriots don't want to see any more U.S. soldiers die in vain.

* * * * *

DAVID E. HICKMAN, R.I.P.

The Iraq War is officially over—for the third time.

The first time the Iraq War ended was on May 1, 2003, when President Bush announced—in front of a "Mission Accomplished" banner—that "the United States and our allies have prevailed" and "major combat operations in Iraq have ended."

Evidently major combat operations had not quite ended since 4,300 more American soldiers then died for a lie while President Bush promised to the families of those killed to "complete the mission so that their child or their husband or wife has not died in vain."

The second ending of the Iraq War was on August 31, 2010, when President Obama proclaimed that "the American combat mission in Iraq has ended" and "Operation Iraqi Freedom is over, and the Iraqi people now have lead responsibility for the security of their country."

Sixty-six more American soldiers then died in vain during "Operation New Dawn."

I hope for the sake of every young man and woman in the U.S. military that the Iraq War is really over this time.

I remember writing about the unconstitutional Iraq War on its third anniversary ("Weapons of Mass Distraction") when 2,317 American soldiers had already died. When I wrote about this unjust war on its fourth anniversary ("Four Years, Four Plans"), that number had risen to 3,218. On the fifth anniversary of this unnecessary war, ("Five Years and Counting"), the number was up to 3,992. On the sixth anniversary of this senseless war ("What Happened to the War?"), it was up to 4,259. On the seventh anniversary of this criminal war ("The Forgotten War"), the death toll was up to 4,385. On the eighth anniversary of this immoral war ("When Will the Iraq War Really End?"), the number of U.S. soldiers who died had "only" increased to 4,439, with 211 of those deaths occurring after Obama took over as the chief war criminal.

I am thankful to God that there will be no ninth anniversary of this horrible war. I am relieved that the death count of U.S. soldiers has ended at 4,487. I am relieved that there will only be 255 U.S. soldiers who died after the inauguration of President Obama.

What Vietnam veteran (and later senator) John Kerry said in testimony before the Senate Foreign Relations Committee (of which he is now chairman) in 1971 about the war in Vietnam is relevant to the Iraq War and especially to its end:

> In our opinion and from our experience, there is nothing in South Vietnam which could happen that realistically threatens the United States of America. And to attempt to justify the loss of one American life in Vietnam, Cambodia or Laos by linking such loss to the preservation of freedom, which those misfits supposedly abuse, is to us the height of criminal hypocrisy, and it is that kind of hypocrisy which we feel has torn this country apart.
>
> We found that not only was it a civil war, an effort by a people

who had for years been seeking their liberation from any colonial influence whatsoever, but also we found that the Vietnamese whom we had enthusiastically molded after our own image were hard put to take up the fight against the threat we were supposedly saving them from.

We found most people didn't even know the difference between communism and democracy. They only wanted to work in rice paddies without helicopters strafing them and bombs with napalm burning their villages and tearing their country apart. They wanted everything to do with the war, particularly with this foreign presence of the United States of America, to leave them alone in peace, and they practiced the art of survival by siding with whichever military force was present at a particular time, be it Viet Cong, North Vietnamese or American.

We found also that all too often American men were dying in those rice paddies for want of support from their allies. We saw first hand how monies from American taxes were used for a corrupt dictatorial regime. We saw that many people in this country had a one-sided idea of who was kept free by the flag, and blacks provided the highest percentage of casualties. We saw Vietnam ravaged equally by American bombs and search and destroy missions, as well as by Viet Cong terrorism—and yet we listened while this country tried to blame all of the havoc on the Viet Cong.

We rationalized destroying villages in order to save them. We saw America lose her sense of morality as she accepted very coolly a My Lai and refused to give up the image of American soldiers who hand out chocolate bars and chewing gum.

We learned the meaning of free fire zones, shooting anything that moves, and we watched while America placed a cheapness on the lives of orientals.

We watched the United States falsification of body counts, in fact the glorification of body counts. We listened while month after month we were told the back of the enemy was about to break. We fought using weapons against "oriental human beings." We fought using weapons against those people which I do not believe this country would dream of using were we fighting in the European theater. We watched while men charged up hills because a general said that hill has to be taken, and after losing one platoon or two platoons they marched away to leave the hill for reoccupation by the North Vietnamese. We watched pride allow the most unimportant battles to be blown into extravaganzas, because we couldn't lose, and we couldn't retreat, and because it didn't matter how many American bodies were lost to prove that point, and so there were Hamburger Hills and Khe Sanhs and Hill 81s and Fire Base 6s, and so many others.

Now we are told that the men who fought there must watch quietly while American lives are lost so that we can exercise the incredible arrogance of Vietnamizing the Vietnamese.

Each day to facilitate the process by which the United States washes her hands of Vietnam someone has to give up his life so that the United States doesn't have to admit something that the entire world already knows, so that we can't say that we have made a mistake. Someone has to die so that President Nixon won't be, and these are his words, "the first President to lose a war."

We are asking Americans to think about that because how do you ask a man to be the last man to die in Vietnam? How do you ask a man to be the last man to die for a mistake?

Army Specialist David E. Hickman, 23, of Greensboro, North Carolina, of the 2nd Battalion, 325th Airborne Infantry Regiment, 2nd Brigade Combat Team, 82nd Airborne Division, Fort Bragg, North Carolina, is that man. He was killed by an IED in Iraq on November 14, 2011. He is the last man to die in Iraq. He is the last man to die for a mistake.

If only Bush hadn't lied us into war. If only Bush had ceased hostilities after the capture of Saddam Hussein. If only Obama had pulled out U.S. troops after his inauguration. If only Obama had really ended the American combat mission in August. If only the war had ended sooner. If only David E. Hickman didn't have to die for a mistake. May he rest in peace.

* * * * *

WAS IT WORTH IT?

Would you sacrifice your firstborn son to establish a democracy in country that had a dictatorship? How about giving up your son to effect a regime change? What about exchanging your son to end the oppression of minorities? How about trading your son in return for a country holding elections?

I don't know of any American mother or father that would do such a thing. I wouldn't give a finger from one of my sons to do any of these things. Some Americans, however, wouldn't mind it if some other American's son came back from some foreign war in a box with only a finger that was recognizable—just as long as it wasn't their son.

Now that the war in Iraq is *officially* over, I keep hearing from apologists for the war about how it was worth it. I keep hearing that because Saddam Hussein is gone, Iraq has a Constitution, Iraqis have freedom, and Iraq holds elections that all the death and destruction was worth it. "We are leaving behind a sovereign, stable and self-reliant Iraq, with a representative government that was elected by its people," President Obama told the troops at Fort Bragg. "I think the price has been worth it, to establish a stable government in a very important region of the world," said Defense Secretary Leon Panetta. Of course, none of Panetta's three sons died in Iraq.

Okay, suppose it's all true—and then some. Suppose it's even better than anyone could have imagined. What if Iraq is now a model democracy for the rest of the world? What if Iraq now has a constitution that rivals our own? What if there is now no more sectarian violence in Iraq? What if Iraq now has a free market? What if Iraq is now an American ally? What if Iraq is now a friend of Israel? What if Iraqis now have freedom of speech and freedom of religion? What if Iraq now respects the rights of women and minorities? What if all Iraqi children are now in school? What if Baghdad is really the best city on earth instead of the worst?

Would it now be worth the life of your son? Can you look your son in the face and tell him that you would have sacrificed him to bring about these changes in Iraq? And if your son had the misfortune of dying in Iraq, how do you think he would feel if he could now hear you say that his death was worth it?

There are a total of 4,487 American sons (and daughters) who died in Iraq. Some of them came home in one piece in a flag-draped coffin; others came home in a box of unidentified fragments and were dumped in a landfill. Hundreds of thousands of Iraq War vets suffer from PTSD or traumatic brain injuries. Many thousands more are missing an arm or a leg—or combinations thereof. Hundreds of vets will need a lifetime of medical and/or psychiatric care. Hundreds have committed suicide, as will hundreds more.

And then there are the thousands of Iraqi defenders (remember, we invaded them) killed, the many thousands of civilians killed, the 1.2

million Iraqis displaced, and the 1.6 million Iraqis made refugees, not to mention the horrendous destruction of infrastructure.

But, of course, none of this matters since these are just dark-skinned foreigners who speak a difficult language, worship a strange god, and wear towels on their head. And besides, they are all terrorists anyway, or would grow up to be one.

So, even though Iraqis paid a terrible price for their "freedom," let's just focus on America and Americans.

I don't think it was worth one drop of blood from one American soldier to bring about anything "good" that happened in Iraq. Not a drop of blood, not an injury, not a headache.

It doesn't matter if Iraq had weapons of mass destruction. It doesn't matter if Saddam Hussein was a brutal dictator. It doesn't matter if Iraqis were not free. It doesn't matter if women in Iraq were oppressed. It doesn't matter if Iraq was a threat to its neighbors. It doesn't matter if Iraq was not a friend of Israel. It doesn't matter if Iraq was not pumping enough oil. It doesn't matter if Saddam Hussein gassed his own people. Nothing that was going on in Iraq mattered.

The United States is not the policeman, fireman, security guard, social worker, mediator, babysitter, guardian, manager, or overseer of the world. Any American concerned about anything going on in Iraq should have gone there and put his own life on the line and on his own dime instead of expecting other Americans to expend their blood and treasure.

I have consistently maintained these views since the beginning of the Iraq War. Yet, although I am the one who didn't want the drop of one American soldier spilled in some senseless foreign war, I am the one who has been labeled un-American and unpatriotic; I am the one who is said to be unsupportive of the troops and a traitor.

The next time some armchair warrior, some warvangelical, some member of Congress, some reich-wing nationalist, some bloodthirsty conservative, some warmongering Republican, some red-state fascist, some neocon, or some theocon beats the drums for war—like they are doing regarding Iran right now—tell him to put his son in uniform, put him on the first plane overseas, and tell his son what a noble cause it is that he is being sent to die for. Let him tell his son how much his death will be worth it. And if he doesn't think it worth the death of his son, then it is not worth the death of any other American's son either.

* * * * *

A DAY OF DISHONOR

The ninth anniversary of the U.S. invasion of Iraq has come and gone, and with little fanfare.

The Iraq War should never have had a first anniversary. President Bush announced on May 1, 2003—in front of a "Mission Accomplished" banner—that "the United States and our allies have prevailed" and "major combat operations in Iraq have ended." If the war had ended then, it would have resulted in the deaths of "only" 140 U.S. soldiers.

But, of course, it didn't end. Just like it didn't end on August 31, 2010, when President Obama proclaimed that "the American combat mission in Iraq has ended" and "Operation Iraqi Freedom is over, and the Iraqi people now have lead responsibility for the security of their country." By that time 4,420 U.S. soldiers had died for a lie.

The war in Iraq did not "officially" end until December 18, 2011, after 4,487 U.S. soldiers had died in vain. The war lasted more than twice as long as the U.S. war against Nazi Germany in World War II.

I first wrote about the Iraq War on its third anniversary ("Weapons of Mass Distraction") when 2,317 American soldiers had already died. When I wrote about the war on its fourth anniversary ("Four Years, Four Plans"), that number had risen to 3,218. On the fifth, ("Five Years and Counting"), the number was up to 3,992. On the sixth ("What Happened to the War?"), it was up to 4,259. On the war's seventh anniversary ("The Forgotten War"), that number had risen to 4,385. Last year, on the war's eighth anniversary ("When Will the Iraq War Really End?"), the number of U.S. soldiers who had died was up to 4,439.

I would not have written anything about the Iraq War this year had not President Obama just proclaimed the ninth anniversary of the U.S. invasion of Iraq to be a National Day of Honor:

> Nine years ago, members of the United States Armed Forces crossed the sands of the Iraq-Kuwait border and began one of the most challenging missions our military has ever known. They left the comforts of home and family, volunteering in service to a cause greater than themselves. They braved insurgency and sectarian strife, knowing too well the danger of combat and the cost of conflict. Yet, through the dust and din and the fog of war, they never lost their resolve. Demonstrating unshakable fortitude and unwavering commitment to duty, our men and women in uniform served tour after tour, fighting block by block to help the Iraqi people seize the chance for a better future. And on December 18, 2011, their mission came to an end.

Today, we honor their success, their service, and their sacrifice. In one of our Nation's longest wars, veterans of Operation Iraqi Freedom and Operation New Dawn wrote one of the most extraordinary chapters in American military history. When highways became mine fields and uncertainty waited behind every corner, service members rose to meet the task at hand with unmatched courage and determination. They learned languages and cultures, taking on new roles as diplomats and development experts to improve the communities where they served. Their strength toppled a tyrant, and their valor helped build opportunity in oppression's place. Across nearly 9 years of conflict, the glory of their service—as well as the contributions of other members of the U.S. Government and our coalition partners—always shone through.

The war left wounds not always seen, but forever felt. The burden of distance and the pain of loss weighed heavily on the hearts of millions at home and overseas. Behind every member of our military stood a parent, a spouse, or a son or daughter who proudly served their community and prayed for their loved one's safe return. For wounded warriors, coming home marked the end of one battle and the beginning of another—to stand, to walk, to recover, and to serve again. And, in war's most profound cost, there were those who never came home. Separated by time and space but united by their love of country, nearly 4,500 men and women are eternally bound; though we have laid them to rest, they will live on in the soul of our Nation now and forever. To them, to their families, and to all who served, we owe a debt that can never be fully repaid.

When we returned the colors of United States Forces-Iraq and the last of our troops set foot on American soil, we reflected on the extraordinary service and sacrifice of those who answered our country's call. Their example embodied that fundamental American faith that tells us no mission is too hard, no challenge is too great, and that through tests and through trials, we will always emerge stronger than before. Now, our Nation reaffirms our commitment to serve veterans of Iraq as well as they served us—to uphold the sacred trust we share with all who have worn the uniform. Our future is brighter for their service, and today, we express our gratitude by saying once more: Welcome home.

NOW, THEREFORE, I, BARACK OBAMA, President of the United States of America, by virtue of the authority vested in me by the Constitution and the laws of the United States, do hereby proclaim March 19, 2012, as a National Day of Honor. I call upon all Americans to observe this day with appropriate programs, ceremonies, and activities that commemorate the return of the United States Armed Forces from Iraq.

IN WITNESS WHEREOF, I have hereunto set my hand this nineteenth day of March, in the year of our Lord two thousand twelve, and of the Independence of the United States of America the two hundred and thirty-sixth.

BARACK OBAMA

The president should have proclaimed a National Day of Dishonor. There is nothing honorable about the War in Iraq. It was unconstitutional, immoral, unjust, senseless, unnecessary, aggressive, irresponsible, and destructive.

Yes, members of the U.S. Armed Forces left "the comforts of home and family," but what was this "cause greater than themselves" that the president is saying they volunteered for? He mentions the U.S. military helping "the Iraqi people seize the chance for a better future," toppling "a tyrant," and building "opportunity in oppression's place."

And those things were worth the deaths of 4,487 American soldiers? Are those things worth hundreds of thousands of Iraq War vets suffering from PTSD or traumatic brain injuries? Are those things worth thousands of U.S. soldiers missing an arm or a leg, or both? Are those things worth the thousands of war veterans who will need a lifetime of medical and/or psychiatric care? Are those things worth the buckets of tears that Americans have shed over the deaths of their loved ones in Iraq? Are those things worth the deaths of more Iraqis than had ever been killed under Saddam Hussein?

The only cause U.S. troops were fighting for was the cause of an aggressive, belligerent, and meddling foreign policy of empire, imperialism, and hegemony.

It doesn't matter what was going on in Iraq. It doesn't matter how brutal a dictator Saddam Hussein was. It doesn't matter if women were oppressed in Iraq. It doesn't matter if religious minorities were persecuted in Iraq. It doesn't matter if Iraq was a threat to Kuwait. It doesn't matter if sectarian violence plagued Iraq. It doesn't matter if Saddam Hussein gassed his own people. It doesn't matter if Iraqis didn't have freedom. It doesn't matter if Iraq had sham elections. It doesn't matter if the Iraqi government tortured Iraqis. It doesn't matter if Iraq didn't have a representative government. It doesn't matter what weapons Iraq had. It doesn't matter if Iraq defied the UN.

Correcting any or all of these things was not worth one drop of blood from one American soldier. Not a scratch, a scrape, or a paper cut. And I am the one who has been called unpatriotic?

Because the U.S. military should be limited to the actual defense of the United States, the anniversary of the invasion of Iraq is not a day of honor. It is a day of infamy, embarrassment, shame, ignominy, and reproach.

* * * * *

THE IRAQ WAR WAS A JUST WAR

The Iraq War began in Iraq on March 20, 2003, at about 5:30 a.m. In the U.S., it was still March 19. So that means that it was ten years ago today that the Iraq War began.

Although the Iraq War is now officially over, it actually ended three times.

The first time was on May 1, 2003, when President Bush announced—in front of a "Mission Accomplished" banner—that "the United States and our allies have prevailed" and "major combat operations in Iraq have ended."

The second time was on August 31, 2010, when President Obama proclaimed that "the American combat mission in Iraq has ended" and "Operation Iraqi Freedom is over, and the Iraqi people now have lead responsibility for the security of their country."

The third time was on December 15, 2011, when a flag-lowering ceremony was held at Baghdad International Airport in which Defense Secretary Leon Panetta said: "The cost was high—in blood and treasure for the United States and also for the Iraqi people, but those lives have not been lost in vain."

I have argued for many years just the opposite—that those lives have been lost in vain (see "They Died in Vain" and "Why They Died in Vain"). But that's not all. I have also said that the War in Iraq was immoral, unconstitutional, unjust, senseless, unholy, unnecessary, unscriptural, aggressive, offensive, and evil. I have also said that the U.S. troops killed in Iraq did not die for anyone's freedoms; they died for a lie.

I wrote about the Iraq War on its third anniversary in 2006 ("Weapons of Mass Distraction"), its fourth in 2007 ("Four Years, Four Plans"), its fifth in 2008 ("Five Years and Counting"), its sixth in 2009 ("What Happened to the War?"), its seventh in 2010 ("The Forgotten

War"), its eighth in 2011 ("When Will the Iraq War Really End?"), and its ninth anniversary in 2012 ("A Day of Dishonor").

But now, on the war's tenth anniversary, I have come to my senses: The Iraq War was a just war.

In its essence, just war theory concerns the use of force: when force should be used and what kind of force is acceptable. The timing of force relates to a country's justification for the initiation of war or military action; the nature of force relates to how military activity is conducted once a country commits to use force. The principle of the just war is actually many principles, all of which must be met for a war to be considered just. A just war must have a just cause, be in proportion to the gravity of the situation, have obtainable objectives, be preceded by a public declaration, be declared only by legitimate authority, and only be undertaken as a last resort.

A war that is not justifiable is nothing short of mass murder. Killing in a war that is unjust or not a war of genuine self-defense is wholesale murder.

Therefore, above all, a just war is a defensive war. As G. K. Chesterton once said: "The only defensible war is a war of defense." This is why I now say that the Iraq War was a just war. Even President Bush once said that the War in Iraq was a defensive war.

In fact, the Iraq War was such a just war that I see no need to write anything else about it again. No more articles on the anniversary of the war. No more articles about the origin of the war. No more articles about the duration of the war. No more articles about the cause of the war. No more articles about the morality of the war. No more articles about the cost of the war. No more articles about the architects of the war. No more articles about the effects of the war. These things are all so unnecessary because the Iraq War was a just war.

The Iraq War was a just war—if you were an Iraqi.

Iraq was not responsible for the 9/11 terrorist attacks—as the U.S. intelligence community briefed Bush ten days after September 11, 2001, and as Bush and Cheney eventually acknowledged.

None of the alleged 9/11 hijackers were from Iraq. And even if one or more of them were from Iraq, that still doesn't justify the Iraq War. If an American citizen hijacked an Air France jet and crashed it into the Eiffel Tower, that wouldn't justify France attacking the United States.

Claims that Iraq had weapons of mass destruction were just a ruse for war. The speech that then Secretary of State Colin Powell gave to the United Nations in 2003 in which he gave a detailed description of what turned out to be Iraq's non-existent weapons programs was later said by

Powell to be a permanent "blot" on his record and said by his chief of staff Lawrence Wilkerson to be "a hoax on the American people, the international community, and the United Nations Security Council." According to the Duelfer Report—the final report on Iraq's weapons of mass destruction by the Pentagon and CIA organized Iraq Survey Group—Iraq had no deployable weapons of mass destruction on the eve of the U.S. invasion in March 2003, and had not produced any since 1991.

The Downing Street Memo (2002), which was made public in 2005, showed Bush's long-standing intent to invade Iraq and his willingness to provoke Saddam Hussein into providing a pretext for war. The necessity of going to war in Iraq was a lie from the very beginning. A student at the University of Illinois documented in 2004 twenty-seven rationales given for the Iraq war by the Bush administration, war hawks in Congress, and the media between 9/11 and the October 2002 congressional resolution to use force in Iraq. It was "the Bush administration, and the President himself" that "established the majority of the rationales for the war and all of those rationales that make up the most prominent reasons for war." A report prepared by the U.S. House of Representatives Committee on Government Reform in 2004 (*Iraq on the Record: The Bush Administration's Public Statements on Iraq*) showed that in 125 separate appearances, Bush, Cheney, Powell, Rumsfeld, and Rice "made 11 misleading statements about the urgency of Iraq's threat, 81 misleading statements about Iraq's nuclear activities, 84 misleading statements about Iraq's chemical and biological capabilities, and 61 misleading statements about Iraq's relationship with al Qaeda." But even before these, Robert Sheer proved, in his 2003 book *Five Biggest Lies Bush Told about Iraq*, that every major assertion the Bush administration put forward to justify the invasion of Iraq was false.

Iraq was never a threat to the United States, and no Iraqi was ever a danger to an American, until Americans invaded and occupied Iraq. U.S. troops were not liberators, peacekeepers, or patriots; they were aggressors, destroyers, and mercenaries. Iraqis were perfectly justified in using whatever means were necessary to repel an invasion and resist an occupation—just like Americans would be fully justified in doing the same. If ever there was a just war, the Iraq War was a just war.

* * * * *

CHAPTER 4
WORLD WAR II

THE EXECUTION OF EDDIE SLOVIK

Every child learns in school that Dwight D. Eisenhower was the thirty-fourth president of the United States. Some Americans also know that Eisenhower was the Supreme Commander of the Allied forces in Europe during World War II. "I Like Ike" was not just a campaign slogan. Many Americans genuinely liked Eisenhower—many Americans except Private Eddie Slovik. And no doubt many Europeans liberated by the Allies also liked Ike—many Europeans except those Russian prisoners of war sent back to the Soviet Union.

Jeffrey Tucker has written about all modern armies being essentially totalitarian enterprises. "Once you sign up for them, or are drafted, you are a slave. The penalty for becoming a fugitive is death. Even now, the enforcements against mutiny, desertion, going AWOL, or what have you, are never questioned."

One notable example of a man who paid the ultimate price for wanting to change his job, a job that he never asked for in the first place, was Edward Donald "Eddie" Slovik (1920–1945). Slovik was a private in the U.S. Army during World War II. Today, January 31, marks the 60th anniversary of his execution by firing squad for desertion. There were 21,049 soldiers sentenced for desertion during WWII, with 49 of them receiving death sentences. However, only Slovik's death sentence was carried out. He was the first U.S. soldier to be executed for desertion since the Civil War. He was also the last, but that may soon change when Rumsfeld and Company decide to make an example of U.S. soldiers who choose to no longer participate in the war in Iraq.

Born in Detroit, Michigan, Slovik was a small-time thief and ex-convict who was originally classified as unfit for military service. But shortly after his first wedding anniversary, in November of 1943, he was drafted anyway. Then, after training for a few months at Camp Wolters in Texas, he was sent to France in August of 1944. Slovik faced impending death in The Battle of Hürtgen Forest, where the American army suffered 24,000 casualties during the battle and an additional 9,000 casualties due to fatigue, illness, or friendly fire. After Slovik's request to be reassigned from the front lines to the rear was refused, he deserted, voluntarily surrendered, and wrote that he would run away again if sent into combat. Confined in the division stockade and facing a court-martial, Slovik refused to return to his unit. On November 11 (Armistice Day), 1944, he was tried and pleaded not guilty, but was convicted of desertion. He wrote a letter to General Eisenhower on December 9 pleading for clemency, but on December 23, during the Battle of the Bulge, Eisenhower confirmed the death sentence.

Slovik's life and death were recounted in the 1954 book *The Execution of Private Slovik*, by William Bradford Huie. The award-winning 1974 NBC-TV movie of the same name, staring Martin Sheen, Ned Beatty, and Gary Busey, is available on video. The trailer can be viewed here.

Captain Benedict Kimmelman, a member of the court martial board, wrote in 1987 that "Slovik, guilty as many others were, was made an example, the sole example, it turned out." He considered the execution a "historic injustice." Colonel Guy Williams, another officer on the panel, said that he didn't think "a single member of that court actually believed that Slovik would ever be shot. I know I didn't believe it."

According to Bernard Calka, the man responsible for bringing Slovik's remains home in 1987 from an army cemetery in France reserved for criminals to Woodmere cemetery in Michigan, "The man didn't refuse to serve, he refused to kill." Calka, a Polish-American WWII veteran who served as an MP during the war and a commander of a VFW post afterward, and later became a commissioner of Macomb County (one of the three counties in Detroit's "tri-county" metro area), spent more than ten years and $8,000 of his own money to have Slovik's remains re-interred next to his wife. Stephen Osinski, a retired judge who filed a formal petition for a Slovik pardon, said that he found "a virtual plethora of significant deprivations of Pvt. Slovik's constitutional rights."

Like Private Slovik, there are others who owe their deaths to Eisenhower. The repatriation of Russian prisoners of war under Operation Keelhaul was another shameful event of World War II. Russian prisoners liberated from German prison camps were to be returned to the Soviet Union—even though they did not want to go back to life under Stalin (our ally in World War II).

One historian with the courage to report this atrocity is Thomas Woods. In his important new book *The Politically Incorrect Guide to American History*, Professor Woods describes how Operation Keelhaul was also carried out on American soil: "At Fort Dix, New Jersey, hundreds of Soviet POWs, who fought with all their strength when they learned that the American government was reneging on its promise not to send them back to the USSR, were drugged in order to calm them down enough for them to be shipped back."

The execution of Eddie Slovik, Operation Keelhaul, and much worse state-sponsored acts of terror during World War II, like the firebombing of cities and the dropping of the atomic bombs, are often dismissed even by opponents of all the U.S. wars and interventions since World War II because it was "defensive" and important that we "stop Hitler." But was it defensive when U.S. forces (the Flying Tigers) attacked Japanese forces before Pearl Harbor? That Japan attacked the United States without provocation is another of the great myths of World War II. And was it so important that 292,131 American soldiers had to die so that the Communists could control Eastern Europe for forty-five years while the United States wasted billions of dollars fighting the Cold War? Our alliance with Stalin and the USSR during World War II was unconscionable, another point made by Professor Woods.

This brings up another question: Who really won World War II? Tragically, the winner was theory and practice of perpetual war for perpetual peace and the rise of the collectivist state, all at the price of true peace and individual liberty.

Does anyone ever "win" a war anyway? Many have thought not:

War is a series of catastrophes that results in a victory. ~ Georges Clemenceau

One is left with the horrible feeling now that war settles nothing; that to win a war is as disastrous as to lose one. ~ Agatha Christie

You can no more win a war than you can win an earthquake. ~ Jeannette Rankin

For the people wars do not pay. The only cause of armed conflict is the greed of autocrats. ~ Ludwig von Mises

The only winner in the War of 1812 was Tchaikovsky. ~ Solomon Short

Randolph Bourne's (1886–1918) dictum that "War is the health of the State" has been quoted many times before, and I am sure that it will be quoted many times hence. But when people will heed the truth of this powerful statement is one of life's great unanswered questions.

* * * * *

THE GREATEST BLUNDER IN BRITISH HISTORY

It was 70 years ago on March 31 when Great Britain committed the fatal blunder that led to World War II: issuing a war guarantee to Poland. This was the war, as Pat Buchanan says in his recent book, *Churchill, Hitler, and the Unnecessary War*, that "led to the slaughter of the Jews and tens of millions of Christians, the devastation of Europe, Stalinization of half the continent, the fall of China to Maoist madness, and half a century of Cold War." Buchanan's book is essential for understanding why World War II was so unnecessary.

Poland was a creature of the Versailles Treaty. After being partitioned several times in history by Prussia, Russia, and Austria, Poland was reconstituted after World War I at the expense of a defeated Germany. But as Buchanan says: "Versailles had created not only an unjust but an unsustainable peace." To give Poland a port on the Baltic, the city of Danzig, which was 95-percent German and had never belonged to Poland, was detached from Germany and made a Free City administered by the League of Nations. A "Polish Corridor" connected Poland to the Baltic and severed East Prussia from Germany.

The regime in Poland, according to contemporary British historian Niall Ferguson, was "every bit as undemocratic and anti-Semitic as that of Germany." Marshal Jozef Pilsudski, the dictator in Poland who had come to power in a coup, considered making a preemptive strike against Germany before signing a 10-year nonaggression pact with Hitler in 1934. Poland had joined in the dismemberment of Czechoslovakia after the Munich Agreement, seizing the coal-rich region of Teschen. Hitler's offer to Polish foreign minister Jozef Beck—a man known for his duplicity, dishonesty, and depravity—to guarantee Poland's borders and accept Polish control of the Corridor in exchange for the return of Danzig and the construction of German roads across the Corridor was rebuffed.

Britain did not object to Danzig being returned to Germany, knowing that a plebiscite would result in an overwhelming vote in favor of return. Lord Halifax, the British foreign secretary, deemed Danzig and the Polish Corridor to be "an absurdity." Hitler wanted an alliance with Poland, not war. He issued a directive to his army commander in chief: "The Fuehrer does not wish to solve the Danzig question by force. He does not wish to drive Poland into the arms of Britain by this."

But then, after false alarms about an imminent German attack on Poland, Prime Minister Neville Chamberlain addressed the British House of Commons:

I now have to inform the House that ... in the event of any action which clearly threatened Polish independence and which the Polish Government accordingly considered it vital to resist with their national forces, His Majesty's Government would feel themselves bound at once to lend the Polish Government all support in their power. They have given the Polish Government an assurance to that effect.

It was March 31, 1939. Germany terminated its nonaggression pact with Poland on April 24, and Poland would cash this "blank check" on September 1, when Hitler invaded Poland. Chamberlain had repeated the blunder made by Kaiser Wilhelm on the eve of World War I.

Former prime minister Lloyd George considered the war guarantee "a frightful gamble" and "sheer madness." The British army general staff "ought to be confined to a lunatic asylum" if they approved this, said Lloyd George. Former First Lord of the Admiralty Cooper recorded in his diary: "Never before in our history have we left in the hands of one of the smaller powers the decision whether or not Britain goes to war." It was "the maddest single action this country has ever taken," said a member of Parliament. Newspaper military correspondent Liddell Hart wrote that the Polish guarantee "placed Britain's destiny in the hands of Polish rulers, men of very dubious and unstable judgment." Only the warmonger Churchill seemed to think the war guarantee was a good idea, foolishly asserting: "The preservation and integrity of Poland must be regarded as a cause commanding the regard of all the world." Buchanan simply calls it "the greatest blunder in British history."

Buchanan refers to modern British historians Roy Denman, Paul Johnson, and Peter Clarke about the folly of the Polish war guarantee:

The most reckless undertaking ever given by a British govern-ment. It placed the decision on peace or war in Europe in the hands of a reckless, intransigent, swashbuckling military dictator-ship.

The power to invoke it was placed in the hands of the Polish government, not a repository of good sense. Therein lay the foolishness of the pledge: Britain had no means of bringing effective aid to Poland yet it obliged Britain itself to declare war on Germany if Poland so requested.

If Czechoslovakia was a faraway country, Poland was further; if Bohemia could not be defended by British troops, no more could Danzig; if the democratic Czech Republic had its flaws, the Polish regime was far more suspect.

Britain could not save Poland any more than it could have saved Czechoslovakia. As Buchanan wrote elsewhere:

> Britain went to war with Germany to save Poland. She did not save Poland. She did lose the empire. And Josef Stalin, whose victims outnumbered those of Hitler 1,000 to one as of September 1939, and who joined Hitler in the rape of Poland, wound up with all of Poland, and all the Christian nations from the Urals to the Elbe. The British Empire fought, bled and died, and made Eastern and Central Europe safe for Stalinism.

Neither Britain nor France had the power to save any nation of Eastern Europe. Yet, Britain was willing to go to war rather than allow Germany to dominate Europe economically, unaffected by a British blockade.

It is the Polish war guarantee for which Neville Chamberlain should be forever judged harshly, not the Munich Agreement for which he is often castigated. (The Munich Agreement essentially ceded to Hitler large sections of Czeckoslovakia in order to reduce the possibility of a European War. This has often been referred to as Chamberlain's "appeasement" of Hitler. Many believe this agreement gave Hitler the resolve to invade Poland, setting off WWII.) It is March 31 that ought to be a day that will live in infamy. The bloodiest conflict in human history was neither good nor necessary.

* * * * *

BUCHANAN'S NECESSARY BOOK

Pat Buchanan and I have some differences—some major differences.

He is a Catholic; I am a Protestant. He is a conservative; I am a libertarian. He is a protectionist; I am a freetrader. He has disparaged Wal-Mart; I spend most of my money there. He believes Alexander Hamilton was one of the greatest of the Founding Fathers; I much prefer Thomas Jefferson. He has worked for Republican presidents; I loathe Republican presidents. He favors a government limited to conservative and Republican policies; I favor a government as limited as possible.

There is one thing, however, that Buchanan and I do agree on, and it is something that I consider to be very important: World War II was an unnecessary war. It was unnecessary for the Treaty of Versailles to enlarge the British, French, Italian, and Japanese empires at the expense of Germany. It was unnecessary for Britain to end its Anglo-Japanese treaty. It was unnecessary for Britain to impose sanctions on Italy, driving Mussolini into an alliance with Hitler. It was unnecessary for Britain to issue a war guarantee to Poland. And most importantly, it was unnecessary for 420,000 American soldiers to die fighting a foreign war.

I am not the only one to express a new-found agreement with Pat Buchanan. Writing in *The Texas Observer*, Josh Rosenblatt explains:

> One of the more disconcerting (if poorly publicized) effects of the last eight years of American foreign policy is that I'm now forced to admit there are things Pat Buchanan and I agree on. It was so much easier during the reign of the first President Bush, when Buchanan was the happy culture warrior, fire-breathing his way across the country attacking gays, feminists, liberals and other degenerate life forms as he went, and I could hate the man and sleep comfortably. Now it seems like every time I turn on MSNBC, there's Buchanan, condemning the second President Bush's Iraq War, railing against his blundering efforts in Afghanistan, bemoaning his cowboy posturing toward Iran and Russia. And before I know what's happening, I'm nodding my head and thinking, "Maybe Pat Buchanan isn't such a bad guy after all." Inevitably I end up turning the TV off in self-disgust, imagining my father turning somersaults in his grave.

There are really five Pat Buchanans.

There is Pat Buchanan the syndicated columnist. God only knows how many newspapers and magazines Buchanan has been published in. He is also a co-founder of The American Conservative magazine.

There is Pat Buchanan the TV commentator. Besides being a regular on *The McLaughlin Group*, Crossfire, and *The Capital Gang*, Buchanan's nationally-recognized face has been seen on countless other news programs.

There is Pat Buchanan the political operative. He was an adviser to Nixon's presidential campaigns, and worked in the Nixon and Ford White Houses. He served under Reagan as the White House Communications Director.

There is Pat Buchanan the politician. In 1992 and 1996, he sought the Republican presidential nomination. He was the Reform Party's presidential candidate in the 2000.

And then there is Pat Buchanan the author. He is the author of the following books:

- *The New Majority: President Nixon at Mid-Passage* (1973)
- *Conservative Votes, Liberal Victories: Why the Right Has Failed* (1975)
- *Right from the Beginning* (1988)
- *The Great Betrayal: How American Sovereignty and Social Justice Are Being Sacrificed to the Gods of the Global Economy* (1988)
- *America Asleep: The Free Trade Syndrome and the Global Economic Challenge: A New Conservative Foreign Economic Policy for America* (1991)
- *A Republic, Not an Empire: Reclaiming America's Destiny* (1999)
- *The Death of the West: How Dying Populations and Immigrant Invasions Imperil Our Country and Civilization* (2002)
- *Where the Right Went Wrong: How Neoconservatives Subverted the Reagan Revolution and Hijacked the Bush Presidency* (2004)
- *State of Emergency: The Third World Invasion and Conquest of America* (2006)
- *Day of Reckoning: How Hubris, Ideology, and Greed Are Tearing America Apart* (2007)
- *Churchill, Hitler, and the Unnecessary War: How Britain Lost Its Empire and the West Lost the World* (2008)

Buchanan's books are not all created equal; e.g., see David Gordon's review of *A Republic, Not an Empire* and *The Death of the West*. There is one book, however, that is not only Buchanan's best and most important book; it is one of the best and most important books ever written. I am referring to his latest book on World War II: *Churchill, Hitler, and the Unnecessary War: How Britain Lost Its Empire and the West Lost the World*.

Now, I realize that my lofty assessment of Buchanan's book might be dismissed as a hyperbolic exaggeration on steroids. But as one who is a student of war and foreign policy, and writes extensively about war-related issues, and especially on the folly of war, I, having read the book very, very carefully, cannot, must not, say otherwise. I don't recall ever having highlighted, dog-eared, written in, read, and reread any book like I have this one.

Since the book came out last year, and has been reviewed—positively (*The American Conservative*), negatively (*The Jerusalem Post*), and savagely (*Newsweek*)—many times already, I am forgoing a formal review. I knew when the book came out last year that it was something I would have to read and write about, but it was only after going through the book for myself that I realized just what a monumental thing it was that Pat Buchanan had done.

This book is so important, so crucial to the cause of peace, because World War II, more than any other war in the history of the world, is considered to be, not only necessary, but just, right, and good. Indeed, World War II is known as the "Good War."

But if this is true then we have a problem, for, as Buchanan writes in his introduction: "It was the war begun in September 1939 that led to the slaughter of the Jews and tens of millions of Christians, the devastation of Europe, Stalinization of half the continent, the fall of China to Maoist madness, and half a century of Cold War." How can a war that resulted in the deaths of 50 to 70 million people be termed a good war? How can a war in which two-thirds of those who died were civilians be termed a good war?

Whenever I write about the folly of war, I inevitably get e-mail from some armchair warrior who says something like: "You [pacifist, appeaser, liberal, communist, traitor, America-hater, peacenik, coward]! Don't you know that if the U.S. military had not intervened to stop Hitler we would all be speaking German right now?"

A greater lie has never been uttered.

Churchill, Hitler, and the Unnecessary War debunks the myths about World War II being necessary and demolishes the arguments offered in defense of World War II as a "good" war.

But this is not just a book on World War II. And it could not be otherwise, for World War II was but the continuation of "the great civil war of the West." "This is not peace," said French Marshal Ferdinand Foch after the "war to end all wars," "it is an armistice for twenty years." "All lines of inquiry lead back to World War I," said American diplomat and historian George Kennan. "Versailles," writes Buchanan, "had created not only an unjust but an unsustainable peace."

Accordingly, the first three chapters of Buchanan's book are about the causes and consequences of World War I. Chapters 4 through 12 likewise treat World War II. Buchanan points out in his introduction the two great myths about these wars: "The first is that World War I was fought 'to make the world safe for Democracy.' The second is that World War II was the 'Good War,' a glorious crusade to rid the world of Fascism that turned out wonderfully well." That first statement is now generally recognized for the myth that it is. The second; however, is still a widely-held opinion—hence the need for this book.

The last three chapters of the book deal with Hitler's real ambitions ("Hitler never wanted war with Britain."), Churchill as a poor choice for man of the century (Churchill's concessions at Moscow were far worse than Chamberlain's at Munich."), and America inheriting Britain's empire ("There is hardly a blunder of the British Empire we have not replicated.").

The book is also a history and geography lesson: Bohemia, the Sudetenland, Alsace, Lorraine, Danzig, Transylvania, Czechoslovakia, Yugoslavia, Abyssinia, the Austro-Hungarian Empire, Moravia, Sarajevo, Trianon, Trieste, the Polish Corridor, Galicia, Tyrol, Ruthenia, Silesia, and the Treaties of Versailles, Trianon, Brest-Litovsk, and St. Germain. And aside from the usual relevant pictures in the center of the book like we see in most books on the world wars, Buchanan's book includes very detailed maps that wonderfully supplement the text.

There are no battle accounts in *Churchill, Hitler, and the Unnecessary War*. No details on troop movements. No information on fighting techniques. No theories about military strategy. No particulars about weapons. The crucial question for Buchanan is: "Were these two devastating wars Britain declared on Germany wars of necessity, or wars of choice?"

Britain? Yes, Great Britain, the United Kingdom, the empire on which the sun never set. You mean you thought both world wars were all the fault of Germany?

Now, we know all about the evils of Hitler and Nazism: the fascism, the murder, the mayhem, the destruction, the aggression, the militarism, the racism, the anti-Semitism, the death camps. Buchanan doesn't excuse Germany in the least: "None of this is to minimize the evil of Nazi ideology, or the capabilities of the Nazi war machine, or the despicable crimes of Hitler's regime, or the potential threat of Nazi Germany to Great Britain once war was declared." And neither does he slight the heroism of the British: "The question this book addresses is not whether the British were heroic. That is settled for all time. But were their statesmen wise?"

When it came to World War I, British statesmen were anything but wise:

British hawks looked to a European war to enhance national prestige and expand the empire.

Unknown to the Cabinet and Parliament, a tiny cabal had made a decision fateful for Britain, the empire, and the world. Under the guidance of Edward Grey, the foreign secretary from 1905 to

1916, British and French officers plotted Britain's entry into a Franco-German war from the first shot.

It was the British decision to send an army across the Channel to fight in Western Europe, for the first time in exactly one hundred years, that led to the defeat of the Schlieffen Plan, four years of trench warfare, America's entry, Germany's collapse in the autumn of 1918, the abdication of the Kaiser, the dismemberment of Germany at Versailles, and the rise to power of a veteran of the Western Front who, four years after the war's end, was unreconciled to his nation's defeat.

Had Britain not declared war on Germany in 1914, Canada, Australia, South Africa, New Zealand, and India would not have followed the Mother Country in. Nor would Britain's ally Japan. Nor would Italy, which London lured in with secret bribes of territory from the Habsburg and Ottoman empires. Nor would America have gone to war had Britain stayed out. Germany would have been victorious, perhaps in months. There would have been no Lenin, no Stalin, no Versailles, no Hitler, no Holocaust.

Buchanan gives five reasons why the Britain government at the time "turned the European war of August 1 into a world war": to preserve France as a great power, to defend British honor, to retain their control of the government, Germanophobia, and imperial ambition and opportunism.

The cost of Britain's folly: 700,000 dead British soldiers, plus 200,000 more from throughout the empire. And for what?

The caricature of Germany as the most militaristic country is just that. Buchanan points out that from Waterloo to World War I, Germany had only been involved in three wars while Great Britain had engaged in ten.

World War I, as Buchanan quotes British historian John Keegan, was "an unnecessary conflict. Unnecessary because the train of events that led to its outbreak might have been broken at any point during the five weeks that preceded the first clash of arms, had prudence or common goodwill found a voice."

And then there is World War II:

Had Britain not given a war guarantee to Poland in March 1939, then declared war on September 3, bringing in South Africa, Canada, Australia, India, New Zealand, and the United States, a German-Polish war might never have become a six-year world war in which fifty million would perish.

Thus did the British government, in panic over a false report about a German invasion of Poland that was neither planned nor prepared, give a war guarantee to a dictatorship it did not trust, in a part of Europe where it had no vital interests, committing itself to a war it could not win.

From 1914—1918, Britain and France, with millions of soldiers, had barely been able to keep the German army out of Paris. Two million Americans had been needed to crack the German lines. Now, with a tiny fraction of the British army of 1918, with former allies Russia, Japan, and Italy now hostile, and with America now neutral, Britain was handling out war guarantees not only to Belgium and Holland, but also to Poland and Rumania.

Buchanan's conclusion will be a tough one for some to swallow: "It was Britain that turned both European wars into world wars."

Churchill, Hitler, and the Unnecessary War is a necessary book.

It is necessary because it tells the real story of British prime minister Neville Chamberlain's "appeasement" of Hitler at Munich. Because the Sudeten Germans in Czechoslovakia—a multiethnic, multilingual, multicultural, Catholic-Protestant conglomerate that had never before existed—"hated the Prague regime and had no loyalty to a nation where they were second-class citizens" (there were more Germans in Czechoslovakia than Slovaks), Chamberlain, correctly, and not alone, "did not believe that maintaining Czech rule over three million unhappy Germans was worth a war."

It is necessary because it shows that the greatest blunder in British history was not Munich, but the Polish war guarantee that committed Britain to fight for a Polish dictatorship that had considered making a preemptive strike against Germany, signed, like Stalin, a nonaggression pact with Hitler, and joined in the dismemberment of Czechoslovakia after the Munich Agreement. Here Buchanan is not alone. Lloyd George considered it "a frightful gamble" and "sheer madness." Former First Lord of the Admiralty Cooper recorded in his diary: "Never before in our history have we left in the hands of one of the smaller powers the decision whether or not Britain goes to war." It was "the maddest single action this country has ever taken," said a member of Parliament. I have written about this foolish Polish war guarantee here.

It is necessary because it demolishes the cult of Churchill. Winston Churchill, rather than being the indispensable man of the century, was "the most bellicose champion of British entry into the European war of 1914 and the German-Polish war of 1939." Among his other crimes,

Churchill appeased Stalin—one of the twentieth century's greatest mass murderers, whose crimes exceeded those of Hitler—by agreeing to his "annexation of the Baltic republics," accepting "his plunder from the devil's pact with Hitler," and turning "a blind eye to the Katyn massacre."

It is necessary because it explains how Hitler never wanted war with Britain. Hitler wanted absolute power in Germany. Hitler wanted to overturn the Versailles Treaty. Hitler wanted to restore lands to Germany. Hitler wanted to enlarge the German empire to the east. Hitler wanted to cleanse Germany of Jews. Hitler wanted to destroy Bolshevism. Hitler wanted Germany to achieve economic self-sufficiency in Europe. Hitler wanted to go down in history as "the greatest German of them all." But Hitler never wanted war with Britain. To Hitler: "Great Britain was Germany's natural ally and the nation and empire he most admired. He did not covet British colonies. He did not want or seek a fleet to rival the Royal Navy. He did not wish to bring down the British Empire. He was prepared to appease Britain to make her a friend of Germany."

It is necessary because it confirms that Hitler was not a threat to the United States. The German Luftwaffe lost the Battle of Britain to the Royal Air Force; the German Navy was no match for Britain's Royal Navy ("The Navy—what need have we of that?," said Hitler in 1936). At the start of the war, Germany had only two battleships. The *Bismarck* had not been built yet—and it would be sunk on its maiden voyage. There were no troopships, landing barges, or transports for tanks and artillery. If Hitler could not cross the English Channel and conquer Great Britain, how could he possibly have been a threat to America? Buchanan dismisses Germany's supposed plans "to build a massive surface fleet, develop a trans-atlantic bomber, and procure naval bases" as "comic-book history." The historical truth is that "there are no known German plans to acquire the thousand ships needed to convey and convoy such an army and its artillery, tanks, planes, guns, munitions, equipment, fuel, and food across the Atlantic." And as Buchanan points out about German bombers: "A trip over the Atlantic and back would require twenty hours of flying to drop a five-ton load on New York." And if even today the U.S. Air Force doesn't have a bomber that can fly round trip from the Midwest to Germany without refueling, how could German bombers in the 1940s have possibly bombed the United States and returned to Germany when air-to-air fueling had not yet been invented?

Was it necessary that tens of millions were slaughtered to prevent Hitler from slaughtering millions?

Certainly not.

But don't take Pat Buchanan's word for it when we have the word of Churchill himself:

> One day President Roosevelt told me that he was asking publicly
> for suggestions about what the war should be called. I said at once,
> "The Unnecessary War." There never was a war more easy to stop
> than that which has just wrecked what was left of the world from
> the previous struggle.

And if World War II was unnecessary, then how much more unnecessary
are the wars in Iraq and Afghanistan?

Churchill, Hitler, and the Unnecessary War—buy it, read it, digest
it, and refer to it often. And the next time someone tries to justify some
U.S. military intervention by appealing to the "Good War," ask him what
was so good about it.

* * * * *

BOMBINGS WORSE THAN NAGASAKI AND HIROSHIMA

The world knows all too well about the atomic bombs the United
States dropped on Hiroshima on Monday, August 6, 1945 ("Little Boy"),
and on Nagasaki on Thursday, August 9 ("Fat Man"). "Dropping the
bombs ended the war," said President Harry Truman.

They may have ended the war, but they did not end the bombing of
Japan.

On August 14, 1945, *after* the two atomic bombs had been dropped
on Japan, and *after* Emperor Hirohito had agreed to surrender because
"the enemy now possesses a new and terrible weapon with the power to
destroy many innocent lives and do incalculable damage," General Henry
Harley "Hap" Arnold, to boost his already over-inflated ego (he was made
a five-star general in 1944), undertook a completely unnecessary act of
terror from the skies over Japan that had never before been seen. In their
1953 book *The Army Air Forces in World War II*, Wesley F. Craven and
James L. Cate state:

> Arnold wanted as big a finale as possible, hoping that USASTAF
> could hit the Tokyo area in a 1,000-plane mission: the Twentieth
> Air Force had put up 853 B-29's and 79 fighters on 1 August, and
> Arnold thought the number could be rounded out by calling on
> Doolittle's Eighth Air Force. Spaatz still wanted to drop the third
> atom bomb on Tokyo but thought that battered city a poor target
> for conventional bombing; instead, he proposed to divide his

forces between seven targets. Arnold was apologetic about the unfortunate mixup on the 11th and, accepting Spaatz' amendment, assured him that his orders had been "co-ordinated with my superiors all the way to the top." The teleconference ended with a fervid "Thank God" from Spaatz. Kennedy had the Okinawa strips tied up with other operations so that Doolittle was unable to send out his VHB's. From the Marianas, 449 B-29's went out for a daylight strike on the 14th, and that night, with top officers standing by at Washington and Guam for a last-minute cancellation, 372 more were airborne. Seven planes dispatched on special bombing missions by the 509th Group brought the number of B-20's to 828, and with 186 fighter escorts dispatched, USASTAF passed Arnold's goal with a total of 1,014 aircraft. There were no losses, and before the last B-29 returned President Truman announced the unconditional surrender of Japan.

This was the largest bombing raid in history. Yet, many timelines of World War II do not even list this event as having occurred.

But although this was the largest bombing raid, it was not the deadliest. In fact, the atomic bombs dropped on Japan were not even the deadliest. Because high-altitude precision bombing was viewed as not effective enough, the Army Air Force began using incendiary attacks against Japanese cities. After months of studies, planning, and several incendiary bombing test runs, Tokyo was firebombed on the night of March 9, 1945, by low-flying B-29's with increased bomb loads. Seventeen hundred tons of bombs were dropped in a densely populated area (an average of 103,000 people per square mile) of twelve square miles. The result was just what one would expect: as many as 100,000 dead, over 40,000 wounded, over 1,000,000 made homeless, over 267,000 buildings destroyed. The water boiled in some small canals because of the intense heat. This was the most destructive air attack in history. It killed more people than the dropping of an atomic bomb.

The Tokyo firebombing raid was followed by larger ones against Nagoya, Osaka, and Kobe, some of Japan's largest cities. Then Nagoya was hit again. All in all, 1,595 sorties had flown in 10 days, dropping over 9,300 toms of bombs. Japanese cities—large and small—were continually hit with conventional and incendiary bombs through the end of the war.

But the bombing of Japanese cities was not war, it was wholesale murder. How, then, does this act of terrorism continue to be defended almost sixty-five years later? Simple. Japan bombed Pearl Harbor. In fact, nothing U.S. forces did to Japan during the war matters because of Pearl Harbor.

But even if FDR didn't have prior knowledge of the Japanese attack on Pearl Harbor and even if the United States didn't provoke Japan into firing the first shot (See Robert Stinnett's excellent book *Day of Deceit: The Truth about FDR and Pearl Harbor*, which persuasively argues that he did have prior knowledge and did provoke Japan into firing the first shot), Japan's attack on Pearl Harbor still doesn't justify bombing the civilian population of Japan. Why is it that the 9/11 attacks on America are considered acts of terrorism but a 1,000-plane bombing raid on Tokyo after the dropping of two atomic bombs isn't?

Pearl Harbor or no Pearl Harbor, the bombing of Tokyo on August 14, 1945, was a despicable act—worse than the firebombing of Tokyo, worse than Hiroshima, and worse than Nagasaki—because it was so unnecessary.

* * * * *

RETHINKING THE GOOD WAR

"Rarely in history has a war seemed so just to so many." ~ Michael Bess

"Participation in the war against Hitler remains almost wholly sacrosanct, nearly in the realm of theology." ~ Bruce Russett

On September 1, 1939—70 years ago—Germany attacked Poland and officially began World War II. Although over 50 million people died in the war—including 405,000 Americans—it is considered to be the Good War. The fact that most of deaths were on the Allied side (the "good" side), the majority of those killed were civilians, hundreds of millions were wounded—including 671,000 Americans—and/or made refugees, homeless, widows, or orphans, hundreds of billions of dollars worth of property was destroyed, hundreds of billions of dollars more were wasted on armaments, and untold millions underwent an incomprehensible amount of suffering, misery, and loss doesn't seem to matter either. World War II is still universally recognized as the Good War.

How is it possible to make such a description of such carnage on a grand scale?

As John V. Denson explains in his essay "Franklin D. Roosevelt and the First Shot" in his book *A Century of War: Lincoln, Wilson, and Roosevelt:*

Part of the mythology that surrounds this war is that it was the "last good war." It was a "just" war because it was defensive. Despite President Roosevelt's supreme efforts to keep America neutral regarding controversies in Europe and Asia, the Japanese launched an *unprovoked surprise attack* at Pearl Harbor, thereby "forcing" America into the fray. It was also a "noble" war because America fought evil tyrannies known as Nazism in Germany and fascism in Italy and Japan.

From the American point of view, World War II is basically considered to be the Good War for two reasons: Pearl Harbor and Hitler.

But setting aside for a moment the facts of Roosevelt's duplicity and culpability, as well as the U.S. provocation of Japan: Was it necessary for 405,000 American soldiers to die to avenge the 2,400 (1,177 were from one ship, the USS *Arizona*) who were killed at Pearl Harbor? Was it moral to incinerate hundreds of thousands of civilians in Japanese cities because Japan bombed the Pearl Harbor Naval Base, a military target? And setting aside for another moment the folly of U.S. intervention in World War I, which prevented a dictated peace settlement and paved the way for the harsh terms of the Treaty of Versailles, thus facilitating the rise of Hitler: Was it necessary that tens of millions were slaughtered to prevent Hitler from slaughtering millions? Was it wise to join forces with a brutal dictator like Stalin, who had already killed millions, with the result that he enslaved half of Europe under communism?

It is time to rethink the Good War.

World War I

"The Second World War," as explained by the widely-published British military historian John Keegan in his book of that name, "in its origin, nature and course, is inexplicable except by reference to the First; and Germany—which, whether or not it is to be blamed for the outbreak, certainly struck the first blow—undoubtedly went to war in 1939 to recover the place in the world it had lost by its defeat in 1918." Not only would World War II never have taken place without World War I: "The first war explains the second and, in fact, caused it, in so far as one event causes another," said British historian A. J. P. Taylor (1906–1990) in his seminal work *The Origins of the Second World War.* "Germany fought specifically in the second war to reverse the verdict of the first and to destroy the settlement that followed it," adds Taylor. "This is not peace," said French Marshal Ferdinand Foch after Versailles, "it is an armistice for twenty years."

World War II as we know it would never have taken place without

U.S. intervention in World War I. Just before the Second Battle of the Marne, only five months before the armistice of November 11, 1918, German armies, as related by John Keegan,

> occupied the whole of western Russia . . . enclosed Kiev . . . and cut off from the rest of the country one-third of Russia's population, one-third of its agricultural land and more than one-half of its industry. . . . German expeditionary forces operated as far east as Georgia in Transcaucasia and as far south as the Bulgarian frontier with Greece and the plain of Po in Italy. Through her Austrian and Bulgarian satellites Germany controlled the whole of the Balkans and, by her alliance with Turkey, extended her power as far away as northern Arabia and northern Persia. In Scandinavia, Sweden remained a friendly neutral, while Germany was helping Finland to gain its independence from the Bolsheviks . . . . In distant south-east Africa a German colonial army kept in play an Allied army ten times its size. And in the west, on the war's critical front, the German armies stood within fifty miles of Paris. In five great offensives, begun the previous March, the German high command had regained all the territory contested with France since the First Battle of the Marne fought four years earlier. A sixth offensive promised to carry its spearheads to the French capital and win the war.

The United States officially declared war on Germany on April 6, 1917. By June of that year, the first U.S. troops landed in France. By March of 1918, 250,000 U.S. doughboys were in France. That number increased to 1 million by the time of the Second Battle of the Marne. But even after this and subsequent victories for the Allies, no battles were ever fought on German soil.

World War I was not our war. In a memo written at the end of World War II, Churchill wrote:

> This war should never have come unless, under American and modernizing pressure, we had driven the Habsburgs out of Austria and the Hohenzollerns out of Germany. By making these vacuums we gave the opening for the Hitlerite monster to crawl out of its sewer onto the vacant thrones. No doubt these views are very unfashionable.

The Revolutionary War was our war. The War of 1812 was our war. The Mexican War was our war. The Spanish-American War was our war. The Philippine-American War was our war. But World War I was not our war.

Had we stayed out of it, another European war would have come to an end—as they had for centuries. The history of Europe is the history of war.

European Wars

The America Founding Fathers, whatever their faults, realized this. Most educated people are familiar with the "isolationist" sentiments of George Washington in his farewell address:

> The great rule of conduct for us in regard to foreign nations is, in extending our commercial relations to have with them as little political connection as possible.

> Europe has a set of primary interests which to us have none; or a very remote relation. Hence she must be engaged in frequent controversies, the causes of which are essentially foreign to our concerns. Hence, therefore, it must be unwise in us to implicate ourselves by artificial ties in the ordinary vicissitudes of her politics, or the ordinary combinations and collisions of her friendships or enmities.

> Why, by interweaving our destiny with that of any part of Europe, entangle our peace and prosperity in the toils of European ambition, rivalship, interest, humor or caprice?

> It is our true policy to steer clear of permanent alliances with any portion of the foreign world.

But it is our third president, Thomas Jefferson, who had spent time in Europe, that over and over and over again warned about getting embroiled in European affairs:

> For years we have been looking as spectators on our brethren in Europe, afflicted by all those evils which necessarily follow an abandonment of the moral rules which bind men and nations together. Connected with them in friendship and commerce, we have happily so far kept aloof from their calamitous conflicts, by a steady observance of justice towards all, by much forbearance and multiplied sacrifices.

> We have seen with sincere concern the flames of war lighted up again in Europe, and nations with which we have the most friendly and useful relations engaged in mutual destruction. While we

regret the miseries in which we see others involved let us bow with gratitude to that kind Providence which, inspiring with wisdom and moderation our late legislative councils while paced under the urgency of the greatest wrongs, guarded us from hastily entering into the sanguinary contest, and left us only to look on and to pity its ravages.

Believing that the happiness of mankind is best promoted by the useful pursuits of peace, that on these alone a stable prosperity can be founded, that the evils of war are great in their endurance, and have a long reckoning for ages to come, I have used my best endeavors to keep our country uncommitted in the troubles which afflict Europe, and which assail us on every side.

You will do what is right, leaving the people of Europe to act their follies and crimes among themselves, while we pursue in good faith the paths of peace and prosperity.

Since this happy separation, our nation has wisely avoided entangling itself in the system of European interests, has taken no side between its rival powers, attached itself to none of its ever-changing confederacies. Their peace is desirable; and you do me justice in saying that to preserve and secure this, has been the constant aim of my administration.

Peace and abstinence from European interferences are our objects, and so will continue while the present order of things in America remain uninterrupted.

I have used my best endeavors to keep our country uncommitted in the troubles which afflict Europe, and which assail us on every side.

Nothing is so important as that America shall separate herself from the systems of Europe, and establish one of her own. Our circumstances, our pursuits, our interests, are distinct. The principles of our policy should be so also. All entanglements with that quarter of the globe should be avoided if we mean that peace and justice shall be the polar stars of the American societies.

I am decidedly of opinion we should take no part in European quarrels, but cultivate peace and commerce with all.

I am for free commerce with all nations, political connection with none, and little or no diplomatic establishment. And I am not for linking ourselves by new treaties with the quarrels of Europe, entering that field of slaughter to preserve their balance, or joining in the confederacy of Kings to war against the principles of liberty.

At such a distance from Europe and with such an ocean between us, we hope to meddle little in its quarrels or combinations. Its peace and its commerce are what we shall court.

Determined as we are to avoid, if possible, wasting the energies of our people in war and destruction, we shall avoid implicating ourselves with the powers of Europe, even in support of principles which we mean to pursue. They have so many other interests different from ours, that we must avoid being entangled in them.

In 1941, Representative Frances Bolton (R–Ohio), in the *Congressional Record*, and historian Charles A. Beard, in the *Chicago Daily Tribune*, each presented lists of the various European wars. John Keegan points out that "Hiram Maxim, the inventor of the first successful machine-gun, is alleged to have given up experiments in electrical engineering in 1883 on the advice of a fellow American who said: 'Hang your electricity! If you want to make your fortune, invent something which will allow those fool Europeans to kill each other more quickly.'"

American Foreign Policy

The United States followed Washington's "great rule" for most of the nineteenth century. In the midst of enthusiasm for Greece in its nationalist struggle against the Ottoman Turks and Latin America against Spain, Secretary of State (and future president) John Quincy Adams delivered a brief address on American foreign policy on the Fourth of July in 1821 in which he argued for a policy of sympathy and example, but not intervention:

Wherever the standard of freedom and independence has been unfurled, there will her [America's] heart, her benedictions, and her prayers be. But she goes not abroad in search of monsters to destroy. She is the well-wisher to the freedom and independence of all. She is the champion and vindicator only of her own. She will commend the general cause by the countenance of her voice, and the benignant sympathy of her example. She well knows that by once enlisting under other banners than her own, were they even the banners of foreign independence, she would involve herself beyond the power of extrication, in all the wars of interest and intrigue, of individual avarice, envy, and ambition, which assume the colors and usurp the standard of freedom.

Likewise, when the Hungarian nationalist Louis Kossuth sought American aid in the struggle for Hungarian independence, Henry Clay remarked that "the cause of liberty" is better served by "avoiding the distant wars of Europe." We should instead "keep our lamp burning brightly on this Western Shore, as a light to all nations, than to hazard its utter extinction, amid the ruins of fallen or falling republics in Europe," said Clay.

When President Grover Cleveland delivered his first inaugural address in 1885, he saw no reason to deviate from a century of non-intervention:

> The genius of our institutions, the needs of our people in their home life, and the attention which is demanded for the settlement and development of the resources of our vast territory dictate the scrupulous avoidance of any departure from the foreign policy commended by the history, the traditions, and the prosperity of our republic.

This does not mean that U.S. forces never landed in Central and South America or that the U.S. Navy never sailed to the Far East. These things happened every year or so, but always to protect U.S. citizens or promote U.S. interests. The acquisitions, absorptions, imperialism, and military expansionism of the United States in the nineteenth century were primarily continental.

The big shift in American foreign policy began with the 1893 overthrow of the Hawaiian monarchy and the 1898 annexation of Hawaii—a de facto American protectorate since the 1850s. (It should be noted that without the annexation of Hawaii there would have been no Pearl Harbor to be bombed by the Japanese; just like without the purchase of Alaska from Russia in 1867 there would have been no fighting with Japan in the Aleutian Islands in 1942–1943, which resulted in the deaths of 1,500 American soldiers.) The seizing of Hawaii was followed by the acquisition of Cuba, Puerto Rico, the Philippines, and Guam from Spain during the Spanish-American War. The United States was fast becoming a global imperial power—like the Europeans.

But after being reelected on the campaign slogan of "He kept us out of war," President Wilson, not five months later, asked Congress for a declaration of war against Germany to make the world "safe for Democracy." The vote was 82–6 in the Senate and 373–50 in the House—in favor of jettisoning the foreign policy of the Founders. The cost in

American lives was 117,000.

The Great War—with its death and destruction on a scale never seen before in history, tremendous expansion of government power, unprecedented violations of civil liberties, artificial creation of countries like Yugoslavia, Czechoslovakia, and Iraq, Carthaginian peace imposed on Germany, and starvation blockade of Germany that former president Herbert Hoover called "a wicked thrust of Allied militarism and punishment"—was the great mistake, as far as America was concerned.

The Interwar Years

All of this was almost universally recognized in the United States in the interim between the world wars. The spirit of peace and nonintervention prevailed. Disillusionment with war spread throughout society. The horrors of war were graphically depicted in literature and film. In 1921, Eugene Debs, who had been sent to prison in 1918 for urging resistance to conscription, had his sentence commuted and was received by President Harding at the White House.

"Revisionist" books, like *The Genesis of the World War* (1926) by Harry Elmer Barnes (1889–1968), were published by the major publishing houses. The German antiwar novel *All Quiet on the Western Front*, which appeared in 1928, was translated in English and made into a movie in 1930. Marine Corps Major General Smedley Butler denounced war after his retirement in his 1935 book *War Is a Racket*.

New peace and pacifist organizations were formed. After winning the right to vote, women turned more of their attention to the peace effort. Women founded the War Resister League in 1924 as a registry for those who refused to participate in war. The Peace Letter campaign of 1925 sought and received signatures on a pledge to "refuse to support or render war service to any Government which resorts to arms." Albert Einstein and other intellectuals actively supported campaigns for conscientious objection and against conscription. Hundreds of college students signed a pledge that they would not "support the United States government in any war it may conduct." There were student strikes in the mid 1930s to protest the growing threat of war. Advocates of strict neutrality called for the embargoing of all belligerents to prevent economic interests from dragging the country into war. As Spain erupted into civil war, the Emergency Peace Campaign sponsored meetings in hundreds of American cities in 1936. The following year the group launched the No-Foreign-War Crusade to bolster the antiwar movement. The Keep America Out of War Congress was formed in 1938. Even many American organizations that supported FDR's domestic agenda opposed his foreign policy.

The Five-Power Treaty, signed by the United States, Britain, France, Japan, and Italy in 1922, was an agreement to voluntarily scrap warships and limit the construction of new ones. The Kellogg-Briand Pact was signed in 1928 by the United States and the other major powers as they pledged to renounce war as an instrument of national policy. The Nye Committee in the U.S. Senate, which met between 1934 and 1935, investigated the munitions industry and documented not only the large profits made by arms manufacturers during World War I, but price fixing, the bribing of public officials, and collusion between U.S. and British firms. The U.S. Congress passed a series of Neutrality Acts beginning in 1935. The proposed amendment to the Constitution by Rep. Louis Ludlow (D-IN), introduced several times in Congress beginning in 1935, called for a national referendum on congressional declarations of war, unless the United States was attacked first. General Smedley Butler recommended a Peace Amendment that would prohibit the removal of the Army from U.S. soil, limit the distance that Navy ships could steam from our coasts, and limit the distance that military aircraft could fly from our borders.

It was the same even after the start of the war in Europe. The America First Committee was formed in 1940 to try to keep the United States out of the war. Membership was over 800,000, with millions of fellow travelers. The AFC regularly published its statement of principles:

1. Our first duty is to keep America out of foreign wars. Our entry would only destroy democracy, not save it.
2. We must build a defense, for our own shores, so strong that no foreign power or combination of powers can invade our country by sea, air or land.
3. Not by acts of war, but by preserving and extending democracy at home can we aid democracy and freedom in other lands.
4. In 1917 we sent our ships into the war zone; and this led us to war. In 1941 we must keep our naval convoys and merchant vessels on this side of the Atlantic.
5. Humanitarian aid is the duty of a strong free country at peace. With proper safeguards for the distribution of supplies we should feed and clothe the suffering and needy people of the occupied countries.
6. We advocate official advisory vote by the people of the United States on the question of war and peace, so that when Congress decides this question, as the Constitution provides, it may know the

opinion of the people on this gravest of all issues.

On the American First Committee, see Bill Kauffman's *America First!: Its History, Culture, and Politics* (Prometheus Books, 1995). On American anti-interventionist thought during the interwar years, see Eric A. Nordlinger's *Isolationism Reconfigured: American Foreign Policy for a New Century* (Princeton University Press, 1995) and David Cortright's *Peace: A History of Movements and Ideas* (Cambridge University Press, 2008). Indispensable on this subject is Justus D. Doenecke's *Storm on the Horizon: The Challenge to American Intervention 1939–1941* (Rowman & Littlefield, 2000).

Both the Democrats and Republicans had antiwar statements in their 1940 political platforms:

> We will not participate in foreign wars and we will not send our army, naval or air forces to fight in foreign lands outside the Americas, except in case of attack.

> The Republican Party is firmly opposed to involving this nation in foreign wars.

Both candidates—Roosevelt and Willkie—campaigned on the promise to stay out of foreign wars:

> While I am talking to you mothers and fathers, I give you one more assurance. I have said this before but I shall say it again and again. Your boys are not going to be sent into any foreign wars.

> If you elect me President, I will never send an American boy to fight in a European war.

Now, we know that presidential candidates, like all other political candidates, will say whatever they think the public wants to hear in order to get elected. Roosevelt, as will be seen, moved the country toward war even while speaking out against getting involved. And Willkie, who openly espoused interventionism and raised money for interventionist causes before his run for the presidency as a weak peace candidate, showed his true interventionist colors after he lost the election. The point here is that what both candidates said about staying out of foreign wars resonated with the American people.

But instead of Americans learning the lesson they should have from World War I, they succumbed to the war propaganda once more and got involved again—going to war in Europe after being attacked by an Asian country. This time, however, there was no turning back. World War II has been viewed as the "great exception" to the "great rule" of George Washington ever since. And not only that, America's entry in the war was, as Murray Rothbard wrote in his obituary for Harry Elmer Barnes:

> The crucial act in expanding the United States from a republic into an Empire, and in spreading that Empire throughout the world, replacing the sagging British Empire in the process. Our entry into World War II was the crucial act in foisting a permanent militarization upon the economy and society, in bringing to the country a permanent garrison state, an overweening military-industrial complex, a permanent system of conscription. It was the crucial act in creating a Mixed Economy run by Big Government, a system of State-Monopoly-Capitalism run by the central government in collaboration with Big Business and Big Unionism. It was the crucial act in elevating Presidential power, particularly in foreign affairs, to the role of single most despotic person in the history of the world. And, finally, World War II is the last war-myth left, the myth that the Old Left clings to in pure desperation: the myth that here, at least, was a good war, here was a war in which America was in the right. World War II is the war thrown into our faces by the war-making Establishment, as it tries, in each war that we face, to wrap itself in the mantle of good and righteous World War II.

But none of this matters because of Pearl Harbor. In fact, *nothing* we did to Japan during the war matters—because of Pearl Harbor. And for that matter, *nothing* we did during the war to Japan, Germany, Italy, or anyone else, including civilians and U.S. citizens, matters—because of Pearl Harbor.

A Date which Will Live in Infamy

The attack on Pearl Harbor was, of course, what *actively* put the United States into the Second World War. Without war against Japan, the conflict with Germany could conceivably have been limited to naval engagements. But was the "sudden and deliberate attack" on Pearl Harbor a surprise?

There have been a slew of books written over the years on the subject of Roosevelt's duplicity and culpability regarding the Japanese attack on Pearl Harbor. I believe the most recent one is George Victor's *The Pearl Harbor Myth: Rethinking the Unthinkable* (Potomac Books,

2007). This is an exceptional book, not only because it is up-to-date and very well documented, but also because the author is an "admirer of Roosevelt" who maintains that "criticism and justification of Roosevelt's acts are outside the purpose of this book."

But before World War II had even ended, Roosevelt's nemesis John T. Flynn (1882–1964) wrote what is probably the first "revisionist" account of the Pearl Harbor attack: *The Truth About Pearl Harbor*. This appeared on the front page of the *Chicago Daily Tribune* on October 22, 1944, "with only a few deletions," under the headline of: "Records Bear Truth about Pearl Harbor." Flynn wrote a sequel in 1945 that was published in the same paper on September 2, 1945, under the three headlines of:

Exposes More Secrets of Pearl Harbor Scandal
Blame for Tragic Delays Fixed; Blunders Bared
John T. Flynn Charges Government Knew Jap Cabinet Intended to Break
Relations

The editor's note preceding the article reads:

John T. Flynn, investigator and publicist, author of "The Truth About Pearl Harbor," has written a second sensational article on this catastrophe. He discloses new and startling information that was in the possession of the United States high command during the final days and hours before the great Pacific base was attacked by the Japanese on Dec. 7, 1941. In this inclusive treatise, he fixes the blame for the disaster squarely upon Franklin D. Roosevelt, then President of the United States.

This was published in booklet form as *The Final Secret of Pearl Harbor*. At the end of his essay in this latter work, Flynn summed up what he saw as the "pathetic tragedy of blunders":

1. By January 1, 1941, Roosevelt had decided to go to war with Japan.
2. But he had solemnly pledged the people he would not take their sons to foreign wars *unless attacked*. Hence he dared not attack and so decided to provoke the Japanese to do so.
3. He kept all this a secret from the Army and Navy.
4. He felt the moment to provoke the attack had come by November. He ended negotiations abruptly November 26 by handing the Japanese an ultimatum which he knew they dared not comply with.

5. Immediately he knew his ruse would succeed, that the Japanese looked upon relations as ended and were preparing for the assault. He knew this from the intercepted messages.

6. He was certain the attack would be against British territory, at Singapore perhaps, and perhaps on the Philippines or Guam. If on the Philippines or Guam he would have his desired attack. But if only British territory were attacked could he safely start shooting? He decided he could and committed himself to the British government. But he never revealed this to his naval chief.

7. He did not order Short to change his alert and he did not order Kimmel to take his fleet out of Pearl Harbor, out where it could defend itself, because he wanted to create the appearance of being completely at peace and surprised when the Japs started shooting. Hence he ordered Kimmel and Short not to do anything to cause alarm or suspicion. He was completely sure the Japs would not strike at Pearl Harbor.

8. Thus he completely miscalculated. He disregarded the advice of men who always held that Pearl Harbor would be first attacked. He disregarded the warning implicit in the hour chosen for attack and called to Knox's attention. He disregarded the advice of his chiefs that we were unprepared.

9. When the attack came he was appalled and frightened. He dared not give the facts to the country. To save himself he maneuvered to lay the blame upon Kimmel and Short. To prevent them from proving their innocence he refused them a trial. When the case was investigated by two naval and army boards, he suppressed the reports. He threatened prosecution to any man who would tell the truth.

[Kimmel and Short were the Pearl Harbor Navy and Army commanders; Knox was the Secretary of the Navy.]

Flynn's works on Pearl Harbor were followed by George Morgenstern's *Pearl Harbor: The Story of the Secret War* (New York: Devin-Adair, 1947) and Rear Admiral Robert A. Theobald's *The Final Secret of Pearl Harbor: The Washington Contribution to the Japanese Attack* (New York: Devin-Adair, 1954). In addition, the following books were also published about the same time that contain valuable chapters relating to Pearl Harbor and/or U.S. foreign policy in relation to Japan in the 1930s: Charles A. Beard's *President Roosevelt and the Coming of the War 1941: A Study in Appearances and Realities* (Yale University Press, 1948), William Henry Chamberlin's *America's Second Crusade* (Henry Regnery,

1950), Charles Callan Tansill's *Back Door to War: The Roosevelt Foreign Policy 1933–1941* (Henry Regnery, 1952), and the edited work by Harry Elmer Barnes, with contributions by Morgenstern, Chamberlin, Tansill, et al., titled *Perpetual War for Perpetual Peace: A Critical Examination of the Foreign Policy of Franklin Delano Roosevelt and Its Aftermath* (The Caxton Printers, 1953).

Nevertheless, the myth of Pearl Harbor was soon well established. Barnes lamented in 1966:

> Despite this voluminous revisionist literature which has appeared since 1945 and its sensational content, there is still virtually no public knowledge of revisionist facts over twenty years after V-J Day. The "man on the street" is just as prone to accept Roosevelt's "day of infamy" legend today as he was on December 8, 1941.

He gives several reasons why this is the case: the country never really had time to cool off after the war like it did following World War I, the American public proved more susceptible to simple brainwashing through propaganda than Orwell could imagine, the conformity of intellectuals whereby individuality and independence all but disappeared, the moderation of the liberals and radicals who had been champions of revisionism after the First World War, the intense hatred of Hitler and Mussolini that blinds people to accept any facts that might diminish their guilt, the rise of the idea that the United States must do battle with any foreign country whose political ideology does not accord with ours, the excessive security measures adopted under the Cold War that have increased the public's fear and timidity, and the lack of major publishers willing to publish revisionist material.

This latter point is especially important because, says Barnes: "No matter how many revisionist books are produced, how high their quality, or how sensational their revelations, they will have no effect on the American public until this public learns of the existence, nature, and importance of revisionist literature."

The last thing Barnes wrote before he died in 1968 was a careful summary of the whole Pearl Harbor controversy. He reasoned that "only a small fraction of the American people are any better acquainted with the realities of the responsibility for the attack than they were when President Roosevelt delivered his 'Day of Infamy' oration on December 8, 1941. The legends and rhetoric of that day still dominate the American mind." "Pearl Harbor After a Quarter of a Century" was published in Murray Rothbard's journal *Left and Right: A Journal of Libertarian Thought* (Vol. IV, 1968, 9-132). It would also be this journal's last article, as it ceased publication with this "special Harry Barnes–Pearl Harbor issue."

Perhaps the most authoritative book on Pearl Harbor is Robert Stinnett's *Day Of Deceit: The Truth About FDR and Pearl Harbor* (Free Press, 2000). Stinnett, who served in the Navy during World War II, spent seventeen years of his life researching in archives, conducting interviews, and examining documents obtained through Freedom of Information Act requests. He concludes that not only did FDR know the attack on Pearl Harbor was coming, he deliberately provoked it. From the White House perspective, the Pearl Harbor attack "had to be endured in order to stop a greater evil—the Nazi invaders in Europe who had begun the Holocaust and were poised to invade Europe." Pearl Harbor was Roosevelt's "back door to war."

The Peruvian minister to Japan reported to the U.S. embassy there in January of 1941—almost a year before Pearl Harbor—that "Japanese military forces were planning, in the event of trouble with the United States, to attempt a surprise mass attack on Pearl Harbor using all their military resources."

In former CIA director William Casey's book *The Secret War Against Hitler* (Regnery, 1988), he claims that "the British had sent word that a Japanese fleet was steaming east toward Hawaii."

Secretary of War Henry Stimson recorded in his diary on November 25—less than two weeks before the Pearl Harbor attack:

> The question was how we should maneuver them into the position of firing the first shot without allowing too much damage to ourselves.
>
> In spite of the risk involved, however, in letting the Japanese fire the first shot, we realized that in order to have the full support of the American people it was desirable to make sure that the Japanese be the ones to do this so that there should remain no doubt in anyone's mind as to who were the aggressors.

On the day the attack took place, he expressed relief: "When the news first came that Japan had attacked us, my first feeling was of relief that indecision was over and that a crisis had come in a way which would united all our people." And testifying after Pearl Harbor, Stimson stated: "If there was war, moreover, we wanted the Japanese to commit the first overt act."

Eleanor Roosevelt didn't seem too surprised either. In an article in the *New York Times Magazine* a few years later, she recalled: "December 7 was just like any of the later D-days to us. We clustered at the radio and waited for more details—but it was far from the shock it proved to the country in general. We had expected something of the sort for a long time."

But even if Pearl Harbor was not in any way a surprise, was it, as Secretary of State Cordell Hull said, "a treacherous and utterly unprovoked attack on the United States"?

Japan had become the dominant power in the Far East after its victory in the Russo-Japanese War of 1904–05. In 1931 Japan began the process of controlling all of Manchuria by seizing Mukden. After a series of skirmishes and "incidents," full-scale war began in 1937 between China and Japan. The Chinese nationalists and the Chinese communists, who had been fighting a civil war since 1927, temporarily united against Japan.

But instead of remaining neutral, the United States sided with China. As William Henry Chamberlin explains:

> There was sentimental sympathy for China as the "underdog" in the struggle against Japan. This was nourished by missionaries and other American residents of China. The "Open Door" policy for China, enunciated by Secretary of State John Hay about the turn of the century, was regarded as a sacrosanct tradition of American diplomacy and was seldom subjected to critical and realistic examination. Considerations of prestige made it difficult to surrender established rights under pressure. The groups which believed in permanent crusade against aggression, in a policy of perpetual war for the sake of perpetual peace, were quick to mobilize American opinion against Japan.

China, of course, is now the boogeyman and Japan is one of our allies.

The United States had already pressured Great Britain to scrap its Anglo-Japanese treaty, thus isolating Japan. The United States supplied munitions, arms, and aircraft to British, Chinese, and Dutch forces in the Pacific. China received millions of dollars worth of loans. Twentyfour U.S. submarines were sent to Manila. Roosevelt sent U.S. naval vessels on cruises into Japanese waters. He refused to meet with the Japanese prime minister, Prince Konoye, leading to the rise of Tojo. Secretary of State Hull issued a provocative ultimatum to Japan on November 26, 1941, that he knew the Japanese government would reject: "The government of Japan will withdraw all military, naval, air and police forces from China and Indochina."

The United States waged economic warfare against Japan. The 1911 Treaty of Commerce and Navigation with Japan was abrogated on January 26, 1940. Based on the Export Control Act of July 2, 1940,

Roosevelt restricted exports of aviation fuels, lubricants, melting iron, and scrap steel beginning on July 31. On October 16, 1940, an embargo took effect on all exports of scrap iron and steel to overseas destinations other than Britain. All Japanese assets in the United States were frozen on July 25, 1941. On August 1, 1941, a final embargo on all oil shipments to Japan was instituted. Japan was allowed to build up its oil reserves just enough to enable it to go to war.

In General Smedley Butler's aforementioned book *War Is a Racket*, he mentions U.S. Navy war games in the Pacific that were bound to provoke Japan: "The Japanese, a proud people, of course will be pleased beyond expression to see the United States fleet so close to Nippon's shores. Even as pleased as would be the residents of California were they to dimly discern through the morning mist, the Japanese fleet playing at war games off Los Angeles."

Then there is the American Volunteer Group (AVG), known as the Flying Tigers. This was the "efficient guerrilla air corps" mentioned in 1940 by Major Rodney Boone (USMC) of the Office of Naval Intelligence. This group of 100 American pilots, who were allowed to resign from their branch of the military with the assurance that they could be reinstated when their one-year contract with a front company called the Central Aircraft Manufacturing Company (CAMCO) was up, were mercenaries who secretly trained in the jungles of Southeast Asia to fly bombing missions for the Chinese Air Force. They sailed from the West Coast as ordinary civilians in order to keep hidden their true mission and mask FDR's secret attempt to support China against Japan. All of the details, supported by government documents, are in Alan Armstrong's *Preemptive Strike: The Secret Plan that Would Have Prevented the Attack on Pearl Harbor* (The Lyons Press, 2006). In 1991, the Flying Tigers were retroactively recognized as members of the U.S. military during their period of mercenary service.

The most damaging piece of evidence that the United States provoked Japan into firing the first shot is the "McCollum memo" of October 7, 1940, written by Lieutenant Commander Arthur McCollum, the head of the Far East desk of the Office of Naval Intelligence. McCollum's five-page, ten-point memorandum proposed eight actions under point nine to provoke Japan into war:

1. Make an arrangement with Britain for the use of British bases in the Pacific, particularly Singapore.
2. Make an arrangement with Holland for the use of base facilities and acquisition of supplies in the Dutch East Indies.

3. Give all possible aid to the Chinese government of Chiang-Kai-shek.

4. Send a division of long range heavy cruisers to the Orient, Philippines, or Singapore.

5. Send two divisions of submarines to the Orient.

6. Keep the main strength of the U.S. Fleet now in the Pacific in the vicinity of the Hawaiian Islands.

7. Insist that the Dutch refuse to grant Japanese demands for undue economic concessions, particularly oil.

8. Completely embargo all U.S. trade with Japan, in collaboration with a similar embargo imposed by the British Empire.

McCollum concludes that "if by these means Japan could be led to commit an overt act of war, so much the better." The Tripartite Pact had just been signed by Germany, Italy, and Japan. Provoking Japan into war was a backdoor way to get the United States involved in the European war. McCollum's proposals were all implemented by Roosevelt. The attack on Pearl Harbor was but the climax of a long series of events. It was neither a surprise nor unprovoked.

To supplement these provocations against Japan, the U.S. Pacific Fleet was moved from the West Coast to Pearl Harbor beginning in April of 1940. The commander of the fleet at the time, Vice Admiral James Richardson, objected because of the lack of training facilities, large-scale ammunition and fuel supplies, support craft, and overhaul facilities. There was also the morale problem of men kept away from their families. FDR relieved Richardson of his command on February 1, 1941. In January of 1941, the Secretary of the Navy, Frank Knox, warned that Pearl Harbor was vulnerable to bombing, sabotage, and submarine attack. In an interview with FDR in June of 1941, the new commander of the Pacific Fleet, Admiral Husband Kimmel, outlined the weaknesses of placing the fleet at Pearl Harbor. In the days before Pearl Harbor, the Pacific Fleet's two aircraft carriers, the *Lexington* and *Enterprise*, and twenty-one modern warships were sent out to sea.

Although the Japanese diplomatic and naval codes were broken, vital information was withheld from the commanders at Pearl Harbor, General Walter Short and Admiral Husband Kimmel. Both men were made scapegoats, relieved of their commands, demoted in rank, and denied an opportunity to defend themselves. Yet, title V, subtitle D, section 546, of the National Defense Authorization Act for fiscal year 2001 reversed nine previous Pearl Harbor investigations and found:

Numerous investigations following the attack on Pearl Harbor have documented that Admiral Kimmel and Lieutenant General Short were not provided necessary and critical intelligence that was available, that foretold of war with Japan, that warned of imminent attack, and that would have alerted them to prepare for the attack.

Although Kimmel and Short were never posthumously restored to their former ranks, Congress concluded that "the losses incurred by the United States" in the attacks on Pearl Harbor "were not a result of dereliction in the performance" of their duties.

Admirers of FDR—past and present—admit that he, as Clare Booth Luce remarked, "lied us into war":

Franklin Roosevelt repeatedly deceived the American people during the period before Pearl Harbor. . . . If he was going to induce the people to move at all, he would have to trick them into acting for their best interests, or what he conceived to be their best interests. He was like the physician who must tell the patient lies for the patient's own good. . . . A president who cannot entrust the people with the truth betrays a certain lack of faith in the basic tenets of democracy. But because the masses are notoriously shortsighted and generally cannot see danger until it is at their throats, our statesmen are forced to deceive them into an awareness of their own long-run interests. This is clearly what Roosevelt had to do, and who shall say that posterity will not thank him for it. (Thomas A. Bailey, *The Man in the Street*, 1948).

As Germany began to prepare for conquest, genocide, and destruction of civilization, the leader of only one major nation saw what was coming and made plans to stop it. As a result of Roosevelt's leadership, a planned sequence of events carried out in the Atlantic and more decisively in the Pacific brought the United States into one of the world's greatest cataclysms. The American contribution helped turn the war's tide and saved the world from a destructive tyranny unparalleled in modern history. (George Victor, *The Pearl Harbor Myth*, 2007).

For those who refuse to believe that presidents lie, see Eric Alterman's *When Presidents Lie: A History of Official Deception and Its Consequences* (Viking, 2004). Truth, it has been said, is always the first casualty of war.

But would Roosevelt really be willing to sacrifice American lives to become a war president? When he sent U.S. naval vessels on "pop-up" cruises into Japanese waters, FDR remarked: "I just want them to keep popping up here and there and keep the Japs guessing. I don't mind losing one or two cruisers, but do not take a chance on losing five or six." According to Robert Stinnett, losing two cruisers would be sacrificing 1,800 men. That is almost as many naval personnel that were killed at Pearl Harbor. And of course, Roosevelt knew that American entry into the war would result in thousands of dead U.S. soldiers.

But even with all the Roosevelt lies and provocations, Japan still attacked us, it is argued. None of our pre-war actions directly killed any Japanese, but they killed 2,400 of our men when they bombed Pearl Harbor. But what did we expect Japan to do? We don't cheer on the bully who taunts another kid for weeks and then beats him up after the kid finally breaks his nose. True, Japan was not just "another kid." Japan was becoming increasingly militaristic. Japan sought to aggressively expand its empire in the Far East. The Japanese brutally treated the Chinese and the Koreans. But none of this should have been the concern of the United States. In fact, previous to this, the United States became increasingly militaristic, sought to expand its control over the Philippines, and brutally treated the Filipinos. The British and Dutch had been expanding their empires in the Far East for many years. Japan wanted to eject the European empires and replace them with its own.

The Japanese may have been short, bucktoothed, slant-eyed, yellow vermin, subhuman apes in khaki (see U.S. wartime propaganda), but they weren't stupid. Japan knew it could not win a war against the United States. Japan in 1941 was not the economic powerhouse it became after the war. It was a small island nation of fishermen and farmers. At the time of American entry into World War II, Japan had less than 4 percent of the world's manufacturing capacity, while America produced more steel, aluminum, oil, and vehicles than all the other major nations combined. Japan had very little of the necessary resources for an industrial war economy. And the United States was the chief supplier to Japan. During the war there were four tons of supplies for each American soldier and two pounds of supplies for each Japanese soldier. Japan did not attack the United States because Japan was "evil" and America was "good." Japan sought to gain control of Southeast Asian resources. The attack on Pearl Harbor would prevent the U.S. Pacific Fleet from interfering. Secretary of War Stimson acknowledged after the war that "if at any time the United States had been willing to concede to Japan a free hand in China there would have been no war in the Pacific."

This is all clear now, or at least it should be. The problem is that the average American at the time knew nothing about the lies and provocations of the Roosevelt administration. The only thing the typical American knew on December 7, 1941, was that Japan had attacked the United States. These things are also true of Americans serving in the military at the time. Should we fault the servicemen who valiantly defended Pearl Harbor? No. Should we dishonor those military personnel who were killed by the Japanese at Pearl Harbor, many of whom are still entombed in the USS *Arizona*? Certainly not. But was it necessary for 405,000 American soldiers to die to avenge the 2,400 killed at Pearl Harbor?

But even if Japan had not been provoked, and the Pearl Harbor attack was a complete surprise, was war with Japan the correct response? This is a question that is rarely, if ever, raised. And here is another question that should be considered: Is it still a defensive war if troops have to travel thousands of miles to engage an "enemy" that attacked and then retreated? The war against Japan was certainly more a war of revenge, vengeance, retaliation, retribution, anger, or rage than a war of defense.

Once again, if Japan had not been provoked, and the Pearl Harbor attack was a complete surprise, what should the United States have done? Regardless of what course of action should have been taken, there is one thing that should have been done immediately: determine why it happened. No country, army, navy, air force, terrorist organization, or individual aggresses against the United States for no reason. We may not like or agree with the reason, but there is always a good reason, at least in the minds of the attackers.

Yet again, if Japan had not been provoked, and the Pearl Harbor attack was a complete surprise, does that justify the atrocities committed against the Japanese during the war? I mean things like the harvesting of gold teeth from dead and not-so-dead Japanese soldiers, boiling the flesh off enemy skulls to make ornaments for military vehicles or to send home as souvenirs, urinating in the mouths of dead Japanese soldiers, carving enemy bones into letter openers, mutilating corpses, attacking and sinking hospital ships, shooting sailors who abandoned ship, shooting pilots who bailed out, killing wounded enemy soldiers on the battlefield, torturing and executing enemy prisoners, massacring unarmed Japanese soldiers who just surrendered, kicking in the teeth of prisoners before or after their execution, and the collecting of Japanese ears. See John W. Dower's *War Without Mercy: Race and Power in the Pacific War* (Pantheon Books, 1986). True, the Japanese committed unspeakable brutalities and atrocities against Allied soldiers and POWs, their own soldiers, and civilians in areas they occupied (see e.g., *The Rape of Nanking: The Forgotten Holocaust of World War II* [Basic Books, 1997]). But it is the Japanese that were considered to be uncivilized, knuckle-dragging brutes, not the

Americans.

And finally, if Japan had not been provoked, and the Pearl Harbor attack was a complete surprise, does that justify terrorizing the civilian population of Japan? The Japanese had the decency to attack a genuine military target instead of dropping bombs on downtown San Diego or Honolulu. After months of studies, planning, and several incendiary bombing test runs, the U.S. Army Air Force firebombed densely- populated Tokyo on the night of March 9, 1945. The results were unprecedented: 100,000 dead, 40,000 wounded, 1,000,000 made homeless, 267,000 buildings destroyed. Further incendiary attacks were made against other Japanese cities for the duration of the war. This was climaxed by the dropping of atomic bombs on Hiroshima and Nagasaki. And then, on August 14, 1945, *after* the two atomic bombs had been dropped on Japan, and *after* Emperor Hirohito had agreed to surrender because "the enemy now possesses a new and terrible weapon with the power to destroy many innocent lives and do incalculable damage," the egotistical General Henry Harley "Hap" Arnold got his big finale: a 1,000-plane bombing mission against Tokyo. This was worse than Nagasaki and Hiroshima because it was so unnecessary. Although this was the largest bombing raid in history, many timelines of World War II do not even list this event as having occurred. Why is it that the 9/11 attacks on America are considered acts of terrorism but a 1,000-plane bombing raid on Tokyo after the dropping of two atomic bombs isn't? (On the atomic bombing of Japan, see Gar Alperovitz's *The Decision to Use the Atomic Bomb: And the Architecture of an American Myth* [Knopf, 1995]).

I have seen documentaries on Pearl Harbor where U.S. servicemen who survived the attack still say that they will never forgive the Japanese and refuse to meet with Japanese pilots who bombed Pearl Harbor, as other survivors have done. But if any of these servicemen support the war in Iraq then they are hypocrites. Japan made a preemptive strike against the United States just like the United States did in Iraq. It can also be argued that the United States certainly provoked Japan more than Iraq provoked the United States. Why should we fault the Japanese pilots who bombed Pearl Harbor? Weren't they just following orders like we expect American troops to do? And why should we fault the Japanese civilians who grew food and built weapons for their soldiers just like American civilians? None of this matters, of course, because of Pearl Harbor. Nothing we did to Japan during the war matters—because of Pearl Harbor.

It is time to rethink Pearl Harbor.

There is nothing "conspiratorial" about Pearl Harbor revisionism.

In addition to the books mentioned thus far in relation to Pearl Harbor, I recommend chapter 3, "A Hobson's Choice for Japan," in Bruce M. Russett's *No Clear and Present Danger: A Skeptical View of the U.S. Entry into World War II* (Harper & Row, 1972); chapter 4, "Myth: The Attack on Pearl Harbor Was a Surprise," in Michael Zezima's *Saving Private Power: The Hidden History of "The Good War"* (Soft Skull Press, 2000), issued in paperback in 2005 as *There Is No Good War: The Myths of World War II*; part 3, "The U.S. Enters the War," in Richard J. Maybury's *World War II: The Rest of the Story and How It Affects You Today* (Bluestocking Press, 2003); and chapter 4, "Franklin D. Roosevelt and the First Shot," in John V. Denson's *A Century of War: Lincoln, Wilson, and Roosevelt* (Mises Institute, 2006). The Independent Institute also maintains a very informative Pearl Harbor Archive.

Hitler

So, what about Hitler? I have answered that question in the context of just war theory in my review of Robert Brimlow's *What about Hitler? Wrestling with Jesus's Call to Nonviolence in an Evil World* (Brazos Press, 2006). Here, however, we are concerned with the questions of the necessity of the United States to fight against Hitler, the wisdom of allying with Stalin against Hitler, the tactics of the U.S. military, the conduct of U.S. troops during and after the war, and, most importantly, the lies, provocations, and other actions of Roosevelt that resulted in the United States getting involved in the deadliest European war in history.

Like Pearl Harbor, it is time to rethink Hitler.

Now, there are many things about Hitler that don't need rethinking. The evils of Hitler and Nazism are beyond dispute: fascism, militarism, racism, anti-Semitism, forced labor, death camps, gruesome medical experiments, murder, genocide, theft, book burning, lies, propaganda, brutal suppression of dissent, deliberate targeting of civilians, horrendous destruction of property, tremendous violations of civil rights, the invasion, conquest, and occupation of other countries, etc., etc., etc.

Still, without excusing any of the horrors of Hitler's regime, the questions remain about the necessity of fighting against Hitler, the wisdom of allying with Stalin, the tactics of the U.S. military, the conduct of U.S. troops, and the activities of Roosevelt that moved the country toward war.

Like Pearl Harbor, nothing we did to Germany during the war matters—because of Hitler. Nothing we did during the war to Germany, Italy, Japan, or anyone else, including civilians and U.S. citizens, matters—because of Hitler. And furthermore, nothing the U.S. military has done since World War II matters—because of the supposed threats of other Hitlers.

After the Japanese attack on Pearl Harbor on December 7, 1941, and the declaration of war against Japan by the United States on December 8, Germany and Italy, signatories of The Tripartite Pact with Japan, declared war on the United States on December 11. This was immediately followed by a declaration of war by the United States against Germany and Italy on the same date (the United States also declared war on the Axis powers of Bulgaria, Hungary, and Romania on June 5, 1942).

Whether Germany declared war on the United States or not, it was not necessary for the United States to fight against Germany. Hitler was not a threat to the United States. On May 20, 1940, German forces reached the English Channel. Yet, the German *Luftwaffe* lost the Battle of Britain to the Royal Air Force; the German *Kriegsmarine* was no match for Britain's Royal Navy, and the German *Heer* could neither invade nor conquer Great Britain. The British Isles were much more secure against a German invasion in 1941 than they were at the beginning of the war. Yet, Roosevelt made a speech on May 27 in which he asserted: "The war is approaching the brink of the western hemisphere itself. It is coming very close to home." If Hitler couldn't conquer Great Britain across the English Channel, how could he possibly have been a threat to the United States across the Atlantic Ocean? This was exactly the argument made at the time by several U.S. senators, including the great Old Right stalwart Robert Taft (R–Ohio).

And looking back from the present time, three other things are clearly evident. If the French in occupied France weren't forced to speak German, how can American's keep repeating the lie that we would all be speaking German right now if the U.S. military hadn't intervened to stop Hitler? If it was unnecessary for Britain and France to fight against Germany, as Patrick J. Buchanan powerfully and compassionately argues in *Churchill, Hitler, and the Unnecessary War: How Britain Lost Its Empire and the West Lost the World* (Crown Publishers, 2008), it was certainly more unnecessary for the United States to do so. And if Switzerland could remain neutral during World War II, then so could the United States.

Hitler never wanted war with Britain. He wanted absolute power in Germany. He wanted to be a great German historical figure like Bismarck. He wanted to overturn the injustices of the Versailles Treaty. He wanted to restore German lands and people. He wanted to enlarge the German empire to the east. He wanted to cleanse Germany of Jews and other inferior races. He wanted to destroy Bolshevism. He wanted Germany to achieve economic self-sufficiency in Europe. Whether these things were right or wrong is immaterial. Hitler never wanted war with Britain, and certainly not with the United States. He never wanted a two-front war, let alone a world war. He wanted Germany to be a world power, not the ruler of the world. He wanted a friendly or neutral Britain, not a hostile or rival Britain.

The greatest blunder in British history was not Munich, where Chamberlain "appeased" Hitler, but the Polish war guarantee that committed Britain to fight for an anti-Semitic Polish dictatorship that had considered making a preemptive strike against Germany, signed, like Stalin, a nonaggression pact with Hitler, and joined in the dismemberment of Czechoslovakia after the Munich Agreement.

Germany did not declare war on Great Britain and France on that fateful day in September of 1939; Great Britain and France declared war on Germany after Germany invaded Poland. Yet, when the Soviet Union invaded Poland from the east just two weeks later, neither Great Britain nor France declared war on the Soviet Union. Why?

On the other hand, just because Germany declared war on the United States doesn't mean that American troops had to cross the Atlantic Ocean and go to war in Europe. Defensive wars are not fought thousands of miles away. It was Japan, not Germany, that attacked Pearl Harbor. The United States didn't go to war with Germany over actual attacks on American ships like the *Robin Moor, Sessa, Steel Seafarer, Greer, Montana, Pink Star, I. C. White, W. C. Teagle, Bold Venture, Kearny, Lehigh, Salinas*, and *Reuben James*—all bombed or torpedoed and in most cases sunk by Germany during the period from May 21 to October 31, 1941.

Another recent book besides Buchanan's that will cause one to question the well-entrenched orthodox view of the beginnings of World War II is Nicholson Baker's *Human Smoke: The Beginnings of World War II, the End of Civilization* (Simon & Schuster, 2008). I agree with a sympathetic revisionist critic of the book that "it is not the book that needs to be written," but for a different reason. That reason is that we don't have to wait "until that book is published," for it, or rather they, have already been published.

I previously mentioned some revisionist books published soon after World War II that contained valuable chapters relating to Pearl Harbor and/or U.S. foreign policy in relation to Japan in the 1930s. These works likewise include much valuable information on the events leading up to World War II in Europe: Beard's *President Roosevelt and the Coming of the War 1941*, Chamberlin's *America's Second Crusade*, Tansill's *Back Door to War*, and the edited work by Barnes, *Perpetual War for Perpetual Peace*. To this I can now add Beard's *American Foreign Policy in the Making 1932–1940: A Study in Responsibilities* (Yale University Press, 1946) and A. J. P. Taylor's *The Origins of the Second World War* (Atheneum, 1962).

To cite but one damning passage from these works, William Henry Chamberlin stated that "the eleven principal steps by which Roosevelt took America into undeclared war in the Atlantic may be briefly summarized as follows":

1. The repeal of the arms embargo in November 1939.
2. The trade of destroyers for bases in September 1940.
3. Enactment of the Lend-Lease Act in March 1941.
4. The secret American-British staff talks, January–March 1941.
5. The institution of "patrols" in the North Atlantic on April 24.
6. The sending of American laborers to build a naval base in Northern Ireland.
7. The blocking of German credits in the United States and the closing of consulates in the early summer of 1941.
8. The occupation of Iceland by American troops on July 7.
9. The Atlantic Conference, August 9–12.
10. The shoot-at-sight orders given to American warships and announced on September 11.
11. Authorization for the arming of merchant ships and the sending of merchant ships into war zones in November 1941.

All the details are in the abovementioned books by Beard, Chamberlin, Tansill, Barnes, and Baker, plus the other books I have mentioned by Russett, Zezima, and Maybury.

There are, of course, many additional actions of Roosevelt that could be added to Chamberlin's list. As Harry Elmer Barnes concluded:

> In regard to American entry into the European war, the case against President Roosevelt is far more serious than that against Woodrow Wilson with respect to the First World War. . . . Roosevelt had abandoned all semblance of neutrality, even before war broke out in 1939, and moved as speedily as was safe and feasible in the face of an anti-interventionist American public to involve this country in the European conflict.

Yet, the same conservatives who denounce FDR for his socialism and interventionism often praise him for his warmongering. I cite here just a few more of FDR's activities that moved the country toward war.

In June of 1940, Roosevelt fired his anti-interventionist secretary of war, Harry Woodring, and appointed a militant interventionist, Republican Henry Stimson, to replace him. Another Republican war hawk, Frank Knox, was named the new Secretary of the Navy. Both supported the massive transfer of munitions and supplies to Great Britain. Stimson endorsed compulsory military training while Knox wanted a million-man army.

The U.S. government began a massive military buildup as a "defensive" measure. Automobile companies were enlisted in the pre-war effort. To take the Ford as an example, in early 1941—long before Pearl Harbor—plans were made by Ford to manufacture the B-24 Liberator bomber for the government at a new plant at Willow Run, west of Detroit. One of the largest manufacturing plants ever constructed, the Willow Run plant was finished in 1942, eventually producing one bomber per hour. Before Pearl Harbor, Ford was already committed to, or had begun the production of, planes, tanks, aircraft engines, jeeps, reconnaissance cars, and anti-aircraft guns (see *Ford: Decline and Rebirth: 1933–1962*). In the five weeks before Pearl Harbor, the U.S. government contracted for $3.5 billion worth of military supplies from automobile plants alone.

A peacetime conscription bill was introduced in June of 1940. This, of course, was another "defensive" measure. It passed both houses of Congress and was signed into law by FDR on September 16. Originally applying to men between 21 and 35, this was expanded after the United States entered the war to all men aged 18 to 65 being required to register. The day had already come in Europe where, as related by John Keegan: "Military service was seen no longer as the token by which the individual validated his citizenship but as the form in which the citizen tendered his duty to the state and took part in its functions." And as Catherine Fitzgibbon of the Women's International League for Peace and Freedom pointed out, it was large conscript armies that allowed Hitler, Mussolini, and Stalin to hold power. It is therefore not surprising that conscription had opponents from across the political spectrum. "Military conscription is not freedom but serfdom; its equality is the equality of slaves," said the socialist Norman Thomas. "Conscription . . . is a road leading straight to militarism, imperialism and ultimately to American fascism and war," he added. Harry Elmer Barnes called conscription "the first step to American fascism." According to Senator Taft, the logical conclusion was "the conscription of everything—property, men, industries, and all labor." Over 16,000 Americans were imprisoned for draft evasion. On November

14, 1940, a group of students stood before a judge and pled guilty to this "crime," maintaining that "war consists of mass murder, deliberate starvation, vandalism, and similar evils." They were each sentenced to a year and a day in prison. Around 40,000 soldiers in the European Theater alone decided that they weren't fighting for our freedoms and deserted.

While all of these things were going on in the United States, and before Hitler broke the Molotov-Ribbentrop Pact and invaded the Soviet Union on June 22, 1941, Stalin was engaged in carving up Europe just like Hitler. After attacking Poland soon after Germany, Stalin attacked Finland on November 30. Then, on June 17, 1941, the Soviet Union invaded and conquered Estonia, Latvia, and Lithuania. These Baltic states thus became part of Russia's pre-war conquests that made up the Soviet Union: Armenia, Azerbaijan, Belarus, Georgia, Kazakhstan, Kyrgyzstan, Moldova, Tajikistan, Turkmenistan, Ukraine, and Uzbekistan—all now independent countries since the fall of the Soviet Union. The Soviet Union's aggressive territorial expansion was greater than that of Germany. In light this, was it wise to ally with Stalin against Hitler?

And not only did the Soviet Union join Germany in the rape of Poland and execute thousands of Polish army officers and intellectuals in what is known as the Katyn Forest Massacre, the Soviets had their own concentration camps. And as contemporary historian Norman Davies relates: "The liberators of Auschwitz were servants of a regime that ran an even larger network of concentration camps of its own." In light of this, was it wise to ally with Stalin against Hitler?

Stalin's body count was also much greater than Hitler's. Stalin, who had once attended seminary and was exceptionally well read, was also an exceptional liar, forger, robber, sadist, adulterer, terrorist, revolutionary, and murderer. One can read all the gory details in a book like Donald Rayfield's *Stalin and His Hangmen: The Tyrant and Those Who Killed for Him* (Random House, 2004). Stalin was a greater threat, and the Soviet Union a greater evil, than Hitler and Germany. After Germany attacked the Soviet Union, Senator Taft remarked that the victory of communism would be far more dangerous to the United States than the victory of fascism. This is because, although each had committed unspeakable horrors, communism had more of a worldwide appeal; fascism of the Nazi variety was racist and nationalistic. Communism, explained Taft, "Is a greater danger to the United States because it is a false philosophy which appeals to many. Fascism is a false philosophy which appeals to very few." In light of this, was it wise to ally with Stalin against Hitler?

More than anything else, World War II was a war between Nazism and Bolshevism. Three-fourths of all the deaths in the war were on the

Eastern Front. Then-senator Harry Truman (D-MO) had the right idea: "If we see Germany is winning we ought to help Russia and if we see Russia is winning we ought to help Germany, and in that way let them kill as many as possible." When the fascists and the communists turned against each other, Great Britain should have withdrawn from the war and watched from the sidelines with the United States as two of the most tyrannical states in history slaughtered each other. Instead, Great Britain and the United States sided with Stalin.

The tactics of the U.S. military during the war were sometimes despicable. The United States joined with Great Britain in bombing civilians in German cities. And just like the United States did to Japan, American planes firebombed German cities, killing civilians by the thousands. The city of Dresden, which was packed with refugees from other German cities, was hit particularly hard. On Wednesday, February 14, 1945, it was Ash Wednesday in more ways than one as Dresden was firebombed by the U.S. Army Air Force, destroying much of the city and incinerating thousands of civilians. This was not war; this was terrorism and wholesale murder.

Even the hallowed D-Day invasion is not untainted. About 3,000 French civilians died on D-Day—about the same number as American soldiers killed in the invasion. All told, hundreds of tons of Allied bombs were dropped during the "liberation" of Normandy, destroying fields and livestock, obliterating towns and villages, and killing 20,000 civilians. On D-Day from the civilian perspective, see William I. Hitchcock's *The Bitter Road to Freedom: A New History of the Liberation of Europe* (Free Press, 2008). But, it is argued, this was all for the greater good: the liberation of Europe from the Nazis. True, but that is the problem with war: The greater good always results in too much collateral damage, destruction of property, and civilian suffering, and too many deadly mistakes, friendly-fire incidents, and unforeseen consequences.

The conduct of American forces during the war, and in some cases after the war, was sometimes shameful. After the D-Day invasion, some members of the "greatest generation" engaged in drunkenness, carousing, vandalism, petty thefts, looting, seizing property as trophies, robbery, trafficking in stolen military goods, wasting scarce food and drink, billeting themselves in private homes, sexual assault, rape, and gang rape of women of all ages, and mistreating, assaulting, and otherwise abusing their power over those they liberated in France, Belgium, and Germany. Venereal disease and prostitution were rampant, as you can imagine. None of this matters, of course, because we were fighting Hitler.

But after we were done fighting Hitler, American soldiers participated in the forced repatriation of hundreds of thousands of Russian POWs to the Soviet Union, where many were killed or sent to the gulag, and the mistreatment and neglect of German POWs. But none of this matters either because we fought against Hitler.

But Hitler was evil, it is argued, and the United States had a moral duty to stop him regardless of whether he was a direct threat, regardless of Great Britain, regardless of Poland, regardless of Stalin, regardless of the tactics of the U.S. military, regardless of the conduct of U.S. soldiers, and regardless of Roosevelt. I will leave it to the philosophers to debate whether one can truly perform a moral duty while acting immorally. The world is full of evil—it always has been and always will be. Any individual or any group of people anywhere in the world who want to confront evil anywhere else in the world are free to do so. But, it is said, Hitler and Nazism were such a great menace that only the might of the U.S. military could bring about their downfall. Even if this were true (it isn't—the Red Army was more responsible for the defeat of Germany), it doesn't mean, in the words of John Quincy Adams, that America should go abroad seeking monsters to destroy. Neither the Bible nor the Constitution appointed the United States to be the world's policeman. And if Hitler had to be stopped because he was so evil, then why did we wait until Japan bombed Pearl Harbor and Germany declared war on us? Hitler was just as evil during the first two years of the war as he was after the German declaration of war.

And why does everyone stop with Hitler? The United States did nothing to stop greater and lesser evils like Stalin in the Soviet Union, Mao in China, Pol Pot in Cambodia, Kim Il-sung in North Korea, and Idi Amin in Uganda. Should the United States have gone to war against these evil rulers as well? If not, then what is it about Hitler that justifies the deaths of 405,000 Americans to make Eastern Europe safe for Stalin?

The reason certainly isn't the Holocaust. Roosevelt was indifferent when asked—just days after *Kristallnacht*—if he would relax immigration restrictions so Jewish refugees from Germany could settle in the United States. On June 6, 1939, the passengers of the MS *St. Louis*, a German ship filled with over 900 Jewish refugees, were denied entry to the United States and forced to return to Europe where many of them later died in the Holocaust. On the recent 70th anniversary of this "voyage of the damned," the U.S. Senate passed a resolution (S. Res. 111) acknowledging the role that the United States played in this tragic event. And how can we forget that the great ally of the United States—the Soviet Union—had a history of Jewish pogroms. And although our other great ally—Great Britain—did not have Jewish blood on its hands, it had the blood of German civilians on its hands thanks to its starvation blockade *after* World War I. According to Harry Elmer Barnes: "Had Hitler tortured and then killed every one of the half million Jews living in Germany in 1933 such a foul and detestable act would still have left him a piker compared to Britain's blockade of 1918-1919." Although Jewish persecution may have continued—as it had throughout history—the Holocaust was not inevitable; it was a consequence of the war.

Conclusion

In addition to World War I being the Great War, it should have also been the Great Example of how utterly and senselessly destructive to life, liberty, and property war on such scale could be. Over 400,000 U.S. soldiers died during World War II because what should have been never was. True, American soldiers fought and bled and died heroically, valiantly, and courageously, but how much greater the "greatest genera-tion" would have been if its members had said "not again" and stayed out of the war altogether.

The legacy of World War II is a gruesome one. The bombing of civilians on a grand scale was adopted as an intentional policy. The killing of innocents at a distance was made part of our national character. The military/industrial warfare state became a permanent fixture in the United States. World War II ushered in the nuclear age of mutually assured destruction. The war also set a precedent for later interventions by the world's new superpower.

But even if World War II were good, just, and necessary, it still doesn't justify any American military action since then—not in Korea, not in Vietnam, not in Iraq, not in Afghanistan, and certainly not in Iran.

The governments of the world cannot be trusted when they say that their soldiers must go to war. The U.S. government is no exception. There is always more to it than this country did *this* so the U.S. military needs to do *that*. So, no matter what happens, the next time the U.S. government says that some military action overseas is necessary—just say no. Say no to loss of liberties. Say no to senseless destruction of property. Say no to flag-draped coffins. Say no to billions of dollars wasted. Say no to supporting the troops. Say no to the warfare state.

Besides the books relating to World War II I have mentioned thus far, I would also recommend Clive Ponting's *Armageddon: The Reality Behind the Distortions, Myths, Lies, and Illusions of World War II* (Random House, 1995), Karl Roebling's *Great Myths of World War II* (Paragon Press, 1985), Thomas Fleming's *The New Dealers' War: FDR and the War Within World War II* (HarperCollins, 2001), Norman Davies' *No Simple Victory: World War II in Europe* (Viking, 2007), and World War II veteran Edward W. Wood's *Worshipping the Myths of World War II: Reflections on America's Dedication to War* (Potomac Books, 2006). On the British propaganda effort to push America into the war, see Thomas E. Mahl's *Desperate Deception: British Covert Operations in the United States, 1939–44* (Brassey's, 1988) or Nicholas J. Cull's *Selling War: The British Propaganda Campaign against American "Neutrality" in World War II* (Oxford University Press, 1995). On Churchill as a power-hungry warmonger see Buchanan's book and Ralph Raico's "Rethinking Churchill" in John V. Denson, ed., *The Costs of War: America's Pyrrhic Victories*, 2nd expanded ed. (Transaction Publishers, 1999). On the absurd idea that World War II is what got American out of The Great Depression, see Robert Higgs' *Depression, War and Cold War: Studies in Political Economy* (Oxford University Press, 2006). And on historical revisionism in general see Jeff Riggenbach's *Why American History Is Not What They Say* (Mises Institute, 2009). The Independent Institute also maintains a very detailed archive on World War II.

It is time to rethink the Good War. Rather than being good, just, and necessary, it was the most destructive thing to life, liberty, and property that the world has ever seen. As Benjamin Franklin once said: "There never was a good War or a bad Peace."

* * * * *

CHAPTER 5
OTHER WARS

THE WAR TO END ALL WARS

One hundred and fifty years ago, France and Great Britain intervened in what was, and should have remained, a dispute between Russia and Turkey. The official beginning of what came to be called the Crimean War was on March 28, 1854, when Great Britain and France declared war on Russia. Coming between Napoleon's defeat at Waterloo in 1815 and the beginning of World War I in 1914, the Crimean War should have been the "war to end all wars" instead of being a precursor to the carnage of the war that made "the world safe for democracy."

There are three things that came out of the Crimean War that most people are familiar with but have no idea that they are connected with it: the nurse Florence Nightingale, the poem "The Charge of the Light Brigade," and the novel *War and Peace*.

Florence Nightingale (1820–1910) was the famed pioneer of nursing and reformer of hospital sanitation methods. After hearing of the deplorable conditions that existed in the British Military Hospital at Scutari, opposite of Constantinople, she arrived in the Crimea with 38 nurses on November 4, 1854, and soon began to improve the conditions at the hospital.

"The Charge of the Light Brigade" was the poem written by Alfred Lord Tennyson (1809–1892) that immortalized the disastrous British cavalry charge which occurred during the Crimean War at the Battle of Balaclava on October 25, 1854.

> "Forward, the Light Brigade!"
> Was there a man dismay'd?
> Not tho' the soldiers knew
> Some one had blunder'd:
> Their's not to make reply
> Their's not to reason why,
> Their's but to do and die:
> Into the valley of Death
> Rode the Six Hundred.

Set in Russia during the Napoleonic Era, *War and Peace*, by the Russian writer Leo Tolstoy (1828–1910), is the epic novel published between 1865 and 1869. Although most people have never read it, because it contains 365 chapters, *War and Peace* is the book usually mentioned when one wants to compare some daunting task to reading an unusually large book. The connection between *War and Peace* and the Crimean War? Tolstoy was a Russian second lieutenant in the Crimean War, and therefore an eyewitness to battle scenes he so realistically describes in this novel.

Located in southern Ukraine, the Crimean peninsula juts into the Black Sea and connects to the mainland by the Isthmus of Perekop. Its area is about 9,700 square miles. Dry steppes, scattered with numerous burial-mounds of the ancient Scythians, cover more than two-thirds of the peninsula, with the Crimean mountains in the south rising to heights of 5,000 ft. before dropping sharply to the Black Sea.

Various peoples have occupied the Crimean peninsula over the years: Goths, Huns, Scythians, Khazars, Greeks, Kipchaks, Mongols. The Ottoman Turks conquered the region in 1475. In 1783, the whole of the Crimea was annexed to the Russian Empire. The Crimea was the scene of some bloody battles in the Second World War. It was also the site of the "Big Three" (Roosevelt, Churchill, and Stalin) Conference held in the former palace of Czar Nicholas at Yalta, a city on the Crimean southeastern shore of the Black Sea. It was here during the week of February 4–11, 1945, that Roosevelt delivered Eastern Europe to Stalin.

The underlying cause of the Crimean War was the Eastern Question—the international problem of European territory controlled by the decaying Ottoman Empire. The immediate causes of the Crimean War were religious. Now, there is nothing the least bit "religious" about war, but, without a complete separation of church and state, religion is often used by the state as a pretext for war. Russia (Orthodox) was engaged in a dispute with France (Catholic) over the guardianship of the "Holy Places" in Palestine, and a dispute with the Ottoman Turks over the protection of the Orthodox Christians subject to the Ottoman sultan. Russia demanded from the Turks that there be established a Russian protectorate over all Orthodox subjects in the Ottoman Empire. After Turkey refused, Russia, in July of 1853, occupied the Ottoman vassal states of Moldavia and Walachia. The czar made the claim that "by the occupation of the Principalities we desire such security as will ensure the restoration of our dues. It is not conquest that we seek but satisfaction for a just right so clearly infringed."

In October of the same year, the Ottoman Turks declared war on

Russia. War between Russia and Turkey was nothing new, as the Russo-Turkish Wars (1768–74, 1787–92, 1828–29) evidence. They had first clashed over Astrakhan in 1569. Although Constantinople had fallen to the Turks in 1453, the Ottoman Empire was in decline, and Russia, since the time of Peter the Great (1672–1725), had wanted to secure a warm-water outlet to the Mediterranean—at the expense of Ottoman territory. This naturally upset France and Great Britain, which saw Russian ambitions as a threat to the balance of power in the Mediterranean. Russia was given an ultimatum demanding the withdrawal of its forces from the principalities. When Russia refused, France and Great Britain, having already dispatched fleets to the Black Sea, declared war on Russia on March 28, 1854. The Anglo-Franco alliance was a precarious one. France and Great Britain had historically been enemies, but, like Herod and Pilate, who "were made friends together" when they allied to condemn Christ (Luke 23:1–12), they united to check the ambitions of Russia, under the guise of defending Turkey.

Most of the subsequent fighting took place in the Crimea because of the strategic Russian naval base at Sevastopol on the southwestern coast. The accession of a new czar in Russia (Alexander II) and the capture of Sevastopol led to the Treaty of Paris (March 30, 1856) that ended the war and the dominant role of Russia in Southeast Europe. Britain and France saved the Ottoman empire, an empire that they would help destroy in World War I.

The Crimean War is known for a number of "firsts": deadly-accurate rifles, significant use of the telegraph, tactical use of railways, life-saving medical innovations, trench combat, undersea mines, "live" reporting to newspapers, and cigarettes.

But there is one other thing that began with the Crimean War that should have made it the war to end all wars: photography.

Although photography had only recently been invented before the Crimean War, it had progressed enough so as to make it possible to photograph the horrors of war. The wet collodion process by Frederick Scott Archer (1813–1857), introduced in 1850, cut exposure times from minutes to seconds.

War correspondents Thomas Chenery and William Russell relayed some of the horrors of war back to *The Times* in Britain. Thomas Agnew, of the publishing house Thomas Agnew & Sons, then proposed sending a photographer to the Crimea as a strictly private, commercial venture. The British government had previously made several official attempts to document the war with photographs. One effort ended in shipwreck, and none of the photographs survive from the other two.

Enter Roger Fenton (1819–1869). Fenton, who had previously photographed the royal family, spent four months in the Crimea (March 8 to June 26, 1855) photographing the war. He had the cooperation of Prince Albert and the ministry of war, as well as the field commanders in the Crimea. After converting a horse-drawn wine merchant's "van" into a mobile darkroom, Fenton, his assistants, horses, photographic van, and equipment were transported to the Crimea courtesy of the British government. He returned to Britain with 360 photographs and cholera.

On September 20th, 1855, an exhibit of 312 of the photographs opened in London. Sets of photographs went on sale in November. Although the pictures were widely reviewed and advertised, when the war ended, interest in photographs of the war ended with it, and the entire stock of unsold prints and negatives were auctioned off by December of 1856. Fenton abandoned photography in 1862, putting an advertisement in the *Photographic Journal* to dispose of his equipment.

In 1944, the Library of Congress purchased 263 of Fenton's prints from one of his relatives. The Roger Fenton Crimean War photographs, thought to be Fenton's proof prints made upon his return, can be viewed online and freely downloaded, including his most well-known photograph, "Valley of the Shadow of Death."

While Fenton's photographs show plenty of scenes of military supplies, camp life, groups of soldiers, the leading figures of the allied armies, and landscape scenes, there are no scenes of combat or devastation. He wrote about scenes of death and destruction that he witnessed, but he did not photograph any of them. At the scene of the Light Brigade's ill-fated charge, he saw "skeletons half-buried, one was lying as if he had raised himself upon his elbow, the bare skull sticking up with still enough flesh in the muscles to prevent it falling from the shoulders." But whether it was because of an explicit directive from, or an implicit understanding with, the British government, the fact remains that Fenton witnessed the horrors of war, and had ample opportunity to photograph them, but didn't. For political or commercial reasons, or both, the war was portrayed in the best possible light. A positive report was needed to counter negative press reports and to encourage the British nation to support the war effort. For this reason, Fenton's photographs can be considered the first instance of photographic propaganda.

The Crimean War destroyed the lives of over 200,000 men. How many Russians could have become another Boris Pasternak or Igor Sikorsky? How many British could have become another Christopher Wren or Isaac Newton? How many French could have become another Victor Hugo or Frédéric Bastiat? How many Turks could have become another Mustafa Kemal or Ali Erdemir. God only knows. The Crimean War could have and should have been the war to end all wars. Instead, as A. N. Wilson remarks in *The Victorians*, it was the greatest blunder of the nineteenth century, setting up animosities and alliances that led to World War I and the continuing turmoil of Eastern Europe, the Middle East, and Central Asia.

For the latest book on the Crimean War, see Trevor Royle's Crimea: The Great Crimean War 1854-1856.

* * * * *

THE HORRORS OF WAR

"It is well that war is so terrible, lest we grow too fond of it." ~ Robert E. Lee

"The evils of war are great in their endurance, and have a long reckoning for ages to come." ~ Thomas Jefferson

Current Conflicts

At the dawning of the year 2004, there were fifteen major wars in progress, plus twenty more "lesser" conflicts. According to Global Security, there are now conflicts raging in the following places:

Afghanistan (Taliban and al-Qaeda)
Algeria (insurgency by Muslim fundamentalists)
Angola (secessionist conflict in Angola's Cabinda enclave)
Burma (insurgency by ethnic minority groups)
Burundi (civil war between ethnic groups)
China (dispute with other countries over ownership of Spratly Islands)
Colombia (insurgency by various guerilla groups)
Democratic Republic of the Congo (Congo War involving nine
   African nations)
Georgia (conflict with Russia, ethnic group conflict)
India (longstanding conflicts in Assam and Kashmir; Naxalite uprising)
Indonesia (conflicts in Aceh, Kalimantan, Maluku, and Papua)
Iraq (occupation by U.S. forces)
Israel (Intifada)
Ivory Coast (civil war)
Liberia (ritual killings and cannibalism)
Moldova (Transdniester independence movement)

Namibia (Caprivi Strip liberation movement)
Nepal (Maoist insurgency)
Nigeria (religious and ethnic conflicts)
Peru (Shining Path terrorist movement)
Philippines (Moro Islamic Liberation Front uprising)
Russia (Chechen uprising)
Somalia (civil war)
Spain (Basque uprising)
Sri Lanka (Tamil uprising)
Sudan (civil war)
Thailand (Islamic insurgency)
Turkey (Kurdish separatist movement)
Uganda (civil unrest)

Although the United Nations was founded "to save succeeding generations from the scourge of war, which twice in our lifetime has brought untold sorrow to mankind," there have been more conflicts in the world since the founding of the UN than during any previous period in history.

The United States maintains a global empire of troops and bases that would make a Roman emperor look like the mayor of a small town.

War

Too much has been written throughout history that glorifies war and the warrior who is sent by the state to do its bidding. Dying for one's country—regardless of the circumstances that brought on the conflict—is seen as the ultimate sacrifice. To protest the war is to be a traitor. Being a professional soldier is viewed as one of the noblest of occupations. The death of enemy combatants is celebrated. Civilian casualties are written off as "collateral damage."

In the current Iraq war, before the phoney transfer of power on June 28, 855 American troops had died. That is 800 young men (and women) who will never gave their parents any grandchildren or who left behind grieving wives and children. Forgotten are the over 5000 military personnel who were injured, many of whom will endure suffering the rest of their life. And that number is just the "official" figure. The thousands of Iraqi troops killed or injured are not much of a concern to anyone—and neither are the Iraqi civilian casualties.

General descriptions of the horrors of war can be read in any military history by John Keegan or Martin Gilbert. But more and more specific accounts of the horrors of war are beginning to see the light of day. *Blood Red Snow: The Memoirs of a German Soldier on the Eastern Front* and *His Time in Hell: A Texas Marine in France* are two recent books that explore the horrors of war from the individual soldier's point of view. Chris Hedges' *What Every Person Should Know About War* is a stinging indictment of the twin evils of the glorification of war and the concealment of its brutality.

Intimate Voices

The recently published *Intimate Voices from the First World War* does all of those things and much more. What makes this book so unique is that the authors—twenty eight men, women, and children from thirteen different nations—because they were not writing for publication, had no particular statement to make other than to describe the effects of war on themselves and their surroundings. This is the ultimate in primary source material. From their research into hundreds of first-hand accounts, the editors of the book, Svetlana Palmer and Sarah Wallis, selected twenty-eight diaries or collections of letters written by soldiers and civilians who lived (and in some cases died) during World War I. Many of the diaries were found decades after the end of the war, and some in the last few years. A few are published here for the first time.

The horrors of war are described here as no historian writing in the twenty-first century could describe them. But in addition to the accounts of death, destruction, and starvation, *Intimate Voices* also gives us an insight into the role of the state in warfare, the religious ideas of the combatants, the war's demoralizing effect on women, and the regrets of soldier and civilian.

The War

The conflict we read about in *Intimate Voices* is the "great war" to "make the world safe for democracy"—the "war to end all wars." The war began when Austria declared war on Serbia after the assassination of Archduke Franz Ferdinand, the heir to the Austro-Hungarian throne, during a state visit to Sarajevo, the capital of the Austro-Hungarian province of Bosnia-Herzegovina. The archduke had recently given an after-dinner toast in which he advocated peace: "To peace! What would we get out of war with Serbia? We'd lose the lives of young men and we'd spend money better used elsewhere. And what would we gain, for heaven's sake? A few plum trees, some pastures full of goat droppings, and a bunch of rebellious killers." His advice went unheeded, and resulted in the slaughter of over a million soldiers who fought for his empire, plus an untold number of ordinary citizens. Overall, 65 million men donned a miliary uniform, over 9.3 million soldiers died, 21 million soldiers were wounded, 7.8 million soldiers were captured or missing, and 6.7 million civilians died.

The Cast of Characters

The writers of the diaries and letters in *Intimate Voices* are a diverse lot.

German soldier Paul Hub is a young recruit sent to make up for the heavy losses suffered by his advancing army. He married his sweetheart, whom he wrote to throughout the war, while home on leave in June of 1918. After a few days with his wife he returned to the front—only to die two months later.

Polish widow Helena Jablonska survived the war and died in 1936.

Austrian doctor Josef Tomann tends to the sick and wounded soldiers in a hospital in Przemysl. He contracted disease and died in May 1915, leaving behind a wife and a baby daughter.

German officer Ernst Nopper, an interior decorator from Ludwigsburg, was killed in action on the Western Front, leaving a wife and two children.

Serbian officer Milorad Markovic is the future grandfather of Mirjana Markovic, wife of Slobodan Milosevic. He survived the war, only to be captured by the Nazis in the next one. He made it through that one as well and died in 1967.

Russian soldier Vasily Mishnin was reunited with his wife and two sons after the war. He went back to work at a furniture shop and died in 1955.

Australian corporal George Mitchell finished the war as a captain. He wrote several books about World War I and served again in World War II. He died in 1961.

Turkish second lieutenant Mehmed Fasih was captured by the Allies and released at the end of the war. He married in 1924 and lived until 1964.

German doctor Ludwig Deppe returned to Dresden after the war. His subsequent fate is unknown.

French captain Paul Truffrau returned to Paris after the war, where he became a teacher. He went on to fight and keep another diary in World War II. He died in 1973.

Russian officer Dmitry Oskin joined the Bolsheviks after the

Russian Revolution. He advanced in the Communist Party but died suddenly in 1934, possibly a victim of a Stalinist purge.

American officer John Clark survived the war and married his sweetheart, a Red Cross nurse.

An unnamed Austrian officer wrote a diary that was found on his dead body in July of 1915. He died in mid-sentence.

Russian soldier Alexei Zyikov was captured by the Germans. His diary was found by a Russian soldier in Germany during World War II.

German schoolgirl Piete Kuhr lived through the war and became a professional performer and then a writer. She and her family fled to Switzerland during World War II. She died in 1989.

French schoolboy Yves Congar lived to become a priest, serve in World War II, and be made a cardinal. He lived until 1995.

Klara Hess was the mother of the future Nazi, Rudolf Hess.

African Kande Kamara was from French Guinea. He fought for the French and returned home to West Africa at the end of the war. Forced to flee his village, he never saw his family again.

British private Robert Cude returned to London after the war. He later appeared as an extra in a James Bond film.

British officer Richard Meinertzhagen became a colonel and attended the Paris Peace Conference. He became an advocate of Zionism and later wrote *Middle East Diary*, about his experiences in the Middle East after World War I. He died in 1967.

Canadian Winnie McClare was killed in May of 1917, within a month of his arrival at the front line. He was nineteen.

The Horrors of War

There is no better description of the horrors of war than an eyewitness description. German soldier Paul Hub writes to his girlfriend:

> I've already seen quite a lot of misery of war. . . . Maria, this sort of a war is so unspeakably miserable. If only you saw a line of stretcher-bearers with their burdens, you'd know what I mean. I haven't had a chance to shoot yet. We're having to deal with an unseen enemy. . . . Every day brings new horrors. . . . Every day the fighting gets fiercer and there is still no end in sight. Our blood is flowing in torrents. . . . That's how it is. All around me, the most gruesome devastation. Dead and wounded soldiers, dead and dying animals, horse cadavers, burnt-out houses, dug-up fields, cars, clothes, weaponry—all this is scattered around me, a real mess. I didn't think war would be like this. We can't sleep for all the

noise.

Polish widow Helena Jablonska writes in her diary:

Vast numbers of wounded are being brought in. Many of them die from severe blood loss, but the death toll would not be half as great were it not for cholera. It is spreading so fast that the cases outnumber those wounded and killed in battle. Everything has been infected: carts, stretchers, rooms, wardens, streets, manure, mud, everything. Soldiers fall in battle, where it is impossible to remove the bodies and disinfect them. They don't even bother.

Austrian doctor Josef Tomann writes in his diary:

Starvation is kicking in. Sunken, pale figures wander like corpses through the streets, their ragged clothes hanging from skeletal bodies, their stony faces a picture of utter despair. . . . A terrifying number of people are suffering from malnutrition; the starving arrive in their dozens, frozen soldiers are brought in from the outposts, all of them like walking corpses. They lie silently on their cold hospital beds, make no complaints and drink muddy water they call tea. The next day they are carried away to the morgue. The sight of these pitiful figures, whose wives and children are probably also starving at home, wrings your heart. This is war.

German officer Ernst Nopper writes in his diary:

There are dead bodies everywhere you look. The villages have been completely destroyed. The fields are covered in so many graves it looks like moles have been at work. There are shell holes everywhere.

Serbian officer Milorad Markovic writes in his diary:

I remember things scattered all around; horses and men stumbling and falling into the abyss; Albanian attacks; hosts of women and children. A doctor would not dress an officer's wound; soldiers would not bother to pull out a wounded comrade or officer. Belongings abandoned; starvation; wading across rivers clutching onto horses' tails; old men, women and children climbing up the rocks; dying people on the road; a smashed human skull by the road; a corpse all skin and bones, robbed, stripped naked, mangled; soldiers, police officers, civilians, women, captives. Vlasta's cousin, naked under his overcoat with a collar and cuffs, shattered, gone made. Soldiers like ghosts, skinny, pale, worn out, sunken eyes, their hair and beards long, their clothes in rages, almost naked, barefoot. Ghosts of people begging for bread, walking with sticks, their feet covered in wounds, staggering. Chaos; women in soldiers's clothes; the desperate mothers of those who are too exhausted to go on. A starving soldier who ate too much bread and dropped dead. A soldier selling anything and everything for bread: his gun, clothes, shoes and boots, coats, horses' feedbags, saddlebags, horses.

Russian soldier Vasily Mishnin writes to his pregnant wife:

We go to the depot to get our rifles. Good Lord, what's all this? They're covered in blood, black clotted lumps of it are hanging off them. . . . It is frightening even to sit or lie down here—the rifle is shaking in my hands. My hand comes down on something black: it turns out there are corpses here that haven't been cleared away. My hair stands on end. I have to sit down. There is no point in staring into the distance—it is pitch dark. All I can feel is fear. I am so frightened of the shells that I want the ground to open up and swallow me. . . . Suddenly a screeching noise pierces the air, I feel a pang in my heart, something whistles past and explodes nearby. My dear Lord, I am so frightened—and I hear this buzzing in my ears. I leave my post and climb into my dugout. It is packed, everyone is shaking and asking again and again, "What's going on? What's going on?" One explosion follows another, and another. Two lads are running, shouting our for nurses. They are covered in blood. It is running down their cheeks and hands, and something else is dripping from underneath their bandages. They're soon dead, shot to pieces. There is screaming, yelling, the earth is shaking from artillery fire and our dugout is rocking from side to side like a boat. . . . Our eyes are full of tears, we wipe them away, but they just keep coming because the shells are full of gas. We are terrified. . . . We will probably never see each other again—all it takes is an instant and I will be no more—and perhaps no one will be able to gather the scattered pieces of my body for burial. . . . A zeppelin attacked Ostrow in the night and dropped a few bombs, many killed. One woman and her two kids got blown to pieces that blew away in the wind.

Australian corporal George Mitchell writes in his diary:

And again I heard the sickening thud of a bullet. I looked at him in horror. The bullet had fearfully mashed his face and gone down his throat, rendering him dumb. But his eyes were dreadful to behold. How he squirmed in agony. There was nothing I could do for him, but pray that he might die swiftly. It took him about twenty minutes to accomplish this and by that time he had tangled his legs in pain and stiffened. I saw the waxy colour creep over his cheek and breathed freer.

Turkish second lieutenant Mehmed Fasih writes in his diary:

Though I keep picking off lice, there are plenty more—I just can't get rid of them and am itching all over. My body is covered with red and purple blotches. . . . When I finally reach our trenches I find a large pool of blood. It has coagulated and turned black. Bits of brain, bone and flesh are mixed in with it.

German doctor Ludwig Deppe writes in his diary:

Behind us we have left destroyed fields, ransacked magazines, and, for the immediate future, starvation. We were no longer the agents of culture; our track was marked by death, plundering and evacuated villages.

French captain Paul Truffrau writes in his diary:

We reach the trench, dug out by joining up the shell-holes and it stinks of bogs and decaying corpses. Stagnant water. . . . The smell of corpses everywhere.

Russian officer Dmitry Oskin writes in his diary:

The battle became so vicious that our soldiers started using spades to split Austrians' skulls. This hand-to-hand fighting went on for at least two hours. Only nightfall stopped the butchery.

American officer John Clark writes to his sweetheart:

I was only beginning to see what war really is. . . . Outside of the enemy fire, it was a terrific strain on our men, for we were firing night and day—on a couple of occasions, for ten hours without any intermission. We spent our spare time burying the infantry dead which were scattered all around us. It was gruesome work, for the bodies had been lying on the battlefield for two, three or more days. On the crest just before us were light "tanks" which had been shattered by German shellfire. They were the most gruesome of all,

for the charred bodies of their crews were still in or scattered about
them.

The unnamed Austrian officer writes his last words in his diary:

> The wounded groan and cry for their mothers. You have to shut
> your ears to it. . . . It is enough to drive you insane. Dead, wound-
> ed, massive losses. This is the end. Unprecedented slaughter, a
> horrific bloodbath. There is blood everywhere and the dead and
> bits of bodies lie scattered about so that

Second only to the horrors on the battlefield are those that one
endures in captivity. Russian soldier Alexei Zyikov writes in his diary:

> Hunger does not give you a moment's peace and you are always
> dreaming of bread: good Russian bread! There is consternation in
> my soul when I watch people hurling themselves after a piece of
> bread and a spoonful of soup. We have to work pretty hard too, to
> the shouts and beatings of the guards, the mocking of the German
> public. We work from dawn till dusk, sweat mingling with blood;
> we curse the blows of the rifle butts; I find myself thinking about
> ending it all, such are the torments of my life in captivity! . . . Then
> there are those of us who eat potato peel: they take it out of the pit,
> wash it and boil it, eat it and say how delicious it is. Some consider
> it the greatest happiness to snatch food from the tub where the
> Germans throw their leftovers.

War and the State

The truth of Randolph Bourne's classic statement, "War is
the health of the state," can be seen throughout the excerpts from the
diaries and letters in *Intimate Voices*. To get a war to work—to get men
to kill other men that have never aggressed against them and that they
don't even know—the state must do two things: convince men to love the
state and to hate the members of other states. The first is always cloaked
in patriot-ism, and leads to an acceptance of interventionism. The second
is always cloaked in nationalism, and leads to hatred toward foreigners
within one's country. German schoolgirl Piete Kuhr writes in her diary:

> At school they talk of nothing but the war now. The girls are
> pleased that Germany is entering the field against its old enemy
> France. We have to learn new songs about the glory of war. The
> enthusiasm in our town is growing by the hour. . . . People wander

through the streets in groups, shouting "Down with Serbia! Long live Germany!" Crowds of people are milling around in the streets, laughing, wishing each other good luck and joining in singing the national anthem. . . . Dear God, just bring the war to an end! I don't look on it as glorious any more, in spite of "school holidays" and victories. . . . At school everyone is so much in favour of the war. . . . They scream so that the headmaster sees what a patriotic school he has. . . . Everyone talks of shortages. Most people are buying in such massive stocks that their cellars are full to bursting. Grandma refuses to do this. She says she doesn't want to deprive the Fatherland of anything. We're not hoarders. The Fatherland won't let us starve. . . . To them [uncle and mother] "the German nation" is still everything. Fall with a cheer for the Fatherland, and you will die as a hero in their eyes.

German officer Ernst Nopper writes in his diary:

At the border post we strike up "Deutschland, Deutschland Über Alles."

French schoolboy Yves Congar writes in his diary:

I can only think about war. I would like to be a soldier and fight. . . . Very well, if they want to starve us then they'll see when, in the next war, the next generation goes to Germany and starves them. They are turning the French people against them and I'm happy about it. I have never hated them so much. . . . The Germans, fiends, thieves, murderers and arsonists that they are, set fire to everything. . . . The Boches' behaviour in France is scandalous. The loot they are taking back to Germany is unbelievable: they'll have enough to refurbish every one of their towns! But one day soon it will be our turn: we will go there and we will steal, burn and ransack! They had better watch out! Over in Germany they are almost as unhappy as we are. There is famine in all the big cities: Berlin, Dresden and Bavaria; I hope they all die!

Russian soldier Alexei Zyikov writes in his diary:

They boast to us that their governments send them bread and parcels from home. But we, Russians, get nothing: our punishment for fighting badly. Or, perhaps, Mother Russia has forgotten about us.

Klara, the mother of Rudolf Hess, writes to her son:

Of course I know that an armistice would mean your safe return, my sons, but your future and that of the Fatherland would be built on shaky foundations. . . . It would be cowardly of us to worry about you. Instead we should be proud that through our sons we are fighting for the salvation of the Fatherland.

Polish widow Helena Jablonska writes in her diary:

The Jews are frightened. The Russians are taking them in hand now and giving them a taste of the whip. They are being forced to clean the streets and remove manure. . . . The Jewish pogrom has been under way since yesterday evening. The Cossacks waited until the Jews set off to the synagogue for their prayers before setting upon them with whips. They were deaf to any pleas for mercy, regardless of age. . . . It pains me to hear the Germans bad-mouth Galicia. Today I overheard two lieutenants asking "Why on earth should the sons of Germany spill blood to defend this swinish country?" We, the Poles, are hated by everyone in this Austrian hotchpotch and are condemned to serve as prey for all of them.

African Kande Kamara writes in his diary:

We black African soldiers were very sorrowful about the white man's war. There was never any soldier in the camp who knew why we were fighting. There was no time to think about it. I didn't really care who was right—whether it was the French or the Germans—I went to fight with the French army and that was all I knew. The reason for war was never disclosed to any soldier. They didn't tell us how they got into the war. We just fought and fought until we got exhausted and died. Day and night, we fought, killed ourselves, the enemies and everybody else.

Australian corporal George Mitchell writes in his diary:

A wounded Turk told us they regard Australians as fiends incarnate.

British private Robert Cude writes in his diary:

I long to be with battalion so that I can do my best to bereave a German family. I hate these swines. . . . It is a wonderful sight and one that I shall not forget. War such as this, on such a beautiful day seems to me to be quite correct and proper! . . . Men are racing to certain death, and jesting and smiling and cursing, yet wonderfully quiet in a sense, for one feels that one must kill, and as often as one can.

The unnamed Austrian officer writes in his diary:

Since yesterday my mind has been troubled by the thought of the many Austrian heroes who have given their lives defending the honour of Austria and the Habsburgs, while I entertained my thoughts of treason, all for the love of an unworthy [Italian] woman. I am disgusted at myself. Habsburg, I live for you and I shall die for you, too! . . . He who gives his life for the Fatherland and the honour of the Habsburgs shall be honoured and remembered for eternity.

Russian officer Dmitry Oskin writes in his diary of his support for the ultimate form of state interventionism. First he records part of a speech he heard given by Lenin in support of Communism: "The main point is that land should be taken immediately from the landowners and given to the peasants without compensation. All ownership of land is to be eliminated." Then he recounts his own comments: "We the soldier-peasants demand that the land be immediately decreed common property. That it is immediately taken from the landowners and given to local land committees."

Religion in War

If there is ever a time when men get religious it is certainly in the midst of a war. The phenomenon of "fox hole religion" is understandable. What is interesting, however, is the religious ideas of some combatants when they go into the war. Men on both sides think that God is on their side. Turkish second lieutenant Mehmed Fasih writes in his diary:

From the rear comes "Allah! Allah!"—the rallying cry of our soldiers. . . . One of his comrades tells us how Nuri said to him when they arrived at the Front together: "I implore God to let me become a martyr!" Oh Nuri! Your prayer was answered. We bury Nuri. It was God's will that I would say the opening verse of the Koran over him.

The African Kande Kamara writes in his diary:

Coming from the background I came from, which was Muslim oriented, the only thing you thought about was Allah, death and life. . . . Whatever we thought was dedicated to the God Almighty alone.

This attitude is not restricted to Muslims. The unnamed Austrian officer writes in his diary:

Dear Lord, come to our aid, for we fight in the name of Justice, the Empire and the Faith. Dear Lord, steer the flight of the double eagle so that these beauteous lands, which had one time belonged to Austria, once again fall under the shadow of its mighty wings. . . . Cases of cholera. This is all we need. Is God no longer on our side? . . . Italy will pay for this, for the Lord sits in judgement up on high and he is wrathful.

German schoolgirl Piete Kuhr writes in her diary:

But we have faith in France and God, and comfort ourselves with the thought that over in Germany they are almost as unhappy as we are.

Klara, the mother of Rudolf Hess writes to her son:

Thank God the German Michael [the patron saint of Germany] has finally had the guts to stand firm until our rights to water and land have been secured.

Women in Wartime

One of the great tragedies of war is its demoralizing effect on women, either through subjugation or whoredom. Austrian doctor Josef Tomann writes in his diary:

And then there are the fat-bellied gents from the commissariat, who stink of fat and go arm in arm with Przemysl's finest ladies, most of who (and this is no exaggeration) have turned into prostitutes of the lowest order. The hospitals have been recruiting teenage girls as nurses, in some places there are up to 50 of them! . . . They are, with very few exceptions, utterly useless. Their main job is to satisfy the lust of the gentlemen officers and, rather shamefully, of a number of doctors, too. . . . New officers are coming in almost daily with cases of syphilis, gonorrhoea, and soft chancre. Some have all three at once! The poor girls and women feel so flattered when they get chatted up by one of these pestilent pigs in their spotless uniforms, with their shiny boots and buttons. .... Anything that can't be carted off or used to pay one of the prostitutes for her services is burnt, so that the Germans don't get it when they march in.

British officer Richard Meinertzhagen writes in his diary:

All the blacks are mad on looting, whether it is the Askaris or the porters, man, woman or child. It is also difficult to stop the blacks from raping women, because they see them as property, like cows or huts.

African Kande Kamara writes in his diary:

The only way to get to town was by sneaking out of camp. There were some white women who had mattresses and beds and invited you to their bedrooms. In fact they tried to keep you there. They gave you clothes, money, and everything. When the inspector came, he never saw you, because you were hiding under the bed or under the bed covers of that beautiful lady. That's how some soldiers got left behind. None of them went back to Africa.

Canadian Winnie McClare writes in a letter to his father:

An awfull lot of fellow that go to London come back in bad shape and are sent to the V.D. hospitals. There is one V.D. hospital near here that has six hundred men in it. It is a shame that the fellows can't keep away from it.

Disillusion and Regret

Occasionally, we read in *Intimate Voices* of the disillusion and regret of soldiers and civilians. The folly of war is sometimes recognized. German officer Ernst Nopper writes in his diary:

And all this time the weather is so beautiful that the shooting seems absurd.

Russian soldier Vasily Mishnin writes to his pregnant wife:

What are we suffering for, what do I achieve by killing someone, even a German? ... It is quite a peaceful scene when it's quiet and no one is firing. This is our enemy? They look like good, normal

people, they all want to live and yet here we are, gathered together
to take each other's lives away.

British officer Richard Meinertzhagen writes in his diary:

It seemed so odd that I should be having a meal today with people
whom I was trying to kill yesterday. It seemed so wrong and made
me wonder whether this really was war or whether we had all
made a ghastly mistake.

German officer Ernst Nopper writes in his diary:

I no longer share most people's enthusiasm for war. I think about
the dying soldiers, not just Germans, but also French, English,
Russian, Italian, Serbian and I don't know who else.

German schoolgirl Piete Kuhr writes in her diary:

I don't want any more soldiers to die. Millions are dead—and for
what? For whose benefit? We must just make sure that there is
never another war in the future. We must never again fall for the
nonsense peddled by the older generation.

And finally, the regret of Russian soldier Alexei Zyikov, who writes
in his diary during Easter of 1916:

Why did I lead such a debauched life? Why did I not cherish my
family and friends? I don't know. I loved adventure and now I am
paying for it. I feel very sad. Must I really die like this, fruitlessly,
with nothing worth repenting of?

The argument that modern warfare has changed so much that these
descriptions of World War I never happen—modern war really isn't all
that bad (unless of course you get killed)—is never made by the soldier
who suffers psychological damage or psychiatric disorders the rest of his
life, the forgotten civilians injured or disfigured in the conflict, or by those
maimed or blown up by land mines years later.
Such are the horrors of war.

* * * * *

THE CHRISTMAS TRUCE

Most American families have some traditions they observe every Christmas, even Jewish families. It might be decorating a tree, singing Christmas carols, shopping for bargains on Christmas Eve, attending church services, reading the biblical account of the birth of Christ, taking the kids to see the grandparents, driving around and looking at Christmas lights, eating at a particular restaurant, or watching *It's a Wonderful Life*, *Miracle on 34th Street*, or *A Christmas Carol*.

As fine as these things are, there is another tradition worth observing this Christmas and every Christmas: reading *Silent Night* (The Free Press, 2001). Not only is "Silent Night" the name of a Christmas carol, it is also the title of the book by historian Stanley Weintraub that tells the story of the World War I Christmas truce.

What makes the World War I Christmas truce even more relevant this Christmas is that we are once again at war on Christmas and it is the 90th anniversary of the famous truce.

The Christmas of 1914 was the first Christmas of the "war to end all wars." The war would drag on through three more. The German, French, Belgium, and British troops engaged in killing each other did not just all of a sudden lay down their arms because it was Christmas. According to Weintraub, neither side had been "firing at mealtimes" and "friendly banter echoed across the lines." The soldiers in their trenches were sometimes so close to each other that "they would throw newspapers, weighted with a stone, across to each other, and sometimes a ration tin." In early December, a British general issued an order that forbade fraternization because "it discourages initiative in commanders, and destroys the offensive spirit in all ranks."

Yet, less than a week before Christmas, a British lieutenant wrote to his mother:

> Some Germans came out and held up their hands and began to take in some of their wounded and so we ourselves immediately got out of our trenches and began bringing in our wounded also. The Germans then beckoned to us and a lot of us went over and talked to them and they helped us to bury our dead. This lasted the whole morning and I talked to several of them and I must say they seemed extraordinarily fine men. . . . It seemed too ironical for words. There, the night before we had been having a terrific battle and the morning after, there we were smoking their cigarettes and they smoking ours.

Brief and localized pre-holiday truces were springing up, usually initiated by the Germans. As Christmas Day approached, some German troops put up small Christmas trees on the parapets of their trenches. On Christmas Eve they began to sing *Stille Nacht* ("Silent Night"). Placards with Christmas greetings were set up by both sides. On Christmas Day, both sides buried their dead who had been lying in "No Man's Land." They chatted, exchanged souvenirs, shook hands, ate and drank together, played football, had joint religious services, and smoked each other's tobacco. They also took pictures.

No one knows for certain where and how the truce officially began. What is known is that men from both sides up and down the front agreed on informal truces for Christmas Eve and Christmas Day. A Bavarian captain recalled that he shouted to his enemies that: "we didn't wish to shoot and that we [should] make a Christmas truce. I said I would come from my side and we could speak with each other. First there was silence, then I shouted once more, invited them, and the British shouted 'No shooting!' Then a man came out of the[ir] trenches and I on my side did the same and so we came together and we shook hands—a bit cautiously!" An English captain wrote to his wife:

> I was in my dugout reading a paper and the mail was being dished out. It was reported that the Germans had lighted their trenches up all along the front. We had been calling to one another for some time Xmas wishes and other things. I went out and they shouted "no shooting" and then somehow the scene became a peaceful one. All our men got out of the trenches and sat on the parapet, the Germans did the same, and they talked to one another in English and broken English. I got on top of the trench and talked German and asked them to sing a German Volkslied, which they did, then our men sang quite well and each side clapped and cheered the other.

A Scottish corporal relates his experiences:

> We shook hands, wished each other a Merry Xmas, and were soon conversing as if we had known each other for years. We were in front of their wire entanglements and surrounded by Germans—Fritz and I in the center talking, and Fritz occasionally translating to his friends what I was saying. We stood inside the circle like street-corner orators. Soon most of our company . . . hearing that I and some others had gone out, followed us; they called me "Fergie" in the Regiment, and to find out where I was in the darkness they kept calling out "Fergie." The Germans, thinking

it was an English greeting, answered "Fergie." What a sight—little
groups of Germans and British extending almost the length of our
front! Out of the darkness we could hear laughter and see lighted
matches. . . . Where they couldn't talk the language they were
making themselves understood by signs, and everyone seemed to
be getting on nicely. Here we were laughing and chatting to men
whom only a few hours before we were trying to kill!

That last sentence alone shows the utter folly of war. It also shows that left
to themselves, men would not naturally engage in such a senseless war
like World War I. It takes the state to get men to hate and kill other men
that have never aggressed against them and that they don't even know.

After a silent night and a day, the war continued—the commanders
saw to it. A British general who visited the front was aghast that
"sufficient attention" was not being paid to fighting the Germans. In a
memorandum to his commanders he stated:

I would add that, on my return, I was shown a report from one
section of how, on Christmas Day, a friendly gathering had taken
place of Germans and British on the neutral ground between the
two lines, recounting that many officers had taken part in it. This
is not only illustrative of the apathetic state we are gradually
sinking into, apart also from illustrating that any orders I issue on
the subject are useless, for I have issued the strictest orders that on
no account is intercourse to be allowed between the opposing
troops. To finish this war quickly, we must keep up the fighting
spirit and do all we can to discourage friendly intercourse. I am
calling for particulars as to names of officers and units who took
part in this Christmas gathering, with a view to disciplinary action.

Weintraub closes the book with a chapter titled "What If—?" But
amid all that the author proposes that might or might not have been, one
statement stands out: "The butchery in which hundreds of thousands of
bodies were ground into the mud of the Western Front, leaving not an
identifiable bone, would not have happened. The more than six thousand
deaths every day over forty-six further months of war would not have
occurred."

And now, ninety years later, we are again engaged in a war. The
casualties may be less, but the state's lies about the war have increased.

The president maintains that the United States and the world are
safer now than before the September 11th attacks. But does the rest of the
world real feel safer? The situation described by Lew Rockwell just after
Christmas two years ago has not changed: "The US remains the only

government in human history to have dropped nuclear weapons on people, it has far more weapons than anyone else, and remains the only country that reserves to itself the right of first strike."

Instead of invading the world, the United States should declare a truce with the world. No more threats. No more bombs. No more troops or bases on foreign soil. No more spies. No more trade sanctions. No more embargoes. No more foreign aid bribes. No more foreign entanglements. No more simultaneously playing the world's bully and policeman. In a word: noninterventionism; that is, the principles of our Founding Fathers. What is wrong with "peace, commerce, and honest friendship with all nations"? What is wrong with avoiding "entangling alliances"? What is wrong with "having as little political connection as possible" with foreign nations? What is wrong with not going abroad "seeking monsters to destroy"? Can anyone honestly say that Bush's principles are better than Jefferson's principles?

Over 1,300 U.S. soldiers won't be celebrating Christmas this year—or any year. They died in vain for an unconstitutional, immoral, senseless war while in the service of a reckless, imperial presidency. They will forever have a silent night.

* * * * *

THEY KNEW NOT WHERE THEY WERE GOING OR WHY

In times of war, people do strange and irrational things. They also do things that they would never think of doing in peacetime—like killing and maiming people that never lifted a finger against them, that they didn't know, and that they had never even spoken to.

It was one hundred years ago that the first war ended in what was to be a very bloody century of war. The Russo-Japanese War began on the night of February 8, 1904, with the Battle of Port Arthur, a port on the Liaotung peninsula in Manchuria that served as the primary base for the Russian fleet in the Pacific. Port Arthur, which took its name from British Royal Navy Lieutenant William C. Arthur, was a strategic seaport coveted by Russian and Japan.

Although the immediate cause of the war was the Japanese naval attack on Port Arthur, the Russo-Japanese War was preceded, as are most wars, by interventionism. Russia and Japan, at the expense of China, wanted control or "influence" in the Far East. After warring against China in the mid 1890s, Japan demanded control of Port Arthur. The European Powers objected, not because they respected Chinese sovereignty, but because they had their own ambitions in the Far East. Within a couple of years, Russia took control of Port Arthur, gaining a valuable ice-free port to supplement Vladivostok. Suppression of the Boxer Rebellion in 1900 resulted in more intervention by Japan and the European powers. Russian troops remained in Manchuria after the fighting ended. It was Russian refusal to make good on its promised withdrawal of Russian troops that led to the Russo-Japanese War.

The outcome of the Battle of Port Arthur was inconclusive, but Japan was victorious when the Siege of Port Arthur ended on January 2, 1905. The Japanese also defeated the Russians at four major land battles and two major sea battles before the war effectively ended on May 28, 1905, with the defeat of the Russian fleet at the Battle of Tsushima. Nearly the entire Russian fleet, which had sailed all the way from the Baltic coast, was destroyed in this battle in the waters of Tsushima Straits (between the Japanese island of Kyushu and South Korea), along with over 4,300 men. The Japanese lost only three torpedo boats and a little over 100 men.

The wasting of the lives of over 4,400 men in this battle is a great tragedy. But the role of the state in sending men off to war and the blind obedience to the state by the men sent off to war is an incredible outrage. The same can be said about almost any war or foreign intervention. In the 1998 Discovery Channel video, *Last of the Czars*, the narrator speaks these solemn words as pictures of Russian troops are shown:

> In 1904 Nicholas had been drawn into a disastrous war with Japan. He dispatched his troops with his blessing. Not that they knew where they were going or why. The Russian people believed the propaganda which promised a short, sharp, victorious war. But the Japanese people believed their propaganda which promised the same and proved to be right. It took the Russian navy's Baltic Fleet six months on the high seas to make the engagement; only to be sunk in a single day at the Battle of Tsushima.

About 130,000 men were killed in the Russo-Japanese War. Although the Treaty of Portsmouth, signed at the Portsmouth Naval Base, New Hampshire, on Sept. 5, 1905, officially ended the war, it did not end the folly of war and intervention that is still with us one hundred years later.

* * * * *

WHO WILL IT BE?

Another milestone will soon be reached in the war on terrorism. No, the Homeland Security threat level will not be lowered to green. No, regular tubes of toothpaste will not be allowed on airplanes. And no, U.S. troops will not be turning everything over to Iraqis and Afghans.

The milestone I am referring to is not a good one. There have been 43 U.S. soldiers killed in Afghanistan so far this year. This brings the total dead up to 990. But if last year is any indication, when 317 soldiers died, the 1,000th U.S. soldier will soon die in Afghanistan.

Who will it be? Who will be the 1,000th U.S. soldier killed in Afghanistan?

Will it be someone from your family? Will it be your father, your brother, your uncle, your grandfather, your nephew, or perhaps your husband? Will it be your mother, your sister, your aunt, your grandmother, your niece, or perhaps your wife?

Will it be someone you know? Will it be your friend, your neighbor, your classmate, your coworker, or just an acquaintance?

Will it be someone from your area? Will it be someone from your state, your county, your city, or maybe even your street?

For those in the military, will it be someone serving with you? Will it be your corporal, your sergeant, lieutenant, your captain, or your colonel? Will it be someone in your squad or platoon? Will it be someone in your barracks or on your ship? Will it be you?

Who will it be? Who will be the 1,000th U.S. soldier killed in Afghanistan?

These deaths are all so senseless. The 9/11 hijackers are all dead. None of them were Afghans. The terrorist attacks were primarily planned in apartments in the United States by individuals legally authorized to be in the county, not in terrorist training camps in Afghanistan. The United States supported the Muslim insurgents and Afghan militants when they were freedom-fighting Mujahideen fighting against the Soviet Union. The president's National Security Advisor, retired Marine Corps general James L. Jones, not only acknowledged that the al-Qaeda presence in Afghanistan was very diminished, but that "the maximum estimate is less than 100 operating in the country, no bases, no ability to launch attacks on either us or our allies." No American was ever harmed by anyone in Afghanistan until the U.S. military invaded and occupied that country.

Obama's escalation of the war in Afghanistan is folly on a grand scale. This primitive country with a long history of ethnic, religious, and factional squabbling is known as the graveyard of empires. The British found this out the hard way, as did the Soviet Union. Why is America the great exception?

According to the Congressional Research Service, the United States spends about $3.6 billion a month in Afghanistan—and that was as of last October when there were fewer U.S. troops in the country than there are now. The 30,000 additional troops that Obama wants to send to Afghanistan will cost another $30 billion. That's another $2.5 billion a month. The Pentagon has acknowledged that it costs about $400 to get a gallon of fuel into the remote areas of Afghanistan to U.S. troops. The trucking and security companies hired by the United States to transport supplies to military bases in Afghanistan have paid hundreds of millions of dollars in protection money to the Taliban and other insurgent groups to keep from being attacked on the roads. Since the U.S. invasion and occupation of Afghanistan, the Army Corps of Engineers has spent more than $4.5 billion on construction projects, most of it building nearly 400 U.S. and coalition bases in that country.

We don't know who will be the 1,000th U.S. soldier to die in Afghanistan. But we do know it will be soon. And there are some other things we know about his upcoming death. We know that his death will be in vain and for a lie. We know he will not die to avenge 9/11. We know he will die, not as a hero, but as a dupe. We know he will not die to protect anyone from terrorists. We know he will not die for anyone's freedoms. We know his death will be senseless, unnecessary, and preventable. We know his death will be a sacrifice for the furtherance of the U.S. global empire.

Who will it be?

* * * * *

THE TWENTY YEAR WAR IN IRAQ

"Why should a single American die for the Emir of Kuwait?" ~ Pat Buchanan

The current war in Iraq—now near the end of its seventh year—did not really begin on March 20, 2003, when George W. Bush ordered the United States military to invade Iraq. It actually began twenty years ago on January 17, 1991, when another Bush, George H.W., ordered the United States military to invade Iraq the first time.

After getting a green light from the U.S. Ambassador to Iraq, April Glaspie, who told Saddam Hussein: "We have no opinion on your

Arab-Arab conflicts, such as your dispute with Kuwait. Secretary Baker has directed me to emphasize the instruction, first given to Iraq in the 1960s, that the Kuwait issue is not associated with America," Hussein invaded Kuwait, on August 2, 1990. But even after John Kelly, the Assistant Secretary of State for Near Eastern Affairs, testified to Congress that the "United States has no commitment to defend Kuwait and the US has no intention of defending Kuwait if it is attacked by Iraq," Bush the elder sent 500,000 U.S. troops to that caldron known as the Middle East.

After imposing sanctions on Iraq in August, the United Nations in November set a date of midnight on January 16 as the deadline for Iraq to withdraw its troops from Kuwait. Congress—ignoring the Constitution and refusing to issue a declaration of war—issued a resolution authorizing the president to use military force against Iraq, "Joint Resolution to Authorize the Use of United States Armed Forces Pursuant to United Nations Security Council Resolution 678." The vote was 52-47 in the Senate and 250-183 in the House. Only two Republicans in the Senate and three in the House voted against the resolution.

When Iraq failed to withdraw its troops from Kuwait by the deadline, the United States commenced bombing as Operation Desert Shield turned into Operation Desert Storm. The 88,500 tons of bombs dropped widely destroyed both military and civilian infrastructure. The U.S. ground assault, Operation Desert Sabre, begin on February 24. A cease-fire was declared four days later. For the United States, there were 148 battle deaths and 145 non-battle deaths. This means that 293 Americans did die for the emir of Kuwait. Among the dead U.S. soldiers were 15 women and 35 killed by "friendly fire." The first American casualty of the war, LCDR Scott Speicher, was actually the last of the U.S. military dead to be identified, and just a couple of years ago.

Tens of thousands of Iraqi soldiers were also killed, plus several thousand Iraqi and Kuwaiti civilians. The current war in Iraq is but a delayed campaign in the war against Iraq. During the intermission there were tensions, threats, missile strikes, enforcement of no-fly zones, bombing raids, brutal sanctions that resulted in the deaths of hundreds of thousands of Iraqi children, infamously said to be "worth it" by U.S. ambassador to the UN (and later Secretary of State) Madeleine Albright, and a continued presence of U.S. troops in Saudi Arabia, which inflamed the Muslim world, created terrorists, and led to the attacks of 9/11.

So, what should the United States have done when one autocratic Muslim state (Iraq) invaded another autocratic Muslim state (Kuwait)? The answer is the same no matter what country invades, bombs, attacks, or threatens another country—absolutely nothing.

It is not the purpose of the U.S. government to be the policeman, security guard, mediator, and babysitter of the world. The preamble to the Constitution mentions providing for the common defense, promoting the general welfare, and securing the blessings of liberty "to ourselves and our Posterity," not to the tired, poor, huddled masses, and wretched refuse on distant shores.

The United States should be a beacon of liberty, leading the world by example, and not intervening or meddling in the affairs of other countries—for any reason. Not isolationism, of course, but in the words of Thomas Jefferson: "Peace, commerce, and honest friendship with all nations—entangling alliances with none," yet doing "what is right, leaving the people of Europe to act their follies and crimes among themselves, while we pursue in good faith the paths of peace and prosperity."

And as I have maintained over and over again, the U.S. military should be engaged exclusively in defending the United States, not defending other countries, and certainly not attacking, invading, or occupying them. The U.S. military should be limited to defending the United States, securing U.S. borders, guarding U.S. shores, patrolling U.S. coasts, and enforcing no-fly zones over U.S. skies instead of defending, securing, guarding, patrolling, and enforcing in other countries. To do otherwise is to pervert the purpose of the military.

The world is full of evil, and conflicts between peoples have existed since the beginning of time. The United States has neither the responsibility nor the resources to resolve every conflict and stamp out all the evil in the world. Any American concerned about oppression, human rights violations, sectarian violence, ill treatment of women, forced labor, child labor, persecution, genocide, famine, natural disasters, or injustice anywhere in the world is perfectly free to contribute his own money to or go and fight on behalf of some particular cause. Just don't expect U.S. taxpayers to foot the bill for and U.S. soldiers to die for your cause.

Freeing Kuwait from Iraq—even if "only" 293 Americans died, even if Saddam Hussein had been deposed, even if it hadn't resulted in brutal sanctions, even if it hadn't led to another war, and even if it had ensured the free flow of oil at market prices—was not worth one cent from the U.S. treasury or one drop of blood from an American soldier.

* * * * *

CHAPTER 6

THE U.S. GLOBAL EMPIRE

THE U.S. GLOBAL EMPIRE

There is a new empire in town, and its global presence is increasing every day.

The kingdom of Alexander the Great reached all the way to the borders of India. The Roman Empire controlled the Celtic regions of Northern Europe and all of the Hellenized states that bordered the Mediterranean. The Mongol Empire, which was the largest contiguous empire in history, stretched from Southeast Asia to Europe. The Byzantine Empire spanned the years 395 to 1453. In the sixteenth century, the Ottoman Empire stretched from the Persian Gulf in the east to Hungary in the northwest; and from Egypt in the south to the Caucasus in the north. At the height of its dominion, the British Empire included almost a quarter of the world's population.

Nothing, however, compares to the U.S. global empire. What makes U.S. hegemony unique is that it consists, not of control over great land masses or population centers, but of a global presence unlike that of any other country in history.

The extent of the U.S. global empire is almost incalculable. The latest "Base Structure Report" of the Department of Defense states that the Department's physical assets consist of "more than 600,000 individual buildings and structures, at more than 6,000 locations, on more than 30 million acres." The exact number of locations is then given as 6,702—divided into large installations (115), medium installations (115), and small installations/locations (6,472). This classification can be deceiving, however, because installations are only classified as small if they have a Plant Replacement Value (PRV) of less than $800 million.

Although most of these locations are in the continental United States, 96 of them are in U.S. territories around the globe, and 702 of them are in foreign countries. But as Chalmers Johnson has documented, the figure of 702 foreign military installations is too low, for it does not include installations in Afghanistan, Iraq, Israel, Kosovo, Kuwait, Kyrgyzstan, Qatar, and Uzbekistan. Johnson estimates that an honest count would be closer to 1,000.

The number of countries that the United States has a presence in is staggering. According the U.S. Department of State's list of "Independent States in the World," there are 192 countries in the world, all of which, except Bhutan, Cuba, Iran, and North Korea, have diplomatic relations with the United States. All of these countries except one (Vatican City) are members of the United Nations. According to the Department of Defense publication, "Active Duty Military Personnel Strengths by Regional Area and by Country," the United States has troops in 135 countries. Here is the list:

Afghanistan	Djibouti
Albania	Dominican Republic
Algeria	East Timor
Antigua	Ecuador
Argentina	Egypt
Australia	El Salvador
Austria	Eritrea
Azerbaijan	Estonia
Bahamas	Ethiopia
Bahrain	Fiji
Bangladesh	Finland
Barbados	France
Belgium	Georgia
Belize	Germany
Bolivia	Ghana
Bosnia and Herzegovina	Greece
Botswana	Guatemala
Brazil	Guinea
Bulgaria	Haiti
Burma	Honduras
Burundi	Hungary
Cambodia	Iceland
Cameroon	India
Canada	Indonesia
Chad	Iraq
Chile	Ireland
China	Israel
Colombia	Italy
Costa Rica	Jamaica
Cote D'Ivoire	Japan
Cuba	Jordan
Cyprus	Kazakhstan
Czech Republic	Kenya
Denmark	Kuwait

Kyrgyzstan
Laos
Latvia
Lebanon
Liberia
Lithuania
Luxembourg
Macedonia
Madagascar
Malawi
Malaysia
Mali
Malta
Mexico
Mongolia
Morocco
Mozambique
Nepal
Netherlands
New Zealand
Nicaragua
Niger
Nigeria
North Korea
Norway
Oman
Pakistan
Paraguay
Peru
Philippines
Poland
Portugal
Qatar
Republic of the Congo

Romania
Russia
Saudi Arabia
Senegal
Serbia and Montenegro
Sierra Leone
Singapore
Slovenia
Spain
South Africa
South Korea
Sri Lanka
Suriname
Sweden
Switzerland
Syria
Tanzania
Thailand
Togo
Trinidad and Tobago
Tunisia
Turkey
Turkmenistan
Uganda
Ukraine
United Arab Emirates
United Kingdom
Uruguay
Venezuela
Vietnam
Yemen
Zambia
Zimbabwe

This means that the United States has troops in 70 percent of the world's countries. The average American could probably not locate half of these 135 countries on a map.

To this list could be added regions like the Indian Ocean territory of Diego Garcia, Gibraltar, and the Atlantic Ocean island of St. Helena, all still controlled by Great Britain, but not considered sovereign countries. Greenland is also home to U.S. troops, but is technically part of Denmark. Troops in two other regions, Kosovo and Hong Kong, might also be included here, but the DOD's "Personnel Strengths" document includes U.S. troops in Kosovo under Serbia and U.S. troops in Hong Kong under China.

Possessions of the United States like Guam, Johnston Atoll, Puerto Rico, the Trust Territory of the Pacific Islands, and the Virgin Islands are likewise home to U.S. troops. Guam has over 3,200.

Regular troop strength ranges from a low of 1 in Malawi to a high of 74,796 in Germany. At the time the most recent "Personnel Strengths" was released by the government (September 30, 2003), there were 183,002 troops deployed to Iraq, an unspecified number of which came from U.S. forces in Germany and Italy. The total number of troops deployed abroad as of that date was 252,764, not including U.S. troops in Iraq from the United States. Total military personnel on September 30, 2003, was 1,434,377. This means that 17.6 percent of U.S. military forces were deployed on foreign soil, and certainly over 25 percent if U.S. troops in Iraq from the United States were included. But regardless of how many troops we have in each country, having troops in 135 countries is 135 countries too many.

The U. S. global empire—an empire that Alexander the Great, Caesar Augustus, Genghis Khan, Suleiman the Magnificent, Justinian, and King George V would be proud of.

* * * * *

THE BASES OF EMPIRE

A global empire like the United States needs overseas bases to accommodate its troops, now in 135 countries. Although the latest "Base Structure Report" of the Department of Defense admits to having 96 military installations in U.S. overseas territories and 702 military installations in foreign countries, it has been documented that this number is far too low.

The official list of countries that we have bases in is as follows:

Antigua	Denmark
Australia	Egypt
Austria	France
Bahamas	Germany
Bahrain	Greece
Belgium	Honduras
Canada	Iceland
Colombia	Indonesia
Cuba	Italy

Japan	Portugal
Kenya	Singapore
Luxembourg	Spain
Netherlands	South Korea
New Zealand	Turkey
Norway	United Arab Emirates
Oman	United Kingdom
Peru	Venezuela

To this must be added the bases that we have in Diego Garcia, Greenland, Hong Kong, Kwajalein Atoll, and St. Helena. This makes a total of 39 foreign locations that the United States officially has bases in, not counting bases in U.S. overseas territories like Guam, Johnston Atoll, Puerto Rico, and the Virgin Islands.

But there are problems with this official list. First of all, it has some notable omissions. The Air Force Technical Applications Center in Thailand is not listed. And neither is Eskan Village and Prince Sultan Air Base in Saudi Arabia. The United States has had a troop presence in the former Soviet Republics of Kyrgyzstan and Uzbekistan since October of 2001, yet they are not listed either. The huge Camp Bondsteel in Kosovo is not even listed, although President Bush has spoken there. According to the Department of Defense publication, "Active Duty Military Personnel Strengths by Regional Area and by Country," the United States has 2,997 active duty military personnel in Qatar. Yet, no base in listed in the Base Structure Report. Incredibly, no bases are even listed in Afghanistan, Kuwait, or Iraq. With critical omissions like these, God only knows how many more foreign bases we have that are not listed.

The issue is not just how many countries the United States has bases in. The issue is U.S. troops on foreign soil. Having an official base just makes our foreign presence worse. It would be better for U.S. troops to patrol our border with Mexico than to patrol the borders of countries half way around the world that most Americans could not locate on a map.

* * * * *

GUARDING THE EMPIRE

When faced with evidence that the U.S. global empire has troops and/or bases in the majority of countries on the planet, apologists for the warfare state and the "military-industrial complex" attempt to dismiss this U.S. global hegemony by claiming that it is the Marine guards at U.S. embassies overseas that account for our presence in so many countries.

It is traditionally believed that the United States has an embassy in every foreign country and that every foreign country has an embassy in the United States. Most people also think that every U.S. embassy has an attachment of Marine guards to provide security for embassy personnel. Both of these assumptions are wrong.

U.S. Embassies in Foreign Countries

Of the 191 "Independent States in the World" besides the United States, there are 29 countries in which we do not have an embassy:

Andorra	Nauru
Antigua and Barbuda	Palau
Bhutan	Republic of the Congo
Comoros	Saint Kitts and Nevis
Cuba	Saint Lucia
Dominica	Saint Vincent and the Grenadines
Grenada	San Marino
Guinea-Bissau	Sao Tome and Principe
Iran	Seychelles
Kiribati	Solomon Islands
Libya	Somalia
Liechtenstein	Tonga
North Korea	Tuvalu
Maldives	Vanuatu
Monaco	

The United States does not have an embassy in the countries of Bhutan, Cuba, Iran, and North Korea because we do not have diplomatic relations with them.

Many small countries in which the United States has no embassy are "covered" by another country. The U.S. ambassador to Spain is accredited to Andorra. The U.S. ambassador to Barbados is accredited to Antigua and Barbuda, Dominica, Grenada, Saint Kitts and Nevis, Saint Lucia, and Saint Vincent and the Grenadines. The U.S. ambassador to Mauritius is accredited to Seychelles and Comoros. The U.S. ambassador to Senegal is accredited to Guinea-Bissau. The U.S. ambassador to the Marshall Islands is accredited to Kiribati. The U.S. ambassador to Switzerland is accredited to Liechtenstein. The U.S. ambassador to Sri Lanka is accredited to Maldives. The U.S. consul general in Marseille, France, is accredited to Monaco. The U.S. consul general in Florence, Italy, is accredited to San Marino. The U.S. ambassador to Papua New

Guinea is accredited to the Solomon Islands and Vanuatu. The U.S. ambassador to Kenya is accredited to Somalia. The U.S. ambassador to Gabon is accredited to Sao Tome and Principe. The U.S. ambassador to Fiji is accredited to Tonga, Tuvalu, and Nauru. The U.S. ambassador to the Philippines is accredited to Palau.

The status of U.S. embassies sometimes changes. In some countries, like Antigua and Barbuda, Guinea-Bissau, Iran, and the Solomon Islands, we used to have an embassy, but it is now closed. The United States has an ambassador to the Republic of the Congo, but the embassy is temporarily collocated with the U.S. embassy in the Democratic Republic of the Congo (formerly called Zaire). The Afghan embassy closed in January 1989 but then reopened in December 2001. In the Central African Republic, the embassy is currently operating with a minimal staff. The United States closed its embassy in Libya in May 1980 and then resumed embassy activities in February 2004 through a U.S. "interest section" in the Belgian embassy. Since June 2004, the United States has maintained a "liaison office" in Libya, but has no immediate plans for an embassy. New embassies had to be built in Kenya and Tanzania after they were bombed in August 1998.

Foreign Embassies in the United States

Just because the United States does not have an embassy in a particular country does not necessarily mean that that country does not have an embassy in the United States. Of the 191 "Independent States in the World" besides the United States, there are 18 countries that do not maintain an embassy in the United States:

Andorra	Monaco
Bhutan	Nauru
Comoros	San Marino
Cuba	Sao Tome and Principe
Iran	Solomon Islands
Kiribati	Somalia
North Korea	Tonga
Libya	Tuvalu
Maldives	Vanuatu

As mentioned above, the United States does not have diplomatic relations with Bhutan, Cuba, Iran, and North Korea. All of these countries that do not maintain an embassy in Washington, D.C. are members of the United Nations and have a representative of some kind at the UN in New York.

There are therefore 11 of these countries that have an embassy in the United States even though we do not have one in their country:

Antigua and Barbuda	Republic of the Congo
Dominica	Saint Kitts and Nevis
Grenada	Saint Lucia
Guinea-Bissau	Saint Vincent and the Grenadines
Liechtenstein	Seychelles
Palau	

There are no countries in which the United States has an embassy that do not likewise have one on U.S. soil.

Marine Security Guards

The question of Marine guards providing security at our embassies is not an easy one to answer. All of our embassies have security measures of some kind, but all are not guarded by U.S. Marines. For security reasons (isn't that always the excuse?), the government does not like to reveal which embassies have Marine guards and which embassies do not.

Marine security guards are members of the Marine Security Guard Battalion headquartered at the Marine Corps base in Quantico, Virginia. Quantico is also the location of the Marine Security Guard School, where guards are trained to react to terrorism, fires, riots, demonstrations, and evacuations.

The stationing of Marine Security Guards at U.S. embassies can be traced to The Foreign Service Act of 1946, which authorizes the Secretary of the Navy, "upon the request of the Secretary of State, to assign enlisted members of the Navy and the Marine Corps to serve as custodians under supervision of the Principal Officer at an Embassy, Legation or Consulate." The first Marine security guards went to Tangier and Bangkok on January 28, 1949. By the end of May 1949, 303 Marines had been assigned to foreign posts. By 1953, this number had increased to 6 officers and 676 enlisted men. By 1956, the number of enlisted men was up to 850.

There are currently over 1,200 Marines serving at over 130 posts abroad, in over 100 countries. Exact figures are not available, but in a report "Concerning the Role of Marine Security Guards in Securing U.S. Embassies and Government Personnel" given before the House Armed Services Committee Special Oversight Panel on Terrorism on October 10, 2002, by W. Ray Williams, the Deputy Assistant Secretary for Countermeasures and Information Security, the number of Marine security guards was given as 1,029 "at 131 US Missions abroad, soon to be 132 with the reactivation of a Marine Security Guard Detachment in Belgrade scheduled for January 2003." He further stated that 19 additional detachments of Marine guards were to be added in the next five years, with a long-term goal of 1,352 Marine guards at 159 detachments. According to the U.S. State Department, as of August 2003, the United States had "over 1,200 Marines for the internal security of 132 U.S. embassies, missions, and consulates worldwide."

Marine security guards are organized into 7 regional companies. Company A headquarters is located in Frankfurt, Germany, and is responsible for 20 detachments in Eastern Europe. Company B headquarters is located in Nicosia, Cyprus, and is responsible for 18 detachments in northern Africa and the Middle East. Company C headquarters is located in Bangkok, Thailand, and is responsible for 18 detachments located in the Far East, Asia, and Australia. Company D headquarters is located in Ft. Lauderdale, Florida, and is responsible for 26 detachments in Central and South America and the Caribbean. Company E headquarters is also located (with Company A) in Frankfurt, Germany, and is responsible for 16 detachments in Western Europe and Ottawa, Canada. Company F headquarters is located in Nairobi, Kenya, and is responsible for 11 detachments in Sub-Saharan Africa. Company G headquarters is located in Abidjan, Cote d'Ivoire, and is responsible for 12 detachments in West and Central Africa.

Marine security guard companies are commanded by a lieutenant colonel. At each diplomatic post, there is a minimum of one detachment commander and five Marine security guards. This allows them to maintain one security post 24/7. Locations with more than one security post have more than five guards. About 40 percent of detachments have the 1/5 ratio of commander to guards, another 40 percent are between 1/6 and 1/10, and the remaining 20 percent have something greater than 1/10. After graduating from security guard school, a Marine can usually expect two fifteen-month duty tours.

The U.S. Global Empire

What, then, do embassies and Marine guards have to do with the U.S. global empire of troops and bases that garrison the planet? As mentioned at the onset of this article, apologists for the U.S. global empire attempt to dismiss our troop presence in so many countries by claiming that including Marines guarding embassies inflates the total number of countries in which we have a troop presence. The truth, however, is that whether Marine guards are counted or not, the United States still has a global empire that now encompasses 136 countries.

The source for information on U.S. troops stationed abroad is the quarterly publication titled "Active Duty Military Personnel Strengths by Regional Area and by Country." This is published by a Department of Defense organization called the Directorate for Information Operations and Reports (DIOR). The latest edition that will be referenced in this article is dated March 31, 2004. Previous editions can be seen here. According to the DIOR, the information contained in its report of personnel strengths is provided directly by each branch of the U.S. Armed Forces; that is, the DIOR merely reports the information it receives. The DIOR publication does not indicate *why* troops are in a particular country, it merely reports the fact that they are there.

The issue here is whether the Marine Corps troops listed as deployed on foreign soil includes Marine guards at embassies. If the figure given for Marines in each country *does not* include embassy guards, then the United States *does* in fact have troops in 136 countries. Case closed. There is no need for this article other than to point out that the United States has added one more country (Guyana) since the first time I addressed the subject of the U.S. global empire. But if the figure given for Marines in each country *does* include embassy guards, then what apologists for the U.S. global empire are saying is that the United States *does not* have troops in 136 countries because Marine guards should not be included. Therefore, so they say, the number of countries in which the U.S. has troops should be limited to those countries in which we actually have bases. Of course, that is a problem as well, but it is not under consideration here since I have previously addressed the subject of the bases of the U.S. empire.

Although the case could be made that these guards are what Lew Rockwell calls "armed servants for the spies and bureaucrats," I am willing to agree with apologists for the U.S. global empire that Marine guards should not be counted when determining whether the United States has troops in other countries. This is also assuming that the "Active Duty Military Personnel Strengths by Regional Area and by Country" document is accurate.

The issue cannot be settled by merely asking the Marine Corps how it determines the number of Marines it has in each country. No one I spoke with in the DOD or the Marine Corps ever heard of the "Active Duty Military Personnel Strengths by Regional Area and by Country" document. And no one in the DOD or the Marine Corps that I sent the document to ever responded. Furthermore, when you start asking questions about Marines guarding U.S. embassies, DOD and Marine Corps officials get nervous (and sometimes downright belligerent) and start asking you questions about why you want the information.

After studying the "Active Duty Military Personnel Strengths by Regional Area and by Country" document, and after determining which countries have a U.S. embassy, it looks as though the figures given for Marines deployed to foreign countries do not include Marine guards at embassies.

Of the 55 countries in which the United States does not have any troops (not just Marines), the following have a U.S. embassy:

Angola	Mauritania
Armenia	Mauritius
Belarus	Micronesia
Benin	Moldova
Brunei	Namibia
Burkina Fasco	Panama
Cape Verde	Papua New Guinea
Central African Republic	Rwanda
Croatia	Samoa
Equatorial Guinea	Slovak Republic
Gabon	Sudan
Gambia	Swaziland
Holy See (The Vatican)	Tajikistan
Lesotho	Uzbekistan
Marshall Islands	

If the figures include Marine guards, then this would mean that no U.S. embassy in any of these 29 countries had Marine security guards.

Some countries in which the United States has Army, Navy, and/or Air Force troops have a U.S. embassy but no Marines are listed as being in the country:

Belize	Malawi
Cambodia	Mongolia
Eritrea	New Zealand
Guyana	Suriname
Lebanon	Ukraine
Madagascar	

If the figures include Marine guards, then this would mean that no U.S. embassy in any of these 11 countries had Marine security guards.

Other countries in which the United States has troops including

Marines have a U.S. embassy but do not have the minimum number of 6 Marines necessary for embassy security guard duty.

Albania	Mexico
Botswana	Morocco
Bulgaria	Romania
Cameroon	Serbia and Montenegro
Demo. Republic of the Congo	Sri Lanka
Guinea	Sweden
Iceland	Tanzania
Laos	Zambia
Luxembourg	Zimbabwe
Malaysia	

If the figures include Marine guards, then this would mean that no U.S. embassy in any of these 19 countries had Marine security guards.

There are 13 countries in which the only troops listed are Marines:

Azerbaijan	Mozambique
Burundi	North Korea
Fiji	Sierra Leone
Kyrgyzstan	Trinidad and Tobago
Latvia	Togo
Mali	Turkmenistan
Malta	

The countries of Azerbaijan, Burundi, Fiji, Sierra Leone, and Trinidad and Tobago do not have the minimum number of 6 Marines necessary for embassy security guard duty. If the figures include Marine guards, then this would mean that no U.S. embassy in these 5 countries had Marine security guards. We do not have an embassy in North Korea for Marines to guard. Likewise, there are 167 Marines in Cuba but the United States has no embassy there either.

But supposing that the figure given for Marines in each country does include Marine security guards at embassies, we still have a problem. Most of the countries with a U.S. embassy that have the minimum number of 6 Marines that are necessary to provide embassy security guard duty also have Army, Navy, and/or Air Force troops as well. So whether the figures include Marine guards is irrelevant. The following countries have a U.S. embassy, troops from the Army, Navy, and/or Air Force, and at least 6 Marines:

Afghanistan
Algeria
Argentina
Australia
Austria
Bahamas
Bahrain
Bangladesh
Barbados
Belgium
Bolivia
Bosnia and Herzegovina
Brazil
Burma
Canada
Chad
Chile
China
Colombia
Costa Rica
Cote D'lvoire
Cyprus
Czech Republic
Denmark
Djibouti
Dominican Republic
Ecuador
Egypt
El Salvador
Estonia
Ethiopia
Finland
France
Georgia
Germany
Greece
Guatemala
Guinea
Haiti
Honduras
Hungary
Iceland
India
Indonesia/East Timor
Iraq

Israel
Italy
Jamaica
Japan
Jordan
Kazakhstan
Kenya
Kuwait
Liberia
Lithuania
Macedonia
Nepal
Netherlands
Nicaragua
Niger
Nigeria
Norway
Oman
Pakistan
Paraguay
Peru
Poland
Portugal
Qatar
Russia
Saudi Arabia
Senegal
Singapore
Slovenia
South Africa
South Korea
Spain
Switzerland
Syria
Thailand
Tunisia
Turkey
Uganda
United Arab Emirates
United Kingdom
Uruguay
Venezuela
Vietnam
Yemen

The "Personnel Strengths" document includes the country of East Timor under Indonesia so it is impossible to determine exactly how the 10 Marines in that region are divided between the countries.

Of the 13 countries in which the only troops listed are Marines, 6 were previously eliminated because either the United States did not have an embassy in the country or there was not the minimum number of 6 Marines necessary for embassy security guard duty. This leaves only the following seven countries as *potential* examples of countries with a U.S. embassy guarded by Marines that should not be included in the total of 136 countries in which the United States has troops:

Kyrgyzstan	Mozambique
Latvia	Togo
Mali	Turkmenistan
Malta	

But a comparison of the current "Personnel Strengths" document with the previous quarterly editions shows that this is not the case. For example, Kyrgyzstan, which is now listed as having 8 Marines, had 14 Marines three months ago and 27 Marines six months ago. And Malta, which is now listed as having 4 Marines, had 7 Marines three months ago and 3 Marines six months ago. This could not possibly be just Marine embassy guards. The next quarterly report of "Active Duty Military Personnel Strengths by Regional Area and by Country" is sure to have similar changes.

So the fact remains: Marine guards or no Marine guards, the United States has troops in 136 countries.

But even that figure is too low, for the United States also has troops in Dependencies and Areas of Special Sovereignty. These are territories controlled by countries that may be located thousands of miles away from the mother country. For example, the United States has troops in Great Britain and areas controlled by Great Britain such as Gibraltar (on the southern coast of Spain), Diego Garcia (an atoll in the Indian Ocean), and St. Helena (an island in the South Atlantic Ocean). The United States has a 234,022-acre Air Force Base in Greenland, a region controlled by Denmark since 1721. Then there is Kosovo (an autonomous province of Serbia) and Hong Kong (a special administrative region of China).

Aside from the 50 states of the United States, there are also U.S. troops in areas we control like Guam (an island in the Pacific Ocean), Johnston Atoll (an atoll in the Pacific Ocean), Puerto Rico (an island commonwealth in the Caribbean Sea), and the U.S. Virgin Islands (islands between the Caribbean Sea and the North Atlantic Ocean, east of Puerto

Rico).

According to the "Personnel Strengths" document, the United States also maintains 23 army personnel in the Trust Territory of the Pacific Islands. After World War II, these island groups in the Pacific Ocean came under the control of the United States. This "Trust Territory" now consists of three sovereign countries (Marshall Islands, Micronesia, and Palau) and the Commonwealth of the Northern Mariana Islands, a commonwealth of the United States.

If these additional areas that have U.S. troops are counted, then it could be said that the United States has troops in 150 countries or territories. It is now easier to list the countries in which the United States does not have troops instead of the other way around. So, although this list could change tomorrow, the following countries are not officially reported as having any U.S. troops:

Andorra	Dominica
Angola	Equatorial Guinea
Armenia	Gabon
Belarus	Gambia
Benin	Grenada
Bhutan	Guinea-Bissau
Brunei	Holy See (The Vatican)
Burkina Faso	Iran
Cape Verde	Kiribati
Central African Republic	Lesotho
Comoros	Libya
Croatia	Liechtenstein
Maldives	Samoa
Mauritania	San Marino
Mauritius	Sao Tome and Principe
Moldova	Seychelles
Monaco	Slovak Republic
Namibia	Solomon Islands
Nauru	Somalia
Panama	Sudan
Papua New Guinea	Swaziland
Republic of the Congo	Tajikistan
Rwanda	Tonga
Saint Kitts and Nevis	Tuvalu
Saint Lucia	Uzbekistan
Saint Vincent and the Grenadines	Vanuatu

U.S. Foreign Policy

In his Farewell Address, George Washington warned against "permanent alliances with any portion of the foreign world" and said that the United States should have "as little political connection as possible" with foreign nations. But he also warned us about "those overgrown military establishments which, under any form of government, are inauspicious to liberty, and which are to be regarded as particularly hostile to republican liberty."

If any country ever had an overgrown military establishment, it is the United States and its military juggernaut. Before the recent Iraq war, the United States outspent the "evil" rogue nations of Iraq, Syria, Iran, North Korea, Libya, and Cuba on defense spending by a ratio of twenty-two to one. The actual amount that the United States spent on "defense" during fiscal year 2004 has been estimated by Robert Higgs to be about $695 billion. The United States is also the biggest arms exporter, accounting for about half of all global arms exports.

Most of this spending could be eliminated if the United States returned to the foreign policy ideas of the Founders. Current U.S. foreign policy can only be described as reckless, interventionist, militaristic, and belligerent. This can lead to severe consequences, as Chalmers Johnson has pointed out in his incredible book *Blowback: The Costs and Consequences of American Empire*, "The suicidal assassins of September 11, 2001, did not 'attack America,' as political leaders and news media in the United States have tried to maintain; they attacked American foreign policy."

The U.S. Empire is greatly overextended. Buried on page 362 of the 9/11 Commission Report is an admission that the entire planet is our manifest destiny:

> Now threats can emerge quickly. An organization like al Qaeda, headquartered in a country on the other side of the earth, in a region so poor that electricity or telephones were scarce, could nonetheless scheme to wield weapons of unprecedented destructive power in the largest cities of the United States. In this sense, 9/11 has taught us that terrorism against American interests "over there" should be regarded just as we regard terrorism against America "over here." In this same sense, the American homeland is the planet.

The 9/11 attacks were just the beginning of a worldwide revolt against the current U.S. foreign policy of a global empire. Only a

Jeffersonian foreign policy of peace, commerce, friendship, and no entangling alliances can arrest the menacing U.S. Empire.

* * * * *

WHAT'S WRONG WITH THE U.S. GLOBAL EMPIRE?

Some questions are not meant to be answered. They are really requests phrased as questions. Here are a couple that I have received, followed by what is really being requested if one reads the entire contents of what was written:

Question: "Why do you write for that Rockwell fellow?"
Request: "You should not write for Lew Rockwell because he is a libertarian nut who hates the state and the military."

Question: "Why don't you move to another country?"
Request: "You should move to another country (like France) because you are anti-American for not supporting the president and the war in Iraq."

Some questions, however, are genuine:

I was wondering if you could please give me a few reasons why you think it is a negative thing to have a US presence in that many countries around the world.

I recently received the above question, which is apparently a belated response to my articles last year on the U.S. global empire: "The U.S. Global Empire," "The Bases of Empire," and "Guarding the Empire." There I documented that the U.S. has an empire of troops and bases the world over and explained that what makes U.S. hegemony unique is that it consists, not of control over great land masses or population centers, but of a global presence unlike that of any other country in history.

The question raised is an important one, and since the question seemed genuine—the questioner did not preface or conclude his question with the charge that I was a pacifist, a liberal, a communist, or a traitor because I don't support the war in Iraq and don't think it is right for our military to have troops in almost every country on the planet—I am now answering it in the form of this article.

So what's wrong with the U.S. global empire? In answer to the above query, I came up with ten things. The responses are not in any particular order, and could certainly be expanded upon further.

1. What's right about it? This is perhaps the most important response because it puts the question right back where it should be—on those who support the U.S. global empire. If someone is going to advocate some activity, he should be responsible to explain why it is necessary or why it is a positive thing. It should not be left up those who don't advocate that particular activity to explain what the potential negative effects are. Are there any really positive things that result from the United States having its troops scattered around the globe? I mean things that could never be achieved by some other way. I can't think of any. This does not mean that no one benefits from the U.S. global empire. The military industrial complex benefits. Nationals contracted by the U.S. military in their country to work on U.S. military installations benefit. Stockholders in companies that serve as defense contractors might benefit. But do the American people as a whole benefit?

2. It is unnatural. It is not natural for the United States (or any country) to have an empire of troops and bases that encircles the globe. Why should any U.S. troops ever leave American soil or American territorial waters? Suppose that the countries of Tunisia, Sweden, and Kenya announced that they were going to build military bases in the United States. Or suppose that the countries of Pakistan, Cameroon, and Bolivia announced that they were sending troops to the United States. These would be viewed as acts of aggression. Yet, why is it that the American people think nothing of the United States garrisoning the planet?

3. It is very expensive. The money factor cannot be ignored. Even without fighting a war, it costs a lot of money (the American taxpayers' money) to pay, house, feed, and provide medical care for thousands of American soldiers. Then there are the expenses for weapons, ships, tanks, fuel, etc. Robert Higgs has recently estimated that "the government's total military-related outlays in fiscal year 2006 will be in the neighborhood of $840 billion—or, approximately a third of the total budget." In Old Right conservative John T. Flynn's "A Rejected Manuscript," from *Forgotten Lessons*, a collection of his essays, he explains that "the oldest of all rackets for spending the people's money is the institution of militarism. It creates a host of jobs—at low wages—in the armed services plus the far better paid and numerous jobs and dividends in the industries which produce the arms, provide the sailors and soldiers with food, clothes, medical care, and, juiciest of all, the weapons of war."

4. It is against the principles of the Founding Fathers. Sending troops overseas, building military bases in foreign countries, and making alliances is foreign interventionism, pure and simple. The Founding Fathers recommended a noninterventionist foreign policy, and for good reason. George Washington warned against "permanent alliances with any portion of the foreign world." He also said: "The great rule of conduct for us in regard to foreign nations is, in extending our commercial relations to have with them as little political connection as possible." Thomas Jefferson stated: "I am for free commerce with all nations, political connection with none, and little or no diplomatic establishment. And I am not for linking ourselves by new treaties with the quarrels of Europe, entering that field of slaughter to preserve their balance, or joining in the confederacy of Kings to war against the principles of liberty." John Quincy Adams would certainly not have approved of current U.S. foreign policy since he said that "America . . . goes not abroad seeking monsters to destroy." Were they transported to the twenty-first century, would Washington, Jefferson, and Adams even recognize the American republic today as the same country in which they served as president?

5. It fosters undesirable activity. As I pointed out in my article "Should a Christian Join the Military?" Chalmers Johnson, of the Japan Policy Research Institute, in his seminal work *Blowback: The Costs and Consequences of American Empire*, has described the network of bars, strip clubs, whorehouses, and VD clinics that surround U.S. bases overseas. The former U.S. naval base at Subic Bay in the Philippines "had no industry nearby except for the 'entertainment' business, which supported approximately 55,000 prostitutes and a total of 2,182 registered establishments offering 'rest and recreation' to American servicemen." At the annual Cobra Gold joint military exercise in Thailand: "Some three thousand prostitutes wait for sailors and marines at the South Pattaya waterfront, close to Utapao air base." Johnson has also chronicled the excessive crime rates among American servicemen stationed in Okinawa—"the 58-year-long record of sexual assaults, bar brawls, muggings, drug violations, drunken driving accidents, and arson cases all committed by privileged young men who proclaim they are in Okinawa to protect the people from the dangers of political 'instability' elsewhere in East Asia."

6. It increases hatred of Americans. One need look no further than the "welcome" our troops have received in Iraq. Of the 1,569 American military deaths in Iraq, 1,102 of them have occurred *since* the capture of Saddam Hussein. (The actual figures may in fact be higher—which means that more senseless deaths of Americans have occurred since the writing of this article). Why was Osama bin Laden so upset with the United States? He was outraged by the U.S. military presence in Saudi Arabia. In

2002, after two U.S. soldiers were acquitted by a U.S. military court in South Korea of negligent homicide in the deaths of two Korean school-girls, Koreans demonstrated, burned American flags, chanted anti-American slogans, and demanded that U.S. troops leave the country. Hatred of the United States is not a result of our freedoms and our values, it is a direct result of our intervention into the affairs of other countries and our military presence around the world.

 7. *It perverts the purpose of the military.* The purpose of the U.S. military should be to defend the United States. That's it. Nothing more. Using the military for any other purpose perverts the purpose of the military. The U.S. military has no business attempting to bring democracy to the world, remove dictators, spread goodwill, fight communism or Islam, guarantee the neutrality of any country, change a regime that is not friendly to the United States, train the armies of other countries, open foreign markets, protect U.S. commercial interests, provide disaster relief, or provide humanitarian aid. The U.S. military should be engaged exclusively in defending the United States, not defending other countries, and certainly not attacking them. What are U.S. troops doing overseas when the border between Mexico and the United States is not even secure?

 8. *It increases the size and scope of the government.* There is no way a country can have hundreds of bases and thousands of troops overseas without a substantial and onerous bureaucracy at home. Cold warrior William F. Buckley admitted as much in his 1952 article in the *Commonweal*, "A Young Republican View": "We have to accept Big Government for the duration—for neither an offensive nor a defensive war can be waged given our present government skills except through the instrumentality of a totalitarian bureaucracy within our shores." Buckley went on to recommend that we support "large armies and air forces, atomic energy, central intelligence, war production boards and the attendant centralization of power in Washington." It is no wonder that the "conservative" Buckley was branded by Murray Rothbard as "a totalitar-ian socialist," and rightly so, for intervention abroad cannot but follow intervention at home. The practice of "national greatness" conservativism abroad and "leave us alone" conservatism at home, as espoused by Michael Barone, Andrew Sullivan, and assorted neoconservatives, is an impossibility. As Justin Raimondo explains: "It doesn't work that way. We can't have an Empire abroad, and a Republic at home (except in name only) for the simple reason that the tax monies it takes to build mighty fleets and bases all around the world, to police the earth and humble the wicked, must be enormous. Furthermore, the sheer power it takes to direct

these armies, to say whether there shall be war or peace on a global scale, is necessarily imperial, and cannot be republican in any meaningful sense of the word. For this sort of power, i.e. military power, must be highly centralized in order to be effectively wielded: an interventionist foreign policy necessarily turns the President into an Emperor, as Congress has learned partly to its relief and often to its sorrow."

9. It makes countries dependent on the presence of the U.S. military. This is especially true in countries where U.S. troops have had a presence for decades. Consider the case of Germany. The United States recently sought to punish Germany for leading international opposition to the war in Iraq by withdrawing some U.S. troops from German soil. The planned withdrawal of troops was designed to harm the German economy and make an example of Germany. But even if troop withdrawals are not retaliatory in nature, the fact remains that the local economies in the occupied countries suffer because they become dependent upon the presence of the U.S. military. The threat or even the mention of troop withdrawals causes unnecessary contention between nations.

10. The United States is not the world's policeman. It's a dirty job. It's a thankless job. It's an impossible job. And no, someone does not really have to do it. Why, then, do we even try? We cannot police the world. We have no right to police the world. It is the height of arrogance to try and remake the world in our image. Most of what happens in the world is none of our concern and certainly none of our business. If the people in a country don't like their ruler, then they should get rid of him, not look to the United States to intervene. Actually, though, most of the time it is the United States that institutes a regime change. If Sunni and Shi'ite Muslims want to terrorize each other—it is a tragic thing, but nothing the United States should get involved in. If India and Pakistan want to endlessly debate the Kashmir Question, then let them endlessly debate it. Why should we get involved? What would we think if India or Pakistan tried to intervene in a border dispute between the United States and Mexico? If the Hutus and the Tutsis battle it out in Africa—it is a terrible thing but none of our business. If an individual American feels that strongly about either side, he can pray for peace, he can send money to the side he favors, or he can go to Africa and enlist in the Hutu or Tutsi army and fight. If North and South Vietnam have a quarrel—it is not worth the lives of over 58,000 Americans (the Vietnam Veterans Memorial in Washington, DC now lists 58,245 names), the wounding of 304,000 Americans, and the disabling of 75,000 of those wounded (over 23,000 were totally disabled) to intervene. It is not worth the life of one American. It is strange how advocates of U.S. wars, interventions, and militarism consider opponents of these things to be un-patriotic and anti-American when those who are for nonintervention are the ones concerned about the life of even one American being used as cannon fodder for the state. Being the world's policeman also entails bribing countries with foreign aid—a subject I have explored elsewhere.

Does this U.S. global presence mean that the United States has an empire? It is an empire in everything but name. Supposedly sovereign, free, and independent countries can't even have an election without the United States intervening. Yes, there is a high probability of fraud in some foreign elections. But not only are foreign elections none of our business, how would we feel if China, Kenya, Belarus, or Botswana sent "observers" to supervise our elections because of the high probability of fraud?

"Today," as neoconservative Charles Krauthammer maintains, "the United States remains the preeminent economic, military, diplomatic, and cultural power on a scale not seen since the fall of the Roman Empire." Yes, and if we are not careful we will go the way of the Roman Empire. The U.S. government's foolish interventions have caused much of the world to view America as the new evil empire. Krauthammer also claims that "the international environment is far more likely to enjoy peace under a single hegemon. Moreover, we are not just any hegemon. We run a uniquely benign imperium." Until, of course, a country disagrees with us—then it is bombs away.

What's wrong with the U.S. global empire? Everything.

* * * * *

TODAY IRAQ, TOMORROW THE WORLD

"We don't seek empires. We're not imperialistic." ~ Donald Rumsfeld (2003)

"If we want Iraq to avoid becoming a Somalia on steroids, we'd better get used to U.S. troops being deployed there for years, possibly decades, to come. If that raises hackles about American imperialism, so be it. We're going to be called an empire whatever we do. We might as well be a successful empire." ~ Max Boot (2003)

"We're an empire now." ~ a senior adviser to President Bush (2004)

The number in Germany is 69,395. The number in Japan is 35,307.

The number in Korea is 32,744. The number in Italy is 12,258. The number in the United Kingdom is 11,093.

I am not speaking of the number of car accidents last year in Germany, Japan, Korea, Italy, or the United Kingdom. And neither am I speaking of the number of poisonings, suicides, or armed robberies in any of these countries.

No, I am speaking of something far more lethal: the continued presence of U.S. troops.

According to the latest edition of the "Active Duty Military Personnel Strengths by Regional Area and by Country," published by the Defense Department's Directorate for Information Operations and Reports (DIOR), the U.S. has troops in 142 countries. This is up from the figure of 136 countries that the government was reporting the last time I addressed the subject of the number of countries under the shadow of the U.S. Global Empire. Additions to the list are Armenia, Republic of the Congo, Gabon, Iran, Malawi, Moldova, Slovak Republic, and Sudan. Subtractions are Eritrea and North Korea. Only 49 countries to go and the United States will have hegemony over the whole world. But it is worse than it appears. Counting the U.S. troops in territories, the officially reported number of countries or territories that the United States has troops in is now 155. It is not without cause that the twentieth century's greatest proponent of liberty, and the greatest opponent of the state, Murray Rothbard (1926–1995), said that "empirically, taking the twentieth century as a whole, the single most warlike, most intervention-ist, most imperialist government has been the United States."

This foreign troop presence is, of course, directly opposite the foreign policy of the Founding Fathers:

> George Washington: "The great rule of conduct for us in regard to foreign nations is, in extending our commercial relations to have with them as little political connection as possible."

> Thomas Jefferson: "Peace, commerce, and honest friendship with all nations—entangling alliances with none."

> John Quincy Adams: "America . . . goes not abroad seeking monsters to destroy."

In his Farewell Address, George Washington also warned against "permanent alliances with any portion of the foreign world." Could he have ever imagined the commitment of the United States to be the world's policeman?

Since the Spanish-American War of 1898, the foreign policy of the United States has been one of interventionism, which is always followed by its stepchildren belligerency, bellicosity, and jingoism. When televangelist Pat Robertson recently said that the United States government should "take out" the president of Venezuela, Hugo Chavez, he had a history of CIA assassinations and assassination schemes to go by. This certainly doesn't excuse his remarks, but it is important to note that U.S. intervention abroad has not always been masked under the noble purposes of humanitarian relief or making the world safe for democracy.

Because we live in an imperfect world of nation-states that is not likely to change anytime in the near future, the question of U.S. foreign policy cannot be ignored. Many libertarians make the mistake of expending all of their energies in an attempt to downsize the state by freeing the market and society from government interference while forgetting that "war," in the immortal words of Randolph Bourne (1886–1918), "is the health of the state." Libertarians who disparage the welfare state while turning a blind eye to the warfare state are terribly inconsistent.

So, as Rothbard again said, since "libertarians desire to *limit*, to whittle down, the area of government power in all directions and as much as possible," the goal in foreign affairs should be the same as that in domestic affairs: "To keep government from interfering in the affairs of other governments or other countries." We should "shackle government from acting abroad just as we try to shackle government at home."

The state's coercive arm of foreign intervention is the military. U.S. troops don't "defend our freedoms." As the Future of Freedom Foundation's Jacob Hornberger has so courageously pointed out, U.S. troops

> serve not as a defender of our freedoms but instead simply as a loyal and obedient personal army of the president, ready and prepared to serve him and obey his commands. It is an army that stands ready to obey the president's orders to deploy to any country in the world for any reason he deems fit and attack, kill, and maim any "terrorist" who dares to resist the U.S. invasion of his own country. It is also an army that stands ready to obey the president's orders to take into custody any American whom the commander in chief deems a "terrorist" and to punish him accordingly.

To say that U.S. troops "defend our freedoms" is to say that my freedom to write this article right now that is critical of the U.S. government's foreign policy is a direct result of the recent U.S. invasions of

Afghanistan and Iraq. That may sound ridiculous, but it is no more ridiculous than saying that U.S. troops "defend our freedoms" when what they actually do is bomb, invade, and occupy other countries.

"Well," I can hear the retort, "if it wasn't for U.S. troops halting the German menace we would all be speaking German right now." I suppose this is the same Germany that couldn't cross the English Channel and invade Great Britain. And how does that justify keeping 69,395 U.S. troops on German soil over sixty years later?

There is, therefore, one element of foreign policy that I would like to touch on: the role of the U.S. military in foreign affairs. It should be quite obvious from my writings on the U.S. empire ("The U.S. Global Empire," "The Bases of Empire," "Guarding the Empire," and "What's Wrong with the U.S. Global Empire") that I don't agree with Max Boot's statement that "on the whole, U.S. imperialism has been the greatest force for good in the world during the past century." That being said, the subject to be addressed is what should be done with the U.S. military in order to dissolve the U.S. empire and return to the nonintervention policy of the Founders.

Today Iraq, tomorrow the world.

The first thing that needs to be done is to get out of Iraq before the blood of one more American is shed on Iraqi soil. I have elsewhere shown that it is a simple matter to withdraw from Iraq in not only a safe, reasonable, and timely manner, but also in a just manner. That was back on August 8, when the number of wasted American lives was "only" 1,827. Three hundred more American soldiers have died since then. And for what? Three hundred more sets of American parents have suffered the loss of a child. And for what? Six hundred more sets of grandparents have suffered the loss of a grandchild. And for what? Many hundreds more brothers and sisters have lost a brother, or in some cases, a sister. And for what? Untold numbers of friends and acquaintances have lost the same. And for what?

It is the warmongers who are anti-American, not us "antiwar weenies." We never considered the shedding of the blood of even one American to be "worth" whatever it is that U.S. troops are now dying for. As I have elsewhere said: "Bringing democracy to Iraq and ridding the country of Saddam Hussein is not worth the life of one American. What kind of government they have and who is to be their 'leader' is the business of the Iraqi people, not the United States."

We should withdraw our forces, not because the war is going badly, not because too many American troops are dying, and not because the war is costing too much. We should withdraw our troops because the war was a monstrous wrong from the very beginning.

Withdraw from Iraq today, and withdraw from the rest of the world tomorrow.

After the withdrawal of U.S. troops from Iraq, the rest of the world should be put on notice: you're next. Instead of listening to the BRAC Commission recommendations about which bases to close in the United States, Congress should close all foreign bases first. Instead of reading documents like Defense Planning Guidance or Rebuilding America's Defenses, Congress should have read Murray Rothbard:

> The primary plank of a libertarian foreign policy program for America must be to call upon the United States to abandon its policy of global interventionism: to withdraw immediately and completely, militarily and politically, from Asia, Europe, Latin America, the Middle East, from everywhere. The cry among American libertarians should be for the United States to withdraw now, in every way that involves the U.S. government. The United States should dismantle its bases, withdraw its troops, stop its incessant political meddling, and abolish the CIA. It should also end all foreign aid—which is simply a device to coerce the American taxpayer into subsidizing American exports and favored foreign States, all in the name of "helping the starving peoples of the world." In short, the United States government should withdraw totally to within its own boundaries and maintain a policy of strict political "isolation" or neutrality everywhere.

This is certainly a policy that could be implemented. How many countries in the world do the countries of Italy, Argentina, and Iceland have troops and bases in? How about Switzerland, Mongolia, and Lithuania? Are any of these countries in danger of being attacked because they don't have an empire of troops of bases? There is absolutely no reason why the United States has to have an empire of troops and bases that encircles the world that it presently has.

This policy is one of political isolation. It doesn't mean that the United States should refuse to participate in the Olympics, refuse to issue visas, refuse to trade, refuse to extradite criminals, refuse to allow travel abroad, or refuse to allow immigration. It is a policy, not of isolationism, but of noninterventionism.

It is also the policy of the Founding Fathers, like Thomas Jefferson:

> No one nation has a right to sit in judgment over another.

> We wish not to meddle with the internal affairs of any country, nor

with the general affairs of Europe.

I am for free commerce with all nations, political connection with none, and little or no diplomatic establishment.

We have produced proofs, from the most enlightened and approved writers on the subject, that a neutral nation must, in all things relating to the war, observe an exact impartiality towards the parties.

No judgment, no meddling, no political connection, and no partiality. What is wrong with the wisdom of Jefferson?

Today Iraq, tomorrow the world—and then what?

Once American troops are withdrawn from garrisoning the planet, they should be prevented from doing so again. One way to do this would be to adopt the Amendment for Peace, proposed by U.S. Marine Corps Major General Smedley Butler (1881–1940):

1. The removal of members of the land armed forces from within the continental limits of the United States and the Panama Canal Zone for any cause whatsoever is hereby prohibited.
2. The vessels of the United States Navy, or of the other branches of the armed service, are hereby prohibited from steaming, for any reason whatsoever except on an errand of mercy, more than five hundred miles from our coast.
3. Aircraft of the Army, Navy and Marine Corps is hereby prohibited from flying, for any reason whatsoever, more than seven hundred and fifty miles beyond the coast of the United States.

This amendment is a great starting point. Obviously, the Panama Canal Zone statement is now irrelevant. And whether the government could be trusted to not use "an errand of mercy" as a covert operation is now very debatable.

Major Butler believed that his amendment "would be absolute guarantee to the women of America that their loved ones never would be sent overseas to be needlessly shot down in European or Asiatic or African wars that are no concern of our people."

He also reasoned that because of "our geographical position, it is all but impossible for any foreign power to muster, transport and land sufficient troops on our shores for a successful invasion." In this Butler was echoing Jefferson, who recognized that geography was one of the great advantages of the United States:

The insulated state in which nature has placed the American continent should so far avail it that no spark of war kindled in the other quarters of the globe should be wafted across the wide oceans which separate us from them.

At such a distance from Europe and with such an ocean between us, we hope to meddle little in its quarrels or combinations. Its peace and its commerce are what we shall court.

But even without the advantage of geography, a policy of nonintervention is sufficient, as Congressman Ron Paul (R–Tex.) has pointed out: "Countries like Switzerland and Sweden who promote neutrality and nonintervention have benefited for the most part by remaining secure and free of war over the centuries."

What, then, would become of our military if a strict noninterventionist policy of peace and neutrality were adopted? For starters, perhaps the Department of Defense could then actually do something to "defend our freedoms" like guard our borders and patrol our coasts. The military could be scaled back considerably (along with what Robert Higgs has estimated to be its $840 billion budget), with militias picking up the slack, as William Lind has recently pointed out here and here.

Some say that Jefferson's ideals are not practical in a post-9/11 world. To them I offer the wisdom of Representative Paul, who has described a foreign policy for peace in these words:

Our troops would be brought home, systematically but soon.

The mission for our Coast Guard would change if our foreign policy became non-interventionist. They, too, would come home, protect our coast, and stop being the enforcers of bureaucratic laws that either should not exist or should be a state function.

All foreign aid would be discontinued.

A foreign policy of freedom and peace would prompt us to give ample notice before permanently withdrawing from international organizations that have entangled us for over a half a century. US membership in world government was hardly what the founders envisioned when writing the Constitution.

The principle of Marque and Reprisal would be revived and specific problems such as terrorist threats would be dealt with on a contract basis incorporating private resources to more accurately target our enemies and reduce the chances of needless and endless war.

The Logan Act would be repealed, thus allowing maximum freedom of our citizens to volunteer to support their war of choice. This would help diminish the enthusiasm for wars the proponents have used to justify our world policies and diminish the perceived need for a military draft.

If we followed a constitutional policy of non-intervention, we would never have to entertain the aggressive notion of preemptive war based on speculation of what a country might do at some future date. Political pressure by other countries to alter our foreign policy for their benefit would never be a consideration. Commercial interests and our citizens investing overseas could not expect our armies to follow them and protect their profits.

A non-interventionist foreign policy would not condone subsidies to our corporations through programs like the Export/Import Bank and the Overseas Private Investment Corporation.

A non-interventionist foreign policy would go a long way toward preventing 9/11 type attacks. The Department of Homeland Security would be unnecessary, and the military, along with less bureaucracy in our intelligence-gathering agencies, could instead provide the security the new department is supposed to provide. A renewed respect for gun ownership and responsibility for defending one's property would provide additional protection against potential terrorists.

Today Iraq, tomorrow the world. The sooner we adopt this policy the better. How many more U.S. soldiers have to needlessly die in Iraq before Americans realize this?

* * * * *

UPDATE ON THE EMPIRE

If it is true, as Ambrose Bierce (1842–1914) said, "War is God's way of teaching Americans geography," then empire must be God's way of making Americans masters of the subject since the United States now has troops in 159 different regions of the world.

We know this is true, not because some opponent of U.S. imperialism says so, but because the Department of Defense publishes a quarterly report called the "Active Duty Military Personnel Strengths by Regional Area and by Country." Although these reports used to be issued by the Defense Department's Directorate for Information Operations and Reports (DIOR), they are now prepared by the Statistical Information Analysis Division of the Defense Manpower Data Center. The latest report is dated September 30, 2006. Previous reports can be seen here.

I first reported on this in an article published on March 16, 2004, and called "The U.S. Global Empire." There I documented that the U.S. had troops in 135 countries, plus 14 territories that were not sovereign countries—some controlled by the United States and some controlled by other countries. I then showed on October 4, 2004, in "Guarding the Empire," that the U.S. empire had increased to 150 different regions of the world. The last time I reported on the extent of the empire, December 5, 2005, in "Today Iraq, Tomorrow the World," it had grown to encompass 155 different regions of the world. Today it pains me to report that the U.S. empire has now extended its tentacles to 159 regions of the world: 144 countries and 15 territories.

To the original list of 135 countries I gave in "The U.S. Global Empire" can now be added:

Angola	Rwanda
Armenia	Slovakia
Gabon	Somalia
Guyana	Sudan
Moldova	Uzbekistan

North Korea can be removed from the list. Yes, the "Active Duty Military Personnel Strengths by Regional Area and by Country" document that I originally used in 2004 said that there were four U.S. Marines stationed in the Democratic Peoples Republic of Korea.

Since there are 192 countries in the world besides the United States, this means that the U.S. military has troops in over 70 percent of the world's countries. And this doesn't include territories that are not sovereign countries.

The fifteen territories in which the United States now has troops are:

American Samoa	Hong Kong
Diego Garcia	Kosovo
Gibraltar	Marshall Islands
Greenland	Micronesia
Guam	Northern Mariana Islands

Palau	Virgin Islands
Puerto Rico	Wake Island
St. Helena	

The Marshall Islands, Micronesia, Palau, and the Northern Mariana Islands make up the Trust Territory of the Pacific Islands. American Samoa, Guam, the Northern Mariana Islands, Puerto Rico, the Virgin Islands, and Wake Island are all territories of the United States. Here we might ask, not why does the United States have troops in these areas, but why does the United States have control of these territories to begin with?

Although Donald Rumsfeld once claimed that the United States is not imperialistic and doesn't seek empires, what else are you going to call this global presence in 159 regions of the world? Do all these countries want U.S. troops on their soil? Is there really any reason why the United States still has 64,319 troops in Germany, 33,453 troops in Japan, and 10,449 troops in Italy—sixty years *after* World War II? And what are we doing with 1,521 troops in Spain, 414 troops in Honduras, and 347 troops in Australia? And why do we have 31 soldiers in Cote D'Ivoire? Cote D'What? Cote D'Where? How many Americans can locate Cote D'Ivoire on a map or have ever heard of it? How many even care? (For the record, Cote D'Ivoire is next to Burkina Faso.)

Scholarly advocates of American imperialism, like CFR Senior Fellow Max Boot, reject the term imperialism, but hold, like Boot, that the United States "should definitely embrace the practice." Boot subscribes to what can be called twenty-first-century gunboat diplomacy. He believes that the United States should impose the rule of law, property rights, and free speech on Iraq "at gunpoint if need be." Since "Iran and other neighboring states won't hesitate to impose their despotic views on Iraq; we shouldn't hesitate to impose our democratic views."

Less sophisticated apologists for U.S. interventionism and imperialism, along with the usual assortment of chickenhawks, armchair warriors, Bush lovers, Christian warmongers, Republican Party loyalists, and other "conservatives" who defend the military and the warfare state, attempt to dismiss U.S. global hegemony over the majority of the planet by claiming that many of the U.S. troops stationed abroad are just embassy guards. Since I have already showed in "Guarding the Empire" that it definitely is *not* the Marine guards at U.S. embassies overseas that account for the U.S. troop presence in so many countries, I will not address that point again here.

The other argument is that the presence of U.S. troops in so many countries is really not an issue because in some countries the United States has only a handful of its soldiers. Now, it is true that the United States only has a handful of troops stationed in some countries (e.g., 9 in Albania, 7 in Latvia, 3 in Laos), but focusing on how few troops are actually in some countries misses the point entirely. The issue is U.S. troops on foreign soil. They have no business there. Period. No bases, no troops, and no military advisors.

Echoing the inscription on the Liberty Bell, President Bush closed his Second Inaugural Address with the statement that "America, in this young century, proclaims liberty throughout all the world, and to all the inhabitants thereof." But rather than proclaiming liberty, the stationing of soldiers in 159 different regions of the world and garrisoning the planet with military bases does just the opposite. Instead of proclaiming liberty, it proclaims imperialism, interventionism, militarism, and jingoism—all with devastating consequences for those countries that dare to question American hegemony.

* * * * *

THE BEGINNINGS OF EMPIRE

> "We don't seek empires. We're not imperialistic. We never have been. I can't imagine why you'd even ask the question." ~ Donald Rumsfeld (April 2003)

And we can't imagine why Rumsfeld is so ignorant of American military history, especially since Vice President Dick Cheney calls him "the finest Secretary of Defense this nation has ever had," and especially since the Department of Defense, *which he ran for six years*, publishes a quarterly report that reveals the extent of America's global troop presence, now up to 159 different regions of the world.

I have referred to this report ("Active Duty Military Personnel Strengths by Regional Area and by Country") in several previous articles. The DOD now has these quarterly reports online for the years 1950 and 1953 through the present. What they show is that the U.S. global empire is not a recent phenomenon. One would think that after World War II, all U.S. forces would have been brought home—or at least brought home from every place except Western Europe and Japan.

Think again.

The U.S. global empire was well in place soon after World War II. According to the "Personnel Strengths" document for 1950 (the oldest available), the United States had troops in about 100 different countries and territories. Here is the list:

Alaska	India
Afghanistan	Indo-China (Vietnam, Laos, Cambodia)
Algeria	Indonesia
Argentina	Iran
Australia	Iraq
Austria	Ireland (Eire)
Azores	Israel
Belgium	Italy
Bermuda	Japan
Bolivia	Jerusalem
Brazil	Johnston Island
British West Indies Federation	Korea
Bulgaria	Lebanon
Burma	Liberia
Canada (including Newfoundland)	Libya (Tripoli)
Canal Zone	Luxembourg
Caroline Islands (Truk, Palau)	Mariana Islands
Ceylon	Marshall Islands
Chile	Mexico
Colombia	Midway
Costa Rica	Morocco
Cuba	Netherlands
Cyprus	New Zealand
Czechoslovakia	Nicaragua
Denmark	Norway
Dominican Republic	Pakistan
Ecuador	Panama (Republic of)
Egypt	Paraguay
El Salvador	Peru
Eritrea	Philippines
Ethiopia	Poland
Finland	Portugal
France	Puerto Rico
Germany	Rumania
Greece (& Crete)	Ryukyus (Okinawa)
Greenland	Samoan Islands
Guatemala	Saudi Arabia
Haiti	Singapore
Hawaii	Spain
Honduras	Sweden
Hong Kong	Switzerland
Hungary	Syria
Iceland	Taiwan

Thailand	USSR (Russia)
Trieste	Venezuela
Turkey	Virgin Islands
Union of South Africa	Volcano Islands (Iwo Jima)
United Kingdom	Yugoslavia
Uruguay	

We still have troops in some of the same places. And no, they are not all embassy guards, as is explained here and here.

And what has having troops in all of these places since World War II resulted in? Nothing but wars and military interventions. Vietnam veteran and peace advocate James Glaser has documented the sixty-five official foreign military actions since World War II that have been approved by Congress to qualify the combatants for membership in the Veterans of Foreign Wars (VFW). A paper based on extensive research of American military actions in foreign countries that was presented at the 2002 annual meeting of the Southern Political Science Association in Savannah, Georgia, documented these and other unofficial actions, concluding in part:

> Analysis of all United States military actions since the end of World War II show that America has engaged in 263 military actions. A third of these occurred before 1991, while the United States initiated 176 of these between 1991 and 2002.

World War II was not the beginning of the U.S. empire. Between the two world wars, U.S. troops were sent to Cuba, the Dominican Republic, Russia, Panama, Honduras, Yugoslavia, Guatemala, Turkey, and China.

But World War I was not the beginning either. Before we tried to make the world safe for democracy, U.S. troops were sent to Nicaragua, Panama, Honduras, the Dominican Republic, Korea, Cuba, Nicaragua, China, and Mexico.

Although we might begin the U.S. empire with the seizure from Spain of Cuba, Puerto Rico, the Philippines, and Guam during the Spanish-American War of 1898, we need to go back a few years earlier to U.S. intervention in Hawaii. Many Americans know that Hawaii became the 50th state in 1959; few Americans know what led up to the annexing of the island chain in 1898.

A new book by Stephen Kinzer, *Overthrow: America's Century of Regime Change from Hawaii to Iraq* (Times Books, 2006), tells the sordid tale of how Hawaii's white plantation owners conspired with the Harrison administration in Washington and John L. Stevens, the American minister to Hawaii, to overthrow the existing monarchy of Queen Liliuokalani. This was all made possible by the protection of the U.S. Navy, which sent ashore 162 sailors and marines. Concludes Kinzer:

> Although Stevens was an unabashed partisan, he was no rogue agent. He had been sent to Hawaii to promote annexation, and the men who sent him, President Harrison and Secretary of State Blaine, knew precisely what that must entail. It was true, as his critics would later claim, that Stevens acted without explicit orders from Washington. He certainly overstepped his authority when he brought troops ashore, especially since he knew that the "general alarm and terror" of which the Committee of Safety had complained was a fiction. Still, he was doing what the president and the secretary of state wanted. He used his power and theirs to depose the Hawaiian monarchy. That made him the first American to direct the overthrow of a foreign government.

The beginnings of this overthrow actually go back to the 1850s when, "to protect American growers, the United States levied prohibitive tariffs on imported sugar." Hawaiian sugar planters eventually agreed, with the acquiescence of the Hawaiian monarch, to "grant the United States exclusive rights to maintain commercial and military bases in Hawaii" in exchange for a reciprocity treaty that promised free trade in sugar. But as Kinzer explains: "This treaty preserved the façade of Hawaiian independence, but in effect turned Hawaii into an American protectorate."

Neoconservative Max Boot believes that U.S. imperialism "has been the greatest force for good in the world during the past century." Those of us who prefer the noninterventionist foreign policy of the Founders to the gunboat diplomacy of neoconservative warmongers have a different opinion: U.S. imperialism has been the greatest force for evil.

Rather than the presence of the U.S. military guaranteeing peace and stability throughout the world, the presence of the U.S. military more often than not is the cause of war and instability.

It goes without saying that U.S. troops should not be on foreign soil. And not only should the removal and redeployment of U.S. troops from American territory be prohibited, as U.S. Marine Corps Major General Smedley Butler (1881–1940) proposed in his Amendment for Peace, there should be no military advisors, no bases, no entangling alliances, no nation building, no humanitarian relief, no peacekeeping operations, no spreading democracy, no regime changes, no opening markets, no enforcing UN resolutions, no liberations, no bombing, no killing, no policing the world—no intervention whatsoever.

A noninterventionist foreign policy would also mean no foreign aid, disaster relief, or "donations" to the United Nations, the International Monetary Fund, or the World Bank. A noninterventionist foreign policy is simply a Jeffersonian foreign policy:

> I am for free commerce with all nations, political connection with none, and little or no diplomatic establishment.

> Peace, commerce, and honest friendship with all nations—entangling alliances with none.

Rumsfeld can't imagine why anyone would ask about U.S. imperialism. How could anyone *not* ask about U.S. imperialism after studying American military history for more than five minutes?

Rather than being a history of how the military has defended the country, it is a history of aggression, imperialism, empire, invasion, meddling, occupation, hegemony, belligerency, bellicosity, jingoism, gunboat diplomacy, and every other form of interventionism. How can a secretary of defense be so ignorant?

* * * * *

NINETY-FIVE YEARS TO GO

"Make it a hundred." ~ John McCain

Although U.S. troops have been in Iraq for five years now, we have only just begun. We can expect the great grandchildren of the current U.S. soldiers in Iraq to be there as well—if John McCain has his way. This assumes, of course, that these soldiers make it back to the United States breathing and in one piece so that they can have children.

Speaking at a January town hall meeting in New Hampshire, Senator McCain was asked about President Bush's comment about the United States staying in Iraq for fifty years. His reply to "Make it a hundred," although it was harshly criticized, did not keep him from winning primaries and becoming the Republican presidential nominee. After all, said McCain, "We've been in Japan for 60 years. We've been in South Korea 50 years or so. That would be fine with me."

The senator is not the only one to make a statement like that. Someone at *National Review* said last year: "Ladies and gentlemen: Our

Problems are here, there, and everywhere. They will last our lifetime. You have heard of the Thirty Years' War. This is ours—if not our Hundred Years' War."

McCain did go on to condition the U.S. occupation on "as long as Americans are not being injured or harmed or wounded or killed." But when asked about his statement on "Face the Nation," the man who would be president remarked that "Americans aren't concerned" about troops in Iraq for the next 10,000 years. He also told a reporter "that U.S. troops could be in Iraq for 'a thousand years' or 'a million years,' as far as he was concerned."

Now he says that he "will never set a date for withdrawal."

It should come as no surprise that the United States will have troops in Iraq for many years to come. After all, there are still 57,080 U.S. soldiers stationed in Germany, 9,855 U.S. soldiers stationed in Italy, 32,803 U.S. soldiers stationed in Japan, and 27,014 U.S. soldiers stationed in Korea. But even where the United States did not fight a war, there are large numbers of U.S. troops to be found. There are 1,286 U.S. soldiers stationed in Spain and 9,825 soldiers stationed in the United Kingdom.

It should also come as no surprise that the United States has troops in Iraq in the first place. We would probably have U.S. forces there regardless of whether we went to war. You see, there are U.S. soldiers stationed in about 70 percent of the world's countries. The Defense Department freely and publicly acknowledges this. In fact, the DOD issues a quarterly report, the "Active Duty Military Personnel Strengths by Regional Area and by Country," that provides this information. The latest report is dated September 30, 2007. Previous reports can be seen here.

To recap on the extent of U.S. troop presence around the globe, I first reported on this in an article published on March 16, 2004, titled "The U.S. Global Empire." There I documented that the U.S. had troops in 135 countries, plus 14 territories controlled by the United States or some other country. I then showed on October 4, 2004, in "Guarding the Empire," that the U.S. empire had increased to 150 different regions of the world. The third time I reported on the extent of the empire, December 5, 2005, in "Today Iraq, Tomorrow the World," that number had grown to 155. The last time I updated the status of the U.S. global empire, in "Update on the Empire," I revealed that U.S. soldiers were stationed in 159 regions of the world: 144 countries and 15 territories.

Not much has changed since then. The United States has withdrawn its small contingent of military personnel from the British territories of Gibraltar and St. Helena, but now has four sailors stationed in the British territory of Bermuda. New countries with U.S. troops are Belarus, Croatia, and Tajikistan. There is one country that lost U.S. troops—Fiji.

Although the Trust Territory of the Pacific Islands doesn't exit anymore, the DOD has been reporting the presence of American troops there for years. This Trust Territory included what are now the Republic of the Marshall Islands, the Federated States of Micronesia, the Commonwealth of the Northern Mariana Islands, and the Republic of Palau. The DOD now reports U.S. troop presence in what was this Trust Territory differently. Since the DOD used to just report the total number of U.S. troops stationed in the entire region, I was counting this as four territories with U.S. troops. The Marshall Islands, Micronesia, and Palau are technically independent countries, but are associated with the United States under a Compact of Free Association. The United States provides financial aid to these sovereign regions, including many U.S. domestic programs, in exchange for allowing the United States to provide for their defense; that is, allow the United States to build bases, station troops, and otherwise use the islands for "defense-related" purposes. The DOD now just reports that there are seventeen Army personnel stationed in the Marshall Islands. This would be for the U.S. Army's Ronald Reagan Ballistic Missile Defense Test Site.

So, according to the Defense Department's latest "Personnel Strengths" report, the United States now has troops stationed in 147 countries and 10 territories. This is the greatest number of countries that the United States has ever had troops in. These numbers are not the result of Marine embassy guards stationed at U.S. embassies, as I showed in "Guarding the Empire." To avoid giving a complete list, I refer the reader to the original list of 135 countries I gave in "The U.S. Global Empire." From this list should be subtracted Fiji and North Korea, and to this list should be added Angola, Armenia, Belarus, Croatia, Gabon, Guyana, Marshall Islands, Moldova, Rwanda, Slovakia, Somalia, Sudan, Tajikistan, and Uzbekistan. True, U.S. troop presence in some countries and territories is quite small. But what are we doing with 403 soldiers in Honduras, 140 soldiers in Australia, and 126 soldiers in Greenland?

John McCain insists that the issue in Iraq is "not American presence; it's American casualties." Most Americans would probably agree since there is hardly a sound of protest over the U.S. troops that are still in Germany, Italy, Japan, and Korea after fifty or sixty years. The U.S. global empire of troops and bases has been around for so long that it is generally accepted by most Americans. I explained a few years ago in "What's Wrong with the U.S. Global Empire?" exactly what is wrong a foreign policy of empire: it's not right, it's unnatural, it's very expensive, it's against the principles of the Founding Fathers, it fosters undesirable activity, it increases hatred of Americans, it perverts the purpose of the military, it increases the size and scope of the government, it makes countries dependent on the presence of the U.S. military, and finally, because the United States is not the world's policeman.

What would Americans think if Russia or China built bases in the United States and stationed thousands of troops on our soil? They would be outraged, regardless of whether any U.S. citizens were harmed. In fact, most Americans would be incensed if Russian, China, or any other country sent just a handful of troops to the United States—even though the United States does the same thing to scores of other countries. Would it be okay if all of the 147 countries that the United States has troops in sent a contingent of their troops to our country as long as it didn't result in any American casualties? Why not? Why the double standard? What gives the United States the right to garrison the planet with bases, station troops wherever it wants, police the world, and intervene in the affairs of other countries? Does might make right? Even McCain recently remarked that "our great power does not mean we can do whatever we want whenever we want."

U.S. foreign policy is not only aggressive, reckless, belligerent, and meddling, it is extremely arrogant. It is based on the myth of American exceptionalism; that is, the idea that the United States is the indispensable nation, that its government is morally and politically superior to all other governments, that its motives are always benevolent and paternalistic, and that the nations of the world should always conform to its dictates.

Avoiding another ninety-five years in Iraq is merely the tip of the iceberg. It is an arrogant, interventionist U.S. foreign policy that is the real problem—a problem that a McCain, a Clinton, or an Obama administration will simply perpetuate. Jefferson's foreign policy of peace, commerce, honest friendship, and no entangling alliances is needed now more than ever.

* * * * *

MR. OBAMA, TEAR DOWN THIS EMPIRE

Twenty-two years ago, June 12, 1987, President Ronald Reagan made a speech in front of the Brandenburg Gate at the Berlin Wall in which he implored Mikhail Gorbachev to "tear down this wall." Within a year, the wall that symbolized repression and tyranny did in fact come crashing down. But with the demise of the Soviet Union, there is something else that should likewise have been toppled: the U.S. empire of troops and bases that encircles the globe.

Mr. Obama, Tear down this empire.

The kingdom of Alexander the Great reached to the borders of India. The Roman Empire controlled Western Europe and the Hellenized states that bordered the Mediterranean. The Mongol Empire stretched from Southeast Asia to Europe. The Byzantine Empire lasted over a thousand years. The Ottoman Empire stretched from the Persian Gulf in the east to Hungary in the northwest; and from Egypt in the south to the Caucasus in the north. At the height of its dominion, the British Empire included almost a quarter of the world's population.

Nothing, however, compares to the U.S. global empire. It is an empire that would make Alexander the Great, Caesar Augustus, Genghis Khan, Suleiman the Magnificent, Emperor Justinian, and King George V proud. What makes U.S. hegemony unique is that it consists, not of control over great landmasses or population centers, but of a global presence unlike that of any other country in history.

Sure, Donald Rumsfeld maintained: "We don't seek empires. We're not imperialistic. We never have been." Right. Just like Iraq had weapons of mass destruction. Just like the war in Iraq was supposed to be a cakewalk. Just like Bush told us, "we don't torture." Some neocons are a bit more honest, like CFR Senior Fellow Max Boot, who rejects the term "imperialism," but insists that the United States "should definitely embrace the practice."

Those who believe that it is in the national interest of the United States to intervene in conflicts around the globe, attempt to control foreign governments, and spread our political and economic systems to other countries by force argue that we are not an empire because we haven't annexed any country's soil in over a hundred years. But America's unprecedented global presence of troops, bases, and ships clearly says otherwise.

The extent of the U.S. global empire is almost incalculable. The Department of Defense's "Base Structure Report" states that the Department's physical assets consist of "more than 545,700 facilities (buildings, structures and linear structures) located on more than 5,400 sites, on approximately 40 million acres." There are 268 sites in Germany alone. The 316,238 buildings occupied by the DOD comprise over 2.2 billion square feet with a value of over $455 billion. The DOD manages almost 30 million acres of land worldwide. There are over 700 U.S. military bases on foreign soil in 63 countries. The United States has official commitments to provide security to over 35 countries.

In addition to the 1.1 million U.S. military personnel stationed in the United States and its territories, there are almost 300,000 U.S. troops in foreign countries—not even counting the over 200,000 U.S. soldiers in Iraq and Afghanistan. With its geographic command centers (NORTH-COM, CENTCOM, etc.) that cover the globe, the United States apparently views the whole earth as its territory. According to the DOD's quarterly report titled "Active Duty Military Personnel Strengths by Regional Area and by Country," there are U.S. troops stationed in 146 countries and 12 territories in every corner of the globe. This means that U.S. troops occupy about 75 percent of the world's countries.

Although President Obama has talked about removing thousands of U.S. troops from Iraq, it should come as no surprise that the United States will have its forces in Iraq for many years to come. There are 82,460 U.S. soldiers in Europe to face a non-existent Soviet Union. There are still 33,286 troops in Japan—almost seventy years after World War II. But even where the United States did not fight a war, there are large numbers of U.S. troops to be found. There are 1,220 U.S. soldiers stationed in Spain and 9,426 soldiers stationed in the United Kingdom. What are 41 U.S. soldiers doing soaking up the sun in the Bahamas? What strategic interest is there in the United States having soldiers in places like Australia and New Zealand? The United States has troops in places most Americans couldn't even locate on a map—like Tunisia and Cameroon. And in addition to military personnel, the Department of Defense employs 700,000 civilians worldwide, including thousands of foreign nationals.

The DOD's personnel, bases, weapons, and equipment come with a heavy price.

According to economist and historian Robert Higgs, real U.S. defense spending is around $1 trillion. This accounts for over half of the world's military-related spending. The United States is also the world's chief arms dealer, as the residents of Gaza recently discovered.

But instead of all of this being an example of imperialism, empire, and foreign policy on steroids, we are told by neoconservative intellectuals that the United States is merely exercising "benevolent hegemony," that America "has been the greatest force for good in the world during the past century," and that the invasion of Iraq was "the greatest act of benevolence one country has ever done for another."

With troops in about 100 countries and territories, the U.S. empire was firmly in place soon after World War II. But the "Good War" was not the beginning. Between the two world wars, U.S. troops were sent to Cuba, the Dominican Republic, Russia, Panama, Honduras, Yugoslavia, Guatemala, Turkey, and China. But World War I was not the beginning either. Before the "Great War," U.S. troops were sent to Nicaragua, Panama, Honduras, the Dominican Republic, Korea, Cuba, Nicaragua, China, and Mexico. And although we might begin the U.S. empire with the seizure from Spain of Cuba, Puerto Rico, the Philippines, and Guam during the Spanish-American War of 1898, we can actually go back a few years earlier to U.S. intervention in Hawaii *before* we deposed the monarch and annexed the territory.

U.S. foreign policy can only be described as aggressive, reckless, belligerent, and meddling. Its fruits are the destabilization and overthrow of governments, the destruction of industry and infrastructure, the backing of military coups, death squads, and drug traffickers, imperialism under the guise of humanitarianism, support for corrupt and tyrannical governments, brutal sanctions and embargoes, and failed attempts to police the world. U.S. foreign policy results in nothing but discord, strife, hatred, and terrorism toward the United States. U.S. foreign policy is also very arrogant. What would Americans think if some country—any country—stated its intention to construct a naval base in Key West, Florida? They would be outraged. So why the double standard? Does might make right? What gives the United States the right to encircle the world with bases?

Mr. Obama, Tear down this empire.

It is not enough for the president just to close down the Guantánamo prison in Cuba. The Guantánamo Bay Naval Base, which the United States has occupied for over 100 years, should be closed as well. The problem with the Base Realignment and Closure (BRAC) Commission is that military base realignment and closure recommendations are all in the United States. All Status of Forces Agreements should be rescinded, all foreign bases closed, and all troops brought home. Yes, it's a radical proposal, but only because America has long ago rejected the Founding Fathers foreign policy of nonintervention.

Now, we know that one man shouldn't have so much power over so much. But the Congress that hasn't issued a declaration of war since World War II—while funding several major wars and scores of other military interventions since then—isn't going to do anything to significantly change U.S. foreign policy. And historically, it has been the executive branch that drives U.S. foreign policy anyway.

And to ensure that no future president again expands the U.S. empire, we need, not a renewal of the War Powers Act, but something with some real teeth, like Marine Corps Major General Smedley Butler's (1881–1940) proposed peace amendment. This amendment would prohibit the removal of the Army from within the continental limits of the United

States, the Navy from steaming more than 500 miles from the coast, and the Air Force from flying more than 750 miles from American soil. This "would be absolute guarantee to the women of America that their loved ones never would be sent overseas to be needlessly shot down in European or Asiatic or African wars that are no concern of our people."

Butler reasoned that because of "our geographical position, it is all but impossible for any foreign power to muster, transport and land sufficient troops on our shores for a successful invasion." In this he was merely echoing Thomas Jefferson, who recognized that geography was one of the great advantages of the United States: "At such a distance from Europe and with such an ocean between us, we hope to meddle little in its quarrels or combinations. Its peace and its commerce are what we shall court."

But even without the advantage of geography, a policy of nonintervention is sufficient, as Congressman Ron Paul (R–Tex.) has pointed out: "Countries like Switzerland and Sweden who promote neutrality and non-intervention have benefited for the most part by remaining secure and free of war over the centuries."

A policy of nonintervention doesn't mean that the United States should refuse to issue visas, trade, extradite criminals, allow travel abroad, or allow immigration. As Jefferson said in his first inaugural address: "Peace, commerce, and honest friendship with all nations—entangling alliances with none."

Mr. Obama, if you welcome change and openness, there is one sign the United States can make that would be unmistakable, that would advance dramatically the cause of freedom and peace. President Obama, if you seek peace, if you seek relief from bloated military budgets for the United States and the rest of the world, close down the overseas military bases. Mr. Obama, bring the troops home. Mr. Obama, tear down this empire!

* * * * *

SAME EMPIRE, DIFFERENT EMPEROR

Just as Hadrian succeeded Trajan, Domitian succeeded Titus, Nero succeeded Claudius, and Caligula succeeded Tiberius, so Kennedy replaced Eisenhower, Nixon replaced Johnson, Reagan replaced Carter, and Obama replaced Bush.

Same empire, different emperor.

The extent of the U.S. global empire is almost incalculable. We know enough, however, about foreign bases, physical assets, military spending, and foreign troop levels to know that we have an empire in everything but the name.

There are, according to the Department of Defense's "Base Structure Report" for FY 2009, 716 U.S. military bases on foreign soil in thirty-eight countries. Yet, according to the expert on this subject, Chalmers Johnson, the author of *Blowback, The Sorrows of Empire,* and *Nemesis,* that number is far too low: "The official figures omit espionage bases, those located in war zones, including Iraq and Afghanistan, and miscellaneous facilities in places considered too sensitive to discuss or which the Pentagon for its own reasons chooses to exclude—e.g. in Israel, Kosovo, or Jordan." Johnson places the real number of foreign bases closer to 1,000.

This same Base Structure Report states that the DOD's physical assets consist of "more than 539,000 facilities (buildings, structures and linear structures) located on more than 5,570 sites, on approximately 29 million acres." The 307,295 buildings occupied by the DOD comprise over 2.1 billion square feet. The DOD manages almost 30 million acres of land worldwide.

The latest defense budget (Obama's first) is almost as much as the rest of the world's defense spending combined. The U.S. military is the single-largest consumer of oil in the world, officially using 320,000 barrels of oil a day. The U.S. Navy's battle fleet is larger than the next 13 foreign navies combined. And thanks to the work of economist Robert Higgs, we know that total spending for all defense-related purposes is actually about a trillion dollars. And then there are the supplemental appropriation bills not in the Pentagon's budget.

In addition to the over 1.1 million U.S. military personnel stationed in the United States and its territories, there are about 262,000 U.S. troops in foreign countries—not counting the 130,000 soldiers in Iraq and the 68,000 soldiers in Afghanistan, and not counting the other troops deployed in Iraq in support of Operation Iraqi Freedom and in Afghanistan in support of Operation Enduring Freedom. And then there is Obama's new 30,000-man troop surge for Afghanistan. There would be even more troops in Afghanistan if it were not for the 120,000 contractors there on the payroll of the Defense Department, State Department, and USAID.

According to the latest DOD quarterly report titled "Active Duty Military Personnel Strengths by Regional Area and by Country," there are U.S. troops stationed in 148 countries and 11 territories in every corner of the globe. This the greatest number of countries that the United States has ever had troops in. This also means that U.S. troops occupy over 75 percent of the world's countries.

The U.S. global empire was well in place soon after World War II with security alliances, bilateral agreements, status of forces agreements, thousands of military installations, and troops in about 100 different counties and territories. When I first wrote about U.S. troop presence around the globe on March 16, 2004, in "The U.S. Global Empire," I documented that the U.S. had troops in 135 countries, plus 14 territories controlled by the United States or some other country. I then showed on October 4, 2004, in "Guarding the Empire," that the U.S. empire had increased to 150 different regions of the world. The third time I reported on the extent of the empire, December 5, 2005, in "Today Iraq, Tomorrow the World," that number had grown to 155. The fourth time I updated the status of the U.S. global empire, on February 19, 2007, in "Update on the Empire," I revealed that U.S. soldiers were stationed in 144 countries and 15 territories. The last time I visited this subject, on April 7, 2008, in "Ninety-Five Years to Go," I detailed that the United States had troops stationed in 157 regions of the world: 147 countries and 10 territories.

Changes from 2008 consist of the addition of U.S. troops to the countries of Eritrea, Fiji, Iran, Libya, and the territories of the Northern Mariana Islands and St. Helena and the removal of troops from Antigua, Belarus, Iceland, and Suriname. Because of the independence of Kosovo on February 17, 2008, which has been recognized by the United States, I am now counting Kosovo as a country instead of a territory. And as I have said on other occasions, these numbers are not the result of Marine embassy guards stationed at U.S. embassies, as I showed in "Guarding the Empire."

Since it has been six years since I gave a complete list of countries occupied by U.S. troops, I will once again list them here:

Afghanistan	Bangladesh
Albania	Barbados
Algeria	Belgium
Angola	Belize
Argentina	Bolivia
Armenia	Bosnia and Herzegovina
Australia	Botswana
Austria	Brazil
Azerbaijan	Bulgaria
Bahamas	Burma
Bahrain	Burundi

Cambodia
Cameroon
Canada
Chad
Chile
China
Colombia
Congo
Costa Rica
Cote D'lvoire
Croatia
Cuba
Cyprus
Czech Republic
Denmark
Djibouti
Dominican Republic
East Timor
Ecuador
Egypt
El Salvador
Eritrea
Estonia
Ethiopia
Fiji
Finland
France
Gabon
Georgia
Germany
Ghana
Greece
Guatemala
Guinea
Guyana
Haiti
Honduras
Hungary
India
Indonesia
Iran

Iraq
Ireland
Israel
Italy
Jamaica
Japan
Jordan
Kazakhstan
Kenya
Kosovo
Kuwait
Kyrgyzstan
Laos
Latvia
Lebanon
Liberia
Libya
Lithuania
Luxembourg
Macedonia
Madagascar
Malaysia
Mali
Malta
Marshall Islands
Mauritania
Mexico
Moldova
Mongolia
Morocco
Mozambique
Nepal
Netherlands
New Zealand
Nicaragua
Niger
Nigeria
Norway
Oman
Pakistan
Panama

Paraguay	Sweden
Peru	Switzerland
Philippines	Syria
Poland	Tajikistan
Portugal	Tanzania
Qatar	Thailand
Romania	Togo
Russia	Trinidad and Tobago
Rwanda	Tunisia
Saudi Arabia	Turkey
Senegal	Turkmenistan
Serbia	Uganda
Sierra Leone	Ukraine
Singapore	United Arab Emirates
Slovakia	United Kingdom
Slovenia	Uruguay
Somalia	Uzbekistan
Spain	Venezuela
South Africa	Vietnam
South Korea	Yemen
Sri Lanka	Zambia
Sudan	Zimbabwe

The eleven territories where U.S. troops are stationed are: American Samoa, Bermuda, Diego Garcia, Greenland, Guam, Hong Kong, Northern Mariana Islands, Puerto Rico, St. Helena, U.S. Virgin Islands, and Wake Island.

President Obama has been in office a year now and the United States is "the world's sole military superpower" with an inventory of weapons measured in the trillions and a defense budget and global empire of troops and bases that are larger than ever. We are engaged, either openly or covertly, in five fronts in the war on terror (Afghanistan, Pakistan, Iraq, Yemen, and Somalia), plus possible future military action against Iran. Additionally, the president maintains that "the struggle against violent extremism will not be finished quickly, and it extends well beyond Afghanistan and Pakistan." He also announced plans to increase spending on America's arsenal of nuclear weapons—despite saying in his State of the Union speech that he seeks "a world without them." Under commander in chief Obama we have also seen a dramatic escalation of Predator drone strikes, increased arrests and secret detentions of suspected terrorists on the slightest suspicion, and the continuation of the presidential license to order, without judicial oversight, the murder of foreigners and American citizens anywhere in the world based on dubious claims that they are a terrorism threat. And now it has come out that the Army Corps of Engineers has spent more than $4.5 billion on construction projects in Afghanistan, most of it building the nearly 400 U.S. and coalition bases scattered throughout the country.

Obama is the man who, on the campaign trail, on October 27, 2007, pledged: "I will promise you this, that if we have not gotten our troops out by the time I am President, it is the first thing I will do. I will get our troops home. We will bring an end to this war. You can take that to the bank."

Well, Bush didn't get the troops out, Obama became the new commander in chief, and, after over a year, the troops are still there. And not only are U.S. troops still in Iraq, there are still over 50,000 U.S. troops in Germany, over 35,000 in Japan, and over 24,000 in South Korea—decades after the end of World War II and the Korean War.

Not two months after taking office in January of 2009, Obama ordered an additional 21,000 troops dispatched to Afghanistan. Last summer he signed a $106 billion war supplemental appropriations bill. In October Obama quietly ordered another 13,000 soldiers to deploy to Afghanistan. Now the peace-prize laureate wants an additional $33 billion and 30,000 troops to further expand the war in that graveyard of empires known as Afghanistan. And not only will he get what he wants, he will have bipartisan support. Presidential administrations come and go, but the empire remains the same.

Same empire, different emperor.

*　*　*　*　*

THE REAL REASON GUANTÁNAMO SHOULD BE CLOSED

It has been ten years now since the first "terrorists" arrived at the U.S. military prison at Guantánamo Bay, Cuba. Of the 779 people who have been detained at Guantánamo over the years, 171 still remain.

Of those 171 prisoners, 46 are "indefinite detainees" who will neither be charged nor released, 89 are eligible for release or transfer but are still held in the prison camps, 6 face death-penalty trials that may begin this year, 4 are convicted war criminals, and 1 is serving a life sentence.

Although Secretary of Defense Donald Rumsfeld called the detainees at Guantánamo "among the most dangerous, best-trained, vicious killers on the face of the earth" and insisted that all of them "were captured on a battlefield," the majority had to be released when it turned out, after months or years of confinement, abuse, or torture, that most were hapless innocents sold by warlords as terrorists to the U.S. military in order to collect a bounty. An analysis by Seton Hall Law School professor Mark Denbeaux—based on the government's own data—found that only one of the 516 Combatant Status Review Tribunal unclassified summaries of the evidence alleged that a detainee had been captured by the Unites States on a battlefield.

George W. Bush's assurances in a 2006 White House speech that "we have in place a rigorous process to ensure those held at Guantánamo Bay belong at Guantánamo" and that detainees "are in our custody so that they cannot murder our people" were simply ruses for indefinite detention.

Barack Obama pledged to close Guantánamo, both before and after he became president. But like most promises made by politicians, and especially presidential candidates, it never came to pass. Congress, of course, shares in the blame for this injustice, and especially the Republican national-security statists who populate both the House and Senate. Congress has blocked the White House from financing trials of Guantánamo detainees on U.S. soil and the acquisition of a state prison in Illinois to hold detainees currently held who will not be put on trial.

The prison at Guantánamo is the most expensive prison in the world. It is staffed by 1,850 U.S. troops and civilian linguists, intelligence analysts, federal agents, and contract workers at a cost of $800,000 a year per detainee.

The prisoner abuse that has taken place at Guantánamo is well known, and not just from those who have experienced it. The FBI has released documents showing that at least 20 of its agents witnessed aggressive mistreatment and harsh interrogation techniques of prisoners by other government agencies or outside contractors, including the chaining of detainees to the floor, hand and foot in a fetal position for 24 hours with no food or water, and covered in their own filth. Former Army Sgt. Erik R. Saar has disclosed that female interrogators tried to break Muslim detainees by sexual touching, wearing miniskirts, and thong underwear. Ex-Guantánamo guard Brandon Neely has spoken of the violence that was committed against detainees by the U.S. military.

The recently passed National Defense Authorization Act could result in Americans' being declared "enemy combatants" and sent to Guantánamo where they could be detained indefinitely.

The reasons to close the prison at Guantánamo Bay are legion. But there is another reason Guantánamo should be closed that is rarely mentioned. The real reason that the prison at Guantánamo should be closed is that it is at Guantánamo Bay, Cuba.

To understand that we must go back to the Spanish-American War. The United States declared war on Spain on April 25, 1898, intervening in and fighting its first imperial war. When the war ended on August 12, 1898, the United States found itself in possession of Spain's overseas empire of Puerto Rico, the Philippines, Guam, and Cuba.

Prior to that, the U.S. Congress had passed, and William McKinley had signed, the Teller Amendment, in which the United States "hereby disclaims any disposition of intention to exercise sovereignty, jurisdiction, or control over said island except for pacification thereof, and asserts its determination, when that is accomplished, to leave the government and control of the island to its people."

But in 1901, a series of articles known as the Platt Amendment (after Sen. Orville Platt of Connecticut) were drawn up by Secretary of War Elihu Root and incorporated into the new Cuban constitution of 1902. The Platt Amendment made Cuba virtually a U.S. protectorate. It allowed the United States to intervene at will in Cuban affairs and authorized the United States to lease Guantánamo Bay from Cuba perpetually.

After U.S. troops withdrew from Cuba in 1902 (although they returned in 1906–1909, 1912, and 1917–1922), the Cuban-American Treaty was signed in 1903 by the president of Cuba and the new American president, Theodore Roosevelt. This treaty, which is still contested by Cuba, allows the United States to lease a 45-square-mile area of land and water at Guantánamo Bay for "coaling or naval stations only, and for no other purpose."

In 1943, under the Good Neighbor Policy of Franklin Roosevelt, the Platt Amendment was abrogated, but the provisions of the Cuban-American Treaty regarding the leasing of Guantánamo remained in effect. The United States continues to send a monthly rent check to Cuba, but the checks are never cashed. After Fidel Castro came to power, relations between the United States and Cuba deteriorated. Cuban territory outside the U.S. Naval Station Guantánamo Bay has been off-limits to U.S. servicemen and civilians since January 1, 1959.

How many Americans even realize that Guantánamo is located, not in the United States or in a U.S. territory, but 400 miles away in another country?

But Guantánamo is only the tip of the iceberg. According to the Department of Defense's "Base Structure Report" for fiscal year 2011, the Defense Department "manages a global real property portfolio consisting of more than 542,000 facilities (buildings, structures, and linear structures) located on nearly 5,000 sites worldwide covering more than 28 million acres." Officially, there are 611 of these facilities in 39 foreign countries. Unofficially, however, there are hundreds more. Although the Base Structure Report lists 194 sites in Germany, 108 sites in Japan, and 82 sites in South Korea, the report lists no branch of the U.S. military' having any bases in Afghanistan or Iraq, even though we know that there exist hundreds of "sites" in those two countries.

The late Chalmers Johnson, author of *Blowback*, *The Sorrows of Empire*, and *Nemesis*, and one of the foremost authorities on the subject, always maintained that the official Defense Department figures regarding overseas military bases were too low because they "omit espionage bases, those located in war zones, including Iraq and Afghanistan, and miscellaneous facilities in places considered too sensitive to discuss or which the Pentagon for its own reasons chooses to exclude—e.g., Israel, Kosovo, or Jordan." Johnson estimated the number to be closer to 1,000. We know now that he was right about the Defense Department's figures, for Nick Turse, author of *The Complex: How the Military Invades Our Everyday Lives*, has recently confirmed that Johnson's figure of 1,000 foreign bases is actually too low. The number is really closer to 1,100.

The real problem with the Guantánamo prison is not that it is too expensive, that it holds detainees who are not really terrorists, or that prisoners are mistreated there, but that it is located on a U.S. military base on foreign soil.

Although World War II ended in 1945, the United States still maintains scores of bases and tens of thousands of troops in Germany, Italy, and Japan. It is long past time to end the U.S. empire of bases and troops that encircles the globe.

Imagine the outrage of Americans if Russia claimed the authority to build a military base around San Francisco Bay and station thousands of troops there. Imagine the indignation if China took over part of the Florida Keys.

It is the height of arrogance for the U.S. government to insist on building hundreds of military bases in foreign countries and to consider it an act of aggression for other countries to want to do likewise.

The prison at Guantánamo should be closed, the U.S. Naval Station Guantánamo Bay should be evacuated, and all the land currently occupied by the United States should be given back to Cuba.

* * * * *

FACT CHECKING THE *WASHINGTON POST*

> "We don't need to pay all this money to keep troops all over the country, 130 countries, 900 bases. But also, just think, bringing all the troops home rather rapidly, they would be spending their money here at home and not in Germany and Japan and South Korea, tremendous boost to the economy." ~ Ron Paul, February 7, 2012

In a post on February 9th at the *Washington Post*'s The Fact Checker blog, which claims to give "the truth behind the rhetoric," Glenn Kessler writes about "Ron Paul's Strange Claim about Bases and Troops Overseas":

> This comment by GOP presidential aspirant Ron Paul after Tuesday night's caucuses caught the ear of our editor. Paul's phrasing could have left the impression that he thinks there are 900 bases in 130 countries, but normally he makes it clear he is talking about two different things.

> For instance, in the GOP debate Sept. 12, Paul said: "We're under great threat, because we occupy so many countries. We're in 130 countries. We have 900 bases around the world."

> We will lay aside Paul's loose definition of "occupy"—which denotes taking away a country's sovereignty. You could also quibble with the concept of a "base," but we'll accept that he's talking about any military facility.

> Are there any facts to back up these eye-popping figures?

I never read anything by Kessler until this piece on Ron Paul. The Fact Checker blog says that he "has covered foreign policy, economic policy, the White House, Congress, politics, airline safety and Wall Street."

In giving us the facts to evaluate the truth of Dr. Paul's assertions, Kessler refers, but not by name, to two Department of Defense documents: the annual "Base Structure Report" dated September 30, 2011, and the quarterly "Active Duty Military Personnel Strengths by Regional Area and by Country," most recently issued on September 30, 2011.

Regarding the number of foreign bases, Kessler correctly notes that "the DOD list shows a list of 611 military facilities around the world (not counting war zones)." However, he discounts that figure because "only 20 are listed as 'large sites,' which means a replacement value of more than $1.74 billion." He also notes that most (549) of the DOD foreign sites are listed as being small sites.

Regarding the numbers and locations of U.S. troops in foreign countries, Kessler correctly notes that the "Personal Strengths" document lists "53,766 military personnel in Germany, 39,222 in Japan, 10,801 in Italy and 9,382 in the United Kingdom. That makes sense." "But wait," he says, "most of the countries on the list, in fact, have puny military representation." He points out that the U.S. has only nine troops in Mali, eight in Barbados, seven in Laos, six in Lithuania, five in Lebanon, four in Moldova, three in Mongolia, two in Suriname and one in Gabon." Then he says that he counts "153 countries with U.S. military personnel, actually higher than the 130 cited by Paul." But he dismisses both numbers by saying that "the list essentially tracks with places where the United States has a substantial diplomatic presence. (The United States has diplomatic relations with about 190 countries.)." He charges Paul with "counting Marine guards and military attaches as part of a vast expanse of U.S. military power around the globe." And after all, "this document indicates that only 11 countries actually house more than 1,000 U.S. military personnel."

Kessler concludes that "Paul's statistics barely pass the laugh test. He has managed to turn small contingents of Marine guards into occupying armies and waste dumps into military bases. A more accurate way to treat this data would be to say that the United States has 20 major bases around the world, not counting the war in Afghanistan, with major concentrations of troops in 11 countries."

As one who is very familiar with both of the aforementioned DOD documents and has written about these things long before Ron Paul even ran for the Republican presidential nomination the first time, I can say with confidence that it is Glenn Kessler and the *Washington Post* that need some fact checking.

First of all, according to the Base Structure Report, the Defense Department "manages a global real property portfolio consisting of more than 542,000 facilities (buildings, structures, and linear structures) located on nearly 5,000 sites worldwide covering more than 28 million acres." Officially, as Kessler reports, there are 611 of these facilities in 39 foreign countries (excluding war zones). But why dismiss sites that are not "large sites"? Even small sites can have a replacement value of up to $929 million. True, some of the sites are not technically bases, but what about all the foreign bases that are not on the official list?

I recently wrote in "The Real Reason Guantánamo Should Be

Closed":

> The late Chalmers Johnson, author of *Blowback, The Sorrows of Empire*, and *Nemesis*, and one of the foremost authorities on the subject, always maintained that the official Defense Department figures regarding overseas military bases were too low because they "omit espionage bases, those located in war zones, including Iraq and Afghanistan, and miscellaneous facilities in places considered too sensitive to discuss or which the Pentagon for its own reasons chooses to exclude—e.g., Israel, Kosovo, or Jordan." Johnson estimated the number to be closer to 1,000. We know now that he was right about the Defense Department's figures, for Nick Turse, author of *The Complex: How the Military Invades Our Everyday Lives*, has recently confirmed that Johnson's figure of 1,000 foreign bases is actually too low. The number is really closer to 1,100.

Nick Turse's work painstaking work on the number of foreign U.S. military bases can be seen here, here, and here. Although Kessler acknowledges the existence of "106 U.S. military facilities in Afghanistan," Turse has reason to believe that the number is much greater and concludes that the military doesn't even know the true number:

> Last January, Colonel Wayne Shanks, a spokesman for the U.S.-led International Security Assistance Force (ISAF), told me that there were nearly 400 U.S. and coalition bases in Afghanistan, including camps, forward operating bases, and combat outposts. He expected that number to increase by 12 or more, he added, over the course of 2010.

> In September, I contacted ISAF's Joint Command Public Affairs Office to follow up. To my surprise, I was told that "there are approximately 350 forward operating bases with two major military installations, Bagram and Kandahar airfields." Perplexed by the loss of 50 bases instead of a gain of 12, I contacted Gary Younger, a Public Affairs Officer with the International Security Assistance Force. "There are less than 10 NATO bases in Afghanistan," he wrote in an October 2010 email. "There are over 250 U.S. bases in Afghanistan."

> By then, it seemed, the U.S. had lost up to 150 bases and I was thoroughly confused. When I contacted the military to sort out the discrepancies and listed the numbers I had been given—from Shanks' 400 base tally to the count of around 250 by Younger—I

was handed off again and again until I landed with Sergeant First Class Eric Brown at ISAF Joint Command's Public Affairs. "The number of bases in Afghanistan is roughly 411," Brown wrote in a November email, "which is a figure comprised of large base[s], all the way down to the Combat Out Post-level." Even this, he cautioned, wasn't actually a full list, because "temporary positions occupied by platoon-sized elements or less" were not counted.

Along the way to this "final" tally, I was offered a number of explanations—from different methods of accounting to the failure of units in the field to provide accurate information—for the conflicting numbers I had been given. After months of exchanging emails and seeing the numbers swing wildly, ending up with roughly the same count in November as I began with in January suggests that the U.S. command isn't keeping careful track of the number of bases in Afghanistan. Apparently, the military simply does not know how many bases it has in its primary theater of operations.

Turse specifically mentions the countries of Qatar, Pakistan, and Kuwait. Qatar is not listed on the Base Structure Report, but contains Al-Udeid Air Base, a billion-dollar facility where the U.S. Air Force secretly oversees its on-going unmanned drone wars. Pakistan is also not listed on the Base Structure Report, but U.S. drone aircraft, operating under the auspices of both the CIA and the Air Force take off from one or more bases in that country. And then there are the other sites like the "covert forward operating base run by the U.S. Joint Special Operations Command (JSOC) in the Pakistani port city of Karachi," and "one or more airfields run by employees of the private security contractor Blackwater (now renamed Xe Services)." And Kuwait, which has one nameless site on the Base Structure Report, has a number of U.S. military facilities.

Suppose that each of the 39 "official" countries with U.S. military bases decided to build the same number of military bases in the United States that the United States maintained in its country? The DOD claims 194 "sites" in Germany. Would the United States government object if Germany insisted on occupying 194 "sites" in the United States? How about just 94? Would the U.S. military not object because they were just "sites" and not technically bases?

Secondly, Kessler is wrong about U.S. troops being in 153 countries. The United States actually has troops in 148 countries and 11 territories. The last time I gave a complete list of all the countries and territories where the United States had troops was in my article of February 11, 2010, titled "Same Empire, Different Emperor." If you add to the list there the countries of Antigua, Congo (Brazzaville), and Suriname, and subtract from the list the countries of Eritrea, Iran, and Somalia, you will have an updated list. The current eleven territories where U.S. are stationed are: American Samoa, Diego Garcia, Gibralter, Greenland, Guam, Hong Kong, Northern Mariana Islands, Puerto Rico, St. Helena, U.S. Virgin Islands, and Wake Island.

But why does Kessler use the arbitrary number of 1,000 in saying: "This document indicates that only 11 countries actually house more than 1,000 U.S. military personnel." Does this mean that it is okay if the United States has military personnel in a country that number 1,000 or less? And why, after giving the figures of "53,766 military personnel in Germany, 39,222 in Japan, 10,801 in Italy and 9,382 in the United Kingdom," does Kessler remark: "That makes sense"? What makes any sense about the United States stationing all of these troops in Germany, Japan, Italy, and the UK when World War II ended in 1945? What makes any sense about the United States stationing 723 troops in Portugal, 1,205 in Belgium, 163 in Singapore, and 335 in Djibouti? How many Americans have ever even heard of Djibouti? What makes any sense about the United States stationing troops in 75 percent of the world's countries? Kessler makes much of the low figures of "nine troops in Mali, eight in Barbados, seven in Laos, six in Lithuania, five in Lebanon, four in Moldova, three in Mongolia, two in Suriname and one in Gabon." But what makes any sense about any U.S. troops being in those countries? And what makes any sense about the United States sending twenty-two of its military personnel to Ecuador, fourteen to Guatemala, seven to Mozambique, and six to Togo? What makes any sense about U.S. troops being stationed anywhere overseas?

Suppose that each of the 148 countries with a contingent of U.S. military personnel decided to send an equal number of their troops to the United States? Would the United States government and its military tolerate 1,491 troops from Turkey, 2,142 from Bahrain, and 354 from Honduras since those are the numbers of troops the United States has in those countries?

And third, Kessler is just plain wrong in dismissing the U.S. troop presence in foreign countries as "places where the United States has a substantial diplomatic presence" or "Marine guards and military attaches." I did a major study of this back in October 2004 called "Guarding the Empire." It has been online ever since, but rather than doing a little research, Kessler was content to just accuse Dr. Paul of turning "small contingents of Marine guards into occupying armies."

In my article I showed beyond any doubt that the U.S. troop

presence in foreign countries cannot be blamed on Marines guarding embassies. Read the article. I can't tell you how many people have written me after I wrote something negative about the U.S. empire of troops and bases that encircles the globe and dismissed my research as a waste of time since, so they said, most of the U.S. troops stationed abroad were just Marine embassy guards. That is simply not true. I did the research and provided a link to the research, but they were just too lazy to click on the link. Don't be lazy; read "Guarding the Empire." Yes, I know it was written in 2004. Yes, I know that some of the figures have now changed. Yes, I know that some of the links no longer work. But my conclusions still stand:

- The United States has an embassy in some countries, but does not have any troops.
- The United States has an embassy in some countries along with Army, Navy, and/or Air Force troops, but there are no Marines listed as being in the country.
- The United States has an embassy in some countries with troops including Marines, but not the minimum number of six Marines necessary for embassy security guard duty.
- The United States has Marines in some countries, but no embassy to guard.

And if the United States has "diplomatic relations with about 190 countries," then how can Kessler say that the list of 148 countries with U.S. troops "essentially tracks with places where the United States has a substantial diplomatic presence"? That is a difference of 42 countries.

Kessler never gets to the real issue. The real issue has nothing to do with the exact number of foreign bases the United States has or the exact number of countries the United States has troops in or the exact number of troops the United States has stationed abroad or the exact number of foreign sites that are really bases.

The real issue is why the United States has troops and military bases in foreign countries in the first place. Especially since the United States doesn't afford other countries the same privilege.

When I first wrote about U.S. troop presence around the globe in March 2004 in "The U.S. Global Empire," I documented that the U.S. had troops in 135 countries and 14 territories. Both numbers have only changed slightly since then. There was no change in U.S. foreign policy from Bush to Clinton to Bush to Obama. Just like there would have been no change in U.S. foreign policy if John Kerry or John McCain had been elected. Both parties are committed to a foreign policy of aggression, intervention, and meddling. Both parties are committed to a foreign policy of policing the world. Both parties are committed to a foreign policy of bombing and war. Both parties are committed to a foreign policy of empire.

The *Washington Post* ought to be writing about Ron Paul's sane claim about bases and troops overseas.

* * * * *

CHAPTER 7

U.S. FOREIGN POLICY

DR. GATES VS. DR. PAUL

What is the purpose of the military? I think it is beyond dispute that the purpose of any country having a military is to defend the country against a foreign attack or invasion. One would think that someone in the United States called the Secretary of Defense would know this. Yet, in his remarks on October 10, 2007, before the Association of the United States Army (a private, non-profit advocacy group for the U.S. Army), Defense Secretary Robert Gates envisioned a new role for the U.S. Army:

> Army soldiers can expect to be tasked with reviving public services, rebuilding infrastructure and promoting good governance. All these so-called nontraditional capabilities have moved into the mainstream of military thinking, planning, and strategy—where they must stay.

In his speech Secretary Gates also acknowledged that "U.S. forces will play some role in Iraq for years to come."

Anything but actually defend the country.

What the Secretary of Defense is saying is simply this: The United States will take a more active role in rebuilding the infrastructure and restoring the government of countries that it invades, destroys, and occupies. Oh yes, Dr. Gates (he has a doctorate in Russian and Soviet history) did mention that the military defends our freedoms. But as Jacob Hornberger has shown, U.S. troops do just the opposite.

Because U.S. foreign policy is aggressive, reckless, belligerent, and meddling; because it has a history of hegemony, nation building, regime change, and jingoism; because it is the story of interventionism, imperialism, and empire; because it results in discord, strife, hatred, and terrorism toward the United States: the U.S. military—the enforcer of U.S. foreign policy—is the greatest force for evil in the world.

America's military heritage is not one of how our troops have repelled invaders, kept us safe from attack, or defended our freedoms. This is a bitter pill to swallow, especially for soldiers who fought for a lie and the families of soldiers who died for a lie. America's military heritage is unfortunately one of bombs and bullets, death and destruction, intervention and invasion, and occupation and oppression. The purpose of the military has been perverted beyond all recognition. U.S. soldiers serve simultaneously as policemen, firemen, scientists, social workers, and bullies with the world as their precinct, forest, laboratory, client, and playground.

Although the military is engaged in very little defense, it is engaged in very real defense spending. The United States spends more on defense than at least the next twelve countries combined. The official budget may only be in the hundreds of billions, but actual defense spending, according to economist Robert Higgs, is now over $1 trillion. Not a dime from the defense budget should be spent on establishing democracy, spreading goodwill, launching preemptive strikes, changing regimes, enforcing no-fly zones, following UN directives, complying with UN resolutions, removing dictators, containing communism, crusading against Islam, training foreign armies, furnishing security in other countries, opening foreign markets, protecting U.S. commercial interests, providing disaster relief, dispensing humanitarian aid, supplying peacekeepers, building overseas bases, stationing troops in other countries, maintaining an empire, enriching federal contractors, supporting the military-industrial complex, or funding the security-industrial complex.

It is no longer honorable to serve in the U.S. military. Not when the military is engaged in sending its soldiers thousands of miles away to kill people and destroy their property after "liberating" them from their ruler. Not when the military is garrisoning the planet.

The prescription of Dr. Gates is more of the same. In fact, Secretary Gates wants more young cannon fodder: "The Army is expanding by some 65,000 soldiers, and I am prepared to support plans to speed up that process as long as we can do it without sacrificing quality."

As I have maintained over and over and over again, the U.S. military should be engaged exclusively in defending the United States, not defending other countries, and certainly not attacking them. It is U.S. borders that should be guarded. It is U.S. coasts that should be patrolled. It is U.S. skies where no-fly zones should be enforced.

A "kinder, gentler" role for the military will only come about in conjunction with a drastic change in U.S. foreign policy. We need a change in foreign policy from an interventionist policy to a noninterventionist one. We need a change in foreign policy from a militaristic policy to a peaceful one. We need a change in foreign policy from a neocon policy to a policy of the Founders. We need a change in foreign policy from that of Dr. Gates to that of Dr. Paul.

Republican presidential candidate Ron Paul has for decades advocated a return to the noninterventionist foreign policy of the Founders. In a speech on the House floor several months before the United States invaded Iraq, Dr. Paul (he has an M.D. from Duke University School of Medicine) made the case for a foreign policy of peace, prosperity, and liberty:

A proper foreign policy of non-intervention is built on friendship with other nations, free trade, and open travel, maximizing the exchanges of goods and services and ideas.

We should avoid entangling alliances and stop meddling in the internal affairs of other nations—no matter how many special interests demand otherwise. The entangling alliances that we should avoid include the complex alliances in the UN, the IMF, the World Bank, and the WTO.

The basic moral principle underpinning a non-interventionist foreign policy is that of rejecting the initiation of force against others. It is based on non-violence and friendship unless attacked, self-determination, and self-defense while avoiding confrontation, even when we disagree with the way other countries run their affairs. It simply means that we should mind our own business and not be influenced by special interests that have an ax to grind or benefits to gain by controlling our foreign policy. Manipulating our country into conflicts that are none of our business and unrelated to national security provides no benefits to us, while exposing us to great risks financially and militarily.

A foreign policy of peace, prosperity, and liberty would drastically change the role of the U.S. military. In the same speech, Dr. Paul also said:

Our troops would be brought home, systematically but soon.

Defending our country from outside attack is legitimate and is of the highest priority. Protecting individual liberty should be our goal. This does not mean, however, that our troops should follow our citizens or their investments throughout the world.

The mission for our Coast Guard would change if our foreign policy became non-interventionist. They, too, would come home, protect our coast, and stop being the enforcers of bureaucratic laws that either should not exist or should be a state function.

If we followed a constitutional policy of non-intervention, we would never have to entertain the aggressive notion of preemptive war based on speculation of what a country might do at some future date. Political pressure by other countries to alter our foreign policy for their benefit would never be a consideration. Commercial interests and our citizens investing overseas could not expect our armies to follow them and protect their profits.

With a foreign policy like this, it would once again be honorable to enlist in the military. Even I might stop discouraging Christians from joining the military.

What would U.S. foreign policy under a Paul administration look like? Dr. Paul has told us:

Under a Paul administration, the United States would trade freely with any nation that seeks to engage with us. American citizens would be encouraged to visit other countries and interact with other peoples rather than be told by their own government that certain countries are off limits to them.

A Paul administration would see Americans engaged overseas like never before, in business and cultural activities. But a Paul administration would never attempt to export democracy or other values at the barrel of a gun, as we have seen over and over again that this is a counterproductive approach that actually leads the United States to be resented and more isolated in the world.

He has in fact written a whole book on the subject: *A Foreign Policy of Freedom.*

Yes, I know that the promises of presidential candidates are less than worthless. But unlike his fascist opponents, Ron Paul can be believed because he has an impeccable track record to back up what he says. The other candidates have a legacy of evasions, lies, flip-flops, and statism.

So, what is it going to be: The foreign policy of Dr. Gates or the foreign policy of Dr. Paul?

If the views of Gates prevail then we can look forward to more dead and wounded American soldiers, more dead foreigners, more hatred of Americans, more blowback from our evil foreign policy, more terrorism threats, more trillion-dollar defense budgets, more funding of the military-industrial and security-industrial complexes, more overseas military adventures, and more violations of civil liberties in the name of security.

If the views of Paul triumph, then we can look forward to peace, an

America-first foreign policy, the saving of billions of dollars, real free trade and travel, the end of the U.S. global empire, and no more preemptive wars, regime changes, entangling alliances, policing the world, meddling in the affairs of other countries, imperialism, taking sides in civil wars, and dismissing civilian casualties as collateral damage.

One thing is for certain: Robert Gates will not be the Secretary of Defense in the Paul administration.

* * * * *

CAN U.S. FOREIGN POLICY BE FIXED?

The WikiLeaks revelations have shined a light on the dark nature of U.S. foreign policy. As Eric Margolis recently described it: "Washington's heavy-handed treatment of friends and foes alike, its bullying, use of diplomats as junior-grade spies, narrow-minded views, and snide remarks about world leaders."

As much as I, an American, hate to say it, U.S. foreign policy is actually much worse. It is aggressive, reckless, belligerent, and meddling. It sanctions the destabilization and overthrow of governments, the assassination of leaders, the destruction of industry and infrastructure, the backing of military coups, death squads, and drug traffickers, and imperialism under the guise of humanitarianism. It supports corrupt and tyrannical governments and brutal sanctions and embargoes. It results in discord, strife, hatred, and terrorism toward the United States.

The question, then, is simply this: Can U.S. foreign policy be fixed? Although I am not very optimistic that it will be, I am more than confident that it can be.

I propose a four-pronged solution from the following perspectives: Founding Fathers, military, congressional, libertarian. In brief, to fix its foreign policy the United States should implement a Jeffersonian foreign policy, adopt Major General Smedley Butler's Amendment for Peace, follow the advice of Congressman Ron Paul, and do it all within the libertarian framework of philosopher Murray Rothbard.

Thomas Jefferson, our first secretary of state and third president, favored a foreign policy of "peace, commerce, and honest friendship with all nations—entangling alliances with none." This policy was basically followed until the Spanish-American War of 1898. Here is the simple but profound wisdom of Jefferson:

No one nation has a right to sit in judgment over another.

We wish not to meddle with the internal affairs of any country, nor with the general affairs of Europe.

I am for free commerce with all nations, political connection with none, and little or no diplomatic establishment.

We have produced proofs, from the most enlightened and approved writers on the subject, that a neutral nation must, in all things relating to the war, observe an exact impartiality towards the parties.

No judgment, no meddling, no political connection, and no partiality: this is a Jeffersonian foreign policy.

U.S. Marine Corps Major General Butler was the most decorated Marine in U.S. history. After leaving the military, he authored the classic work *War Is a Racket*. Butler proposed an Amendment for Peace to provide an "absolute guarantee to the women of America that their loved ones never would be sent overseas to be needlessly shot down in European or Asiatic or African wars that are no concern of our people." Here are its three planks:

1. The removal of members of the land armed forces from within the continental limits of the United States and the Panama Canal Zone for any cause whatsoever is hereby prohibited.
2. The vessels of the United States Navy, or of the other branches of the armed service, are hereby prohibited from steaming, for any reason whatsoever except on an errand of mercy, more than five hundred miles from our coast.
3. Aircraft of the Army, Navy and Marine Corps is hereby prohibited from flying, for any reason whatsoever, more than seven hundred and fifty miles beyond the coast of the United States.

Butler also reasoned that because of "our geographical position, it is all but impossible for any foreign power to muster, transport and land sufficient troops on our shores for a successful invasion." In this he was echoing Jefferson, who recognized that geography was one of the great advantages of the United States: "At such a distance from Europe and with such an ocean between us, we hope to meddle little in its quarrels or combinations. Its peace and its commerce are what we shall court."

And then there is our modern Jeffersonian in Congress, Rep. Ron Paul, the only consistent voice in Congress from either party for a foreign policy of peace and nonintervention. In a speech on the House floor several months before the invasion of Iraq, Ron Paul made the case for a foreign policy of peace through commerce and nonintervention:

> A proper foreign policy of non-intervention is built on friendship with other nations, free trade, and open travel, maximizing the exchanges of goods and services and ideas.
>
> We should avoid entangling alliances and stop meddling in the internal affairs of other nations—no matter how many special interests demand otherwise. The entangling alliances that we should avoid include the complex alliances in the UN, the IMF, the World Bank, and the WTO.
>
> The basic moral principle underpinning a non-interventionist foreign policy is that of rejecting the initiation of force against others. It is based on non-violence and friendship unless attacked, self-determination, and self-defense while avoiding confrontation, even when we disagree with the way other countries run their affairs. It simply means that we should mind our own business and not be influenced by special interests that have an ax to grind or benefits to gain by controlling our foreign policy. Manipulating our country into conflicts that are none of our business and unrelated to national security provides no benefits to us, while exposing us to great risks financially and militarily.

For the libertarian framework necessary to ensure a foreign policy of peace and nonintervention, we can turn to libertarian political philosopher and theoretician Murray Rothbard:

> The primary plank of a libertarian foreign policy program for America must be to call upon the United States to abandon its policy of global interventionism: to withdraw immediately and completely, militarily and politically, from Asia, Europe, Latin America, the Middle East, from everywhere. The cry among American libertarians should be for the United States to withdraw now, in every way that involves the U.S. government. The United States should dismantle its bases, withdraw its troops, stop its incessant political meddling, and abolish the CIA. It should also end all foreign aid—which is simply a device to coerce the American taxpayer into subsidizing American exports and favored foreign States, all in the name of "helping the starving peoples of the world." In short, the United States government should withdraw totally to within its own boundaries and maintain a policy of strict political "isolation" or neutrality everywhere.

The U.S. global empire with its 1,000 foreign military bases and half a million troops and mercenary contractors in three-fourths of the world's countries must be dismantled. This along with the empire's spies, covert operations, foreign aid, gargantuan military budgets, abuse and misuse of the military, prison camps, torture, extraordinary renditions, assassinations, nation building, spreading democracy at the point of a gun, jingoism, regime changes, military alliances, security guarantees, and meddling in the affairs of other countries.

U.S. foreign policy can be fixed. The United States would never tolerate another country building a string of bases around North America, stationing thousands of its troops on our soil, enforcing a no-fly zone over American territory, or sending their fleets to patrol off our coasts. How much longer will other countries tolerate these actions by the United States? We have already experienced blowback from the Muslim world for our foreign policy. And how much longer can the United States afford to maintain its empire?

It is time for the world's policeman, fireman, security guard, social worker, and busybody to announce its retirement.

* * * * *

MICHAEL MOORE IS RIGHT

> "Terrorists aren't trying to kill us because they hate our freedom.
> They're killing us because we're in their countries killing them."
> ~ Michael Moore

In his new book *Decision Points*, former president George W. Bush complains about a 2004 tape by Osama bin Laden "mocking my response to 9/11 in the Florida classroom." What really upset Bush was that "it sounded like he was plagiarizing Michael Moore."

Moore is the documentary filmmaker and liberal political commentator who harshly criticized Bush in his 2004 film *Fahrenheit 9/11*, which he wrote, directed, produced, and stared in. As Lew Rockwell wrote about the film:

> The movie decries the warmongering of the Bush administration, exposes the fraudulence of his excuses for invading and crushing Iraq, unearths the unseemly ties between the Bush regime and big oil and the Saudis, and blasts the Bush regime for its egregious violations of civil liberties and massive pillaging of the American taxpayer on behalf of the merchants of death.

This, of course, does not mean that Lew Rockwell or I endorse anything else that Michael Moore has ever done.

Like Mr. Rockwell, I am no fan of Michael Moore. He is a radical liberal, a union propagandist, a socialist, a gun grabber, an economic ignoramus, and a hypocrite who criticizes capitalism and poses as a spokesman of the working class while living an upscale life, sending his daughter to an elite private school, and boasting of his wealth. I even agree with Bush that Moore is a "slimeball."

But there is one thing Michael Moore is right about.

In a recent open letter to Juan Williams regarding his firing by NPR, Moore used the courtroom statements of the Times Square car bomber Faisal Shahzad to explain why many in the Muslim World hate us. Moore previously wrote an open letter to Bush on the eve of the Iraq war and to Obama about the war in Afghanistan.

Here is what Moore quotes Shahzad as saying at his June 21, 2010, appearance in the Federal District Court in Manhattan where he pleaded guilty to a ten-count indictment:

> I want to plead guilty, and I'm going to plead guilty 100 times over, because until the hour the U.S. pulls its forces from Iraq and Afghanistan, and stops the drone strikes in Somalia and Yemen and in Pakistan, and stops the occupation of Muslim lands, and stops killing the Muslims, and stops reporting the Muslims to its government, we will be attacking U.S., and I plead guilty to that.

And here is what Moore quotes Shahzad as saying on October 5, 2010, when he was sentenced to life in prison with no possibility of parole:

> [Saladin] liberated Muslim lands ... And that's what we Muslims are trying do, because you're occupying Iraq and Afghanistan... So, the past nine years the war with Muslims has achieved nothing for the U.S., except for it has waken up the Muslims for Islam. We are only Muslims trying to defend our people, honor, and land. But if you call us terrorists for doing that, then we are proud terrorists, and we will keep on terrorizing until you leave our land and people at peace.

The first thing to be determined is whether Moore accurately quotes Shahzad. In the court transcript from June 21, "100 times over" appears as "a hundred times forward." The only other difference between Moore and the official transcript is a few commas. In defense of Moore I should point out that the way he quotes Shahzad is the usual way the quote has been reported. In the court transcript from October 5, we can see that the first and second statements attributed to Shahzad actually come after the third statement. And just to be fair to Shahzad (yes, I know he's a convicted terrorist, but that doesn't give us the right to misquote him), here is what he said without the brackets and ellipsis: "He liberated Muslim lands from the Jewish crusade, Christian crusade. And that's what we Muslims are trying do, because you're occupying Iraq and Afghanistan." Moore quotes the third statement word perfect. So, what Moore quotes Shahzad as saying is essentially correct.

It is at the close of his short open letter that Moore reaches his conclusion I quoted above: "Terrorists aren't trying to kill us because they hate our freedom. They're killing us because we're in their countries killing them."

So if Moore is right—and I have no doubt that he is—then Islamic terrorists don't want to detonate bombs in Times Square or blow up U.S.-bound airplanes because we have a bill of rights or because they think Brittany Spears should wear a burqa.

But Michael Moore is not just right; he is by implication giving us the key to declaring the war on terror over: GET OUT. Get U.S. troops out of Iraq and Afghanistan. Get the CIA out of Yemen and Pakistan. Stop the Predator drone attacks. Cease flying the sorties. I'm not sure about Moore, but I would go even further. Close the overseas bases. Bring all the troops home. Retire as the policeman of the world. Discontinue the foreign wars. Halt the spreading of democracy. Freeze the nation building. End the interventionist foreign policy.

What Moore is saying is not new. The CIA calls it blowback. The Bible calls it reaping what you sow.

The terrible truth is that the war on terror creates terrorists. As the great Glenn Greenwald wrote after Faisal Shahzad entered his guilty plea:

> The great contradiction of American foreign policy is that the very actions endlessly rationalized as necessary for combating Terrorism—invading, occupying and bombing other countries, limitless interference in the Muslim world, unconditional support for Israeli aggression, vast civil liberties abridgments such as torture, renditions, due-process-free imprisonments—are the very actions that fuel the anti-American hatred which, as the U.S. Government itself has long recognized, is what causes, fuels and exacerbates the Terrorism we're ostensibly attempting to address.

But never mind what Glenn Greenwald has to say; never mind what Michael Moore has to say, and never mind what Laurence Vance has to say.

According to a report on strategic communication prepared by the Defense Science Board Task Force, "a federal advisory committee established to provide independent advice to the secretary of defense":

> The information campaign—or as some still would have it, "the war of ideas," or the struggle for "hearts and minds"—is important to every war effort. In this war it is an essential objective, because the larger goals of U.S. strategy depend on separating the vast majority of non-violent Muslims from the radical-militant Islamist-Jihadists. But American efforts have not only failed in this respect: they may also have achieved the opposite of what they intended.

> American direct intervention in the Muslim World has paradoxically elevated the stature of and support for radical Islamists, while diminishing support for the United States to single-digits in some Arab societies.

> Muslims do not "hate our freedom," but rather, they hate our policies. The overwhelming majority voice their objections to what they see as one-sided support in favor of Israel and against Palestinian rights, and the longstanding, even increasing support for what Muslims collectively see as tyrannies, most notably Egypt, Saudi Arabia, Jordan, Pakistan, and the Gulf states.

> Furthermore, in the eyes of Muslims, American occupation of Afghanistan and Iraq has not led to democracy there, but only more chaos and suffering. U.S. actions appear in contrast to be motivated by ulterior motives, and deliberately controlled in order to best serve American national interests at the expense of truly Muslim selfdetermination.

> Therefore, the dramatic narrative since 9/11 has essentially borne out the entire radical Islamist bill of particulars. American actions and the flow of events have elevated the authority of the Jihadi insurgents and tended to ratify their legitimacy among Muslims. Fighting groups portray themselves as the true defenders of an Ummah (the entire Muslim community) invaded and under attack—to broad public support.

But U.S. foreign policy blunders didn't just begin on 9/11. As Sheldon Richman recently explained:

> Contrary to those who think history began September 11, 2001,

U.S. regimes have long pursued policies in the Middle East and Central Asia that have brutalized the Muslim world and cultivated a seething passion for revenge. That explains (though does not excuse) the terrorism against civilians that government officials now say they must spend so much to stop. The threat was created by American policy, and it can be ended by changing that policy to the Washington-Jefferson foreign policy of nonintervention. That will not only make us safer, it also will save the taxpayers money.

Richman ought to know, as he prepared the exhaustive study titled "'Ancient History': U.S. Conduct in the Middle East Since World War II and the Folly of Intervention."

The attacks of 9/11 were political acts. They were not undertaken because of our freedoms, way of life, culture, or religion. The problem is our government and its abominable foreign policy. It is because of our foreign policy that our soldiers are needlessly dying in Iraq and Afghanistan.

Now, to accept the fact that terrorists want to kill us because we're in their countries killing them doesn't mean that those killed on 9/11 deserved to die or that violence is justified or that the Koran is a holy book or that Islam is a religion of peace or that no act of terrorism against the United States would ever take place again if we withdrew our troops.

What it does mean—to anyone except red-state fascists, blood-thirsty conservative chickenhawks, Republican armchair warriors, Religious Right warvangelicals, theocon Values Voters, reich-wing nationalists, God and country Christian bumpkins, and other apologists for the U.S. military and its wars—is that maybe, perhaps, possibly there might be something terribly wrong with U.S. foreign policy, as the heroic Ron Paul has pointed out over and over again.

Michael Moore may be a liberal, he may be a hypocrite, he may be wrong on an innumerable number of issues, he may be overweight, he may even have bad breath, but on the subject of why terrorists want to kill us Michael Moore has never been more right.

* * * * *

EGYPT AND U.S. FOREIGN POLICY

Until very recently, the only things many Americans knew about Egypt were its pyramids they read about in their school history texts, its mummies they saw on display at U.S. museum exhibits or on the screen in Hollywood movies, and the Nile River they marveled at in TV documentaries.

Now they see on TV and the Internet and read in the newspaper accounts of protests, violence, demonstrations, strikes, marches, curfews, military helicopters, tanks, government crackdowns on social media, calls for the Egyptian president to step down, cancellations of flights in and out of Cairo, and evacuations of hundreds of Americans by the U.S. State Department.

The civil unrest in Egypt and the sight of U.S. tanks in the streets of Cairo have brought to light two things about U.S.-Egyptian relations that many if not most Americans have heretofore been ignorant of. I am speaking of U.S. foreign policy in general and foreign aid in particular.

Hosni Mubarak has been the "president" of Egypt since the assassination of Anwar Sadat in 1981. Mubarak's brutal military regime has been characterized by political corruption, sham elections, censorship, imprisonment of political opponents without trials, oppression, torture, murder, kidnapping, socialism, state control of the media, an enriched oligarchy at the expense of the majority of poor Egyptians, the crushing of dissent, and a litany of human rights abuses. But in spite of all this, Mubarak has also been a "close and important ally" of the United States.

The country of Egypt received over $1.5 billion in foreign aid last year. And that was lower than what it usually averages. Aid to Egypt peaked in 2002, when the country received over $2 billion in foreign aid. The only country that receives more U.S. foreign aid is Israel. Since their peace accord in 1979, Egypt and Israel have been the top two recipients of U.S. foreign aid. The two countries together account for about one-third of all foreign aid spending, the majority of which pays for armaments. It is not just demonstrators that can be seen in Egypt. M1A1 American Abrams tanks and tear gas canisters stamped "Made in America" can be seen in the streets of Cairo while American F-16s fly overhead. Much of Egypt's officer corps has been educated at American war colleges.

How many Americans have only just now realized that the United States has been a supporter of oppressive dictatorships in the Middle East? How many Americans have only just now realized that their tax dollars have been supporting the police state that is the Mubarak regime? How many Americans still don't know these things? And even worse, how many Americans do know about these things and either don't care or don't have a problem with them?

U.S. foreign policy is a tangled web of contradictions, lies, incompetence, and incoherence. The United States condemns autocratic rulers and human rights abuses in one country while at the same time supporting or turning a blind eye to autocratic rulers and human rights abuses in another. Every country is in some way vital to American interests. Every conflict is in some way relevant to our national security. Intervention in the affairs of other countries in one form or another has been the historic and customary approach. Neutrality, it seems, is never an option. Not only is our reckless and meddling foreign policy very costly, it often results in hatred of Americans and acts of terrorism toward the United States.

The federal government provides some form of foreign assistance to over 150 countries. Since World War II, our government has dispensed hundreds of billions of dollars in foreign aid in the form of cash, construction projects, food, medicine, armaments, subsidized loans, humanitarian and disaster relief, security guarantees, and peacekeeping forces. We extend foreign aid to corrupt regimes, countries that regularly vote against us in the United Nations, countries that are not "developing" countries, and countries on both sides of conflicts. Political alignment is the main determinant of foreign aid spending. Foreign aid is really just an elaborate system of bribes and rewards. Yet, foreign aid enjoys bipartisan support in Congress. Even Republicans who tout their "conservative" credentials often dismiss spending on foreign aid because, so they say, it is an insignificant part of the federal budget or an infinitesimal percentage of GDP.

Writing in the neoconservative *Weekly Standard* soon after the 9/11 attacks, CFR Senior Fellow Max Boot maintained that rather than the attack being a "payback for American imperialism," it "was a result of insufficient American involvement and ambition; the solution is to be more expansive in our goals and more assertive in their implementation." Compare this with the sentiments of the twentieth century's greatest proponent of liberty and opponent of the state, Murray Rothbard: " Empirically, taking the twentieth century as a whole, the single most warlike, most interventionist, most imperialist government has been the United States."

So who is right? For the answer we need look no further than Thomas Jefferson:

No one nation has a right to sit in judgment over another.

I am for free commerce with all nations, political connection with none, and little or no diplomatic establishment.

We ask for peace and justice from all nations; and we will remain uprightly neutral in fact.

U.S. foreign policy should be one of peace, neutrality, commerce, and nonintervention instead of one of threats, alliances, sanctions, and meddling. Rothbard's plan to restore U.S. foreign policy to what it should be is threefold: "abandon its policy of global interventionism," "withdraw immediately and completely, militarily and politically, from everywhere," and "maintain a policy of strict political 'isolation' or neutrality everywhere." Sounds Jeffersonian to me.

Foreign aid should really be called foreign government aid. The U.S. government doesn't divide the foreign aid for a particular country by the population and send a check for an equal amount to each person. God only knows what percentage of foreign aid actually makes it to foreign peoples in real need instead of lining the pockets of foreign regimes that are corrupt, bureaucratic, interventionist, socialist, and statist to the core. Foreign aid is further camouflaged as U.S. support for the UN, IMF, World Bank, and similar globalist organizations. And although I don't support any form of welfare spending in the United States, it still doesn't make any sense for the U.S. government to send taxpayer money overseas when it could be used here to alleviate poverty, help the unemployed, and invest in education and infrastructure. Don't get me wrong, *I don't support the federal government doing any of these things*, but at least they would provide more of a benefit to Americans than lining the pockets of some miscreant regime like Mubarak's.

The main problem, of course, is that foreign aid is nothing more than the forced looting of American taxpayers. The purpose, recipient, cost, and benefit of the aid are irrelevant. Foreign aid money is simply appropriated by Congress and then confiscated from American taxpayers. If a Jewish American objects to his money being taken from him and given to the government of a Muslim country, then he has no say in the matter. If a Gentile American objects to his money being taken from him and given to the government of Israel (the greatest recipient of U.S. aid), then he is out of luck. If an American objects to his money being taken from him and given to foreigners, then he can't do anything about it. If there is any doubt that the vast majority of Americans oppose foreign aid, then consider what would happen if all the countries in the world that receive U.S. foreign aid instead sent a letter appealing for funds to every American taxpayer. Is there any doubt that they would not receive enough money to cover what they spent on postage?

The bizarre U.S. foreign policy in relation to Egypt is but the tip of the iceberg. Beneath the surface is a foreign policy that is about as far removed from the noninterventionism of the Founders and the early history of our republic as could possible be. It is imperative that the mess that is U.S. foreign policy be cleaned up. And it is just as important to end all foreign aid to Egypt and all the other countries that receive it.

Will the events in Egypt be a wake-up call that results in significant change to U.S. foreign policy or will they lead to more acts of folly, more money thrown away, and more intervention on behalf of the United States?

Because Congress usually leaves foreign policy matters to the president, the prospects of returning to a foreign policy of neutrality and nonintervention don't look good. Since the end of the Cold War we have had two Democratic (Clinton & Obama) and two Republican (Bush & Bush) presidents. There is no perceptible difference in their foreign policies.

In the last presidential election, there was only one candidate from either party who philosophically, consistently, and openly called for dismantling the U.S. empire, closing foreign military bases, withdrawing U.S. troops, terminating foreign aid, and stopping the endless cycle of folly that is U.S. foreign policy. Nothing short of a Ron Paul revolution in foreign policy will bring about any real, lasting, and needed change.

* * * * *

TWO WRONGS ON LIBYA WON'T MAKE A RIGHT

Since the day President Obama began his military escapade against Libya on March 19, members of Congress have expressed indignation because they were not consulted. Not, mind you, because they necessarily oppose any of the wars the United States has been or is currently involved in, but because they were not asked to sign off on the military action.

Now, over three months and hundreds of millions of dollars later, Congress is beginning to take action. But is that a good thing?

House Speaker John Boehner sent a letter to the president warning him that he was out of time under the War Powers Act that says the president must terminate a military mission ninety days after notifying Congress that troops have been deployed into some hostility.

Boehner also says that the president lacks the support of members of the House for authorizing the Libyan military operation.

Several House members are backing measures to cut off funds for the Libyan intervention (with exceptions, of course).

Ten lawmakers (seven Republicans and three Democrats) have filed a lawsuit asking a judge to order the president to pull out of the Libya campaign because Congress didn't authorize it.

A bipartisan resolution in the Senate would allow the Libyan operation to continue for one year.

A similar resolution has also been introduced in the House, along with another resolution that would require withdrawal of U.S. forces from the Libyan operation within fifteen days of passage.

The White House has issued a report asserting the president's authority to continue the Libyan military intervention without congressional approval because American involvement falls short of full-blown hostilities.

Congress, of course, is right in insisting that it is the governmental body that should make the decision to go to war. Something called the Constitution says so. The fact that the Obama administration refuses to call its Libyan foray a war while U.S. drones fire missiles into Libya is ludicrous. Any missile fired by any country at the United States would be considered an act of war.

But Congress errs in two respects.

First, a congressional authorization to use force is not a constitutional declaration of war.

The United States has declared war on other countries only eleven times encompassing five conflicts: Great Britain in 1812 (the War of 1812), Mexico in 1848 (the Mexican War), Spain in 1898 (the Spanish-American War), Germany and Austria-Hungary in 1917 (World War I), and Japan, Germany, and Italy in 1941 and Bulgaria, Hungary, and Romania in 1942 (World War II).

Although the United States has fought many wars and undertaken scores more military interventions since World War II, we haven't actually declared war on a country since that "good war." Congress has instead abrogated its responsibility and issued congressional authorizations for the president to use force: Eisenhower in 1955 (Taiwan) and 1957 (the Middle East), Kennedy in 1962 (Cuba and Berlin), Johnson in 1965 (Vietnam), George H.W. Bush in 1991 (Iraq), and George W. Bush in 2001 (Afghanistan) and 2002 (Iraq).

Sometimes Congress hasn't issued anything, like when Truman fought a full-scale war in Korea in the early 1950s, Eisenhower sent Marines to Lebanon in 1958, Johnson sent Marines to the Dominican Republic in 1965, Nixon invaded Cambodia in 1970, Reagan invaded Grenada in 1983, Bush invaded Panama in 1989, and Clinton sent troops to Bosnia in 1995 and Kosovo in 1999.

And then there are all the other cases of the misuse of the military during and after the Cold War.

But second, and more important, two wrongs on Libya won't make a right.

Even if the president came to Congress and Congress voted to approve of military action in Libya, issue an authorization to use military force, or declare war on Libya—the president's military action in Libya would still be unconstitutional, hypocritical, and wrong.

Where in the Constitution does it authorize the U.S. government to intervene militarily in other countries? The preamble to the Constitution says that one reason the Constitution was "ordained and established" was to "provide for the common defense." To this end, Article I, section 8, of the Constitution gives Congress the power to "raise and support Armies," "provide and maintain a Navy," "make Rules for the Government and Regulation of the land and naval Forces," "provide for calling forth the Militia to execute the Laws of the Union, suppress Insurrections and repel Invasions," and "provide for organizing, arming, and disciplining, the Militia." Getting involved in foreign wars was anathema to the Framers. What does intervening in Libya have to do with providing for the common defense of the United States? Absolutely nothing, of course. The president doesn't even claim it does. Our military mission in Libya is supposed to be to protect civilians, provide humanitarian assistance, and—whether publicly admitted or not—further our diplomatic goal of regime change.

It is the height of hypocrisy for the U.S. government to intervene militarily in Libya for humanitarian concerns. Why Libya and not China? Doesn't China limit its families to having one child? Hasn't this also resulted in countless numbers of abortions, some of them forced? And where was the United States when Chairman Mao was killing his millions? Why Libya and not Saudi Arabia? Women in Saudi Arabia are not allowed to drive a car. Shouldn't we liberate Saudi women from such a blatant violation of their human rights? And where was our humanitarian concern when it came to Darfur and Rwanda? Thousands would still be alive if we had sent in the Marines. And what about when Stalin built the White Sea Canal with slave labor? Where was our humanitarian concern when he worked tens of thousands to their deaths? The terrible truth is that U.S. government humanitarian concerns are very selective. And, of course, untold multitudes of people are poor, oppressed, hungry, persecuted, and in danger all over the world right now. The United States can't possibly alleviate all the suffering and injustice in the world.

But not only can't the United States alleviate all the suffering and injustice in the world, it is neither the purpose of the U.S. military or the U.S. government to do so even if it were possible. Although it would be a terrible thing if Gaddafi imprisoned, beat, starved, tortured, enslaved, or killed any of the Libyan people, it is not the business of the United States.

And the same is true if any other dictator or oppressive regime did the same thing. Individual Americans may be outraged, but that still doesn't make it the business of the U.S. government and its military. And what if more Americans than are outraged are either sympathetic or indifferent? What then? The United States is not morally obligated to intervene in any country, militarily or otherwise. Americans who are troubled over injustice and oppression throughout the world have several options. They can financially support resistance movements or, as the case may be, relief efforts. They can go and fight or provide humanitarian aid themselves. They can pray for the oppressive regime to fall and/or for the safety of children, refugees, or civilians in harm's way. If they feel that strongly, they should do all these things. But one thing they shouldn't do is expect other Americans to pay for it in blood and treasure through government intervention.

Needless to say, the United States should cease any and all military activity, directly or indirectly, that relates to Libya. And while we're at it, stop meddling and intervening in the rest of the world as well. The United States is not the world's policeman, fireman, security guard, or social worker, whether Congress affirms it or not. Two wrongs won't make a right.

* * * * *

WHY THEY HATE US

"Today, our fellow citizens, our way of life, our very freedom came under attack in a series of deliberate and deadly terrorist acts. . . . America was targeted for attack because we're the brightest beacon for freedom and opportunity in the world." ~ George W. Bush, address to the nation, September 11, 2001

"They hate our freedoms: our freedom of religion, our freedom of speech, our freedom to vote and assemble and disagree with each other." ~ George W. Bush, address to Congress, September 20, 2001

Of all the lies of the Bush administration used to justify the wars in Iraq and Afghanistan, this one has proven to be the most enduring—and the most wrong.

According to a 2004 report on strategic communication prepared by the Defense Science Board Task Force, "a federal advisory committee established to provide independent advice to the secretary of defense":

American direct intervention in the Muslim World has paradoxi-
cally elevated the stature of and support for radical Islamists, while
diminishing support for the United States to single-digits in some
Arab societies.

Muslims do not "hate our freedom," but rather, they hate our
policies. The overwhelming majority voice their objections to what
they see as one-sided support in favor of Israel and against
Palestinian rights, and the longstanding, even increasing support
for what Muslims collectively see as tyrannies, most notably
Egypt, Saudi Arabia, Jordan, Pakistan, and the Gulf states.

Furthermore, in the eyes of Muslims, American occupation of
Afghanistan and Iraq has not led to democracy there, but only
more chaos and suffering. U.S. actions appear in contrast to be
motivated by ulterior motives, and deliberately controlled in order
to best serve American national interests at the expense of truly
Muslim selfdetermination.

Therefore, the dramatic narrative since 9/11 has essentially borne
out the entire radical Islamist bill of particulars. American actions
and the flow of events have elevated the authority of the Jihadi
insurgents and tended to ratify their legitimacy among Muslims.
Fighting groups portray themselves as the true defenders of an
Ummah (the entire Muslim community) invaded and under
attack—to broad public support.

A 2006 National Intelligence Estimate concluded that the war in Iraq
increased the threat of terrorism rather than reduced it. "Trends in Global
Terrorism: Implications for the United States" points out the "centrality"
of the U.S. invasion of Iraq in fomenting terrorist cells and attacks and
describes how the American presence in Iraq has helped spread radical
Islam by providing a focal point for anti-Americanism.

According to Michael Scheuer, who headed the CIA's bin Laden
unit from 1996 to 1999: "In the long run, we're not safer because we're
still operating on the assumption that we're hated because of our
freedoms, when in fact we're hated because of our actions in the Islamic
world. There's our military presence in Islamic countries, the perception
that we control the Muslim world's oil production, our support for Israel
and for countries that oppress Muslims such as China, Russia, and India,
and our own support for Arab tyrannies."

Peter Bergen, who produced the first television interview with
Osama Bin Laden in 1997, says "that in all the tens of thousands of words

uttered by bin Laden, he was strangely silent about American freedoms and values. He didn't seem to care very much about the beliefs of the 'crusaders.' His focus was invariably on U.S. foreign policy in the Middle East."

Political scientist James Payne, in a review of twenty-four official pronouncements of Osama bin Laden from 1994-2004, found that 72 percent of the content amounted to "criticism of the United States and other Western countries for their aggression against Muslim lands and the need to defend against and punish this aggression." Only 1 percent criticized American culture or the American way of life.

If we really want to know why American is hated by terrorists, insurgents, jihadists, militants, and Islamofascists, then we should just ask them. Actually, we don't even need to ask, just listen.

Listen to Osama bin Laden, the late leader of al-Qaeda. First, from his 1996 fatwa:

> It should not be hidden from you that the people of Islam had suffered from aggression, iniquity and injustice imposed on them by the Zionist-Crusaders alliance and their collaborators; to the extent that the Muslims blood became the cheapest and their wealth as loot in the hands of the enemies. Their blood was spilled in Palestine and Iraq. The horrifying pictures of the massacre of Qana, in Lebanon are still fresh in our memory. Massacres in Tajakestan, Burma, Cashmere, Assam, Philippine, Fatani, Ogadin, Somalia, Erithria, Chechnia and in Bosnia-Herzegovina took place, massacres that send shivers in the body and shake the conscience. All of this and the world watch and hear, and not only didn't respond to these atrocities, but also with a clear conspiracy between the USA and its' allies and under the cover of the iniquitous United Nations, the dispossessed people were even prevented from obtaining arms to defend themselves.

> The latest and the greatest of these aggressions, incurred by the Muslims since the death of the Prophet (ALLAH'S BLESSING AND SALUTATIONS ON HIM) is the occupation of the land of the two Holy Places—the foundation of the house of Islam, the place of the revelation, the source of the message and the place of the noble Ka'ba, the Qiblah of all Muslims—by the armies of the American Crusaders and their allies.

Second, from his 1997 CNN interview:

> We declared jihad against the US government, because the US

government is unjust, criminal and tyrannical. It has committed acts that are extremely unjust, hideous and criminal, whether directly or through its support of the Israeli occupation of the Prophet's Night Travel Land.

A reaction might take place as a result of the US government's hitting Muslim civilians and executing more than 600,000 Muslim children in Iraq by preventing food and medicine from reaching them. So, the US is responsible for any reaction, because it extended its war against troops to civilians.

And third, from his 1998 fatwa:

The Arabian Peninsula has never—since God made it flat, created its desert, and encircled it with seas—been stormed by any forces like the crusader armies spreading in it like locusts, eating its riches and wiping out its plantations. All this is happening at a time in which nations are attacking Muslims like people fighting over a plate of food. In the light of the grave situation and the lack of support, we and you are obliged to discuss current events, and we should all agree on how to settle the matter.

No one argues today about three facts that are known to everyone; we will list them, in order to remind everyone:

First, for over seven years the United States has been occupying the lands of Islam in the holiest of places, the Arabian Peninsula, plundering its riches, dictating to its rulers, humiliating its people, terrorizing its neighbors, and turning its bases in the Peninsula into a spearhead through which to fight the neighboring Muslim peoples.

If some people have in the past argued about the fact of the occupation, all the people of the Peninsula have now acknowledged it. The best proof of this is the Americans' continuing aggression against the Iraqi people using the Peninsula as a staging post, even though all its rulers are against their territories being used to that end, but they are helpless.

Second, despite the great devastation inflicted on the Iraqi people by the crusader-Zionist alliance, and despite the huge number of those killed, which has exceeded 1 million ... despite all this, the Americans are once against trying to repeat the horrific massacres, as though they are not content with the protracted blockade imposed after the ferocious war or the fragmentation and devastation.

So here they come to annihilate what is left of this people and to humiliate their Muslim neighbors.

Third, if the Americans' aims behind these wars are religious and economic, the aim is also to serve the Jews' petty state and divert attention from its occupation of Jerusalem and murder of Muslims there. The best proof of this is their eagerness to destroy Iraq, the strongest neighboring Arab state, and their endeavor to fragment all the states of the region such as Iraq, Saudi Arabia, Egypt, and Sudan into paper statelets and through their disunion and weakness to guarantee Israel's survival and the continuation of the brutal crusade occupation of the Peninsula.

All these crimes and sins committed by the Americans are a clear declaration of war on God, his messenger, and Muslims. And ulema have throughout Islamic history unanimously agreed that the jihad is an individual duty if the enemy destroys the Muslim countries.

The ruling to kill the Americans and their allies—civilians and military—is an individual duty for every Muslim who can do it in any country in which it is possible to do it, in order to liberate the al-Aqsa Mosque and the holy mosque [Mecca] from their grip, and in order for their armies to move out of all the lands of Islam, defeated and unable to threaten any Muslim.

Because of the many undocumented statements that have been attributed to bin Laden since 9/11, I have deliberately not included any of his purported post-9/11 statements.

Listen to Ramzi Yousef, convicted of bombing the World Trade Center in 1993, and now serving a life sentence. From his January 8, 1998, court appearance:

You keep talking also about collective punishment and killing innocent people to force governments to change their policies; you call this terrorism when someone would kill innocent people or civilians in order to force the government to change its policies. Well, when you were the first one who invented this terrorism.

You were the first one who killed innocent people, and you are the first one who introduced this type of terrorism to the history of mankind when you dropped an atomic bomb which killed tens of thousands of women and children in Japan and when you killed over a hundred thousand people, most of them civilians, in Tokyo with fire bombings. You killed them by burning them to death. And you killed civilians in Vietnam with chemicals as with the so-called Orange agent. You killed civilians and innocent people, not soldiers, innocent people every single war you went. You went to wars more than any other country in this century, and then you have the nerve to talk about killing innocent people.

And now you have invented new ways to kill innocent people. You have so-called economic embargo which kills nobody other than children and elderly people, and which other than Iraq you have been placing the economic embargo on Cuba and other countries for over 35 years.

The Government in its summations and opening statement said that I was a terrorist. Yes, I am a terrorist and I am proud of it. And I support terrorism so long as it was against the United States Government and against Israel, because you are more than terrorists; you are the one who invented terrorism and using it every day. You are butchers, liars and hypocrites.

Yousef and his co-conspirators (Mohammed Salameh, Nidal Ayyad, Mahmud Abouhalima, Ahmad Ajaj, and Abdul Rahman Yasin) sent a letter to the *New York Times* after the bombing that spelled out their motive:

We are, the fifth battalion in the LIBERATION ARMY, declare our responsibility for the explosion on the mentioned building. This action was done in response for the American political, economical, and military support to Israel the state of terrorism and to the rest of the dictator countries in the region.

OUR DEMANDS ARE:

1—Stop all military, economical, and political aid to Israel.

2—All diplomatic relations with Israel must stop.

3—Not to interfere with any of the Middle East countries interior affairs.

IF our demands are not met, all of our functional groups in the army will continue to execute our missions against the military and

civilian targets in and out the United States. For your own information, our army has more than hundred and fifty suicidal soldiers
ready to go ahead. The terrorism that Israel practices (Which is
supported by America) must be faced with a similar one. The
dictatorship and terrorism also supported by America) that some
countries are practicing against their own people must also be
faced with terrorism.

The American people must know, that their civilians who got
killed are not better than those who are getting killed by the
American weapons and support.

The American people are responsible for the actions of their
government and they must question all of the crimes that their
government is committing against other people. Or they—
Americans—will be the targets of our operations that could
diminish them.

LIBERATION ARMY, FIFTH BATTALION

Listen to Richard Reid, the convicted "shoe bomber." From his
2003 court appearance:

With regards to what you said about killing innocent people, I will
say one thing. Your government has killed 2 million children in
Iraq. OK? If you want to think about something, 20 against 2
million, I don't see no comparison. OK?

Your government has sponsored the rape and torture of Muslims in
the prisons of Egypt and Turkey and Syria and Jordan with their
money and with their weapons. OK? I don't know, see what I done
as being equal to rape and to torture, or to the deaths of the 2
million children in Iraq. OK? So for this reason, I think I ought not
apologize for my actions.

I am at war with your country. I'm at war with them not for
personal reasons but because they have murdered so many children
and they have oppressed my religion and they have oppressed
people for no reason except that they say we believe in Allah. This
is the only reason that America sponsors Egypt. It's the only reason
they sponsor Turkey. It's the only reason they back Israel. OK?

Listen to Faisal Shahzad, the Times Square car bomber. First, from
his June 21, 2010 court appearance:

I want to plead guilty and I'm going to plead guilty a hundred times forward because until the hour the US pulls it forces from Iraq and Afghanistan and stops the drone strikes in Somalia and Yemen and in Pakistan and stops the occupation of Muslim lands and stops killing the Muslims and stops reporting the Muslims to its government, we will be attacking US, and I plead guilty to that.

Well, I am part of that. I am part of the answer to the US terrorizing the Muslim nations and the Muslim people, and on behalf of that, I'm avenging the attacks, because only—like living in US, the Americans only care about their people, but they don't care about the people elsewhere in the world when they die.

And second, from his October 5, 2010, court appearance:

My statement should take about five minutes to ten minutes, and I hope that the judge and the Court will listen to me before they sentence me. In the name of Allah, the most gracious, the most merciful, this is but one life. If I am given a thousand lives, I will sacrifice them all for the sake of Allah fighting this cause, defending our lands, making the word of Allah supreme over any religion or system. We Muslims don't abide by human-made laws, because they are always corrupt. And I had a firsthand experience when on the second day of my arrest I asked for the Miranda. And the FBI denied it to me for two weeks, effecting harm to my kids and family, and I was forced to sign those Mirandas. The sentence by the judge will not mean anything to me, for how can I be judged when the Court does not understand the suffering of my people. They don't understand my side of the story, where the Muslim life of is no value. Therefore, the only true judgment will be on the day of resurrection when Allah will judge between me and you as to who is fighting for the just cause. So decree whatever you desire to decree, for you can only decree regarding the life of this world. The crusading U.S. and NATO forces who have occupied the Muslim lands under the pretext of democracy and freedom for the last nine years and are saying with their mouths that they are fighting terrorism, I say to them, we don't accept your democracy nor your freedom, because we already have Sharia law and freedom. Furthermore, brace yourselves, because the war with Muslims has just begun. Consider me only a first droplet of the flood that will follow me. And only this time it's not imperial Japan or Germany, Vietnam or Russian communism. This time it's the war against people who believe in the book of Allah and follow the commandments, so this is a war against Allah. So let's see how you can defeat your Creator, which you can never do. Therefore, the defeat of U.S. is imminent and will happen in the near future, inshallah, which will only give rise to much awaited Muslim caliphate, which is the only true world order. Soon the bailout money which is holding your fragile economy will run out and soon you will not be able to afford the war costs.

So, the past nine years the war with Muslims has achieved nothing for the U.S., except for it has waken up the Muslims for Islam. We are only Muslims trying to defend our, people, honor, and land. But if you call us terrorists for doing that, then we are proud terrorists, and we will keep on terrorizing until you leave our land and people at peace. But if you don't, then I remind you that we have watches and we have time. We will defeat you with time.

Listen to Najibullah Zazi, who pled guilty to conspiring to undertake a suicide attack on the New York subway system. From his 2010 court appearance: "I would sacrifice myself to bring attention to what the United States military was doing to civilians in Afghanistan by sacrificing my soul for the sake of saving other souls."

Listen to Anwar al-Awlaki, an American citizen living in Yemen. From his 2010 "Call to Jihad":

We the Muslims do not have an inherent animosity towards any racial group or ethnicity. We are not against Americans for just being Americans. We are against evil and America as a whole has turned into a nation of evil. What we see from America is the invasion of [inaudible] countries, we see Abu Ghraib, Baghram and Guantanamo Bay, we see cruise missiles and cluster bombs and we have just seen in Yemen the death of 23 children and 17 women. We cannot stand idly in the face of such aggression and we will fight back and incite others to do the same.

I for one was born in the U.S., I lived in the U.S. for 21 years. America was my home. I was a preacher of Islam involved in non-violent Islamic activism. However, with the American invasion of Iraq and continued U.S. aggression against Muslims I could not reconcile between living in the U.S. and being a Muslim.

And finally, listen to a statement from al-Qaeda's American-born spokesman, Adam Gadahn, released last year:

The fact is, Barack, if you ever decide to get serious about improving America's security, protecting the American people and preventing a sharp rise in the number of American casualties at home and abroad and in the air, at sea and on land, then there are a number of simple, sound and effective steps which you can take which can go a long way towards achieving those goals. The Muslim Mujahideen defending their faith and brethren against your nation's evildoing have repeatedly made clear these steps, but because I suspect you have been living in the ivory tower and information vacuum in which arrogant Washington insiders like you often live, I shall summarize these steps here. I strongly suggest you heed and implement them, for your own good and the good of your people.

First, you must pull every last one of your soldiers, spies, security advisors, trainers, attaches, contractors, robots, drones and all other American personnel, ships and aircraft out of every Muslim land from Afghanistan to Zanzibar.

Second, you must end all support—both moral and material—to Israel and bar your citizens from traveling to Occupied Palestine or settling there, and you must impose a blanket ban on American trade with the Zionist regime and investment in it. Your security will not be improved by empty threats like those your special envoy made about the possible suspension of American loans, in and of itself a largely meaningless gesture. As Shaykh Usama told you, if you don't heed our warnings and stop your support of Israel, we will have no choice but to continue to use other ways to get our message across.

Third, you must stop all support and aid—be it military, political, economic or otherwise—to the hated regimes of the Muslim world. This includes the so-called "development aid" which your secretary of state recently identified as being one of the most important elements of future American efforts to combat the Islamic renaissance and Jihadi awakening sweeping the Muslim world.

Fourth, you must cease all interference in the religion, society, politics, economy and government of the Islamic world. This means putting an immediate stop to the deployment of your economic hit men, CIA jackals, Peace Corps volunteers, USAID employees, and UN-and-US-sponsored non-governmental organizations, all of which, put together, represent the vanguard of American interference in our region and the world.

Fifth, you must also put an end to all forms of American and American sponsored interference in the educational curricula and information media of the Muslim world, and you must end all broadcasts targeting our region, especially those designed to alter or destroy the faith, minds, morals and values of our Muslim people.

And sixth, you must free all Muslim captives from your prisons, detention facilities and concentration camps, regardless of whether they have been recipients of what you call a "fair" trial or not. As our heroic brother Abu Dujaanah al-Khorasaani told you with his words and actions, we will never forget our prisoners.

Instead of listening or asking questions, the reaction of the United States has been bomb first, don't listen or ask questions, and then bomb later—and invade, occupy, torture, maim, kill, incarcerate, rendition, assassinate, and destroy property and infrastructure. And as Glenn Greenwald recently pointed out:

The fact that victims of American violence over the last two decades have easily outweighed, and continue to outweigh, those of the Dictators and Terrorists whom we so vocally despise is nonetheless an extremely important fact that should shape our understanding of 9/11.

The cry of the Muslim masses in Tunisia, Egypt, Libya, and elsewhere in the Middle East was not for Islamofascism, global Islamic conquest, a global Caliphate, the worldwide establishment of Sharia law, a new holocaust, suicide bombers, and terrorists attacks, but for more freedom—something they supposedly hate us for.

Muslims seem to be more interested in killing other Muslims than in killing Americans who aren't bombing and occupying their countries—just look at the history of Sunni versus Shiite violence since Muhammad died in 632 and a disagreement ensued over whom should be his successor.

The U.S. government has learned absolutely nothing since 9/11. Instead of the occasion being a time to reassess a century of bad foreign policy, it was used as an excuse to start two wars against countries that had nothing to do with 9/11 and accelerate the destruction of American freedoms. And now, ten years later, the anniversary of 9/11 will be used to lionize the police state, the warfare state, and the national security state while justifying even more wars.

The U.S. foreign policy is an abomination in the sight of God, and I don't mean Allah.

* * * * *

KOREA SHOWS ALL THAT IS WRONG WITH U.S. FOREIGN POLICY

The tension on the Korean peninsula escalated late last year when South Korea began live-firing drills off its coastline. That was after North and South Korea shelled each other for the first time since the 1953 armistice that ended the Korean War. U.S. forces in the area went on high alert even as the nuclear-powered aircraft carrier USS *George Washington* joined South Korean naval forces in exercises in the Yellow Sea. That carrier had just concluded drills with Japan involving 400 aircraft, 60 warships, and more than 40,000 U.S. and Japanese troops. South Korea was an official observer during the drills.

Korea shows all that is wrong with U.S. foreign policy.

After World War II, the United States and its allies—against the wishes of most Koreans—divided the country at the 38th parallel. After North Korea invaded the South in 1950, Harry Truman intervened with U.S. combat troops in a "police action." The result was the senseless death of more than 36,000 American soldiers for Truman's foolish policies, for the United Nations, for the failed diplomacy of World War II, and for the division of Korea in the same place it was divided before the war started. Since that time, a day has not gone by when the United States has not had thousands of troops stationed in South Korea, some no doubt the grandchildren of the soldiers who fought in the Korean War. There are at least 25,000 U.S. soldiers currently in Korea. There are also more than 35,000 U.S. troops stationed in Japan.

There was no U.S. declaration of war against North Korea. On five different occasions, the United States has declared war on a total of eleven other countries: Great Britain in 1812 (the War of 1812), Mexico in 1848 (the Mexican War), Spain in 1898 (the Spanish-American War), Germany and Austria-Hungary in 1917 (World War I), Japan, Germany, and Italy in 1941 (World War II), and Bulgaria, Hungary, and Romania in 1942 (World War II).

Only a few Republicans in Congress dared to object to Truman's clearly unconstitutional intervention in Korea. Most notable was Sen. Robert Taft, who maintained, "The president is usurping his powers as commander in chief. There is no legal authority for what he has done. If the president can intervene in Korea without congressional approval, he can go to war in Malaya or Indonesia or Iran or South America." The Korean intervention set a terrible precedent, for no declaration of war has ever been issued since, even though the United States has been involved in many military conflicts since then, some of them being major wars, such as Vietnam, Iraq, and Afghanistan.

The personal army

But not only was there no declaration of war in Korea, there was not even a congressional authorization to use force. Such a resolution has been issued eight times in U.S. history: under Eisenhower in 1955 and 1957 to defend Formosa and check Soviet expansionism in the Middle East; twice under Kennedy in 1962 in response to the threat of Cuban communism and the crisis in Berlin; the infamous 1964 Tonkin Gulf Resolution under Johnson; under Bush the elder in 1991 when he ordered the first U.S. invasion of Iraq; and twice under Bush the younger for launching the Afghanistan war in 2001 and the Iraq war in 2002. The lack of any congressional authorization for the Korean conflict shows that U.S. foreign policy is really at the whim of whoever is the president. Americans are expected to support or demonize a country at the word of the president.

The lack of any congressional input in the decision to go to war in Korea signals the beginning of the U.S. military as merely the president's personal army, as Jacob Hornberger has pointed out:

> Thus, as a practical matter the troops serve not as a defender of our freedoms but instead simply as a loyal and obedient personal army of the president, ready and prepared to serve him and obey his commands. It is an army that stands ready to obey the president's orders to deploy to any country in the world for any reason he deems fit and attack, kill, and maim any "terrorist" who dares to resist the U.S. invasion of his own country. It is also an army that stands ready to obey the president's orders to take into custody any American whom the commander in chief deems a "terrorist" and to punish him accordingly.

The misuse of the military since the Korean War is so prevalent and wide-ranging that the majority of what the military now does has nothing to do with the defense of *this* country and everything to do with intervening in *foreign* countries. The U.S. military performs most of its duties outside the United States providing disaster relief, dispensing humanitarian aid, supplying peacekeepers, enforcing UN resolutions, nation-building, spreading "goodwill," launching preemptive strikes, establishing democracy, changing regimes, assassinating people, training armies, rebuilding infrastructure, reviving public services, "opening markets," maintaining no-fly zones, occupying countries, and, of course, fighting foreign wars.

The U.S. military should be engaged exclusively in defending the United States, not defending other countries, and certainly not attacking, invading, or occupying them. Using the military for any purpose other than the actual defense of the United States perverts the purpose of the military.

The misuse of the military results in needless deaths of U.S. soldiers. The most unnecessary job in the world is that of the Casualty Assistance Calls Officer, who must go knocking with a message that no military family wants to hear. In addition to the more than 36,000 soldiers lost in Korea, there are the more than 58,000 soldiers who lost their lives in Vietnam, and the more than 4,450 soldiers in Iraq and 1,750 in Afghanistan who paid the ultimate price fighting in those places. Every one of those deaths was unnecessary and preventable and can be charged to a reckless and meddling U.S. foreign policy.

Where the boys are

The continued U.S. military presence in South Korea with thousands of troops at 87 different sites (if you include golf courses) is but a small part of the U.S. global empire of troops and bases. According to the Department of Defense's "Base Structure Report" for FY 2009, there are 716 U.S. military bases on foreign soil in 38 countries. Yet, according to the expert on this subject, the late Chalmers Johnson, that number is actually closer to 1,000 because "the official figures omit espionage bases, those located in war zones, including Iraq and Afghanistan, and miscellaneous facilities in places considered too sensitive to discuss or which the Pentagon for its own reasons chooses to exclude—e.g., in Israel, Kosovo, or Jordan." This same report lists the DOD's physical assets as "more than 539,000 facilities (buildings, structures and linear structures) located on more than 5,570 sites, on approximately 29 million acres."

But not only does the United States have thousands of troops in South Korea, Japan, Germany, and Italy decades after World War II and Korea, there are, according to the DOD report titled "Active Duty Military Personnel Strengths by Regional Area and by Country," U.S. troops stationed in 147 countries and 11 territories in every corner of the globe. That means that U.S. troops have a presence in more than 75 percent of the world's countries. All told, there are more than 300,000 U.S. troops in foreign countries—not counting the 50,000 troops in and around Iraq in support of Operation Iraqi Freedom or the 100,000 troops in and around Afghanistan in support of Operation Enduring Freedom. Those numbers would be even higher were it not for the thousands of DOD contractors.

The United States is committed to the defense not only of South Korea, but of many other countries as well, thanks to various security alliances and bilateral agreements. That, in spite of the warnings of Washington and Jefferson to stand clear of permanent and entangling alliances.

The real issue about Korea, as Congressman Ron Paul recently explained, is that "the American taxpayer is still forced to pay for the U.S. military to defend a modern and wealthy South Korea." According to the CIA, the economy of South Korea is 34 times larger than the centrally planned economy of its northern neighbor. South Korea has twice the population of North Korea. Per capita GDP in the South is 15 times what it is in the North. North Korea faces chronic shortages of food and fuel and its "industrial capital stock is nearly beyond repair as a result of years of underinvestment and shortages of spare parts." It makes no sense, financially or otherwise, for the United States to guarantee the defense of South Korea against a country where malnutrition and poverty are the rule rather than the exception.

Korea shows all that is wrong with U.S. foreign policy: disregard for the Constitution, departure from the wisdom of the Founders, unaccountable presidential power, misuse of the military, a global empire of troops and bases, callous disregard for the lives of American soldiers, meddling in the affairs of other countries, and wasting billions of dollars taken from American taxpayers. U.S. foreign policy is hopelessly interventionist—no matter which party controls the Congress or the White House.

* * * * *

IS RON PAUL AN ISOLATIONIST?

The word *isolationist* is a pejorative term used to ridicule advocates of U.S. nonintervention in foreign affairs, intimidate their supporters, and stifle debate over U.S. foreign policy.

Throughout the twentieth century, opponents of U.S. intervention in foreign wars were smeared as isolationists.

Conservative and Republican opponents of Congressman and presidential candidate Ron Paul, although they may argue and fight among themselves, are all agreed on one thing: Ron Paul is an isolationist and espouses a dangerous foreign policy of isolationism.

Actor and conservative activist Chuck Norris insists that "Texas

Representative Ron Paul's bent toward being an isolationist who wants to bring home every one of our 572,000 troops abroad makes the anti-terror, pro-military hairs on the back of my neck stand."

Speaking in South Carolina just before Christmas, Newt Gingrich "sharply criticized Mr. Paul for what he said were his isolationist views on foreign policy."

While stumping in Iowa the week before the Iowa caucuses, Rick Santorum "urged Republicans to carefully study Mr. Paul's isolationist foreign policy views."

Tune in to the leading conservative talk-show hosts or read the comments posted by their followers on right-wing websites and you will hear and see Ron Paul regularly described as an isolationist.

Okay, so what would an isolationist America look like? What if the United States really retreated from the world stage, avoided engagement with the rest of the world, and actually did isolate itself from every other country?

Under a real foreign policy of isolationism, the United States would refuse to participate in the Olympics, refuse to make treaties, refuse to issue visas, refuse to allow foreign goods to be imported, refuse to allow U.S. goods to be exported, refuse to allow foreign students to study at American universities, refuse to allow American students to study at foreign universities, refuse to allow foreign investment, refuse to extradite criminals, refuse to exchange diplomats, refuse to allow cultural exchanges, refuse to participate in disaster-relief efforts, refuse to allow travel abroad, refuse to engage in diplomacy, refuse to deliver mail to or receive mail from foreign countries, refuse to allow emigration, and refuse to allow immigration.

Under a real policy of isolationism, living in the United States would be about as bad as living in East Germany, North Korea, or Myanmar.

Is that the kind of America that Ron Paul envisions?

The last time Ron Paul ran for president, he made it perfectly clear that he espoused anything but isolationism:

> Under a Paul administration, the United States would trade freely with any nation that seeks to engage with us. American citizens would be encouraged to visit other countries and interact with other peoples rather than be told by their own government that certain countries are off-limits to them.
>
> American citizens would be free to spend their hard-earned money wherever they wish across the globe, not told that certain countries

are under embargo and thus off limits. An American trade policy would encourage private American businesses to seek partners overseas and engage them in trade.

A Paul administration would see Americans engaged overseas like never before, in business and cultural activities.

No one has ever accused Dr. Paul of changing his position.

Why, then, is Ron Paul accused of being an isolationist? When his critics hurl this epithet at him, they know full well that he is not an isolationist at all. Here is Rick Santorum on Ron Paul's "dangerous" foreign policy: "One thing he can do as commander in chief is he can pull all our troops home. He can shut down our bases in Germany. He can shut down the bases in Japan. He can pull our fleets back." According to Santorum and his fellow conservative and Republican warmongers Gingrich, Rick Perry, Michele Bachmann, Herman Cain, Mitt Romney, Rush Limbaugh, Mark Levin, Sean Hannity, and the *Weekly Standard*, Ron Paul is an isolationist, not because he wants America to be isolated from the rest of the world, but because he wants to terminate the empire, stop fighting foreign wars, close the foreign military bases, cut the bloated military budget, end foreign aid, halt all offense spending, bring all the troops home, limit the military to the actual defense of the United States, and stop being the policeman of the world.

The foreign policy of Ron Paul is a foreign policy of noninterventionism. In a speech on the House floor several months before the United States invaded Iraq, Paul made his case for a noninterventionist foreign policy of peace, prosperity, and liberty:

> A proper foreign policy of nonintervention is built on friendship with other nations, free trade, and open travel, maximizing the exchanges of goods and services and ideas.

> We should avoid entangling alliances and stop meddling in the internal affairs of other nations—no matter how many special interests demand otherwise. The entangling alliances that we should avoid include the complex alliances in the UN, the IMF, the World Bank, and the WTO.

> The basic moral principle underpinning a noninterventionist foreign policy is that of rejecting the initiation of force against others. It is based on nonviolence and friendship unless attacked, self-determination, and self-defense while avoiding confrontation, even when we disagree with the way other countries run their

affairs. It simply means that we should mind our own business and not be influenced by special interests that have an ax to grind or benefits to gain by controlling our foreign policy. Manipulating our country into conflicts that are none of our business and unrelated to national security provides no benefits to us, while exposing us to great risks financially and militarily.

Ron Paul is merely echoing the foreign policy of Thomas Jefferson, who said,

No one nation has a right to sit in judgment over another.

We wish not to meddle with the internal affairs of any country, nor with the general affairs of Europe.

I am for free commerce with all nations, political connection with none, and little or no diplomatic establishment.

Peace, commerce, and honest friendship with all nations—entangling alliances with none.

A noninterventionist foreign policy is a policy of peace, commerce, travel, cultural exchange, diplomacy, neutrality, and free trade.

A noninterventionist foreign policy means no preemptive strikes, invasions, occupations, bombings, threats, sanctions, embargoes, foreign aid, assassinations, imperialism, meddling, bullying, regime changes, nation building, entangling alliances, spreading democracy, NATO-like commitments, peacekeeping operations, forcibly opening markets, policing the world, and no foreign military bases.

It is a sad day for America and Americans when not supporting an aggressive, belligerent, interventionist, and meddling foreign policy means that you are an isolationist.

Is Ron Paul isolationist?

Is France isolationist because its navy doesn't patrol our coasts? Is Canada isolationist because it doesn't have military bases below the 49th parallel? Is Germany isolationist because it doesn't have tens of thousands of troops stationed in the United States? Is Brazil isolationist because it doesn't kill Americans with drone strikes? Is Russia isolationist because it doesn't build military bases in scores of countries? Is Moldova isolationist because it doesn't send its soldiers to fight foreign wars? Was Ronald Reagan an isolationist because he pulled U.S. troops out of Lebanon?

Noninterventionism is not isolationism. It is practical, sane, moral, just, and right. It is the foreign policy of the Founding Fathers—and Ron Paul.

* * * * *

SUPPOSE

"My point is, if another country does to us what we do to others, we're not going to like it very much. So I would say that maybe we ought to consider a golden rule—in foreign policy. Don't do to other nations what we don't want to have them do to us." ~ Ron Paul

The war-crazed conservatives in the crowd at one of the Republican presidential debates recently held in South Carolina booed and jeered when Ron Paul called for a golden rule in U.S. foreign policy. "We endlessly bomb these other countries and then we wonder why they get upset with us?" added Dr. Paul.

Naturally, the bloodthirsty warmongers at Frontpagemag.com consider Paul's foreign policy to be absurd, dangerous, and clueless.

But just for a minute, let's suppose a few things—

Suppose that a presidential candidate in another country said that the U.S. president needs to be taken off this planet. How would Americans feel about it?

Suppose that a presidential candidate in another country said that the U.S. president would go to hell if he died. How would Americans feel about it?

Suppose that the government of another country said that the U.S. president needed to step down. How would Americans feel about it?

Suppose that the government of another country forbade its citizens from traveling to the United States. How would Americans feel about it?

Suppose that the government of another country imposed sanctions on the United States. How would Americans feel about it?

Suppose that the government of another country had a secret program to develop nuclear weapons for offensive purposes. How would Americans feel about it?

Suppose that the military of another country insisted that it had the right to build over 1,000 military bases in foreign countries. How would Americans feel about it?

Suppose that the military of another country insisted that it had the right to station hundreds of thousands of troops on foreign soil. How would Americans feel about it?

Suppose that the military of another country insisted that it had the right to build bases and station troops on American soil. How would Americans feel about it?

Suppose that the government of another country spent more on defense than all the governments of the rest of the world combined. How would Americans feel about it?

Suppose that the government of another country claimed it had the right to assassinate anyone in the United States. How would Americans feel about it?

Suppose that the intelligence agencies of another country insisted on infiltrating the U.S. government and its intelligence agencies to spy on them. How would Americans feel about it?

Suppose that the government of another country spent a trillion dollars on defense, most of which was really for offense. How would Americans feel about it?

Suppose that the government of another country said that the United States must get rid of its nuclear weapons. How would Americans feel about it?

Suppose that the military of another country bombed American soil. How would Americans feel about it?

Suppose that the military of another country invaded the United States. How would Americans feel about it?

Suppose that the military of another country occupied the United States. How would Americans feel about it?

Suppose that the president or secretary of state of another country said that the United States needed a regime change. How would Americans feel about it?

Suppose that the intelligence agencies of another country flew drone planes at will over the United States. How would Americans feel about it?

You know exactly how Americans would feel about these things. So why is it that foreigners aren't expected to feel the same way?

It is U.S. foreign policy that is absurd, dangerous, and clueless. Ron Paul is the only sane voice that one will hear in the remaining Republican presidential debates.

* * * * *

NO MORE ENTANGLING ALLIANCES

Would the United States go to war over marine life illegally harvested in the South China Sea? The very thought of such a thing sounds ludicrous. But under the U.S. Mutual Defense Treaty with the Philippines, it is a possibility.

For the past month, China and the Philippines have traded threats over a disputed area in the South China Sea after Philippine authorities seized what they said was illegally harvested marine life from Chinese ships, only to be blocked by Chinese ships when a Philippine navy warship tried to tow the Chinese vessels.

Chinese state media have talked of military action while its government has warned Chinese citizens in the Philippines that they may be at risk because of nationalistic sentiment there.

The disputed area is the resource-rich Scarborough Shoal, about 130 miles from the Philippine mainland. The group of reefs, rocks, and small islands are named after the East India Company ship *Scarborough* that was wrecked there in 1784.

China, which calls the shoal Huangyan, maintains that it has been Chinese for centuries; the Philippine government, which calls the area Panatag, claims that it has appeared as part of the Philippines on maps dating back to the 1700s.

Although State Department spokeswoman Victoria Nuland said the United States was "urging restraint from all parties" and "discouraging any kind of escalation of tensions," Secretary of State Hillary Clinton and Defense Secretary Leon Panetta—during recent talks in Washington with their Philippine counterparts—maintained that the United States was not taking sides in the territorial dispute but would honor its treaty obligations.

At the same time, U.S. troops have begun training exercises in Australia. "We have no better ally or friend in the world than Australia, and we have no area in the world which is as important or dynamic over the next 50 years as the Asia Pacific," said Jeffrey Bleich, the U.S. ambassador to Australia.

The 1951 Mutual Defense Treaty between the United States and the Philippines is a short agreement consisting of eight articles. Article IV and V read as follows:

> Article IV. Each Party recognizes that an armed attack in the Pacific area on either of the Parties would be dangerous to its own peace and safety and declares that it would act to meet the common dangers in accordance with its constitutional processes. Any such armed attack and all measures taken as a result thereof shall be immediately reported to the Security Council of the United Nations. Such measures shall be terminated when the Security

Council has taken the measures necessary to restore and maintain international peace and security.

Article V. For the purpose of Article IV, an armed attack on either of the Parties is deemed to include an armed attack on the metropolitan territory of either of the Parties, or on the island territories under its jurisdiction in the Pacific Ocean, its armed forces, public vessels or aircraft in the Pacific.

Article VIII says that the treaty "shall remain in force indefinitely," although either party may terminate it "one year after notice has been given to the other party."

The treaty clause in the U.S. Constitution (Art. II, Sec. 2, Para. 2) states that the president "shall have power by and with the advice and consent of the Senate to make treaties, provided two thirds of the Senators present concur."

Most Americans probably have no idea that such a treaty to defend the Philippines exists. But it is just one of many. The United States has similar treaties with Japan, South Korea, and Australia, as well as many "security arrangements" and "status of forces agreements" that clarify the terms under which U.S. troops are stationed in other countries.

The most well-known U.S. military alliance is the North Atlantic Treaty Organization (NATO) between the United States, Canada, Iceland, and 24 other European countries and Turkey. A few years after the fall of the Soviet Union, NATO was expanded to include 10 former members of the Warsaw Pact. That means that the United States is committed to going to war over Poland, just as the British were when they committed the greatest blunder in their history in giving Poland a "blank check" that drew them into World War II.

Military alliances are dangerous things, especially when they are misinterpreted. Article III of the Tripartite Pact of 1940 between Germany, Japan, and Italy committed the three powers "to assist one another with all political, economic, and military means if one of the Contracting Powers was attacked by a Power at present not involved in the European War or in the Japanese-Chinese conflict." On November 30, 1941, Japanese foreign minister Tojo said to Eugen Ott, the German ambassador to Japan before World War II, that "he hoped in the event of Japan being at war with the USA, Germany and Italy would, according to the Tripartite Pact, stand by her side" (Nicholas Henderson, "Hitler's Biggest Blunder," *History Today*, 43:4 [April 1993], 35–43). After Japan attacked the United States at Pearl Harbor on December 7, Germany declared war on the United States on December 11.

And of course, World War II would have never happened had it not been for World War I and the military alliances that existed among the Great Powers: the Entente cordiale between Britain and France, the Anglo-Russian Convention, and the Franco-Russian Alliance on the one hand; and the Triple Alliance of Germany, Austria-Hungary, and Italy on the other.

Although U.S. foreign policy had become increasingly intervention-ist since the Spanish-American War, the United States generally steered clear of entangling alliances until the end of World War II. That was in keeping with the insight of the Founding Fathers. In his Farewell Address, George Washington famously warned against "permanent alliances with any portion of the foreign world." He also said, "The great rule of conduct for us, in regard to foreign nations, is in extending our commercial relations to have with them as little political connection as possible." In both of those ideas he was echoed by America's third president, Thomas Jefferson:

> I am for free commerce with all nations, political connection with none, and little or no diplomatic establishment. And I am not for linking ourselves by new treaties with the quarrels of Europe, entering that field of slaughter to preserve their balance, or joining in the confederacy of Kings to war against the principles of liberty.

And most famously, from his first inaugural address of March 4, 1801, "Peace, commerce, and honest friendship with all nations—entangling alliances with none."

But the United States today is far removed from the nonintervention of the Founders. As philosopher Robert Nisbet wrote in *The Present Age* at the bicentennial of the Constitution,

> Of all faces of the present age in America, the military face would almost certainly prove the most astounding to any Framers of the Constitution, any Founders of the Republic who came back to inspect their creation on the occasion of the bicentennial.... The returned Framers would not be surprised to learn that so vast a military has inexorable effects upon the economy, the structure of government, and even the culture of Americans; they had wit-nessed such effects in Europe from afar, and had not liked what they saw. What would doubtless astonish the Framers most, though, is that their precious republic has become an imperial power in the world, much like the Great Britain they had hated in the eighteenth century....

The current U.S. foreign policy of maintaining entangling alliances is hazardous to American blood and treasure. And not just because they are all grossly one-sided (can you imagine the Philippine or Albanian navies steaming to America in the event of an attack on the United States?). Nothing that happens in the South China Sea is worth one drop of American blood or one dollar from the U.S. treasury.

Conflict, injustice, and oppression throughout the world are unfortunate things. But the United States cannot right every wrong or correct every injustice in the world. It is not the job of the United States to police the world, put out fires around the world, or be the world's hall monitor, social worker, parole officer, or peacekeeper.

* * * * *

THE JAPAN PROBLEM

There were no issues of any real substance debated by Mitt Romney and Barack Obama in the presidential campaign leading up to the recent election. With foreign wars raging, the USA PATRIOT Act and the NDAA threatening Americans' civil liberties, the police state and surveillance state increasing, drone attacks killing foreign civilians, the drug war destroying Americans' freedoms, the TSA out of control, and the imperial presidency in full force, it's not like there was nothing serious to talk about.

Instead we had to endure endless back-and-forth over how many billions of dollars Obamacare cuts or doesn't cut from Medicare and how much more each candidate wants to "invest" in the space program.

Sure, Romney talked about repealing Obamacare, but only because he wanted to replace it with Romneycare or Republicare, where it would fit nicely alongside of Bushcare.

The reason there was no real debate is that Romney and Obama are much more alike than they are different: foreign aid, foreign wars, drone strikes, targeted killings, bailouts, stimulus programs, the drug war, the police state, the welfare state, the warfare state, the national-security state, and varying degrees of socialism, corporatism, and fascism. Someone even put together a list of "100 Ways Mitt Romney Is Just Like Barack Obama."

But not only did Romney and Obama not debate any issues of substance, they each focused on an issue that was no issue at all: the Iran problem. In his 2012 State of the Union address, Obama stated, "America is determined to prevent Iran from getting a nuclear weapon, and I will take no options off the table to achieve that goal." Romney said that if you, elect *him*, "Iran will not have a nuclear weapon" because "a nuclear-armed Iran is not only a threat to Israel, it is a threat to the entire world." And should sanctions fail to halt Iran's nuclear ambitions, "there's nothing else we could do besides take military action."

All the bluster about Iran is nonsense, of course, considering that Iran (which, unlike Israel, is a signer of the nuclear Non-Proliferation Treaty) is not developing a nuclear weapon and is no threat to the United States or Israel. Even the Supreme Leader of Iran (who is *not* President Mahmoud Ahmadinejad, who leaves office next year) has said that the possession of nuclear weapons is "pointless, dangerous, and is a great sin from an intellectual and a religious point of view."

A real problem with a country that neither Romney nor Obama ever mentioned is a serious issue that has been boiling for years: the Japan problem.

Thousands of Japanese recently protested the deployment of American Osprey military aircraft on a southern Japanese island. Citing safety concerns and recent crimes committed by U.S. military personnel, protesters chanted "Ospreys out! Marine Corps out!" as they called for the removal of 12 MV-22 Osprey hybrid aircraft from Okinawa, where more than half of the troops in Japan are stationed. The protest came just days after an alleged assault by a U.S. airman on a teenage boy and just two weeks after a curfew was imposed on U.S. troops in Japan after the arrest of two Navy sailors in the alleged rape of a local woman. Even before these latest alleged crimes, all active-duty U.S. sailors in Japan were, and are, barred from drinking in public from midnight to 6 a.m. between Monday and Friday and between 2 a.m. and 6 a.m. on Saturdays, Sundays, and holidays.

These embarrassing episodes for the U.S. military in Japan are not isolated incidents by a few bad apples. Crimes against Japanese by American soldiers have been taking place for years (see the works of Chalmers Johnson).

But there is an even bigger crime against the Japanese people: the continued U.S. occupation of Japan. The U.S. government has maintained bases and stationed thousands of troops in Japan since it defeated the Japanese in World War II.

According to the Department of Defense's "Base Structure Report" for fiscal year 2012, the U.S. military has 109 military "sites" in Japan with 9,436 buildings totaling 33,736,309 sq. ft. on 126,450 acres. And according to the latest edition of the DoD's "Active Duty Military Personnel Strengths by Regional Area and by Country," the United States has 36,708 military personnel stationed in Japan.

And then there are the two other major countries that the United States defeated in World War II: Germany and Italy. The same DoD "Personnel Strengths" report lists 53,526 U.S. military personnel in Germany and 10,817 in Italy.

Does anyone really think it is necessary to keep so many American troops in Japan, Germany, and Italy so that they don't try to wage war against the United States again?

The "Japan problem" is not limited to Japan or other Axis powers in World War II. There are still 9,317 U.S. troops in Great Britain—one of the Allied powers in the war.

But World War II was not the beginning. Since the Spanish-American War of 1898, the foreign policy of the United States has been one of interventionism. Even before World War I, U.S. troops were sent to Nicaragua, Panama, Honduras, the Dominican Republic, Korea, Cuba, Nicaragua, China, and Mexico. Between the two world wars, U.S. troops were sent to Cuba, the Dominican Republic, Russia, Panama, Honduras, Yugoslavia, Guatemala, Turkey, and China.

The United States currently has troops in about 160 countries and territories—about 75 percent of the world. It doesn't matter which party controls the Congress or the presidency; both parties are firmly committed to a foreign policy of interventionism. When "incidents" in foreign countries with U.S. military personnel occur, both parties always miss the real issue.

The commander and top officers of a San Diego-based Navy frigate were recently relieved of duty after a rowdy, booze-fueled three-day port visit to Vladivostok, Russia. Their actions will result in reprimands, reassignments, investigations, and the issuance of guidelines to make sure things like that don't happen again, or rather, don't get made public again. The real issue, of course, is, what is the U.S. Navy doing in Vladivostok in the first place?

As part of his Amendment for Peace, U.S. Marine Corps Maj. Gen. Smedley Butler (1881–1940), the author of *War Is a Racket*, proposed the following:

> 1.The removal of members of the land armed forces from within the continental limits of the United States and the Panama Canal Zone for any cause whatsoever is hereby prohibited.
> 2.The vessels of the United States Navy, or of the other branches of the armed service, are hereby prohibited from steaming, for any reason whatsoever except on an errand of mercy, more than 500 miles from the U.S. coast.

3.Aircraft of the Army, Navy, and Marine Corps are hereby prohibited from flying, for any reason whatsoever, more than 750 miles beyond the coast of the United States.

That rules out military advisors, foreign bases, entangling alliances, nation-building, regime changes, spreading democracy, enforcing UN resolutions, drones, policing the world, invasions, occupations, bombing, maiming, killing—and stationing Marines in Japan or sending the Navy to Vladivostok.

Even though Romney lost the election, Republicans will continue to push for, and pressure Obama to push for, solutions to a nonexistent Iran problem while ignoring real difficulties such as the Japan problem. And they will do so to our peril.

* * * * *

THOMAS JEFFERSON VS. JOHN MCCAIN

There is no question that Syria has been ruled by the authoritarian al-Assad family since 1971, that the country's human rights record is dismal, and that over 40,000 Syrians have been killed in a civil war that has been ongoing for almost two years.

The question is what the United States should or shouldn't do about any of these things.

Senator John McCain thinks he knows the answer.

John McCain (born 1936) graduated from the Annapolis Naval Academy in 1958. After flight training, he spent some time on aircraft carriers in the Caribbean and Mediterranean Seas before volunteering for combat duty in Vietnam. In 1967 Lieutenant Commander McCain began bombing runs over North Vietnam. He was shot down on his twenty-third bombing mission and held as a prisoner of war for five years. After his release in 1973, McCain resumed his naval service until his retirement in 1981. While in the Navy, he earned the Silver Star, Bronze Star, Legion of Merit, Purple Heart, and the Distinguished Flying Cross. After leaving the military, McCain began his career in politics. He was elected to the U.S. House of Representatives in 1982. After two terms there, he was elected to the U.S. Senate in 1986, and has been there ever since.

McCain has been in the news of late because while on a trip to the Middle East to meet with officials from Egypt and Lebanon, speak at the World Economic Forum in Jordan, and visit American troops in Turkey, he also met with leaders of the Syrian opposition in Turkey and inside the

Syrian border. McCain, who never met a war or a troop surge he didn't like, wants to expand the 2001 Authorization to Use Military Force (AUMF) that has been used by Presidents Bush and Obama to justify all manner of military interventions. If it were up to McCain, the United States would already be bombing Syria on behalf of the allies of al-Qaeda.

It doesn't matter what has taken place in Syria; it doesn't matter what one side has done to the other side. The simple fact is this: McCain is not only taking sides in a civil war, he is trying to get the U.S. government to take sides as well. McCain's proposals could be dismissed as the ravings of a mad man but for the facts that he is not the only member of Congress who favors regime change in Syria, many interventionists on the left and the right feel the same way, and millions of American are willing to "support the troops" no matter where they go, what they do, or how long they stay.

Contrast McCain's foreign policy proposals with those of Thomas Jefferson.

In addition to being the president of the United States for two terms (1800 & 1804), Thomas Jefferson (1743–1826) was a member of the Virginia House of Burgesses (1769), a delegate to the Continental Congress (1775), the governor of Virginia (1779), a minister to France (1785), the first Secretary of State (1789), the vice president of the United States (1796), and the founder of the University of Virginia (1810).

Jefferson not only believed in a foreign policy of nonintervention, he believed in a foreign policy of neutrality:

I have used my best endeavors to keep our country *uncommitted* in the troubles which afflict Europe, and which assail us on every side.

The satisfaction you express, fellow citizens, that my endeavors have been unremitting to preserve the peace and independence of our country, and that a faithful *neutrality* has been observed towards all the contending powers, is highly grateful to me.

Since this happy separation, our nation has wisely avoided entangling itself in the system of European interests, has *taken no side* between its rival powers, attached itself to none of its ever-changing confederacies.

No one nation has a right to sit in *judgment* over another.

In the course of this conflict, let it be our endeavor, as it is our interest and desire, to cultivate the friendship of the belligerent nations by every act of justice and of incessant kindness; to receive their armed vessels with hospitality from the distresses of the sea, but to administer the means of annoyance to none; to establish in our harbors such a police as may maintain law and order; to restrain our citizens from embarking individually in a war in which their country *takes no part*.

We ask for peace and justice from all nations; and we will remain uprightly *neutral* in fact.

No nation has strove more than we have done to merit the peace of all by the most rigorous *impartiality* to all.

We have produced proofs, from the most enlightened and approved writers on the subject, that a *neutral* nation must, in all things relating to the war, observe an exact impartiality towards the parties.

I have used my best endeavors to keep our country *uncommitted* in the troubles which afflict Europe, and which assail us on every side.

Neutrality was the foreign policy of the Founding Fathers. Whatever their shortcomings, foreign policy was not one of them. Neutrality is an "America first" foreign policy. Neutrality is a moral foreign policy. Neutrality preserves American blood and treasure. Neutrality ensures a noninterventionist foreign policy. Neutrality is a sane foreign policy.

Not neutrality unless one side uses some particular weapon; not neutrality until one side commits some particular atrocity – neutrality no matter what.

If Senator McCain feels so strongly in favor of one side in Syria's civil war, then instead of pulling a public relations stunt he should go to Syria *and fight*—like Nicole Lynn Mansfield did.

Senator McCain is a third generation Navy man. His son, John McCain IV, graduated from the U.S. Naval Academy in 2009, and is a helicopter pilot. If McCain feels so strongly in favor of one side in Syria's civil war, then let his son lead the way. American families have lost enough of their sons in the senseless wars Iraq and Afghanistan that McCain has always supported.

The foreign policy of Jefferson or McCain – only one puts America first, only one is moral, only one preserves American blood and treasure, only one ensures a noninterventionist foreign policy, only one is sane, and it is not McCain's.

* * * * *

FOR FURTHER READING

Alperovitz, Gar. *The Decision to Use the Atomic Bomb and the Architecture of an American Myth.* New York: Alfred A. Knopf, 1995.

Bacevich, Andrew J. *American Empire: The Realities and Consequences of U.S. Diplomacy.* New ed. Cambridge: Harvard University Press, 2004.

_____. *The Limits of Power: The End of American Exceptionalism.* New York: Metropolitan Books, 2008.

_____. *The New American Militarism: How Americans Are Seduced by War.* Oxford: Oxford University Press, 2005.

_____. *Washington Rules: America's Path to Permanent War.* New York: Metropolitan Books, 2010.

Baker, Nicholson. *Human Smoke: The Beginnings of World War II, the End of Civilization.* New York: Simon & Schuster, 2008.

Bandow, Doug. *Foreign Follies: America's New Global Empire.* Longwood: Xulon Press, 2006.

Blum, William. *Freeing the World to Death: Essays On The American Empire.* Monroe: Common Courage Press, 2004.

_____. *Killing Hope: U.S. Military and CIA Interventions Since World War II.* Updated ed. Monroe: Common Courage Press, 2003.

_____. *Rogue State: A Guide to the World's Only Superpower.* Monroe: Common Courage Press, 2000.

Bovard, James. *Terrorism and Tyranny.* New York: Palgrave Macmillan, 2003.

_____. *The Bush Betrayal.* New York: Palgrave Macmillan, 2004.

Buchanan, Patrick J. *A Republic, Not an Empire: Reclaiming America's Destiny.* Washington, D.C.: Regnery Publishing, 1999.

_____. *Churchill, Hitler, and the Unnecessary War: How Britain Lost Its Empire and the West Lost the World.* New York: Crown Publishers, 2008.

_____. *Where the Right Went Wrong: How Neoconservatives Subverted the Reagan Revolution and Hijacked the Bush Presidency.* New York: Thomas Dunne Books, 2004.

Butler, Smedley D., and Adam Parfrey. *War Is a Racket: The Anti-War Classic by America's Most Decorated General, Two Other Anti-Interventionist Tracts, and Photographs from the Horror of It.* Los Angeles: Feral House, 2003.

Carpenter, Ted Galen. *Peace & Freedom: Foreign Policy for a Constitutional Republic.* Washington, D.C.: Cato Institute, 2002.

Carr, Caleb. *The Lessons of Terror: A History of Warfare against Civilians: Why It Has Always Failed and Why It Will Fail Again.* New York: Random House, 2002.

Carroll, James. *Crusade: Chronicles of an Unjust War.* New York: Metropolitan Books, 2004.

Chomsky, Noam. *Hegemony or Survival: America's Quest for Global Dominance.* New York: Metropolitan Books, 2003.

Cortright, David. *Peace: A History of Movements and Ideas.* Cambridge: Cambridge University Press, 2008.

Denson, John V. *A Century of War: Lincoln, Wilson & Roosevelt.* Auburn: Ludwig von Mises Institute, 2006.

_____., ed. *The Costs of War: America's Pyrrhic Victories.* 2nd expanded ed. New Brunswick: Transaction Publishers, 1999.

Doenecke, Justus D. *Nothing Less than War: A New History of America's Entry into World War I.* Lexington: The University Press of Kentucky, 2011.

Ebeling, Richard M., and Jacob G. Hornberger, eds. *The Failure of America's Foreign Wars.* Fairfax: The Future of Freedom Foundation, 1996.

_____. *Liberty, Security, and the War on Terrorism.* Fairfax: The Future of Freedom Foundation, 2003.

Ekirch, Arthur A. *The Civilian and the Military.* New York: Oxford University Press, 1956.

Eland, Ivan. *The Empire Has No Clothes: U.S. Foreign Policy Exposed.* Oakland: The Independent Institute, 2004.

Engelhardt, Tom. *The End of Victory Culture: Cold War America and the Disillusioning of a Generation.* Rev. ed. Amherst: University of Massachusetts Press, 2007.

Fleming, Thomas J. *The Illusion of Victory: America in World War I.* New York: Basic Books, 2003.

Folsom, Burton W., and Anita Folsom. *FDR Goes to War: How Expanded Executive Power, Spiraling National Debt, and Restricted Civil Liberties Shaped Wartime America.* New York: Threshold Editions, 2011.

Greenberg, Amy S. *A Wicked War: Polk, Clay, Lincoln, and the 1846*

U.S. Invasion of Mexico. New York: Alfred A. Knopf, 2012.

Hedges, Chris. *War Is a Force that Gives Us Meaning*. New York: Public Affairs, 2002.

_____. *What Every Person Should Know about War*. New York: Free Press, 2003.

Higgs, Robert. *Neither Liberty Nor Safety: Fear, Ideology, and the Growth of Government*. Oakland: The Independent Institute, 2007.

_____. *Resurgence of the Warfare State: The Crisis Since 9/11*. Oakland: The Independent Institute, 2005.

Higgs, Robert, ed. *Arms, Politics, and the Economy: Historical and Contemporary Perspectives*. New York: Holmes & Meier Publishers, 1990.

Holmes, Stephen. *The Matador's Cape: America's Reckless Response to Terror*. Cambridge: Cambridge University Press, 2007.

Hoppe, Hans-Hermann, ed., *The Myth of National Defense*. Auburn: Ludwig von Mises Institute, 2003.

Hoover, Herbert. *Freedom Betrayed: Herbert Hoover's Secret History of the Second World War and Its Aftermath*. Edited with an Introduction by George H. Nash. Stanford: Hoover Institution Press, 2011.

Johnson, Chalmers. *Blowback: The Costs and Consequences of American Empire*. New York: Owl Books, 2004.

_____. *Nemesis: The Last Days of the American Republic*. New York: Metropolitan Books, 2006.

_____. *The Sorrows of Empire: Military, Secrecy, and the End of the Republic*. New York: Metropolitan Books, 2004.

Kinzer, Stephen. *All the Shah's Men: An American Coup and the Roots of Middle East Terror*. Hoboken: John Wiley & Sons, 2003.

_____. *Overthrow: America's Century of Regime Change from Hawaii to Iraq*. New York: Henry Holt and Co., 2006.

Kolko, Gabriel. *Another Century of War?* New York: The New Press, 2002.

_____. *Century of War: Politics, Conflicts, and Society Since 1914*. New York: The New Press, 1994.

_____. *The Age of War: The United States Confronts the World*. Boulder: Lynne Rienner Publishers, 2006.

Loveland, Anne C. *American Evangelicals and the U.S. Military, 1942–1993*. Baton Rouge: Louisiana State University Press, 1996.

O'Huallachain, D. Liam, and J. Forrest Sharpe, eds. *Neo-CONNED! Again: Hypocrisy, Lawlessness, and the Rape of Iraq*. Norfolk: Light in the Darkness Publications, 2005.

Olson, Lynne. *Those Angry Days: Roosevelt, Lindbergh, and America's*

Fight over World II, 1939–1941. New York: Random House, 2013.

Opitz, Edmund A., ed. *Leviathan at War.* Irvington-on-Hudson: Foundation for Economic Education, 1995.

Overby, Richard. *1939: Countdown to War.* New York: Viking, 2010.

Palmer, Svetlana, and Sarah Wallis, eds. *Intimate Voices from the First World War.* New York: William Morrow, 2003.

Powell, Jim. *Wilson's War: How Woodrow Wilson's Great Blunder Led to Hitler, Lenin, Stalin, and World War II.* New York: Crown Forum, 2005.

Porter, Bruce D. *War and the Rise of the State: The Military Foundations of Modern Politics.* New York: The Free Press, 1994.

Quigley, John B. *The Ruses for War: American Interventionism Since World War II.* Rev. ed. Buffalo: Prometheus Books, 2007.

Raico, Ralph. *Great Wars & Great Leaders: A Libertarian Rebuttal.* Auburn: Ludwig von Mises Institute, 2010.

Ryn, Claes. *America the Virtuous: The Crisis of Democracy and the Quest for Empire.* New Brunswick: Transaction Publishers, 2003.

Schaffer, Ronald. *America in the Great War: The Rise of the War Welfare State.* New York: Oxford University Press, 1991.

Scheer, Christopher, Robert Sheer, and Lakshmi Chaudhry. *The Five Biggest Lies Bush Told Us About Iraq.* New York: Seven Stories Press and Akashic Books, 2003.

Solomon, Norman. *War Made Easy: How Presidents and Pundits Keep Spinning Us to Death.* Hoboken: John Wiley & Sons, 2005.

Stone, Geoffrey R.. *War and Liberty: An American Dilemma: 1790 to the Present.* New York: W. W. Norton & Co., 2007.

Tanaka, Yuki, and Marilyn B. Young, eds. *Bombing Civilians: A Twentieth-Century History.* New York: The New Press, 2009.

Thomas, Evan. *The War Lovers: Roosevelt, Lodge, Hearst, and the Rush to Empire, 1898.* New York: Little, Brown and Co., 2010.

Turse, Nick. *Kill Anything that Moves: The Real American War in Vietnam.* New York: Metropolitan Books, 2013.

_____. *The Complex: How the Military Invades Our Everyday Lives.* New York: Metropolitan Books, 2008.

Zezima, Michael. *Saving Private Power: The Hidden History of the "Good War."* New York: Soft Skull Press, 2000.

_____. *The Seven Deadly Spins: Exposing the Lies Behind U.S. War Propaganda.* Monroe: Common Courage Press, 2004.

Zunes, Stephen. *Tinderbox: U.S. Middle East Policy and the Roots of Terrorism.* Monroe: Common Courage Press, 2002.